Living Theatre

HISTORY OF THE THEATRE

Fifth Edition

Edwin Wilson
Graduate Center, CUNY, Emeritus

Alvin Goldfarb
Western Illinois University

Mc Graw Hill

Boston Burr Ridge, IL Dubuque, IA Madison, WI New York
San Francisco St. Louis Bangkok Bogotá Caracas Kuala Lumpur
Lisbon London Madrid Mexico City Milan Montreal New Delhi
Santiago Seoul Singapore Sydney Taipei Toronto

The McGraw-Hill Companies

Higher Education

Published by McGraw-Hill, an imprint of The McGraw-Hill Companies, Inc., 1221 Avenue of the Americas, New York, NY 10020.

This book is printed on acid-free paper.

3 4 5 6 7 8 9 0 DOC/DOC 0 9

ISBN-13: 978-0-07-351412-3
MHID: 0-07-351412-8

Editor in Chief: *Emily Barrosse*
Publisher: *Lisa Moore*
Sponsoring Editor: *Christopher Freitag*
Editorial Assistant: *Marley Magaziner*
Marketing Manager: *Pamela Cooper*
Developmental Editor: *Caroline Ryan*
Media Producer: *Stacy Bentz*
Project Manager: *Brett Coker*
Manuscript Editor: *Susan Gamer*
Interior and Cover Designer: *Marianna Kinigakis and Jeanne Calabrese*
Art Editor: *Emma Ghiselli*
Photo Researcher: *Inge King*
Photo Research Coordinator: *Sonia Brown*
Production Supervisor: *Tandra Jorgensen*
Composition: *Professional Graphics*
Printing: *45# Publisher's Matte by Shenzhen Donnelley Printing Co., Ltd.*

Cover image: *Actors from the Commedia Dell'arte on a Wagon in a Town Square by Jan Miel (1620–1663)*
Credit: © *Christie's Images/Corbis*

Library of Congress Cataloging-in-Publication Data
Wilson, Edwin.
Living theatre: history of the theatre / Edwin Wilson, Alvin Goldfarb.
p. cm
Includes bibliographical references and index.
ISBN-13: 978-0-07-351412-3
ISBN-10: 0-07-351412-8
1. Theater—History. I. Goldfarb, Alvin II. Title.

PN2101.W54 2004
792.09—dc22

2006048156

www.mhhe.com

About the Authors

Edwin Wilson, as teacher, author, director, and critic, has worked in many aspects of theatre. Educated at Vanderbilt University, the University of Edinburgh, and Yale University, he received a master of fine arts degree from the Yale Drama School, as well as the first doctor of fine arts degree awarded by Yale. He has taught at Yale, Hofstra, Vanderbilt, Hunter College, and the CUNY Graduate Center. At Hunter he served as chair of the Department of Theatre and Film and head of the graduate theatre program. At CUNY he has been Executive Director of the Martin E. Segal Theatre Center.

From 1972 to 1994 he was the theatre critic of *The Wall Street Journal.* He is the author of *The Theater Experience* and a coauthor, with Alvin Goldfarb, of *Theater: The Lively Art,* as well as coeditor of *The Anthology of Living Theater,* all published by McGraw-Hill. He edited and wrote the introduction for *Shaw on Shakespeare,* a new edition of which appeared in 2002. He has been a member of the New York Drama Critics Circle, of which he served as president, and has been on the selection committees of the Pulitzer Prize in drama and the Tony awards. He serves on the board of the Susan Smith Blackburn Prize and the John Golden Fund and for many years served on the board of the Theatre Development Fund, of which he was president for two terms.

Alvin Goldfarb is president and professor of theatre at Western Illinois University. Dr. Goldfarb also served as vice president and holds a Ph.D. in theatre history from the City University of New York and a master's degree from Hunter College.

He is the coauthor of *Theater: The Lively Art* and coeditor of *The Anthology of Living Theater* with Edwin Wilson. Dr. Goldfarb is also the coeditor, with Rebecca Rovit, of *Theatrical Performance during the Holocaust: Texts, Documents, Memoirs,* which was a finalist for the National Jewish Book Award. He has published numerous articles and reviews in scholarly journals and anthologies.

Dr. Goldfarb served as a member of the Illinois Arts Council and president of the Illinois Alliance for Arts Education. He has received service awards from the latter organization as well as from the American College Theatre Festival. Dr. Goldfarb also received an Alumni Achievement Award from the City University of New York Graduate Center's Alumni Association.

To the Memory of Our Parents

Preface

By definition, any history is a chronicle—a recapitulation or reconstruction of events from the past. It cannot, therefore, be a contemporary, spontaneous occurrence. And yet, that is precisely what theatre is—an event that exists not in the past but in the present. In fact, theatre exists only at the moment when it occurs. The essence of theatre is an immediate exchange between the audience and what unfolds onstage: performances, words of a text, and visual effects of sets, lights, and costumes.

The first challenge, therefore, of writing histories of theatre is to bring theatre from the past to life today. In *Living Theatre,* we have taken a number of steps to achieve this. The fifth edition of *Living Theatre* retains all the features that have been well received by students and professors in the past. At the same time, it represents an important advance over the previous editions by adding a number of significant elements.

Organization

Each theatrical era is set in a broad social, political, and economic context. The opening section of each chapter establishes the framework for theatre practitioners: playwrights, performers, managers, architects, and designers.

The different approaches with respect to how history should be viewed and analyzed—revisionism, feminism, deconstructionism, multiculturalism, semiotics, Marxism, and postmodernism—are carefully presented in the Introduction, and noted where appropriate in the text.

Features

Biographical sections are an integral part of the text. These highlight the artists who created theatre, and provide students with interesting information that makes these individuals come alive. A photograph or painting of the person highlighted is included at the start of each section. Where possible, production photos are also included to further bring these artists' work to life.

Debates in Theatre History are boxes designed to help foster critical thought, and give students an awareness of the ever-changing nature of theatre history. In these boxes we focus on some point of disagreement among scholars and historians, to underscore the fact that no single view of history should be taken as immutable.

Maps are presented in many chapters, in recognition of the importance of geographical context. Along with maps of the important theatre sites of Europe, we also include a map depicting the theatrical centers of Asia.

Appendixes include our glossary of theatrical terms, a pronunciation guide, and an updated bibliography.

Online Learning Center. Visit *www.mhhe.com/livingtheatre5* for a wealth of instructor and student resources, including an instructor's manual, test bank, interactive timeline, glossary, multiple choice quizzes, and more.

New to the Fifth Edition

New Design

The most obvious change in this fifth edition is the new design, which for the first time incorporates full color throughout the text. This is an important change, as it enables us to bring the world of theatre even closer to students. As always, we have chosen photographs that not only illustrate the concepts discussed but also are beautiful, lively, and indicative of the vibrancy of theatre. The full-color design showcases the photos better than ever before. In addition, the new design was carefully crafted not just to be attractive, but to make this text even more user-friendly. Signature elements of the text, such as the biography sections and *Debates in Theatre History,* are easily recognizable but do not break away from the conversational flow of the prose. In recognizing the visual world today's students live in, we are pleased to present a text that is so appealing, accessible, and useful in its design.

Content

In Part One, we've included more information on historiography. Also, in light of new research, we've increased our coverage of theatre's origins.

In Part Four, we've updated Chapter 15 to include recent trends in the contemporary theatre of the United States. Also, Chapter 16 has been retitled "Global Theatres." We've added coverage of Canadian and Australian theatre, and we have enhanced our coverage of Latin American theatre.

In addition to the specific changes listed above, the fifth edition has been revised and updated throughout. We have taken special care to highlight the important contributions made by women and minority playwrights, actors, and directors. The latest research, new approaches to studying history, and new theories have been taken note of and explained.

Milestones

With this new feature, we've revised and improved on an idea that was first presented in the fourth edition. The *Milestones* at the end of each chapter serve as a visual summary and a contextual reference for students. These can be used like timelines at the end of each chapter, for summary and review. The thumbnail photos embedded in them depict important people and events from both theatre and the cultural and historical world of each time period. These will help today's visually oriented students review and remember the improtant figures and events from each period.

Acknowledgments

Retained from earlier editions is the excellent material provided by Professor James V. Hatch on African American theatre. For the information in the chapter on Asian theatre, we are deeply indebted to Professors J. Thomas Rimer and Samuel Leiter. Much of the original biographical information was developed by Dr. Rita Plotnicki, Professor J. K. Curry, Thom Thomas, Michelle Sullivan, and Susan Tenneriello. For most of the African American figures, material was furnished by George C. Wolfe. Ann Haugo contributed invaluable information on Native American theatre, and Angie Balsamo provided additional information on Latin American theatre, as well as some updates to Chapters 15 and 16. Edward Dee compiled a comprehensive list of plays for each period. The pronunciation guide was compiled by Kurt Taroff.

There is no way we can adequately express our gratitude to two people who have added in such an incalculable way to the creation of our books, including this edition of *Living Theatre.* The incomparable, inspired, indefatigable Inge King has located and helped select each one of thousands of photographs and illustrations that has appeared in twenty four editions of our books. As far as we are concerned, she is the best photo editor and researcher on the planet. Equally, we wish to thank Susan Gamer, copy editor supreme. Again, she has worked on many editions of our books and her work is always exceptional, in fact, unbelievable in its thoroughness, insight, and intelligence. At the same time, Susan Tenneriello, as so often before, has proved invaluable in preparing the index. At McGraw-Hill, we offer sincere thanks for our hardworking team: our development editor, Caroline Ryan; our production editor, Brett Coker; our designer, Marianna Kinigakis; and our sponsoring editor, Chris Freitag.

We are grateful for the important contributions of all of our instructor reviews over the course of five editions. We thank the following people for their advice and suggestions during the development of the fifth edition of *Living Theatre:*

C. Patrick Tyndall, *University of Arkansas*

David S. Escofferty, *Southwest Missouri State University*

Jennifer Cavenaugh, *Louisiana State University*

Leigh Clemons, *Louisiana State University*

Paul Backer, *University of Southern California*

Jerry Dickey, *University of Arizona*

Peter A. Davis, *University of Illinois*

Robyn Quick, *Towson University*

Randy L. Wonzong, *California State University, Chico*

Terry Allen, *University of Wisconsin—Eau Claire*

Randi Hard, *Parkland College*

Brief Contents

Contents

PART THREE

THEATRES FROM 1660 TO 1875 257

CHAPTER 10

CHAPTER 14 THEATRES FROM 1945 TO 1975 452

Introduction

Throughout the United States on any given day, audiences attend hundreds of theatre events. They may see an outdoor production in a large open space such as the Shakespeare festival in Ashland, Oregon; or they may see an indoor production in a small theatre like the many off-off-Broadway theatres in New York's Greenwich Village. They may see a new play at one of the many regional professional theatres scattered across the country; or they may see a classic—a tragedy by Shakespeare or a comedy by Molière—at one of the hundreds of college or university theatres in the United States and Canada. They may see a lavish Broadway musical or a simple play set on a bare stage; they may see a formal, stylized kabuki production by a visiting Japanese troupe, or a modern American play set in a family's kitchen.

The experiences audiences have at these events are almost as diverse as the events themselves, and the works staged often come from past historical eras. A young woman sees a production of Shakespeare's *Romeo and Juliet* and is amazed at how this 400-year-old play illustrates the problems she is having with her parents, who are trying to prevent her from going out with a young man from a different background. A young man sees *The Miser* by the seventeenth-century playwright Molière and identifies with the son in the play, whose father disinherits him and also tries to steal his girlfriend. An older couple see a revival of the musical *My Fair Lady*—filled with melodies they know—and are thrilled not only with the music but also with the lavish scenery and costumes. Someone who works hard at a job sees a farce or a family comedy, presented just for fun, and enjoys escaping from problems and stress at the end of the day. A young woman who relishes puzzles and clever language sees a play by a writer like the contemporary British dramatist Tom Stoppard or the early twentieth-century Italian Luigi Pirandello and takes pleasure in being challenged intellectually. A young man sees a production of *Fences* by August Wilson and is caught up in the plight of its young hero, who is struggling with his own identity and with the prejudice his black family must face. Many people who identify with specific groups see plays about problems of race, gender, or politics and feel a kinship with the characters portrayed onstage and the challenges those characters face.

The myriad of theatrical events and experiences open to us have their roots in the theatre we have inherited—2,500 years of western theatre and nearly 2,000 years of Asian theatre. What are these many kinds of theatre, and where did they come from? These are questions that *Living Theatre* will address.

Clues to Theatre's Origins: Theatre in Everyday Life

Before we begin our study of theatre history, we should note that theatre has a number of first cousins or near relations in everyday life. Many human activities—both personal and communal—have a theatrical component. Theatre historians, anthropologists, and sociologists often point to these everyday theatrical activities as possible explanations for the origins of theatre. They note that, to a considerable extent, our everyday human interactions have many qualities of theatrical performances and thus may offer clues to how theatre began.

Imitation, Role Playing, and Storytelling

Imitation is universal among children. A child sees an older person walking upstairs or opening a door and learns to do the same by imitation. Role playing is universal among young and old alike, and it too has a theatrical component. People assume family roles—father, mother, grandfather, sister, brother—and also social roles, such as doctor, lawyer, salesperson, and social worker. In playing these roles, individuals adopt behaviors required by their society. Both imitation and role playing involve aspects of acting. The Greek philosopher Aristotle, whom we shall discuss later, suggested that theatre may have originated in the human instinct to imitate.

Another everyday activity with a theatrical element is storytelling, found in cultures throughout the world. Experienced storytellers are able to create suspense, evoke laughter or tears, and keep alive traditions of their culture. They often adopt the voices of characters in their stories; they take on the personalities of old men, young warriors, innocent maidens, or ghosts and other supernatural creatures. At these moments, storytellers become actors or actresses not unlike those we see onstage. You might think of times when you have heard a story read to a young child and how the reader tried to make the rendition more theatrical.

In societies that had not developed written language, the storyteller, known as a *shaman,* kept alive the history of the people, in a fashion that was highly theatrical and, again, may have led to the development of theatre. In recent years, performance artists such as Spalding Gray, Eric Bogosian, Anna Deveare Smith, John Leguizamo, Lisa Kron, and Sarah Jones, many of whom will be discussed later in this book, present one-person theatrical pieces that remind audiences of the close connection between storytelling and theatre.

Thus a child who imitates the gestures and voice patterns of older people, a judge who fills a prescribed role by acting a certain way toward people appearing in a courtroom, a tribal elder who relates a story to a group gathered around a campfire—all are, in some sense, engaging in a form of acting, and these activities all seem to provide clues to the origins of theatre.

Popular Entertainment

Certain types of group activities with a strong theatrical component are referred to as *popular entertainment.* They include a wide range of performance events: singing, dancing, pantomime, juggling, magic, acrobatics, dramatic sketches, and even some kinds of storytelling. In almost every culture and every age, individuals or small groups with acrobatic, musical, or other skills have entertained others. Again, these types of popular performative arts contain the seeds of theatre. We might also note that according to some theorists, these forms of entertainment should be considered *non–text-based* theatre, or sometimes performance art, which is discussed later.

At times and in places where there is no organized traditional theatre, popular entertainment is frequently the chief means of perpetuating theatrical activity. A good illustration is the long period in European history from the end of the Roman empire in the fourth century C.E. until medieval theatre took form almost 1,000 years later. There was no formal theatre during these centuries, but groups of troubadours, jugglers, dancers, and mimes crisscrossed parts of Europe, entertaining at large manor houses—often during banquets and on other special occasions—and at public locations where people congregated, such as markets and religious centers.

Ceremonies and Rituals

Theatrical Aspects of Ceremonies and Rituals

Ceremonies and rituals are found in every human society, and they invariably have important theatrical elements. A *ceremony* is a formal religious or social occasion, usually led by a designated authority figure such as a priest or chief; examples would include a graduation, an inauguration, and a marriage ceremony. A *ritual* is the acting out of an established, prescribed procedure; rituals can range from a family event such as Thanksgiving or Christmas dinner to elaborate religious events—such as the Roman Catholic mass and the Jewish Yom Kippur service during the High Holy Days. Both ceremonies and rituals are observances that follow a prescribed course; thus they are closely related to each other.

People in the west are most familiar with the kinds of ceremonies and rituals just mentioned, but important examples are also found in nonwestern cultures, and these too have theatrical elements. Throughout central and western Africa, for instance, striking and imaginative costumes and masks are used in a variety of ceremonies. In a ceremony performed by the Guro tribe on the Ivory Coast, a dancer depicting an animal figure wears a large mask that combines antelope horns, an abstracted human face, and a large toothed beak. The costume consists of orange netting on the arms and bamboo reeds on the body. Other dancers wear masks and costumes appropriate to their roles.

The costumes and masks used for ceremonies in Africa are among the most beautiful to be found anywhere in the world, but theatrical elements are also found in the actions of the celebrants. Frequently, participants enact someone or something —a bird, an animal, or a spirit. In many cases, people who take part in these rituals

(© Richard T. Nowitz/Corbis)

THEATRE AND RELIGION

Religious celebrations, such as the Jewish bar mitzvah—the one shown here is at the Western Wall in Jerusalem—have many things in common with theatre: ritual, a form of costumes, exchanges of dialogue. Often music and other theatrical elements are also included. In fact, religious processions were actually a part of theatre in ancient Greece. But a religious ceremony, which is intended for worship, is essentially different from theatre, which is an end in itself—an art form that focuses on human concerns.

believe that a performer is actually inhabited by the animal or spirit being portrayed, that the performer is transformed during the ceremony and becomes the figure represented. In addition, leaders and their assistants, as well as other celebrants who play key roles in a ceremony, have definite, assigned tasks and perform in a prescribed manner.

The actions of ceremonial leaders thus bear a certain similarity to those of actresses or actors in dramatic presentations, who learn specific movements and repeat dialogue from a script. Also, rituals and ceremonies generally follow a set sequence of events: the same words and actions are repeated each time, often exactly reproducing previous presentations. This sequence of events corresponds to the "script" and dramatic structure of a theatrical production. Also, the costumes and properties used in ceremonies and rituals reflect the theatrical nature of these events. Thus, many historians and anthropologists argue that theatre grew out of religious rituals and ceremonies. We can turn to an example from Egyptian society to show the close historical connection between religious ceremony and ritual and theatre.

The Abydos Ritual in Ancient Egypt

One ritual containing theatrical elements was enacted in ancient Egypt for nearly 2,000 years, from around 2500 to 550 B.C.E., at a sacred place called Abydos. The evidence suggests that every year thousands of Egyptians made their way to Abydos to see this ceremony. The ritual drama performed at Abydos deals with the Egyptian god Osiris, who became the ruler of Egypt and married his sister Isis. Osiris's brother later became jealous of him and killed him, scattering the parts of his body throughout the Egyptian kingdom. Isis recovered the pieces and, with the aid of another god, brought Osiris back to life. Osiris could not remain on earth, however, and so his body was buried at Abydos. His spirit then went to dwell in the underworld, where he became the most human of the Egyptian gods, the god who judged people's souls.

The tale of Osiris is a virtually universal religious story, recurring in societies throughout the world: a story of betrayal, death, and life after death. We do not have the actual text of the Abydos ritual, but we do have a partial account by someone named Ikhernofret, who participated in it sometime between 1887 and 1849 B.C.E. It is clear from this account that the ceremony had unmistakable theatrical elements: people played the roles of characters in the story and acted out episodes from the life of Osiris.

Indigenous Latin American Ritual

Contemporary Latin American theatre—which we will discuss later—is heavily indebted to the cultures of the indigenous peoples who populated the region before the European conquests. These indigenous peoples took part in performative activities, also often associated with religious rituals. Most notable among these indigenous groups were the Maya, Incas, and Aztecs in what is present-day Central and South America.

A survey of Aztec festivals reveals that these religious and civic rituals contained recognizable theatrical elements. The Aztec festivals, like those of the Egyptians, revolved around the agricultural calendar. The Aztecs would perform staged rituals that celebrated the seasons as part of these festivals. They also staged ceremonies dedicated to their deities, particularly to honor their war gods and to seek the gods' favor.

Among the most theatrically developed of these ceremonies were the Flowery Wars. These battles were carefully staged in full war garb. The theatrical combats concluded with human sacrifices in order to gain the goodwill of various deities.

Nontheatrical Elements of Ceremonies and Rituals

We should also point out that there are some significant differences between religious rituals and ceremonies and theatre.

Efficaciousness One noteworthy aspect setting religious ceremonies and rituals apart from dramatic presentations is that religious ceremonies and rituals are *efficacious;* that is, they are intended to achieve results. Some of the best-known dances of Native Americans, for example, are carried out in the hope of bringing rain to water the crops. Throughout the world, ceremonies have been used to entreat the gods to provide a plentiful harvest, to alleviate suffering, or to bring victory in battle. Formal religions—Catholicism, Protestantism, Judaism, Islam, and others—also have ceremonies intended to serve some purpose: to ask forgiveness, to plead for help, to request a better life in this world and beyond it.

(© Erich Schlegel/Dallas Morning News/Corbis)

CEREMONY AND THEATRE
The Tewa dancers of the North performing an eagle dance during the Eight Northern Indian Pueblos Arts and Crafts Show at San Juan Pueblo, Colorado. Many historians believe that theatre originated in such ceremonial or dance performances, which have many theatrical components. The primary difference is that these ceremonies were believed to be efficacious—to affect the environment and even the gods.

The efficacious nature of a religious ceremony—whether it is a ritual in Africa or a service in a church, synagogue, or mosque—reminds us that an essential difference between theatre and religion lies in their purpose and focus. Religion centers on the worship of a deity or deities, and the intent of a religious ceremony is to pray to the deity: to ask forgiveness, seek help, or offer praise. The focus of theatre, by contrast, is not worship. Theatre acts as a mirror or a celebration of life here on earth. Theatre can serve a number of purposes: it can challenge people to think, transport them to the past, entertain them, take them outside themselves, make them cry, and make them laugh. But its focus is always on human beings—their suffering, their pain, their frustrations, their hopes, their joys, their laughter. Even when theatre deals with a religious subject, it concerns itself with how religion affects human lives.

Methexis: Group Sharing Religious ceremonies often have another quality that distinguishes them from theatrical performances. In the theatre with which we are familiar, there is a clear separation between performers and audience. A space is set aside—the stage—where the performance takes place, and audience members observe the action as spectators. Audiences may become engrossed in what happens onstage and may be emotionally involved, but their involvement is always vicarious. Audience members experience the emotions—the heartaches and joys—of characters onstage empathically, by identifying in their own imaginations with the characters. Spectators may cry real tears and give way to uncontrollable laughter; but this participation occurs at a distance: in the minds and hearts of the spectators, who remain in their seats.

The experience of many tribal ceremonies is different from this kind of theatrical experience, as we can see in certain ceremonies in Africa. To understand the difference, we should consider for a moment how earlier African societies viewed themselves in the world. They did not see the universe as a series of dichotomies such as good versus evil or spiritual versus material; rather, they saw it as a vast, intricate harmony of people, nature, and gods, each having some element of spiritual as well as material existence. Human beings, because they have consciousness and the invocative power of the spoken word, were responsible for maintaining a balance with nature. If this balance was violated through stupidity, greed, or folly, both people and nature suffered. One very important means of maintaining the balance was religious ritual, which embraced song, dance, and drama.

Partly as a result of this philosophy, rituals in many African societies had an aesthetic or artistic principle different from that of the theatre which originated in Europe and was adopted in North and South America and elsewhere. Traditional European theatre is based primarily on *mimesis:* imitation or representation of an action. It also stresses the importance of individual creativity by performers, playwrights, and others, and a set text from which little variation is permitted. And, as we have just seen, audience members in European theatre are spectators rather than participants.

The African tradition, on the other hand, is generally based on *methexis:* group sharing. It emphasizes audience participation, group creativity, and improvisation. As a result, whereas European theatre is meant to affect the audience—to entertain or to teach—the purpose of the African tradition is to embody or to *be.* African ceremonies, although set, offer opportunities for improvisation, and not only the leader or priest but everyone participates, entering into the action and also into transformations of body and spirit.

A New World version of such an African ritual can be found in the Caribbean, where the African gods were integrated with the practices of the Catholic church through religious rituals such as *vodun* in Haiti and *santería* in Trinidad, Puerto Rico, and Cuba. For instance, the Afro-Cuban ritual drama *Shango de Ima,* a mystery play, is a re-creation of the life of the Yorub god Shango, who is known in Cuba as Saint Barbara. This drama, still performed today, contains many Yoruba words and chants; its power sometimes "possesses" the "performers" so that they "become" *orishas* (gods), thus bringing both worshippers and performers into a community of gods and nature.

"Participatory" Theatre

In addition to imitation, role playing, storytelling, popular entertainments, and ceremonies and rituals, theatrical elements can be found in many contemporary educational and therapeutic activities that stress active participation by the people involved. Many of these contemporary activities are similar to earlier participatory rituals and ceremonies.

Good examples are psychodrama, sociodrama, and classroom exercises or therapy groups using dramatic improvisations. Psychodrama focuses on individuals and sociodrama on groups. In both cases, the aim is for participants to engage in deliberate "role playing" as a means of understanding the dynamics and emotional tensions in a situation.

Interestingly, in the United States in past years there were also examples of "participatory theatre" in theatre itself—attempts to remove the barrier between performers and spectators. During the 1960s a number of avant-garde organizations invited spectators to move from their seats in the auditorium and become part of the action. Before a presentation began, audience members might be "initiated" or "indoctrinated" by being led to their seats by performers, or engaged by performers in conversation. During a performance they would be invited to come to the playing area to take part in the action, or perhaps to participate in the aisles of the auditorium.

Prohibition of Theatre

We now consider one additional—and paradoxical—aspect of theatre in daily life: prohibitions against theatre. These prohibitions clearly have had an impact on the extent to which theatre can exist in certain societies. Wherever complex social organizations and population centers develop, theatre is likely to emerge. When it does not, the explanation may be that a society stresses other forms of communal activity —religion or art, say—rather than theatre. But sometimes a society specifically forbids theatre.

One of the strongest deterrents to the emergence of theatre in an advanced society is religious opposition. We have noted the close relationship between theatre and religion: religion has theatrical elements, and theatre has at times evolved from religious ceremonies. The connection between the two, however, has often taken the form of a love-hate relationship, and there have been times when religion has bitterly opposed theatre.

The early Christians, for example, repeatedly denounced Roman theatre and at one point issued an edict that any Christian attending a theatre on a holy day would be excommunicated. In England, when the Puritans came to power under Oliver Cromwell and took control of Parliament in 1642, one of the first things they did was to close all the theatres in London. Two other important examples are found in ancient Judaism and Islam.

Considering the contributions of Jewish people to theatre in later times, it may seem puzzling that the ancient Hebrew nation did not produce theatre. There is evidence of poetic and narrative skills in the Old Testament, and we know from the psalms and other sources that there was singing as well as dancing; but no separate theatre developed. However, there were both social and political reasons for this. The ancient Jews were a nomadic people, moving from place to place, who did not at first develop permanent centers of population like those in Greece and elsewhere. And even after they had established a kingdom and settled in urban centers like Jerusalem, they did not develop theatre, apparently because of their religious beliefs. David S. Lifson, in a book on Yiddish theatre in the United States, has noted that during the biblical period Jews were forbidden to attend pagan theatres. A prayer from the period underlines this fact: "I thank thee, my Lord, that I spend my time in the temples of prayer instead of in the theatres."[1] Some commentators believe that this injunction against theatre stems from the Second Commandment in the Bible: "You shall not make a graven image, or any likeness of anything that is in heaven above or in the earth beneath." According to this theory, "any likeness" was interpreted to include a performer impersonating a character onstage.

In Islam, the prohibition of theatre is equally explicit. Islam, founded by the prophet Muhammad in 610 C.E., became the dominant religion in regions stretching from beyond Persia (now Iran) in the east to Spain in the west. It included all of the middle east, the eastern Mediterranean, North Africa, and southern Spain. Islam forbids the personification of God—that is, showing a person who might embody God—and this rule has remained steadfast from its earliest days to the present.

No permanent theatre as such emerged in Islamic countries; however, it is significant that despite this strong deterrent, theatre crept into Islamic societies. There is archaeological evidence of circuses and other entertainments, and there are indications of popular plays in the eastern part of the Persian empire. Even more noteworthy is the *Taziya* "passion play," a religious drama performed each year as part of the festival of Muharram in areas where the Shiite sect of Islam prevails. The play recounts the survival of Zain, a grandson of Muhammad, after the other members of his branch of the family were slaughtered. The Shiites consider Zain the legitimate successor of Muhammad.

There are many versions of the *Taziya* passion play; an Englishman living in Persia in the 1860s found fifty-two, and in 1878 he had thirty-seven of them published. The *Taziya* has been performed regularly in Baghdad (Iraq) and Tehran and Isfahan (Iran), and it was considered part of a religious festival through all of its early history. Except for isolated instances such as the *Taziya,* theatre was not allowed to develop independently in Islamic countries. In most Islamic countries ruled by religious leaders, there is no theatre whatsoever, although, again, there have been many dissident theatre artists who have written and presented plays, even in the midst of oppressive circumstances.

The subject of theatre in daily life—including "role playing" in all its aspects, as well as the whole range of religious, educational, and celebratory rituals and ceremonies —is clearly important and worthy of detailed study. Prohibition of theatre, of course, is also significant. The subject of this book, however, is the history of theatre where it has evolved, free from outside strictures, as a separate art form, not as a component of other practices. We must examine, therefore, how theatre operates as a separate activity with its own principles, functions, and aesthetics and try

[1]David S. Lifson, *The Yiddish Theatre in America*, Thomas Yoseloff, New York, 1965, p. 18.

to answer questions about theatre itself as we review its various elements through the course of its history. We should note that many contemporary theorists argue against the artificial separation of theatre from ritual activity or popular arts. But in order for us to chronicle the complex history of this ever-changing art form, we will focus primarily on the traditional definition and characteristics of theatre at the same time that we note other approaches.

How Historians Reconstruct the Elements of Theatre

As we have indicated, no one knows exactly how theatre originated. We know *where* it emerged: in Greece in the fifth century B.C.E., in India in the fourth century C.E., and—after being dormant in western civilization—again in Europe in the Middle Ages. But precisely how it developed in each case has been hotly debated by scholars.

Some scholars argue that theatre emerges from religious ceremonies; as we have pointed out, there are significant similarities between such ceremonies and theatre. Others have suggested that theatre evolves from storytelling. Still others argue that in certain instances theatre—especially comedy and farce—has come from various forms of popular entertainment or from secular pagan celebrations. Our purpose here is not to attempt to settle this argument, or even to take one position against another. We are concerned not with the origins of theatre but with how it develops once it becomes established.

We can point to certain characteristics by which we identify theatre as an art form. When something has these characteristics, we traditionally define it as theatre. Let us examine these requirements or elements briefly. In addition, we should also discuss the kinds of questions historians ask when they—and we—try to reconstruct the characteristics of these theatrical elements from past eras.

A Playing Space

Theatre requires a *playing space* where people can come together to watch a performance. As we try to reconstruct historic playing spaces, we will be exploring a number of key issues. What was the relationship between performers and audiences in these spaces? How large were the spaces? What was the configuration of the stage? Where was the audience? Were the spaces permanent or temporary? What building materials were used? Were there areas for selling tickets, changing costumes, storing scenery, and so on? What did the quality of the space suggest about the status of theatre? Did the arrangement of spectators signal an ideological or political positioning of the viewers?

The Audience

In order to understand the makeup of *audiences* of past historic eras, we will need to answer a number of questions. What was the social, economic, political, and gender configuration of the audience? Were any people excluded from the theatre because of gender, race, or economics? Why did audiences attend the theatre? What function did theatre serve in the lives of audience members? How did audiences behave during the course of a production?

The Performers

Equally important are the *performers:* the other half of the actor-audience relationship. Performance is the essence of theatre. For that matter, a Polish theatrical artist-theorist, Jerzy Grotowski, who will be discussed in Chapter 14, defined the essential elements of theatre as the audience and the performers.

Many of the questions we will ask about acting will be similar to those we ask about audiences. Who were the actors? What was their social and economic standing within their society? Were people excluded from performing because of gender, race, or economics? Did the roles assigned to performers reflect ideological or political points of view? How did a person become an actor? How were productions rehearsed, and what was expected of performers during rehearsals?

Possibly the most difficult question we will try to answer is: What was the style of acting in a given historical period? This question is nearly impossible to answer because acting is the most ephemeral of the theatre arts: it disappears as soon as a performance is over. In addition, we consider performance in terms of our own contemporary biases. As we discuss acting throughout this text, we will try to describe the unique conventions and techniques of various historical periods in order to create a flavor of what acting was like in the past.

Visual Elements

Another traditional component of theatre is the *visual elements:* scenery, lighting, and costumes. In reconstructing how visual elements were used in the past, we will confront a number of key issues. What materials were used to create the visual elements? Who was responsible for designing and providing the visual elements? How unified were these elements? What functions did they serve? What kinds of machinery were used to create scenic and lighting effects?

Texts

Throughout the course of theatre history, texts have been performed by actors for their audiences. The most common type of text is a play, written by a playwright or dramatist. However, there have been other kinds of theatrical materials, such as those created by actors or by a director or through collaboration. There have also been texts created at the moment of performance; these are referred to as *improvisatory* presentations.

As we consider the texts of past eras—their subject matter and their structure—we will need to answer some of the following questions. Who created the dramatic materials? How were these materials structured? What was their dominant subject matter? What types of texts were presented in theatres, and were there any recurring characteristics? Were any specific ideological points of view represented within the texts? How were marginalized groups represented in the texts?

Coordination of the Elements

Finally, these various elements must be combined; throughout theatre history someone has had to oversee the process of staging and financing a production. As we discuss the history of directing, we will ask if there was an individual who served the function of director, and—if so—whether this person also had other production duties. What were this person's responsibilities? How unified and coordinated were productions during each of the historical periods? How were productions rehearsed? Who was responsible for rehearsals? Who provided the funds for staging a production? How did economic facors impact the theatre?

Social Requirements

Even if the elements outlined above are in place, theatre has still other requirements. For one thing, it is a communal art calling for the collaboration of many individuals and groups, and those involved must be highly trained and highly skilled. This requires a theatre tradition in which training can take place. It also calls for organization of a kind that can be found only in societies that have developed a complex social structure. Usually this requires a population center—a place where a number of people have gathered together. A population center such as a village, town, or city is important, too, in providing an audience. Without a population center, there would be no audience to attend an event.

Lack of population centers may partly explain why theatre did not develop in certain cultures—among Native Americans, for example, or societies in Africa. These people were nomadic; they developed religious rituals and other ceremonies, but it would have been difficult for them to create a structured theatre.

As noted earlier, theatre emerges wherever complex social organization develops and population centers exist; societies that prohibit theatre, such as ancient Judaism and Islam, are exceptions to this rule. The subject of this study will be those places where theatre has emerged. We will focus mainly on the western tradition, because it is out of that tradition that modern American and European theatre primarily comes. But we will also look at Asian theatre, and at African and Caribbean influences on modern African American theatre.

The Study of Theatre History

Traditional Chronological Narratives

In *Living Theatre,* we will look at theatre as it has unfolded through the ages. In western history, theatre began in Europe and later spread to North and South America. We will also trace theatre as it emerged in Asia. In doing so, we will note what kinds of theatre emerged—tragedy, comedy, melodrama, and various other forms. We will look at dramatic structure and also at acting, production, and visual elements—all aspects of performance. We will note how one country may have built on the experience of another or appropriated from another: seventeenth-century French theatre, for example, was greatly influenced by the Italian theatre that immediately preceded it.

We will point out threads that seem to be woven through several periods and several countries. For instance, domestic comedies began with Greek New Comedy in the third century B.C.E., were continued by Roman writers in the centuries that followed, were picked up by playwrights in Europe in the Renaissance, and have persisted to the present time on the stage, in films, and as situation comedies on television.

In presenting theatre history, we will, for the most part, take what is often called a *positivist* or *narrative* approach, which suggests that history can be explained logically, chronicled objectively, and reconstructed. In *Living Theatre,* we attempt to describe what has happened; to relate the present to the past and show how it might have an impact on the future; to look in depth at the people who have created theatre by perfecting traditional forms or developing new ones; and to look at the full range of theatrical activity—not just dramatic literature, but every aspect of theatrical production, including performance, scene design, and theatre architecture. In order to present this chronicle, we will have to develop a historical narrative.

(Staatliche Antikensammlungen und Glyptothek, Munich)

RESOURCES FOR THEATRE HISTORY
Theatre historians use a variety of sources in attempting to establish the nature of theatres from the past. For classic Greek theatre, for example, one resource is vase paintings. Shown here is a vase depicting the story of Medea. In the lower part is Medea. In the upper part, King Creon laments the death of his daughter, Creusa, whom Medea has killed. From such visual material we learn about costumes, props, and perhaps even the way in which plays were staged.

However, before moving into this chronicle we will note some recent developments and departures in the way theatre history is studied and taught, since in the course of this book we will frequently find it appropriate to call attention to these trends.

Recent Historical Approaches

How theatre history is studied and analyzed, a discipline known as *theatre historiography,* has become a particular concern of certain scholars. In addition, some scholars study *metahistory. Meta* is a Greek term that means "beyond" or "after."

Metahistory is the study of how and why scholars create their historic narratives; it forces us to recognize that history can never be completely objective.

Many contemporary historians argue that there have been fallacies in the traditional representation of history that need to be rectified. These historians remind us that all history is constructed—that is, created by scholars with their own points of view. They warn us that there have been *erasures* of certain peoples and groups by historians who represent majority viewpoints. They argue that such historical errors are a result of flawed methodologies or flawed approaches. They particularly disagree with attempts to create a linear presentation focusing on cause and effect. An example of linear development would be church drama in the Middle Ages leading directly to medieval theatre, and medieval theatre in turn leading directly to the Renaissance theatre of England and Spain. To clarify many of the scholarly debates that we will discuss later in this text, we need to point out some of the new approaches to studying theatre history.

Revisionist Historians

Revisionist historians stress that history has usually been told from the point of view of a social elite; they also suggest that significant "mainstream" phenomena have been ignored because historians focus on what is revolutionary. For example, in

(© Donald Cooper/Photo*stage*, England)

APPROACHES TO THEATRE HISTORY: GENDER STUDIES

Among the many new ways of studying theatre, one involves a reappraisal of gender, feminism, cross-dressing, and similar topics. Cross-dressing might range from Elizabethan theater, in which boys played female roles, to modern theatre. One recent example is Shakespeare's *Richard III,* directed by Barry Kyle with an all-female cast at the Globe in London. Here we see Kathryn Hunter as Richard III and Amanda Harris as Buckingham.

theatre history popular entertainments are frequently disregarded as unworthy of study; only in recent times has there been significant scholarly examination of the popular arts.

Revisionists also force us to revise our usual analysis of historical documents and sources, frequently pointing out misreadings resulting from cultural and social biases. The trend toward revisionism has led to reevaluating the place of women and minorities, for example, in the theatre.

In recent years, the term *revisionism* has taken on a negative connotation, because of its association with racist theorists who call into question the genocide of Jews by Nazi Germany during World War II and who are referred to as "Holocaust revisionists." Of course, these authors are not true revisionists; actual revisionists are knowledgeable historians questioning how history has been presented, but the Holocaust revisionists call into question irrefutable historic events in order to further their racist point of view. Similarly, other so-called revisionists have doubted the injustices of American slavery in the eighteenth and nineteenth centuries.

In this volume we are not concerned with such negative applications of revisionism, where clear, indisputable facts of history are distorted or denied to fit a political agenda. Rather, we focus on the positive approaches of revisionist history. A good example is the work of feminist historians.

Feminist Historians

Feminist historians, for example, are revisionists who argue that the place of women in theatre history has not been carefully explored. They assert that women have been "invisible" in male-centered history and that a reevaluation of history, with a focus on the role of women, is needed.

Feminist historians rediscover women who have been ignored in historic chronicles. These historians also analyze differing feminist approaches to representation and theatrical creation. The work of such historian-theorists as Sue-Ellen Case and Jill Dolan focuses on reading past texts in light of feminist theory, rediscovering marginalized female figures, and examining unique feminist approaches to dramatic structure and representation.

Deconstructionists

Deconstructionists argue that history is written and taught by people in power and therefore needs to be analyzed in terms of who is empowered by history and who is not. The deconstructionists oppose the concept of linear development; instead, they often see history as a series of ruptures. They argue against the traditional evolutionary or cause-and-effect approach to historical events.

To provide a simple example, we can review the geographical history of New York theatres. Positivist historians have pointed to the constant movement of theatres in Manhattan farther uptown, or north, during the nineteenth and twentieth centuries. However, a deconstructionist would point out a number of examples of theatres that developed downtown, even after the majority of New York playhouses were already in midtown.

Deconstructionists have greatly influenced feminist, multicultural, and gay and lesbian historians, who argue that history has been written from the majority perspective of our society and thus ignores the accomplishments of underrepresented groups.

(George Karger/Pix Inc./Time Life Pictures/Getty Images)

MULTICULTURALISM IN THEATRE HISTORY
An important aspect of theatre history is multiculturalism—a fresh look at groups that were not focused on in the past. Examples are Native Americans, Asian Americans, Hispanics, and African Americans. For instance, black stage actors in the nineteenth and twentieth centuries in the United States were often not given the attention they deserved. Shown here is the actress Ethel Waters (center), who finally emerged as a Broadway star in both musicals and straight plays. The scene here is from the musical *Cabin in the Sky* in 1943.

Multicultural Historians

Multicultural historians focus on groups that have been underrepresented in the course of history. For example, in theatre history they emphasize the contributions of Asian Americans, American Indians, African Americans, and Latino-Latina Americans to contemporary American theatre. In addition, they review the ideological and political perspectives of these marginalized groups.

Recent examples include reexamination of the careers of such notable African American figures as the author, director, and theatre educator Owen Dodson and the performer Ethel Waters. Theatrical works by the diverse American Indian, Latino-Latina American, and Asian American populations have received more significant attention. In addition, multicultural historians often argue that there are unique approaches to theatrical arts within these cultures, because of their histories and their interactions with the majority society.

Gay and Lesbian Theatre Historians

Gay and lesbian theatre historians have reevaluated the place of gays and lesbians in theatre history as well as the influence of their sexual orientation on theatrical representation and creation. Furthermore, these historians also review the marginalization of gay and lesbian sensibilities by the majority theatre.

A study of the lesbian actress and director Eva Le Gallienne and the impact of her sexual orientation is an example of such historiography. Historians have also reviewed the portrayal of gays and lesbians in drama throughout theatre history as well as theatrical works created by gay and lesbian artists.

Semioticians and Iconographic Historians

Semioticians argue that theatre historians should focus on the response of audiences to the various elements of a production, which function as signs and thus have inherent meaning for the viewer. They believe that performance has been undervalued in the study of theatre history and that there has been too much emphasis on the literary text and on descriptions of individual elements of theatre—descriptions that fail to take audiences' reactions into account.

Semioticians are primarily interested in audiences' responses to the elements of theatrical events—much as contemporary literary analysts have become interested in the multiplicity of readers' responses to literary texts. All audience members react to scenery, costumes, and acting; however, few historians have discussed the impact of these elements on audiences during important historical periods.

Semioticians also ask what various elements signify to the audience. For example, in discussing theatre architecture historians have almost never described lobby spaces. Yet a lobby often reveals characteristics of an audience and the nature of a theatrical event. Contrasting the rough, tiny lobbies of off-off-Broadway theatre spaces in New York with the spacious, luxurious lobbies of new, large arts complexes in some other American cities clearly underlines differences in their productions and their audiences.

The term *iconography* is Greek in origin and means image writing. Historians who are interested in the iconography of the theatre are those who review the symbolic meaning of the various theatrical elements. These can be as obvious as scenery or costumes or as overlooked as programs, playbills, or statuary in theatre spaces. Iconographists read those meanings in relationship to contemporary society and to the theatrical event itself.

Marxist and Class-Oriented Historians

Marxist and class-oriented historians focus on how theatre reflects economic and political oppression. These historians are interested in *hegemonic theory,* that is, how historic phenomena reflect power structures in a given society. For example, a number of theatre historians have explored how past audiences and their experiences reflect class and issues of political power.

Marxist historians and class-oriented historians explore how the profit motive and capitalism affect the theatrical arts. Class-oriented historians review how certain classes were privileged and others excluded from the theatre in different societies. They often examine how theatre artists broke class boundaries.

There are, of course, still other recent approaches to theatre history. Furthermore, theatre history and historiography have been greatly influenced by new approaches in literary theory, anthropology, cultural studies, and media studies. We should also note that the approaches just described are not mutually exclusive. Feminist historians, for instance, frequently acknowledge the influence of the deconstructionists and the semioticians.

One further comment: there are historians who argue that theatre history is an outdated construct and that a more appropriate new focus is performance studies.

The idea of performance studies is that we should examine the histories and theories of all that is performative in past and current societies and not limit ourselves just to the study of the theatrical arts.

In this text, we will try to point out areas in which theatre historians disagree as well as the points on which they agree. We will attempt to illustrate some of the current debates engendered by these new approaches to the study of theatre history. We will also spend time in each chapter reviewing key issues connected to either multiculturism or gender, in order to highlight some contemporary views of theatre history. In this process, we hope to convey the complexity of theatre history and the way in which our understanding of the past is still evolving.

Why Study Theatre History?

Why should we study theatre history? In most universities, theatre history is a requirement for students who are hoping to become theatre practitioners. In some schools, it is part of the general education requirement for all students. Yet few students ask why this requirement is appropriate or what purpose it serves.

Theatre history is a discipline that serves a multitude of functions. To begin with, it can help future professionals understand their artistic heritage. Theatre history also presents techniques, conventions, and ideas which can be borrowed by contemporary practitioners. We will see, in our discussion of modern theatre, how often contemporary artists adapt historic conventions to create productions that speak to their own audiences. We should note that this is different from re-creating historically accurate productions—another possible use of theatre history.

If theatre is a reflection of its society, then theatre history can also give us insights into societies of the past. We can learn significant information about the major issues and concerns of a historical period by studying its theatre; we can learn about the conventions and norms of a society by analyzing its theatrical presentations.

Theatre history is also an exciting and unique discipline worthy of study purely for the sake of scholarly exploration. Because theatre is an ephemeral art, theatre history is immensely difficult to study. But this difficulty leads to exciting debates and constant reevaluation. Like the art form it tries to examine, theatre history itself—as we noted when discussing the various approaches to theatre historiography—is constantly being reexamined.

How Do Scholars Study Theatre History?

Theatre historians take a variety of approaches in developing their studies. Most traditional historians begin by raising a specific issue or focusing on a specific subject. They are trying to answer a specific question, such as: What types of scenery did classical Greek theatre use? Or: What was acting like during the English Restoration? Sometimes they are researching a specific topic, such as the biography of Ira Aldridge, the nineteenth-century African American actor.

In recent years, theatre historians have taken a more theoretical approach to constructing history. These historians pose a hypothesis, or make an educated guess, about a theatrical phenomenon and then set out to prove it. Frequently they use theoretical points of view regarding the hypothesis they are exploring to place the theatrical phenomenon within a broader historical or theoretical context. These contemporary historians do not believe that it is enough simply to present facts or historical chronicles. Theoretical analysis is also necessary. For example, the November 2004 issue of *Theatre Survey,* published by the American Society for Theatre Research (a learned organization of theatre historians), was entitled "Theatre History in the New Millennium" and contained many essays dealing with the problems related to theatre historiography and writing theatre history.

In order to write theatre history, the theatre historian must, of course, do arduous research. The historian must scour primary sources—that is, original documents from the time period that he or she is studying. Historians must also examine secondary works that touch on their topics. Secondary works are those written by earlier historians who have already done primary research.

Theatre historians are trying either to discover new phenomena that have not received previous historic attention or to provide new insights into phenomena already studied. For example, one of the authors of this textbook published an article on American radio plays written during World War II that touched on the Jewish Holocaust. The article served two purposes. One was to explore a previously ignored topic: these World War II–era radio plays. The other was to prove a hypothesis: that the United States was aware of what was happening to Europe's Jewish population but chose to ignore it.

Where Do Theatre Historians Present Their Work?

Historians present their works in many scholarly journals. These journals are published to share new knowledge with other scholars as well as to make the information available to interested wider audiences. The best-known scholarly journals that publish articles dealing with theatre history are *Theatre Journal, Theatre Survey, Theatre History Studies, Journal of American Drama and Theatre, Nineteenth-Century Theatre Research, Restoration and Eighteenth-Century Theatre Research, Theatre Research International, Theatre Notebook, Latin American Theatre Review, Modern Drama,* and *Women and Peformance.* Of course, theatre historians also publish in journals that are connected to other scholarly organizations and disciplines, such as *Journal of Popular Culture, Journal of the Modern Language Association,* and journals dedicated to the study of Shakespeare.

Theatre historians also belong to many professional organizations, which organize conferences where theatre scholars present their most recent research. Among the national organizations are the Association for Theatre in Higher Education, the American Society for Theatre Research, and the Mid-America Theatre Conference. In addition, theatre scholars present their work at the conventions of the Popular Culture Association and the Modern Language Association, to name just two. In most instances, it is these scholarly organizations that publish the journals mentioned above.

Many theatre historians publish full-length studies with academic and scholarly presses. Among the best-known are Routledge, Palgrave/St. Martin's, Cambridge University Press, University of Iowa Press, University of Michigan Press, Johns Hopkins University Press, and University of Indiana Press.

Theatre in History: Points to Remember

Living Theatre is a journey, an exploration of the theatres of the past that form a rich heritage—the many kinds of theatre experience open to us today. As we begin this adventure, we should make a few additional observations.

First, anyone studying theatre history tends to focus on periods when theatre reached a high point: the Renaissance in Europe, for example, when theatre architecture and scene design were revolutionized in Italy and a form of improvisatory theatre—commedia dell'arte—was perfected; and when there was an outpouring of inspired drama in Spain and England. It is important to remember, though, that there are significant accomplishments in the years that precede and follow such achievements, and also that a great deal of other theatre activity surrounds them. In the Renaissance, other playwrights were active and countless productions were taking place which we do not have time or space to document.

Also, there are frequently lengthy periods between high points when few new developments occur in scene design, playwriting, or acting; but theatrical activity at these times does not cease—it may, in fact, be vigorous. We tend not to focus on periods between high points, because we place such a premium on the innovative and the new. Similarly, what of those countries where there is a lively theatre but no playwright who enters the history books as a pioneer? Those countries should not be ignored; but again, because of limited time and space, they are not always given their full due. The key point to remember is that when historians highlight certain countries during certain periods, this does not mean that theatre did not exist before or after those periods, or in other places at the same time.

Second, it is important to keep in mind that the theatre achievements we discuss in *Living Theatre* are only a small part of what actually happened. For instance, during the fifth century B.C.E. in Greece, approximately 900 tragedies were produced at the City Dionysia festival held each spring in Athens—three tragedies by each of three dramatists each year. But today we have only a small sampling: 7 plays by Aeschylus, who we believe wrote about 90 plays; 7 out of perhaps 125 plays by Sophocles; and 18 out of about 90 plays by Euripides. That is a total of 32 plays out of 900; thus the sample we have is far from offering a complete picture. The same would be true of any other historical period, such as English, Spanish, and French theatres during the Renaissance: we have only a small percentage of the plays that were written then.

Moreover, we often have little or no idea of the acting styles of earlier periods. We do not know, for instance, what the singing or dancing of Greek choruses was like. Nor do we know what acting styles were characteristic when Sanskrit drama in India was in its golden age. For that matter, we are not at all certain about performance styles in the theatre of Shakespeare or Molière.

It should be remembered, too, that although we present theatre as if it were a constant activity, there are times and places where little formal theatre exists. There are also periods when theatre appears to have remained somewhat the same over many years. The first comedies of the Roman playwright Plautus were presented in the third century B.C.E., and Roman comedy was altered by Terence half a century later; but thereafter, we assume that a similar type of comedy was the mainstay of Roman theatre for the next 500 years. What happened during that time? Did comic acting change? Did playwriting change? Were there major alterations in acting styles and dramatic composition, or only minor shifts? We do not know. But if we assume 500 years of a fairly stable form of theatre, we have a situation drastically different from the 500 years from 1500 to 2000 C.E., during which a continual series of shifts, innovations, and mutations has occurred.

Third, we should keep in mind that commentators designate specific achievements from the past—in playwriting, acting, stage design, or some other aspect of theatre—as outstanding. But we must pause on the word *outstanding*. These judgments were made by observers in the last part of the twentieth century and at the beginning of the twenty-first. Plays and performers we now consider exceptional may not have been considered so in their own day, or in some subsequent period.

To take one example, Georg Büchner, a young playwright in Germany in the early nineteenth century, wrote two plays and fragments of a third that were not considered particularly noteworthy when they first appeared and were not even performed until after 1900. In the twentieth century, though, Büchner's plays were rediscovered and produced frequently; people in the twentieth century felt that these plays—*Danton's Death, Leonce and Lena,* and *Woyzeck*—speak to the alienation and pessimism of the modern world. We say of Büchner that he was "ahead of his time," that he anticipated the future. But which judgment is correct—the judgment of the early nineteenth century, when the plays were written but never produced; or that of the late twentieth century, when they were applauded? And what will be the judgment at the end of the twenty-first century?

In contrast, of course, theatre history is replete with examples of plays that were praised in their own day but later came to be considered dated or out of fashion: certain nineteenth-century melodramas such as *Uncle Tom's Cabin* are examples. In addition, racial minorities and women were often overlooked or forgotten as critics created what is known as the *canon* of outstanding works.

Not only plays but styles of acting as well are viewed quite differently in different periods. Approaches to acting that are praised in one period may be damned in another. During the twentieth century, notions of what constitutes outstanding acting moved from a more formal approach early in the century, to emphasis on earthy psychological realism in midcentury, and back to an appreciation of eloquent speech and graceful stage movements toward the end of the century.

The point here is that no judgment is final or definitive. Each age has its own standards of excellence, its own yardstick for measuring theatre, and its own biases. When we point out that certain plays or playwrights are superior, or that specific performers in the past were exemplary, we are presenting the consensus of today's scholars and commentators. We are looking at events and accomplishments through the lens and with the biases of the early twenty-first century. The assessment half a century from now may be different.

Fourth, a key factor to be considered is the audience for which theatre is intended. Once again, there is no uniformity from one period to another. In some ages and places, theatre has been strictly for royalty or the upper classes. This was true of the theatres that emerged in ancient India and China and of theatre in England during the Restoration of the late sixteenth century. At other times, however, theatre has been for mass audiences. Two examples are the medieval period, when plays depicting scenes from the Bible were presented to everyone in a town and the surrounding countryside; and the nineteenth century in England and the United States, when theatre was embraced by a broad spectrum of the middle class.

Fifth and finally, it is important to realize that in different places and at different times, different aspects of theatre have been treasured. In some eras comedy has been the most highly valued form; in other eras, tragedy. There have also been periods when neither form was valued as highly as melodrama. Equally significant is whether written drama—the script itself—was of paramount importance, rather than acting or scenic spectacle. During certain ages, the emphasis is not on playwriting or new drama, but on how plays are interpreted. At other times, neither text nor performance is paramount, but rather the visual splendor of the scenery, lighting, and costumes.

Now that we have called attention to some perspectives on theatre history, we are ready to begin the journey: to strike out and look at the numerous manifestations of theatre which have surfaced through the ages and of which we are the fortunate inheritors today.

SUMMARY

Today's vast variety of theatre experiences has its roots in 2,500 years of western theatre and nearly 2,000 years of Asian theatre.

Many everyday personal and communal human activities—imitation, role playing, storytelling, popular entertainments, ceremonies and rituals, and "participatory theatre" such as psychodrama and sociodrama—have a theatrical component. Though religious ceremonies and rituals have striking theatrical aspects, they differ from theatre in at least two important ways: they are meant to be efficacious, and they emphasize group sharing—audience participation and collective creativity. One significant aspect of theatre is prohibitions against it, as in ancient Judaism and Islam.

The subject of this text is theatre where it has emerged as a separate art form. Elements of theatre—characteristics by which we identify it—are a playing space, an audience, performers, visual elements (scenery, lighting, and costumes), texts, and coordination of these elements. In addition, there are social requirements for theatre: tradition, social structure, and population centers.

While much of this text takes a positivist approach to theatre history, references will be made to other approaches such as revisionism, feminism, deconstructionism, and multiculturalism. Theatre history as a discipline serves a number of functions but is also intrinsically valuable.

In beginning a study of theatre history, it is important to bear several points in mind. Although theatre history focuses on "high points," this does not mean that theatre did not exist between high points; and what theatre history takes up is only a part of what actually happened. Also, there are differences between cultures with regard to judgments of what is "superior" in theatre, the intended audience for theatre, and which aspects of theatre are most highly valued.

Part One | Early Theatres

The theatres we refer to as *early theatres*—Greek, Roman, Asian, and medieval—actually cover a period of nearly 2,000 years: from Greek theatre in the fifth century B.C.E. through medieval theatre, which began 1,500 years later; and from Indian and Chinese theatres, which came to flower, respectively, in the fourth and seventh centuries C.E., to the emergence of Japanese theatre.

In western theatre—that is, in Greece, Rome, and medieval Europe—this is a long time span to encompass the beginnings of theatre. But it is important to remember that in Europe, for nearly 1,000 years—from the declining years of the Roman empire until the emergence of medieval theatre—there was no formal theatre: in the Middle Ages, theatre had to begin all over again. It was also during this thousand-year period that Indian and Chinese theatre began.

The Greek, Roman, and medieval theatres can legitimately be called *early theatres* because they established the foundations on which all subsequent western theatre was built. Not only in theatre, but in virtually every area of life, these cultures formed the basis of western civilization. Their accomplishments are monumental: the classical Greeks developed democracy, philosophy, the study of science and mathematics, and architecture; the Romans were great conquerors, architects, and lawmakers; the medieval Europeans organized methods of farming and established trade guilds.

We do not want to oversimplify the relationship among the theatres of these three societies, but there are important common elements. One is the significant connection in all three between theatre and religious and civic celebrations. It is often argued that the roots of theatre lie in religious rituals, and this seems to be substantiated by the initial connection between Greek theatre and the rites honoring the god Dionysus, the relation between Roman theatre and the festival of Jupiter (Zeus), and the close tie between medieval theatre and the Roman Catholic church. At the same time, a strong secular element permeated all three theatres; there was a desire to treat human as well as religious subjects. This is the natural development of theatre in any society; when theatre becomes an art form on its own, it concentrates on human problems and aspirations.

Another common element is that in each of these cultures, theatre was a significant civic and social event. This is reflected in the huge open-air theatres of Greece and Rome as well as in the spectacular outdoor medieval stage settings. We have large outdoor theatres today—for summer Shakespeare festivals and rock concerts, among other events—but in these earlier societies a large proportion of the population became involved in theatre to a degree that has never been equaled in modern times.

In Asia, the theatres of India, China, and Japan reached a high point of artistic achievement when religion and philosophy were also central in each culture. This level of excellence kept traditional theatre allied to religion and philosophy even when society changed and became more secular. Like culture in the west, the great Asian civilizations we will consider became the foundations for later societies.

As we begin to survey these early theatres, we should remember how much of their drama has survived and is still performed in our own day. Greek tragedies and comedies are still produced; plays of the Roman dramatist Plautus have been adapted as Broadway musicals; and there are modern versions of the medieval morality play *Everyman*. In Japan, the traditional theatres, such as nō, bunraku, and kabuki, are kept alive even today, and there is an almost unbroken line from past to present.

In Part One, as we explore theatre from its origins to a time several centuries later, we should not view it as a remote activity; rather, we should search for elements that continue to be part of our theatre today.

Bacchai, a new version of *The Bacchae* by Euripides, directed by Peter Hall. Left to right: William Houston (Agave), Greg Hicks (Dionysus), and David Ryall (Cadmus). Lighting by Peter Mumford; National Theatre, London, 2002.

CHAPTER 1

Greek Theatre

Western Drama Begins

The roots of western theatre can be found in the fifth century B.C.E. in Athens, Greece. This is where playwriting, acting, and theatre production began. The works of Aeschylus, Sophocles, and Euripides were presented in the Theatre of Dionysus, where a good percentage of the population attended theatre festivals each year. One of the plays from that period is *Hecuba* by Euripides. Shown here is the British actress Vanessa Redgrave as the title character in a production of *Hecuba* by the Royal Shakespeare Company at the Brooklyn Academy of Music.

(© Richard Termine)

Background: The Golden Age of Greece

There are times in history when many elements come together to create a remarkable age. Such a time was the fifth century B.C.E. in Athens, Greece, when there were outstanding achievements in politics, philosophy, science, and the arts. As a part of this culture, western theatre was born.

A number of events had prepared the way. Long before 500 B.C.E., impressive civilizations had developed around the eastern part of the Mediterranean Sea: in Egypt, in Persia (which included present-day Iran, Iraq, Turkey, and other countries), and in Greece. Advances had been made in art—in pottery, for example, and in the performance of elaborate ceremonies such as the one at Abydos in Egypt—as well as in science, astronomy, and mathematics. Athens carried this tradition forward.

Greece at this time was not an empire or even a united country but a series of independent city-states occupying parts of the Greek peninsula and nearby islands: at the start of the fifth century B.C.E., the most important city-state was Athens. Early in the century the Persians had attempted to conquer the Greeks, but in 490 B.C.E., the Greeks had won a decisive battle against them at Marathon. Later in the century—from 431 to 404 B.C.E.—there was a costly conflict between Athens and Sparta known as the Peloponnesian Wars. Between these two events, however, Athens enjoyed a period of remarkable achievements—a time known as the *classical period* and also as the *golden age* of Greece. There are good reasons for calling it a "golden age," because there were important accomplishments in so many fields.

Athens is credited, for example, with being the birthplace of democracy. In 510 B.C.E., the rulers of Athens established a democracy of free citizens, which means that all male citizens—men who were not slaves or of non-Athenian origin—were given a voice in politics and government. Though there were slaves in Athens, and women were subservient, it should be remembered that the United States, also founded on democratic ideals, once suffered from similar limitations: slavery was not abolished until 1865, and women could not vote until 1920. Despite these drawbacks in ancient Athens, it was an admirable achievement to establish democracy for such a large portion of the population.

There were advances in other areas as well. Greek philosophers, such as Socrates and Plato, tried to explain the world around them; and Herodotus transformed history into a social science. A number of important scientific discoveries were made: the Greek mathematician Pythagoras formulated a theory that remains one of the cornerstones of geometry, and the physician's oath written by Hippocrates is the one still taken by doctors. The classical Greeks were also remarkable artists and architects: Greek sculpture from this period is found in museums around the world, and the Parthenon, the temple on the Acropolis, has withstood time and natural catastrophes—its columns and proportions remain models for architects even today. Obviously, this was a time conducive to developments in many fields, and one of the most significant was theatre.

Origins: Greek Theatre Emerges

Theatre is a complex art that requires the coming together of many elements: a story to be told, a dramatization of the story (the script by the playwright), a meeting place for performances, performers to enact the drama, costumes for the performers, some form of stage, perhaps scenery, and an audience for the performance.

In different ways, these elements had been developing in Athens before the fifth century B.C.E. Important forerunners of theatre in Greece were religious ceremonies, which were a prominent feature of Greek society: funeral services, festivals celebrating the seasons, and ceremonies honoring the gods.

GREECE
YEAR, B.C.E.

Theater	Year	Culture and Politics
	800	Age of Homer (800 B.C.E.)
Arion, harpist and poet, develops the dithyramb (c. 600 B.C.E.)	600	
		Thales of Miletus begins natural philosophy (physics) (c. 585 B.C.E.)
	575	
		Peisistratus, tyrant of Athens (560 B.C.E.)
Thespis, supposedly first "actor" in dithyramb (mid–sixth century)	555	
Play contests begin in Athens (534 B.C.E.)		
	525	Pythagoras flourishes; Doric temples of southern Italy and Sicily (c. 525 B.C.E.)
		Athenian democracy (510 B.C.E.)
Comedy introduced to City Dionysia (c. 486 B.C.E.)	500	Pindar begins to write odes (500 B.C.E.)
Aeschylus introduces second actor (c. 471 B.C.E.)		Persian Wars (499–478 B.C.E.)
		Battle of Marathon (490 B.C.E.)
Sophocles introduces third actor (c. 468 B.C.E.)	475	Socrates born (470 B.C.E.)
		Pericles begins rise to power: age of Pericles (462–429 B.C.E.)
Aeschylus's *Oresteia;* introduction of *skene* (458 B.C.E.)	450	Hippocrates born (460 B.C.E.)
Prizes awarded for tragic acting (449 B.C.E.)		Beginning of Parthenon; Herodotus flourishes (447 B.C.E.)
Dramatic activities incorporated into Lenaia (c. 442 B.C.E.)		Phidias dies (500–435 B.C.E.)
Sophocles's *King Oedipus* (c. 430 B.C.E.)	425	Peloponnesian Wars (431–404 B.C.E.)
		Athenian fleet destroyed (404 B.C.E.)
Euripides's *Trojan Women* (415 B.C.E.)		Spartan hegemony begins (404 B.C.E.)
Aristophanes's *Lysistrata* (411 B.C.E.)	400	Trial and execution of Socrates (399 B.C.E.)
		Aristotle born (384–322 B.C.E.)
	375	Plato's *Republic* (c. 375 B.C.E.)
		Spartan hegemony ends (404–371 B.C.E.)
		Theban hegemony ends (371–362 B.C.E.)
	350	Philip II, king of Macedonia (352 B.C.E.)
Professional actors replace amateurs at City Dionysia (c. 350 B.C.E.)		Alexander succeeds Philip II; in 335 B.C.E. occupies Greece
Aristotle's *Poetics* (c. 335–323 B.C.E.)	325	Hellenistic culture spreads throughout eastern Mediterranean (c. 320 B.C.E.)
Theater of Dionysus completed (c. 325 B.C.E.)		
From this period to c. 100 B.C.E., Greek theatres built throughout Mediterranean (320 B.C.E.)	300	
Menander's *Dyskolos* (316 B.C.E.)		
Artists of Dionysus recognized (277 B.C.E.)	275

Of particular significance to theatre were the ceremonies honoring Dionysus, the god of wine, fertility, and revelry; later Greek drama was presented in honor of Dionysus, and a number of historians, though not all, believe that Greek drama originated in the dithyrambic choruses presented to honor Dionysus. *The dithyramb* was a long hymn, sung and danced by a group of fifty men. Its format may have been similar to a modern-day choral presentation: the leader of the chorus recited

THE WORLD OF CLASSICAL GREECE
Greece was divided into a number of city-states. During the fifth century B.C.E., Athens (near the center of the map) was the most powerful of these. It was during this period that Greek drama was first performed at the City Dionysia and other festivals and reached a high point of development. Other cities important to Greek drama are Thebes (northwest of Athens), where the mythical events surrounding Oedipus and his family took place; and Delphi (northwest of Thebes), the site of an oracle visited by the Greeks and referred to in several plays. On the Hellespont (to the northeast) is the legendary city of Troy; the Trojan War figures prominently in plays about Agamemnon and others. Sparta (southwest of Athens, on the Peloponnesus) is the city that finally conquered Athens, at the end of the Peloponnesian Wars in 404 B.C.E.

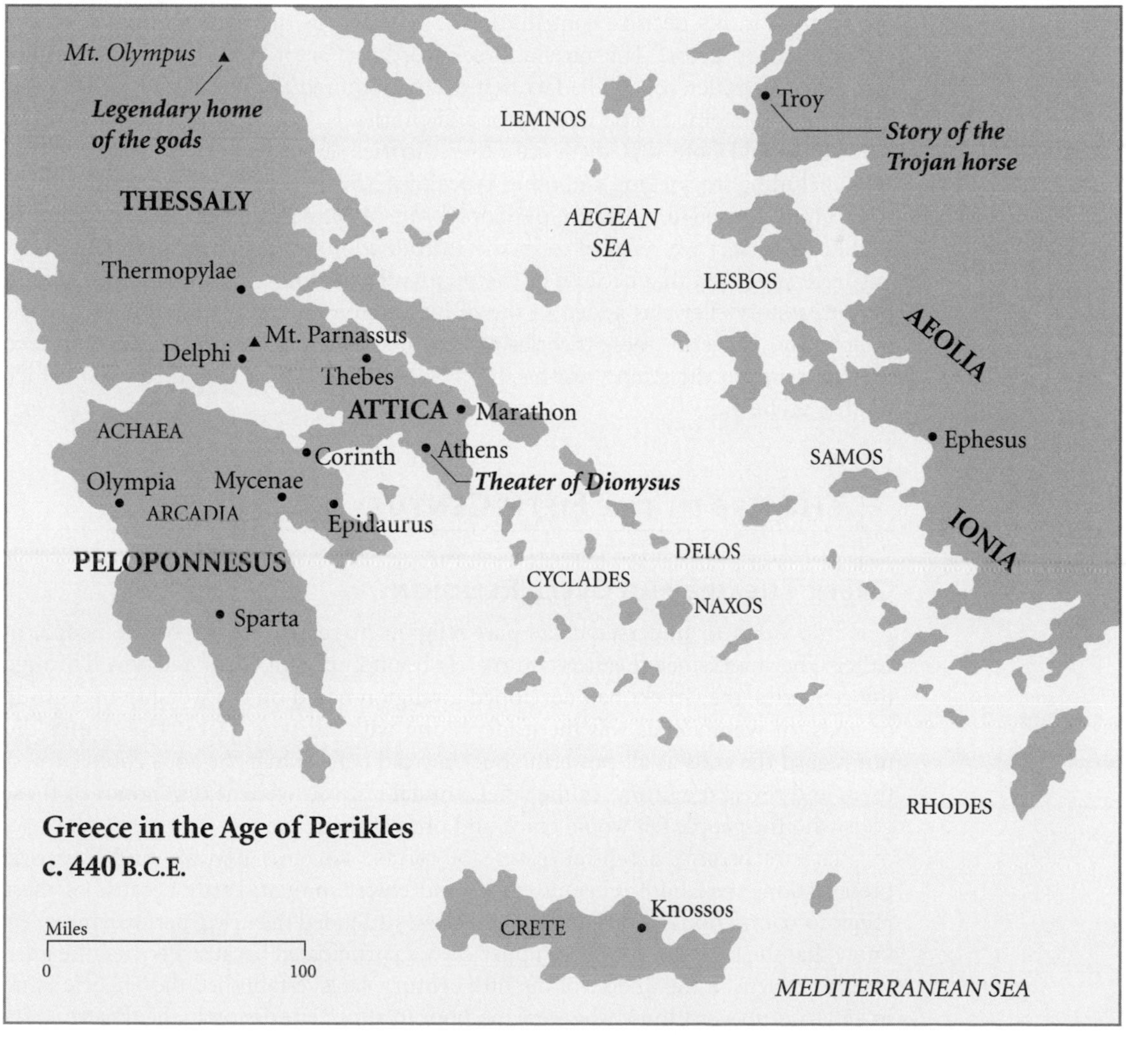

or sang an improvised story while the other members sang a popular refrain. By about 600 B.C.E., the dithyramb became a literary form, detailing heroic stories.

Arion, a talented harpist and poet who had been born in Lesbos but lived in Corinth at the end of the seventh century and the beginning of the sixth century B.C.E., is thought to have been an influential figure in the development of the dithyramb. According to the historian Herodotus, Arion made significant changes in the dithyramb and moved it toward a dramatic form by interspersing spoken sections with the musical portions; these spoken segments were supposedly more dramatic than the songs.

Even more than Arion, a performer named Thespis, in the sixth century B.C.E., is customarily credited with transforming the dithyramb into tragedy by stepping out of the dithyrambic chorus and becoming an actor. Thespis delivered a prologue and presented dialogue that required him to impersonate a character: thus a purely narrative or storytelling form became a dramatic form in which characters exchanged lines. Thespis is said to have been the first writer of tragedy as well as the first actor; his decisive contribution is reflected in the modern term *thespian*, a synonym for "actor." The ancient Greek word for "actor" was *hypokrite*—literally, "answerer"—underscoring the fact that drama required the verbal give-and-take of dialogue and interaction between actor and chorus.

We should note that there are other theories about the origin of Greek theatre, including storytelling and other types of performance. The Greek philosopher Aristotle suggested that theatre developed out of human beings' natural desire to imitate, a subject we referred to in the Introduction. Some contemporary historians have suggested that because of the popularity of storytellers before the classical period, a storyteller was added to the dithyrambic presentation, creating dramatic interaction. However, these theories are not necessarily mutually exclusive; in fact, they all point to the strong relationship between Greek theatre and religion, which we discuss below.

Theatre in the Fifth Century B.C.E.

Greek Theatre and Greek Religion

It is important to understand the part religion played in the life of the people of Athens, because Greek theatre is intimately bound up with Greek religion. Through the centuries, the Greeks had developed a religion based on the worship of a group of gods, of whom Zeus was the leader along with his wife, Hera. The Greeks did not regard the gods as all-powerful, but they did believe that the gods could protect them and reveal the future. In the cities, annual festivals were held in honor of those gods who the people felt would guide and protect them.

Theatre became a central feature of certain religious festivals, and theatrical presentations were both religious events and entertainment. Partly because of these religious connections, people of all social classes attended theatrical performances. We know that the lower as well as the upper classes participated because Pericles, the great ruler of Athens in the middle of the fifth century B.C.E., established the Theoric Fund in 450 B.C.E. to assist those who were too poor to afford admission to the theatre.

(© Michael Nicholson/Corbis)

THE THEATRE OF DIONYSUS

The theatre where the plays of Aeschylus, Sophocles, Euripides, and all the early Greek dramatists were first performed was the Theatre of Dionysus in Athens. It had semicircular seating cut into a hillside, surrounding a circular orchestra, with a wooden stage area at the rear. Today remnants of a later version of the theatre (with stone seats replacing the original wooden ones) remain on the same site in Athens.

Festivals and the City Dionysia

The significance of the "religious-theatrical" event in Greek society gave theatre a far more important place than it occupies in our society. Business came to a standstill during dramatic festivals; wars ceased; political concerns were ignored. Today, certain televised events—such as the Super Bowl and the election returns after a presidential race—attract the attention of millions of Americans. But the total cessation of a society's activities for religious purposes, as practiced by the Greeks, has no present-day equivalent; moreover, obviously, the Greeks attended their festivals in person as opposed to watching them on a television screen.

One festival in particular became important for theatre in Athens. This was the *City Dionysia*, a festival honoring the god Dionysus. The City Dionysia was a signal event in Athens; it was held toward the end of March, when spring had arrived and the port near Athens, which was closed for the winter, had reopened and visitors began pouring into the city. This was also the season when trees and flowers began to come to life again. In 534 B.C.E., tragedy was incorporated into the City Dionysia, and by 486 B.C.E., two other forms of drama—comedy and the satyr play—had been added. (The *satyr play,* a brief comic parody, discussed below, was added in 501 B.C.E.)

The City Dionysia in Athens lasted for several days. Before the opening of the festival, all the major theatrical participants paraded and appeared in the *proagon,* a preliminary presentation designed to advertise and provide information about the coming plays. On one or two other days, there were parades and sacrifices honoring Dionysus. Five days were then assigned to dithyrambs and plays. On two of these days, ten dithyrambic choruses were presented: probably, one day was assigned to choruses made up of men and one day to choruses of boys. Three days were allotted to tragedies and satyr plays, with three tragedies and one satyr play by a single playwright being presented each day; these four plays by one dramatist were called a *tetralogy.*

There has been considerable debate over when the comedies, which were added to the City Dionysia c. 486 B.C.E., were staged. At one time, historians believed that a separate day of the festival was devoted to five comedies, each by a different playwright. Some scholars now suggest that a comedy was added on the five days in which dithyrambs and tragedies were performed.

A few days after the festival, awards were given, the festival operation was reviewed by a representative body, and people who had behaved improperly or disrespectfully were judged and penalized. We are told, for example, that punishment would be meted out to a festivalgoer who used violence to prevent someone else from taking a seat in the theatre or who carried a whip and struck an enemy with it while intoxicated. (Like most accounts passed down through the ages about misconduct in the theatre, these are difficult to date or prove, but they provide a flavor of the event.)

The Greeks were great proponents of competition; the Olympic Games, for example, originated during the classical era. At the end of the City Dionysia, the best tragic and comic playwrights were awarded prizes; in 449 B.C.E., the best tragic acting in the festival was also recognized with an award. (Modern counterparts are the Tony awards in theatre, the Oscars in film, and the Emmys for television.)

Since theatre was both a religious and a civic event, the organization of the dramatic presentations was undertaken by the city-state. The *archon,* an appointed government official, chose the plays 11 months before the next festival.

The archon appointed a *choregus,* the equivalent of a modern-day producer, for each of the selected playwrights. In commercial theatre today, the producer raises funds for a production. In the fifth century B.C.E., the choregus, a wealthy individual, provided the money himself and paid all major expenses connected with the chorus: rehearsals, costumes, and musicians. The city provided the theatre space, the awards, and the playwrights' and actors' salaries. While it is true that a stingy choregus could hurt a playwright's chances of winning the contest, usually the choregus would strive to produce a winner because winning was a source of great prestige. When their productions won, for example, some choregoi erected monuments in their own honor.

During the classical era, theatre became part of other festivals, though not to so great an extent as with the City Dionysia. Before the end of the fifth century B.C.E., theatrical activities were added to the Lenaia, a festival celebrated at the end of January in the city of Athens; and to the Rural Dionysia, celebrated in December by the rural areas of the Athenian city-state.

DEBATES IN THEATRE HISTORY | Did Women Attend Dramatic Festivals?

There is no way of knowing for certain if women attended the Athenian dramatic festivals in the fifth century B.C.E. The question has been debated by historians because it is known that women did not participate fully in the Greek democracy of the golden age and did not act in tragedies or comedies.

One historian of classical Greek theatre, Peter Arnott, notes in *Public and Performance in the Greek Theatre,* "It is still not certain . . . whether or not women were admitted (though it is a reasonable surmise that they were)."* J. Michael Walton, in *Greek Theatre Practice,* lists sources which argue that women were present at classical Greek performances. He cites an account by a contemporary choregus indicating that men and women were impressed by his dress for the theatre and an often-repeated tale that some women in attendance at Aeschylus's *Oresteia* suffered miscarriages.† In Aristophanes' comedy. *The Frogs,* the character of Aeschylus states, satirically, that all decent women committed suicide after seeing one of Euripides' plays; although this comical remark is obviously not to be taken literally, it does indicate that women attended the theatre. Walton suggests that women were probably segregated in separate sections in the theatre, a seating process which would have been facilitated if (as some scholars believe) tribes were also seated in distinct areas.

The question whether or not women were part of the classical Greek audience reminds us, of course, that women did not have equal status with men. Some contributions to this debate also remind us that scholars themselves have sometimes made "sexist" generalizations. For example, Victorian historians believed that Greek women could not have attended comedies because these were bawdy and sexual, but that they could attend tragedies. In many of his plays, however, Aristophanes jokes about women in attendance at performances, demonstrating the fallacy of this reasoning. Moreover, if women were present at tragedies, then they would also have been present for the satyr plays—which, as we will see, were as sexual as the early comedies.

*Routledge, London and New York, 1991, p. 5.
†Greenwood, Westport, Conn., 1980.

The concept of the Dionysian theatre festival still inspires contemporary theatre producers and directors. Various international theatre festivals, for instance, have been held in cities throughout the world. The many Shakespeare festivals held throughout the United States each year are also in the tradition of these ancient events. These modern versions are not religious festivals or contests, but the idea of regularly scheduled festivals, highlighting significant playwriting and theatrical accomplishments, is an attempt to remind audiences of the centrality of theatre in our lives and of its ability to establish a sense of community.

Greek Theatre and Greek Myths

The sources of the subject matter of most of the plays written for the festivals were Greek myths. The stories found in the myths provided the action, the characters, and the conflicts.

Along with festivals and the move from dithyrambic choruses to drama, other aspects of theatre had been developing before the fifth century B.C.E. One was the accumulation of a group of stories on which much of Greek drama, particularly tragedy, was based. In the centuries before the golden age, a number of myths had become an important part of the Greek heritage.

A *myth* is a story or legend—sometimes invented, sometimes based loosely on fact—that is handed down from generation to generation. Frequently, a myth is an attempt to explain natural and human events: the changing of the seasons, for example, or a cataclysmic occurrence like an earthquake or a civil war. Myths may also deal with extreme family situations: one branch of a family opposing another, or a difficult relationship between a husband and wife or between parents and children. In each culture, certain myths are seized on because they seem to sum up its view of human relationships and of the problems and opportunities life presents to individuals.

In Greece, there were a multitude of myths. Good examples are the poet Homer's accounts of the Greek war with the Trojans in the *Iliad* and the hero Odysseus's return from the Trojan War in the *Odyssey.* These and other myths furnished many of the stories for Greek drama, but before they could be performed at the theatre festivals, they had to be transformed by a playwright into dramatic form.

Greek Tragedy

Tragic Playwrights

The first Greek writers of whom we are aware who attempted to create dramatic pieces appeared in the sixth century B.C.E. Though their works have not survived, we know the names of a few writers, including Arion and Thespis. It was in the fifth century B.C.E. that the drama which we still read and perform took shape. The three best-known writers of Greek tragedy in this period were Aeschylus, Sophocles, and Euripides.

AESCHYLUS

Of writers whose works still exist, Aeschylus (525–456 B.C.E.) was the first to develop drama into a form separate from singing, dancing, or storytelling. For this reason he is often considered the founder of Greek drama and therefore of all western drama.

Aeschylus's plays dealt with noble families and lofty themes and were praised for their superb lyric poetry as well as their dramatic structure and intellectual content. They won a number of first prizes in the drama contests, and Aeschylus was the acknowledged master of the tetralogy—four plays that can stand separately but are united by a single story or theme. In addition, he used the chorus more extensively and more effectively than the playwrights who came after him. The power of his poetry and the majesty of his themes are often expressed most fully in the choral sections of his plays.

(Bettmann/Corbis)

Aeschylus.

Before Aeschylus, a drama would have only one actor, who interacted with the chorus. Aeschylus added a second actor; this was an important development in theatre practice, since it allowed for a true dialogue. He also reduced the size of the chorus, perhaps from fifty to twelve, making it more manageable. Later, Sophocles introduced a third actor, and Aeschylus then incorporated this new feature into his own plays. Aeschylus's theatrical work included directing and acting as well as playwriting. He was fond of theatrical spectacle and is sometimes credited with having developed new forms of stage scenery, painted scenery, and elaborate costumes.

In Aristophanes's comedy *The Frogs*, Aeschylus was caricatured as pompous and rhetorical. In the same play, however, he was also judged a dramatist superior to Euripides.

Aeschylus was born of a noble family in Eleusis, near Athens, and was highly regarded not only as a playwright and poet but also as a soldier and prominent citizen. Among his other military exploits, he fought for Athens against the Persians at the battle of Marathon in 490 B.C.E. Ten years later he served with the Athenian fleet during a second Persian invasion and was present at the important victory at Salamis. He died in 456 B.C.E. at the age of 69.

Aeschylus is believed to have written ninety plays. The titles of seventy-nine are known, indicating a diversity of subject matter. However, only seven of his plays still exist (the dates given here indicate when the plays are known or thought to have been first produced): *The Suppliants* (c. 490 B.C.E., but possibly considerably later); *The Persians* (c. 472 B.C.E.); *Seven against Thebes* (c. 469 B.C.E.); *Prometheus Bound* (c. 460 B.C.E.); and *The Oresteia* (458 B.C.E.), a trilogy consisting of *Agamemnon, The Choephori* (*Libation Bearers*), and *The Eumenides.* Aeschylus competed in the City Dionysia drama contest for the first time in 499 B.C.E.; he won first prize for the first time in 484 B.C.E.

SOPHOCLES

Sophocles (c. 496 B.C.E.–406 B.C.E.) developed Aeschylus's dramatic techniques even further. He was particularly noted for his superb plot construction: he introduces characters and information skillfully and then builds swiftly to a climax. The Greek philosopher Aristotle used Sophocles' *King Oedipus* as the model for his own analysis of tragedy. Exploration of character and a focus on the individual are also characteristic of Sophocles' plays. In addition, his poetry is widely admired for both its beauty and its lucidity.

(Réunion des Musées Nationaux, Paris)

Sophocles.

As a boy, Sophocles performed in a public celebration of the victory of the Athenians over the Persians at the battle of Salamis. As an adult, in addition to being a playwright, he acted in his own early dramas. His first victory as a dramatist came when he defeated Aeschylus in the contest of 468 B.C.E. From his very first play, Sophocles was a popular success. Over the years he evidently wrote more than 100 plays, winning first prize eighteen times and never finishing lower than second.

Aristotle credits Sophocles with realistic innovations in scene painting. Sophocles also increased the tragic chorus from twelve to fifteen members and is credited with introducing a third actor to Greek tragedy—a development which, by increasing the number of characters in a play, enlarged the possibilities for conflict and interaction.

Sophocles told his stories as single dramas instead of extending them into the traditional trilogy of three connected plays; this change added more action to the plot. Today, three of Sophocles' surviving plays—*King Oedipus, Antigone,* and *Oedipus at Colonus*—are sometimes grouped as a trilogy because they all concern the fate of the same family; but they were originally written and performed as parts of different trilogies.

As a general, a civic leader, an ambassador, and a priest, Sophocles participated fully in Athenian life during the Greek golden age. He was born near Athens at Colonus (where Oedipus received sanctuary in his final years), the son of a wealthy Athenian factory owner. He was devoted to his native city-state, Athens, and refused many invitations to live at the courts of foreign kings. He died, age 90, in 406 B.C.E. and thus was spared the sight of the defeat of his beloved Athens by Sparta. Throughout his long life, he was known for his good nature, a fact noted by Aristophanes in *The Frogs.*

Though Sophocles wrote over 120 plays, only seven complete tragedies have survived: *Ajax* (c. 450 to 440 B.C.E.); *Antigone* (c. 441 B.C.E.); *King Oedipus* (c. 430 to 425 B.C.E.); *Electra* (c. 418 to 410 B.C.E.); *Trachiniae* (c. 413 B.C.E.); *Philoctetes* (409 B.C.E.); and *Oedipus at Colonus* (c. 406 B.C.E.). Fragments of some of his satyr plays also survive, including a large portion of *The Trackers*.

EURIPIDES

Of the three great tragic playwrights of ancient Greece, Euripides (c. 480–406 B.C.E.) is considered the most "modern." This description is particularly telling because Euripides actually was a contemporary of Sophocles and died a few months before him. There are several reasons why Euripides is often thought of as a more modern writer: his sympathetic portrayal of women, the greater realism of his plays, his mixture of tragedy with melodrama and comedy, and his skeptical treatment of the gods.

(Bettmann/Corbis)
Euripides.

In fact, Euripides was often criticized for "modernism" during his own time: his characters behaved as people do in everyday life, and such realism was not considered appropriate for tragedy. His plays were also criticized for other reasons, such as their plots (which were held to be weak), their diminished use of the chorus, and their sensational subject matter. His mixing of comedy and tragedy was derided (though it became a model for the tragicomedy and melodrama of later periods). The most controversial element of Euripides' plays was his portrayal of the gods as human and fallible, a treatment that was said to undermine the traditional moral order.

Unlike Aeschylus and Sophocles, Euripides took no active part in the political or social life of Athens. He was probably born on the Athenian island of Salamis and was the son of a wealthy citizen. But though his family background and education prepared him for public life, he was by temperament reclusive and moody, interested in observing society and examining the philosophical and scientific movements of the day. It was often said that he had marital problems and disliked women; these reports about his personal life may have developed because many of his plays focus on strong-willed, passionate women. As a dramatist, Euripides created believable female characters and showed a greater understanding of women than his contemporaries.

The comic playwright Aristophanes frequently parodied scenes from Euripides, ridiculing both his philosophy and his dramatic methods. Only five of Euripides' ninety-two plays received prizes during his lifetime, but his reputation grew rapidly after his death. He came to be much admired for his originality and independence of thought, and many of his dramatic methods were copied by both ancient and modern playwrights.

Eighteen plays by Euripides still exist: *Alcestis* (438 B.C.E.); *Medea* (431 B.C.E.); *Hippolytus* (428 B.C.E.); *The Children of Heracles* (c. 425 B.C.E.); *Andromache* (c. 424 B.C.E.); *Heracles* (c. 421 B.C.E.); *The Suppliants* (c. 420 B.C.E.); *Hecuba* (c. 417 B.C.E.); *The Trojan Women* (415 B.C.E.); *Electra* (c. 412 B.C.E.); *Helen* (412 B.C.E.); *Ion* (c. 411 B.C.E.); *Iphigenia in Tauris* (c. 410 B.C.E.); *The Phoenician Women* (c. 409 B.C.E.); *Orestes* (408 B.C.E.); *The Bacchae* (c. 406 B.C.E.); and *Iphigenia in Aulis* (c. 406 B.C.E.), as well as *The Cyclops*, a satyr play whose date is unknown.

THE CHORUS

All the Greek playwrights of the fifth century B.C.E. included a chorus in their plays. In fact, the chorus, which sang and danced as well as recited, was an integral and

THE GREEK CHORUS
The chorus in classical Greek theatre served many functions. It provided exposition, narrated the action, interacted with the other actors, and added spectacle. Shown here is a production of *The Bacchae* by Euripides. It was called *The Bacchai* and was directed by Peter Hall at the National Theatre in London. The chorus added a visual component to the drama. The costumes and masks were designed by Alison Chitty; the lighting was by Peter Mumford.

unique feature of classical Greek drama. Its importance is seen in the fact that a *chorodidaskalos*—a choral trainer—was employed for all festival productions. It is thought that at the time when Aeschylus began writing, there were fifty men in the chorus; this is an assumption based on the fact that there were fifty men in the dithyrambic chorus. As we have pointed out, Aeschylus is said to have reduced the number to twelve, which would be much more manageable, but, again, the actual number is conjectural. It is further believed that Sophocles increased the number to fifteen, where it remained—again, this number is based on a certain amount of speculation, but most commentators agree on it.

One fact to keep in mind about the chorus is that its importance in Greek tragedy decreased during the fifth century. In the plays of Aeschylus, fully half the lines are often given to the chorus. That number is reduced in the plays of Sophocles and diminished even further in the works of Euripides.

In comedy, there were twenty-four men in the chorus. Greek comedy often employed a double chorus, with the twenty-four members divided into two groups of twelve. In *Lysistrata*, there are choruses of old men and old women. Chorus members probably intoned or sang their lines in unison; on occasion, the choral leader delivered his lines independently.

The Greek chorus performed a number of dramatic functions. It provided expository or background information, commented on the action, interacted with other characters, and described offstage action. In tragedy, the chorus often represented the common people of the city-state ruled by the tragic hero or heroine; audience members could identify with the feelings and ideas of these people. Since choruses sang and danced, they also provided spectacle, as choruses do today in musical theatre. In Old Comedy, the chorus was frequently fantastical; for example, chorus members appear as birds in *The Birds* and as frogs in *The Frogs*.

Of the various Greek dramatic conventions, it is the chorus that is probably most difficult for modern audiences to envision; a group of performers speaking in unison, chanting, and dancing is hard for modern spectators to imagine.

Aristotle and the Tragic Form

The first critic who tried to identify the characteristics of the Greek tragedies written by the great dramatists of the fifth century B.C.E. was the philosopher Aristotle. Aristotle wrote nearly 100 years after the golden age and thus was describing a type of drama that had flourished long before his own lifetime, but his work on the subject—*The Poetics* (c. 335 B.C.E.)—is still the best starting point for a discussion of tragedy.

In addition to being a philosopher, Aristotle was a scientist who described and catalogued the world he saw around him. In analyzing tragedy, he followed the same careful, sensible approach that he brought to other fields; and though *The Poetics* is loosely organized and incomplete—it may have been based on a series of lecture notes—it is so intelligent and penetrating that it remains today one of the most important pieces of dramatic criticism we have.

According to Aristotle, drama has six elements, which he ranked in order of priority:

1. Plot—the arrangement of dramatic incidents
2. Characters—the people represented in the play
3. Thought or theme—the ideas explored
4. Language—the dialogue and poetry
5. Music
6. Spectacle—scenery and other visual elements

The implication in *The Poetics* is that tragedy deals with the reversals in fortune and eventual downfall of a royal figure. In "complex" tragedies, which Aristotle feels are the best type, the suffering hero or heroine makes a discovery and recognizes what has led to his or her downfall. There are also a number of what Aristotle calls "simple" tragedies, in which there is no such scene of recognition.

Though there are variations in the structures of the thirty-one Greek tragedies that still exist, many follow the same pattern in the unfolding of their scenes. First comes the *prologos*, the opening scene, which sets the action and provides background information. Next comes the *parodos*, in which the chorus enters. This is followed by the first *episode,* a scene in which the characters confront each other and the plot starts to develop. Next there is a *choral ode* performed by the chorus. Throughout the body of the play, episodes alternate with choral odes until the *exodos,* the final scene, in which all the characters exit from the stage. Aristotle suggests that Greek tragedy usually focuses on one major plot without bringing in subplots or unrelated secondary concerns, though some plays do have subplots.

Several points raised by Aristotle have been subject to different interpretations because his language is sometimes ambiguous; it is difficult to know exactly what he meant. Below, for instance, are two translations of his definition of *tragedy,* neither of which gives a fully satisfactory explanation of his meaning:

(© Donald Cooper/Photo*stage*, England)

A TRAGIC FIGURE
Greek playwrights perfected tragedy, which is described by Aristotle in *The Poetics*. One of the best-known tragic heroines is Euripides' *Medea,* played here by Fiona Shaw in a production in London, carrying the child she has killed. Jason (Jonathan Cake), her unfaithful husband, is in the background.

> Tragedy, then, is an imitation of an action that is serious, complete, and of a certain magnitude; in language embellished with each kind of artistic ornament, the several kinds being found in separate parts of the play; in the form of action, not of narrative; through pity and fear effecting the proper purgation of these emotions.[1]

> Tragedy, then, is an imitation of an action which is serious, complete, and has bulk, in speech that has been made attractive, using each of its species separately in the parts of the play; with persons performing the action rather than through narrative carrying to completion, through a course of events involving pity and fear, the purification of those painful or fatal acts which have that quality.[2]

Parts of this definition are clear enough: tragedy presents a complete story (an action) that is serious and important (has magnitude and bulk) and is dramatized for presentation on the stage rather than recounted by a narrator. When we come to the last part of the definition, though, there is disagreement. Aristotle says that tragedy produces the emotions of pity and fear but that there is a catharsis (in Greek, *katharsis*) of these emotions. One of the translators above calls catharsis a "purgation" of emotions and the other a "purification."

The most widely accepted explanation of catharsis is the one suggested by the first translation: members of the audience feel pity for the suffering tragic hero and fear that a similar fate could befall them. If a king or queen suffers so greatly, how much more probable it would be for an ordinary person to confront similar tragic circumstances. These emotions, however, are purged by the drama because the audience acknowledges them, and by doing so cleanses itself of their deleterious effects.

[1]S. H. Butcher, *Aristotle's Theory of Poetry and Fine Art,* 3d ed. Macmillan, London, 1902, p. 23.
[2]Gerald F. Else, *Aristotle's Poetics: The Argument,* Harvard University Press, Cambridge, Mass, 1957, p. 221.

Some critics, however, would not define catharsis in this way. They suggest that the tragic character, rather than the audience, is purged of pity and fear by discovering the reason for his or her suffering and downfall; this is the implication of the second translation above. Still others suggest that catharsis occurs in the chorus, as it is confronted with the tragic details of the plot, and that the audience is meant to identify with the emotional impact on the chorus. What Aristotle does make clear, however, is that changes occur as a result of the strong emotions associated with tragedy.

There is another debate, concerning Aristotle's discussion of the tragic hero, often called the *protagonist,* who is usually a royal figure. Tragic heroes almost invariably suffer, often as a result of some terrible calamity or turn of events. Why does the tragic hero suffer? The traditional interpretation of Aristotle's commentary suggests that the hero suffers because of a tragic flaw, or *hamartia,* in his or her character. Scholars see the flaw of *hubris,* or excessive pride, in many of the Greek tragic figures. There is, however, a great deal of disagreement over what Aristotle actually means by *hamartia.* The literal translation is "missing the mark," which has suggested to some scholars that hamartia is not so much a character flaw as an error of judgment made by the protagonist. Other critics have suggested that the "flaw" is often not in the leading character but in the tragic world represented by the play, a world that is temporarily disordered or "out of joint." The characters themselves may act nobly but are damned by circumstances or fate.

Despite the debates about the meaning of certain passages in *The Poetics,* Aristotle's analysis of tragedy is still considered one of the most important documents ever written on the subject.

ARISTOTLE

Born at Stagira in northern Greece, Aristotle (384–322 B.C.E.) was the son of a doctor who became court physician to the king of Macedon. Aristotle's lifelong interest in the sciences, especially biology, may be a reflection of his upbringing. As a young man he went to Athens to study with Plato at his Academy, where he remained for 20 years. There he began to develop his own philosophic system, at first by suggesting improvements in Plato's ideas. After Plato died in 347 B.C.E., Aristotle left the Academy and spent 13 years away from Athens, including 3 years as tutor to the young Alexander the Great in Macedon.

(Bettmann/Corbis)

Aristotle.

Aristotle returned to Athens in 335 B.C.E. and opened his own school, the Lyceum. He remained in Athens until a wave of hostility against Macedon—the region where he was born—swept Athens following Alexander's death in 323 B.C.E. Aristotle left Athens and died the following year on a nearby island.

Aristotle's *Poetics,* the work in which he outlines his views on literature, is incomplete and (as we mentioned above) may have originally been written as notes for a series of lectures. Most of the treatise is on tragedy; comedy, epic poetry, and other forms of literature are mentioned only briefly. Aristotle's discussion of tragedy, however, is of supreme importance. Plato had charged that drama, especially tragedy, is a danger to society because it encourages irrationality. As if answering Plato, Aristotle argues in *The Poetics* that tragedy is positive and helpful because it not only arouses pity and fear but also purges these emotions, restoring harmony to the soul.

In *The Poetics,* rather than formulating rules, Aristotle carefully observed classical Greek tragedy and described it in detail. Aristotle, Socrates, and Plato are recognized as the most influential Greek philosophers, but Aristotle was the only one of the three to include an analysis of drama in his philosophic writings.

The Poetics was little studied by the Greeks and Romans, but it became the basis of dramatic criticism when it was rediscovered by Renaissance scholars. During this period, Aristotle's descriptions and suggestions were often misinterpreted as inflexible rules for the writing of tragedies; Aristotle never intended that, but certain of the distortions have unfortunately persisted to modern times.

Climactic Drama

Aristotle's analysis of tragedy emphasizes plot. The Greeks developed an approach to dramatic structure that became the prototype—in an altered form—for plays written in the Renaissance (in Italy and France) and the modern period (the well-made plays of Ibsen, Strindberg, and others). We will refer to this structure as *climactic drama.* At various times this form of dramatic structure has also been referred to as *crisis drama, intensive drama,* and *drama of the catastrophe.* Though not every Greek play conformed to it, its elements were first developed in Greece and are evident in a number of dramas, particularly those by Aeschylus and Sophocles.

In climactic drama the action begins near the climax, or high point, of the story, with the characters already in the midst of their struggles. There are very few characters, and there is only one main action; the play occurs within a short span of time (frequently 24 hours or less) and usually takes place in one locale. Dramatic tension is increased because calamities befall the characters in a very short time. Since the play begins in the midst of the crisis, the audience must be provided with a great deal of background information, which is known as *exposition.* Thus the plot of a crisis drama often unravels like a mystery.

King Oedipus

To understand the structure of Greek tragedy, it will be helpful to examine a single play, Sophocles' *King Oedipus,* which was first presented around 430 B.C.E. There are structural similarities among all extant Greek tragedies, but it should be noted that *King Oedipus* is the only one that conforms exactly to Aristotle's description.

Like most Greek tragedies, *King Oedipus* is based on a myth. In this case, the myth tells how the infant Oedipus, son of the king and queen of Thebes, is left on a mountaintop to die because of a prophecy that he will murder his father and marry his mother. He is rescued by a shepherd, however, and taken to be raised by the king and queen of Corinth. When he grows up, Oedipus hears about the prophecy that he will murder his parents and, not knowing that he is adopted, leaves home so that he will not kill the king of Corinth, the man he thinks of as his father. On the road he encounters a stranger, argues with him, and subsequently kills him, unaware that it is actually his own father whom he has slain. Later, Oedipus becomes king of Thebes and, still in ignorance, marries the woman who is really his mother, Jocasta. When a plague strikes Thebes, Oedipus sets out to find the cause.

Following the pattern of climactic drama, Sophocles begins his play near the major crisis in the story. He also structures his plot by using the basic elements of

(Pier Paolo Cito/AP Images)

KING OEDIPUS

In Sophocles' *King Oedipus*—one of the most famous Greek tragedies—Oedipus becomes king of Thebes after unknowingly killing his father and marrying his mother. Upon learning what he has done, Oedipus puts out his eyes. According to Aristotle, *King Oedipus* represents the quintessential Greek tragedy. In the scene here, from a production in Rome, Oedipus (Grigoris Valtinos) appears in front of his palace after he has blinded himself.

classical Greek tragedy. The play opens with a prologue in which Oedipus learns about the plague and also learns from his brother-in-law, Creon, that an oracle has said that the plague will end when the murderer of the former king is found and punished. Next comes the parodos: the appearance of a chorus of elderly men, who pray to the gods to end the plague. Then begins the first episode. Oedipus proclaims that he will find and punish the guilty person. The blind prophet Teiresias arrives and professes ignorance of past events, but when accused by Oedipus of conspiring with Creon against him, Teiresias hints that the guilty person is Oedipus himself. Oedipus is incensed at the suggestion. Following this, in the first choral song, the chorus asks who the murderer can be and expresses doubt that it is Oedipus.

In the second episode, Creon defends himself against an angry Oedipus, who accuses him of conspiring with Teiresias. Jocasta, Oedipus's wife, enters to tell her husband to ignore the oracle; it had predicted that her first husband would be killed by his son, but according to all reports he was killed by thieves at a crossroads. Oedipus, remembering that he has killed a man at a crossroads, begins to fear that he is the murderer; but he is reassured by Jocasta, who urges him to ignore his fears.

(Notice how skillfully Sophocles alternates good news and bad news for Oedipus, carrying him from the heights to the depths and back again time after time.)

In the next choral song, the chorus—beginning to have doubts about Oedipus's innocence—says that reverence for the gods is best; prosperity leads to pride, which will be punished. In the third scene, or episode, a messenger from Corinth announces that the king of Corinth is dead. Jocasta is jubilant, for this means that the oracle cannot be trusted: it had said that Oedipus would kill his father, but the father has died of natural causes. The messenger then reveals that Oedipus is not the son of the king of Corinth. Fearing the worst, Jocasta tries to persuade Oedipus to cease his search for the facts. When he will not, she rushes into the palace. Oedipus sends for a shepherd who knows the full story of his origins and forces the shepherd to tell it. Learning the truth, Oedipus then goes into the palace himself.

In the following choral song, the chorus says that all life is sorrowful and bemoans the fall of Oedipus. In the exodos, or final scene, a messenger from the palace describes how Jocasta has killed herself and Oedipus has put out his own eyes. The blind Oedipus reappears to recite his sad story, courageously accepts his fate, and goes into exile. One of the features of Greek tragedy is that violence, such as murder or suicide, generally occurs offstage; rarely does it take place in view of the audience. The death of Jocasta and the blinding of Oedipus are no exception.

King Oedipus is admired for several reasons. One is the masterful way in which Sophocles unfolds the plot; it is like a detective story in which Oedipus is the detective tracking down a murderer. Another is the beauty of Sophocles' language. Though most modern readers do not understand ancient Greek, even in translation we can often appreciate the effectiveness of Sophocles' poetic expressions. For example, here are the words of the chorus just after Oedipus has discovered his fate; the chorus is saying that life is only a shadow and happiness often an illusion.

> Alas, you generations of men, I count your life as nothing more than a shadow. Where, where is the mortal who wins more of happiness than just the appearance, and, after the appearance, a falling away? Yours is a fate that warns me, unhappy Oedipus, to call no earthly creature blessed.

King Oedipus is also admired because of the religious and philosophical questions it raises. Why does a man like Oedipus suffer? Is it because of some flaw in his character—his pride, for example—or because of an error in judgment? Is it, perhaps, to test Oedipus, as Job is tested by God in the Bible? Or is it because the world is a place where life is sometimes cruel and unjust and the innocent must suffer?

King Oedipus also affects audiences because of the tragic fall of the protagonist. Oedipus not only loses his kingdom; equally affecting is his loss of his family—dramatized by his separation from his children at the close of the play—and of his community as he goes into exile. We should note that in the great classical tragedies, the playwrights frequently dramatized the political, familial, and social suffering of their protagonists, possibly to heighten catharsis.

People have been studying *King Oedipus* for over 2,000 years, and they continue to find profound and complex meanings in what its characters say and do. The psychoanalyst Sigmund Freud, for instance, developed a theory that each man subconsciously wishes to murder his father and marry his mother; Freud called this desire the *Oedipus complex.*

Antigone

Antigone, another play by Sophocles based on the Oedipus myth, features a female as the leading character. It too follows the form of crisis drama, with limited characters, limited locales, and a single action. In the myth, Antigone is the daughter of King Oedipus. After her father's death, her two brothers, Eteocles and Polynices, become involved in a war against each other to see who will be king of Thebes, and they kill each other. Antigone's uncle, Creon, then becomes king of Thebes. Creon blames one of the two dead brothers, Polynices, for the conflict, and he issues an edict that Polynices is not to be given an honorable burial. Antigone decides to defy Creon's order and bury her brother Polynices.

The above information serves as background to the action. As the play begins, two actors, each wearing the mask and costume of a woman, appear in the playing area: they represent Antigone and her sister, Ismene. As the scene begins, Antigone tells Ismene that she means to defy their uncle, the king, and give their brother Polynices an honorable burial. Ismene, unlike her sister, is timid and frightened, and she argues that women are too weak to stand up to a king. Besides, Ismene points out, Antigone will be put to death if she is caught. Antigone argues, however, that she will not be subservient to men, even the king.

When the two women leave, a chorus of fifteen men enters. These men represent the elders of the city, and throughout the play—in passages that are sung and danced—they will fulfill several functions: providing background information, raising philosophical questions, and urging the principal figures to show restraint. As in other Greek tragedies, the choral sections alternate with scenes of confrontation between the main characters—in this case, Antigone, Creon, and others.

Antigone does attempt to bury her dead brother, is caught, and is brought before the king. When the showdown between Antigone and Creon comes, Antigone defies him, and as punishment is put into a cave to die. In the end, not only is she dead, but so too are Creon's wife and son, who have killed themselves. In the final scene, we see Creon standing alone, wearing his tragic mask, bereft of all those he held dear.

Satyr Plays

As was mentioned earlier, on the days devoted to tragedy at the dramatic festival, three tragedies by a single playwright were presented. (*King Oedipus* would have been performed as one of three tragedies by Sophocles, as would *Antigone.*) When the three tragedies presented were linked to form a connected dramatic whole—for example, *The Oresteia* of Aeschylus—they were called a *trilogy.* Following the presentation of the three plays, whether they formed a trilogy or were independent, a short play by the same author, called a *satyr play,* was given as an afterpiece.

A satyr play was a comical play involving a chorus of satyrs, mythological creatures who were half-goat and half-man. It was structured like a Greek tragedy but parodied the mythological and heroic tales that were treated seriously in tragedies. Satyr plays poked fun at honored Greek institutions, including religion and folk heroes, and often had elements of vulgarity. For example, these plays often included explicit sexual material, and the costumes worn by the actors usually consisted of a short tunic, below which protruded a false erect phallus. The only complete satyr play still in existence is *The Cyclops* by Euripides.

(© Erich Lessing/Art Resource)

SATYRS
Because we have few visual records of Greek theatre itself, we rely on evidence from artifacts such as vases. This vase painting depicts Prometheus and a satyr—one of the mythical half-man, half-goat creatures who appeared in short plays presented after a set of three tragedies.

Old Comedy

The third type of drama presented at Greek festivals was comedy. The comedies of this period are called *Old Comedies;* the only ones that survive are all by Aristophanes and have certain recurring characteristics. Most Old Comedies do not follow the pattern of climactic drama: they do not take place in a short span of time, are not restricted to one locale, and have a large cast of characters. Old Comedy always makes fun of society, politics, or culture, and frequently its characters are recognizable contemporary personalities. In *The Clouds,* for instance, the philosopher Socrates is shown as a character suspended in midair in a basket—in other words, his head is always in the clouds. A present-day equivalent might be the kind of television variety-show sketch that caricatures political figures, such as the president of the United States.

Old Comedy uses fantastical and improbable plots to underline its satire. In *The Birds,* two characters who are unhappy with their earthly existence leave for Cloud-cuckooland to observe the lives of the birds and discover ludicrous parallels between bird society and human society. In *Lysistrata,* Aristophanes uses a comic premise, a parable, in order to condemn the Peloponnesian Wars, which were then raging in Greece. The Greek women in this comedy go on a sex strike, refusing to sleep with their husbands until the men cease warring. Miraculously, the scheme works.

Old Comedies employ a chorus and have sections similar to those in tragedy: prologos, episodes alternating with choral odes, and the exodos. There are, however, certain unique episodes in Old Comedy. One is the *agon,* a scene with a debate between the two opposing forces in a play—each representing one side of a social or political issue. Another is the *parabasis,* a scene in which the chorus speaks directly to the audience, makes fun of the spectators and specific audience members, or satirizes other subjects.

Religious and political officials attended dramatic festivals and were seated in the front row of the theatre; during the parabasis, the chorus would single them out for ridicule. (A counterpart today would be television or standup comics who attack their audiences.)

ARISTOPHANES

The best-known comic playwright of the Greek golden age was Aristophanes (c. 448–380 B.C.E.). In his play *The Clouds,* Aristophanes complains that other playwrights are copying his plots and ideas; if this was true, it suggests that his comedies were very popular. Written in the style of Old Comedy, Aristophanes' plays reflect the social and political climate in Athens as it declined in power toward the end of the fifth century B.C.E.

(Bettmann/Corbis)

Aristophanes

The son of a wealthy citizen, Aristophanes was a member of the prosperous, conservative Athenian middle class. His plays indicate that he came from a cultured, old-fashioned home. Life in Athens was changing rapidly during his lifetime—greed for an empire was undermining the traditional simplicity, stability, and moral order—and he used his plays to ridicule the ideas and people that he felt were leading Athens to ruin. One of his targets was the Peloponnesian Wars with Sparta, a conflict that drained Athens of wealth and destroyed its social order. His death came after these wars had reduced Athens to poverty and disarray.

In spite of his conservative outlook, Aristophanes' plays are full of bawdy wit—a reflection of the open attitude toward sex in Athenian society. Since Old Comedy did not emphasize plot or character, Aristophanes' plays are distinguished for their inventive comic scenes, witty dialogue, and pointed satire. Because of their many references to contemporary people and events, his plays are difficult to translate into playable modern versions.

Besides what we know about him from his plays, an incident recorded in Plato's *Symposium* reveals that Aristophanes was very much involved in the daily life of Athens, including attending parties with friends. Plato reports that after outdrinking and outtalking all the guests at an all-night party, Aristophanes left with the philosopher Socrates, debating whether one man could write both comedy and tragedy.

(© Richard Feldman)

GREEK COMEDY

The counterpart to Greek tragedy was Greek comedy, and the most famous writer of Greek comedy was Aristophanes. A prime example of his work is the satirical comedy *Lysistrata*. This play, which is the story of Greek women who go on a sex strike against their husbands in order to get the men to stop a war, is timeless, even though it was written nearly 2,500 years ago. The scene here is from a production at the American Repertory Theatre in Cambridge. In the center, as the title character, is the actress Cherry Jones.

(© Paul Kolnik)

GREEK OLD COMEDY
The comedy of Aristophanes, known as Old Comedy, was a form that has never appeared in quite the same way since. Usually there was a "comic premise," which might have been quite fantastical. In this scene from a musical adaptation of *The Frogs,* we see Nathan Lane in the center in a production of the play at Lincoln Center Theatre. In the play, Dionysus goes to the underworld to bring back the dead Euripides. Typical of Old Comedy, the play is full of political commentary as well as literary criticism.

Though he wrote approximately forty plays, Aristophanes did not feel competent to stage his own works and usually turned his plays over to a producer-director. Eleven of the plays survive. Among the best known are *The Archanians* (425 B.C.E.), *The Knights* (424 B.C.E.), *The Clouds* (423 B.C.E.), *The Wasps* (422 B.C.E.), *Peace* (421 B.C.E.), *The Birds* (414 B.C.E.), *Lysistrata* (411 B.C.E.), and *The Frogs* (405 B.C.E.). Aristophanes' last plays—in particular, *Plutus* (388 B.C.E.)—are often categorized as *Middle Comedies,* transitional works that led to the development of the nonpolitical New Comedy. (New Comedy is described later in this chapter.)

Greek Theatre Production

The Theatre Building

An important element of Greek theatre was the kind of space in which plays were presented. Since tragedies, comedies, and satyr plays were offered at religious festivals, huge theatres were necessary: the classical Greek theatre probably accommodated 15,000 to 17,000 spectators. The most noted of these theatres was the Theatre of Dionysus in Athens.

Greek theatres were outdoor amphitheatres with illumination provided by the sun, and the Greeks were often resourceful in the use of natural lighting in their dramas; if a play required a "sunrise effect," for example, it would be presented as the first drama of the day, at dawn.

There were three separate parts in a Greek theatre: the *theatron* (literally, "viewing place"), which was the seating area for the audience; the *orchestra,* or playing area for the actors; and the *skene*, or scene building. These three units were adjacent but unconnected architectural entities.

The audience sat in the theatron. The Greeks ingeniously built their theatres into hillsides, which provided naturally sloped seating and excellent acoustics. During the classical period the hillside theatron probably had temporary wooden bleachers, but these were replaced by stone seats during the later Hellenistic period (336–146 B.C.E.). Some historians believe that a specific seating plan was followed in the Greek theatron; they suggest that the various Greek tribes were segregated and that men and women (if women were present) sat separately.

Front-row seats, known as the *proedria,* were reserved for political and religious dignitaries. The theatres, though huge, could not accommodate everyone, and therefore in the fifth century B.C.E. entrance fees were charged. It is important to remember, though, that (unlike a theatre event today) each play was seen by a substantial portion of the population. (Today, it would be as if virtually the entire population of a small town took part in a single event—truly a communal occasion.)

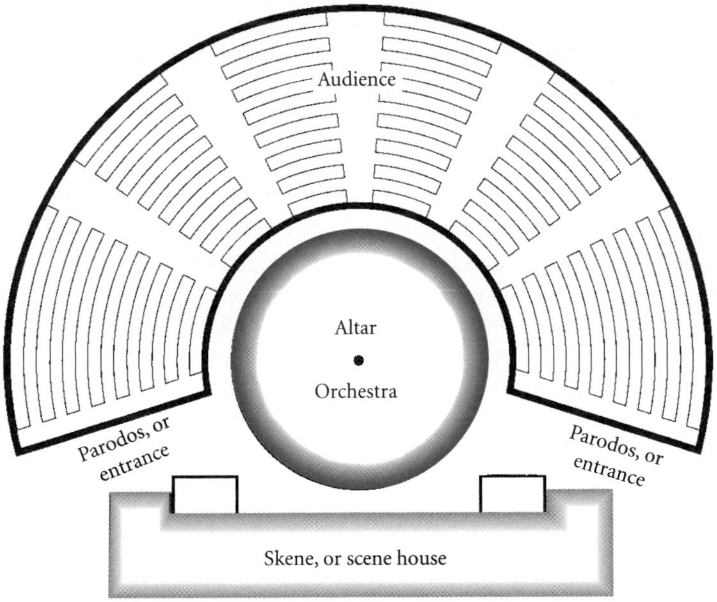

GROUND PLAN OF A TYPICAL GREEK THEATRE

The theatres of ancient Greece were set into hillsides which made natural amphitheatres. At the base of the seating area was a circular space (orchestra) in which the chorus performed; at the center of the orchestra was an altar (thymele). Behind the orchestra was a temporary stage house (skene), at each side of which was a corridor (parodos) for entrances and exits.

DEBATES IN THEATRE HISTORY | The Greek Stage

The difficulty of reconstructing the classical Greek theatre building can be seen in the debate among historians over whether there was an elevated stage in front of the skene, or stage house. Many of the arguments have to do with the appearance of the scene building because no skenes from the classical era survive.

Margarete Bieber, a renowned historian of the Greek and Roman theatres, states categorically, "The most important thing to bear in mind when reading Greek plays is that in the classical age there was no such thing as a raised stage."* The Roman architect Vitruvius, on the other hand, argued that there was a stage, 10 to 12 feet high—although this was probably not true of the classical era but is more accurately a description of the Hellenistic stage. Other historians argue that there was a slightly raised platform (or possibly a flight of stairs) in front of the skene, which would spatially separate the actors from the chorus. These scholars base their argument on needs implied by texts of plays, on contemporary references to staging, and on analysis of excavations of the Theatre of Dionysus.

These differing views lead historians to form different ideas about how the Greek tragedies and comedies were originally staged and about how the skene was used. There is also disagreement about whether there were doors in the skene and if so, how many. Ultimately, these arguments demonstrate how little we actually know about the configuration of this key element in classical Greek theatre architecture. They also indicate that most of our theories are based on later historical commentaries rather than on primary sources from the classical era itself.

*Margarete Bieber, *The History of the Greek and Roman Theatre,* 2d ed., Princeton University Press, Princeton, N.J., 1961, p. 73.

In commercial American theatres, the orchestra is the audience seating area on the ground floor. In the classical Greek theatre, the orchestra was the playing area. The orchestra was the first permanent structural element in the Greek theatre; it was a circle probably about 66 feet in diameter, paved with stone. Here again, there had been a transformation from earlier practices. In ceremonies of earlier days, it is believed, a circle was beaten down in a field of grain to serve as an area for presentations, and this circle was the forerunner of the orchestra. (We should note that some historians, on the basis of studies of excavations of the Theatre of Dionysus, suggest that the first orchestra may have been a rectangle.)

The acting area was surrounded on three sides by audience members—a configuration similar to the modern thrust theatre or three-quarter-round theatre. In this type of theatre, the stage juts out into the auditorium and the audience sits around the stage in a semicircle or on three sides. In the center of the orchestra there was probably a *thymele,* an altar; this is a reminder that Greek drama was a part of religious rituals. Some scholars believe that the thymele may have been used as a scenic element. (For example, in *King Oedipus* Jocasta makes an offering, suggesting one possible use of the thymele.) Other commentators, however, argue that the altar was too holy to have been used in dramas; and still others doubt that the altar was included in the orchestra at all.

The third element in the classical Greek theatre building was the skene, or scene building, located behind the orchestra. Our knowledge of the skene is sketchy, but we do know that it contained dressing space for actors who needed to change costumes and was used to store properties. (A *property,* or *prop,* in the theatre is any object used by the actors during a play, such as a sword or shield in a battle scene.) It is also believed that the skene building was used as the basic setting for all plays after 458 B.C.E.

What the skene looked like is another major point of contention among theatre historians: how tall was it, for example, and how many doors did it have? At first it was a temporary wooden structure; after the classical period, it became a permanent stone edifice. In the earlier classical period, the building was probably one story high, but it later became a two-story structure. The skene also had side wings (*paraskenia*). Since the most common setting for Greek tragedies is a palace, the skene had to be patterned after such an edifice. There were doorways—probably three, although some historians think there was only one—for entrances and exits.

There is another controversy surrounding the architectural configuration of the playing area. Some scholars believe that there was a raised stage area in front of the skene and directly behind the orchestra; others strongly reject the idea of a raised stage. We do know that after the classical period, huge raised stages were constructed in Greek theatres. A possible compromise is the suggestion that there was a slightly raised platform in front of the skene.

Scenery and Special Effects

The standard setting for Greek tragedy, with its royal heroes and heroines, was a palace; but there are some tragedies with other scenic requirements, and the comedies require a wide variety of locales. How, then, did the Greeks transform the facade of the skene so that it might appear to be a different setting for different plays?

We have no definite knowledge about the methods used during the classical period, but some scholars believe that the scene-changing techniques of the later Hellenistic period were adopted from classical theatre. One device was the *pinake,* a type of flat—a wooden frame covered with stretched fabric. Another was the *periaktoi,* a triangular stage device which consisted of three painted flats hinged together, each showing a different scene. Rotating these flats would reveal one new scene to the audience while hiding the other two.

What should be kept in mind is that scene changes in classical Greek theatre were not realistic. Modern audiences expect the environments of different plays to be markedly distinct; but in Greek theatre there were only hints that the setting had changed—and frequently these hints were provided only by the dialogue. Because of the vast size of the theatres and the limitations imposed by an outdoor space, it was impossible to create a unique environment for every tragedy, comedy, and satyr play. Also, many historians argue that such devices as the pinakes and periaktoi were not used at all in the classical era but appeared much later in Greek theatre. (Part of the debate revolves around the interpretation of Aristotle's statement that Sophocles introduced scene painting to Greek theatre.)

The skene also masked the mechanisms for special effects. If modern audiences are hypnotized by technological wonders in theatre, the classical Greeks were no different. The two most popular special-effects devices were the *mechane,* or "machine," and the *ekkyklema.*

Greek dramas often reached a climax with the sudden appearance of a deity who resolved all the dramatic problems. The *mechane,* a crane hidden behind the upper level of the skene, was used to effect the entrance of the actor playing the god or goddess in such a way as to suggest a descent from the heavens; hence the later Latin term *deus ex machina,* which means "god from a machine." (In subsequent

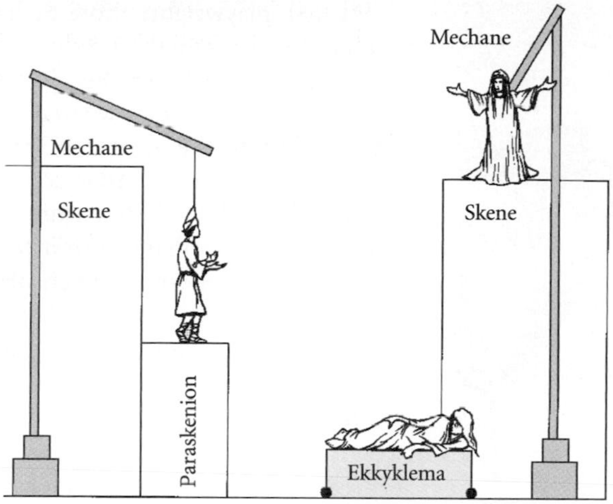

GREEK MECHANE AND EKKYKLEMA
A conjectural reconstruction of Greek stage machinery: on the left, a crane used for flying in characters located on a side wing (paraskenion) of the scene building. On the right, a mechane higher up on the roof of the skene. The ekkyklema below was a plateform on wheels used to bring out characters from inside the building.

usage, of course, this term has been broadened; today, any arbitrary dramatic device used to unravel a plot is referred to as a *deus ex machina.*)

Since the Greeks did not present violence onstage, stage machinery was needed to reveal climactic offstage deaths. One such machine was the ekkyklema, a wagon that would be wheeled from behind the skene. A character who had died offstage would be laid out on the ekkyklema, which would be rolled out from behind the scenes into the full view of the audience.

Acting in Greek Theatre

Actors may or may not have been paid for their participation in festivals during the classical period; but even if they were paid, there were not enough of these events for them to make a living by acting, and so they could not have been full-time professionals. At first, when tragedy had only one actor, the role was usually performed by the playwright; both Thespis and Aeschylus wrote plays and performed in them. As far as we know, Sophocles was the first playwright to give up acting.

As we have seen, Aeschylus is credited with introducing a second actor, and Sophocles supposedly introduced a third actor. Sophocles also introduced a "three-actor rule" in tragedy, calling for no more than three actors, excluding the chorus; this rule seems to have been followed by other Greek dramatists. (Comedy was not restricted by the three-actor rule.) The rule was bent to allow additional performers to portray mute roles, that is, minor characters who did not speak lines. Since one actor could *double*—play more than one part in a play—there could be more than three characters in a play, though never more than three onstage at one time. Sophocles' *King Oedipus,* for instance, has seven speaking parts, and the same actor might play several minor parts.

At first, playwrights chose their own performers and also oversaw the production of their own plays. The tragic playwrights, in particular, functioned as directors; they worked with the chorus and also assisted the actors, conferring with them about roles and scripts. After acting contests were introduced in 449 B.C.E., to ensure fairness the state conducted a lottery that determined which star performers would appear in which plays. Greek dramatists—like today's playwrights, directors, and producers—were aware that it is difficult to discern the quality of a play when the acting is poor.

To imagine the acting style of the fifth century B.C.E. is almost impossible. It could not have been very realistic—that is, it could not have conformed to everyday speech and gestures—because many of the conventions of classical theatre seem to argue against such realism. For example, in many plays (such as *Lysistrata*), it is important for the audience to believe that the female characters are sexually alluring; but women were not allowed to perform, and men played the female roles. Furthermore, all forms of Greek drama required dancelike movement and chanting.

(Bettmann/Corbis)

COSTUMES AND MASKS
We know that in Greek theatre, the performers wore masks covering the entire head. They also wore costumes considered appropriate to the sex, the social status, and the occupation of the character they were portraying. Shown here is an engraving of Greek actors wearing masks.

Costumes and Masks

The major element in Greek costuming was the mask. All Greek performers wore masks, which covered the entire head and included hair, beards, and other distinctive facial features. These helped the audience identify characters and allowed the actors to perform multiple roles. During the classical period, the facial coverings were not highly exaggerated, and in tragedies, the masks for all the chorus members were probably the same. Comic choruses, on the other hand, often required unusual masks; in two of Aristophanes' plays, as we've seen, chorus members represented frogs and birds.

Greek costuming, for the most part, was fairly conventional. Our knowledge of costumes comes mostly from scenes painted on Greek vases. Tragic characters of Greek origin, regardless of historical period, probably wore a very ornate tunic and a short or long cloak. Illustrations often depict Greek performers wearing a thick-soled boot known as a *kothornos,* but this was not used until the later Hellenistic period; in the classical period, soft-soled footwear was used. (There is, however, much debate over the validity of drawing conclusions from vase paintings about costuming during the classical era.)

Comic costumes, which were based on everyday clothing, were often cut tight to create a humorous effect by emphasizing certain physical features. As mentioned earlier, a unique element in comic costuming was the phallus, an exaggerated penis which all male characters wore around the waist. It has been suggested that this use of the phallus originated in the fertility rites out of which comedy possibly originated. Some historians believe that the phallus was a foot long, made of leather, and stuffed. At times, it was probably rolled up and concealed; at other times, it hung loose for a comic effect.

Theatre in the Hellenistic Age

The Athenians had defeated Persia at the battle of Marathon in 490 B.C.E. Later, toward the end of the century, the Peloponnesian Wars, between Athens and Sparta, began in 431. In the 60-year period between 490 and 431, Athens ruled supreme in the Greek world, and it was during this time that the classical theatre took shape and achieved greatness. The war with Sparta was to last off and on for 37 years, until 404 B.C.E., when Sparta decisively defeated Athens. Both during and after the Peloponnesian Wars, however, the theatre at Athens continued to flourish. And after 404, though Athens itself was no longer the power it had been, the theatre which originated there continued to have influence throughout that part of the world. Athenian actors were sought by other nations, and the plays of the best-known writers were presented in a variety of places.

At the same time, we do not hear of important playwrights emerging in the six decades between 404 and 336 B.C.E. Rather, there seem to have been changes under way in the importance accorded to actors, and in the physical characteristics of theatre spaces. We mention the year 336 because that is when Alexander the Great, as he came to be known, began his reign as king of Macedonia, a region that included northern Greece. Though he was only 20 years old when he became king, Alexander established himself as probably the greatest general in the ancient world. Within a few short years he had conquered not only southern Greece but much of the known world in that area, including Egypt, Asia Minor, central Asia, and parts of India. He died in 323 when he was only 32.

Alexander identified strongly with the intellectual achievements, art, and culture of Greece. Wherever he went he carried these values with him and therefore was said to have made the entire area Greek, or "Hellenistic." Thus the period from when he began his reign until Greece was conquered by the Romans in 146 B.C.E. is known as the Hellenistic era.

Among Alexander's other activities was the initiation of a number of theatre festivals to honor his many military victories. During and after his reign, dramatic festivals proliferated throughout the Hellenistic world. Theatrical presentations were no longer confined to such festivals as the Dionysian and the Lenaia but took place on many other occasions.

This increase in festivals was part of a number of changes that took place in theatre during the Hellenistic period. There were changes as well in theatre architecture, acting, and writing.

Hellenistic Theatres

Between 400 and 150 B.C.E. a number of changes took place in the structure and characteristics of Greek theatres. We do not know at what points over this time period the various alterations occurred. We do know two things, however. One is

THE THEATRE AT EPIDAURUS
One Hellenistic theatre still standing is at Epidaurus. Note the semicircular seating area in the hillside and the circular orchestra. However, only remains of the skene's foundation have survived.

that by 150 B.C.E. a definite shape had developed for Hellenistic theatre spaces. The other is that theatres of this type were built throughout the Hellenistic world—over forty locations that we know about, stretching from Asia Minor in the east to Italy in the west. The size of the theatres ranged from seating for 3,000 to more than 20,000.

One significant alteration was in the audience area: the substitution of stone seats for the wooden seats we believe were used during the classical period of the fifth century B.C.E. The stone seats are one reason why so many theatre sites from the later Hellenistic period have survived. Gradually, though, between 400 and 150 B.C.E., other changes took place. One was in the development of the stage itself. Eventually it was quite high: anywhere from 8 to 13 feet. It was also long, stretching at times to 140 feet. The depth was anywhere from 6 feet to 14 feet. The side pieces of the classic stage, the paraskenia, were eliminated. This larger, higher stage was in sharp contrast to the modest stage house used for the first productions of Aeschylus, Sophocles, and Euripides.

The stage house, or proskenion, at the back of the stage went through a series of transformations. At first it seems to have been a relatively simple one-story structure with several openings at the back known as *thyromata.* Later this stage house became increasingly elaborate, with columns separating the openings. One question raised by the developments is just what scenic elements were used. Were various pinakes, or painted panels, placed between the columns? Were they used at all? We are not certain. Another unanswered question concerns the use of the orchestra, the circular area between the stage house and the audience. How much was it used, and for what? Possibly when the classics were performed, it was used for the chorus as it had been originally. But what of newer plays such as those referred to as New Comedy? We do not know the exact answers. What we do know is that this type of theatre was built throughout the ancient world, and so there was doubtless an enormous amount of theatrical activity taking place.

The large, raised stage suggests that the actors were given more and more prominence in the Hellenistic theatre, and there is other evidence of this as well.

Hellenistic Acting

The Rise of the Actor

Throughout theatre history, there are shifts in focus from one theatrical element to another: from script, for instance, to performers to visual effects. Such a shift occurred during the Hellenistic period as new scripts—which had been a prominent feature of the classical era—became less important and the work of performers became more prominent. This is similar to the focus of much of contemporary film and television, which, like Hellenistic theatre, is actor-centered: scripts take second place to star performers.

As we have pointed out, in the Hellenistic era there was a general increase in both number and kind of theatrical activities. Worship of Dionysus was no longer the sole reason for staging drama, and plays were therefore included in other festivals, such as those honoring military victories. With more productions, a need for professional actors developed.

The ascendancy of the actor led to the establishment, by 277 B.C.E., of a guild known as the Artists (*technitai*) of Dionysus. Actors, chorus members, playwrights, and various other theatre personnel belonged to it; and if a local government wanted to stage a play, local members of the Artists of Dionysus had to be hired. The Artists of Dionysus—an early ancestor of the Actor's Equity Association, the union of American professional actors—provided actors with professional security. (Wealthy individuals were no longer expected to produce plays, probably because there was a decrease in personal wealth in Greece at this time. Instead, the government became the producing agency, with a government official, the *agonthetes,* in charge of production details.)

During times of war, actors, who were not expected to take part in military service, could travel unhindered, and performers were called on to serve as ambassadors and messengers.

Developments in costumes also indicate the ascendancy of the actor. Unlike actors in the classical Greek period, actors in the Hellenistic era wore masks that were larger than life and had exaggerated facial features. Tragic characters wore a large, exaggerated headdress known as the *onkos,* and according to some scholars, the shoes (*kothornoi*) worn by tragic characters were extremely elevated. Because the actor was costumed to look bigger than life and performed on a raised stage, he became the clear focus of the audience's attention.

Social Position of Actors

Though the actor was the center of Hellenistic theatre, this should not obscure the fact that he was viewed as less than socially acceptable. In the classical period, the actor had been a semiprofessional involved in religious activity. Yet even in the early fourth century B.C.E., the philosopher Plato, in *The Republic,* expressed his disapproval of theatrical performers, concluding that they should not be allowed to enter the ideal state. Plato's distrust was rooted in his fear that actors would use their chameleon-like personalities to harm society.

In the Hellenistic era, this distrust intensified, and even Aristotle, a great admirer of drama, considered actors disreputable. (The belief that actors are "less moral" than the average citizen still persists; today's gossip columnists feed the public's obsession with "immorality" in Hollywood and on Broadway.) It was because Hellenistic performers wanted to avert public hostility and remind audiences of their ties with religion that they named their guild the Artists of Dionysus.

Mimes

The disrepute of actors was reinforced by the lifestyle of the *mimes,* who were probably the earliest professional performers in Greece. The mimes were not originally involved in religious festivals; they were traveling players who presented a variety of entertainments, including juggling, acrobatics, wordless dances dramatizing fables, and sketches with dialogue. (Greek mimes, who spoke and engaged in varied entertainment activities, were not the equivalent of modern mimes, who perform without words.) Many of the mime troupes originated in southern Italy, and their most popular dramatic pieces were satires of the great tragedies.

Their lifestyle seems to have earned them general condemnation. These performers were nomads who entertained at banquets and probably in the streets on temporary stages. After 300 B.C.E., they were allowed to perform at festivals, but they were never given recognition in the Artists of Dionysus. The traveling mime troupes were also criticized because they included women. The Greeks—and many succeeding civilizations—considered theatre an unsuitable profession for women, and women involved in theatrical endeavors were castigated as licentious and immoral.

Nevertheless, mimes represent an early recorded instance in western theatre of popular entertainment. Throughout theatre history, performances without intellectual or moral pretentions that appeal to ordinary people, as well as to the more affluent, have played an important role in keeping theatre alive. As we move through time, we will take note of these popular entertainments, along with those that have been noted and written about by theatre historians.

New Comedy

For 75 years after the end of the fifth century B.C.E., Greek theatre continued to follow classical conventions. The major change in Greek drama in the fourth century B.C.E. occurred in comedy. By 336 B.C.E., Old Comedy had given way to a form called *New Comedy.* The only playwright of New Comedy whose work still exists is Menander.

Written a hundred years after Aristophanes and Old Comedy, New Comedy differs from its predecessor in a number of important ways. Gone are the fantasies, the political satire, the sharp topical observations of the plays of Aristophones. Gone, too, is the vital role of the chorus in its flights of fancy and its active participation in the contemporary political debates of Old Comedy.

In place of these was another kind of play: a subtle comedy of manners and well-wrought intrigue which focused on domestic—that is, family—situations and bourgeois life in the cities. In short, New Comedy was more realistic, more down-to-earth, and its comedy arose not from satire and extreme exaggeration but from the foibles, pretenses, and complications of the everyday life of Greek citizens. A typical romantic plot can be summarized as "boy meets girl, boy loses girl, boy gets girl." A domineering parent usually comes between the young lovers, and the romantic complications are resolved by sudden dramatic coincidences and discoveries. The plots are usually ingeniously contrived. The characters in New Comedy are recognizable stock types, such as domineering parents, romantic young lovers, and comic servants. The plays are usually written in five acts.

The reduction in the role of the chorus had already begun in the plays of Euripides, and in this as well as in other ways Menander's work echoes the later, nontragic plays by Euripides. The only remnant of the chorus is that singing and dancing interludes occur between the acts.

The influence of New Comedy is almost incalculable. Not only did the Roman comic writers Plautus and Terence borrow heavily from Menander; beyond that, there is a line of domestic comedy stretching from Menander through Roman comedy all the way to the films of the 1930s, 1940s, and 1950s to today's situation comedies on television, which also focus on domestic and romantic complications.

MENANDER

Menander (c. 342–291 B.C.E.), the best-known writer of Greek New Comedy, studied philosophy with Theophrastus, who had been a pupil of Aristotle. Though

(© Werner Forman/Art Resource, N.Y.)

MENANDER Shown here is a Roman copy of a Greek relief showing Menander, on the right. Menander was the well-known writer of Greek New Comedy, who worked in the fourth century B.C.E.

Menander was urged to come to Egypt by the court of Ptolemy I, he preferred to stay in Athens.

For a long time he was known mostly by reputation and through the plays of Plautus and Terence. Three plays by Plautus and four by Terence were based on Menander's works, but no complete, original plays by Menander were known to exist. In 1905 a papyrus scroll was found (it is now in Cairo), which contains a large part of four plays by Menander and a fragment of a fifth. Parts of other plays have been added in subsequent years. Among the plays, portions of which have been recovered, are: *Samia (The Girl from Samos), Aspis (The Shield), Epitrontes (The Men Who Went to Arbitration), Perikeiromene (The Girl Who Had Her Hair Cut), Sicyonius (The Sicyonian),* and *Misoumenos (The Chief Aversion).* In 1957 a complete play, *Dyskolos (The Grouch),* was discovered on papyrus. It is believed that *Dyskolos* was an early play, written when Menander was about 25 and first performed in 317 B.C.E.

While theatre continued to flourish in Greece long after 146 B.C.E., it was no longer purely Greek but, rather, theatrical art influenced by the omnipresent Roman civilization. Therefore, we turn next to Rome in our study of the unfolding of the dramatic arts.

Summary

Greek theatre set the stage for all western theatre to follow. A dramatic form known as *climactic structure* evolved during the classical era, and the tragedies of Aeschylus, Sophocles, and Euripides—which dramatize the downfall of a royal figure caught in a difficult or impossible situation—set a standard for all subsequent tragedy. Aristotle's *Poetics* began the development of serious critical consideration of drama and theatre. The Greeks were leaders in comedy as well: Aristophanes' Old Comedies, which poked fun at contemporary political, social, and cultural events as well as personalities, are forerunners of later satire.

Classical Greek theatre buildings were large outdoor spaces built into hillsides; they accommodated audiences attending religious festivals in honor of the god Dionysus. Behind the orchestra, which was a circular playing space, the scene building served as the basic scenic unit. The performers, all of whom were males, almost certainly acted in a style that did not conform to everyday life. The chorus was an integral element of all classical Greek drama and theatre.

Major changes took place during the Hellenistic period. New Comedy, which was concerned with domestic and romantic situations, prepared the way for almost all popular comedy to follow; in fact, it continues to influence contemporary playwrights. The drama of the Hellenistic period was not as noteworthy as that of the classical era, but the ascendancy of the actor was an important development, prefiguring today's star system. The huge raised stage in theatres, the distinctive footwear and large headdresses in costuming, and the founding of the Artists of Dionysus—a theatre guild for actors—all indicate a new focus on the performer. The permanent stone theatre structures suggest the permanent hold that theatre was to have in western civilization.

Mimes, who toured and presented various forms of amusement—juggling, acrobatics, dances, and dramatic sketches—provided popular entertainment for audiences in many locales.

MILESTONES CHAPTER 1 GREEK THEATRE [C. 1000 B.C.E.–146 B.C.E.]

Geometric [c. 1000–700 B.C.E.]

Cultural and Historical Developments
- Age of Homer (800 B.C.E.): *Iliad; Odyssey*

Archaic [c. 640–490 B.C.E.]

Theatre History
- Arion, harpist and poet, develops dithyramb (c. 600 B.C.E.)
- Thespis, considered first "actor" in dithyramb
- Tragedy incorporated into City Dionysia, spring festival honoring Dionysus in Athens (534 B.C.E.)
- Satyr plays added to City Dionysia (501 B.C.E.)

Cultural and Historical Developments
- Thales of Miletus begins natural philosophy (c. 585 B.C.E.)
- Peisistratus, tyrant of Athens (560 B.C.E.)
- Pythagoras, mathematician, flourishes; Doric temples of southern Italy and Sicily (c. 525 B.C.E.)
- Athenian democracy established (510 B.C.E.)
- Pindar begins to write odes (500 B.C.E.)

Classical [c. 490–336 B.C.E.]

Theatre History

- Comedy introduced to City Dionysia (486 B.C.E.)
- Aeschylus (525–456 B.C.E.) *(right)*, trilogy *The Oresteia*
- Skene in use as scenic setting by 458 B.C.E.

Cultural and Historical Developments
- Olympic festival flourishes (fifth century B.C.E.)
- Persian Wars (499–478 B.C.E.)
- Battle of Marathon (490 B.C.E.)
- Herodotus, historian (c. 484–425)
- Socrates (c. 470–399 B.C.E.) *(right)*

Golden Age [c. 450–400 B.C.E.]

Theatre History

- Prizes for tragic acting awarded (449 B.C.E.)
- Sophocles (c. 496–406 B.C.E.), *King Oedipus*
- Euripides (c. 480–406 B.C.E.) *(above), The Bacchae*
- Aristophanes(c. 448–380 B.C.E.), *Lysistrata*

Cultural and Historical Developments
- Age of Pericles; rise of Athenian power (462–429 B.C.E.)
- Hippocrates, physician (c. 460–377 B.C.E.)
- Pericles establishes Theoric Fund (450 B.C.E.)
- Beginning of Parthenon (448–432 B.C.E.) *(right)*
- Death of Phidias, artist (500–435 B.C.E.)
- Peloponnesian Wars (431–404 B.C.E.)
- Athenian fleet destroyed; Spartan hegemony begins (404 B.C.E.)

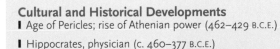

continued

PHOTO CREDITS: Aeschylus. (Bettmann/Corbis) / Euripides. (Bettmann/Corbis) / Raphael's *School of Athens.* (Scala/Art Resource, N.Y.) / The Parthenon. (© Adam Crowley/Getty Images)

MILESTONES CHAPTER 1 GREEK THEATRE [C. 1000 B.C.E.–146 B.C.E.] *continued*

Late Classical [c. 400–336 B.C.E.]

Theatre History

- Theatres built throughout Mediterranean (400–150 B.C.E.)

Cultural and Historical Developments

- Trial and execution of Socrates (399 B.C.E.)
- Plato's *Republic* (c. 375 B.C.E.) *(right)*
- Spartan hegemony ends (404–371 B.C.E.)
- Philip II, king of Macedonia (352 B.C.E.)

Hellenistic [c. 336–146 B.C.E.]

Theatre History

- New Comedy (336 B.C.E.)
- Aristotle's *Poetics* (c. 335 B.C.E.)
- Theater of Dionysus completed (c. 325 B.C.E.)
- Menander (342–291 B.C.E.) *(below)*, *Dyskolos*

- Artists of Dionysus established (277 B.C.E.)

Cultural and Historical Developments

- Alexander the Great succeeds Philip II; occupies Greece (336 B.C.E.)
- Hellenistic culture spreads throughout eastern Mediterranean (c. 320 B.C.E.)
- Greece conquered by Romans (146 B.C.E.)

PHOTO CREDITS: Menander. (© Werner Forman/Art Resource, N.Y.) / Plato and Hippocrates. (Scala/Art Resource, N.Y.)

CHAPTER 2

Roman Theatre

Roman Comedy

The scene here is from a first-century marble relief of a Roman New Comedy. This kind of comedy focuses on domestic situations. In this scene, a young man, second from the right, is on his way home, having become drunk at a tavern. He is being held up by his slave, at the far right. Meanwhile, disaster awaits him in the form of his angry father (second from the left), who has come out of his house with a stick to beat his recalcitrant son.

(Scala/Art Resource, N.Y.)

As Greece declined in power and importance, another civilization began to emerge in Europe, on the Italian peninsula. Its center was the city of Rome, from which it took its name.

Background: The Republic and the Empire

According to legend, Rome was founded around 750 B.C.E. and for over 200 years was ruled by a series of kings from its northern neighbor, Etruria. Around 500 B.C.E. the kings were overthrown and a republic was established, which was to last nearly 500 years. During the early years of the republic, there were three main classes in Rome: patricians, the rich upper class who ruled the country through the Senate; plebeians, ordinary citizens who gradually gained an equal voice in government through a people's assembly; and slaves, who made up roughly half the population. For those who were free, the republic offered a representative form of government.

After the republic was established and had extended its control over much of Italy, it was challenged by Carthage, a nation based in a seaport in North Africa. During the third and second centuries B.C.E. (from roughly 264 to 146 B.C.E.), Rome and Carthage engaged in a lengthy conflict, the Punic Wars, from which Rome finally emerged victorious. As a result, Rome controlled large parts of the central and western Mediterranean, including Spain, Sicily, Sardinia, and some of North Africa. At this time, Rome came into contact with Greece and saw firsthand Greek art and culture, including theatre.

During the first century B.C.E., the Roman republic began to show signs of strain. For one thing, it faced difficulties in maintaining the checks and balances of its own political system. For another, Rome now had control of far-flung territories, and the problems of governing so vast an area led to upheavals and wars. In the midst of this turmoil, Julius Caesar made himself dictator; he was subsequently assassinated by a group led by Brutus, who in turn was defeated in battle by Mark Antony and Octavius. (These events are the basis of Shakespeare's play *Julius Caesar*.)

The republic could not survive these shocks, and in 27 B.C.E. Rome became an empire with one supreme ruler. This form of government continued for several centuries, during which most of the civilized western world was unified under Roman rule. The Roman empire included most of the lands bordering on the Mediterranean Sea and all of Europe through what is now Spain, France, Britain, and the Balkans.

Throughout their long history, the Romans were always practical. Their laws dealing with property, marriage, and inheritance still continue to influence western civilization. The Romans were also great engineers and architects, developing aqueducts and roadways. Today—2,000 years later—modern highways throughout Europe are built on the foundations of roads laid by the Romans; and a number of Roman aqueducts, though no longer in use, are still standing.

Religion was of the utmost importance in Roman history. The Romans worshipped gods who were counterparts of the Greek deities, and also a large number of other divinities: to their own pantheon, they continually added gods worshipped by peoples they conquered. The Romans also staged religious festivals that incorporated elements of theatre.

The emergence of Christianity had a profound influence on the Roman world. The Romans persecuted the early Christians, but in the fourth century C.E. the emperor Constantine (founder of Constantinople, the capital of the eastern empire) was converted to the new belief; thus began the eventual conversion of much of the Roman world to Christianity. The original religions of Greece and Rome had condoned theatre, but the early Christians considered it pagan and therefore evil; the church was to be a contributing factor in the decline of theatre during the later years of the Roman empire.

Rome
Year, B.C.E.–C.E.

Theatre

- Regular comedy and tragedy added to Ludi Romani (240 B.C.E.)
- Plautus's *Pseudolus* (191 B.C.E.)
- Terence's *Phormio* (161 B.C.E.)
- Vitruvius's *De Architectura* (90 B.C.E.)
- First permanent theater in Rome (55 B.C.E.)
- Horace's *Art of Poetry* (24 B.C.E.)
- Romans build theatres and amphitheaters throughout the empire (c. 30–200 C.E.)
- Seneca (c. 4 B.C.E.–65 C.E.) writes Roman tragedies
- Theatrical presentations approximately 100 days per year
- Council of Carthage decrees excommunication for those who attend theatre rather than church on holidays; actors forbidden sacraments (398 C.E.)

Culture and Politics

- Traditional date for the founding of Rome (753 B.C.E.)
- First Punic Wars (Greek influence on Roman culture) (264–241 B.C.E.)
- Second Punic Wars (218–201 B.C.E.); Hannibal's victories (218–216 B.C.E.)
- Rome defeats Philip V of Macedonia (200–197 B.C.E.)
- Censorship of Cato; 1,000 talents spent on sewers (184 B.C.E.)
- Roman citizens freed of direct taxation (167 B.C.E.)
- Rome annexes Macedonia (147 B.C.E.)
- First high-level aqueduct in Rome (144 B.C.E.)
- Slave revolts in Sicily (135 B.C.E.)
- Pompey suppresses piracy (67 B.C.E.)
- Golden age of Roman literature (c. 58–50 B.C.E.)
- Caesar's conquest of Gaul (55 B.C.E.)
- Jesus crucified (30 C.E.)
- Marcus Aurelius rules (161–180 C.E.)
- Severan dynasty; Augustan order disintegrates (193–235 C.E.)
- Extensive persecution of the Christians (c. 250–300 C.E.)
- Constantine rules; empire reunited (324–337 C.E.)
- St. Augustine born (354 C.E.)
- Julian the Apostate restores paganism (361 C.E.)
- Theodosius I forbids pagan worship (391 C.E.)
- Sack of Rome by Visigoths (410 C.E.)
- Death of Attila the Hun (453 C.E.)
- Fall of western Roman empire (476 C.E.)

The Development of Roman Theatre: Popular Influences

Let's now look at the theatre that flourished in Rome and note why it is significant for us today.

Whereas Greece had been noted for creativity and imagination—in art, architecture, and philosophy—Rome came to be known for mastery of more practical arts: law, engineering, and military conquest. And just as the achievements of Rome as a civilization were more down-to-earth than those of Greece, so too was its theatre.

Instead of concentrating on high-minded tragedy, Roman theatre focused on comedy and other popular entertainments, comparable to our own movies, television, and

THE ROMAN EMPIRE

Note how extensive the Roman conquests were: the Romans conquered much of the eastern and western world. The centers of the empire were the cities of Rome and Constantinople, known today as Istanbul.

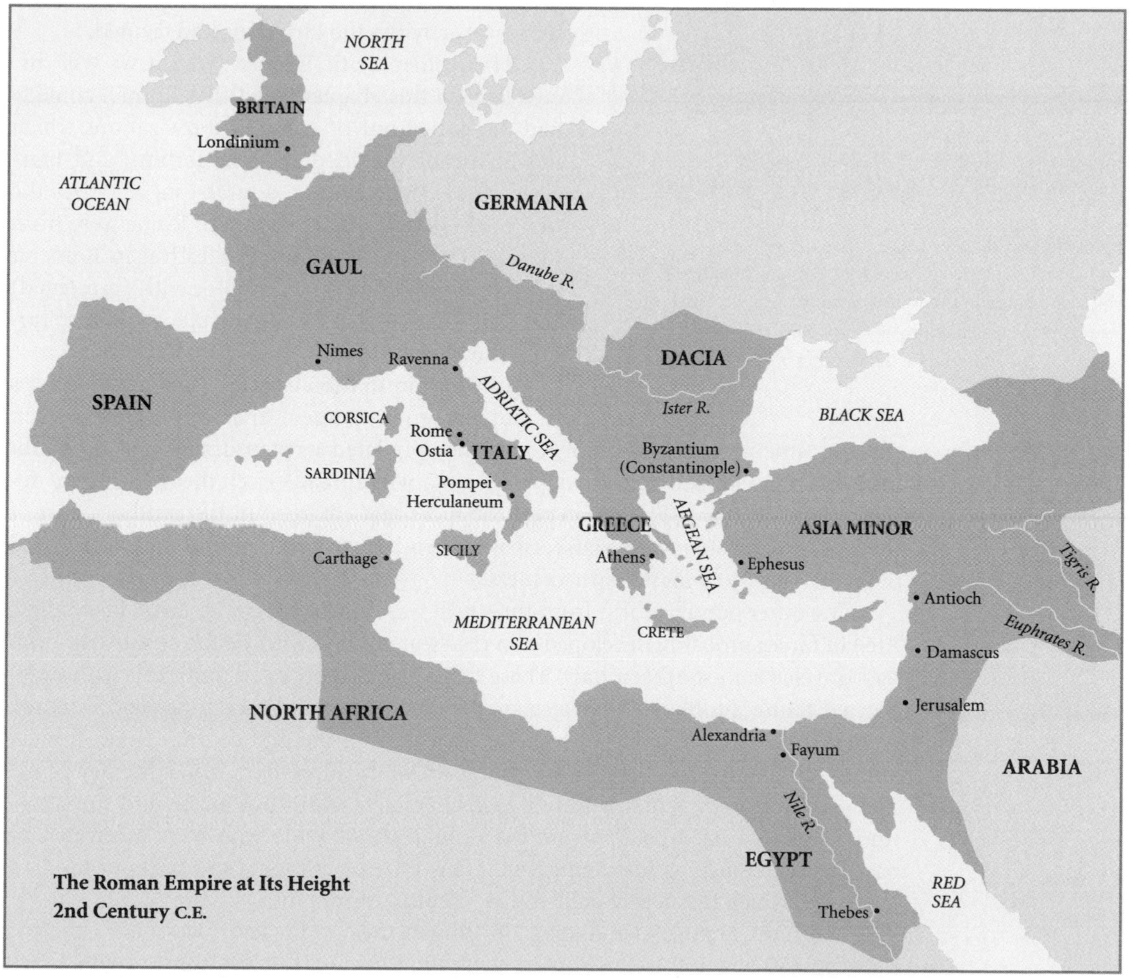

ATELLAN FARCE
One of the tributaries that fed into Roman comedy was farce which originated in the Atellan section north of Rome. This scene, from a wall painting in Pompeii, shows an Atellan farce, with the man on the left wearing a slave's mask and two women on the right.

rock concerts. Taking off from Greek New Comedy, the Romans developed a form of domestic farce that was the prototype of this kind of entertainment—and has continue to have an influence straight through to today's situation comedies on television.

Several threads were woven together to create Roman theatre. Its first source was the Etruscans. Etruria—from which the term *Etruscan* comes—was a civilization northwest of Rome that flourished from about 650 to 450 B.C.E. It included modern-day Pisa and Siena. The Etruscans placed great emphasis on religious festivals. As part of their worship of the gods, their ceremonies included chariot races, gladiatorial battles, prizefighting, and other competitive sports, as well as acting, dancing, juggling, and flute playing. The Romans incorporated the Etruscan festivals into their own culture, including the many sporting and theatrical activities the Etruscans had favored.

The Roman critic Horace (whom we will discuss later in this chapter) held that Roman comedy had developed out of comic improvisations which the Etruscans included in their fertility and marriage rites. Other Roman sources suggest that the first professional actors to come to Rome were from Etruria. The Ludi Romani (the festival in Rome at which Greek drama was subsequently presented) was established by an Etruscan ruler of Rome, Tarquin the Elder (616–579 B.C.E.).

In addition to the Etruscans, two other sources of popular entertainment that influenced Roman theatre came from the south of Rome; they predated written drama and no doubt influenced it. One was mime, adapted from a widespread Greek theatre practice described in Chapter 1. The mime performances that emerged in the southern part of the Italian peninsula were coarse, ribald, often improvised entertainments provided by a small group of masked performers.

The other popular form from the south was known as *Atellan farce.* Like mime, Atellan farces probably developed as a result of contact with Greek performers who had traveled into southern Italy. These farces were improvised and dealt with exaggerated family problems; they also made fun of historical or mythological figures. At first they were presented by touring actors, but in the first century B.C.E., Roman authors began to write these comic pieces down, turning them into a literary genre. The plays featured recurring stereotyped characters who wore masks and stock costumes; they satirized people from the Roman countryside who were motivated by base instincts, such as lust and greed. (This type of humor also occurs in modern comedies, which frequently poke fun at "country bumpkins.")

The most important influence on Roman theatre, however, was Greek theatre. Between 250 and 150 B.C.E., Roman civilization came into close contact with Greek culture. In sculpture, architecture, art, and virtually all other forms of culture, the Romans were strongly affected by the Greeks and borrowed freely from them. The Romans were aware of Greek theatre practices and Greek forms such as tragedy, but—as we will see—it was Greek New Comedy with which Roman writers felt a special affinity.

The Romans are not known for innovations in theatre or for fostering theatre as a high art. Rather, they adapted theatrical practices derived from the Greeks, the Etruscans, and Atellan farces and used these for their own purposes. The Romans are significant, then, because of their development of theatre as popular entertainment.

This entertainment was designed in large measure to meet the demands of Roman audiences. Rome's many conquests led to prosperity for its citizens, who, because of their wealth and slave labor, had an abundance of leisure time. To help fill that time, theatre was offered not just at a few festivals but many times during the year.

The first major Roman festival to incorporate theatre, the Ludi Romani (mentioned above), was dedicated to Jupiter, the Roman equivalent of Zeus. The Ludi Romani, although it dated back to the sixth century B.C.E., did not include drama until 240 B.C.E., which was just about when the Romans came into contact with Greek culture. Additional festivals eventually incorporated theatre, and more days were set aside for minor festivities and theatrical activities during the republic and the empire. Historians estimate that after 250 C.E., theatrical presentations were staged on 100 days of the year.

Despite this extensive theatrical activity—and despite the fact that Roman theatre flourished for nearly seven centuries—the works of only three Roman playwrights have survived: Plautus, Terence, and Seneca. About the playwrights who preceded them, we have only scant, inconsistent bits of information. The first known dramatist to write in Latin—the language of Rome—was Livius Andronicus (fl. 240–204 B.C.E.), who created both tragedies and comedies; but he may have been born in one of the Greek territories rather than in Rome itself. It is believed that the first playwright who was born a Roman citizen was Gnaeus Naevius (c. 270–c. 201 B.C.E.). Gnaeus was especially noted for his comedies, which dramatized Roman subject matter.

Roman Comedy

As we noted above, Roman playwrights had a special affinity for Greek New Comedy. They took this Greek form and perfected their own brand of comedy, which became immensely popular with the masses. Though others were written, the comedies that survive (called *fabula pallieta*) are all based on Greek models. The changes Roman comic writers made in the plays of their predecessors included: (1) elimination of the chorus (which Greek writers had used to divide the action into episodes); (2) addition of musical accompaniment to much of the dialogue (quite possibly an Etruscan influence); (3) an emphasis on eavesdropping, which led to frequent misunderstandings and complications.

Interestingly, Roman New Comedy is the direct ancestor of all western situation comedy; these Roman comedies set a pattern that continued through many centuries and reappeared in Hollywood "screwball" comedies of the 1930s, in Broadway comedies of the same period, and in the situation comedies we see on television today.

Plautus and Terence—two of the three Roman playwrights whose works have survived—are both noted for comedy and are key figures in its history.

PLAUTUS (TITUS MACCIUS PLAUTUS)

(New York Public Library, Picture Collection)

Plautus.

Plautus (c. 254–184 B.C.E.), who worked in the last part of the third century and the first part of the second century B.C.E., was the most popular of all Roman comic writers. According to the Roman critic Cicero, Plautus was "choice, urbane, talented, and witty." His plays were written to entertain, and they delighted Romans for a long time. During the empire, mime became the favorite form of entertainment; but even when Plautus's plays were no longer being produced, they were still read and admired for their farcical situations and their mastery of colloquial Latin. In modern times, adaptations of plays by Plautus have continued to be extremely popular.

Plautus was born in Umbria but went to Rome at an early age and became an actor. When he began writing his own plays, Plautus took song, dance, and native Italian farce—with which he was very familiar—and combined these elements with characters and plots from the New Comedy of Hellenistic Greece. His comedies, like Greek New Comedy, did not have a chorus and did not deal with contemporary

(© Richard Termine)

THE BOYS FROM SYRACUSE

Roman comedies have often been adapted by later playwrights. Plautus's *The Menaechmi*—about lost twin brothers who are mistaken for each other and their slaves—was transformed by Shakespeare into *The Comedy of Errors*, and by Rodgers and Hart in the twentieth century into the musical *The Boys from Syracuse*. The scene here is from the Roundabout Theatre production of the musical.

political or social issues. Instead, they depict the trials and tribulations of romance. In performance, Plautus's plays may have resembled modern musical comedies, because it is believed that a good portion of the dialogue was sung.

Because of his reputation as the master of comedy, over 100 plays were attributed to Plautus, but no more than 45 are now considered authentic. Twenty of his plays and fragments of one more have survived and have been used as models by playwrights from the Renaissance to the present day, including Shakespeare, Ben Jonson, and Molière. Shakespeare's *Comedy of Errors* and Rodgers and Hart's musical *The Boys from Syracuse* are based on *The Menaechmi*. In his *Miles Gloriosus*, Plautus established the braggart soldier as a type—a blustering, pompous man who is secretly a coward. Material from *Miles Gloriosus* and another of Plautus's plays, *Pseudolus*, is included in the musical comedy *A Funny Thing Happened on the Way to the Forum*.

Plautus's *Amphitryon* was the basis of comic versions of that myth by numerous later writers, including Molière and Jean Giraudoux. Plautus's other best-known plays are *The Merchant, The Carthaginians, The Rope, Casina, The Pot of Gold, The Captives, The Haunted House, The Churl,* and *The Girl from Persia*. (The dates of individual plays by Plautus are unknown, but they are all presumed to have been written between 205 and 184 B.C.E.) However, his best-known work is *The Menaechmi*.

The Menaechmi

The Menaechmi, a play about mistaken identity involving a set of twins, is a typical comedy by Plautus. Many stock Roman characters can be found in *The Menaechmi*. Peniculus or "Sponge" is a parasite; Erotium is a comic courtesan; Messenio is a comic servant. The minor characters include a domineering wife, a doddering father-in-law, and a quack doctor.

The setting of the play calls for two doors on the stage: one opens on the house of Menaechmus of Epidamnus (the Greek city in which Plautus has set his play); the other is the door to the house of Erotium, a woman with whom Menaechmus is having a love affair that he is trying to keep secret from his wife. The stage represents the street in front of the two houses; at one end is an exit to the port, and at the other end is an exit to the center of town.

At the beginning of the play, an actor comes onstage to deliver a prologue, spoken directly to the audience. He asks the audience to pay careful attention to what Plautus has to say, and then he outlines the background of the story: how the Menaechmi twins were separated when they were infants and how the twin from Syracuse is just now returning to try to find his long-lost brother.

When the action of the play begins, Menaechmus of Epidamnus and a friend, the hanger-on known as "Sponge," have a conversation in which they establish a number of plot threads. For example, under his outer clothes Menaechmus is wearing one of his wife's prettiest dresses, which he is going to give to his mistress, Erotium. Later, Erotium sends the dress out to be altered, and when Menaechmus's wife looks for the dress and cannot find it, all kinds of complications develop. A bit later Menaechmus's twin from Syracuse comes on the scene and is mistaken for his brother by both the wife and the mistress, at which point Menaechmus of Syracuse becomes hopelessly confused. The play continues with numerous plot complications until all is resolved at the end.

TERENCE (PUBLIUS TERENTIUS AFER)

After Plautus, the most important Roman comic writer was Terence (c. 185–159 B.C.E.). Whereas Plautus's plays were robust and broadly entertaining, Terence stressed characterization, subtlety of expression, and elegant language.

(New York Public Library, Picture Collection)

Terence (Publius Terentius Afer).

Like Plautus, Terence based most of his work on Greek models. Accused of plagiarizing materials from Greek comedies, Terence wrote that he did "not deny having done so" and added that he "meant to do it again." Actually, reworking Greek comedies was a common practice among other Roman authors (including Plautus, as we have seen), so it is likely that this criticism of Terence was motivated by other reasons—perhaps by envy of his talent and his rapid rise in social status.

It was Terence's practice to combine plot elements from two Greek plays to create one new work. Terence provided his defense of his work in his spoken prologues. In this regard, he broke with the tradition of using the prologue to provide background information or to summarize the plot.

Terence's life was itself dramatic. He was born in Carthage and brought to Rome as a slave. The *Afer* in his name may indicate that he was an African, and therefore he may have been the first major black playwright in western theatre. His owner, a senator, educated the young playwright, freed him, and may have introduced him to a literary circle that included a group of prominent writers and philosophers.

Terence's association with high society is reflected in his comedies, which are noted for their subtle humor and cultivated Latin. His plots are more carefully constructed than those of Plautus; and he often used a double plot, placing two characters in similar romantic situations and examining their differing reactions. Though his plays were admired by his learned friends, the populace preferred more lively entertainments. Terence had to present his play *The Mother-in-Law* three times before he could get an audience to sit through the whole performance. On the first two tries, audience members were distracted by nearby circus-type entertainments, which they left the theatre to attend.

While Terence's plots are as complicated as Plautus's, Terence's style is different: more literary and less exaggerated. Terence's *Phormio* dramatizes the attempts of two cousins, Antipho and Phaedria, to overcome their fathers' objections to their lovers. Both young men are aided by Phormio—a tricky parasite—and by dramatic coincidences. The plot complications and stock characters are similar to those in Plautus's *The Menaechmi*, but *Phormio* is less farcical and less slapstick. Much of its humor is verbal; there is less physical comic action but more sparring with words—which makes Terence's work less theatrical than Plautus's. It should also be noted that whereas much of Plautus's dialogue was meant to be sung, Terence's dialogue was spoken.

Subsequent periods, such as the Middle Ages and the Renaissance, held the plays of Terence in great esteem. His plays—more than those of any other Roman dramatist or any Greek dramatist—were used as literary models in medieval convents and monasteries and in Renaissance schools. Hrosvitha of Gandersheim, for example, was called a "Christian Terence." (Hrosvitha is discussed in Chapter 4.) The simple style of Terence's Latin and the high moral tone of his plays made them popular with teachers and scholars.

(North Wind Picture Archives)

STOCK CHARACTERS The comedies of Terence feature a number of stock characters, such as the two shown in the basic drawing seen here—the Parasite (on the left) and the Soldier. Stock characters in Roman comedy had predictable traits and were usually dressed in the same type of costume in every drama.

Terence wrote six plays, all of which have survived: *Andria* (166 B.C.E.); *The Mother-in-Law* (165 B.C.E.); *The Self-Tormentor* (163 B.C.E.); *The Eunuch* (161 B.C.E.); *Phormio* (161 B.C.E.); and *The Brothers* (160 B.C.E.).

We have no idea what happened to Roman comedy after Terence's death; no works survive from that period. We assume, however, that because no plays have been preserved, there was a decline in the quality of comedies.

Roman Tragedy

References to only a few Roman tragic playwrights survive. They include Quintius Ennius (239–169 B.C.E.), Marcus Pacuvius (c. 220–130 B.C.E.), and Lucius Accius (170–c. 86 B.C.E.). Their work appears to have been well regarded when it first appeared, but since no plays survive, it must be assumed that they fell out of favor. Many scholars believe that tragedies written after the first century B.C.E. were not meant for large public performances, because Roman society became much more interested in spectacular popular entertainments. The only tragic playwright of note in the Roman period was Seneca.

DEBATES IN THEATRE HISTORY | Was Terence the First Black Playwright?

There are many scholarly debates about Roman theatre, one of the more intriguing being the ethnic background of the playwright Terence.

Most of the biographical details about this comic playwright come from *The Life of Terence,* written after his death by the Roman author Suetonius. Suetonius states that Terence, whose full name was Publius Terentius Afer, was born in Carthage and brought to Rome as a slave. Suetonius also remarks that Terence was dark-complexioned, and some scholars have suggested that this indicates that he was a black African. The use of *Afer* as part of his name was a reference to North Africa; in a Latin name, it frequently denoted a person from Libya.

This interpretation has become more prominent in recent years, as historians try to identify Afrocentric rather than Eurocentric origins of cultural achievements. (An Afrocentric approach to history suggests that scholars explore the African origins of many accomplishments usually credited to European cultures.)

However, Walter E. Forehand, in *Terence,* notes that there is little evidence that Terence was a black slave from Africa.* He argues that many biographers of the time embellished their subjects' life stories to make them more interesting literary figures. In addition, he argues that while Terence may have been from Carthage or Libya, it is unlikely that he was from an area south and east of them, and it is those areas which had black populations.

The debate over whether Terence was a black African slave—and therefore the first black playwright in western theatre—is not easily resolved. As Forehand states, "As interesting as the question may be, nothing in our biographical sources suggests an answer."†

*Twayne, Boston, Mass., 1985.
†Ibid., p. 6.

SENECA (LUCIUS ANNAEUS SENECA)

(New York Public Library, Picture Collection)

Seneca (Lucius Annaeus Seneca).

The chief Roman tragic writer whose plays have survived is Seneca (c. 4 B.C.E.–65 C.E.). Though there is no absolute proof of his identity, it is generally believed that he is the Roman writer by that name who served as tutor to the emperor Nero.

Seneca's life was somewhat contradictory. As a writer, he espoused Stoicism, a philosophy of moderation and calm acceptance of whatever happens. In his personal life, though, he was an epicure and something of a voluptuary, enjoying the pleasures of the flesh which Stoics were supposed to forgo. These extremes reflect the contradictory forces that characterized Roman life during his time.

Seneca was born in Cordoba, Spain, and was sent to Rome at an early age. He explored a number of philosophies, including one based on a vegetarian diet, before beginning to write his essays on Stoicism and launching his career in politics. By 32 C.E., he was a noted orator. Caligula, the mad Roman emperor, was so envious of Seneca's oratorical skills that he considered executing Seneca and actually did exile him for 2 years, hoping that he would die abroad. Seneca was later exiled again, for 7 years, by Messalina, wife of the emperor Claudius, probably for political reasons, though the charge was adultery with the emperor's niece.

In 49 C.E., Seneca was recalled to Rome by Agrippina, Claudius's new wife, to be tutor to her son, Nero. When Nero became emperor in 54, Seneca became one of his chief advisers, running the government for 5 years and amassing a fortune. Seneca fell from power in 62, and in 65 the emperor ordered him to commit suicide (being ordered by a ruler or a court to take one's own life was a common practice in Greece and Rome). Seneca the Stoic obeyed calmly, discussing philosophy to the end.

Nine plays by Seneca—*The Trojan Women, Medea, Oedipus, Phaedra, Thyestes, Hercules on Oeta, The Mad Hercules, The Phoenician Women,* and *Agamemnon*—are the only surviving examples of Roman tragedy; all are based on Greek myths. (Individual dates for his plays are not known.) Scholars continue to debate whether Seneca's dramas were staged during his lifetime or whether he wrote them as "closet dramas" intended not for production but rather for recitation at banquets or other special events attended by royalty and the nobility.

On the surface, Seneca's plays appear to be similar to Greek tragedies. His plots are reworkings of Greek tales, and—like the Greeks—he uses a chorus. But his tragedy is quite different. His choruses are not integral to the dramatic action, and unlike Greek dramatists, he emphasizes violent spectacle. Scenes that the Greeks would have banished from the stage—stabbings, murders, suicides—are often the climactic onstage moments in Seneca's works. In his *Thyestes,* for example, Thyestes eats the flesh of his children and drinks their blood in full view of the audience; and in his *Oedipus,* Jocasta cuts out her womb and Oedipus blinds himself onstage. This interest in violent spectacle has later historical parallels, of course. Today, there are numerous examples of suspense films that emphasize brutally realistic moments of violence. Some of these—such as the films of Alfred Hitchcock (like *Psycho* and *The Birds*)—are artistically interesting. The majority, however, exploit sensational violence: hatchet murders, animals and insects that prey on humans, demonic forces let loose. Seneca, by contrast, does not exploit violence; he relates it to his themes and to the tragic circumstances of his characters.

Seneca's plays also differ from Greek tragedy in that his characters do not have a tragic flaw; instead, they are obsessed by an overwhelming emotion. In *Thyestes,* for instance, Atreus is obsessed with revenge.

Because Seneca's characters are consumed by one motive, his plays seem highly melodramatic. Supernatural beings often appear in the dramatic action, adding to this melodramatic quality. Seneca's scripts include long, detailed monologues, and his characters frequently spout moralistic axioms.

Although Seneca's popularity has never matched that of the Greek tragic dramatists, his influence on later periods is noteworthy. Seneca's tragedies, written in Latin—and therefore more accessible than the works of the Greek golden age—had a tremendous influence on Renaissance playwrights. His structure of five episodes separated by choral odes became the basis for five-act tragedy. Other elements of Senecan tragedy admired in the Renaissance included the use of supernatural characters, such as ghosts and witches; the depiction of violence onstage; and the use of soliloquies and asides. Shakespeare, for example, was greatly influenced by Seneca's dramatic style; *Hamlet*—which presents much onstage violence, includes soliloquies, and has a supernatural character, the ghost of Hamlet's father—is often described as a Senecan revenge tragedy.

Dramatic Criticism in Rome

Like Roman drama, Roman dramatic criticism was based on the work of others, especially Aristotle. The best-known writer of dramatic theory and criticism in the Roman period was Horace, who is sometimes referred to as the "Roman Aristotle."

Horace's *Ars Poetica* (*The Art of Poetry;* 24–20 B.C.E.) is the only Latin treatise on dramatic criticism still in existence. Horace's work, known to Renaissance scholars and writers before the rediscovery of Aristotle, had a tremendous impact on Renaissance dramatic theory and on the structure of Renaissance plays.

HORACE (QUINTUS HORATIUS FLACCUS)

Son of a freed slave, Horace (65–8 B.C.E.) was a poet who became the friend of Virgil and other leading literary figures of the early Roman empire. He was famous for his lyric poetry—the *Satires* and the *Epodes*—as well as *The Art of Poetry.*

Horace was born in Venusia, an Italian town that had once been a Greek colony. His father, a government collector of market dues, sent the young writer to study in both Athens and Rome so that he might qualify for a high government post. During the civil war that followed the assassination of Julius Caesar, Horace fought with Brutus's army at Philippi. Pardoned by Augustus, the new emperor, Horace went to Rome, obtained a government post, and began writing.

(Culver Pictures)
Horace (Quintus Horatius Flaccus).

At that time, wealthy Romans, following the lead of the emperor, supported literature and the arts; Horace's literary patron gave him a farm, which freed him from financial worries so that he could concentrate on writing. His careful craftsmanship, humor, and use of language attracted the attention of the emperor, who commissioned him to write a fourth book of odes. When he died, Horace was the leading lyric poet of his time.

In his essay on poetic form, Horace surveys the history and theory of dramatic poetry. Less profound and less focused on detail than Aristotle, Horace stressed rules, such as his rule that comedy and tragedy must never be combined. He held that a play should have five acts, that only three speaking characters should appear at the same time, and that gods should not be brought in unless absolutely necessary to resolve a plot. The chorus should be used to forward the action, set a high moral tone, and give "good and sage counsel." Horace felt that the purpose of drama was "to profit and to please"; in other words, writers should both entertain and instruct their audience. Though this opinion was not found in Aristotle, Renaissance critics made it a rule of drama.

Another of Horace's concerns emphasized during the Renaissance was *decorum.* Basically, decorum meant that the language and actions of characters must fit traditional ideas of suitable behavior for their age, gender, social status, and emotional state. Horace wanted writers to avoid extremes of emotion and to attempt to be truthful. Anything overly offensive or overly marvelous (fantastical) should be kept offstage.

THEATRE PRODUCTION IN ROME

ACTORS AND ACTING COMPANIES

Roman production practices differed slightly from those of Greece. Festivals were under the jurisdiction of a local government official who hired an acting troupe. The *dominus,* or head, of a troupe—who was usually the leading actor—made financial arrangements, bought dramas from playwrights, hired musicians, and obtained costumes. Since several companies were hired for each festival, there was an atmosphere of "unofficial" competition, with popular performers vying for rewards from prestigious audience members. Popular entertainments, however, frequently overshadowed the traditional dramatic presentations.

Acting companies hired to stage drama consisted of at least six male members; the Romans ignored the Greek "three-actor rule" even though it was endorsed by Horace. Roman acting technique emphasized detailed pantomime and broad physical gestures, which were necessitated by the size of the Roman theatres; it also stressed beautiful vocal delivery. As noted earlier, probably about two-thirds of the lines in Plautus's comedies were sung.

In today's theatre, actors who play the same kinds of roles over and over again are less esteemed than those who perform a variety of roles. The Romans, however, admired performers who specialized in playing one type of role and who refined a stock characterization. Facial expression was unimportant, since full linen head masks were worn. The masks included an attached wig and therefore covered the entire head. Only mimes performed without masks. The costumes worn by performers followed practices inherited from the Greeks.

The position of actors in Roman society continues to be debated by theatre historians. Some believe that actors were usually slaves and that the dominus who organized a troupe was a free man who purchased his performers. Other historians note that "stars" in Roman theatre were highly respected, well rewarded financially, and accepted socially. Aesopus and Roscius were two such stars. Claudius Aesop (known as Aesopus), who died in 54 B.C.E., left an estate estimated to have been worth the equivalent of perhaps $1 million. Quintus Roscius Gallus (Roscius) was so well connected socially that his friends included the statesman and orator Cicero; when Roscius died in 62 B.C.E., his estate was evidently worth more than the equivalent of $1 million. Still, the majority of actors were probably slaves or unesteemed members of Roman society, barely able to survive financially.

Theatre Buildings and Scenic Elements

To make theatre available to large numbers of people, the Romans built many impressive theatres throughout the empire. They redesigned the Greek amphitheatre but, ironically, did not construct a permanent theatre until 55 B.C.E.; thus, during the lifetime of Plautus and Terence—the best playwrights Rome produced—there were no permanent spaces for presenting their works. Temporary wooden structures, probably similar to the later permanent theatres, were originally erected for theatrical presentations.

Although these structures were temporary, it should not be inferred that they were not elaborate. Many were built by powerful figures, both in and out of government, who wished to impress others with their wealth and grandeur; thus the temporary theatres may well have been sizable and quite ornate. Officials of Rome were opposed to building permanent theatres because, it was argued, they might pose a danger to public morals. This ban was broken by Pompey the Great, who built an impressive stone theatre in 55 B.C.E. He insisted that it was a religious

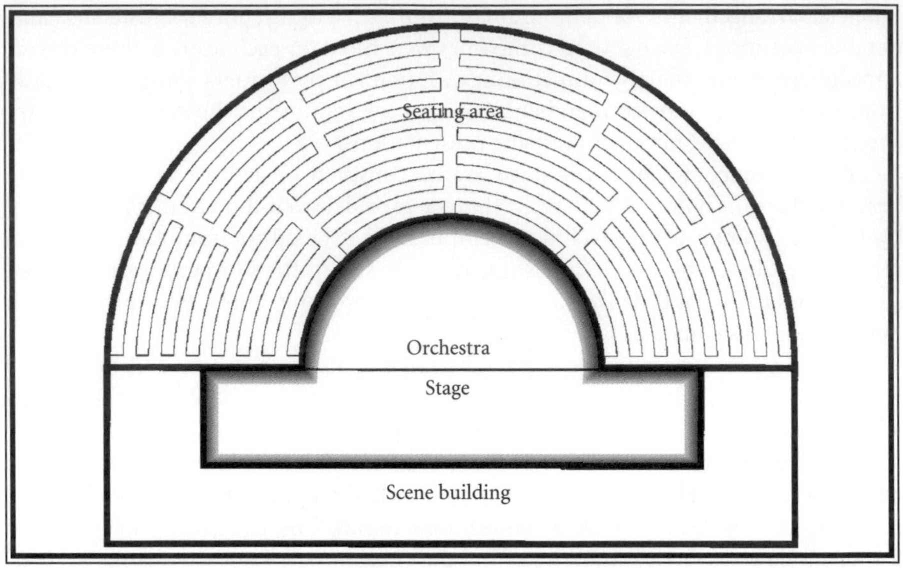

GROUND PLAN OF A TYPICAL ROMAN THEATRE
Roman theatres, in contrast to Greek theatres, were freestanding structures—all one building—with the stone stage house connected to the seating area, known as the cavea. The orchestra was a semicircle instead of a full circle as in Greek theatres. The stage was long and wide, and the stage house was several stories high with an elaborate facade.

edifice, not a theatre, because he had placed a religious shrine near the top. From then on, permanent stone theatres were gradually built throughout the empire.

Roman theatres had the same three units found in the Greek buildings: the *cavea* (the Roman version of the *theatron,* or audience seating area), the *orchestra,* and the *scaena* (the Roman version of the skene, or scene house).

The Roman structures, however, were different from those of classical Greece. The Romans had developed the arch and other engineering techniques that allowed flexibility in construction, and they put this knowledge to good use in building theatres. Roman theatres were usually not built into hillsides but were freestanding structures with a tiered audience section connected to the scene house. The cavea, the audience seating area, was often larger than the Greek theatron; some Roman theatres could hold up to 25,000 spectators. (The seating capacity of Roman theatres varied, however; for example, one of the three permanent theatres constructed in Rome accommodated only 8,000 spectators.) Roman planners also attempted to make audiences comfortable: to protect the spectators from intense heat, awnings were set up and fans blew air over cooled water—a primitive form of air conditioning.

The orchestra was semicircular rather than circular. It was rarely used for staging, but instead was used for seating government officials and for the flooding required for sea battles. In front of the scaena was a large raised stage, about 5 feet high, called the *pulpitum;* its dimensions varied from 100 feet by 20 feet to 300 feet (the length of a football field) by 40 feet. Few of today's performers will have an opportunity to act on a stage that huge.

(© Vanni/Art Resource, N.Y.)

ROMAN THEATRES
The Romans built theatres throughout their empire, which circled the Mediterranean Sea. Shown here is the Roman theatre at Orange, France, near the center of town. It was built in the first or second century C.E. and is one of the best-preserved of all Roman theatres. Note the semicircular orchestra, the large stage area, and the stage house at the back, with its ornate facade with niches for statues and other adornments.

The scaena itself was a unique feature of the Roman theatre. Two or three stories high, it was used for storage and dressing space, and a roof extended out from the scene building over the stage to protect the actors from the elements. Two side wings enclosed the pulpitum and connected the scaena to the cavea. The *scaena frons*—the facade of the scaena—was elaborate and ornate, with statuary, columns, recesses, and three to five entrances; the central entrance was the largest and had stairs leading up to it. The facade was meant to represent a typical Roman street scene, the basic scenic requirement of Roman comedy; it could also represent a palace, the customary tragic setting.

The scaena frons could serve as the basic setting because the Romans, following the Greek tradition, did not require a unique environment for each play. (At the beginning of *The Menaechmi,* for example, the actor who speaks the prologue points out that it is up to the audience's imagination to turn the playing space into the town of Epidamnus.) The Romans, however, did try to alter the scaena frons slightly by using periaktoi, three-sided scenic units described in Chapter 1. Where the periaktoi were located on the high pulpitum or scene house is a matter of conjecture; possibly one was placed in each of the doorways on the sides of the large central portal.

The Romans also used curtains to alter the scenic environment. There were two types of curtains: the *auleum* and the *siparium.* The auleum was a front curtain which was raised and lowered on expandable poles from a trench in front of the stage. Given the size of the scaena, the auleum could not mask the entire facade; instead, its function was to conceal actors before they were revealed to the audience, much as front curtains in theatres are still used. The siparium, a painted backdrop placed against the scaena frons, slightly altered the appearance of the facade. Because of the size of the scaena frons, the siparium could never completely mask the permanent three-dimensional background.

Much of what we know about Roman theatre architecture comes from Marcus Vitruvius, who lived in the first century B.C.E. and whose ten-volume work *De Architectura* indicates that much of Roman architecture was based on Hellenistic models. Vitruvius's massive treatise, which includes a discussion of theatre buildings, became particularly influential when it was rediscovered in the Italian Renaissance. We can also reconstruct the characteristics of Roman theatre buildings by examining those which have survived the ravages of time, in such diverse locations as France, Libya, and Israel.

Popular Entertainment in Rome

A thread of popular entertainment runs throughout theatre history, and theatrical activity in Rome is a good place to introduce the notion of popular entertainments. These are presentations often of a more transitory or basic nature than theatre based on a written text or performed by an established theatre organization. At the same time, popular entertainments frequently have strong theatrical elements such as dancing, pantomime, costumes, and impersonation. Even when the performances do not conform to theatre as we know it—as would be the case with juggling, acrobatics, or the exhibition of trained animals—these presentations can be viewed as related to theatre.

There have been periods when these presentations were the only form of theatrical activity available. A good example would be the medieval period in Europe, when organized theatre had disappeared, and traveling troupes that featured juggling, dancing, or mime kept alive the notion of performances before an audience. In other eras, popular entertainment flourished alongside more formal theatrical presentations. One example is the Elizabethan period in England, when bullbaiting and bearbaiting were popular spectator sports, often taking place in the same theatre space as organized, formal theatre. Another example is the nineteenth century in the United States, when the circus, minstrel shows, and vaudeville operated alongside theatre.

Because most of the works of Plautus and Terence were based on Greek models and the plays of Seneca are not outstanding examples of tragedy, the Romans are not considered originators of great drama. However, they did develop a variety of popular entertainments, many of them adopted from Greek sources—mime and the Atellan farces mentioned earlier—and from Etruscan culture. Popular entertainments appeal to all levels of society, and no educational, social, or cultural sophistication is required to appreciate them. Some historians say that American culture of the past 100 years, with its highly developed popular entertainments—television, film, rock concerts, and other less sophisticated dramatic arts—is much like Roman culture.

(© Vanni Archive/Corbis)

POPULAR ENTERTAINMENT IN ROME
The Romans were famous for all manner of popular entertainments, which they enjoyed at the same time that they attended theatrical presentations. Among Roman favorites were trained animal acts, gladiatorial battles (sometimes to the death), staged sea battles, and chariot races. This votive plaque shows a victory in a chariot race.

Many Roman entertainments correspond to the modern circus. Chariot racing (today's equivalent would be automobile and stock car races) was popular from the seventh century B.C.E. throughout the history of the Roman empire. Equestrian performances, gymnastics, and various forms of hand-to-hand combat were also popular.

Gladiatorial combats were included in festivals at the close of the second century B.C.E. These were not necessarily make-believe fights; in some cases they were actual battles to the death. The *naumachiae* were sea battles staged on lakes, on artificial bodies of water, or in flooded arenas; the first one was organized by Julius Caesar in 46 B.C.E. Trained animals were often used in popular entertainments; they were also put on display and used in combat with unarmed humans. This interest in blood sports also has modern counterparts: in parts of the United States, illegal cockfights still take place, and in Spain and Mexico bullfighting continues to attract large numbers of spectators.

In ancient Rome, special buildings were constructed to house sporting and other spectacles. The Circus Maximus, constructed in 600 B.C.E. for chariot races and frequently remodeled thereafter, seated over 60,000 people. The most renowned Roman amphitheatre was the Colosseum, built in 80 C.E. The caverns beneath the Colosseum may have held Christians waiting to be sacrificed to wild beasts; the slaughter of early Christians by lions was viewed by the Roman populace as a spectacular diversion.

Again, this interest in human executions is not confined to the Romans; throughout the eighteenth and nineteenth centuries in England and elsewhere, public hangings drew huge crowds.

The Romans also developed popular entertainments that were more truly theatrical. Roman mime, like Greek mime, included gymnastics, juggling, songs, and dances, and became popular in the third century B.C.E. The variety of entertainments referred to as *mime* during Roman times makes this form difficult to define. Short, risqué (that is, sexually suggestive) comedic skits were frequently part of mime performances. (The Romans enjoyed sexually provocative dramatic material, and the emperor Heliogabalus, in the first part of the third century C.E., is said to have forced mimes to perform actual sexual acts.)

The mimes performed in found spaces, that is, spaces in town squares or open courtyards that could be used for performances even though not specifically designed for them. Mimes provided the primary theatrical entertainment at the Roman fertility festival, the Ludi Florales, starting about 238 B.C.E. But even though mime troupes were allowed to entertain at festivals, they, like the Greek mimes, were castigated for being transients and for including women in their ranks.

A unique Roman stage presentation was the pantomime. Some scholars believe that pantomime, which is distinct from mime, may have developed during the first century B.C.E. It required a single dancer, a chorus, and musical accompanists and might be compared to ballet. The major performer in Roman pantomime danced a mythological, historical, or occasionally comical story; the chorus chanted the narrative and explained the action. Pantomime performers were often supported by emperors and wealthy individuals.

The Decline of Roman Theatre

In the fourth century C.E., it was clear that the Roman empire was beginning to fall apart. In 330, the emperor Constantine established two capitals: Rome in the west and Constantinople in the east. From that point on, the center of gravity moved from the west to the east, toward Constantinople, and Rome became less and less of a factor.

The downfall of Rome, marked by the unseating of the western Roman emperor by a barbarian ruler in 476 C.E., was caused by the disintegration of the Roman administrative structure and the sacking of Roman cities by northern barbarians. Not all of Rome, however, fell. The eastern part, known as the Byzantine empire, continued to exist until 1453, when it was conquered by the Islamic Turks.

The decline of Roman theatre coincided with the downfall of the western empire. Yet the fall of Rome is not the only explanation for the deterioration of its theatre. Theatre itself had become less of an art form and more of an entertainment, to the point where distinguishing between theatrical offerings and circuses, or between gladiatorial contests and pantomimes, often became difficult.

Another important factor in the decline of Roman theatre was the rise of Christianity. From the outset, the Christian church was opposed to theatre. Early Christians saw a connection between theatre and pagan religions, and the church fathers argued that the evil characters portrayed onstage taught immorality. Church leaders were offended by the sexual content of Roman entertainments and by their frequent satirical attacks on Christianity. As a result, the church issued various edicts condemning theatre and its participants. In 398 C.E., a church council decreed that anyone who went to the theatre rather than to church on holy days would be excommunicated, and performers were not allowed to take part in holy rites.

These attacks had far-reaching historical ramifications. As late as the seventeenth century, the French playwright Molière was refused Christian burial because he had been an actor and dramatist. Ironically, the institution that condemned theatre to perdition was to revive it five centuries later: the Roman Catholic church was the impetus in the rebirth of western theatre. But this was later; the early Christian church opposed theatre, and that was one reason why theatre as an organized institution disappeared for the time being.

Another important reason was the disintegration of Roman civilization. The invaders from the north plundered the cities of the Roman empire, and after a time no large centers of culture remained. People scattered, and in many places the buildings that had housed government offices, schools, and performing spaces were abandoned. The plays of the Greek and Roman dramatists and the writings of Aristotle and Horace were lost or forgotten. The tradition of theatre that had stretched virtually unbroken for nearly 1,000 years, from the Greeks in the fifth century B.C.E. through the early centuries of the Christian era, was at an end.

The dispersal and destruction of educational, political, and cultural institutions led later historians to call the period after the fall of the Roman empire the *dark ages*. Many present-day historians, however, believe that this term is simplistic and too negative. The fall of the Roman empire did not occur overnight; the empire had been deteriorating from within for many years. By the seventh and eighth centuries the medieval system of self-contained, church-centered communities had begun to emerge—though it would be some time before theatre was again a full-fledged institution in Europe.

Meanwhile, in the same period during which theatre was dormant in the west, it began to emerge in Asia, to which we turn in Chapter 3.

SUMMARY

The Romans borrowed many Greek conventions, including the introduction of drama and theatre into religious and civic festivals, but modified them so that they became uniquely Roman. The Romans did not produce great original plays, but the New Comedies of Plautus and Terence, as well as the tragedies of Seneca, are noteworthy because of their influence on later playwrights. Instead of significant drama, Roman civilization developed sophisticated forms of popular entertainment.

Horace's *Ars Poetica* was an attempt to establish dramatic rules for Roman dramatists.

Roman theatres were usually huge outdoor buildings. In Roman playhouses (unlike Greek theatres) all elements were connected. The most significant elements were the ornate facade of the scene house and the huge raised stage. The Romans were the first to use curtains for scenic variety. The male actors who performed in these playhouses, unlike the Greeks, were professionals.

MILESTONES CHAPTER 2 ROMAN THEATRE [C. 650 B.C.E.–476 C.E.]

Etruscan [c. 650–450 B.C.E.]

Theatre History

- Circus Maximus (600 B.C.E.)
- Ludi Romani, by Etruscan ruler, Tarquin the elder (sixth century B.C.E.)
- Mime and Atellan farce emerge in southern Italy *(right)*

Cultural and Historical Developments

- Traditional date for the founding of Rome (753 B.C.E.)

Republic [500–27 B.C.E.]

Theatre History

- Mime performances popular in Rome (third century B.C.E.)
- Comedy and tragedy added to Ludi Romani (240 B.C.E.)
- Gnaeus Naevius (c. 270–c. 201 B.C.E.), credited as first Roman playwright
- Livius Andronicus (fl. 240–204 B.C.E.), first known dramatist to write in Latin
- Comic genre *fibula pallieta* develops
- Plautus (Titus Maccius Plautus, c. 254–184 B.C.E.), *The Menaechmi*
- Tragic playwrights: Quintius Ennius (239–169 B.C.E.); Marcus Pacuvius (c. 220–c. 130 B.C.E.); Lucius Accius (170–c. 86 B.C.E.)
- Terence (Publius Terentius Afer, c. 185–159 B.C.E.), *(right) Phormio*

- *Pantomime* performed (first century B.C.E.)
- Marcus Vitruvius, *De Architectura* (90 B.C.E.)
- Actors Roscius (d. 62 B.C.E.) and Aesopus (d. 54 B.C.E.)
- First permanent theater built in Rome by Pompey (55 B.C.E.)
- Julius Caesar organizes *naumachiae* (46 B.C.E.)

Cultural and Historical Developments

- Greek influence on Roman culture (250–150 B.C.E.)
- Punic Wars between Rome and Carthage (246–146 B.C.E.)
- Hannibal, Carthaginian general, achieves military victories (218–216 B.C.E.) *(right)*

- Rome defeats Philip V of Macedonia (200–197 B.C.E.)
- Censorship of Cato; 1,000 talents spent on sewers (184 B.C.E.)
- Roman citizens freed of direct taxation (167 B.C.E.)
- Rome annexes Macedonia (147 B.C.E.)
- First high-level aqueduct in Rome (144 B.C.E.)
- Slave revolts in Sicily (135 B.C.E.)
- Pompey suppresses piracy (67 B.C.E.)
- Caesar's conquest of Gaul (58–50 B.C.E.)
- Golden age of Roman literature (c. 50–10 B.C.E.)
- Jesus crucified (30 C.E.) *(right)*

continued

PHOTO CREDITS: Atellan farce. (© Erich Lessing/Art Resource, N.Y.) / Terence. (New York Public Library, Picture Collection) / *Hannibal Fighting a Roman Legion in the Alps*, from the school of Raphael. (© Araldo de Luca/Corbis) / *The Holy Trinity* by Tiepolo. (© Cameraphoto/Art Resource, N.Y.)

MILESTONES CHAPTER 2 ROMAN THEATRE [C. 650 B.C.E.–476 C.E.] *continued*

Empire [27 B.C.E.–476 C.E.]

Theatre History

- Horace, *Art of Poetry* (*Ars Poetica,* 24–20 B.C.E.)
- Romans build theaters and amphitheaters throughout the empire (c. 30–200 C.E.)
- Seneca (Lucius Annaeus Seneca, c. 4 B.C.E.–65 C.E.), *Thyestes*
- Colosseum built (80 C.E.) *(below)*

- Council of Carthage decrees excommunication for those who attend theater rather than church on holy days; actors forbidden sacraments (398 C.E.)

Cultural and Historical Developments

- Marcus Aurelius rules (161–180 C.E.)
- Extensive persecution of the Christians (c. 250–300 C.E.)
- Constantine rules (324–337 C.E.) *(right)*
- St. Augustine born (354 C.E.)
- Julian the Apostate restores paganism (361 C.E.)
- Theodosius I forbids pagan worship (391 C.E.)
- Sack of Rome by Visigoths (410 C.E.)
- Death of Attila the Hun (453 C.E.)
- Fall of western Roman empire (476 C.E.)

PHOTO CREDITS: The Roman Colosseum. (Royalty-Free/Corbis) / Constantine the Great. (Bildarchiv Preussischer Kulturbesitz/Art Resource, N.Y.)

CHAPTER 3
EARLY ASIAN THEATRES

KABUKI

Much of Asian theatre is highly stylized and uses well-established gestures, music, dance, and often masks. Moreover, Asian theatre often perpetuates theatrical customs, styles, and stories that have been in use for hundreds or even thousands of years. Shown here is a kabuki theatre as depicted in a color woodblock print by Utagawa Toyokuni. Note the characteristic costumes, the two levels of the stage, and the musicians seated on the upper level.

(Réunion des Musées Nationaux/Art Resource, N.Y.)

For 1,000 years, from approximately 350 to 1350 C.E., there was no organized theatre in the west. But on the continent of Asia, thousands of miles away, theatre had begun to emerge. The development of theatre began in India over 2,000 years ago, and theatre later became well established in China while formal theatre was still moribund in the west. Theatre in Japan followed not long after. These traditions of Asian theatre, established centuries ago, continue to the present day.

Background: The Theatres of Asia

The people who created theatre in Asia knew nothing of the theatres of Greece or Rome. In the Introduction, we discussed the universal tendency toward theatre and observed that except where theatre is expressly forbidden by religious or other laws, it is likely to emerge in any civilization. This was true in India, China, and Japan—the countries we will focus on in this chapter—and also in other Asian countries, such as Indonesia.

Each of the Asian theatres is unique, but these theatres also have aspects in common that set them apart from western theatre. To mention two: they rely much more on dance than western theatre does (in many instances, Asian theatrical presentations could be called *dance dramas*), and they emphasize symbolism. All the great Asian traditions—including those of India, China, and Japan—have created and sustained one form or another of what has been described as *total theatre.* In this type of theatre there is a synthesis or integration of elements—acting, mime, dancing, music, and text—more complete than in traditional western theatre. Though each of the Asian theatrical traditions is unique and self-contained, all have qualities that may seem familiar to westerners who have been exposed to opera, in which a colorful blending of ideas, art, and technique is crucial.

One reason why this kind of synthesis developed in Asia and found continued support lies in the fact that the religious roots of theatre are still kept alive there. Each of the three Asian traditions on which we will focus—Indian, Chinese, and Japanese—reached a high point of artistic excellence at a time when religion and philosophy were central in its culture. This level of excellence has kept the focus of traditional theatre at least allied to religion and philosophy, even when society itself changed and became modernized.

We can speculate on the antecedents of theatre in India, China, and Japan, but the actual origins of theatre in each culture often remain obscure. The high point, however, usually occurred when writers of poetic and intellectual ability began to create a dramatic tradition in which the text assumed a central place. (Some scholars suggest a connection among the three traditions, noting that Chinese theatre may have been influenced by Indian theatre, which in turn may have influenced Japanese theatre.)

What remained in later years was usually the words rather than the production style; this is, of course, partially explained by the fact that anything written, such as a script, has some permanence, whereas a performance is ephemeral. Thus little is known of early performance practices in China or India. Japan, on the other hand, is unique in having preserved many of the ancient techniques of acting, dancing, and singing. Still, in all three theatres the ancient traditions—interpreted and reinterpreted as these cultures developed and changed—have continued to color and shape many later experiments.

Indian Theatre

Indian history has been characterized as a succession of immigrations into the Indian subcontinent. Early traces of civilization there go back to 3000 B.C.E. The Aryans, who came into southern India 1,000 years later, left behind works in Sanskrit that constitute the basis of the great Indian literary traditions. Scholars believe that by 1000 B.C.E., certain fundamental aspects of Indian civilization were already established; one of these is the

Asia
Year, c.e.

300 · 500 · 700 · 900 · 1100 · 1300 · 1500 · 1700

Theatre

- *Natyasastra*, major critical work of Indian Sanskrit drama (c. 200 B.C.E.–100 C.E.)
- Sanskrit drama highly developed in India (320–600)
- *Shakuntala*, famous Sanskrit drama by Indian author Kalidasa (fifth century)
- *The Little Clay Cart*, Indian Sanskrit drama attributed to King Shudraka (fifth century)
- Academy of the Pear Garden, school for dancers and singers, founded in China (714)
- Development of professional theater companies in China (960)
- Decline of Sanskrit drama (1150)
- Indian dance drama, puppet plays, and folk plays (late twelfth century)
- Scholars and artists work in popular theater in China (thirteenth century)
- Zeami Motokiyo (1363–1444); development of nō drama
- Literary and romantic drama develops during Ming period in China (1368–1664)
- In Japan, kabuki first performed in Kyoto (1600–1610)
- Nō becomes an aristocratic entertainment and rigidly codified (1650)
- Kabuki becomes popular form of theater (1675–1750)
- Chikamatsu Monzaemon begins writing for bunraku (puppet theater) (1684)
- Bunraku formalized in Japan (1685)

Culture and Politics

- In India, spread of Buddhism; trade with China, Egypt, Rome, southeast Asia; gandhara school of art flourishes (180 B.C.E.–150 B.C.E.)
- Golden age of classical Sanskrit in India (300–500)
- Earliest known use of zero and decimals occurs in India (600)
- Tang dynasty in China (618–907)
- Travels in India of Xuan Zang, Chinese pilgrim and chronicler (630–644)
- Song dynasty in China (960–1279); flowering of arts, literature, and scholarship
- Civil strife in Japan leads to military government (1100)
- Beginning of Muslim rule in India (1192)
- Marco Polo visits court of Kublai Khan, Beijing, China (1271); Polo visits Kayal, southern India (1288)
- Yuan dynasty in China (1279–1368)
- Rule of Yoshimitsu (rules 1395–1408) in Japan; years of stability followed by civil wars
- Ming dynasty in China (1368–1644)
- First Europeans visit Japan (1542)
- Period of national unification in Japan (1568–1600)
- Rule of Shah Jahan in India; construction of great buildings, including Taj Mahal (1628–1657)
- Qing (Ching) dynasty in China (1644–1911)

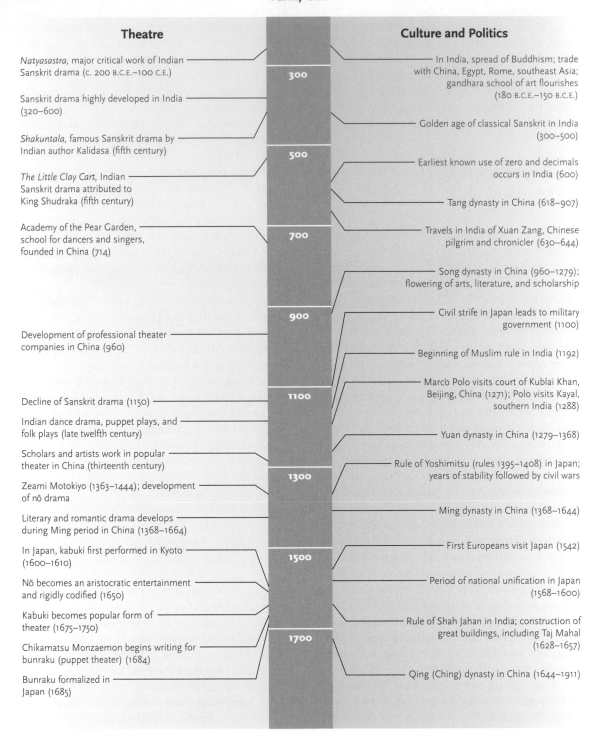

caste system, under which people are classified by heredity: a person must remain in the caste to which he or she is born, and people are forbidden to change occupations.

Around 400 B.C.E., Buddhism, which had its origins in India, reached a peak of development, and soon it became a major force throughout eastern and central Asia. Based on the ideas of Gautama Buddha (c. 563–483 B.C.E.), Buddhism teaches that suffering is inherent in life but that human beings can be liberated from suffering by mental and moral self-purification. King Asoka, who ruled in India about 240 B.C.E., managed to unite the whole nation under Buddhist rule, but a period of disorder and confusion followed until the Gupta dynasty began to unite the nation again around 320 C.E.

It was at this time that another important thread in Indian history, Hindu culture, entered a golden age; and it was during the following centuries that the great Sanskrit dramas were written and performed. Hinduism stresses the belief that soul or spirit is the essence of life; that the goal of all people is to achieve oneness with the supreme world-soul, known as *Brahman;* and that the things of this life do not exist in the same way as Brahman, which is eternal, infinite, and indescribable.

Sanskrit Drama

What remains from the tradition of the Indian golden age is a group of plays that were written in Sanskrit, the language of the noble classes, to be performed in various court circles. There are between fifty and sixty plays that can be reliably assigned to this period, and the greatest of them are among the finest works of classical Indian literature.

We have been provided a great insight into this early Indian theatre by a remarkable document called the *Natyasastra* (translated as *The Study of Theatre* or *The Art of Theatre*). The *Natyasastra* has been attributed to Bharata Muni but may well be by someone else, possibly by several people. Written sometime during the 300-year period between 200 B.C.E. and 100 C.E., it describes the mythological origin of theatre in India and also presents important material about the nature of Indian drama; it even includes a description of the theatre space in which performances took place.

In the course of this complex treatise, the author defines a quality called *rasa,* or "flavor," which permits spectators to surrender themselves to a dramatic situation corresponding to some powerful feeling that they themselves possess. Theatre can thus serve as a means toward enlightenment; art becomes a way to move toward metaphysics and the divine.

The *Natyasastra* also serves as a kind of encyclopedia of theatrical practice. In an abstract way, every element of the complex ancient theatre is treated, from gesture and posture to music, dance, voice, and so forth. Types of characters and categories of plays are discussed, and all this specific information is related in turn to a series of metaphysical principles, which, although perhaps difficult for the modern reader to grasp, are nevertheless challenging, even humbling, to read.

Although we do not know exactly how plays were performed, we learn from the *Natyasastra* that each early troupe presenting Sanskrit theatre had a leader, the *sudtradhara,* who was the chief actor and also managed all others involved in production. Men were the main performers, but women played important roles too. Acting in this type of theatre was a skill that combined voice, body, emotions, costume, and makeup in an integrated whole.

(© Lindsay Hebberd/ Woodfin Camp and Associates)

SANSKRIT DRAMA

The great early drama of India was Sanskrit, and it appears to have first developed between 200 B.C.E. and 100 C.E. Sanskrit drama reached its high point between 300 C.E. and 600 C.E. Shown here is a performance, in the Shri Shri-Govindaji Temple in Imphal, of a drama illustrating episodes from the great Sanskrit epic *The Mahabharata*. Five Vaishnavite Manipuri boys are made up to represent the Pandava brothers.

The typical theatre in which Sanskrit drama was performed was 96 feet long and 48 feet wide, divided equally into stage and auditorium, and its seating capacity was probably between 200 and 500. There were four pillars in the auditorium—colored white, yellow, red, or blue—indicating where members of different castes were to sit. A curtain divided the stage into two parts: one part for the action, and the other for dressing rooms and a behind-the-scenes area. The few records available from the later period of Sanskrit drama indicate that most performances were given by troupes invited to the courts of the nobility, and performing spaces were arranged in courtyards and similar areas.

Scenery was evidently not used, although elaborate costumes probably were. Dance, symbolic gestures, and music played an important part in the productions; but again, we have no specific information about performance practices. The plays often make use of fixed characters, such as a narrator and a clown; once again, there are no details concerning how these performers appeared onstage.

From comments in a book entitled *Mahabhasya,* some scholars believe that the main elements of Sanskrit drama, as described in the *Natyasastra,* were in place by 140 B.C.E. However, this is speculative and has not yet been proved. There are also those who believe, again without definite proof, that Greek practices, possibly brought to India by Alexander the Great during the Hellenistic period, may have had some influence on early Indian theatre. The earliest plays that survive, from the first and second centuries C.E., were written by Asvaghosa.

As we have noted, these plays were written in Sanskrit, the classical language of the nobility, though some of the lover characters in the later plays speak a hybrid of Sanskrit and local dialect. Thus they had little following among the general public, who could not understand them. The plays usually draw on themes from Indian epic literature.

From what we know, the most productive playwright of classical India was Bhasa, who may have lived around 400 C.E. Thirteen surviving plays have been attributed to him, but it is not certain they are all his. Among the best-known plays of this general era is *The Little Clay Cart,* attributed to King Sudraka, although his identity and dates have not been clearly established. He is thought by many to have lived in the fifth century C.E. *The Little Clay Cart* concerns the love between a ruined merchant and a courtesan; its style is enlivened and enriched by politics and humor. The most famous Sanskrit play, however, comes from the fourth or fifth century: this is *Shakuntala,* which is usually considered the finest classical Indian drama and whose author, Kalidasa, is the greatest of the playwrights from the classic period.

KALIDASA

Though *Shakuntala* is an acknowledged masterpiece of Indian drama, almost nothing is known about its author, Kalidasa (373?–415 C.E.). Many scholars have attempted to establish his date of birth and to learn some details of his life, but they have had little success. At one point, it was thought that he lived in the ninth century C.E., but recent studies have placed his writings in the late fourth or early fifth century. It is possible that he lived at the court of King Chandragupta II, in the city of Uj Jain.

There is no doubt that *Shakuntala* is a masterwork of Sanskrit drama. In seven acts, the play recounts the romance of King Dushyanta and Shakuntala, the foster daughter of a hermit, who secretly marry and are then subjected to a long separation brought about by the curse of an irate sage. After many trials, the lovers are reunited and the king finally meets his son and heir.

Shakuntala, which is subtitled *The Recovered Ring,* has story elements similar to Wagner's *Ring of the Nibelung:* a secret marriage, forgetfulness caused by a curse, and a magic ring. It also has ideas from Indian philosophy, religion, aesthetics, and psychology. Like all Sanskrit drama, it has both serious and comic elements and includes a large number of locations and characters. It also includes supernatural elements. In addition, *Shakuntala* has a recognition scene, in which the lovers confirm their identity through signs; this recognition through signs bears some resemblance to scenes in classic Greek tragedy.

Kalidasa's power as a lyric poet is shown in his description of the king's journey in a chariot and in his account of Shakuntala caring for her plants and a pet fawn. In fact, while *Shakuntala* follows traditional patterns of Sanskrit drama, it is set apart by Kalidasa's delicate lyricism. Kalidasa also wrote several poems that mingle love, nature imagery, and religion; and two other plays: *Malavike and Agnimitra,* a courtly comedy about a king's love for one of the palace serving women, and *Vikrama and Urvashi,* a heroic mythological drama focusing on the love of a king and a nymph.

Shakuntala is known in the west through many translations—beginning in the eighteenth century, when the German playwright Goethe found himself profoundly inspired by it. It was first translated into English in 1798 by William Jones and became well known to the literary elite throughout western Europe. It has been widely performed as a play, an opera, and a ballet.

Later Indian Drama

Sanskrit drama—both the plays themselves and dramatic criticism—had faded by the end of the ninth century. By the twelfth century, the Arabs had begun to invade India, and in 1206 they established the sultanate of Delhi. With this series of invasions, the Hindu Sanskrit tradition disappeared. Under Islamic rule, theatrical activities were not encouraged and the old ways of performing were no longer maintained among educated people.

However, folk dramas in the many vernacular languages of India had always been popular, and the continued performances of such works, while they may not have achieved a very high artistic level, helped to keep certain traditions alive. Many of these folk plays have continued to the present day. They used the same traditional epic materials as Sanskrit dramas, but most of them were created by dramatists whose names are now unknown, and the scripts—assuming that these dramas were written down—have not been preserved. Folk plays were extremely eclectic and emphasized spectacle rather than metaphysical profundity.

Also popular with the public were dance dramas that took up aspects of Indian myths. In the performance of such dramas, movement, rather than the spoken word, was strongly emphasized. These and other developments in later Indian theatre, including a well-known dance-drama form called *kathakali,* will be discussed in detail in Chapter 16.

Chinese Theatre

The civilization of China can be traced back to at least 2000 B.C.E., when a unified culture spread over large parts of the area that is now the People's Republic of China. The Shang dynasty represents the first period that can be authenticated through artifacts and documents. The period following the Shang dynasty was a turbulent era known as the Zhou dynasty. The dates of both dynasties are somewhat disputed. Traditionally, the Shang was thought to have been from 1766 to 1122 B.C.E., but some scholars suggest either 1600 or 1523 to 1028 B.C.E. The Zhou dynasty was dated from 1122 to 256 B.C.E., but alternative dates have been offered: 1027 to 256 B.C.E. In any event, during the later Zhou dynasty, Confucius, Lao-tzu, and Mencius—three of the greatest Chinese philosophers—lived and wrote. They formed part of the general background of religions, philosophies, and religious practices out of which later Chinese theatre developed.

Confucianism was based on the teachings of Confucius (551–479 B.C.E.), whose ideas about the perfectibility of human beings were never wholly embraced in his lifetime but were widely adopted by later generations. Confucianism emphasized the responsibility of one individual or group to others: a ruler to his subjects, family members to one another, friends to friends. Taoism began in the sixth century B.C.E. with the teachings of Lao-tzu (born c. 604 B.C.E.), who believed in the importance of the *tao,* or path. Taoism stresses simplicity, patience, and nature's harmony; following the tao, the path of the cosmos, leads to self-realization. A key element in the philosophy of Mencius (c. 371–288 B.C.E.) is that all people are good. Their innate moral sense can be cultivated, or it can be perverted by an unfavorable environment.

Another movement that was to influence the later development of theatre was shamanism, whose rituals combined costume, song, dance, and gesture. Shamans were spiritual leaders who were thought to have magical powers to communicate with the dead and to ward off evil spirits. Buddhism, too, found its way from India to China and was added to the religious thought and practice of the time.

In terms of political developments, by 200 B.C.E. the centralized imperial system had been developed, and China was provided with a central government that continued to remain effective through many long periods of stability down to modern times.

Early Theatre in China

The early development of theatre in China—as with many other forms of Chinese art—was linked to the patronage of the imperial court. Popular forms of theatre may also have flourished, of course, though no records of early folk performances survive. Records of court entertainments, however, go back as far as the fifth century B.C.E., and such diverse activities as skits, pantomimes, juggling, singing, and dancing are frequently mentioned in ancient chronicles.

The court of the emperors during the Tang period (618–906 C.E.) was one of the high points of human culture. At this time there was a kind of actors' training institute in the capital; it was called the Pear Garden and had been founded in 714. Details of activities and performances at the Pear Garden have not been preserved, but it firmly established a tradition of training theatrical performers.

In the Song dynasty (960–1279), which preceded the coming of the Mongols, various court entertainments contributed to the development of what are known as *variety plays.* In addition to court records, there are other documents recording the existence of traveling theatrical troupes, some permanent playhouses, and theatrical activity that involved not only actors, dancers, and singers but also shadow puppets and marionettes. Low comedy was popular as well, and its effect must have been something like our vaudeville.

A form that emerged in the province of Zhejiang, possibly in the early twelfth century, was called *nanxi,* which means "southern drama," after the region where it developed. Indications are that at this time four types of characters were predominant in Chinese theatre: the *sheng,* or male character; the *dan,* or female character; the *jing,* or painted face; and the *chou,* or clown. These were to remain staples of Chinese theatre in subsequent works.

A significant synthesis of art and popular tradition was to come in the dramas of the Yuan period, which followed the Song.

(National Palace Museum, Taipei, Taiwan, Republic of China)

EARLY CHINESE THEATRE
Detail from a silk scroll depicting, at the center on the right-hand side, a Chinese theatre set up for a festival in the twelfth century at Kaifeng, the northern capital during the Ching dynasty. (This scroll is an eighteenth-century copy of the original.) Note the covered stage on which performers appear, and the audience members standing on three sides of the stage observing the action.

Theatre in the Yuan Dynasty

The Yuan dynasty (1279–1368) was well known in the west through the writings of the Italian explorer Marco Polo. The ruler at this time was not a Chinese emperor but a Mongol, Kublai Khan, whose grandfather Genghis Khan had come down from the north to conquer China.

The Mongols, although they tolerated many Chinese customs, nevertheless dismantled much of the traditional bureaucracy. Ironically, this turned out to be an important impetus for the development of Chinese theatre. Earlier, the highly educated literati—literary intellectuals—had composed essays and poetry of the highest quality but had disdained plays as beneath their dignity. With the coming of the Mongols, many of the literati were no longer employed by the government and took up literary and theatrical work to make a living. In this way, high art and the popular theatrical tradition met. Because the complex mixture of cultural influences produced such a rich outpouring during the Yuan dynasty, scholars have compared its theatre to that of Greece in the fifth century B.C.E. and to that of Elizabethan England.

The form of drama perfected in the Yuan dynasty, often referred to as *zaju*, usually had four acts or—perhaps more accurately, since these plays used a great deal of music—four song sequences. Rather than writing specifically for the dramas, playwrights composed their texts to suit the rhythms and meters of popular music already known to the audience. Usually the protagonist sang all the music in any act. Unfortunately, none of the music has survived.

The poetic content of these plays was considered the central factor in their success. Because of their lyrical nature, these dramas had only a few characters and avoided subplots and other complications. Accounts from the Yuan period tell us that topics chosen by the playwrights ranged from love and romance to religion and history, domestic and social themes, crimes and lawsuits, and bandit heroes like the western Robin Hood.

Important Plays from the Yuan Period

Though we do not know exactly how many plays were produced during the Yuan period, there are records indicating that over 500 dramatists were writing at this time; and we know the titles of some 700 plays, of which 168 survive.

Perhaps the most famous of the plays surviving from this period is *The Romance of the Western Chamber,* actually a cycle of plays, by Wang Shifu (fl. late thirteenth century). These dramas chronicle the trials of two lovers—a handsome young student and a lovely girl of good family—who have been models for thousands of imitations down to the present century. The plays contain a certain amount of adventure and a good deal of superlative poetry.

Another popular play that has survived is *The Orphan of Chao,* which deals with vengeance, sacrifice, and loyalty. *The Orphan of Chao* was one of the first Chinese plays known in the west, as a version of it was translated into French in 1735 and was adapted for the French stage by Voltaire.

Another popular Yuan drama, *The Circle of Chalk,* is an excellent example of the lawsuit-and-trial genre in which a clever, Solomon-like judge frees an innocent person accused of a crime. When the twentieth-century German playwright Bertolt Brecht saw a version of this play (it had been freely adapted and translated into German), he was so intrigued with the theme that he created his own version: *The Caucasian Chalk Circle.*

Theatre Production in the Yuan Period

Despite the fact that many Yuan texts survive and have been admired down to the present day, relatively little is known about how they were performed. Contemporary spectators left few records of their reactions, perhaps because theatregoing was regarded as beneath the notice of highly educated people. Nevertheless, in recent years careful scholarship has managed to piece together a certain amount of information on theatre presentations.

Professional actors and actresses performed in Yuan dramas, and both would on occasion play male and female roles. Some of the actresses performed for private entertainments at the palace, and stories of their affairs in high society were as eagerly sought out as stories about the activities of today's film and television stars. The performers were organized into troupes, some of which were run by women.

Only meager information remains about the theatres used for these performances. Evidently, there was a bare stage with two doors on each side at the rear, and a painted cloth hanging between the doors. (This arrangement is shown in a wall hanging from northwestern China painted about 1324.) Most stages seem to have been built for

DEBATES IN THEATRE HISTORY — Did Playwrights in the Yuan Period Create Tragedies?

In his book *A History of Chinese Drama,* William Dolby writes: "Such plays as *Dream of Two on a Journey, Autumn in the Han Palace,* and *Rain on the Paulownia Tree* raise the perennial question of whether early Chinese drama ever contained tragedy."*

The question arises because though most Yuan plays end happily, a few of them are predominantly serious. These serious works are considered by some scholars and commentators to be the equivalent of tragedies in the west such as those of the Greeks, the Elizabethans, and the French neoclassical playwrights. The serious Yuan plays have a perfunctory or formal "happy" ending, but many scholars are not convinced that this is the ultimate outcome intended by the playwright.

As Dolby points out, *Rain on the Paulownia Tree* ends on a "purely sad note." *Dream of Two on a Journey* is, in Dolby's words, "consistently gloomy." It ends on a note of revenge, which could be considered "happy," but Dolby feels that there are circumstances which might have led the audience to feel otherwise. Knowing the history and background behind the story of *Dream of Two on a Journey,* they would realize that the revenge called for in the play actually occurred and resulted in a national disaster.†

In other words, it is argued—with some strength—that when we consider both the content and the context of several key plays, they can be seen to embody many of the characteristics of dramas which in the west have long been classified as tragedy.

At the same time, there are arguments against considering these Yuan dramas tragedies. One argument, of course, is the "happy" endings. It may be said that these endings merely conform to custom and do not indicate the true intentions of the dramatist; nevertheless, the endings are there. They would make these plays consistent, not with tragedy, but with what has been called in the west *heroic drama.* There is another argument that fascinates linguists and other scholars of language: the Chinese of the Yuan period had no character or symbol for *tragedy.* If there was not even a "word" to denote tragedy, how could anyone have written plays containing the tragic spirit or the tragic point of view? This question is posed by scholars who oppose considering these plays an Asian version of tragedy.

Thus the question whether we can justifiably think of these plays as tragedies remains undecided.

*Harper and Row, New York, 1976, p. 47.
†Ibid., pp. 47–48.

outdoor use and were not roofed over. Curtains and such properties as swords and fans were used, but there is no evidence of any scenery. Much of the color of performances came from elaborate costumes. Some of the stylized robes, which are illustrated in artworks of the time, resemble those in modern Peking (or Beijing) opera. Makeup was also important and was evidently applied heavily, in a stylized manner.

Theatre in the Ming Dynasty

By the end of the Yuan period, the level of accomplishment in theatre was very high and drama had become firmly established as a respectable art form. With the overthrow of the Mongols, however, and the establishment of the Ming dynasty (1368–1644), a Chinese emperor was restored to the throne. At this point, the traditional patterns of social behavior were restored; highly educated scholars were still able to write plays, but they tended to confine their efforts more and more to dramas that would please the elite. The theatre, because of its very legitimacy, tended to become ornate and artificial; it lost contact with the broad mass of the public, which had originally supported it.

What had been an active theatre in the Yuan dynasty, responsive to general audiences, now became a kind of "literary drama" which emphasized poetry and was

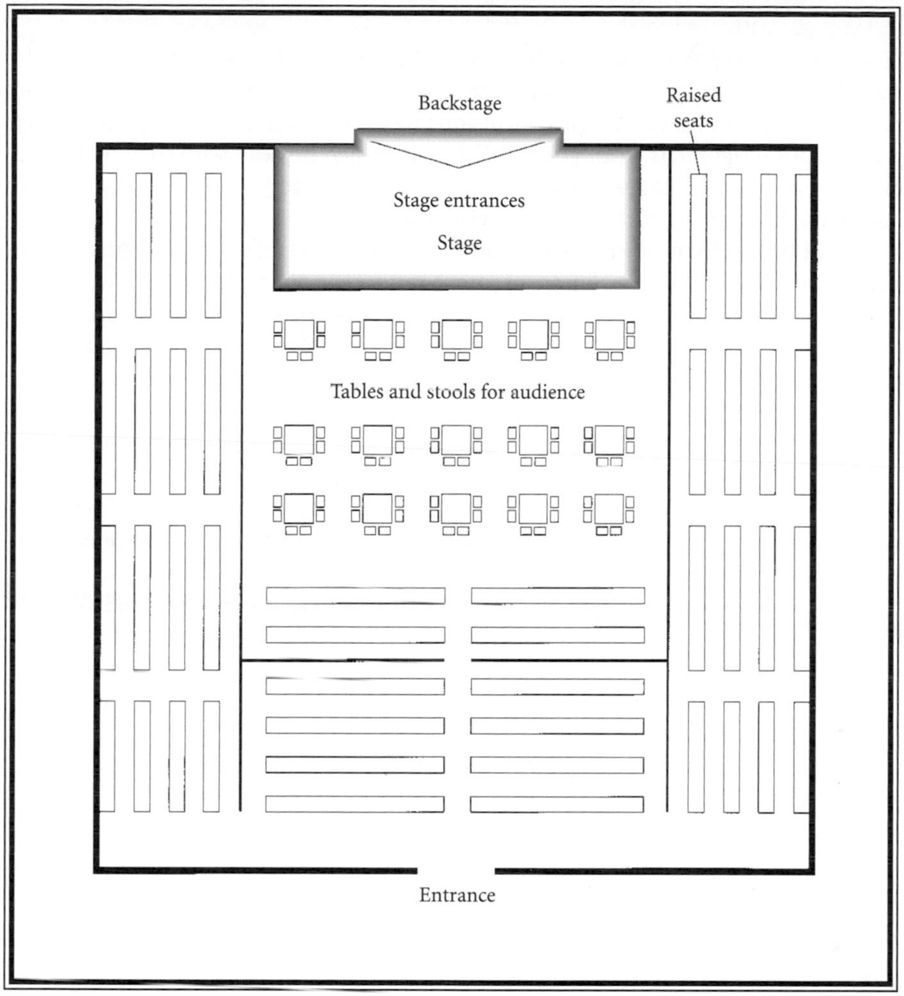

GROUND PLAN OF A TRADITIONAL CHINESE THEATRE Diagrammed here is the arrangement for seating in Chinese theatre for the period from the seventeenth through the nineteenth centuries. Before that, performances were held in teahouses; when permanent theatres were built, tables with chairs around them were retained in the section nearest the stage. Women and commoners sat at the sides and back.

averse to sustained or powerful dramatic action. The structure of Ming plays often became far more complex than that of Yuan plays. Also, only one actor had sung in each act of a Yuan play, but several actors were now permitted to sing during an act, and the instrumental accompaniments became very elaborate.

One of the earliest and best plays written in this expanded form is *Lute Song* by Gao Ming (c. 1301–1370), dealing with questions of family loyalty in a woman whose husband has abandoned her for political reasons. *Lute Song* contains strong characterizations and beautiful poetry and has been popular ever since its composition; this story of a faithful wife even reached Broadway in a musical theatre version, also called *Lute Song,* written for Mary Martin in 1946.

Attempts to create drama of distinction during the Ming dynasty culminated in the works of Li Yu, a scholar who failed his examinations and became instead a playwright, theatre critic, and impresario.

LI YU

Li Yu (1611–c. 1685), China's first important drama critic, believed that a playwright should write clearly, with a mass audience in mind, and should be well versed in practical stage knowledge. These conclusions were based on his own experience as a popular playwright. His writings on theatre—in which he dealt with such matters as plot construction, dialogue, music, and versification—are among the most important in the history of Chinese dramatic criticism.

Li Yu turned to the theatre to earn a living after he had failed several times to pass the provincial examinations for government service. To support his forty wives and his numerous concubines and children, he and his company of singing girl actresses traveled around the country, seeking the patronage of local mandarins. Because of the beauty and skill of his young actresses, his troupe was often charged with corrupting the morals of young men. Though he had many influential friends, he was forced to sell his home and worked from time to time as a landscape gardener to pay his debts.

As a playwright, Li Yu was criticized by contemporary Chinese literary figures for his dramatic style. He wrote his plays for entertainment and placed little emphasis on the poetic songs that other playwrights favored. Instead, he developed well-made situation comedies with intricate plots and sophisticated dialogue. Rather than borrow his material from standard literary sources, Li created original plots based on the lives of common people. He was particularly skilled at writing strong characters for his young female performers. Most of his notable plays, including *Ordained by Heaven, Be Circumspect in Conjugal Relationships,* and *The Error of the Kite,* revolve around romantic themes.

In his dramatic criticism, Li championed the methods and knowledge he had gained as a practicing playwright; but he had little influence on other dramatists. He is said to have been an expert on painting, music, poetry, architecture, feminine charm, the sexual arts, travel, recreation, diet, hygiene, and furniture. Li Yu's plays and his extensive knowledge made him a popular author in both China and Japan.

Later Chinese Theatre

At the end of the Ming dynasty, theatre, which was patronized almost entirely by the rich, began to lose any real contact with the larger public, and its vitality seeped away.

Events in Chinese theatre following the Ming dynasty and into the modern period will be covered in Chapter 16.

Japanese Theatre

Although the civilization of Japan is younger than that of China, the Japanese heritage is long and complex. The origins of the Japanese people are obscure, but anthropologists have found artifacts suggesting migrations from such diverse areas as Siberia, Korea, south China, and southeast Asia. We know that by the fifth century C.E. the southern portions of Japan were consolidated and a series of capitals were established in the vicinity of present-day Kyoto. At the time, the Japanese followed a religion called Shinto, or the Way of the Gods, closely allied to nature and spirit worship.

With the growing influence on the Japanese aristocracy of the Tang dynasty in China (618–906 C.E.) Buddhism, a religion that was more sophisticated than Shinto in both ritual and doctrine, became a prevailing influence, first in court circles and then in the country as a whole. Influences from both Shinto and Buddhism were strong in the development of theatre in Japan.

Early Theatre in Japan

The earliest recorded theatrical activities in Japan are the court entertainments of the Heian period (794–1195 C.E.). These entertainments were influenced by Chinese models, but that is the only link—a very remote one—between the two traditions. Later, similar kinds of performances formed part of annual Shinto and Buddhist ceremonies. These were usually of a popular nature and included juggling, skits, dancing, and the like.

The first great period in Japanese theatre occurred in the fourteenth century, not long after similar developments in China. The sudden and remarkable development of *nō* (it is also spelled *noh*)—one of the three principal forms of traditional Japanese theatre—came about when popular stage traditions were combined with serious scholarly pursuits. Despite similarities in theatrical developments, however, there was no direct connection between Japan and China at this time; and there are significant differences in how theatre emerged in the two cultures. In the Yuan period the Chinese upper classes often disdained theatre; but well-known, powerful people—in both politics and the arts—shaped Japanese nō. For this reason, the development of nō is far better documented than the development of Yuan drama.

Nō

In the fourteenth century in Japan, there were a number of roving troupes of actors who performed in a variety of styles; some of their presentations were simply popular entertainment, but some aspired to art. One of the more artistic troupes was directed by the actor Kan'ami (1333–1384), who was also a playwright. A typical, well-known play by Kan'ami is *Sotoba Komachi* (*Komachi at the Stupa*), which was based on a familiar legend of the time. In this legend, Komachi, a beautiful but cruel woman, is pursued by a man named Shii no Shōshō. She tells him that he must call on her for 100 nights in a row, and for 99 nights he comes, in all kinds of weather. But on the hundredth night he dies.

At the beginning of the play, two priests enter, discussing the virtues of following Buddha. They then come upon an old woman—the leading actor in the mask and wig of Komachi in old age. She says that she was once beautiful but has grown old and lost her beauty. She argues with the priests about religion and then reveals who she is. She recounts the story of what she did to Shōshō.

At one point in the play, the spirit of Shōshō takes over Komachi's body, an action carried out in pantomime to musical accompaniment. At another time, Komachi is dressed as Shōshō and actually becomes him, feeling his death agony. At the end of the play, the spirit of Shōshō leaves Komachi, and she prays to Buddha for guidance and for a peaceful life in the hereafter.

A presentation by Kan'ami's troupe was seen by the shogun Ashikaga Yoshimitsu (1358–1408), a man of wealth, prestige, and enormous enthusiasm for the arts.

Fascinated by what he saw, he arranged for Kan'ami's son, Zeami, who was then 11 years old, to have a court education in order to improve the quality of his art.

When Zeami succeeded his father as head of the troupe, it remained attached to the shogun's court in Kyoto. With a patron of this caliber, Zeami was freed from financial problems and could devote himself to all aspects of theatre: writing plays, training actors, and constantly refining his own acting style, whose outlines had been inherited from his gifted father.

ZEAMI MOTOKIYO

Over 500 years after his death, Zeami Motokiyo (1363–1443) is still considered the most important figure in the history of Japanese nō theatre, a complex form of classical dance drama favored by the aristocracy. A gifted actor, Zeami brought new prestige to nō, and his plays remain an important part of the nō repertoire. He was most influential, however, as a theorist; in his writings, he established the aesthetic and philosophical basis of nō.

Zeami became the director of his father's troupe when Kan'ami died in 1384. He continued to improve nō, borrowing elements of other, earlier, forms of dance drama. His 200 plays, 124 of which remain in the active nō repertory, incorporated his innovations.

Zeami also began writing on the theory and philosophy of nō, presenting ideas that were heavily influenced by his study of Zen. In his several volumes of theoretical works, Zeami developed the concept of *yūgen,* the mysterious inner heart or spirit behind outward form. Yūgen is the aim of nō performances; another definition of it might be philosophical and physical gracefulness. Zeami's theoretical writings remained secret, however; they were written to instruct his own son and pupil, Motomasa. The writings were first made public when they were published in the early twentieth century.

Though Zeami was at the height of his acting powers in 1408, he and his troupe lost the patronage of the court when his friend the shogun Yoshimitsu died. Zeami continued to perform and to write until 1422, when he gave the troupe to his son and became a Buddhist monk.

A new shogun made Zeami chief court musician in 1424, but he lost that post to his nephew in 1429 when another shogun took office. Motomasa died young, leaving Zeami with no direct heir to his theoretical writings on nō. At the age of 72, he was exiled to the island of Sado for political reasons, but three years later he returned to Kyoto, where he died in 1443.

Characteristics of Nō Theatre

Under Zeami's direction, nō became the dominant form of serious theatre in his generation, and it remained dominant well past 1600, until it was supplanted in the popular taste by bunraku and kabuki.

Nō, as perfected by Zeami, was and is a remarkably successful synthesis of various theatrical forms into a single, total experience. Nō actors (there were no actresses in Zeami's theatre) trained from childhood and became adept at singing, acting, dancing, and mime. The plays they performed were remarkably sophisticated in language and content and were all constructed around a definite series of organizational principles based on musical, psychological, and mimetic—or imitative—movements, which change gradually from a slow to a fast tempo. Many of the greatest nō plays were written by Zeami himself.

The stories considered appropriate for nō plays were often from literary or historical sources. One important source was a famous novel of Heian court life, Lady Murasaki's *Tale of Genji,* written around 1000. Another important source was *The Tale of the Heike,* a chronicle of the devastating civil wars that destroyed the power of the aristocracy in Japan at the end of the Heian period in 1185. Nō characters were generally based on literary or historical figures already familiar to the audience. A nō play reveals some working out of passions felt by a character, who often appears as a ghost or spirit.

The major roles in nō are the *shite,* or main character, who is often masked; the *waki,* a supporting character; and the *tsure,* an accompanying role. There may be various smaller parts as well, including a *kyōgen,* or comic character.

There are two typical no plays. One type, known as the "phantasmal," is divided into two parts. In the first part, for example, a Buddhist priest on a pilgrimage might visit a famous site, such as a tree or a gravestone, related to the life of the main character. The priest may find there a local person who will say something about the legend of the chief character and then disappear. In the second part of the play, the chief character will appear, revealing to the priest that the local person in the first part was actually himself or herself in disguise, and then describing some profound experience in his or her life. Usually, this recitation will end with a dance or in some other powerful way. Generally, the second half of the finest phantasmal plays provides an unusual combination of poetry with stirring movements and music.

(Courtesy of Inoue Corp. U.S.A.)

NŌ PERFORMANCE TODAY
Traditional nō theatre is still performed in Japan and other parts of the world, and it still retains its stylized acting, minimalist settings, ornate costumes, and distinctive makeup. The traditions of acting, speaking, singing, and gestural movement have been handed down from one generation to the next for several centuries. Shown here is a performer in a production of *Taihei Shojo,* staged in Kyoto, Japan.

A second type of nō play is more realistic than the "phantasmal" type. Sometimes called the "present existence" type, it features action that occurs to living characters in present, stage time. This second type is important not only on its own terms, but also because it would have a strong influence on the more realistic kabuki theatre, discussed below.

Producing Nō Theatre

The elegance, mystery, and beauty of nō have fascinated the Japanese since the time of Zeami, and the nō tradition, passed on from teacher to disciple, has been carried on to this day. In most of the larger Japanese cities, nō can be seen in excellent performances by troupes whose traditions go back to the fourteenth century—a remarkable legacy. There have been some changes in performance practice since Zeami's time; for one thing, scholars have established that today's performances are much more stately and take a good deal more time than those of Zeami's day. Still, the general effect of a modern performance is certainly in consonance with Zeami's intentions.

Even the nō stage has remained roughly the same since the time of Zeami and his immediate successors. There is a bridge, called the *hashigakari,* which leads from the actors' room offstage to the stage. The bridge is normally about 20 feet long; the main playing space to which it leads is about 18 feet square, is roofed, and has a ceremonial pine tree painted on the rear wall. At the back of the playing space is a narrow section for four musicians who accompany the play on flute, small hand drum, large hand drum, and stick drum. Nō theatres were originally outdoors, and the audience sat on three sides of the stage. The modern nō theatre is built inside a larger shell as though it were a giant stage set itself, and the audience sits on two sides.

The temple roof above the stage is supported by four columns or pillars, each of which serves a definite purpose in the staging. For instance, the second pillar on the right in the front is the pillar of the second actor (*waki*) in nō plays; the left, rear pillar diagonally opposite it is for the first actor (*shite*). In addition to the actors and musicians, in nō there is a chorus of ten men who serve as a very rough equivalent of the chorus in Greek theatre.

Nō actors move in a highly stylized fashion that involves important elements of both dance and pantomime. During the performance of a nō text, the actors alternate sections of chanting with a kind of heightened speech that might best be compared to recitative in western opera. The costumes made for nō are usually of great elegance, and the masks worn by the shite are among the most beautiful, subtle, and effective created for any theatre.

There are occasional comic elements in nō, and these elements eventually developed as a separate form called *kyōgen.* Originally, kyōgen plays were short farcical interludes performed between the acts of nō plays; later, they became an independent genre, although still performed on most nō programs. Kyōgen plays, which use a good deal of folk humor and slapstick, are still performed and appreciated today.

The kyōgen are usually performed without costumes, masks, or wigs, except when a nō play is being parodied, in which case the appropriate nō mask is used. Parody and satire are common in kyōgen, and no subject is sacrosanct or exempt from being treated comically. A feudal lord, monk, or friar can be the main figure; so might a drunken or stupid servant, a braggart, a shrew, or a gallant.

Bunraku

Nō remained the most popular form of theatre during Japan's medieval period. During the sixteenth century, civil wars and other disturbances caused political disarray of increasing gravity, until in 1600 a general, Tokugawa Ieyasu, unified the country. All through the long Tokugawa period (1600–1868), which bears his family name, Japan was unified and at peace, but this calm was purchased at a price. Alarmed at the political maneuvering of Japan's growing number of Christians, who had been converted by European missionaries, the Tokugawa family outlawed Christianity and cut Japan off from any extensive contact with either China or Europe until the middle of the nineteenth century.

Peace did bring a rapid development of commerce and trade that led to increasingly sophisticated urban life. As the merchant class grew, its members' wealth and their increasing leisure time allowed them to patronize various entertainments. The aristocracy and the Tokugawa family continued to support nō as a kind of private state theatre, but the merchants supported theatrical arts that more closely mirrored their own world. These entertainments flourished in large cities, such as Osaka, Kyoto, and Edo (now Tokyo).

Before we turn to puppet theatre—bunraku—and to the later kabuki, it is worth noting that both forms of theatre can be understood more fully if one takes into account certain tenets of neo-Confucianism. These tenets form the basis of rigid codes of behavior regarding such matters as sacrifice, loyalty, and revenge as found in the class system and the samurai code of the warrior aristocracy of Japan. These strict codes of behavior, in turn, are reflected in the theatrical presentations of bunraku and kabuki.

Of the new popular forms of theatre that developed in Japanese cities, puppet theatre was the first. Since the nineteenth century, this puppet theatre has been called *bunraku,* a name that derives from a famous puppeteer. It developed in a most unusual way. One widespread form of entertainment in the medieval period was the art of the chanter—who, with his *biwa* (a kind of large lute), would travel around the countryside intoning chronicles of wars and tales of romantic heroes and heroines.

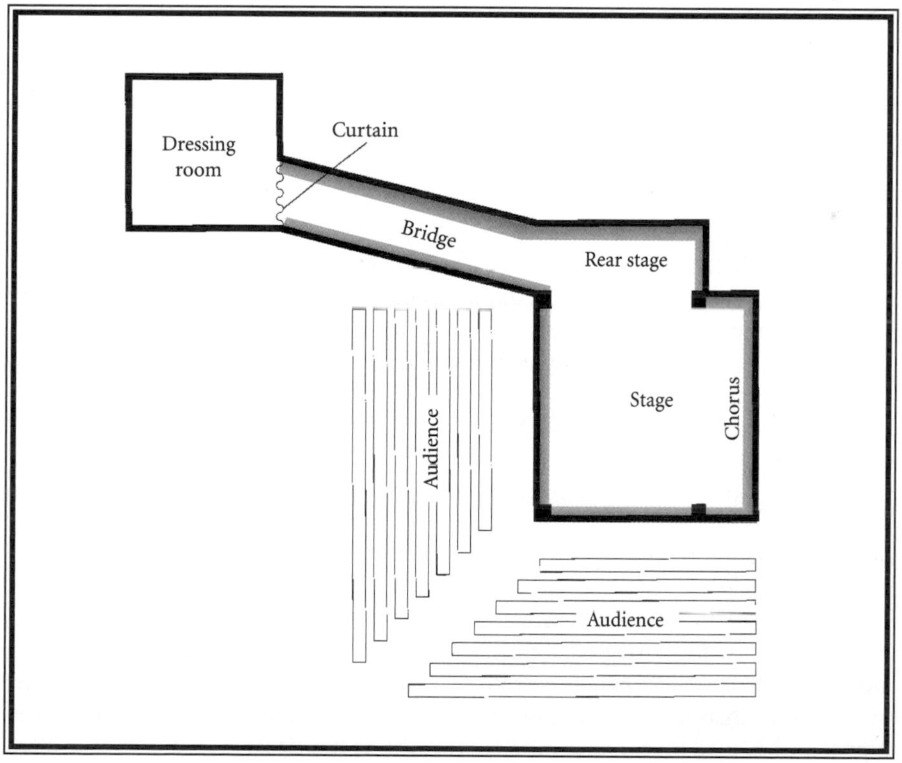

GROUND PLAN OF TRADITIONAL NŌ THEATRE

The nō theater of Japan—a stylized theatre originally for the upper classes—began nearly 600 years ago. It was performed outdoors; a ramp at the left led from a dressing room to the wooden platform stage. Spectators sat on two sides of the stage, to the left and in front.

(Mark Phillips/AP Images)

BUNRAKU: PUPPET THEATRE

Shown here is a scene from a well-known bunraku puppet play, *The Love Suicides at Sonezakui.* Bunraku—which is still popular in Japan today—has a number of uniquely theatrical conventions not present in most western puppet theatre. For example, the handlers, seen here at each side of the puppet figures and dressed in black, are in full view of the audience, but are considered invisible. Part of the excitement of bunraku comes from watching the great skill of those who manipulate the puppets, which are roughly two-thirds life-size.

Between 1570 and 1600 the *samisen,* a three-stringed instrument something like a banjo, replaced the biwa as the chief instrument accompanying the chanter. By around 1600, it became customary to add to these performances, as a kind of extra attraction, companies of puppeteers who would act out the stories, "illustrating" the chanter's music. The introduction of the samisen and the puppeteers made possible the development of bunraku.

The chanted texts are called *jōruri,* after the name of a popular female character in one of the recited tales. The chanters, down to the present day, have been regarded with the kind of awe reserved for opera singers in the west. The chanters perform all the voices in a play, as well as the narration, and set the general mood. Originally, they also wrote their own scripts. Eventually, however, it became customary to ask someone else to write the text.

In bunraku, the puppets representing important characters are manipulated by three people: one for the legs, one for the left arm, and the chief handler for the head and right arm. The chief handler is often dressed in an elaborate, gorgeous costume, but the other handlers are dressed in black and are assumed to be invisible. The puppets, which today are approximately two-thirds life-size, were originally smaller.

of them still active. A kabuki dynasty that lasted through twelve generations was founded by Ichikawa Danjuro (1660–1704), who became known as Danjuro I and who began a bravura acting style known as *aragato.* Danjuro I was also a playwright, writing under the name Mimasuya Hyōgo, and created a great many of the plays that became kabuki classics. His son, the actor Danjuro II (1688–1758), was famous for developing his father's *aragato* techniques. Another well-known actor in this tradition was W. Danjuro VI (1778–1799). Many actors came to fame in *Chushingura* or *The Forty-Seven Rōnin,* a frequently revived play originally written for puppets. It is perhaps Japan's most popular history play. The play is based on an actual historical incident in which a provincial lord was provoked into an act of violence and forced to commit ritual suicide. It traces the vendetta or revenge of the forty-seven retainers who are left behind and is a remarkable blend of adventure, pathos, and romance. Ghost stories, too, were popular dramas in the kabuki repertoire.

(© Asian Art and Archaeology/Corbis)

THE ONNAGATA: A KABUKI TRADITION
In kabuki, female roles are played by men, who are known as *onnagata.* In a stylized manner, onnagata performers convey the delicacy, grace, and subtle movements of the female characters they portray. Through the years, many have been praised for being exceedingly skillful and convincing. Shown here is an onnagata actor in full costume, depicted in a nineteenth-century print by Utagawa Yoshiiku.

Producing Kabuki

Kabuki actors are trained from childhood in vocal technique, dancing, acting, and physical versatility. The male actors who play women's parts (these actors are called *onnagata*) are particularly skillful at imitating the essence of a feminine personality through stylized gestures and attitudes. Costumes and makeup in kabuki are elegant and gorgeous, although they may often be strikingly gritty and realistic. The effect of an actor's performance is frequently quite theatrical and a bit larger than life. Again, however, it must be emphasized that, for all its theatricality, kabuki actually expresses a wide range of styles, from the fantastical to the realistic.

The stage used for kabuki performances underwent various changes during the history of this art, but the fundamental arrangement was reached in the mid-nineteenth century and then altered somewhat after Japan was opened to the west after 1853. The stage is wide and has a relatively low proscenium. Musicians—sometimes onstage, sometimes offstage—generally accompany the stage action. Kabuki features elaborate and beautiful scenic effects, including the revolving stage, which was developed in Japan before it was used in the west. Another device used in kabuki is the *hanamichi,* or "flower way," a raised narrow platform connecting the rear of the auditorium with the stage. Actors often make entrances and exits on the hanamichi and occasionally perform short scenes there as well.

Some kabuki plays use a second or temporary hanamichi down the aisle on the audience's opposite side. The stage is also well equipped with large and small elevator

A KABUKI THEATRE Kabuki, a 400-year-old Japanese theatre, is performed today in elaborate spaces with staging devices that include onstage turntables for shifting scenery. As shown in this ground plan, the stage covers the entire front of the theatre and is approached by a ramp—the hanamichi—on which performers make dramatic entrances and exits.

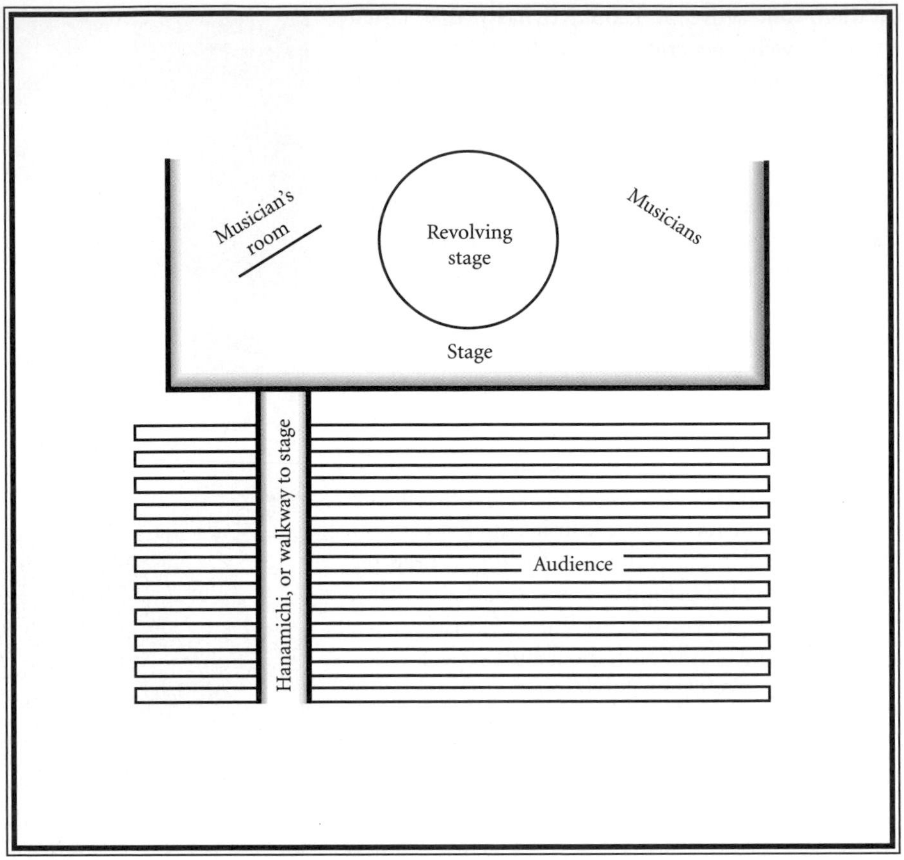

traps, used to lift actors in tableaux as well as spectacular settings, which come into view as the audience watches. There is even a small trap on the hanamichi that allows supernatural characters to emerge (or disappear) in the midst of the audience.

Southeast Asia: Shadow Plays

Though we have focused on theatre in India, China, and Japan, it is important to remember that considerable theatre activity has occurred in other parts of Asia, such as Korea and the southeastern countries of Burma, Cambodia, Laos, Indonesia, Malaysia, Thailand, and Vietnam. Though each of these southeastern nations has its own theatrical history and tradition, all of them share certain characteristics. Most of their theatrical styles were influenced by the theatre of India, and in some instances by that of China. In virtually every one of these countries we note the influence of two epics from India, the *Ramayana* and the *Mahabharata.* These stories and others are almost always performed as dance drama, classical dance, or puppet theatre. As is true in other Asian countries, theatrical presentations combine dance, song, move-

(© Michael Freeman/Corbis)

SHADOW PUPPETS
Shadow puppets are a longtime theatrical tradition in southeast Asia. The figures are manipulated by puppeteers holding sticks attached to the puppets, which themselves are intricately carved flat figures made of leather that create patterns of light and shadow when projected on a screen. The performance here is a Wayang Golek play being presented at a puppet workshop in Java, Indonesia.

ment, and recited text with elaborate costumes. It is worth noting that most of these countries do not even have a word in their language that denotes a dramatic form which is only written or spoken.

One type of theatrical activity that came to prominence in southeast Asia in the eleventh century is particularly significant. This was the *shadow play,* which is widely performed in Thailand, Malaysia, and Indonesia. It appears to have been developed most fully in Java, an Indonesian island.

A shadow play uses flat puppets made of leather. These figures are intricately carved to create patterns of light and shadow when their image is projected on a screen. The puppets are manipulated by sticks attached to the head, the arms, and other parts of the body. The person manipulating the puppets also narrates the drama and speaks the dialogue of the characters. Shadow plays usually take place at night—sometimes they last all night long—and are accompanied by music and sound effects.

In various places, other theatrical forms have been developed from shadow puppets. One variation uses three-dimensional doll puppets; another uses human performers wearing masks.

In this chapter we have looked at the early development of theatre in India, China, and Japan. These theatres were formed independently of theatre in the west; in some cases, they emerged when formal theatre in Europe was dormant. We have covered a period that goes up to approximately 1700. Though this is several centuries beyond the time when theatre reemerged in the west, there was little or no contact between the two theatre traditions until considerably later.

Later we will look at further developments in Asian theatre: for example, Peking opera in China. We will also note the significant exchanges between Asian and western theatre that began at the end of the nineteenth century and continued through the twentieth century and into the twenty-first. In the meantime, however, we return to the theatre of the west in the medieval period .

Summary

The traditional theatres of Asia originated from religious ceremonies and concepts. Most of these theatres are highly theatrical and stylized and fuse acting, mime, dance, music, and text.

In India in the fourth and fifth centuries C.E., a theatre of a very high order—Sanskrit drama—came to full flower. Its origins and dramatic rules were outlined in a revealing document called the *Natyasastra.*

In China, an acting school called the Pear Garden flourished in the early eighth century, and professional theatre companies flourished in the tenth century. The first significant Chinese theatre from which we have surviving manuscripts emerged during the Yuan dynasty from 1271 to 1368. During the succeeding Ming dynasty, from 1368 to 1644, theatre became more "literary" and less in touch with ordinary people.

In Japan, the first important theatre form was nō, which emerged in the fourteenth and fifteenth centuries and is still performed today. Bunraku—puppet theatre—came on the scene in Japan in the seventeenth century, followed closely by kabuki. Both bunraku and kabuki are still performed in Japan today. Like most Asian theatres, nō, kabuki, and bunraku are complex forms; to understand them, audiences need to be aware of their intricate conventions.

Considerable theatre activity has also taken place elsewhere in Asia; one example is the shadow plays performed in Thailand, Malaysia, and Indonesia.

India

Theatre History

- Ancient Hindu epics *Ramayana (below), Mahabharata; Natyasastra* (c. 200 B.C.E.–100 C.E.)

Cultural and Historical Developments

- Gautama Buddha (c. 563–483 B.C.E.)
- Buddhism develops (c. 400 B.C.E.)
- King Asoka, Buddhist *(below)*, unites nation (c. 240 B.C.E.)

- Spread of Buddhism in India; trade with China, Egypt, Rome, southeast Asia; Gandhara school of art flourishes (180–150 B.C.E.)

Gupta [320–647 C.E.]

Theatre History

- Sanskrit drama (320–600 C.E.)
- Bhasa (c. 400), *The Vision of Vasavadatta*
- Kaildasa (373?–415 C.E.), *Shakuntala*
- *The Little Clay Cart,* attributed to Sudraka (fifth century)

Cultural and Historical Developments

- Golden age of Hindu culture
- Earliest known use of zero and of decimals occurs in India (600 C.E.)

Medieval [647–1310]

Theatre History

- Sanskrit drama declines (ninth century)
- Theatrical activities discouraged under Islamic rule; Indian dance drama, puppet plays and folk plays continue (late twelfth century)

Cultural and Historical Developments

- Sultanate of Delhi established; beginning of Islamic rule in India (1206)

continued

PHOTO CREDITS: *Mahabharata* performance. (© Baldev/Corbis) / King Asoka. (© Mary Evans Picture Library/The Image Works)

China
Tang Dynasty [618–906 C.E.]

Theatre History

- Academy of the Pear Garden founded (714 C.E.)

Cultural and Historical Developments

- Confucius (551–479 B.C.E.) *(right)*
- Lao-tzu (born c. 604 B.C.E.); Taoism
- Mencius (c. 371–288 B.C.E.)
- Travels in India of Xuan Zang, Chinese pilgrim and chronicler (630–644 C.E.)

Song Dynasty [960–1279]

Theatre History

- Variety plays; shadow puppets *(right);* marionettes; *nanxi,* "southern drama," emerges in province of Zhejiang (twelfth century)

Cultural and Historical Developments

- Flowering of arts, literature, and scholarship

Yuan Dynasty [1279–1368]

Theatre History

- *Zaju,* lyrical dramatic form composed of song sequences
- Wang Shifu (fl. late thirteenth century), *The Romance of the Western Chamber*
- *The Orphan of Chao; The Circle of Chalk*

Cultural and Historical Developments

- Marco Polo *(right)* visits court of Kublai Khan, Beijing, China (1271); visits Kayal in southern India (1288)

Ming Dynasty [1368–1644]

Theatre History

- Literary and romantic drama
- Goa Ming (c. 1301–1370), *Lute Song*
- Li Yu (1611–c. 1685), *The Error of the Kite*

Cultural and Historical Developments

- Ching dynasty (1644–1911)

continued

PHOTO CREDITS: Confucius. (Snark/Art Resource, N.Y.) / Javanese shadow puppet. (© Shelley Gazin/Corbis) / Marco Polo. (© The Art Archive/Corbis)

MILESTONES CHAPTER 3 EARLY ASIAN THEATRES [320–1868] *continued*

Japan
Heian [794–1185]

Theatre History

- Lady Murasaki's *Tale of Genji (below)*

Medieval [1200–1600]

Theatre History

- Nō drama flourishes (fourteenth century)
- Kan'ami (1333–1384), *Sotoba Komachi*
- Zeami Motokiyo (1363–1443)

Cultural and Historical Developments

- Rule of Yoshimitsu (r. 1395–1408); years of stability followed by civil wars

Tokugawa or Edo [1600–1868]

Theatre History

- Kabuki first performed in Kyoto (1600–1610); Okuni (c. 1596), female dancer, credited with first public performances (1603)
- Women's kabuki banned (1629); boys' troupes banned (1652)
- Nō becomes aristocratic entertainment, rigidly codified (1650)
- Ichikawa Danjuro (Danjuro I, 1660–1704), kabuki actor, *aragato* style
- Bunraku (puppet theater) flourishes (1685) *(below)*

- Chikamatsu Monzaemon (1653–1725), *The Love Suicides at Sonezaki*

Cultural and Historical Developments

- First Europeans visit Japan (1592)
- Period of national unification (1568–1600)
- Meiji restoration (1869); new ruler sponsors exchanges with west

Photo Credits: Scene from *The Tale of Genji.* (© Archivo Iconografico, S.A./Corbis) / Bunraku puppet theatre. (Mark Phillips/AP Images)

CHAPTER 4

Medieval Theatres in Europe

Popular Entertainment in the Middle Ages

The illustration shown here, "Charivaris," is a miniature in the *Roman de Fauvel*. It shows many forms of popular entertainment provided by traveling troupes during the Middle Ages. Note, for example, the musicians, the dancers, the characters in animal costumes, and the different costumes and headdresses.

(Cliché Bibliothèque Nationale de France, Paris)

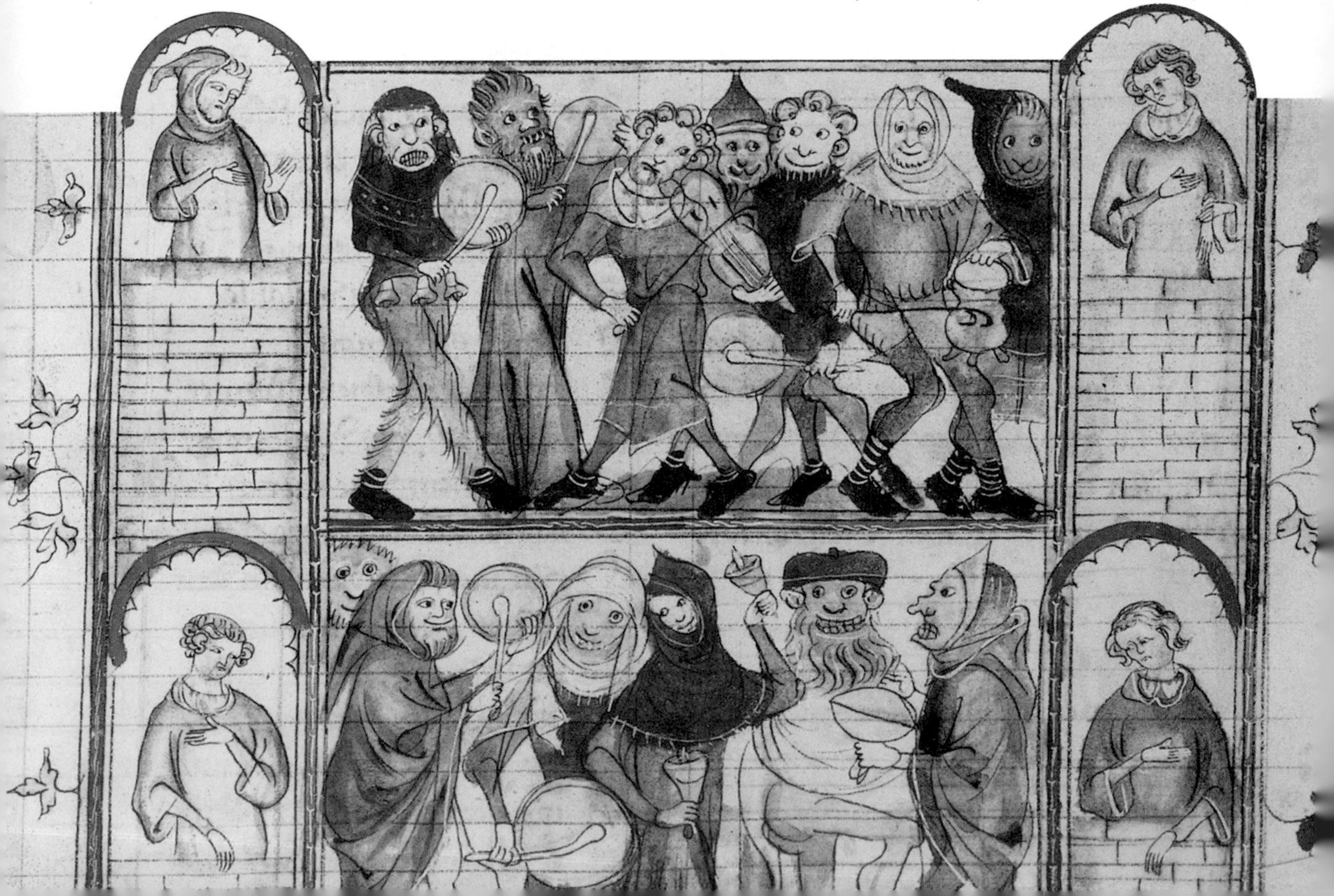

As we begin to examine the Middle Ages—or the *medieval* period, as this era is also called—it is important to remember that divisions of history are artificial and are used primarily so that historical developments will be easier to discuss. This is certainly the case with the medieval era.

Background: The Middle Ages

In western culture, the period from 500 through 1400 C.E. is referred to as the *Middle Ages,* and the years between 1400 and 1650 are known as the *Renaissance*—the era when the classics of Greece and Rome were rediscovered. But these dates are arbitrary: in some cases the Middle Ages are extended to 1450 or 1500; and in some cases the Renaissance is said to have begun by 1350. This is often a matter of which country or which form of art is being studied; developments vary from one country and one branch of art to another. Thus the Renaissance came to Italy before it came to France and England, and Renaissance painting had emerged while theatre was still in its medieval phase: the greatest medieval drama was created between 1350 and 1550, a period when Renaissance painting and sculpture were already established. Medieval theatre, therefore, extends through 1550—well past the time when most cultural historians would say that the Renaissance had begun.

This overlap between the Middle Ages and the Renaissance points up the fact that developments in theatre often seem to lag behind other cultural developments. This suggestion, of course, is not meant to demean theatre. Theatre is a reflection of society and is particularly concerned with people and their relationships to each other and to society. It takes time for shifts in these relationships to be absorbed, and therefore it is not surprising that theatre needs time to take in and mirror societal transformations. Another reason why theatre sometimes reflects cultural changes more slowly than other art forms is that in order to survive it must usually have wide appeal: it must attract a broad cross section of society. A single patron can commission a painting or a sculpture; but a theatre performance needs an audience.

Byzantium: Popular Arts and Theatrical Preservation

Before examining western society and theatre during the Middle Ages, we should turn our attention briefly eastward. When Rome fell in 476 C.E., only the western Roman empire collapsed. The eastern empire, centralized in 330 C.E. by Constantine in Constantinople (today Istanbul, Turkey), continued to function until 1453. Withstanding expansion by Islamic peoples, Byzantium, as the eastern empire was known, synthesized three important influences: ancient Greece, Rome, and Christianity. The western world came into contact with Byzantium during the Crusades—the religious wars of the twelfth and thirteenth centuries that were undertaken to prevent the expansion of Islam. The western world, however, had always looked on the eastern empire as a secondary civilization, and a sharp split between east and west occurred in 1054, when eastern Christianity broke from western Christianity, refusing to acknowledge the supremacy of the papacy.

The theatre of Byzantium was reminiscent of theatre during the Roman empire. The Hippodrome, a large arena in Constantinople, was the Byzantine equivalent of the Circus Maximus or the Colosseum, and popular entertainments like those of Rome flourished in the east. Thus, one contribution of the Byzantine empire to the continuity of theatre consists of these popular presentations. Another important contribution lies in the fact that Byzantium was the preserver of the manuscripts of classical Greek drama: the plays of Aeschylus, Sophocles, and Euripides and the criticism of Aristotle were saved because eastern scholars recognized their importance and made certain that they were not destroyed. When the eastern empire fell in 1453, these manuscripts were transferred to the western world and became part of the rediscovery of the past that influenced the Renaissance.

Middle Ages
Year, c.e.

Theatre

- Traveling performers (c. 500–925)
- Byzantine theater (similar to Roman theater (fifth through seventh centuries)
- Trulian synod attempts to end performances in Byzantium (692)
- Traveling performers on European continent (500–975)
- *Quem quaeritis* trope (c. 925)
- Hrosvitha, a nun, writes Christian comedies based on Terence (c. 970)
- Vernacular religious drama flourishes; peak of medieval theater (c. 1350–1550)
- *Second Shepherds' Play* (c. 1375)
- *Pride of Life* (c. 1400)
- *The Castle of Perseverance* (c. 1425)
- Actor playing Judas at Metz almost dies while being hanged (1437)
- *Pierre Patelin* (c. 1470)
- Hans Sachs born (1494)
- *Everyman* (c. 1500)
- Cycle staged at Mons (1510)
- Jean Bouchet, pageant master, directs cycle at Poitiers (1508)
- John Heywood's *Johan Johan* (1533)

Year

475 · 525 · 575 · 675 · 725 · 775 · 825 · 875 · 925 · 975 · 1025 · 1075 · 1125 · 1175 · 1225 · 1275 · 1325 · 1375 · 1425 · 1475 · 1525

Culture and Politics

- "Dark ages" (476–1000)
- Justinian becomes Byzantine emperor (527)
- Muhammad born (c. 570)
- Charles Martel defeats Muslims near Poitiers (732)
- Charlemagne crowned Holy Roman Emperor (800)
- Beginning of Romanesque architecture (c. 830)
- Earliest European reference to a collar in the harness of a horse which would allow the drawing of heavy loads and plow (920)
- *Beowulf* (1000)
- Norman Conquest (1066)
- First Crusade (1095)
- Beginning of Gothic architecture (1140)
- English Magna Carta (1215)
- Oxford University flourishes (c. 1260)
- Roger Bacon's *De Computo Naturali* (1264)
- Black death apparently originates in India (1332)
- Boccaccio's *Decameron* (1353)
- Pope Urban VI in Rome; Clement VII at Avignon (1378)
- Peasant revolt in England (1381)
- Chaucer dies (1400)
- Gutenberg invents printing by movable type (c. 1450)
- Constantinople falls to the Turks (1453)
- Copernicus born (1473)
- Martin Luther born (1483)
- Columbus crosses the Atlantic (1492)

The Middle Ages in Western Europe

Most discussions of medieval society are concerned with western developments from the early Middle Ages (500 to 1000 C.E.) through the High Middle Ages (about 1000 to 1400). The years from 500 to 1000 were traditionally called the *dark ages*, because historians originally viewed this period as one in which few cultural or historical advances were made. Most historians now argue that this era actually laid the groundwork for the advances of the High Middle Ages, and we will therefore refer to it as the early Middle Ages.

During the early Middle Ages, the vestiges of the Roman empire were overrun by barbarians, primarily from northern Europe, and institutions established by the Romans were toppled; Roman towns and roadways fell into disuse. The institution

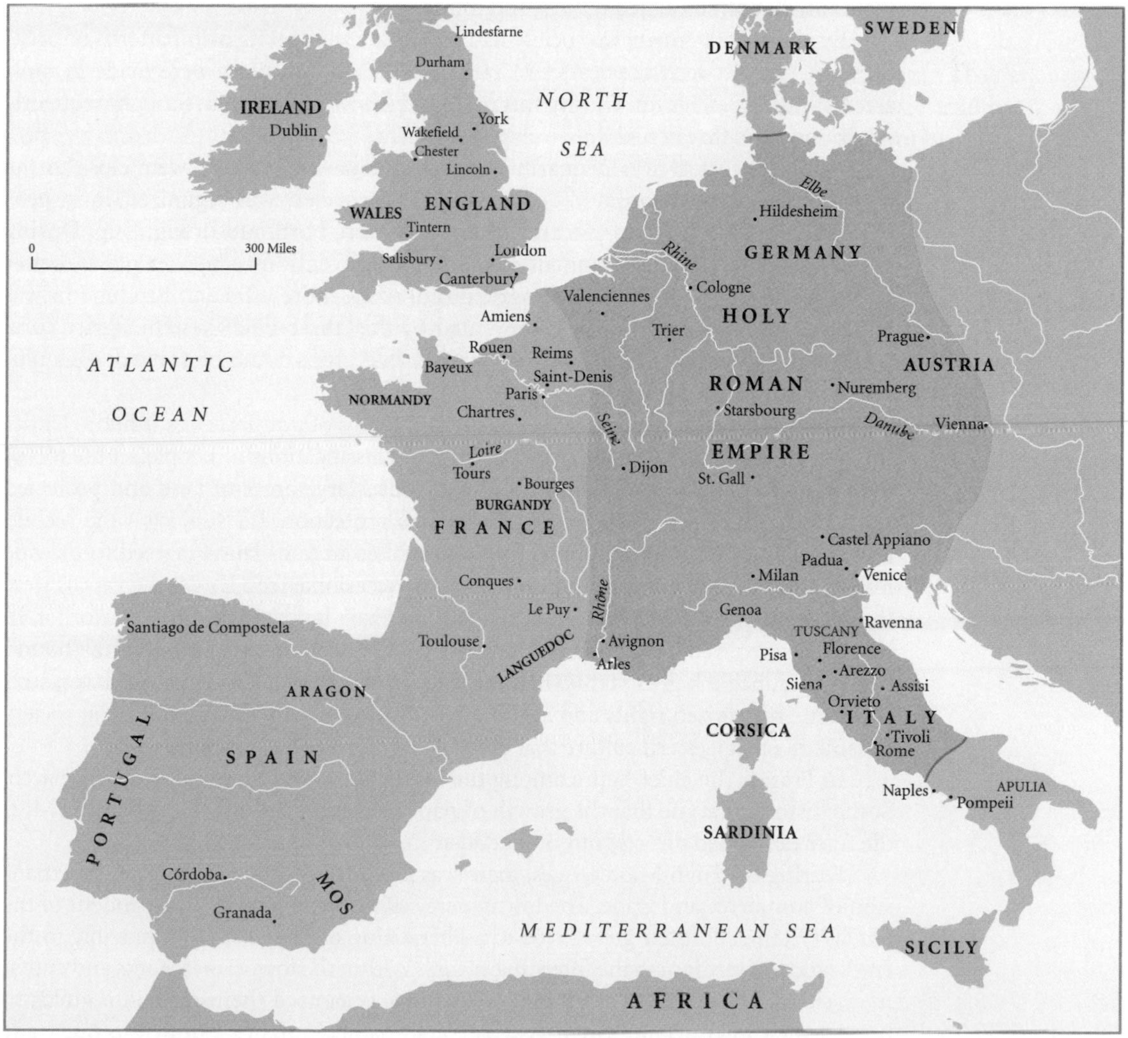

Medieval Europe

that stepped in to provide a semblance of order to the chaotic society was the Roman Catholic church. As noted in Chapter 2, the Roman empire had been Christianized before its fall, and when the pagan barbarians invaded, many of them were converted to the new belief. The church's power was centralized in Rome under the pope; when Charlemagne became the most powerful secular ruler in Europe, during the early part of the ninth century, he was crowned emperor of the Holy Roman Empire. Secular rulers were always subject to the church's influence.

During these early years of the Middle Ages, there probably were troupes of traveling popular performers who presented comic, acrobatic, and circus-like entertainments. These performers were most common in areas closest to Rome and were frequently attacked by church officials. There were also traveling singers and storytellers, particularly in the north; and festivals that had been popular before the advent of Christianity were staged as well. These festivals contained performative elements, including dance, simulated battles, and mime.

By about 1000, medieval society had begun to establish its own patterns of organization, and between the years 1000 and 1400 major advances were made in most areas of human endeavor. During this period, the powerful church, though frequently questioned and threatened, was ever-present.

Medieval society was primarily agrarian; people everywhere were close to the land. For financial reasons and because of the way society was organized, most people rarely strayed far from the area where they were born and brought up. During the Middle Ages, the development of mechanical inventions—heavier plows, better harnesses, and windmills—made agricultural work more efficient. Production was increased and soil depletion was prevented by the "three-field" system: agricultural landholdings were divided into three parts so that crops could be rotated; each plot remained unplanted once every 3 years.

Medieval society developed feudalism as a means of political organization. Under this system there were three major categories or classifications of people. At the top of the hierarchy were *lords* or *counts,* who controlled large areas of land and protected less wealthy landholders. In return for a lord's protection, his subjects—the second level, *vassals* or lesser lords, who controlled smaller areas of land—agreed to provide military service, consult with him, and pay him occasional fees. Under the vassals were the *peasants,* or *serfs,* who were attached to their lord's land and required to work it. In return they received protection and a very small financial reward. Serfs, though bound to the land, had a higher status than the slaves of earlier societies. Unlike slaves, serfs had some recognized rights and at times could move to other areas. Medieval society became the first western culture that did not practice slavery on a large scale.

In France, the chief figure among the important lords came to be the monarch. Some historians argue that the growth of national monarchies at the end of the Middle Ages developed directly out of feudalism.

During the High Middle Ages, there was a rebirth of towns as a result of expansion of commerce and trade. The towns were self-governing units, independent of the feudal system, and their growth led to a liberalizing of feudalism and possibly to the eradication of serfdom in the fifteenth century. Within the towns, merchants and craftsmen, such as butchers, weavers, and goldsmiths, organized themselves into guilds to protect their interests and privileges. (A rough parallel might be drawn to our trade associations.) Under the guilds, vocational training was organized: to become a master craftsman, for instance, one would have to serve first as an apprentice and then as a journeyman. The guilds controlled the number of people entering the various professions.

An important aspect of the medieval period was the spread of knowledge. By the year 1500—after the end of the High Middle Ages—there were over 100 universities in Europe. Earlier, in the twelfth century, the writings of Aristotle and other classic texts were rediscovered by scholarly monks in monasteries in western Europe. However, despite a new awareness of ancient philosophy and the arts in the High Middle Ages, the "queen of sciences" remained theology—the study of religion—which had been the main intellectual pursuit of the early Middle Ages. Monks copied influential manuscripts; and as a result, the monasteries were centers of learning. As early as the tenth century, a nun in a convent in Germany, Hrosvitha of Gandersheim, wrote plays patterned on those of the Roman dramatist Terence.

HROSVITHA

Hrosvitha (c. 935–1001), the earliest known female dramatist, flourished during the tenth century in northern Germany. During this phase of the Middle Ages, religious communities served as centers of scholarship and intellectual life. Hrosvitha was a nun who lived and worked in one of these—Gandersheim, a Benedictine abbey in Saxony led by women of noble families. Gandersheim was an influential center.

Hrosvitha of Gandersheim.
(From Johann Georg Leuckfeld, *Antiquitates Gandersheimenses*, Wolfenbüttel, 1709, courtesy of Das Roswitha-Jahr in Bad Gandersheim, edited by the Bad Gandersheim Council, 1973.)

There are indications that Hrosvitha was of noble birth and had more access to the world than the other nuns at Gandersheim. One of the scholars who have written about Hrosvitha, Sister Mary Marguerite of Mercy College, finds evidence that she was a "canoness" and therefore not completely cloistered—that is, not completely confined to the abbey.

Hrosvitha read and wrote in Latin, the language of the Roman Catholic church and of western scholarship during the Middle Ages. Like other medieval scholars, she studied classical Roman texts for their form and style. During the Middle Ages, one Roman writer admired for his style was the playwright Terence; Hrosvitha particularly admired Terence's plays, but she feared that his subject matter was not suitable for Christian readers. To provide dramas that students could read without risk of corruption, Hrosvitha wrote six plays in the Terentian manner but using Christian stories. In the preface to her collected plays, she noted that her purpose was to glorify Christian virgins.

Martyrdom of devout Christians, hard-won conversions of nonbelievers, renunciations of past sins, and strict penance for the past are the recurring dramatic actions in Hrosvitha's plays. Her plays *Paphnutius* and *Abraham* both concern a woman's redemption from sexual sins. Another, *Dulcitius,* depicts the martyrdom of three Christian virgins: Agape, Chionia, and Irena. This play has a surprisingly comic scene, in which the captor Dulcitius visits the sisters in the middle of the night and mistakenly makes love to some dirty pots and pans. Other plays by Hrosvitha are *Gallicanus, Callimachus,* and *Sapienta.*

There is no evidence that Hrosvitha's plays were intended for performance or ever received performances in her own time. Without an active theatre tradition, it is unlikely that Hrosvitha had much knowledge of dramatic performance. On the other hand, it is possible that the plays were read aloud at Gandersheim.

In addition to her plays, Hrosvitha wrote poetry, biographies of saints, and history. Her work was not widely known until it was rediscovered and published in 1501.

In retrospect, Hrosvitha's plays are of interest because of their connection to both the formal composition of classical drama and the themes and subject matter of medieval mystery and morality plays as well as their relationship to contemporary feminist theory.

Liturgical Drama

Development of Medieval Liturgical Drama

During the Middle Ages, the church was omnipresent; it is not surprising, therefore, that medieval drama was mostly religious. Moreover, much of the drama of this period was actually presented in the sanctuaries of churches and cathedrals. How could this be? How could the church, which had attacked theatre so vehemently during the late Roman empire and the early Middle Ages, become the instrument of its rebirth?

There are several possible explanations for the development of church, or liturgical, drama. We noted in the Introduction that religious rites have theatrical elements, and the rituals of Roman Catholicism are no exception. Roman Catholic rituals had many elements that contained the seeds of the rebirth of theatre. The mass and the hours, the vestments worn by the clergy, the church space, the musical accompaniment, and the annual symbolic events (such as the burial of the cross on Good Friday and its resurrection on Easter Sunday) are all inherently theatrical.

Church drama seems to have developed along with changes in liturgical music. A popular form of early medieval music had two groups responding to each other in song, almost suggesting dramatic interaction. By the ninth century, extended musical passages, called *tropes,* had been added to services; later, lyrics were written for these passages. The mass was the most rigid of the numerous daily services; for that reason, tropes were most often interpolated into other services, such as the hours, which varied from day to day and also had special texts for occasions like Christmas and Easter. These tropes, which were sung or chanted in Latin to musical accompaniment, were in most cases performed in monasteries.

Medieval records indicate that in certain localities a trope called the *Quem quaeritis* was added to the introductory section of the Easter service around the year 925. The Latin words *Quem quaeritis*—meaning "Whom do you seek?"—are the first words spoken in this trope: they are the question asked by an angel when the three Marys visit the tomb of Christ. When the women reply that they are seeking Christ, the angel announces that Christ is not in the tomb but has risen. We do not know whether the trope of 925 was acted out by performers playing the three Marys and the angel, but between 965 and 975 it definitely became a tiny play. We know this because those are the dates of the *Regularis Concordia,* a book by Ethelwold, bishop of Winchester, England. *Regularis* was intended to establish clear goals and rules of conduct and procedure for monasteries. Among other things, it described how the *Quem quaeritis* trope was to be performed.

It is a reasonable assumption that around 965—and certainly soon after—tropes on other parts of the Bible had also begun to be staged, and more than 400 plays dealing with the visit of the Marys to the tomb have been found in various places in Europe. By the year 1000, then, liturgical dramas—short plays on this story

DEBATES IN THEATRE HISTORY | Why Was Hrosvitha Ignored for So Long?

Hrosvitha is considered the first female playwright in the history of theatre and is at least the first female playwright of whom we have any record. However, until the 1970s and 1980s she had received very little attention from theatre historians. Why?

The feminist critic Sue-Ellen Case, in her essay "Re-Viewing Hrotsvit,"* tries to explain why Hrosvitha had been ignored by scholars and why her plays have rarely been produced. Case argues that Hrosvitha was too often depicted as a poor imitator of the Roman playwright Terence, whose plays she adapted. Furthermore, it was too often assumed that, if she was cloistered, Hrosvitha must have created these dramas only as a monastic exercise. Case suggests that these ideas came from a male-oriented view of dramatic technique and history. She has reinterpreted Hrosvitha's scripts: according to Case, Terence presents female characters who are manipulated by men, are controlled by the institution of marriage, and have little onstage presence; but Hrosvitha represents women as controlling the dramatic action and as responding to male aggression. In addition, Case argues that Hrosvitha used a variety of uniquely feminist dramatic techniques and for that reason has never been well received critically. Case also asserts that Hrosvitha created her plays for the community of women who lived with her in the convent.

Case's analysis of Hrosvitha's work forces us to consider that because of the biases of historians, key figures and their works may be ignored; it also leads us to ask whether the traditional list of great dramatists and their works—known as the *canon*—needs revision. In addition, it forces us to reevaluate traditional ideas that we have come to accept as historic reality.

**Theatre Journal*, vol. 35, no. 2, December 1983, pp. 533–542.

of the visit to the tomb as well as other biblical events—had been incorporated into the services of churches in England and on the European continent. At first, as we noted above, these were presented primarily in monasteries; but as urban centers began to emerge in the eleventh and twelfth centuries and larger churches were built, services incorporating the small dramas of the tropes were produced in churches and cathedrals.

During this early period of the Middle Ages, a German nun named Hildegard von Bingen (1098–1179) wrote short musical plays, which were probably performed in the convent that she oversaw. Hildegard wrote liturgical songs that were accompanied by texts. These dramatic musical pieces honored saints and the Virgin Mary and were written for performance on religious days. Hildegard also created a play in Latin, *Ordo Virtutum (Play of Virtues)*, that seems to foreshadow the later vernacular morality plays.

Producing Liturgical Drama

Liturgical dramas were written in Latin and presented by members of the clergy with the assistance of choirboys. At first, these dramas were staged in monasteries; the general population did not attend. Between 1000 and 1300, however, several significant changes took place. Urban centers developed where large groups of people congregated and where sizable churches began to be built. It was during this period that church architecture changed from Romanesque to Gothic; the Gothic style, with its pointed arches and buttressed walls, allowed for larger, more sweeping interior spaces. With the development of centers of population and the construction of Gothic churches and cathedrals, the liturgical plays were no longer confined to monasteries but came to be produced more widely.

DEBATES IN THEATRE HISTORY

The Origins of Medieval Theatre and the Role of Quem quaeritis

Michal Kobialka, in *This Is My Body: Representational Practices in the Early Middle Ages*,* provides a postmodernist reading of medieval theatre history. In his introduction, Kobialka forces the reader to confront contradictions in the best-known histories of early medieval theatrical practices.

Kobialka cogently argues that there is significant disagreement among historians regarding the origins of medieval theatre and drama. As he notes, "Even this brief discussion of the origins of medieval drama and theatre indicates that there is no consensus among scholars concerned with the issue. The interpretations vary from nonecclesiastical to ecclesiastical origins, from ritual to literary origins, or from forensic discourse to Marxist labor relations."*† Kobialka is suggesting that there are varied interpretations of possible origins, ranging from mime to religious liturgical additions to public recitations to legal rhetorical delivery, and to connections to the development of towns and changes in work practices. Each theory embodies a historian's bias and unique point of view regarding interpretation of surviving texts and documents.

In addition, Kobialka points out that there is no agreement regarding the place of *Quem quaeritis* in the development of medieval theatrical and dramatic practices, citing many of the leading medieval theatre historians:

> Thus to establish the identity of the *Quem quaeritis*, the scholars utilize seven different theatrical forms: (1) liturgicaldrama (Chambers), (2) play (Young, Sticca, Anderson, Axton), (3) play of ritual drama (Hardison), (4) dramatic office (Craig), (5) liturgical music dr ama (Smoldon), (6) dramatic resurrection ceremony (Bjork), and (7) performance ceremony (Norton).‡

Clearly each of these theories reflects an individual historian's interpretation and contextualization of *Quem quaeritis*, how that historian interprets documents pertaining to it (or excludes other sources), and how that scholar draws parallels to known theatrical practices. Given the diversity of opinions, clearly there is no one prevailing theory.

Postmodernist historians have forced all of us to realize that the historical narratives we study are laden with biases and contradictory methodologies. The attempt to evaluate the theories regarding the origins of medieval theatrical and dramatic practices underscores the postmodernists' arguments.

*University of Michigan Press, Ann Arbor, 1999.
†Pp. 17–18.
‡P. 24.

Two basic spatial elements were used for staging liturgical dramas within the church: the *mansion* and the *platea.* The platea was the central, open space, such as the nave. The mansion was a scenic structure depicting some locale needed for a biblical tale. Such a scenic unit could be specially—sometimes elaborately—constructed, or it could be an existing area within the church, such as an altar or the crypt. Mansions were set up around the larger central playing area, the platea. Since a mansion was much too small to perform in, it was used only to indicate a locale; once an action had been initiated at a mansion, it would move to the platea; the entire platea then became associated with the originating mansion for the duration of the scene.

The mansions in a church (or, later, in an outdoor space) were all on view at the same time. This convention of multiple simultaneous settings is not one with which modern audiences are likely to be familiar. We are accustomed to seeing only one locale at a time; if various locales are set up on a modern stage, lighting will be used to focus our attention on a particular area. In the medieval church, since the various mansions were visible simultaneously, the audience had to focus on one at a time and ignore the others. Interestingly, some twentieth-century avant-garde theatre companies have designed theatre spaces where several playing areas are used simultaneously. In today's theatre, however, this technique has most often been meant to shatter the

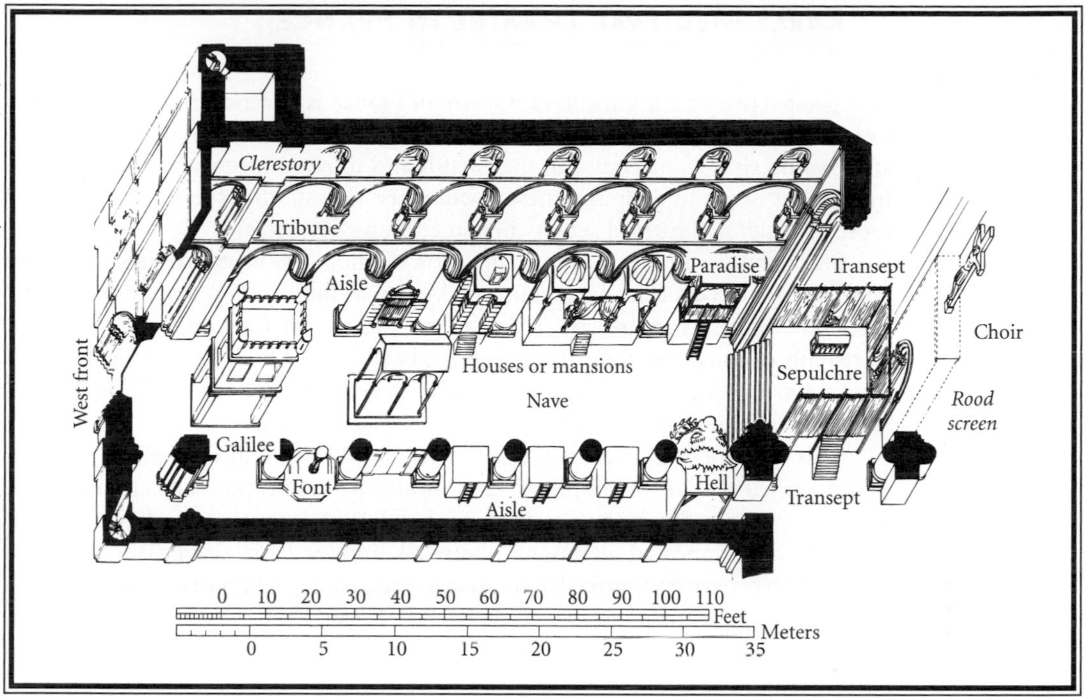

(Richard Leacroft, *The Development of the English Playhouse*, Cornell University Press, Ithaca, N.Y., 1973. By Permission of Reed Book Services/Methuen London.)

STAGING LITURGICAL DRAMA
This reconstruction shows how the interior of a medieval church was used for staging liturgical plays. In addition to the specially created mansions, existing areas within the church were used; note the open space used for the platea.

theatrical illusion of realistic drama and force audiences to become aware of the fact that they are watching a play. Medieval theatre, which was highly conventional, did not use, or need, its simultaneous settings for this purpose. In early English liturgical dramas, for example, males performed all roles and church vestments served as costumes. Acceptance of multiple settings was in keeping with these conventions; it was also in keeping with the medieval worldview: the concept that all times and places were tied together in God's scheme of things.

As we have said, liturgical drama was written and performed in Latin, the language of scholarship and the church. When people attended a church service, there were many Latin words they understood—phrases from the mass, for example, such as *In nomine Patris, et Filii, et Spiritus Sancti,* which means, "In the name of the Father, the Son, and the Holy Spirit." Still, Latin was not the language people spoke every day, and therefore most of the dialogue of liturgical plays would not have been understood by the audience. In the thirteenth century, however, dramas began to be written and presented in the languages spoken by ordinary people: Italian, French, Spanish, English, and so forth. The language of these plays could be understood by everyone; thus the plays became more meaningful and immediate. The term for everyday speech is *vernacular,* and so this new form of drama—to which we turn below—is called *religious vernacular drama.* But first we should examine some unique developments in early medieval French theatre.

Early Medieval Theatre in France

Our perspective on early medieval theatre in France is different from our perspective on England or other European countries. This is because we have more records and manuscripts from France in the twelfth and thirteenth centuries than we have from other areas. In addition, these documents indicate that there may have been more diversity in theatrical activity in France than elsewhere.

From the twelfth century in France, for example, we have two versions of the biblical story of Daniel, and a manuscript known as the *Play of Adam* or the *Mystery of Adam* which features stories of Adam and Eve and of Cain and Abel. From the thirteenth century, there are six surviving plays. Two of these offer religious messages, sometimes presented in comic terms. Several dramas from this period mix serious Christian subject matter with comic, secular material.

This mixture is characteristic of early medieval theatre in France. For instance, it is assumed that in many places Latin liturgical drama preceded drama in the vernacular—everyday language. In France, however, vernacular religious drama seems to have appeared at roughly the same time as Latin drama, and in a few instances may have even preceded it. Thus in the theatre of France at this time, Latin and vernacular drama, and low comedy and serious works, existed alongside one another. In fact, there may also have been more of this blending in other parts of Europe than is generally recognized.

Still, by the end of the fourteenth century a fairly clear division had been drawn between liturgical drama and secular drama, and it is to the origin and development of vernacular theatre that we will turn next.

The Development of Religious Vernacular Drama

Historians continue to debate how medieval vernacular drama originated. The earliest historians of medieval theatre suggested that church dramas performed in Latin simply metamorphosed—were transformed—into the vernacular. Scholars who held this evolutionary theory also believed that in addition to changing from Latin to the vernacular, religious plays moved from inside church buildings to stages erected outside. Among the reasons suggested for this move are the following: (1) The productions were becoming increasingly elaborate and were therefore difficult to stage in churches. (2) The cost of staging these dramas was becoming burdensome to the church. (3) Church officials were opposed to using holy spaces for theatre. One play that supports the notion of a move from inside the church building to outside it is *The Mystery of Adam* (c. 1150), whose stage directions clearly indicate that it was performed outdoors, alongside the church.

Most contemporary scholars believe that later vernacular drama developed independently from the liturgical plays—that there was no evolutionary relationship, though there were similarities in dramatic style and subject matter. As we have noted, the evidence from early medieval theatre in France suggests that vernacular drama did not come after liturgical drama but may have developed alongside it. Whatever its origin, however, between 1350 and 1550 religious vernacular drama presented outside church buildings flourished in a number of European countries, including

England, France, Spain, Germany, Switzerland, and the Netherlands.

In describing religious vernacular drama, it is important to remember that attempts to categorize various types have been made only long after these plays were actually performed. But to help us understand what kinds of plays were produced, scholars have separated religious vernacular dramas into two general categories: *mystery* or *cycle* plays and *morality plays,* which are difficult to categorize as religious or secular.

Mystery or Cycle Plays

The term *mystery* comes from *ministerium,* meaning a religious service or office; this suggests the religious origin of mystery dramas. The mystery plays dramatized series of biblical events, from the creation to the last judgment. The cycle plays sometimes dramatized other stories connected to biblical figures, the lives and miracles of saints, and contemporary church doctrines. They were distinct from the brief liturgical plays: first, they were not presented as part of a religious ceremony but were staged independently as drama; second, they were not small, individual scenes, but short dramas sometimes presented as part of a sequence. When a number of plays were presented in sequence, they constituted a "cycle"—which is how the term *cycle plays* originated.

(© Marilyn Kingwill/ArenaPAL/The Image Works)

MYSTERY PLAYS
The mystery plays depicted scenes from the Bible, both the Old Testament and the New Testament. These plays were frequently presented in cycles, a series of short dramas each of which dramatized an episode from the Bible. They were strung together over several hours or several days. The scene here shows Edward Woodward as God in a production of a mystery play at Canterbury Cathedral in England.

Spring and summer were the most popular times for the presentation of vernacular drama, primarily because of the weather. A favorite occasion for cycle plays was the feast of Corpus Christi. This festival, which was recognized officially by the church in 1311, was observed in the week after Trinity Sunday. Trinity Sunday occurs eight weeks after Easter Sunday; thus Corpus Christi took place sometime between the last week in May and the last week in June. It was intended to remind laypeople of the doctrine that the bread and wine of the mass become the body and blood of Christ; but it went farther than that—it incorporated the mystery that, in Roman Catholicism, gives meaning to existence: the union of human and divine in the person of Christ and the promise of redemption made possible by his sacrifice. It was because of this breadth of meaning, and because the festival took place in late spring, that Corpus Christi became a favorite occasion for cycle plays. But cycle plays were also presented at other times and in conjunction with other festivals. Though no exact parallel can be drawn, it is interesting to note that Greek and Roman drama was also presented in conjunction with religious observances or festivals. These appear to be natural times—times when people are gathered together and are in a celebratory mood—for dramatic presentations.

Since cycle plays were written in the vernacular and staged outdoors, they were meant to appeal to large audiences and to popular tastes. The mysteries are often set in biblical or earlier times, but the characters are medieval types; Abraham and Isaac, for example, are dramatized not as Old Testament Jews but as medieval Christian serfs. Old Testament characters in the cycle plays speak of saints who have not yet been born. Such a displacement in time is called an *anachronism,* and mystery plays are filled with anachronisms. Presenting characters and events outside their proper historical sequence made the biblical characters more identifiable to audiences and also drew parallels between past eras and medieval times. Abraham and Isaac, Noah, Joseph, and the Virgin Mary were depicted as ordinary men and women just like the friends and neighbors of medieval audiences. The charm and directness of these characterizations are still evident when we read the plays today.

(© Donald Cooper/Photo*stage*, England)

A "MODERN" MYSTERY PLAY
A modern version of the mystery plays was based on the English Chester cycle of plays. The version here by the Broomhill Opera Company, featuring a multiracial cast and a good deal of music, met with great success first in South Africa, where it originated, and then in England and the United States, as well as elsewhere.

To popularize these religious dramas, medieval dramatists also highlighted the spectacular. (Even today, audiences can be mesmerized by biblical spectacle, as is evidenced by the popularity of biblical epic films.) A good example of special effects was a production of a play about Noah in 1501 in the town of Mons, in present-day Belgium. In this play, Noah is commanded by God to build an ark to save his family and all the animals because it will soon rain for 40 days and 40 nights and a great flood will come. When the moment of the deluge arrived, the Mons production provided a spectacular effect. On the roofs of houses behind the "Noah" stage area in the town square, water had been stored in wine barrels and men were standing by, waiting for a signal to open the barrels. When the signal was given, the deluge began and torrents of water fell onto the stage. Enough water had been stored to provide a steady rain for 5 minutes. In the presentation, water rose all around, but Noah, his family, and his animals were safe in the ark.

Comedy was also introduced to make the cycle plays more appealing. A good example is found in this play about Noah and his wife. As Noah begins building, his neighbors make fun of him, and his carping wife argues with him. The wife is caricatured as a shrew, always nagging her husband. She does not want to board the ark, and the byplay between her and Noah is highly humorous. In other words, though the story is serious, both the character and the actions of Noah's wife are comic.

At the close of this discussion, we should emphasize that there is much controversy surrounding the "cycle" plays of the Middle Ages. Current scholarship suggests that the cycles were probably not as extensive as previously thought and that few actual cycles may have been staged. In addition, while Corpus Christi became most associated with the cycle plays, historians now point out that these plays were staged at many other times as well. We will see later in this chapter that there is also considerable disagreement about the staging of the cycles.

The Second Shepherds' Play

In order to understand the themes and dramatic structure of vernacular plays, we can look at a specific example: *The Second Shepherds' Play* (c. 1375), from England's Wakefield cycle. (The English vernacular plays are grouped in a series of cycles, named for the places where they were performed: York, Chester, Wakefield, and "N." The last has only an initial; we do not know which of the 125 towns in England where cycle plays were performed is designated by it.)

The Second Shepherds' Play dramatizes the biblical story of the shepherds who are told by an angel of the birth of Christ and are instructed to visit the manger where he has been born. Its first section comically depicts the stealing of a sheep from three shepherds by a rogue, Mak. When the three shepherds search for the missing sheep in Mak's home, Gil, his wife, puts it in a crib and pretends that it is her newborn child. When the shepherds return a second time to offer gifts to Mak's "child," they discover that the infant is the stolen sheep. Though thievery was a capital offense in medieval law, the lenient shepherds merely toss Mak in the air in a blanket.

The humble and just shepherds are then called by the angel to visit the newborn Christ child, to whom they bring gifts in the second section of the play. The farcical "birth" of the first section, therefore, sets the stage for the holy nativity. Parallels are drawn between these two plots: the "child" in the first section is a sheep, just as Christ is the lamb of God; and in both sections there are scenes of adoration and gift-giving.

The Second Shepherds' Play uses most of the standard dramatic techniques of medieval cycle plays. It is written in the vernacular and in verse and is filled with anachronisms. The shepherds are characters out of the Middle Ages, not the Bible: they complain about their lords and feudal conditions, and even though Christ is not born until the close of the play, they pray to him and to various saints throughout the first section. Though the play dramatizes the birth of the Christian savior, this event is preceded by an extended comic section that reflects the influence of secular farce. The mixture of comic and serious elements itself indicates the two strains of medieval theatre—religious and secular.

The Emergence of Episodic Form

In Chapter 1, we examined the first important dramatic form that emerged in western theatre, the climactic drama developed in Greece and Rome. The second major dramatic form to develop in the western tradition is *episodic* structure. Early traces of episodic structure can be found in medieval religious drama.

Episodic drama stands in marked contrast to climactic drama. The "crisis" structure of Greek drama is formal and somewhat rigid. In a typical Greek play, the plot begins near the climax of the story, there are very few major characters, the locale of the action is limited (often to one place), and comedy and tragedy are not mixed in the same play. In the religious drama that emerged in the Middle Ages, the dynamics are quite different.

In *The Second Shepherds' Play,* as we have seen, the action shifts abruptly from a field to Mak's hut and then to Christ's manger some distance away; and comic and serious elements are freely intermingled. Obviously, a play about the birth of Christ should be serious; but the taste for earthy farce was irrepressible in English drama of this period, and so comedy also became a part of the drama.

Moreover, *The Second Shepherds' Play*—unlike climactic drama—does not have a single plot; it has two separate, though related, stories: Mak and the theft of the sheep, and the visit to the Christ child. The fact that two stories are followed simultaneously suggests how these plays achieved unity and advanced a theme. The method is to juxtapose two stories, two plot threads, and two sets of characters so that they reverberate with and thus reinforce one another. A theme is looked at from two or more points of view so that the whole becomes greater than its parts. In *The Second Shepherds' Play,* Mak steals a lamb, and we recall that Christ is often called the *lamb of God.* As we move from the story of Mak to the story of Christ's birth, we are aware of two babies and two lambs; and the echoes and resonances of these two ideas bring the parts of the drama together to create a forceful image.

Frequent changes in time and place occur in *The Second Shepherds' Play;* but this did not bother medieval audiences, who were not concerned with a realistic or literal rendition of a story. In a series of cycle plays, the story would unfold from beginning to end and would often involve a great many characters.

In the cycle plays, then, instead of the economy and compression of Greek drama, we find expansiveness and a juxtaposition of elements. We switch from one element to another: from one group of characters to a different group; from one historical period to another; from one story line to another; from comedy to serious drama. Tension and excitement, as well as meaning, are often created by this shifting back and forth.

Episodic structure was logical for the cycle plays, given the medieval worldview—the concept of all time as part of God's continuum. The past was considered part of the medieval present; therefore, anachronisms and sudden changes in time and place were not seen as incongruous. A parallel can be drawn with medieval triptych paintings: many of these paintings were designed as church altarpieces and show three separate religious scenes side by side.

Episodic drama was in its infancy in the medieval period, but in later years it became the foundation for highly complex plays, such as those of English playwrights like Shakespeare and Spanish dramatists like Lope de Vega. The episodic approach entered the mainstream of western drama; it and the Greek climactic form became the two predominant dramatic structures from the sixteenth to the early twenty-first century.

Producing the Cycle Plays

Liturgical drama, as we noted earlier, was produced within the church building. For the mystery plays, production techniques varied throughout Europe.

On the continent, mystery plays were produced by religious guilds or clubs called *confraternities.* In northern England, they were produced by trade guilds. In England, plays were often assigned to the trade guild that seemed "appropriate." The last supper, for example, might have been presented by the bakers' guild because of the bread served by Christ; the Noah play by the shipbuilders' guild; and the visit of the magi (in which the three wise men bring gold, frankincense, and myrrh to the Christ child) by the goldsmiths' guild. Because of the guilds' participation, the presentations were often civic and commercial events; the cycle plays provided an opportunity for trades and craftsmen to display their abilities. Frequently, town councils assisted in financing and scheduling, although the church continued to oversee outdoor religious theatrical events.

Cycle plays were usually produced once every 2 to 10 years, and some were extremely elaborate. A passion play presented at Valenciennes in France in 1547 lasted 25 days; and *The Acts of the Apostles,* given in 1536 at Bourges (also in France), lasted for 40 days and had a cast of 300 performers. Probably, these were exceptions and most productions took place over a shorter period of time; nevertheless, productions were often complex to mount. The Noah play was part of a cycle at Mons that involved 150 actors playing approximately 350 roles. A total of 48 rehearsals were held, and the productions lasted for four days. Performances of the cycle plays often began early in the day and, after a break for lunch, continued until late afternoon. Depending on the locale, this went on for 2, 3, or many more days.

Most people knew about forthcoming performances because so many members of a community were involved, but those who were not aware would be informed by announcements and processions a few days beforehand. Practices on charging spectators varied. In England most productions were free; for certain productions on the continent, a fee was charged.

Performers

Both on the continent and in England, the actors in cycle plays were amateurs. As the productions became more complex, however, professionals may have supplemented the amateur casts. Customs regarding women performers varied: women performed in France, for instance, but were excluded in England. Because of the extensive scope of the cycle plays, doubling—having a performer play two or more different parts—was not unusual. Rehearsal time was minimal; typically, there were fewer than five rehearsals for an individual cycle. Amateur actors agreed under oath to perform and were fined for missing or disrupting a rehearsal. Since nonprofessionals were used, they were usually typecast and were requested to repeat their roles when a cycle was restaged. *Typecasting* means choosing people who have certain qualities in real life to play characters with similar qualities. A tough-looking man with a strong voice, for instance, would be cast as Cain, who kills his brother Abel; an innocent-looking young woman would play the Virgin Mary.

The financial burden on the individual performer could be great, but the task was undertaken as a religious duty. If, for example, an actor was unable to attend work because of his obligations in the production, he would have to hire a replacement at his job.

Costumes

Actors in the cycle plays provided their own costumes. They would be assisted, however, if they needed unusual costumes: God, for example, would be costumed as a pope (the pope being God's earthly representative), and angels wore church vestments with wings attached.

The assumption has usually been that the common characters in medieval mystery plays wore contemporary clothing: such costuming would be in keeping with the anachronistic nature of these plays and with the desire to let audience members identify with biblical characters.

Recent scholarship, however, questions this traditionally accepted view. Some costume historians point out that in medieval art there is considerable interest in representing clothing from earlier periods, although most of these representations are historically inaccurate. In addition, lists of props and costumes which survive from certain pageants, as well as stage directions in some of the plays, suggest that costuming was not contemporary. For example, the "N Town" passion play requires one character to be costumed as a Jewish high priest.

What is most likely is that the approach to costuming in medieval theatre was not uniform—just as there was no single approach to staging. This uncertainty about costumes again reminds us that to try to establish a single, uniform concept of "medieval theatre" is to diminish a vital, robust art form which flourished in many parts of Europe in a number of individual configurations.

Pageant Masters

Because of the complexity of cycle plays, there developed, both on the continent and in England, a practice of having one person organize and oversee a production. In

England, there are records of someone referred to as a *pageant master,* who supervised the mounting of plays on wagons. This might include advance preparations—both for the wagons and for the rehearsals of plays to be presented on them—and the logistics of seeing that the plays unfolded on schedule.

In the 1500s on the continent—in France, Spain, Belgium, Switzerland, and Austria—men were hired to oversee the elaborate production of cycle plays, and some of these men's names are known. One of them, a Frenchman named Jean Bouchet, outlined the duties of the manager or director. These responsibilities, Bouchet said, included finding people to construct scenery as well as seating for the audience; supervising the building of the stage (or stages); positioning machines and scenery; selecting and rehearsing performers; disciplining performers and fining those who violated the rules; assigning people to collect money at the entrances; and serving as a narrator between plays—describing what had happened before and arousing interest in what was to come.

The duties and responsibilities of managers or pageant masters varied a great deal from place to place. As we have mentioned, the plays were organized in some areas by guilds and in other places by committees. But in many instances there was a single person who oversaw and managed the production. Such people did not perform the same duties as modern directors—they did not, for instance, develop an interpretation of the text or an overall concept to guide the production. But in terms of organization and management, the pageant masters anticipated the director, who was to come very much to the forefront several centuries later. Also, the pageant masters could be said to anticipate modern-day producers.

(Cliché Bibliothèque Nationale de France, Paris)

MEDIEVAL THEATRE "DIRECTOR"
This illustration, "Meneur du Jeu," is from a miniature of the *Mystère de la Passion.* This is one of the earliest depictions of a "director" at work during a rehearsal of a medieval passion play. Note that he is holding a script in one hand and a baton in the other.

Stages

Processional and Stationary Staging Two traditions developed for staging the cycle plays: processional and stationary. The English, Spanish, and Dutch seem to have used processional staging for some of their mystery plays; the rest of Europe used mainly stationary staging. Recent research suggests, however, that both forms of staging were probably used in most countries.

In *processional staging,* audiences would assemble in various places and the cycle play would be set up on a wagon which moved from locale to locale, so that the play could be presented separately for each audience area along its route. Numerous

(Cleveland State University, Theatre Arts Area)

PAGEANT WAGONS
One form of staging medieval religious plays was the pageant wagon, which could be rolled into a town or a nearby field. A wagon or wagons would be set up to serve as a stage, with a backstage area for costume changes. We do not know exactly how these pageant wagons worked, but two possibilities are shown here. At the top is a model of a pageant wagon in a town square: the wagon has a platform with a cloth covering its lower part (from which devils could emerge). At bottom is a drawing of two wagons side by side, one serving as a stage platform and the other as a place for changing costumes and hiding special effects.

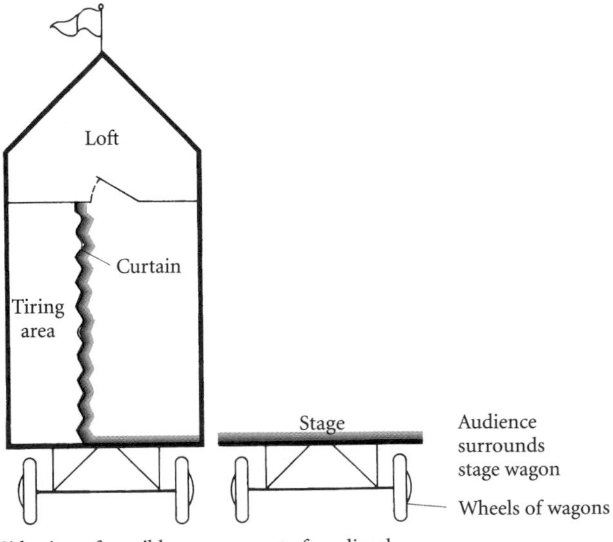

Side view of possible arrangement of medieval pageant wagon behind a second wagon

questions remain unanswered regarding processional staging in England. For example, what did a pageant wagon look like? One theory is that the wagon was a two-story structure on four to six wheels, with the bottom level serving as a curtained dressing area, and the second level containing scenery and acting space.

This theory has been challenged, though, because such wagons might have been too large and unwieldy to move through the narrow streets of medieval English towns and would not have provided a large enough area for acting. A second theory is that one-story wagons carrying scenery were used in conjunction with bare scaffold carts for acting; costume changes would take place in a curtained-off back area of the scenery cart. This theory is based on the Spanish practice of pulling scenery wagons up to a platform for performances; however, the Spaniards used two, three, or four scenery carts for each play.

The most radical theory is that true processional staging was too complicated: a town that had set aside only one day for a religious theatrical event could not have staged a complete cycle at a series of locales; also, since the plays were not uniform in length, it would have been difficult to coordinate a processional production. Therefore, some scholars believe that the pageant wagons, carrying scenery and possibly actors in a mute tableau, were paraded through a town (much like floats in a modern parade) and then pulled up to a stationary stage for the actual performance.

Though there is debate about precisely what form processional staging took, there is no question that it was an accepted type of theatre presentation during the Middle Ages, particularly in England, Spain, and the Netherlands.

The second major form of production for cycle plays was *stationary staging*. In this form—which predominated throughout Europe—a series of small scenic mansions stood side by side, like those for liturgical drama. Usually, a huge platform stage was erected in an open courtyard of a town or in a town square. On occasion, the pulpitum—or stage area—of an abandoned Roman amphitheater was used. The platforms were usually outdoors, but smaller indoor stages were sometimes used. In certain places, existing sites provided a setting for performances. In Rome, Italy, and Bourges, France, there were amphitheaters remaining from Roman days;

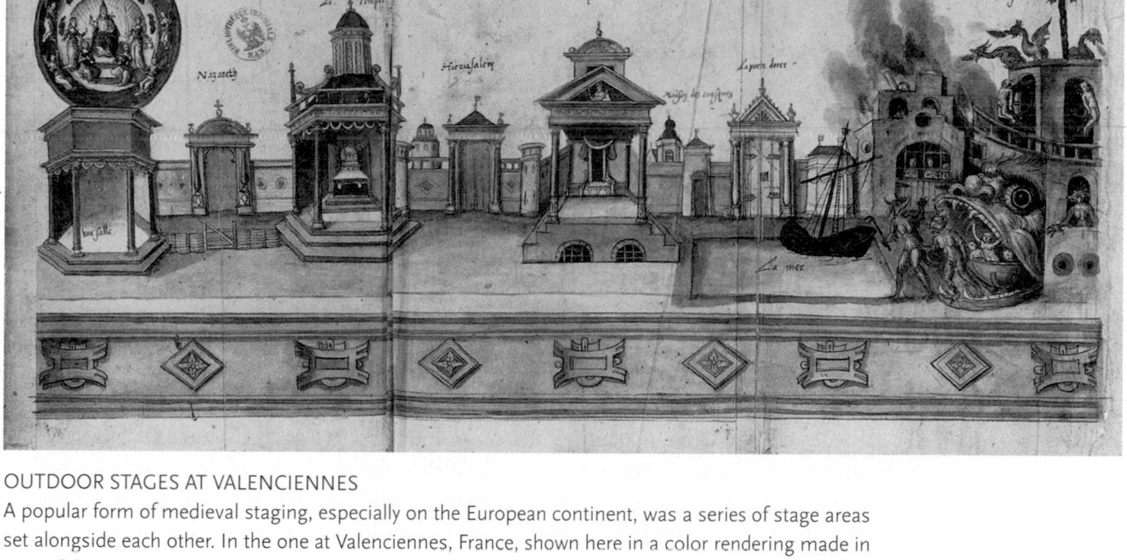

(Bibliothèque Nationale de France)

OUTDOOR STAGES AT VALENCIENNES

A popular form of medieval staging, especially on the European continent, was a series of stage areas set alongside each other. In the one at Valenciennes, France, shown here in a color rendering made in 1547 of the original stage set by Cailleau, the action would move from one area to the next. At the far left is heaven or paradise; at the right is hell with a mouth out of which devils came. In between are other "mansions" representing various locales.

and in Cornwall, England, there was a circular structure, known as the *Cornish round,* with earthen embankments approximately 10 feet in diameter surrounding various stage areas.

Scenic units—the mansions—were placed side by side on the stage or, in some instances, directly on the ground. At times, a cycle would be divided into sections by intermissions, some of them as long as 24 hours, during which the mansions could be changed or rearranged.

The most popular and most spectacular mansions, representing heaven and hell, were placed at opposite ends of the playing area or platform. Heaven was elevated and frequently contained flying machinery—that is, equipment to lift performers aloft. The entrance to hell was most often depicted as the head of a monster, which spewed forth fire and smoke. Between heaven and hell were less intricate mansions representing various earthly locales.

The relationship between the audience and the stage varied; occasionally, spectators viewed the action from all sides, in what was almost theatre-in-the-round, but sometimes they were on three sides or only one side. Seating was temporary: people closest to the stage stood, and farther back scaffolding and box seats were erected. Rooms in nearby houses and on adjoining roofs held additional spectators; in some instances, no doubt, these choice locations were sold to people who wanted the best possible view.

The Neutral Platform Stage One aspect of medieval staging that was to have important ramifications for the theatres of England and Spain in the years to come was the concept of a neutral, nonlocalized platform stage. A pageant wagon might have a specific scenic background, and stationary settings might have mansions for individual scenes, but in both cases the most important playing area was a stage platform in front of these settings. (It will be recalled that dramas presented inside churches also used a generalized area where most of the performance took place—the central platea.)

We know from the texts of many cycle plays that action would often move instantaneously from one locale to another. In *The Second Shepherds' Play,* for instance, at one moment the shepherds are in a field, at the next moment they are in Mak's house, and a few minutes later they are at Christ's manger. In *Abraham and Isaac,* at one point the characters are preparing to go on a journey to a mountaintop; after a few steps across the stage, they have arrived there. To accept such abrupt, sudden transitions, the audience had to regard the platform itself as a neutral area, not a specific locale. In the audience's imagination, the stage could be transformed instantaneously into whatever the play indicated it was: a field, a room in a house, a mountaintop.

As with dramatic structure, this concept of stage space differs from Greek and Roman practice. Instead of a specific locale, such as the palace of Oedipus or Agamemnon, the medieval stage was like a slate from which writing can be erased. A place could be designated, and then the slate could be "wiped clean" so that another locale could be assigned to it. Shifts of locale could be created in the imagination of the spectators rather than by changes of scenery—an arrangement that we sometimes find in today's theatre.

Secrets: Early Experiments with Technology

Special stage effects, called *secrets,* were enormously popular and ingeniously worked out. They were so important that a *secrets master* was hired to oversee them. The flood for the play about Noah is an example of an elaborate stage effect. On stationary stages, actors impersonating heavenly beings could be "flown in" on lines or ropes from the roofs of adjoining buildings. On movable stages, characters could be flown in from the tops of the wagons; trapdoors also allowed actors to be raised and lowered. Shiny surfaces were used to reflect light and create "halo" effects; the halo was quite common in medieval religious painting and was also popular in religious theatre. Between 1350 and 1550, religious drama devised many innovations for special effects.

(© Bettmann/Corbis)

SECRETS: SPECIAL EFFECTS IN MEDIEVAL THEATRE
Theatres in the Middle Ages used a number of visual and sound effects. In the scene depicted here, for instance, when characters were entering the infernal regions, the stage manager orchestrated an array of sounds and sights. A thunder barrel, partially filled with pebbles, was turned vigorously, horns were blown, guns were fired, and characters gave forth unearthly howls.

Morality Plays

Thus far in this chapter we have focused on religious drama, and particularly on the cycle plays. We now turn to another important form of medieval drama, the *morality play.* A morality play attempts to teach a moral lesson through the use of allegorical characters. In allegory, people represent ideas: one character stands for charity, another for integrity, another for greed, and so forth. In morality plays, characters often undertake a journey through which they learn the moral lesson. Some scholars describe morality plays as *station dramas* because during the journey the protagonist is confronted by a series of crises that can be seen as analogous to Christ's journey through the "stations of the cross."

Scholars debate whether to categorize morality plays as religious or secular. It is true that the main characters in morality plays are ordinary men and women, rather than the saints or biblical figures of the miracle and cycle plays. However, the morality plays dealt with moral issues and were deeply rooted in Christianity—and this is the important thing to remember about them.

One key aspect of the morality play reappears in plays of the Renaissance, particularly in England. Frequently, the basis of these dramas is a struggle between two forces, one good and the other evil, for the soul of the main character. This struggle could be between God and Satan, or between a good angel and a bad angel; the crucial element is a battle between two sides for a person's soul. In the English Renaissance, we will see this idea refined by the playwright Christopher Marlowe and developed still further by Shakespeare in several of his plays.

(Andreas Schaad/AP Images)

EVERYMAN

The best-known medieval morality play—shown here in a German adaptation by Hugo von Hofmanstahl staged annually outside the cathedral in Salzburg, Austria—is the story of Everyman, who is summoned to die. In the play, whose main object is to teach a lesson, abstract ideas become characters: Death, Good Deeds, and so on. Everyman tries to forestall dying, and then tries to get others to come with him, but all refuse except Good Deeds. In this scene, we see (left to right) Elisabeth Schwarz as Faith, Ulrike Folkerts as Death, Peter Simonischek as Everyman, and Elisabeth Rath as Good Deeds.

Everyman

Everyman remains the most popular example of a morality play. In this drama, the character of Everyman—who represents humanity—is suddenly and unexpectedly told by Death, a messenger of God, that his earthly life is over. Unprepared for death and afraid to journey to the next world alone, Everyman seeks a companion to accompany him. He speaks to a number of characters, each representing an abstract idea—Worldly Goods, Kin, Beauty, and others—but none of them except Good Deeds will accompany him to the afterlife. The lesson that Everyman, along with the audience, learns is that only Good Deeds can be of any assistance when one is summoned by Death.

Producing the Morality Plays

Though the subject of medieval morality plays was religious, by the early sixteenth century they were probably staged by professional performers—unlike mystery or miracle plays. The introduction of professional actors was in keeping with a transition from religious to secular theatre which is reflected in the morality plays of the late Middle Ages. The text of *Everyman,* however, suggests that staging techniques for moralities were similar to those for the cycle plays and were based on the same concept of a neutral platform stage.

Secular Theatre in the Middle Ages: Popular Forms

A battle between secular and religious studies unfolded slowly in the High Middle Ages, leading to an explosion in the Renaissance. One reflection of this struggle is found in medieval theatre: during the centuries in which liturgical drama and, later, mystery and morality plays were developing, nonreligious or *secular* drama was also emerging. Secular theatre, which could be classified as popular entertainment, was often comic and sometimes irreverent.

Throughout the early Middle Ages and into the High Middle Ages, the tradition of professional theatre was kept alive by wandering minstrels, mimes, jugglers, and rope dancers. These performers, who were attacked by the church as pagan and sacrilegious, continued a tradition of touring players that can be traced back to ancient Greece. Other secular entertainments inspired by festivals, such as May Day games, were enjoyed by the conquering barbarians. Many of these festivals, which featured phallic maypoles and the like, celebrated fertility and sensual freedom. The church was unable to coerce the pagans into renouncing these activities even after they were converted to Christianity.

These forms—indicative of a desire to keep the theatrical impulse alive—came to fruition in the High Middle Ages. Out of the festival celebrations came two types of secular drama: folk plays, dramatizing the heroic exploits of folk heroes; and farce, which comically depicts universal human weaknesses. Secular farce seems also to have been influenced by such church-related events as the Feast of Fools and the festival of the Boy Bishop. During the Feast of Fools, young clergymen selected a mock "bishop" or "pope of fools," who was allowed to misuse his religious power; they also sang and danced indecently, burlesqued sermons and services, and staged plays satirizing the church. The festival of the Boy Bishop was similar, though tamer.

Such popular festivities, which were criticized by the church's hierarchy, contained the seeds of farce. There was something earthy and basic about these comic pieces; as a result, they had an appeal that continued for many years, and eventually they found their way into the plays of Shakespeare and other writers of his time.

Nonreligious comic pieces of the Middle Ages contrast sharply with religious drama. Religious drama, obviously, focuses on the significance of religion—the importance of the Bible, the rewards of virtue, the punishment of vice. Comic drama emphasizes the imperfections and scandals of everyday human behavior; adultery, hypocrisy, and other forms of misbehavior form its subject matter. Also, this subject matter is presented in a strongly satirical or comic light.

We have records of secular drama and farces dating from the thirteenth century. One extant drama, *The Play of Greenwood* by Adam de la Halle of Arras in France, dates from about 1276. This play combines folk material about fairies and supernatural events with satirical material about people living in Arras. There is even more native material in *The Play of Robin and Marion,* written about 1283 by the same author. The popularity of brief secular comedies and farces grew steadily during the fourteenth century.

Among plays surviving from the fifteenth century is a French farce called *Pierre Pathelin,* which dates from around 1470 and was so popular that it went through thirty editions in the next 130 years. Its story concerns a lawyer—Pathelin—who cheats a merchant out of a roll of cloth and then, proud of his success, tells a peasant how to get out of paying his debts, whereupon the peasant turns the tables on the lawyer and cheats him out of the fee the peasant owes him.

A German writer of farce who emerged in the sixteenth century was Hans Sachs (1494–1576). A shoemaker and also a singer, Sachs learned a great deal about drama in his wide travels. A prolific author, he wrote nearly 200 plays. A good example of his work is *The Wandering Scholar from Paradise.* The play is about a woman who, because her second husband is a brute, dreams fondly of her deceased first husband. When a traveling student tells her that he is from Paris, she thinks he has said *paradise.* She assumes that he can contact her dead husband, and asks him to take clothes and money to her first husband when he returns to "paradise." The student readily agrees and goes on his way with his spoils. When the second husband returns and hears the story, he chases after the student to recover the money; but when he overtakes the student, he too is fooled and the student escapes not only with the woman's money but with the second husband's horse.

In England, farce also developed in the sixteenth century. John Heywood (c. 1497—c. 1580) wrote a play called *Johan Johan* in which a henpecked husband's wife is having a love affair with a priest. When the husband is ridiculed by his wife and her lover, he sends them both away from home but then realizes that he has made a mistake—he has actually thrown them into each other's arms.

In France, a first cousin to native farce was the *sottie.* In French, *sot* means "stupid," "foolish," or "absurd," and *sottise* means "foolishness" or "nonsense." These short sketches, which frequently had the figure of a fool as a central character, were often critical of the church or religious figures. A sense of native fun as well as satire predominated in the *sottie.*

At the same time that farce was developing, vagabond players began organizing into troupes and finding wealthy patrons among monarchs, lords, and merchants. They found that this was the best way to develop some continuity and stability in their transient, unreliable profession. The type of entertainment they often presented to their patrons was the *interlude,* a short dramatic piece staged between the courses of a banquet. For their performances, a large banquet hall was used rather than a theatre space. European professional players, who toured a great deal, were accustomed to performing in such improvised spaces.

With the rise of the monarchy in parts of Europe, nonreligious court entertainments became more popular. An intriguing medieval dramatic form staged for royalty was the *street pageant.* By the fifteenth century, allegorical, biblical, and mythological dramatizations, honoring visiting monarchs, were staged along town routes. These were pantomimed tableaux with occasional narration.

It is important to remember that nonreligious drama was being performed at the same time as the mystery plays. These satiric pieces, farces, and folk plays in which ordinary people were the heroes no doubt had some influence on religious drama, and vice versa: the way in which religious plays were written and performed must have affected secular drama, and the down-to-earth comic quality of nonreligious plays affected the cycle plays. Much of what is popular in the medieval mysteries is reminiscent of folk plays and farces. The fact that so many of the cycle plays contain farcical characters and scenes is an indication of the interaction between religious and secular drama.

The Decline of Religious Theatre

The weakening of the church in the sixteenth century, culminating in the widespread Protestant Reformation, was one reason for the demise of religious theatre. Roman Catholicism withdrew its support from religious theatre, which it accused of having weakened the church; for example, it outlawed religious drama in Paris in 1548. Protestantism considered religious drama a tool of Catholicism; thus Elizabeth I, as head of the Anglican church, banned religious drama in England in 1559.

Another reason for the decline of religious drama was that its secular qualities finally overwhelmed the religious material. The farce within *The Second Shepherds' Play* and the focus on the human struggle in *Everyman* were steps in the development of the great secular drama of the English Renaissance.

Medieval religious theatre—in the form of drama it developed and in its staging practices—was to be a major influence on later theatre and drama, particularly in Elizabethan England and the Spanish golden age. In Spain, religious drama continued to flourish alongside secular drama until well into the Renaissance. Furthermore, religious theatre continues to thrive in many parts of the world today. A significant example is the controversial community-staged Oberammergau Passion Play, which is produced annually in Germany. (Debate rages over whether the play's portrayal of Jewish characters is anti-Semitic. In medieval cycle plays dealing with the life of Christ, Jews were often presented negatively.) Still, although religious theatrical works remain important spiritual experiences for some audiences, after the Middle Ages religion was no longer the central concern of most theatre.

In Part Two, we will begin to see how western theatre developed after the Middle Ages, as we take up the theatres of the Renaissance.

SUMMARY

During the early Middle Ages, touring minstrels kept the theatrical tradition alive. Later in the Middle Ages, theatre was reborn in the Roman Catholic church. Musical and dramatic interpolations added to religious services grew into liturgical dramas; these plays, written in Latin and dramatizing biblical events, were staged in churches by the clergy.

In the fourteenth century, plays in the language of the people—religious vernacular drama—developed. Mystery or cycle plays, which depicted a series of biblical tales, were staged and acted outdoors by guilds in northern England and by confraternities on the continent. In England, Spain, and the Netherlands, mystery plays were usually presented on pageant wagons, which probably traveled through towns. In other parts of the continent, a large open playing space with a series of scenic mansions set side by side was common. A medieval dramatic form difficult to categorize is the morality play, which presents allegorical characters and moral lessons and was staged by professional performers.

Medieval plays used simple, direct dramatic techniques that called on the imagination of the spectators. They frequently used symbols and exercised great freedom in shifts in time and space.

Secular theatre also flourished in the Middle Ages. During the High Middle Ages, folk drama and farce developed, and professional performers were employed at the courts of the emerging monarchs. The influence of secular theatre can be seen in the farcical and folk elements of the cycle plays.

Cultural and Historical Developments

- Byzantine empire centralized in Constantinople by Constantine (330)
- Fall of Rome (476)

Early Middle Ages [500–1000]

Theatre History

- Festival entertainments (c. 500–925)
- *Quem quaeritis* trope (c. 925)
- Hrosvitha (c. 935–1001) *(below)*, *Dulcitius*

- Hildegard von Bingen (1098–1179), *Ordo Virtutum*
- Liturgical drama (first century)

Cultural and Historical Developments

- Justinian becomes Byzantine emperor (527)
- Muhammad born, founder of Islam (c. 570)
- Charles Martel defeats Muslims near Poiters (732)
- Charlemagne crowned emperor of Holy Roman Empire (800) *(right)*

- Earliest European reference to a horse collar that allowed the drawing of heavy loads and plowing (920)
- Beginning of Romanesque architecture (c. 1000)

High Middle Ages [1000–1400]

Theatre History

- Liturgical drama spreads outside monasteries (1000–1300)
- Biblical drama *Mystery of Adam* (c. 1150)
- Adam de la Halle, *The Play of Robin and Marion* (c. 1283)
- Feast of Corpus Christi (1311)
- Vernacular religious drama: mystery or cycle and morality plays flourish in Europe (c. 1350–1550)
- *Second Shepherds' Play* (c. 1375), from Wakefield cycle

Cultural and Historical Developments

- Expansion of commerce and trade
- Anglo-Saxon epic *Beowulf* (c. 1000)
- First Crusade (1095) *(right, top)*

- Beginning of Gothic architecture (1140)
- Black death apparently originates in India (1332)
- Chaucer (c. 1343–1400), *The Canterbury Tales*
- Boccaccio's *Decameron* (1353) *(right, bottom)*

- Urban VI in Rome; Clement VII at Avignon (1378)
- Peasant revolt in England (1381)

continued

MILESTONES CHAPTER 4 MEDIEVAL THEATRES IN EUROPE [500–1400] *continued*

High Middle Ages [1000–1400]

Theatre History

- *Pierre Patelin*, French farce (c. 1470)
- Hans Sachs (1494–1576), *The Wandering Scholar from Paradise*
- *Everyman*, morality play (c. 1500) *(right, top)*
- Cycle staged at Mons with spectacular effects (1510)
- Pageant master Jean Bouchet directs cycle at Poitiers (1508)
- John Heywood (c. 1497–c. 1580), *Johan Johan* (1533)
- Traveling troupes perform at banquets for wealthy patrons; street pageants *(right, bottom)* staged for royalty along town routes (sixteenth century)

Cultural and Historical Developments

- Gutenberg invents printing by movable type (c. 1450)
- Constantinople falls to the Turks (1453)
- Copernicus born (1473)
- Martin Luther born (1483)
- Columbus crosses the Atlantic (1492)

Photo Credits: Everyman. (Andreas Schaad/AP Images) / Medieval pageant wagon. (Cleveland State University, Theatre Arts Area)

Part Two Theatres of the Renaissance

The Renaissance was an age of humanism, discovery, and exceptional art, including a flowering of theatre. *Renaissance* is a French word meaning "rebirth," and during this historical period—from roughly 1400 to 1650—European culture is said to have been reborn. Its rebirth included a rediscovery of earlier cultures, but equally important was a new view of human possibilities. In the Middle Ages, human beings had been seen as part of a group. Individually, they were often considered insignificant figures on the lower rungs of a sort of universal ladder, with the deity and other divinities at the top. In the Renaissance, people began to regard the individual as important and as having enormous potential.

A significant aspect of the Renaissance was, of course, the rediscovery of the civilizations of Greece and Rome. For the first time in several centuries, the heritage of these civilizations—their art, literature, and philosophy—became available, largely through the rediscovery of ancient manuscripts. The achievements and ideas of Greece and Rome struck a sympathetic chord in men and women living in fourteenth-century Italy and France, and they hoped to create a new classical civilization that would equal the old.

Other things were happening in addition to this rediscovery of the past. The major distinction between the Middle Ages and the Renaissance was a secularization of society—that is, a move away from religion. The dominance of the Roman Catholic church was eroded as Renaissance society became more concerned with "this world" than with the "next world," the afterlife in heaven.

There was a great sense of experimentation and discovery during the Renaissance, and several parallels with our own times are striking. The exploration of the new world in the Renaissance created the same kind of excitement as our own first attempts to open the frontier of space: Columbus's voyage across the Atlantic to the Americas was like the astronauts' first landing on the moon. The discovery of gunpowder in the Renaissance transformed military strategy, as the development of the atomic bomb did in our own day. Gutenberg's printing press opened up the world to the masses, as film, television, telecommunication, and computers do today. There is also a parallel in economics: at the end of the Renaissance in the seventeenth century, societies suffered from severe inflation, just as many countries suffered in the twentieth century. And the questions that shook the Renaissance world—questions about God, rulers, and the place of humanity in the universe—continue to reverberate in our own time.

Throughout Europe, the Renaissance brought a burst of theatrical activity. Italian innovations such as opera, commedia dell'arte, the proscenium stage, painted-perspective scenery, and the neoclassical rules for playwriting would affect theatre for the next 200 years. *Neo* means a new or different form of something; thus *neoclassical* refers to the revival or adaptation in the Renaissance period of practices of Greece and Rome. French neoclassical drama in the late seventeenth century was greatly influenced by Italian neoclassicism. The theatres of the English Renaissance and the Spanish golden age were distinctly different from those of Italy and France but were no less active and innovative.

The impact of the Renaissance is still apparent in theatre today. When we sit in a proscenium-arch theatre or enjoy a Shakespearean play produced at a festival, we are taking part in the rich theatrical heritage of the Renaissance.

Tom Nelis as Oberon and Christina Rouner as Titania in Shakespeare's *A Midsummer Night's Dream,* directed by Kim Rubinstein, Long Wharf Theatre, 2005. Set and costume design by G. W. Mercier; lighting by Joel Moritz.

CHAPTER 5

The Theatre of the Italian Renaissance

Entertainment at an Italian Villa

The painting shown here, dated 1566, is one of the earliest known representations of a theatrical event at the time of the Italian Renaissance. Titled *A Court Festival Set in a Garden of an Italian Villa,* it depicts several activities that might have provided entertainment in this period, including acrobatics, tableaux, and processions.

(William F. Reilly, photo courtesy of Trinity Fine Art Ltd, London)

During the Renaissance, European culture advanced dramatically, and the first center of cultural activity was Italy. At that time, Italy (like classical Greece) was not a unified nation but a group of independent city-states.

Background: The Renaissance in Italy

European politics changed markedly during the Renaissance, as the autocratic rule of kings and princes superseded the decentralized feudal system and the dominance of the church. The means by which a ruler maintains control were outlined by Niccolò Machiavelli (1469–1527), an Italian author, statesman, and political philosopher. Machiavelli looked on politics as a science and argued in his book *The Prince* (1513) that to protect their subjects rulers must do whatever is necessary and practical—even if it borders on the unethical.

Because of the extensive growth in trade in Italy, the entrepreneur, or enterprising merchant, became the key economic figure. The merchant class grew in strength and power, and as the merchants' wealth increased, they had leisure time to fill; they were also eager to display their fortunes. As a result, a patronage system developed, in which wealthy merchant-princes, such as the Medici family in Florence, gave financial support to artists.

Renaissance art is quite different from the art of the Middle Ages, as can be seen when paintings by Renaissance artists such as Michelangelo and Leonardo da Vinci are compared with medieval art. During the Middle Ages, paintings—such as Giotto's *Madonna Enthroned* (c. 1310)—had religious subjects. Many Renaissance artists also took inspiration from religion: good examples are Michelangelo's *David* and *Moses* and his ceiling in the Sistine Chapel, and Leonardo's *Last Supper*. Renaissance artists, however, treat religious subjects secularly: no longer are the religious figures idealized; instead, they are human beings with whom we can identify.

Artistic techniques also changed dramatically during the Renaissance. Through the use of new materials and skills, paintings became more "natural"; what was reflected on canvas was closer to what people saw in life as they looked about them. The introduction of oil paints made portraits more lifelike, and perspective was introduced and refined. *Perspective* is a convention for representing depth on a flat surface—that is, for approximating the way a scene looks to the human eye: objects in the distance are smaller than those in the foreground, and parallel lines—such as a pair of railroad tracks—converge in the distance. Perspective gives an illusion of depth because the eye is attracted to a vanishing point; with perspective, the human subjects in Renaissance art were placed in realistic backgrounds.

In Renaissance literature, the major movement was *humanism*. The humanists focused on people rather than gods; they were preoccupied with describing humanity and human powers, and they studied and imitated the Greeks and Romans. The Italian poet Dante Alighieri (1265–1321), in the early fourteenth century, composed the first important literary work written not in Latin but in the vernacular, the everyday language of the people. Called *The Divine Comedy,* it was an imaginary journey through hell, purgatory, and heaven, inspired by the Roman poet Virgil. Dante's younger contemporary Petrarch (1304–1374) argued for an emphasis on human over theological subjects and for the study of Greek and Roman classics. A more earthy approach was taken by Boccaccio (1313–1375) in his collection of ribald tales, *The Decameron.*

Later, in the mid-fifteenth century, the invention of the printing press by the German Johannes Gutenberg made literature available to great numbers of people; this, like humanism, aided the spread of literature rediscovered from the past.

The Renaissance was also a period of invention and exploration. People moved away from the otherworldly concerns of the Middle Ages and became anxious to explore and conquer the world around them. Sailing expeditions brought discoveries in many parts of North and South America and contributed new wealth to the Old World. Although the Renaissance began in Italy, other European countries initiated the exploration and exploitation of the New World. Columbus, who reached America in 1492, was

Italian Renaissance

Year

Year
1325
1400
1425
1450
1475
1500
1525
1550
1575
1600
1625
1650

Theatre

- Twelve of Plautus's lost plays rediscovered (1429)
- Vitruvius's *De Architectura* published (1486)
- Plays by Aristophanes published by Aldine Press in Venice (1498)
- Ariosto's *I Suppositi* (1509)
- Machiavelli's comic play *Mandragola* (c. 1513)
- Bibbiena's *La Calandria* (1513)
- Beolco begins writing and performing (c. 1520)
- Serlio's *Architettura* (6 vols.) (1545)
- Peak of commedia dell'arte (1550–1650)
- First performances of I Gelosi (the Andreinis) (c. 1569)
- Castelvetro requires unities (1570)
- Teatro Olimpico built (1584)
- Sabbioneta theatre built (1588)
- Peri's *Dafne* (1597)
- I Gelosi troupe disbands on the death of Isabella Andreini (1604)
- Aleotti uses flat wing (c. 1606)
- Teatro Farnese built (1618)
- Sabbatini's *Manual for Constructing Theatrical Scenes and Machines* (1638)
- Torelli's pole-and-chariot system (c. 1645)

Culture and Politics

- Death of Dante (1321)
- Antonio Laschis, *Achilles* (c. 1390)
- Manuel Chrysoloras opens Greek classes in Florence; beginning of revival of Greek literature in Italy (1396)
- Cosimo de' Medici rules Florence (1432)
- Founding of Platonic Academy in Florence (1440)
- Gutenberg invents movable type (c. 1450)
- Leonardo da Vinci born (1452)
- Manuscripts of Greek plays brought to Italy after fall of Constantinople (1453)
- Lorenzo de' Medici rules Florence (1469)
- Michelangelo born (1475)
- *Birth of Venus* by Botticelli (1484)
- Columbus discovers America; Leonardo da Vinci draws a flying machine (1492)
- Italian wars spread Italy's cultural influence but weaken Italy politically (1494)
- Leonardo da Vinci's *Mona Lisa* (1503)
- Michelangelo's *David* (c. 1504)
- Sistine Chapel (c. 1512)
- Machiavelli's *The Prince* (1513)
- Leonardo da Vinci dies (1519)
- Verrazano discovers New York Bay and Hudson River (1524)
- Uffizi Museum at Florence founded (1560)
- Galileo born; Michelangelo dies (1564)
- Palladio's *I quattro libri dell'architettura* (1570)
- Catherine de Médicis, queen mother of France, dies (1589)
- Mannerism begins to appear in Italy (1600)
- Galileo dies (1642)

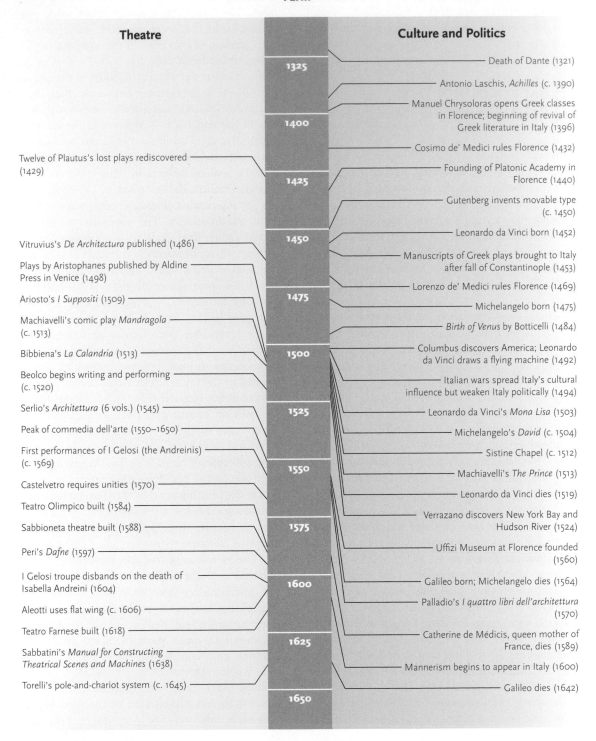

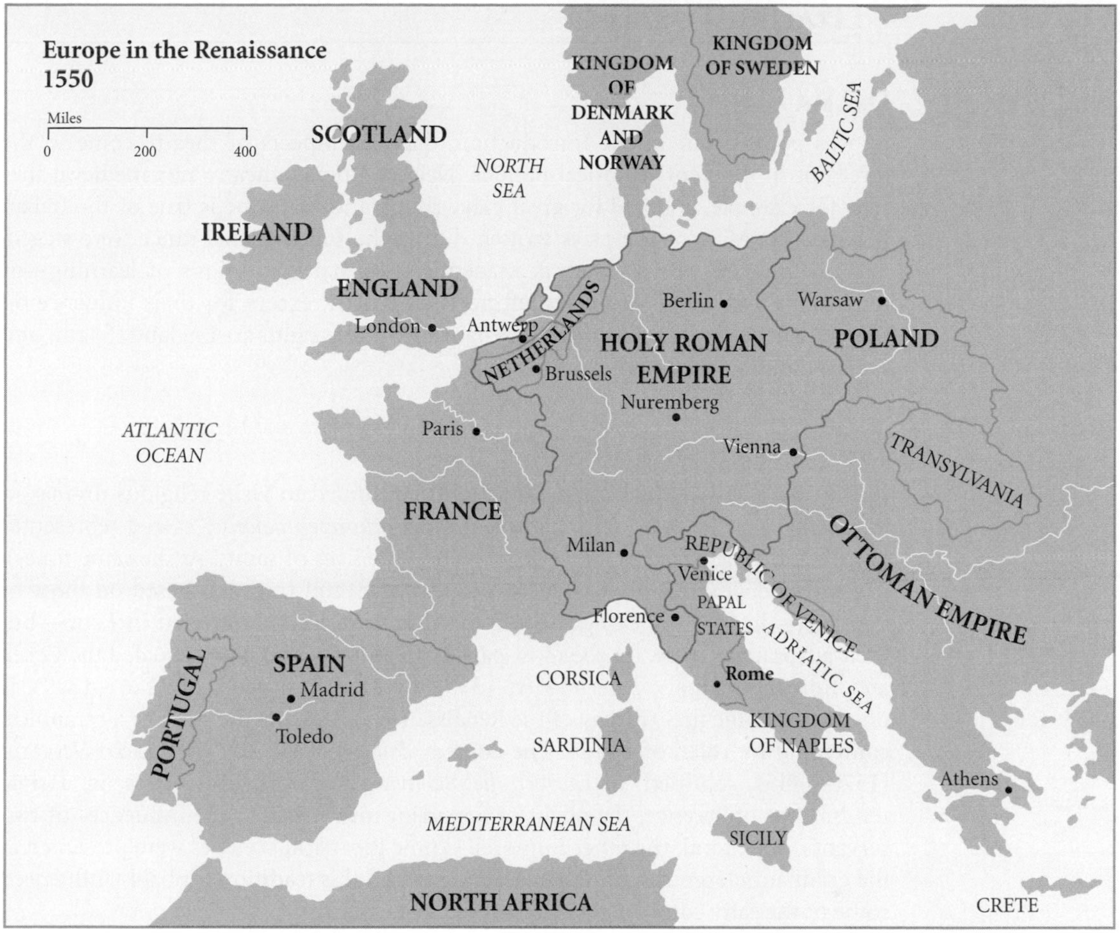

Renaissance Europe

sponsored by the monarchy of Spain; Portugal led in the circumnavigation of Africa and the development of a sea route to India; and the English, the Dutch, and the French were also successful explorers.

Scientific advances revolutionized the perception of humanity's place in the universe. The Italian astronomer Galileo, the Polish scientist Copernicus, and the German mathematician Kepler proved that the sun, not the earth, is the center of the solar system. These men demystified the cosmos by developing mathematical formulas for astronomical phenomena. (The invention of the telescope, of course, was a factor in these scientific breakthroughs.) Though Galileo was condemned by many philosophers and theologians because his theories questioned long-held beliefs—and he was forced by the church to recant—his ideas eventually won out. In 1992, the Roman Catholic church revoked the charges which had been brought against Galileo during the Renaissance.

As a part of this general cultural and social revolution, theatre in Italy was transformed radically between 1550 and 1650. The Italian Renaissance witnessed major innovations in four areas of theatre arts—acting (in commedia dell'arte), dramatic criticism, theatre architecture, and scene design.

Italian Theatre

Drama

As was pointed out in the Introduction, different aspects of theatre come to the forefront in different historical periods. Neither Roman theatre nor medieval theatre, for example, is noted for great playwriting, and the same is true of the Italian Renaissance. Most of the plays written during the Italian Renaissance were staged, or sometimes just read aloud, at academies—formal institutions of learning—or for wealthy patrons. These plays left no lasting mark except for their influence on writers who were to follow: some Renaissance playwrights in England, Spain, and France did draw on Italian plays.

Tragedies and Comedies

In the 1300s and 1400s, Italian playwrights continued to write religious dramas in the medieval style; these were known as *sacra rappresentazioni* ("sacred representations") and were based on biblical stories and the lives of saints. At the same time, a few early Renaissance playwrights wrote comedies and tragedies based on those of antiquity—in fact, the earliest secular dramas were actually written in Latin—but their adaptations were, for the most part, staid and dry and never equaled the Greek and Roman originals. *Eccerinus* (c. 1315), by Albertino Mussato (1261–1329), is often cited as the first tragedy of the Renaissance; it presents the story of a tyrannical contemporary ruler of Padua. The comedy *Paulus* (1350) by Pier Paolo Vergerio (1370–1445), subtitled *To Correct the Behavior of Youth,* dramatizes, in a style reminiscent of Terence, the plight of a student torn between the influences of two servants: one moral, the other immoral. Comic theatrical sketches were presented at the graduation exercises of Italian academies, and this tradition probably influenced some of the early comic playwrights of the Renaissance.

The renewal of interest in classical dramatic traditions was inspired by several developments: (1) a revival of the teaching of Greek by such noted scholars as Manuel Chrysolaras at the close of the 1300s; (2) a transfer in 1453 of surviving Greek and Roman manuscripts to Italy after the fall of Constantinople, which had been the center of the eastern Roman empire; (3) the publication of all the extant plays attributed to Aeschylus, Sophocles, Euripides, Aristophanes, Plautus, Terence, and Seneca; and (4) the dissemination of the writings of Aristotle and Horace. The publication of some influential works was made possible by Gutenberg's printing press; early examples include the works of Aristophanes (published in Venice in 1498), Sophocles (in 1502), Euripides (in 1503), and Aeschylus (in 1518).

Beginning in the early 1500s, Italian plays were written not in Latin but in Italian; they were still, however, based on classical models. For example, *La Cassaria* (*The Chest,* 1508) and *I Suppositi* (*The Counterfeits,* 1509) by Ludovico Ariosto (1474–1533) and *La Calandria* (1513) by Cardinal Bernardo Dovizi da Bibbiena (1470–1520) are clearly indebted to plots and techniques popularized in Roman New Comedy. Two Renaissance tragedies of the early sixteenth century were *Sofonisba,* which was written in 1515 by Giangiorgio Trissino (1478–1550) and published in 1518 but not produced until 1562, at the Olympic Academy in Vicenza;

DEBATES IN THEATRE HISTORY | Adaptations as Sources of Drama

Adaptations by Italian Renaissance dramatists of Greek and Roman models raise the general question of adaptations as sources of theatre. Italian Renaissance dramatists were not the first or the last to turn to other sources for stylistic inspiration or content. As we noted in Chapter 1, the Greek tragedies were based on myths and other fictionalized accounts of Greek history. The Roman playwright Seneca turned to Greek drama for the plotlines of many of his melodramatic tragedies; Plautus and Terence borrowed a great deal of their comic technique and subject matter from Menander. During the Middle Ages, amateur playwrights turned to the Bible as a source of stories.

In later eras, dramatists often borrowed from playwrights who had preceded them or adapted materials from other literary forms. Shakespeare appropriated many of his plotlines and characters from popular stories of the Italian Renaissance, from English history, and from classical sources; his *Comedy of Errors,* for example, is a reworking of Plautus's *The Menaechmi.* The French comic dramatist Molière used techniques of commedia dell'arte. Jean Racine turned to the Greek tragedies; his *Phaedra* is a retelling of Euripides' *Hippolytus.* In the eighteenth century, many authors rewrote Shakespeare in an attempt to make his plays adhere to the neoclassical ideals or to expand certain roles for leading performers; the actor David Garrick, for example, adapted *Macbeth* for his own performances. In the nineteenth century, many dramatists turned to popular novels—as many screenwriters do today—and adapted the story lines. The novels of Charles Dickens were often staged, and the most successful play of the nineteenth-century American theatre was an adaptation of Harriet Beecher Stowe's novel *Uncle Tom's Cabin.*

In the twentieth century, in the period between the two world wars there were numerous attempts to imitate and adapt techniques and story lines of Greek and Shakespearean drama. Like Italian Renaissance playwrights, some twentieth-century authors believed that copying the style and subject matter of earlier periods would enhance the artistic worth of their own works. The American playwright Maxwell Anderson (1888–1959), in *Elizabeth the Queen* (1930), *Mary Queen of Scotland* (1933), and *Winterset* (1935), used verse reminiscent of Shakespeare's, trying to create a modern equivalent of Shakespearean history plays; but Anderson's plays do not have the unique linguistic brilliance of Shakespeare's, nor does Anderson dramatize historic events as imaginatively as Shakespeare. Among other playwrights who were contemporaries of Anderson and used classical story lines were Jean Cocteau, Jean Giraudoux, and Eugene O'Neill.

American and British musical theatre has a long history of borrowing from popular dramas and novels. Two famous examples are Leonard Bernstein's *West Side Story,* which is an adaptation of Shakespeare's *Romeo and Juliet;* and Andrew Lloyd Webber's *Phantom of the Opera,* based on a nineteenth-century novel that had already been dramatized and filmed in several other versions.

Some critics have argued that playwrights' frequent reliance on adaptation reflects the fact that there are only a limited number of plotlines, which must therefore be used and reused throughout theatre history. In addition, of course, playwrights who must work quickly to create new drama for popular theatre will have to turn to other sources for inspiration. What is most intriguing is to try to identify the differences between authors who copy unimaginatively and those who use sources creatively, building on the originals to produce great works of drama. Shakespeare, of course, is a prime example of the latter.

and *Orbecche* (1541) by Giambattista Giraldi Cinthio (1504–1574). Trissino's play borrowed many structural elements from classical Greek tragedy; Cinthio's was modeled on Seneca's more melodramatic tragic style. Trissino also wrote an adaptation of Plautus's comedy *The Menaechmi,* entitled *I Simillimi* (1547).

Intermezzi and Pastorals

Two other popular dramatic forms developed in the Renaissance which were influenced by classical subject matter and dramatic techniques were intermezzi and pastorals. (Another form—opera—which also reflects classical influences is discussed below.)

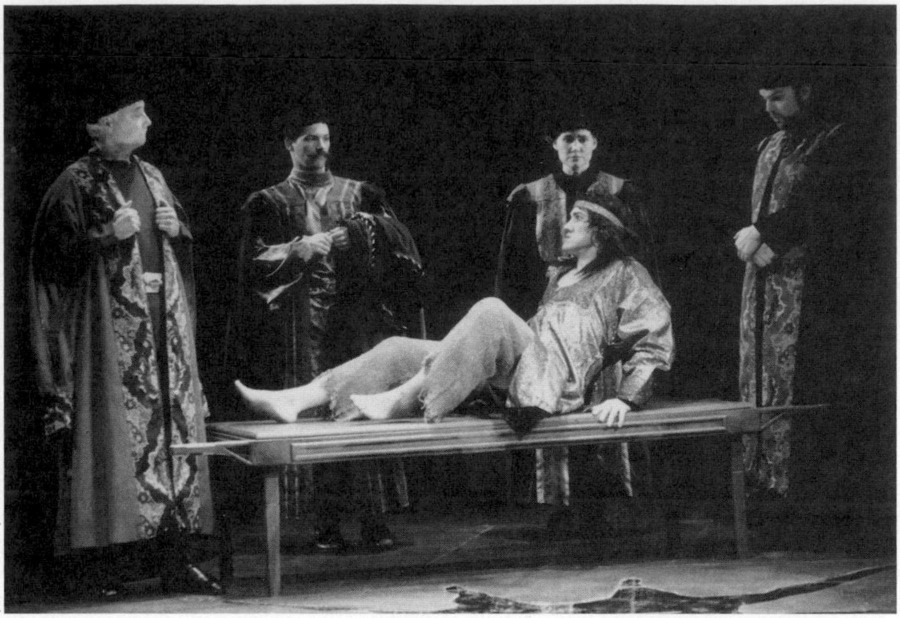

(Chris Drew)

THE MANDRAKE
One of the few Italian Renaissance plays still produced today is *Mandragola—The Mandrake*—by the political philosopher Niccolò Machiavelli. It is very reminiscent of Roman New Comedy and reflects the influence of the classical era on the Renaissance. Shown here is a recent production by the Sacramento Theatre Company.

Intermezzi were short pieces depicting mythological tales; they were presented between the acts of full-length plays and were often thematically related to the full-length works they accompanied. These short works had developed out of popular court entertainments. Intermezzi often required spectacular scenic effects. Although popular in the sixteenth century, this form disappeared in the 1600s.

The Italians also imitated Greek satyr plays—short, ribald comic pieces that had been presented as a follow-up to Greek tragedies—in a form they called a *pastoral*. The subject matter of a Renaissance pastoral is romance; the characters are usually shepherds and mythological creatures who inhabit the forests and countryside. Unlike the Greek satyr plays, the Italian pastorals were not overtly bawdy or sexual in style or subject matter. These pastorals usually deal with lovers who are threatened and often at odds with each other; although the action is serious, the endings are happy, with the lovers being reunited.

The most famous example of a pastoral play is *Aminta* (1573) by Torquato Tasso (1544–1595). Aminta, a shepherd, is passionately in love with Sylvia, who does not love him. Even after Aminta saves her from an evil satyr, she refuses to return his affection. When Aminta hears a false report that Sylvia has been killed by a lion, he throws himself off a hillside. Sylvia's heart is finally moved when she is told of Aminta's suicide, and she sets off to give him an appropriate burial, hinting that she too will commit suicide. However, in the final act it is reported that Aminta was saved when his fall was broken by bushes and has been revived by a kiss from his beloved Sylvia. The classical influences on Tasso's pastoral are quite clear. Its characters are reminiscent of those in satyr plays. Also, a chorus is used to reflect on the action and interact with the characters. All the violent actions—including Sylvia's being threatened by the villainous satyr and Aminta's jumping off the hill—occur offstage and are simply described.

Because Italian Renaissance authors were usually more interested in copying Greek and Roman dramatic forms and plotlines than in imaginatively adapting or building on these earlier traditions, their dramas are of little interest to contemporary theatre practitioners and are rarely revived. The one most frequently produced today is *Mandragola* (*The Mandrake,* c. 1513–1520). This play is a bawdy comedy by Machiavelli that depicts a gullible husband hoodwinked by his wife and her lover.

Opera

Opera was the only theatrical form of the Italian Renaissance to survive. It was developed at a Florentine academy at the end of the sixteenth century. By the mid-seventeenth century, several public opera houses had been constructed in Venice, indicating the widespread popularity of the new form. Its inventors, in keeping with the Renaissance desire to revive classical forms, believed that they were re-creating the Greek tragic style, which had fused music with drama. The earliest operas were based on Greek mythology and ancient history. Jacopo Peri's *Euridice* (1600) and Claudio Monteverdi's *Orfeo* (1605), for example, dealt with the Greek myth of Orpheus, who went to the underworld—Hades—to try to bring back his wife, Eurydice.

Opera is quite dramatic and could be considered a form of drama, but it is usually studied as a form of music because most operas are completely sung, and dramatic action, mood, and characters are created through song and music. The text of an opera, called the *libretto,* is often secondary to the music. One clear indication of the primacy of music is that operas are invariably identified in terms of composers, not librettists. For example, *Don Giovanni* has a libretto by Lorenzo da Ponte, but it is never spoken of as being by da Ponte; it is always described as Mozart's *Don Giovanni*. In the same way, *Falstaff* is based on Shakespeare's *The Merry Wives of Windsor,* but it is known only as Verdi's *Falstaff*. In opera, the composer reigns supreme.

The basic elements of opera are the purely musical sections and the recitative. Included in musical segments are the *aria,* a solo song accompanied by the orchestra; and duets, trios, and quartets: songs by two, three, and four persons respectively. A *recitative* is sung dialogue.

The stories of opera moved from myth to history to contemporary fictional and real events as source material.

A key figure in the history of opera was the Italian Alessandro Scarlatti (1659–1725), who established the supremacy of the aria. Having begun in Florence, Italy, around 1600 as drama set to music, opera spread to other parts of Italy during the seventeenth century. For three centuries, from 1600 to 1900, it spread and developed throughout not only Italy, but France, Germany, and much of the European continent, as well as England. In the middle of the seventeenth century, the French created their own operas, modifying Italian opera to suit their tastes. French opera insisted on textual clarity and incorporated ballet. The first master of French opera was the Italian-born composer Jean-Baptiste Lully (1632–1687). The subject matter of most seventeenth-century opera was historical or mythological.

One of the great composers of eighteenth-century opera was Wolfgang Amadeus Mozart (1756–1791), who was born in Salzburg, Austria, but lived much of his short life in Vienna. He brought comic opera to the peak of perfection.

The nineteenth century was the era of grand opera: major works with powerful, melodic arias and full choral and orchestral elements. Two of the best-known composers in this form are Richard Wagner (1813–1883), a German composer who imposed on opera his ideas of monumental works based on legends and myths, with sweeping scores, all joined together in a unified theater piece; and the Italian composer Giuseppe Verdi (1813–1901), a superb musician with mastery of orchestral techniques and an impressive instinct for dramatic effect.

In the modern period, in addition to such works as Alban Berg's *Wozzeck* (1921) and *Lulu* (1934), contemporary American and British musical theatre includes works that some commentators have categorized as opera. George Gershwin's *Porgy and Bess* (1935), Stephen Sondheim and Hugh Wheeler's *Sweeney Todd* (1978), Andrew Lloyd Webber and Tim Rice's *Jesus Christ Superstar* (1971) and *Evita* (1978), and Webber's *Phantom of the Opera* (1987) are operatic, using recitative instead of dialogue to move the dramatic action along. Hit songs in operatic-style musical comedies are the modern-day equivalent of arias. Because their music has popular appeal, these shows are more accessible to contemporary audiences than the grand opera of earlier centuries.

Commedia dell'Arte: A Popular Theatrical Form

In contrast to opera, which is chiefly a musical form, another equally popular type of entertainment in Renaissance Italy was a type of pure theatre. This is *commedia dell'arte,* which is Italian for "play of professional artists."

Commedia companies usually consisted of ten performers—seven men and three women, though sometimes the numbers varied. They were traveling troupes, possibly the successors of Greek and Roman mimes. Although there were instances when commedia performers staged serious forms of drama, they usually staged comedies, and through the years the term *commedia dell'arte* has come to be associated primarily with comedy.

Commedia thrived in Italy over a considerable period of time, from 1550 to 1750. It was not a written, literary form, but rather consisted of improvised presentations. Scenarios—short scripts without dialogue—were written by members of a company, and these scripts provided plot outlines; in other words, the performers had no set text but invented the words and actions as they went along. Over 1,000 such scenarios survive from the Italian Renaissance. Using these outlines, actors would create the dialogue and would be expected to move the action along through improvisation.

Conventions of Commedia dell'Arte

The conventions of commedia dell'arte made the actors' task simpler than its improvisatory nature would suggest. For one thing, commedia actors played the same stock characters throughout most of their careers. Among the popular comic figures were a lecherous, miserly old Venetian, *Pantalone;* a foolish pedant who was always involved in his neighbors' affairs, *Dottore;* a cowardly, braggart soldier, *Capitano;* and servants known as *zanni,* who were sometimes sly and sometimes foolish. *Arlecchino,* or *Harlequin,* was the most popular of the comic servants. Commedia scenarios also included serious young lovers whose romances were often blocked by Pantalone and Dottore. Since the performers fused their own personalities with those of their characters, improvisation was easier. And since the

(© Christie's Images/Corbis)

COMMEDIA DELL'ARTE

The most important development in acting during the Italian Renaissance was the emergence of commedia dell'arte, in which the performers improvised dialogue around a fixed scenario. Commedia had stock characters, who wore unchanging costumes and masks. This form also became popular outside Italy, particularly in France. Shown here is a painting from the period showing commedia players, along with other entertainers, performing outdoors.

performers worked together, playing the same characters, for extended periods of time, they became adept at creating comic interaction on the spur of the moment.

Improvisation was also made easier because all the commedia characters used standard *lazzi*—repeated bits of physical comic business. Capitano, for example, would get entangled with his sword so that it often would emerge from between his legs as a ludicrous phallic symbol. A lazzo from Florence—dating from 1612—shows how bawdy these comic physicalizations could be: "Hearing about the physical perfection of a certain woman, Pantalone's (or the Captain's) dagger begins to rise between his legs."[1] (Twentieth-century film and television comics had their own lazzi; the great film clowns—such as Laurel and Hardy, the Marx Brothers, and the Three Stooges—had pieces of physical business that they repeated in all their performances.)

[1] "The Comic Routines of the Commedia dell'Arte," Mel Gordon (ed. and trans.), *Performing Arts Journal*, New York, 1992, p. 32.

TWO FAMOUS COMMEDIA CHARACTERS
Commedia dell'arte was noted for stock characters who reappeared regularly in its popular scenarios. These characters can usually be categorized as *zanni,* or comic servants; lecherous old men; and young lovers. The two seen here are (right) Pantalone, a miserly old Venetian merchant who chases after younger women; and (left) Pulcinella, a Neapolitan servant.

In addition, commedia actors used conventional entrance and exit speeches as well as prepared musical duets. Surviving from the Renaissance are manuscripts put together by commedia actors which contain jokes, comic business, and repeated scenes and speeches. (These books were referred to by many different names, but the most common term for them was *zibaldoni.*)

Costuming also facilitated improvisation. Commedia characters all wore traditional costumes, such as Harlequin's patchwork jacket and Dottore's academic robe, so that audiences could recognize them immediately. Usually, each character would always wear the same outfit, and its exaggerated details reflected his or her comic personality. A significant addition to Harlequin's costume was the slapstick, a wooden sword used in comic fight scenes. Sometimes the slapstick consisted of two thin slats of wood, one on top of the other; when a performer was thwacked with it, the effect was greatly exaggerated by the sound of the two pieces of wood smacking together. Today we use the term *slapstick* for comedies emphasizing physical horseplay. Masks, covering either the whole face or part of the face, were an essential element of commedia costumes. Pantalone's mask, for example, always had a huge hooked nose. The young lovers, however, did not wear masks.

Commedia Companies

Commedia dell'arte was enormously popular with audiences. One measure of its success is its popularity outside Italy, particularly in France.

The most successful commedia companies were often organized by families and chose names which were meant to characterize them: *I Gelosi* (The Zealous), *I Fideli* (The Faithful), *I Confidenti* (The Confident), and *I Accesi* (The Inspired). Most companies were based on a profit-sharing plan: members of the company shared in its profits as well as its expenses and losses. Commedia performers were flexible in terms of spaces where they performed: they could play in town squares, in unused theatre spaces, in the homes of wealthy merchants, or at court.

I GELOSI

I Gelosi (The Zealous, c. 1569–1604) became the most acclaimed commedia dell'arte troupe in Europe through the talents of two performers: Francesco and Isabella Andreini. I Gelosi was formed about 1569 from the remnants of another noted company; after 1578, when Francesco Andreini became one of the group's leaders and married Isabella, it reached its greatest renown.

Francesco Andreini (1548–1624) had acted with the troupe for several seasons before his marriage. Originally, he played the *innamorato,* or male lover, but then he switched to his most famous role, the military figure Captain Spavento. As a young man he had been a professional soldier, and it is likely that this experience helped to shape his performance. Francesco was also a poet, musician, and linguist. At the age of sixteen Isabella Canali (1562–1604) married Francesco Andreini and began her stage career as the company's *innamorata,* or female lover. The leading poets of Italy and France wrote verses praising Isabella's beauty and charm, but she was equally renowned for her wit, intelligence, and virtue. A Latin scholar, she also wrote her own sonnets, songs, and pastorals.

(photos12.com-ARJ)

COMMEDIA DELL'ARTE PERFORMERS
One of the most famous family troupes of commedia dell'arte, the improvisational Italian theatre, was known as "I Gelosi." Performers from the troupe are seen here with the leading actress, Isabella Andreini, in the center. Isabella and her husband, Francesco Andreini, were the leading performers in the Gelosi troupe.

Friends of the Andreinis included members of the Italian and French nobility and even royalty—the prince of Mantua was godfather to one of their seven children. In 1600, Henri IV of France invited the troupe to Paris for his wedding to Marie de' Medici. They stayed in Paris for 4 years, winning the esteem of both Henri and Marie. On the journey back to Italy, Isabella had a miscarriage, and she died at Lyon in France; the entire city turned out for her funeral.

After Isabella's death, Francesco disbanded the troupe and retired from the stage. One of their sons, Giambattista (c. 1578–1654), became a renowned commedia actor and an author. Around 1605, he organized a company known as *Comici Fedeli* (Faithful Players) with several actors who had been members of I Gelosi. The Comici Fedeli troupe survived until 1652, though it never quite matched the fame and high reputation of I Gelosi. Giambattista Andreini usually took the role of Harlequin or that of Lelio, an innamorato. He married twice, both times to women who played the innamorata in his company.

Influence of Commedia dell'Arte

The historical significance of commedia dell'arte is seen in its influence on later theatre practitioners. Its stock characters—who seem to have evolved from figures in ancient mime, from the plays of Plautus and Terence, and from medieval farces—were further refined by later playwrights. The miserly merchant Pantalone, for instance, is the ancestor of the avaricious Harpagon in the late-seventeenth-century French play *The Miser* by Molière, and the comic servant Pulcinella evolved into Punch in the English Punch and Judy puppet shows. The improvisatory nature of commedia influenced many avant-garde twentieth-century theatre companies, including the politically oriented San Francisco Mime Troupe, popular in the 1960s and 1970s and still performing today; and contemporary performers like Bill Irwin and David Shiner, who brought their commedia clowning to Broadway several times in the 1990s in a show called *Fool Moon.*

As noted earlier, comparisons can also be drawn between commedia performers and many of the classic film comics—including Charlie Chaplin, Laurel and Hardy, the Marx Brothers, Abbott and Costello, and the Three Stooges. The zany films of the Marx Brothers, for example, used many techniques reminiscent of commedia.

DEBATES IN THEATRE HISTORY | **Women Performers in Commedia dell'Arte**

In their classic textbook *A History of the Theatre,* George Freedley and John A. Reeves remark: "One of the most important achievements of the commedia dell'arte was the introduction of women onto the stage on equal (frequently even more favorable) terms with men. Occasionally they appeared as themselves in the Middle Ages but the widespread use of them in female parts sprang out of Italian comedy."* It is clear that women were significant members of Italian commedia troupes at a time when they were excluded from the English stage. (The exclusion of women from English acting troupes during the Shakespearean period will be discussed in Chapter 6.) But why women were accepted as performers in commedia companies is still debated, as is their actual status in these companies.

Some historians point to the fact that theatrical forms which may have been forerunners of commedia dell'arte—such as Greek and Roman mime presented by traveling troupes—included women. Others note that many women in commedia dell'arte were married to male performers; this meant that there was less likelihood that their morality would be called into question. The status of women in commedia, therefore, would have been similar to that of actresses in companies of the Spanish golden age, who were required to be married or otherwise related to a male member. (We will discuss this in Chapter 7.) Some commedia actresses were greatly admired; Isabella Andreini, who, along with her husband Francesco, was head of the famous I Gelosi commedia troupe, was idolized during her lifetime and greatly mourned when she died. Nevertheless, the female characters she played were often stereotypical, and most of the praise she received from poets focused not on her acting but on her beauty and her high sense of morality. For that matter, Pierre Louis Duchart notes that the roles played by all the women in commedia dell'arte were recurrent types: "innamoratas, servants, *ingenues,* mistresses, wantons, and matrons."†

Thus while Freedley and Reeves are correct in pointing out that women were significant figures in commedia dell'arte, research still needs to be done on several key points: why women were initially employed in commedia troupes, what their financial status was in these companies, what their social status was, and how female characters were represented in the scenarios of commedia dell'arte. The question whether, as Freedley and Reeves argue, women were "on equal (frequently even more favorable) terms with men" needs more analysis.

*Crown, New York, 1941, p. 81.

†*The Italian Comedy,* Randolph T. Weaver (trans.), Dover, New York, 1966, p. 20.

Groucho, Harpo, and Chico portrayed the same kinds of characters, with only slight deviations, in all their movies; that is, they created stock characters. Groucho was an unsuccessful, pedantic gigolo; Harpo was a lecherous, musically inclined mute; Chico was a scheming immigrant. Much of their action and dialogue—to the chagrin of their screenwriters—was improvised. Also, the Marx Brothers used standard lazzi and stock costumes. Groucho walked with a stoop and toyed with a cigar; Harpo always wore a long trench coat, carried a horn, and mimed messages. Audiences enjoyed seeing repetitions of these characters' wildly comic business as they became involved in different complicated situations.

Italian Theatre Architecture

Theatre Buildings

While academic writers were following classic models and groups of actors were developing commedia, architects in the Italian Renaissance were revolutionizing theatre design and scenic effects. Since much of the drama written during the

(© Dennis Marsico/Corbis)

TEATRO OLIMPICO

Completed in 1584, the Teatro Olimpico in Vicenza, Italy, is the oldest theatre surviving from the Renaissance. The stage attempted to duplicate the facade of the Roman scene house and had five alleyways leading off it. Down each alleyway, small models of buildings were created to give the illusion of disappearing perspective. This photo shows the ornate facade, a holdover from Roman theatres, with the five alleyways, two on each side of the central alleyway.

Renaissance was staged at academies, changes in theatre architecture frequently developed within these institutions. Three buildings in particular showed a move toward a new kind of theatre architecture, and, remarkably, all three are still standing.

Teatro Olimpico

The oldest surviving theatre constructed during the Italian Renaissance, the Teatro Olimpico in Vicenza, was initially designed by the architect Andrea Palladio (1518–1580) for the Olympic Academy in that city. When Palladio died, Vincenzo Scamozzi (1552–1616) completed the building in 1584. The premiere production in the Olimpico was Sophocles' *King Oedipus* in 1585.

Palladio was influenced by his reading of the Roman Vitruvius, and therefore the Olimpico was designed as a miniature indoor Roman theatre. Its auditorium, accommodating 3,000 spectators, consisted of elliptical benches connected to the scaena, or stage house; this arrangement created a semicircular orchestra. There was a raised stage, about 70 feet wide by 18 feet deep, in front of the scaena. The ornate facade of the scene house, patterned after the Roman scaena frons, was designed to look like a street. There were five openings in the facade—three in the back wall and one on each side. Behind each opening was an alleyway or street scene that seemed to disappear in the distance. To achieve the effect of depth, in each alleyway there were three-dimensional buildings—houses and shops—which decreased in size as they were positioned farther and farther away from the opening onstage.

THE THEATRE AT SABBIONETA

In 1588, Scamozzi constructed a tiny 250-seat theatre in Sabbioneta, Italy. This theatre, paid for by the duke of Mantua, was erected for the Academia dei Confidenti. It had only one background vista, which extended from one side of the stage to the other. The vista was a perspective scenic view painted on the sides and back of the stage area. In some ways Sabbioneta is a smaller, much more intimate version of the Teatro Olimpico. Set in a rectangular building, it has a small colonnade around the horseshoe-shaped auditorium, which has a flat floor and no fixed seating. However, the raised stage with a painted panorama at the back has none of the complex features of the Olimpico stage. Rather, it is simplicity itself. One idea is that Sabbioneta forms a transition between the Teatro Olimpico and the Teatro Farnese.

(Federico Arborio Mella)

THE THEATRE AT SABBIONETA
A significant milestone in the development of theatre architecture, the small, 250-seat theatre at Sabbioneta, Italy, is still standing. Designed by Scamozzi, it was conceived as a single unit, with semicircular seating (shown here) facing an open stage that used angled wings for scenery. It represented a clear step toward later proscenium theatres.

Teatro Farnese and the Proscenium Stage

Some historians believe that the single-vista design at Sabbioneta influenced the architect Giovan Battista Aleotti (1546–1636), who was responsible for the most notable theatre building of the Italian Renaissance, the Teatro Farnese in Parma. The Farnese was completed in 1618. It had a typical court and academic theatre auditorium, with raised horseshoe seating accommodating 3,500 spectators and a semicircular orchestra in front of the stage. The orchestra could be used for additional seating, or it could be flooded—a spectacular practice adopted from the Romans—for aquatic scenes such as naval battles.

What was revolutionary in the Teatro Farnese was its proscenium-arch stage. The Farnese was probably not the first space in Italy with a proscenium; it is believed that temporary arches were used earlier at court performances and that another permanent proscenium stage may have been constructed earlier. But the Farnese is the most famous because it is still standing—though it required extensive renovation after it was damaged during World War II. Actually, very few performances took place in the Farnese; it is significant because it is the prototype of the proscenium-arch theatre.

The *proscenium-arch stage*—also known as the *picture-frame, fourth wall,* or *conventional stage*—is still among the best-known types of theatre space. The audience, facing in one direction, views the action through the arch, which frames the stage picture. (In most modern theatres, the "arch" is not rounded but rectangular.) The proscenium hides from the audience the stage mechanisms for scene changes and special effects, increasing theatrical illusion. The proscenium arch, along with Renaissance innovations in scene design (discussed below), was an impetus for the development of greater realism in the theatre.

Audience Seating

Along with developments in the stage arrangement, there were also changes in the auditorium where the spectators sat. The Italian revolution in auditorium design occurred in the public opera houses of Venice, four of which had been constructed by 1641. These were proscenium-arch houses, and, as commercial ventures, they needed as many paying customers as possible; thus they required a larger audience area than the academy theatres. The opera houses were therefore designed with "pit, boxes, and galleries," an auditorium style that had already been used in France, England, and Spain. Combining a "pit, box, and gallery" auditorium with a proscenium-arch stage made the Venice opera houses innovative.

The *pit,* in which audience members stood, was an open area on the house floor extending to the side and back walls. Built into the walls were tiers of seating. The lower tiers were usually the most expensive; they were divided into separate private *boxes* frequented by the upper classes. The upper tiers, called *galleries,* had open bench seating. The pit—a raucous area where the spectators ate, talked, and moved around—and the galleries were the least expensive accommodations. The proscenium-arch theatre with pit, box, and gallery seating was to become the standard theatre space throughout the western world for over 300 years.

(Hulton Archive/Getty Images)

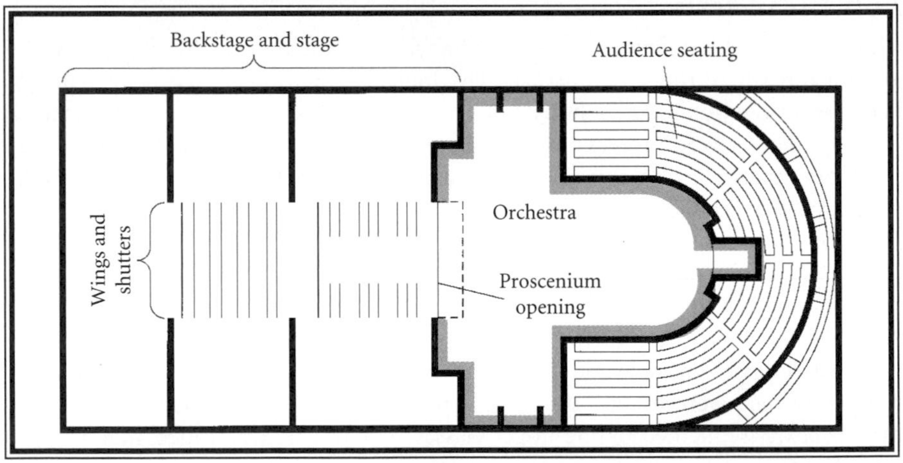

TEATRO FARNESE

Completed in 1618, the Teatro Farnese was the first theatre with a proscenium arch—the opening behind which scenery and stage machinery are concealed. (Note the large backstage area.) The horseshoe-shaped auditorium held 3,500 spectators, and a semicircular orchestra was placed between the audience and stage. The scene shown at the top is a drawing of around 1730, showing the proscenium opening and the stage of the Farnese with spectators standing below.

(© Arne Hodalic/Corbis)

VENETIAN THEATRE DESIGN
The revolution in theatre architecture that began with the Olimpico, Sabbioneta, and the Farnese was carried forward with opera houses in Venice. The proscenium stage became standard, particularly in the auditorium with "pit, boxes, and galleries." The drawing here shows a performance, with an audience watching a scene onstage, in a Venetian theatre in the latter part of the seventeenth century. The theatre illustrates the features in the auditorium that had become standard. Also, note the audience members wearing face masks, large hats, and black coats, in the spirit of a masked ball.

Scene Design and Early Theatre Technology

Advances in scene design during the Italian Renaissance were no less impressive than those in theatre architecture. Again, the initial impetus came from the rediscovery, in 1414, of a classical source—Vitruvius's *De Architectura,* a Roman text on architecture which deals extensively with theatre design. Historians believe that the earliest designs in Italy during the late 1400s were attempts to create a Roman stage and to replicate Vitruvius's suggestions for comic, tragic, and pastoral settings.

Perspective in Scene Design

The most significant innovation in scenic design was perspective drawing, which had become an important part of Renaissance painting. With the use of perspective,

DEBATES IN THEATRE HISTORY

What Is the Exact Origin of the Proscenium Arch?

Why did the Italians develop the proscenium arch? There is continuing debate over *when* the proscenium-arch space was first used; but *what* influences led to this design may be an even more significant question, because of all Renaissance innovations, the proscenium arch has had the most lasting impact. The proscenium-arch stage has been traced to several sources, and there is no universal agreement among Renaissance scholars about its origin.

Given the significant influence of classical theorists and the desire to revive classical theatrical traditions, some historians have argued that the *thyromata*—the large openings in the stage house of Greek Hellenistic theatres and the large central portals of Roman theatres—may have been the inspiration for the Italian theatre designers who introduced the proscenium arch.

Other historians have pointed to medieval traditions, which were popular at court. These scholars suggest that triumphal arches, which were used for medieval pageantry and were frequently set up in the streets of medieval cities for the grand entry of a visiting dignitary, were the ancestors of the proscenium arch. Since there were an immense number of theatrical presentations at courts in the Italian Renaissance—and since the first proscenium arch may have been used in a temporary space at an Italian court—this medieval influence seems logical.

Another theory is that the frames in which perspective paintings were placed in the Italian Renaissance were copied by designers who introduced painted-perspective scene designs; thus the proscenium would be the theatrical equivalent of the frame of a painting.

The definitive explanation of the origin of the proscenium arch therefore remains unresolved. Though its origins are debatable, however, there is no question that the development of the proscenium arch is of immense importance in western theatre.

scenes onstage, although painted on flat surfaces (such as backdrops), could achieve an illusion of depth—a three-dimensional quality. While there is debate over when perspective painting was first used to create a theatrical setting, most historians believe that it was used as early as 1508, for a court performance of Ariosto's *La Cassaria.*

Many artists wrote treatises about perspective in drawing and painting in the first half of the sixteenth century. The person who detailed many of the early methods for creating perspective settings was Sebastiano Serlio, in his book *Architettura* (1545).

SEBASTIANO SERLIO

The Italian architect, painter, and designer Sebastiano Serlio (1475–1554) is an important figure in the history of scene design. In the second book of his work on architecture, published in 1545, Serlio devoted only a small portion to theatre, but that section was to influence European theatre for the next 100 years.

Serlio helped introduce perspective—with its sense of visual realism—into scene design. He also believed that there should be three basic settings for drama: (1) a tragic setting, showing a street of stately houses; (2) a comic setting, showing a common street scene; and (3) a pastoral setting, showing trees, hills, and cottages.

To create these settings Serlio recommended using a series of *angled wings*—flats hinged in a fixed position and painted in perspective—placed one behind another on both sides of the stage. Each wing would give the appearance of a house and would have some three-dimensional ornamentation. To increase the illusion of depth, the tops of these painted houses were constructed so that they slanted downward. The set was enclosed in the back by either a painted *backdrop* or two painted *shutters* that met in the middle.

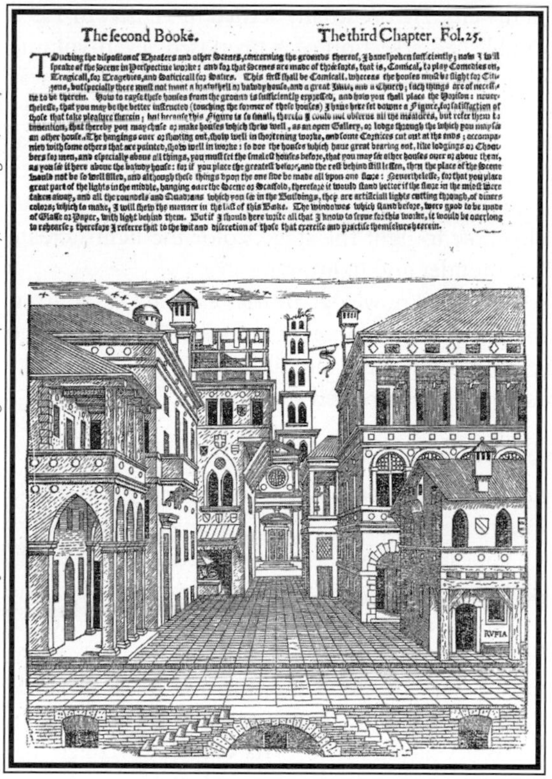

(From *The Second Booke of Architecture*, The Folger Shakespeare Library, Washington, D.C.)

(From Serlio's *Architettura*, Book 2, 1606, Amsterdam edition, The Folger Shakespeare Library, Washington, D.C.)

(From Serlio's *Architettura*, Book 2, 1584, Italian edition, The Folger Shakespeare Library, Washington, D.C.)

SERLIO'S THREE SETTINGS
The Italian architect and designer Sebastiano Serlio developed the use of perspective—a convention for representing three-dimensionality—in scene design. In a book on architecture, he set forth three basic settings, shown here: tragic (above), pastoral (above right), and comic (below right). Note how the scenes disappear into the distance.

The back area of the stage, according to Serlio, was to be *raked*—that is, slightly inclined or slanted—so that the bottoms of the wings slanted upward; this too would enhance the illusion of depth. Later in the Italian Renaissance, theatres were designed with permanently raked stages. Today, in describing stage areas, we still refer to the area farthest from the audience as *upstage.* In Renaissance theatres, this area was literally "up," or higher; the front of the stage was "down." In modern theatres, stages are usually not raked; instead, the seating for the audience is.

Before writing his treatise on architecture, Serlio—who was the son of an Italian ornament painter—had studied extensively and had worked as both a painter and an architect. He went to Rome to work with Baldassare Peruzzi, the first designer to apply principles of perspective to the stage. In Rome, Serlio also studied the many examples of classical architecture in the city. He eventually settled in Venice. In 1537, the year of Peruzzi's death, Serlio published a section of a proposed seven-volume work on architecture. Serlio used ideas from Vitruvius, the Roman architect who was the source for classical architectural theory, and from Peruzzi's unpublished notes and designs, but he combined these sources in a new way. He fused architectural theory with detailed, practical instructions on building.

Serlio's method can be seen in his passages on theatre, in which he tells how to construct a theatre building and also how to light the stage, color the lights, create mobile heavenly bodies, and produce thunder and lightning.

Serlio became a court architect, and his knowledge in that capacity came from practical experience; he served many princes, most notably Francis I of France at the palace of Fontainebleau. His books were translated and circulated throughout Europe, where they became basic texts for architecture and stage design.

Advances in Scenic Techniques: From Serlio to Torelli

The problem posed by Serlio's angle-wing setting was that it was virtually impossible to shift scenes during a performance. In the period after 1550, various solutions were attempted, one of the first of which appears to have been the *periaktoi.* This, it will be remembered, was the three-sided device used by the Greeks: when one face of the periaktoi is shown to the audience, the other two are invisible. Rotating the device on a central axis allows three different scenes to be shown.

An early application of the periaktoi in the Italian Renaissance was by Aristotile de San Gallo (1481–1551) in 1543 at Castro. By 1569, periaktoi were in use in Florence. In his *Two Rules of Perspective Practice* (1583), Giacomo Barozzi da Vignola suggested that variations of the periaktoi, with from two to six sides, could be used to change scenery.

In the half century after 1585, other methods of scene changing were developed. For example, in his book *Manual for Constructing Theatrical Scenes and Machines* (1638), Nicola Sabbattini (1574–1654) refers to three methods of changing scenery: one is the periaktoi; a second is to place new wings around those already in place; and a third is to pull painted canvases around wings to conceal the previous scene.

The reference to painted canvas introduces the notion of the flat wing, that is, one not angled in the manner of Serlio. The development of the flat wing in the early seventeenth century was made possible by advances in art, specifically in perspective painting and drawing. An indication that this approach was already being advanced is the fact that in 1600 a method for painting a perspective scene on a flat wing was outlined in *Six Books of Perspective,* by Guido Ubaldus. Once the illusion of depth—of three-dimensional space—could be created on a flat surface, it was no longer necessary to have angle wings, and by 1650 they seem to have been abandoned.

Flat wings were a series of individual wings on each side of the stage, parallel to the audience, placed in a progression from the front to the back of the stage and enclosed at the very back by two shutters that met in the middle. The final element in these perspective settings was an overhead border—a strip across the top of the stage—to complete the picture. The first use of flat wings is usually credited to Giovan Battista Aleotti in 1606; Aleotti was also the designer of the Teatro Farnese, the famous proscenium-arch theatre mentioned earlier in this chapter.

The earliest method of scene shifting for flat-wing settings is often referred to as the *groove system.* Wings and shutters were placed in grooves in and above the

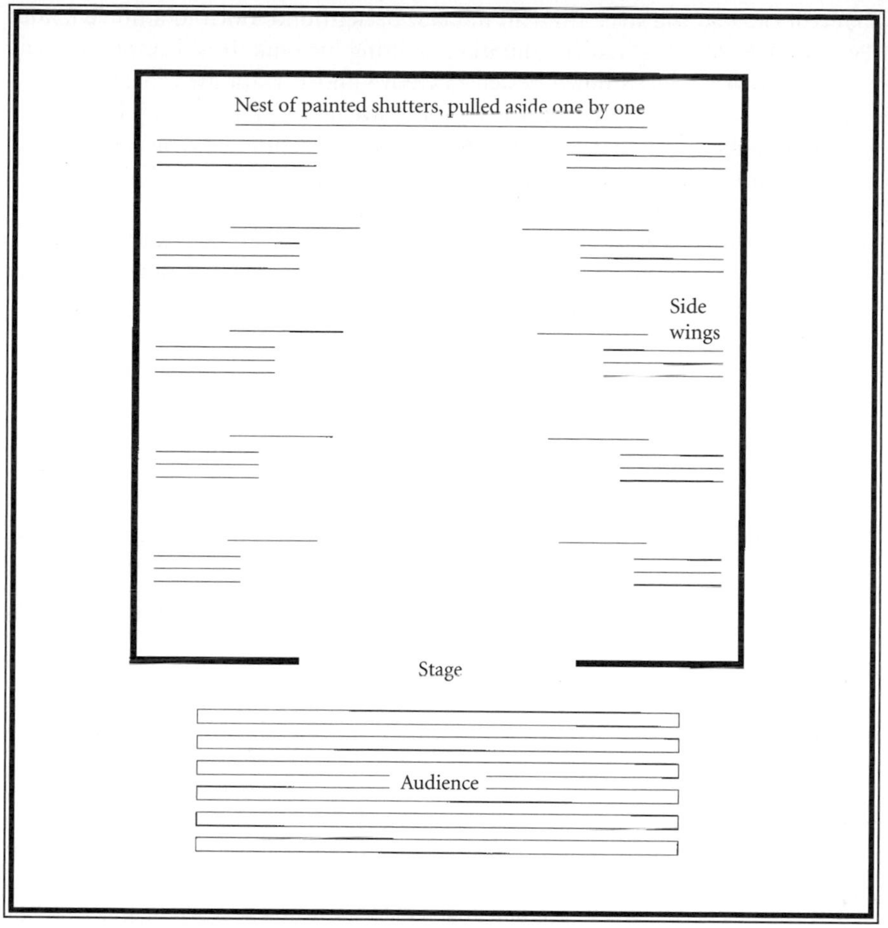

GROOVE SYSTEM OF SCENE CHANGES During the Italian Renaissance, the groove method of shifting scenery was perfected. Along the sides of the stage, in parallel lines, scenery was set in sections. At the back, two shutters met in the middle. Together, these pieces formed a complete stage picture. When one set of side wings and back shutters was pulled aside, a different stage picture was revealed.

stage floor; the grooves allowed these elements to slide offstage easily and quickly so that a new series of wings and shutters—in place behind the original set—would be immediately revealed to the audience. In this fashion, a number of sets were positioned one behind the other, allowing for rapid scene changes. The major problem with this system was coordinating the removal of the flat wings by scene shifters at each groove position. (Renaissance theatres had curtains, but since they were raised and lowered only at the beginning and end of a presentation, scene changes were not hidden.) A later innovation facilitated scene changing when, between 1641 and 1645, Giacomo Torelli developed the *pole-and-chariot* system.

GIACOMO TORELLI

For his many spectacular stage settings and scene changes, Giacomo Torelli (1608–1678) was nicknamed the "great wizard." His elaborate stage machinery and designs were influential in both Italy and France, and his method of shifting scenery became standard throughout continental Europe.

Torelli came to the stage from an unlikely background. Born to a noble family of Fano in Italy, he was given an education befitting his rank. It is possible (though not certain) that he also studied design in Pesaro and Ferrara, two theatrical centers near his home. At some point, Torelli must have offended his family, because he was disinherited in his father's will. By 1640, he was designing in Venice, which was developing into a center of opera, and it was at the Teatro Novissimo in Venice that he developed the staging methods which were to make him famous.

At the Teatro Novissimo, Torelli perfected the pole-and-chariot method of scene shifting. In Torelli's system, poles were attached to scene flats; these poles went below the stage floor, where they were connected to wheels—the "chariots"—that ran in tracks. In this way, flats could be moved offstage smoothly; with a series of connected ropes and pulleys, an entire set of flat wings could be removed simultaneously by turning a single winch.

The pole-and-chariot system was adopted widely throughout the western world (the only exceptions were England, the Netherlands, and later the United States). Audiences were astounded by the many variations of scene changes Torelli explored with the new system. Another of his innovations was occasional use of cutout flats that produced an effect of three-dimensional trees and shrubs.

In 1645, Torelli—now internationally renowned—was invited to Paris to stage an opera sponsored by the royal family. When he found that he was expected to work on this opera with an Italian commedia dell'arte troupe, he considered it an indignity and—unavailingly—protested to the queen. Ironically, the opera, *La Finta Pazzo,* was a great success at court and hastened the adoption of Torelli's scenic inventions in Paris.

Though he married a French noblewoman and staged many successful productions for the French court—notably, Corneille's *Andromède*—Torelli was disliked in France because of his Italian background and his association with Cardinal Mazarin, the king's Italian minister. When Mazarin died in 1661, Torelli was ordered to leave France, and most of his French designs were destroyed by Gaspare Vigarani, a rival Italian designer at court. Torelli returned to Fano, his birthplace, where in 1677 he staged his last production at the theatre he had designed there.

Special Effects and Lighting

Italian Renaissance theatre, which emphasized spectacle, developed many ingenious special effects. For example, there were flying machines, called *glories;* trapdoors; and primitive sound-effects devices to create thunder and wind.

There were also some primitive attempts to deal with stage lighting. Since Italian Renaissance theatres were indoors, artificial lighting was needed; candles and oil lamps were used, but these produced a smoky, hazy atmosphere. Candles—the primary means of illumination—were placed at the front of the stage as well as in chandeliers and on poles above and along the sides of the stage. There were also some attempts to control the intensity of onstage lighting; for example, open canisters would be used to cover some of the candles, to diminish the amount of light. Because it was difficult to provide sufficient illumination, the auditorium as well as the stage was always lit.

(Bibliothèque Nationale de France, Paris)

A DESIGN BY TORELLI

Giacomo Torelli, a master scene designer during the Italian Renaissance, continued the use of painted-perspective scenery; he also improved scene shifting by inventing the pole-and-chariot system for wings and shutters. The setting shown here would have been created from wings and shutters, with some three-dimensional ornamentation, and shifted by the pole-and-chariot method. Torelli's work was so highly esteemed that he was invited to France to design for the court.

Italian Dramatic Criticism

The Neoclassical Ideals

If the written drama of Renaissance Italy was of limited historical significance, the same cannot be said of its dramatic criticism. The rules formulated by Italian critics, known as the *neoclassical ideals,* dominated dramatic theory in most of Europe for nearly 200 years.

The neoclassicists believed that they were formulating rules which would force dramatists to imitate the Greeks and Romans; and they insisted that their ideals were derived from their examination of Greek and Roman models and from their interpretations of—and on occasion, their deviations from—Aristotle and Horace. These claims need to be looked at with a certain skepticism, however, because the neoclassicists were far more rigid than Aristotle; they had many more rules and applied these rules more strictly. In fact, Aristotle did not actually prescribe rules; he

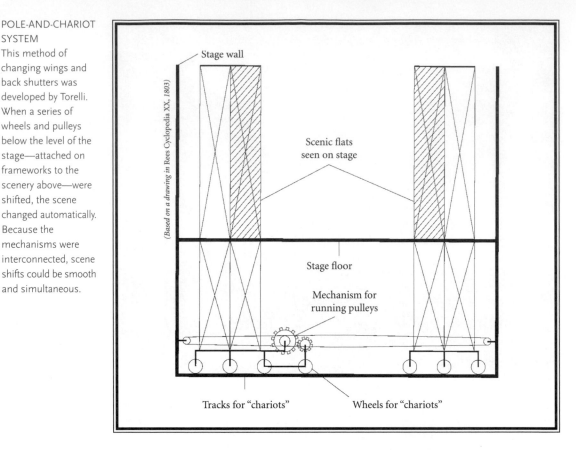

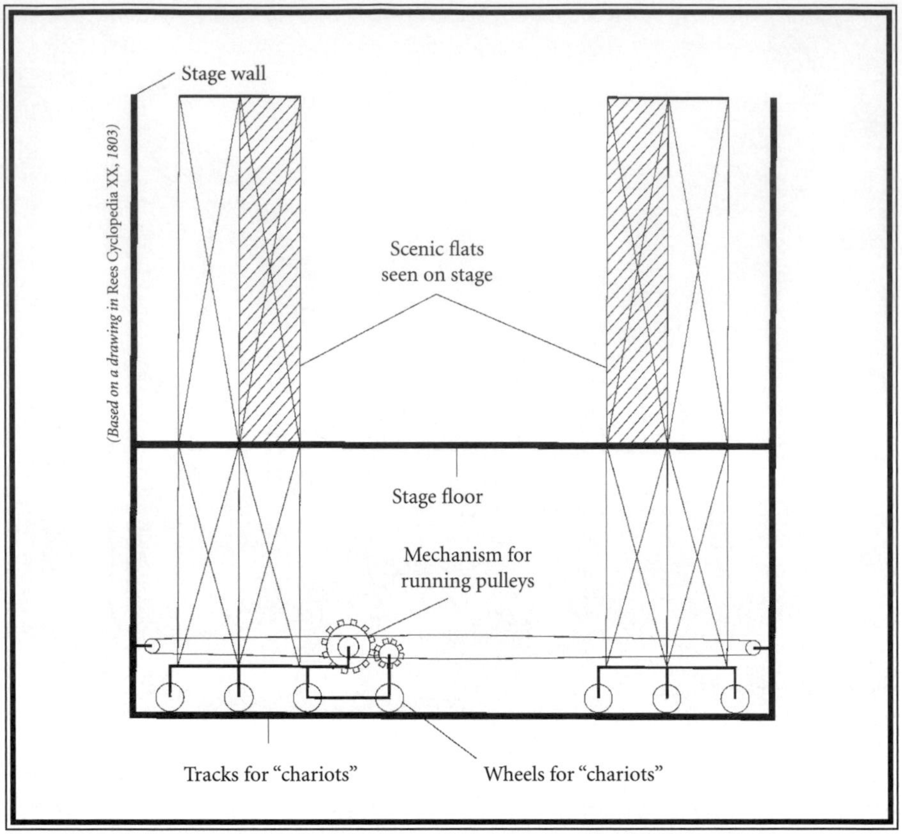

POLE-AND-CHARIOT SYSTEM
This method of changing wings and back shutters was developed by Torelli. When a series of wheels and pulleys below the level of the stage—attached on frameworks to the scenery above—were shifted, the scene changed automatically. Because the mechanisms were interconnected, scene shifts could be smooth and simultaneous.

analyzed what Greek dramatists had done. The neoclassicists, by contrast, wanted to establish mandates for playwrights. (Thus some historians have argued that the Italian neoclassicists were really influenced more by the Roman critic Horace than by Aristotle.) Three of the major neoclassical critics were Julius Caesar Scaliger (1484–1558), Lodovico Castelvetro (1505–1571), and Antonio Minturno (d. 1574).

Julius Caesar Scaliger and Lodovico Castelvetro, two of the most important and influential dramatic critics of the Italian Renaissance, distinguished themselves from their ancient predecessors. Although their theories varied in details, they were in general agreement on the basic principles that constituted the neoclassical ideal.

Scaliger's scholarly interests extended from botany and zoology to grammar and literary criticism. He studied medicine in Padua and in 1525 left Italy for France, where he served as a physician to the bishop of Agen, eventually marrying and becoming a French citizen. His massive *Poetics Libri Septem* (1561), written in Latin, was a comprehensive attempt to standardize literary form and content by relating Aristotle's *Poetics* to existing literary tradition based on Latin writers, especially Horace's *Art of Poetry.*

Castelvetro, who was trained in law, became a prominent literary critic in Italy. Around 1560, he became involved in a theological controversy that resulted in his excommunication by the Inquisition for doctrinal deviance. His final years were spent in exile in France and Vienna. In 1570, Castelvetro published the first translation and commentary on Aristotle in Italian, *Poetica d'Aristotele vulgarizzata e sposta* (*Aristotle's Poetics Translated into the Vernacular and Explicated*), which reached a wide audience.

Scaliger's highly didactic critical system consolidated the concepts of *decorum* and *verisimilitude* as aspects of imitation that contribute to moral edification. The purpose of drama, he says, is to teach, move, and delight. He stresses that theatrical events need to approximate actuality as closely as possible in order to be persuasive and that characters should consistently adhere to accepted norms of social behavior or they will appear implausible. Castelvetro draws more radical conclusions than Scaliger. He argues that theatre was invented to "please the ignorant multitude," and he puts greater emphasis on the theatrical experience than on the literary value of drama. His insistence on pleasure over moral intent is unusual in neoclassical doctrine. In fact, according to Castelvetro, the physical needs and practical demands of the spectators dictate that the dramatic action mirror the actual time of the performance and that a change of location would appear ludicrous to an audience aware of being in one place themselves. He made the actual conditions of theatre—the limitations imposed by space, time, and audience—a central argument in his dramatic theory. Castelvetro's formulation of the unities of time, place, and action was the first coherent statement of the "rules" that became a cornerstone of neoclassical criticism.

Decorum and Verisimilitude

One of the neoclassical ideals was *decorum,* a term which meant that all dramatic characters should behave in ways based on their age, profession, sex, rank, and the like. Each character, in other words, was expected to follow set behavior which was deemed appropriate.

An even more important ideal of the neoclassicists, however, was *verisimilitude:* all drama was to be "true to life." Thus, because they were not observed in everyday life, such things as ghosts, apparitions, and supernatural events were forbidden. At the same time, the neoclassicists' concept of verisimilitude was not the kind of "realism" we find in modern drama, in which characters and situations are like observed reality and are individualized—a real family shown in a real living room or kitchen, for example. The neoclassicists had in mind what we would now consider stock dramatic situations and stock characters, but they insisted that these be recognizable and verifiable from real life.

The Unities: Time, Place, and Action

The most famous mandate of the neoclassicists grew out of their desire for verisimilitude: this was their insistence on observance of three unities—time, place, and action. The critic who was most responsible for codifying the unities was Castelvetro.

Unity of time required that the dramatic action in a play should not exceed 24 hours. A few radical neoclassicists argued that time should be limited to 12 hours; the most radical wanted the dramatic action to match the time provided for the presentation: if, for instance, a play lasted 2 hours, its action should cover 2 hours. Most neoclassicists, however, insisted only on the 24-hour rule. Their argument for unity of time was based on their belief that audiences could not accept a long passage of time as "truthful."

Unity of place restricted the action of a play to one locale. Again, there were varying interpretations of this rule; liberal neoclassicists argued that "one locale" would permit a dramatist to present scenes within the same general location—for example, it would be allowable to dramatize various scenes within one city. Again, the rationale for this rule was that audiences could not accept as "truthful" a representation of more than one place within the confines of a theatre.

Unity of action required one central story, involving a relatively small group of characters. This meant there could be no subplots, such as we find in Shakespeare's *King Lear,* where the main plot is the story of King Lear and his three daughters, and the story of the Duke of Gloucester and his two sons is a subplot.

(It should be pointed out and emphasized that Aristotle, a Greek model invoked by neoclassical critics, included only the unity of action in his writings; he made no mention of the unities of time and place.)

Genre and Other Rules

The neoclassicists also defined *genre*—a French word meaning "type" or "category"—very narrowly. Tragedy dealt with royalty, comedy dealt with common people; tragedy must be resolved calamitously, comedy must be resolved happily. The two genres must never be mixed, and the function of all drama was to teach a moral lesson. In short, all drama must be didactic.

There were numerous minor rules. Characters must act decorously, and their actions must be morally acceptable to the audience. Onstage violence was forbidden. Since the neoclassicists were obsessed with verisimilitude, they condemned several Greek and Roman dramatic conventions for not being true to life. For instance, the neoclassicists banished the chorus and the *deus ex machina,* and for the same reason they opposed the soliloquy—a monologue through which a character reveals thoughts by speaking them aloud. Playwrights who ignored these precepts were vigorously attacked by the neoclassicists.

The Neoclassicists' Influence

As noted earlier, the Renaissance was a time when there was a widespread desire to analyze and explain the world. Just as the great advances in science and exploration grew out of a desire to map the universe, so too the neoclassical ideals came from a desire to map the workings of classical drama. The neoclassicists considered themselves proper authorities to develop rules and regulations for theatre through their analysis of rediscovered drama. We should note, however, that the neoclassicists were exceedingly literal-minded in applying their ideas to drama.

Despite the extreme rigidity of the neoclassical ideals, they were closely adhered to in many European countries. In France in 1636, for example (as we will see in Chapter 8), Cardinal Richelieu—the power behind the throne of Louis XIII—gave his blessing to the French Academy, which strictly enforced the neoclassical principles, censuring playwrights who deviated from them.

There were, of course, countries in which the neoclassicists were largely ignored—Elizabethan England and Spain in its golden age—but the ideals were an important influence during the Renaissance; and beyond that, they established dramaturgic rules which would be sharply debated for several centuries to come.

Issues of Dramatic Criticism

We have now looked at several important figures in dramatic theory and criticism: Aristotle, Horace, and the neoclassicists of the Italian Renaissance. When we study the history of western theatre, we find three key issues that divide theoreticians, and all three had emerged by the time of the Renaissance, in the works of these critics. These issues continue to influence western criticism.

The Nature of Criticism: Descriptive and Prescriptive Criticism

The first issue is that some criticism is *descriptive,* or analytical, while other criticism is *prescriptive.* Descriptive criticism analyzes what has gone before. Thus Aristotle in the fourth century B.C.E. wrote about the Greek drama of the previous century. Modern critics who examine the works of a dramatist like Eugene O'Neill or a period like the American theatre of the 1940s and 1950s are usually writing descriptive criticism. They attempt to tell us what type of drama was written, how it was put together, what it means, and so forth.

Prescriptive criticism, on the other hand, argues for a certain point of view, sets down rules, and prescribes formulas. This approach is often referred to as *didactic,* that is, intended for instruction. Most neoclassic critics of the Italian Renaissance were didactic, telling playwrights what to write and what not to write. So, too, were the writers and theoreticians of the French Academy in the seventeenth century. In the nineteenth century, the French writer Émile Zola (1840–1902) set forth a program for naturalism in theatre. Zola argued that drama must adhere closely to the laws of nature as they were understood at that time. In the twentieth century, the German playwright Bertolt Brecht argued for a theatre that would instruct its audience, especially in political matters; and in the late twentieth century there were several critics who could be considered prescriptive or didactic: good examples are Marxist critics and politically oriented feminist critics.

It is important to note that both kinds of critics—descriptive and prescriptive—make important contributions.

The Nature of Drama: Should Theatre Be Didactic?

A second issue that has divided critics through the centuries has to do not with the nature of criticism but rather with the nature of the artwork being criticized. This issue is whether or not drama should be didactic. The question here is not whether critics should instruct their readers but whether a play itself should teach a lesson and be morally uplifting.

Many critics feel that art need not—indeed, should not—be didactic; they hold that art is its own excuse for being. These critics would argue that in distilling life and presenting its essence, art provides a unique mirror in which we can see ourselves. If we learn from that—as we may very well do—so much the better, but it is not incumbent on art to teach a lesson; teaching is the job of people like educators and the clergy. Critics who take this position would argue that in some cases making art didactic might distort it beyond recognition. How, for example, could you make a simple landscape painting or an abstract design morally instructive?

On the other side are critics who say that art should be didactic. The Roman writer Horace, who first raised this issue, did not insist on instruction in drama, but he did say that entertainment joined with instruction was the best kind of drama. In certain periods—for example, in seventeenth-century England and France—theatre was attacked as immoral; writers like Molière in France and Ben Jonson in England defended it on the basis that it is a lesson.

This controversy continued into the twentieth century. We have already mentioned Bertolt Brecht, and in the 1950s there was a famous debate on this question between the absurdist playwright Eugène Ionesco (1909–1994) and the critic Kenneth Tynan (1927–1980). Ionesco took the view that didacticism is not a primary function of art; Tynan argued that it is.

The Form of Drama: Neoclassical Structure

A third issue that engaged critics for several centuries concerns dramatic structure. This debate was set in motion by the Italian neoclassical critics and carried forward by the French Academy; it concerns the neoclassicists' strict rules of structure: verisimilitude and the unities of time, place, and action.

As we will see in Chapters 6 and 7, the plays of Shakespeare and other Elizabethan playwrights and those of Spanish playwrights like Lope de Vega have a very different structure—the episodic form. Lope de Vega wrote a spirited defense of his approach to structure, and in the eighteenth century the German critic Gotthold Lessing questioned the neoclassical rules and praised the dramaturgy of Shakespeare. This issue of neoclassical structure raged for several hundred years, but unlike the debate over didacticism, it had subsided by the nineteenth century.

The Legacy of the Italian Renaissance

Almost all of western theatre was eventually influenced by Italian dramatic criticism and by the advances in theatre architecture and scenic design initiated during the Italian Renaissance. This influence was felt first in France and later in other countries such as England, Spain, and Germany. With regard to performance, commedia dell'arte similarly influenced theatre in France in a very direct way and other nations less directly. The long-range effect of commedia continues, in some respects, to the present.

We turn next to two countries which did not look immediately to developments in Italy, but rather looked to their own roots in medieval theatre and to the effect of their own interpretation of rediscovered Greek and Roman classics. These countries are England and Spain.

Summary

The innovations of the Italian Renaissance in theatre architecture and scene design have been unparalleled in theatre history. For the next 200 years, anyone attending a theatre anywhere in Europe would be in a proscenium-arch playhouse watching the stage action from either the pit, a box, or a gallery. The scenery would consist of painted-flat wings and shutters that could be shifted either by Torelli's mechanized pole-and-chariot system or—as in England, the Netherlands, and the United States—by stagehands who pulled them off in grooves.

The Italian Renaissance also produced opera, commedia dell'arte, and the neoclassical rules of dramatic structure. Although this period left us few significant plays, these rigid neoclassical rules shaped much of the world's drama through the eighteenth century. The improvisatory actors' theatre known as *commedia dell'arte* remained popular into the 1700s and has influenced many contemporary theatrical experimenters.

The Italian Renaissance was more than the rebirth of a theatre; in many respects, it was a period that witnessed the restructuring of theatre.

MILESTONES CHAPTER 5 THE THEATRE OF THE ITALIAN RENAISSANCE [1400–1650]

Cultural and Historical Developments

- Dante Alighieri (1265–1321), *The Divine Comedy*
- Petrarch (1304–1374)
- Giotto, *Madonna Enthroned* (c. 1310)
- Boccaccio, *The Decameron* (1353)
- Manuel Chrysoloras revives teaching of Greek (late fourteenth century)

Early Renaissance [1400–1500]

Theatre History

- *Sacra rappresentazioni* (fourteenth–fifteenth century)
- Albertino Mussato (1261–1329), *Eccerinus*
- Pier Paolo Vergerio (1370–1445), *Paulus*
- Vitruvius's *De Architectura* rediscovered (1414)
- Twelve of Plautus's lost plays rediscovered (1429)

Cultural and Historical Developments

- Cosimo de' Medici rules Florence (1432)
- Filippo Brunelleschi, Dome of Florence Cathedral completed (1426) *(below)*

- Founding of Platonic Academy in Florence (1440)
- Gutenberg movable type (c. 1450)
- Transfer of Greek and Roman manuscripts to Italy after fall of Constantinople (1453)
- Lorenzo de' Medici rules Florence (1469)
- Copernicus (1473–1543)
- Botticelli, *Birth of Venus* (1484) *(below)*

- Columbus reaches America (1492)
- Italian wars spread Italy's cultural influence; weaken Italy politically (1494)

PHOTO CREDITS: Dome of the cathedral in Florence. (Punchstock) / Botticelli's *The Birth of Venus.* (Scala/Art Resource, N.Y.)

continued

MILESTONES CHAPTER 5 THE THEATRE OF THE ITALIAN RENAISSANCE [1400–1650] *continued*

High Renaissance [1500–1550]

Theatre History

- Julius Caesar Scaliger treatise, *Poetics Libri Septem* (1561)
- *Intermezzi* and *pastorals* popular throughout sixteenth century
- Neoclassical critics Lodovico Castelvetro (1505–1571) and Antonio Minturno (d. 1574)
- Ludovico Ariosto (1474–1533), *La Cassaria*
- Giangiorgio Trissino (1478–1550), *I Simillimi*
- Giambattista Giraldi Cinthio (1504–1574), *Orbecche*

Cultural and Historical Developments

- Plays by Aristophanes published by Aldine Press in Venice (1498); followed by plays of Sophocles (1502), Euripides (1503), Aeschylus (1518)
- Leonardo da Vinci, *Mona Lisa* (1503–1505) *(below)*
- Michelangelo, *David* (1501–1504); Sistine Chapel (1508–1512)
- Raphael, *School of Athens* (1510–1511)
- Machiavelli, *The Prince* (1513)
- Titian, *Venus of Urbano* (1538)
- Verrazano discovers New York Bay and Hudson River (1524)
- Sebastiano Serlio, *Architettura* (1545)

Baroque [1550–1650]

Theatre History

- *Commedia dell'arte* thrives in Italy (1550–1750)
- First performance of I Gelosi (c. 1569) with Francesco Andreini *(below, right)* (1548–1624) and Isabella Andreini *(below, left)* (1562–1604)

- Teatro Olimpico built (1584), designed by Andrea Palladio (1518–1580)
- Early operas: Jacopo Peri's *Euridice* (1600), Claudio Monteverdi's *Orfeo* (1605)
- Teatro Farnese built (1618), designed by Giovan Battista Aleotti (1546–1636)
- Nicola Sabbattini, *Manual for Constructing Theatrical Scenes and Machines* (1638)
- Public opera houses in Venice designed with "pit, boxes, and galleries" (c. 1641)
- Giacomo Torelli develops pole-and-chariot system for scene changes (1641–1645)

Cultural and Historical Developments

- Uffizi Museum at Florence founded (1560)
- Galileo (1564–1642) *(below)*

- Palladio's *I quattro libri dell'architettura* (1570)
- Kepler (1571–1630)
- Catherine de Médicis, queen mother of France, dies (1589)
- Paolo Veronese, *The Rape of Europa* (c. 1580)
- Gianlorenzo Bernini, *The Ecstasy of Saint Teresa* (1645–1652)

PHOTO CREDITS: Leonardo da Vinci's *Mona Lisa.* (Réunion des Musées Nationaux/Art Resource, N.Y.) / Isabella Andreini. (Harvard Theatre Collection, The Houghton Library, Fredric Woodbridge Wilson, Curator) / Francesco Andreini. (The Folger Shakespeare Library, Washington, D.C.) / Galileo Galilei. (Nimatallah/Art Resource, N.Y.)

CHAPTER 6

The Theatre of the English Renaissance

The Reconstructed Globe

In terms of Elizabethan theatre production, one of the most exciting developments in recent years has been the discovery of the sites of the Globe and Rose theatres on the south bank of the Thames River in London. The findings at the Rose location led to confirmation of the original dimensions of the stage and other elements. These were used, along with other elements, to create the replica of the Rose used in the film *Shakespeare in Love.* The Globe was completely reconstructed at a place near the original site. Productions, such as the one shown here, are presented regularly during the warm summer months each year.

(© Andrea Pistolesi/Image Bank/Getty Images)

The English Renaissance, though it began later than the Renaissance in Italy, was equally explosive and led to major developments in English society and culture, especially theatre. When speaking of developments in England at this time, some scholars prefer the term *early modern England* rather than *English Renaissance.* The English Renaissance is also sometimes called the *Elizabethan* period, because the major political figure during this time was Queen Elizabeth I, who reigned for 45 years, from 1558 to 1603. Actually, the English Renaissance began sooner than Elizabeth's reign and lasted longer: it began during the reign of Henry VII, who became king in 1485, and ended with the Puritans' takeover of England. This takeover occurred in 1642, when civil war broke out in England and Charles I was forced to leave London. (The war continued until 1649, when the Puritans, under Oliver Cromwell, triumphed and Charles was beheaded.) During the 150-year period from the late fifteenth century to 1642, English culture rose to unequaled heights.

Background: The Renaissance in England

A secularization of English society which had begun at the end of the Middle Ages was reinforced when Henry VIII broke with the Roman Catholic church. Henry wanted to have his marriage to Catherine of Aragon annulled so that he could marry Anne Boleyn; in 1534, when the pope refused, Henry declared that the papacy no longer had any authority in his kingdom, and he established the Church of England (also known as the Anglican church) as an independent entity with himself as its head. The establishment of Anglicanism was part of the Protestant Reformation that was sweeping through Europe and cutting away the power of Roman Catholicism.

After Henry VIII's death and the brief reign of his only son Edward VI, his daughter Mary became queen. Mary attempted to reinstate Catholicism in England; because of the numerous executions during her 5-year reign, she was nicknamed Bloody Mary. After her death, however, Henry's daughter by Anne Boleyn became Elizabeth I. As queen, Elizabeth strengthened the Anglican church; and with the execution of another Mary—her cousin Mary Stuart (known as Mary, Queen of Scots)—she ended the Catholic claim to the English throne. It was during the reign of Elizabeth I that the English Renaissance reached its peak. One reason was Elizabeth's ability to unite the English people with regard to both internal affairs and the rejection of Catholicism.

Another step in England's break with Catholicism came in 1588, with the defeat of the Spanish armada; with this victory England proved that it was not to be ruled by Spanish Catholics. The defeat of the armada also brought England to ascendancy on the seas, and this naval superiority allowed England to take full advantage of the age of discovery—the period of intense exploration of new lands, especially in the Americas.

Throughout the English Renaissance, language and literature flourished. One landmark of the early Renaissance in England was the publication of Thomas More's *Utopia.* It appeared in Latin in 1516 and in English in 1551. *Utopia* is a political romance describing an ideal country. The English were intrigued by language, and Queen Elizabeth herself was an amateur linguist. But at the heart of the English Renaissance in literature and arts was theatre.

The Early Drama of the English Renaissance

During the first three-quarters of the sixteenth century, a number of developments prepared the way for an explosion of theatrical activity in the Elizabethan era. Under Henry VII and Henry VIII, *interludes*—brief dramatic entertainments written and staged by professionals—were presented at court and in the homes of the nobility. Also, from the early 1500s through about 1580, English *school drama* became increasingly popular. These plays, written at the universities and presented at schools and colleges rather than for the general

English Renaissance Year

Theatre

- Sackville and Norton's *Gorboduc:* first English tragedy (1561)
- Master of revels made licenser of plays and companies; James Burbage's Earl of Leicester's Men founded (1574)
- The Theatre built by James Burbage; first Blackfriars opened (1576)
- Kyd's *Spanish Tragedy* (c. 1587)
- Marlowe's *Doctor Faustus* (c. 1588)
- Alleyn's Lord Admiral's Men and Burbage's Lord Chamberlain's Men, the major companies in London (1594)
- Second Blackfriars built by James Burbage (1596)
- Globe Theatre built (1599)
- Shakespeare's *Hamlet* (c. 1600)
- Lord Chamberlain's Men become the King's Men (1603)
- Jonson's *Volpone* (1606)
- Webster's *Duchess of Malfi* (c. 1613)
- Inigo Jones designs masques (c. 1620)
- Jacobean playwrights flourish (c. 1620)
- John Ford's *'Tis Pity She's a Whore* (c. 1630)
- Parliament closes British theatres (1642)

Year

1450, 1475, 1500, 1525, 1550, 1575, 1600, 1625, 1650

Culture and Politics

- 100 Years' War (1338–1453)
- War of Roses (1455–1485)
- Henry VIII reigns (1509–1547)
- Thomas More's *Utopia* (1516)
- Elizabeth I, queen of England, rules (1558–1603)
- Sir Walter Raleigh's expedition to Virginia (1584)
- Execution of Mary, queen of Scots (1587)
- Defeat of Spanish armada (1588)
- James I begins reign (1603)
- Jamestown, Virginia, founded (1607)
- Hudson claims part of North America for United Provinces (1609)
- King James Bible (1611)
- Thirty Year's War begins (1618)
- Francis Bacon's *Novum Organum* (1620)
- Charles I begins reign (1625)
- Charles I dissolves Parliament (1629)
- English civil war (1642)
- Charles I beheaded (1649)

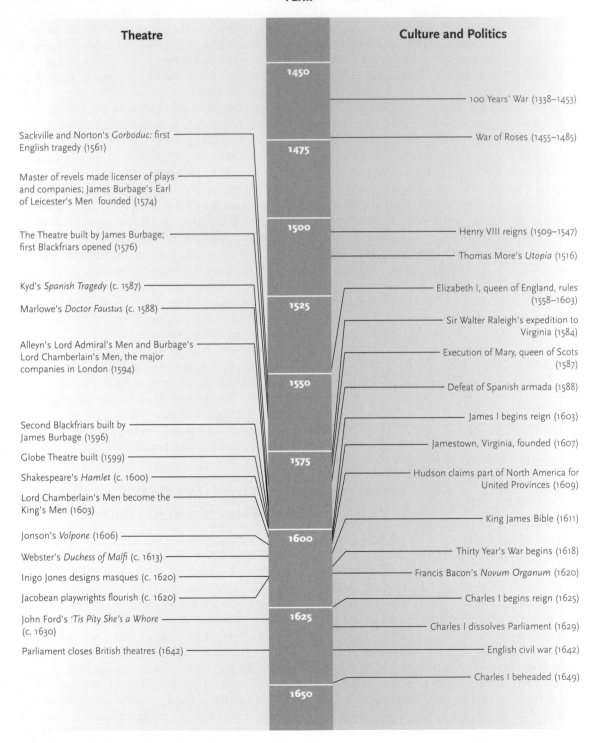

(Cleveland State University, Theatre Arts Area)

A MEDIEVAL UNIVERSITY STAGE
This is a model of a stage set up at a university for a production of Terence's *Andria* in the late Middle Ages. Medieval universities had a profound impact on writers of the early English Renaissance: many early Elizabethan dramatists were known as university wits because they were trained at the universities and had contact with drama there.

public, usually reflected some Greek and Roman influence, but they also used many medieval dramaturgical techniques. Two of the best-known school dramas were *Ralph Roister Doister*, written in the late 1530s; and *Gammer Gurton's Needle*, written in the late 1550s. Both were rollicking comedies which, though based on Roman models, were written in English and incorporated medieval elements.

Ralph Roister Doister was written by Nicholas Udall, who served as headmaster at two schools: Eton and Westminster. Strongly influenced by a play by the Roman dramatist Plautus, it indicates the interest in drama at schools and colleges in England during this time. In 1546, Queen's College at Cambridge University instituted a policy requiring that a play be presented at the college every year. We also know that *Gammer Gurton's Needle* was presented at another Cambridge college, Christ's College, sometime in the decade after 1552.

The popularity of drama in the schools is frequently cited as a reason for the later development of boys' acting companies. These companies were first established by Elizabeth I for court entertainments. In 1576, one of the boys' masters, Richard Farrant, who had received permission from the queen to allow his company to give plays to the public, began presentations. For these productions, the boys' companies used an indoor hall in Blackfriars (a former ecclesiastical building), and many major playwrights provided them with dramas.

Among the playwrights who provided boys' companies with scripts were members of a group known as the university wits. The "wits," almost all of whom were university graduates and professional dramatists, included Christopher Marlowe, Thomas Kyd (1558–1594), John Lyly (1554–1606), and Robert Greene (1588–1592). They and others, who had attended universities or studied law at the Inns of Court, wrote plays based on Roman models and also introduced medieval elements into them. These full-length dramas paved the way for Shakespeare and his contemporaries.

Elizabethan Drama

We noted in Chapter 1 that there are certain times in history when a number of elements come together to make important achievements possible. The fifth century B.C.E. in Greece was such a period; another was Elizabethan England. During the Elizabethan age, many elements—politics, exploration, literature, learning—converged to produce a favorable climate for England and for English playwrights, who included not only William Shakespeare but also Christopher Marlowe, Ben Jonson, and a number of others.

Many influences contributed to the art of Shakespeare and his contemporaries. For example, we can see important Roman influences on Elizabethan drama. Seneca's revenge-obsessed characters, his presentation of violence onstage, and his use of supernatural beings were freely imitated by Elizabethan playwrights. Plautus's and Terence's comic plots and techniques were also adapted by the English; Shakespeare's *Comedy of Errors,* for instance, was an adaptation of Plautus's *The Menaechmi.* In some instances, Elizabethan dramatists took stories from Roman and English history and also borrowed plotlines from Italian Renaissance literature. (Shakespeare reworked Italian novellas in several of his plays.)

In Chapter 4, we discussed medieval plays in which the beginnings of episodic structure began to emerge. This structure involves many characters and many scenes ranging through time and shifting from place to place. Drama of the English Renaissance followed this pattern; thus it was almost totally counter to the Italian neoclassical ideals described in Chapter 5. The Italians attempted to resurrect Greek crisis drama; the Elizabethans used the episodic form, which grew out of medieval drama.

English dramatists rarely observed the neoclassical unities of time, place, and action; and rather than tell only one story, they often had parallel plots or subplots related to the main dramatic action. They presented violence onstage and filled their plays with supernatural characters. The soliloquy, attacked by the Italians, was a popular dramatic convention in England. Like the Italians, the Elizabethans featured royal or noble characters in tragedies and lower-class characters in comedies; but the English were not as rigid as the Italians about such distinctions: they often mixed higher and lower characters and included comic scenes in serious plays. A good example is Thomas Preston's *Cambises,* written about 1561. Its subtitle describes the mixture of serious and comic: *A Lamentable Tragedy Mixed Full of Pleasant Mirth.*

As written drama was taking shape, there were also significant developments in theatre production. The stage that had been developing in England was well suited to Elizabethan episodic plays. In Chapter 4, we noted that a neutral platform stage was used for medieval mystery plays; this could become any place the dramatist designated. In the English Renaissance, the neutral platform stage had evolved to a point where it was ideal for plays in which scenes moved freely from one place to another and from one time to another. Thomas Kyd's *The Spanish Tragedy,* written around 1587, is an example: in Acts I and II, we move from the court of Spain to the court of Portugal, then back to the court of Spain, then to the palace of a nobleman, then to a garden, and so forth.

In fact, *The Spanish Tragedy* was an important forerunner of later plays in more ways than one; it skillfully incorporated a number of devices that had come to the forefront during the sixteenth century, such as episodic structure, ghosts, soliloquies, and the theme of revenge. Stories chosen by Kyd and his contemporaries established material that would be used shortly thereafter by Shakespeare and his colleagues. We should add that *The Spanish Tragedy* was also the most popular play of its time—all through the late 1580s and early 1590s.

From accounts of the professional performances that gave life to these plays, we can assume that actors were improving their craft during the sixteenth century. Also, it seems reasonable to assume that they were becoming increasingly accomplished at creating both comic and serious characters, at speaking verse effectively, and at mastering such physical activities as sword fighting. Moreover, the organization of the acting companies that would mount the plays of Marlowe, Shakespeare, and Jonson was beginning to take shape.

In short, the ground had been prepared for both playwrights and performers. Let us now look at the two most important Elizabethan playwrights; we'll then consider theatres and acting companies.

(© Donald Cooper/Photo*stage*, England)

DOCTOR FAUSTUS

The most important Elizabethan playwright before Shakespeare was Christopher Marlowe, whose best-known play is *Doctor Faustus,* about a man who sells his soul to the devil. In this modern-dress production at the Young Vic Theatre in London, Richard McCabe (left) plays Mephistopheles and Jude Law (right) portrays Faustus.

Elizabethan Playwrights

Marlowe and the Mighty Line

The most famous of the "university wits" was Christopher Marlowe, who set a standard for dramatic structure and contributed a gallery of interesting characters to English theatre.

Marlowe also focused on another element that was to be central in later Elizabethan plays—dramatic poetry. Critics speak of Marlowe's "mighty line," the power of the dramatic verse he developed. For example, the title character in his play *Doctor Faustus* makes a pact with the devil, Mephistopheles, to give up his soul if the devil will grant him a number of wishes, one of which is to be with the beauteous Helen of Troy. When Faustus meets Helen, Marlowe gives him these lines:

Was this the face that launched a thousand ships,
And burnt the topless towers of Ilium?
Sweet Helen, make me immortal with a kiss.

This verse is *iambic pentameter;* that is, it has five beats to a line, with two syllables to each beat and the accent on the second beat. In Marlowe's hands, dramatic verse in iambic pentameter developed strength, subtlety, and suppleness, as well as great lyric beauty.

Another element which Marlowe developed had originated in medieval morality plays. In *Everyman,* as we saw in Chapter 4, good and bad forces vie for the soul of the main character. This struggle became an accepted theme in English drama, and Marlowe used it in *Doctor Faustus:* a good angel and a bad angel attempt to influence Faustus. Thus an abstract notion from the morality plays was incorporated into a full-length Elizabethan drama.

CHRISTOPHER MARLOWE

The plays of Christopher Marlowe (1564–1593), the first significant dramatist to emerge in the Elizabethan period, include *Tamburlaine, Parts I and II* (c. 1587), *The Tragical History of Doctor Faustus* (c. 1588), *The Jew of Malta* (c. 1588–1589), *The Massacre at Palis* (c. 1592), and *Edward II* (c. 1592). Among his other accomplishments, Marlowe perfected the chronicle play, a history play that emphasizes important public issues.

(© Bettmann/Corbis)

Christopher Marlowe.

As was usual in his day, Marlowe wrote for production rather than for publication. His *Doctor Faustus,* for example, was not published until 1604, more than 10 years after his death. Though it is a serious play, it includes many comic scenes, some perhaps not written by Marlowe. Thus there has been some dispute over how the text should be edited to reflect Marlowe's intentions.

Marlowe's verse and subject matter, as well as some of his dramatic techniques, influenced Shakespeare. *The Massacre at Paris* and *The Jew of Malta* show Marlowe's interest in exploring Machiavellian characters. *Edward II* is an exploration of the personal tragedy of a king; *Doctor Faustus* explores the tragedy of the damnation of a human soul. All his plays are noted for the beauty of their dramatic verse.

The son of a Canterbury shoemaker, Marlowe attended Corpus Christi College, Cambridge, on a scholarship. He received his B.A. in 1584 and continued studying for his M.A., although by then he appears to have become a secret government agent. A letter from the queen's privy council, submitted to explain his frequent absences, thanked him for his service to the country and requested that he be granted his degree, which he received in 1587.

Marlowe's writing career began at Cambridge, and when he moved to London, he became one of the "university wits," a circle of young writers who had studied at Oxford or Cambridge. With Thomas Nashe, another member of the group, he is listed as coauthor of *Dido, Queen of Carthage.* The first drama he wrote alone, *Tamburlaine the Great, Part I,* was performed in 1587; it was so successful that he wrote *Part II,* which was produced the following year. Marlowe continued working as a government agent; in 1589, he spent 2 weeks in Newgate Prison for his participation in a fight that resulted in a man's death.

Little is known about Marlowe's personal life, but it was said that he held unorthodox religious views and had difficulties with the law. For instance, in May of 1593, the queen's privy council ordered his arrest on a charge of atheism. Before he could be arrested, however, Marlowe was stabbed to death in a brawl in a private house by a man named Ingram Frizer. Two government agents were accessories to the killing, and Frizer was acquitted on the ground that he had acted in self-defense; it is possible that Marlowe's stabbing was a planned assassination related to his government activities. In any case, it cut short the life of one of Elizabethan England's most talented playwrights.

WILLIAM SHAKESPEARE

When William Shakespeare (1564–1616) appeared on the theatre scene around 1590, the stage for great drama had been set. He took established elements—Senecan devices; episodic plot structure; the platform stage; powerful dramatic verse; and stories from English history, Roman history, Roman drama, and Italian literature—and fused them into one of the most impressive bodies of plays ever created.

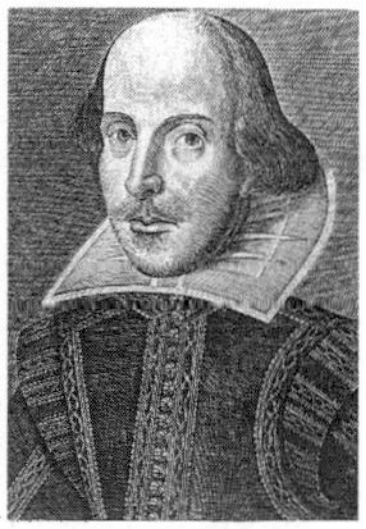
(Victoria and Albert Museum, London)

William Shakespeare.

Shakespeare was born in Stratford-upon-Avon, a town about 85 miles northwest of London. Though he spent many years in London as a member of an acting company, he never cut his ties to Stratford. Most of his land investments were in or around his birthplace; they included New Place, one of the largest houses in the town, which he bought in 1597. He also used his money to pay his father's debts and restore his family to prosperity and honor.

When Shakespeare was born, in 1564, his father—John Shakespeare—was a prosperous glover and town alderman; his mother, Mary Arden, was the daughter of a yeoman farmer and landowner. As the son of a burgess—a town official—young William was entitled to a free education at the King's New School in Stratford, an institution that prepared students for the university. When he was 13, however, his father suffered business losses, and so he was probably withdrawn from school and apprenticed to a trade. Town records mention William Shakespeare in November 1582, when he married Anne Hathaway, who was several years older. Their daughter Susanna was born in March 1583; Hamnet and Judith, twins, were born in 1585. Shakespeare's actions and whereabouts between 1585 and 1590 are not recorded, but by 1590 he was in London working as an actor and playwright.

For the next 23 years—except for 1593–1594, when the theatres were closed because of a plague and he wrote his narrative poems—Shakespeare was a working member of a London acting company. From 1595 until his retirement, he was associated with London's leading troupe, first called the Lord Chamberlain's Men and after 1603 known as the King's Men. As an actor, he was said to play small but important roles, such as the Ghost in *Hamlet.* His duties as a playwright probably took up most of his time; besides writing plays for the company, he was also expected to help stage them. As a shareholder in the company and a part owner of the theatre, he was also involved with the management of the troupe.

The following are Shakespeare's best-known plays, with the approximate dates when they were first presented. Tragedies: *Romeo and Juliet* (1595), *The Merchant of Venice* (1596–1597), *Julius Caesar* (1599), *Hamlet* (1601), *Othello* (1604), *Macbeth* (1605–1606), *King Lear* (1605–1606), *Anthony and Cleopatra* (1606–1607), *Coriolanus* (1607–1608). Comedies: *Comedy of Errors* (1592), *Two Gentlemen of Verona*

(1594–1595), *Love's Labour's Lost* (1594–1595), *A Midsummer Night's Dream* (1595), *Much Ado about Nothing* (1598), *As You Like It* (1599), *Twelfth Night* (1601), *All's Well That Ends Well* (1602–1603). Histories: *Richard II* (1595–1596), *King John* (1596–1597), *Henry IV, Parts I and II* (1597–1598), *Henry V* (1599). Romances and problem plays: *Troilus and Cressida* (1601–1602), *Measure for Measure* (1604–1605), *Pericles* (1608–1609), *Cymbeline* (1609–1610), *A Winter's Tale* (1610–1611), *The Tempest* (1611–1612).

The Globe Theatre, where his later plays were produced, burned in 1613. Though the theatre was rebuilt, Shakespeare retired in 1613 to Stratford and became one of its leading citizens. He died 3 years later.

Shakespeare's Skill and Diversity

Shakespeare excelled in many aspects of theatre. As an actor and a member of a dramatic company, he understood the technical elements of theatre. His plots, in episodic form, are exemplary; his verse—especially in the power of his metaphors and the music of his language—is extraordinary; his characters are so well-rounded and so carefully detailed that they often seem like living people.

Another hallmark of Shakespeare's work is his diversity. As can be seen in the list of his plays above, he excelled in tragedies, comedies, histories, and other categories that are difficult to label and thus are sometimes called *problem plays.*

Shakespeare's plays illustrate how influences from earlier drama came together during the English Renaissance, and how complex those influences were. To begin with, there are the many sources, techniques, and stories used in the plays. Shakespeare's *Hamlet*, for example, is reminiscent of Seneca's plays, particularly in its use of revenge as a theme (Hamlet, Laertes, and Fortinbras are all seeking revenge), its onstage violence, a supernatural apparition (the ghost of Hamlet's father), feigned and real madness, and soliloquies in which Hamlet reveals his inner thoughts.

Because Elizabethan playwrights were expected to turn out dramas quickly for the popular theatre, they often used a variety of sources: other dramas, literary pieces, and history. Many scholars believe that Shakespeare's *Hamlet* is a reworking of an earlier version, perhaps written by Thomas Kyd; this earlier version was itself based on thirteenth-century Danish history and a French adaptation from 1576. Other plays by Shakespeare were based on Roman history, Italian novellas, and English chronicles.

Following a tradition that had developed in Elizabethan drama, Shakespeare made no attempt to observe the structural rules of the Italian neoclassicists. His episodic structure derives from medieval drama rather than from the neoclassical unities. The action frequently shifts from one locale to another, short scenes alternate with longer ones, and comic episodes punctuate serious scenes. Examples of comic scenes are the scene with the drunken porter in *Macbeth* and the scene with the gravedigger in *Hamlet.*

Shakespeare, like other Elizabethan dramatists, was not simply reacting against the neoclassical rules. He and others were developing a new and powerful dramatic form based on different rules. Like his contemporaries, Shakespeare uses episodic structure to create a forceful, imaginative drama that has its own dynamics. Again, *Hamlet* is an example: the scenes in the play shift from one locale to another. We

(© Donald Cooper/Photo*stage*, England)

HAMLET
The continuing popularity of Shakespeare is obvious from the many productions of his plays around the world. Ever since it was written, Shakespeare's *Hamlet* has been staged by great actors and directors. Along with offering great roles and great scenes, the play raises a number of intriguing and complex questions. Here, on the right, is Simon Russell Beale as Hamlet. Denis Quilley, holding the skull, is the gravedigger. The production was at the Royal National Theatre in London.

move from private episodes to public episodes, from scenes in which Hamlet is alone giving a soliloquy or is in conference with a friend to scenes of pageantry in the throne room. Shakespeare skillfully alternates scenes so that each episode illuminates or forms a counterpoint to the one just before it and just after it. Also, there is a subplot in *Hamlet,* as there is in other plays such as *King Lear.* In *Hamlet,* Fortinbras, the prince of Norway, attempts to avenge his own father's death by fighting the Danes, who he believes have wronged his father. In *King Lear,* the title character mistakenly thinks his evil daughters are good, and in the subplot Gloucester mistakenly thinks his good son is evil.

In these plays Shakespeare shows tremendous skill in creating rich tapestries, pulling many diverse elements together to form a unified picture. One unifying element is thematic; another has to do with tone and texture.

Another accomplishment of Shakespeare's is the creation of a fascinating group of characters. Not only the title characters—Macbeth, Lear, Othello, Hamlet, Richard III, Julius Caesar, Henry V—but a host of others, including Falstaff, Iago, Bottom, and Prospero, are among the most memorable stage individuals ever created. Volumes have been written about each one; in many cases they have been discussed and analyzed more thoroughly than actual historical figures.

Still another achievement of Shakespeare is his use of language. Entire volumes are filled with quotations from Shakespeare, and innumerable phrases used in everyday

DEBATES IN THEATRE HISTORY | Who Wrote Shakespeare's Plays?

For well over a century there has been a debate over the authorship of the plays attributed to William Shakespeare. Most theatre scholars have accepted the idea that they were written by the man known as Shakespeare—the man born in Stratford-upon-Avon, who went to school there and later showed up in London in 1590 as an actor, who became a shareholder in the Lord Chamberlain's Men, whose name appeared on quarto editions of the plays and later on the published folio of twenty-three plays. But there have long been others—lawyers, intellectuals, other skeptics—who have questioned that this person could be the author.

The plays attributed to Shakespeare are a remarkable body of work. They display a range of knowledge about the past, a genius for creating memorable characters, a mastery of dramatic construction, a gift for developing profound themes, and an incomparable talent for poetic expression. The chief objection to the idea of Shakespeare as the author of the plays is that a person with Shakespeare's limited education and background could not possibly have accomplished all this. The plays must have been written by someone with a university education, someone who went to Oxford or Cambridge. They must also have been created by someone extremely worldly: a member of the upper classes who had traveled widely on the continent, for instance, and who had been exposed to a diverse group of people of all classes.

Taking this as a premise, those who question Shakespeare's authorship set about trying to identify who this person might be. A number of names have surfaced through the years: the statesman and philosopher Francis Bacon; the playwright Christopher Marlowe; and Edward de Vere, the seventeenth Earl of Oxford. Others have suggested that the plays were the result of a collaboration—between Marlowe and Shakespeare, for instance—or were written by a committee.

Each candidate put forward has certain credentials that make him a possibility. For most candidates, however, there are problems to be dealt with. Marlowe, for example, was killed in 1593, well before the bulk of Shakespeare's plays were written. Those who still think Marlowe was the author (or a collaborator) say that he was not really killed, that the announcement of his death was a conspiracy which allowed him to continue writing uninterrupted. This argument has not won widespread support, however.

Recently the most vigorous support has been given to de Vere, the earl of Oxford. Oxford's candidacy was launched in 1920 by Thomas Looney in a book, *Shakespeare Identified*. Oxford, Looney argued, had all the qualifications: a classical education, sympathy for the house of Lancaster in the War of the Roses, Roman Catholic leanings, a love-hate attitude toward women, and so forth. Since Looney's book, others have taken up the cause. There is a Shake-

speech (including some we are not even aware of) come from his plays. Moreover, it is not only the sense of the words and their imagery and rhythm that are so impressive, but also their sound. The speeches, after all, were written to be spoken onstage, and to be heard by audiences. This aural aspect of Shakespeare's language was described by George Bernard Shaw as "word music."

The fact that the plays were written to be performed reminds us that the practice at the time was not to publish plays in the way they are published today. Certain of Shakespeare's plays appeared individually in quarto editions and later in folio editions, and there is often much disagreement as to which version is the most reliable. This is because most playwrights, as we have noted, did not supervise the publication of their plays. (The chief exception among playwrights of this period was Ben Jonson.) Shakespeare's complete works did not appear in printed form until 1623, seven years after his death, when two colleagues who had been fellow actors, John Hemminges and Henry Condell, edited what is known as the First Folio.

How were Shakespeare's plays first staged? This brings us to the subjects of theatres and acting in the English Renaissance, which we'll consider in the next sections.

speare Oxford Society which publishes a journal and holds annual conferences mostly devoted to supporting the candidacy of de Vere. One piece of evidence which de Vere's supporters advance is that he marked passages in his copy of the Geneva Bible that correspond to passages in Shakespeare's plays. On the other side of the argument about de Vere is the fact that the poetry de Vere is known to have written is not particularly noteworthy.

The arguments continue and show no signs of abating. If anything, they are now more virulent than ever. In 1987, a moot court trial was held in which three Supreme Court justices took part: *Earl of Oxford* v. *Shakespeare.* At first the justices voted for Shakespeare, but later they seem to have wavered. A play by Amy Freed, *The Beard of Avon,* suggested a collaboration between Marlowe and Shakespeare; and a film by Michael Rubbo, *Much Ado about Something,* posited several theories, all designed to question Shakespeare's authorship.

In recent years the controversy has continued unabated. In a volume entitled *"Shakespeare" by Another Name: The Life of Edward de Vere, Earl of Oxford, the Man Who Was Shakespeare* (2005), the author Mark Anderson argues once again that Edward de Vere, not Shakespeare, wrote the plays. At the same time, works by three other scholars in one way or another support the position that Shakespeare was indeed the author of the plays. These include *1599: A Year in the Life William Shakespeare* (2005) by James Shapiro; *Will in the World: How Shakespeare Became Shakespeare* (2004) by Stephen Greenblatt; and *Shadowplay: The Hidden Beliefs and Coded Politics of William Shakespeare* (2005) by Clare Asquith.

What is the answer? Who really wrote the plays? Probably, we will never have a definitive solution. No one can prove unequivocally that someone other than Shakespeare wrote the plays, but then neither can the proponents of Shakespeare offer irrefutable proof of his authorship. One thing is certain: for those who would topple Shakespeare from his perch, several formidable obstacles remain. One is the fact that he was unquestionably an actor and shareholder in the theatre company that produced the Shakespearean plays. Another is that his name is the only one to appear on the published quartos of individual plays and on the folio edition of the collected plays put together by his colleagues Hemminges and Condell. Finally, there is the fact that if this man, who was not an aristocrat, not a university graduate, and not well traveled, and who was seemingly unsophisticated, did write the plays, it is not the first time in history that a genius emerged from unlikely circumstances. There have always been a few people who take everything they see, or read, or hear, and not only absorb it completely but magically transform it into art. This has happened before, with Mozart and others, and it might well have happened here.

ELIZABETHAN THEATRES

THEATRES AND PRODUCTION PRACTICES: PROBLEMS OF RESEARCH

There is considerable confusion—and controversy—surrounding the appearance of Elizabethan playhouses. At this point, therefore, it is appropriate to pause in our examination of the English Renaissance theatre and discuss the reasons for this uncertainty. To understand the situation, we need to become familiar with certain problems of theatre research.

In order to reconstruct earlier theatrical events and production techniques, historians consult *primary sources*—that is, materials surviving from the period under study. Imagine, for example, what kinds of materials might help scholars of the early twenty-second century reconstruct the theatre of the early twenty-first century. These materials might include surviving playhouses; scripts; sketches of costumes; models of sets; reviews; promptbooks; contracts with performers, playwrights, and builders; autobiographies; videotapes; and photographs. Of course, all such sources would have to be carefully examined and interpreted; future historians would have to ask, for example, whether the people who reviewed a Broadway opening in, say, 2006 had any biases that colored their opinions, and whether or not to take at face value the autobiography of an actor who represented himself as having been of crucial importance in certain productions. Evaluating the reliability of sources is an essential aspect of the theatre historian's job. History is not simply accumulating information but analyzing its validity and significance.

Only a few sources have survived that can help us reconstruct the theatres of ancient Greece or Rome, the Middle Ages, or most early Asian cultures. Vase paintings are a visual source for classical Greek drama; ruins like those at Epidaurus and Delphi are sources for Hellenistic theatre. The theatre at Orange in France is a well-preserved Roman playhouse. From the tenth century C.E. there is a description by Bishop Ethelwold of Winchester of the staging of the *Quem quaeritis* trope. Medieval town documents are sources for some of the arrangements for producing cycle plays. Drawings by Serlio are sources for developments in scene design during the early Italian Renaissance.

Of course, conclusions about theatrical practices drawn from these materials vary, because the sources are open to various interpretations: they do not tell us everything. To take just one example, no skenes (stage facades) have survived from Hellenistic playhouses. In many eras, no special care was taken to preserve theatrical artifacts, because theatre was considered popular and impermanent. The ephemeral nature of live theatre implies that once an event is completed, it disappears; thus the artwork itself will not survive to be studied.

The problem of re-creating the Elizabethan playhouse is an example of the difficulties of theatre research. Few documents survive, and controversy surrounds most of them. A principal visual source, for example, is a copy of a drawing of one of the London theatres, the Swan; the original was made in 1596 by a visiting Dutchman, Johannes de Witt. Because what we have is not the original, and because even the original was done by someone not completely familiar with English stage practices, there are questions surrounding the validity and accuracy of this source.

There are also questions about how it should be interpreted. For example, historians debate what is depicted as going on in the playhouse. The drawing shows three figures onstage. Does this indicate a performance or a rehearsal? If you believe that a performance is shown, you will reach conclusions quite different from those you will reach if you think that what is shown is a rehearsal. Another unanswered question is: Are the people shown in the second level of the tiring house—the stage house—spectators or actors?

In addition to de Witt's drawing, two other important documents survive: contracts for the construction of two theatres, the Fortune in 1600 and the Hope in 1613. These give dimensions and some additional facts about the theatres; yet they too can be frustrating. The Fortune contract, for example, takes for granted a familiarity with other Elizabethan playhouses; often, it calls for some feature of the Globe Theatre of 1599 to be copied. Unfortunately, we do not know exactly what this Globe looked like. And the Hope Theatre is not a representative example; since it doubled as an arena for bearbaiting—a popular recreation of the time—its platform stage and tiring house could be removed to clear the space.

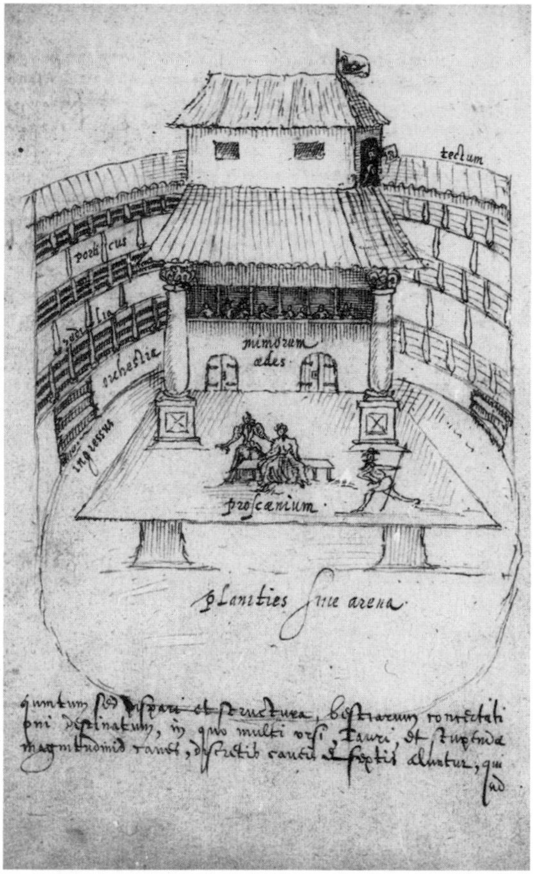

(University Library, Utrecht)

(The Folger Shakespeare Library, Washington, D.C.)

(The Folger Shakespeare Library, Washington, D.C.)

SOURCES OF THEATRE HISTORY

These illustrations are often used as a basis for conjectural reconstructions of the Elizabethan public playhouse. All three also illustrate problems faced by theatre historians. The drawing (upper left) of the Swan Theatre is a copy of a sketch made by a Dutch visitor in 1596. Though it shows the platform stage, tiring house, yard, and galleries, it is controversial. Is the sketch complete? If so, where is the "reveal" space? Who are the people in the gallery? Is this a rehearsal or a performance? The illustration (lower right) from William Alabaster's *Roxana* (1630) seems to show a performance in the late Renaissance. The curtained space could be an "inner below" for "reveal" scenes. But again, who are the people in the gallery above the stage? Also, is this a public playhouse or a converted court hall? The third drawing (upper right) is from Francis Kirkman's *The Wits; or Sport upon Sport* (1672). Obviously, it was drawn after the English Renaissance and is therefore questionable. Does it show a real playhouse, an imaginary one, or perhaps one from the commonwealth period or the early Restoration? Given such questions, it is understandable that there is no definitive reconstruction of the English public theatre.

(Hulton Archive/Getty Images)

THE FORTUNE THEATRE
One of the later theatres to be constructed in the Elizabethan era was the Fortune, which was built in 1600. Two things set it apart from other theatres of the period: it was square in shape, and we have the exact dimensions of its ground plan. The backstage area ran along one side, and the rectangular stage extended halfway into the "yard" where spectators stood. The drawing here shows a scene in the interior around the year 1620, two decades after the Fortune was built.

Legal documents concerning the Red Lion Theatre—possibly the first public playhouse—have also been discovered, and there have been some recent excavations of the Rose and the Globe. But these new sources have led to theories about the Elizabethan playhouse that are in conflict with generally accepted ideas. Finally, there are some drawings relating to indoor theatres converted from cockpits, which were probably by Inigo Jones or his assistant, although we do not know what theatres they represent.

It is clear, then, why so much disagreement exists over the physical appearance of the Elizabethan playhouses. What these sources might tell us, however, is that historians (including the authors of this textbook) too often try to create a homogeneous point of view; in reality, history is not that easily homogenized. In this case, what is most likely is that there was no "standard" Elizabethan playhouse; rather, many different versions of theatre spaces existed.

A similar situation is found with Elizabethan scenery. Debate over how much scenery was used and how complex it was often revolves around interpretations of Philip Henslowe's diary. Henslowe —along with his son-in-law, the actor Edward Alleyn—managed a theatre company called the Lord Admiral's Men, and his diary contains lists of scenic pieces and props. Many of them, however, are not fully or clearly described.

Given the paucity of primary sources and their frequent lack of clarity, it is no wonder that so much debate rages over Elizabethan staging practices. This should be kept in mind as we turn our attention to Elizabethan theatres, scenery, and costumes. As we have seen, Elizabethan drama was distinctly different in structure from Italian Renaissance drama; and Elizabethan playhouses and staging practices also developed differently from those in Italy: in English theatres, the proscenium arch and painted-perspective scenery had not been introduced. There were two types of theatres available to Elizabethan audiences. They have been given different names by different scholars. Some refer to them as *public* and *private;* others describe them as *outdoor* and *indoor;* still others use terms such as *amphitheater* and *hall* playhouses. The point to remember is that the larger theatres such as the Globe and the Fortune were open to the sky in their central area, and they accommodated more people and charged less than the smaller indoor or "hall" theatres, which were therefore more private.

Public or Outdoor Theatres

Many commentators believe that forerunners of the Elizabethan public theatres were bearbaiting rings or inns adapted for performances. In the case of the latter, the enclosed inn yard would become the performance space. At the end opposite the entrance, a stage would be set up, and the rooms overlooking this yard would serve as viewing spaces. Other spectators would stand in the yard. The notion, however, that the inn was a primary model for Elizabethan outdoor theatres has been disputed. It has been pointed out that inns would not want to interrupt their business for sustained performances. Besides, the inns themselves were of different configurations. Inns no doubt were an influence, but there were several sources for what became the standard for permanent theatres: not only inns, but halls owned by royalty or the nobility adapted for performances, spaces at colleges and schools used for their presentations, and the outdoor platform stages of medieval theatre, as well as other public spaces such a bullbaiting and bearbaiting arenas.

Whatever their origin, public theatres designed especially for performances became the primary playing spaces for professional adult companies. Between the 1560s and 1642, at least twelve open-air public theatres were built outside London.

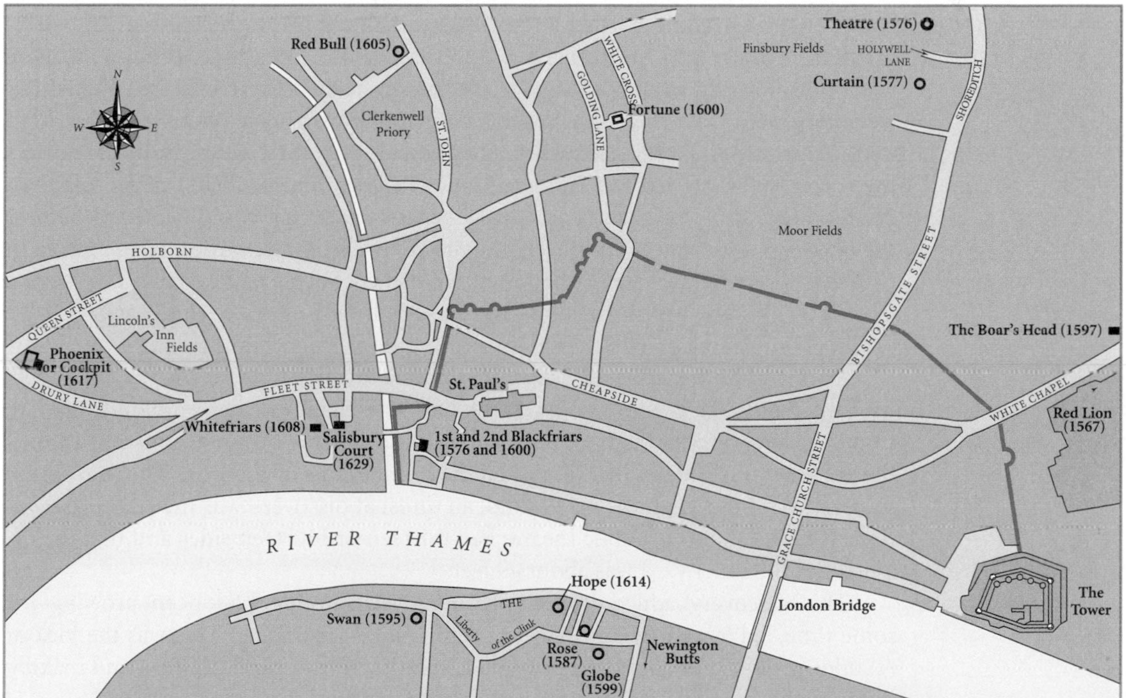

LONDON THEATRES—1575–1630

Above is the map indicating the location of public and private theatres just before and after 1600. Dates indicate the year in which they were built. The black line stretching from the Tower on the right, past St. Paul's on the left, marks the boundary of the City of London. The town fathers forbade the building of theatres inside the City limits; hence, theatres were built outside.

Recent discoveries show that James Burbage (father of Richard Burbage, the great actor in Shakespeare's plays) was operating an outdoor playhouse called the Red Lion as early as 1567.

The public theatres were built outside the city limits of London, to the north or south of the city across the Thames River. The reason was that the London city fathers opposed theatre on moral grounds and forbade it in the city. This opposition was offset by the support of theatre from Queen Elizabeth, members of the nobility, and many ordinary citizens. The queen and the nobility not only enjoyed theatre but also gave financial support in various ways—one way being to pay for performances given at court or in large private homes.

However, it was necessary for public theatres to be located outside the jurisdiction of city officials—and so the Theatre (1576), the Curtain (1577), and the Red Bull (1605) were north of the city boundaries; and the Swan (1595), the Rose (1587), the Globe (1599), and the Hope (1614) were across the Thames to the south. There is no question that the most famous public theatre was the Globe, constructed in 1599 by Richard and Cuthbart Burbage, James's sons, for the Lord Chamberlain's Men.

Because, as we have seen, there is so little primary source material, we can only hypothesize about the nature of the outdoor public theatres; but most historians now believe that there was no single, uniform design. Certain details varied, particularly the external shape of the theatres. One expert insists that the Globe Theatre had twenty sides, while another authority argues that it had eighteen sides. The original Rose Theatre had fourteen sides, and the Fortune Theatre was square. If there was no uniformity in the outward shape, however, there were other elements that were consistent. The stage, for instance, was a platform stage about four feet high that thrust into the audience, which surrounded it on three sides. In most theatres the stage was wide—40 feet in several known cases, and probably never less than 26 feet. Moreover, this playing area was a neutral space that could become whatever the playwright indicated, an inheritance, no doubt, from the notion of the platea in churches where medieval plays had been performed. Such a neutral stage offers great flexibility: it can be transformed instantaneously from indoors to outdoors; it can be as all-encompassing as a battlefield, or as intimate as a bedchamber.

Estimates of the audience capacity of public theatres range from 1,500 to 3,000; the larger number is more widely accepted. The shape of these buildings varied: some buildings are said to have been circular and others polygonal; and at least one, the Fortune, was square. In 1989, when the foundations of the Rose Theatre, on the south bank of the Thames, were found, an unusual discovery was made: the excavations revealed that this public theatre had thirteen or fourteen sides and that the diameter of the inner yard was about 49 feet.

This discovery added impetus to a movement that had been growing for some time, led largely by an American actor, Sam Wanamaker. This was the idea of rebuilding the Globe as near as possible to the site of the original Globe, and making it, in so far as possible, like the earlier Globe theatres.

In the 1990s this dream became a reality. John Orrell was charged with doing most of the research on how the theatre looked and how it was built. Using old maps, drawings, and other data, Orrell came up with a version that had twenty sides and was 99 feet in overall diameter, with the diameter of the yard being 74 feet. (Another expert had suggested an eighteen-sided structure with an outer diameter

(Hulton Archive/Getty Images)

THE GLOBE AND SWAN THEATRES
Two theatres built on the south side of the Thames River, outside the jurisdiction of the London town fathers, were the Swan, on the left, and the Globe. This drawing, made a number of years after the theatres were first built, shows the outer shape and relative positions of these two important Elizabethan theatres. Note the polygonal exterior of the two theatres, with several sides creating a rounded structure. The Globe, of course, was where many of Shakespeare's major plays were first performed.

of 90 feet and a yard diameter of 66 feet; still others suggested a smaller theatre.) Orrell's reconstruction served as the basis for the reconstruction of the Globe on the South bank of the Thames. To the extent possible, the building materials matched those used in the early seventeenth century: a thatched roof, oak beams, joints with wood pegs, and plaster made of lime, sand, and goat hair.

The reconstructed Globe, because it is unroofed at the top, offers performances only in the warmer months. It opened in 1997 and has proved immensely popular with audiences, giving them a sense of what the original experience must have been for those attending Shakespeare's plays when they were first presented.

Audience Seating in Public Theatres

Audiences at public theatres were accommodated in the pit, boxes, and galleries. Usually, there were three tiers of seating around the sides of the theatre. Part of one tier—most likely the bottom one—was divided into boxes, which were known as *lords' rooms* because they were frequented by wealthy people. Indications are that the height of the first tier was usually 12 feet; of the second tier, about 11 feet; and of the third tier, approximately 9 feet.

According to the Puritans—who, however, were opposed to theatre and are therefore not entirely reliable—prostitutes sometimes rented the lords' rooms, giving public theatres a bad reputation. The other tiers, or galleries, were undivided and had bench seating. On the ground floor, in front of and on the sides of the stage, was a standing area known as the *yard;* the lower-class spectators who stood there were known as *groundlings.* All strata of society, then, attended productions at the public theatres.

Before and during performances, food and drink—apples, nuts, water, ale—were sold throughout the playhouse. Some spectators no doubt decided to limit how much they ate or drank, since the only toilet facilities were buckets—or the river, if one wanted to walk there. Many men smoked throughout the play; and it was necessary to avoid sitting behind anyone wearing a large hat, which would obstruct the view of the stage.

The Stage in Public Theatres

The stage was a raised platform surrounded on three sides by the audience; thus it was closer to a contemporary thrust stage than to a proscenium-arch stage. (Some historians have theorized that some public theatres were arena spaces. In at least one outdoor playhouse, the first Boar's Head, the stage may not have been pushed back against the tiring house. In other words, spectators may have stood on four sides, making it an arena stage. Moreover, recent scholarship has shown that in the indoor halls in Cambridge, stages were often set up in the middle of the room, not set against the hall screen at one end.)

In the outdoor theatres, spectators were never very far away from the stage; however, there is a great deal of debate over how far into the yard the platform stage extended. While documents dealing with the Fortune Theatre suggest that its stage extended 27 1/2 feet—or halfway—into the yard (see the drawing on page 196), analysis of the excavations of the Globe and the Rose suggests that stages did not usually extend this far. The excavations at the Rose, for instance, show that when it was built in 1587 its stage was only 16 feet 5 inches deep by 39 feet 9 inches wide at the rear and 36 feet 10 inches wide downstage. When it was altered 5 years later, the stage (though somewhat more rectangular) was still only 17 or 18 feet deep; this means that it went only about a third of the way into the yard. Also, the front half of the yard, where groundlings stood to watch, sloped from the back toward the stage.

There were trapdoors leading below the platform; the gravediggers' scene in *Hamlet,* for instance, was staged with a trap in the Globe Theatre.

The Tiring House

Behind the raised platform was a stage house, known as a *tiring house,* which functioned much like a Greek skene. The tiring house was probably a three-story building that served as a place for changing costumes as well as storing properties and set pieces. Its facade was the basic scenic element in the Elizabethan public theatres. Exits into the tiring house and entrances from it indicated scene changes.

There is a great deal of controversy regarding the exterior appearance of the tiring house. To begin with, some historians debate whether the tiring house was built into the back wall of the playhouse or set up as a separate unit on the stage,

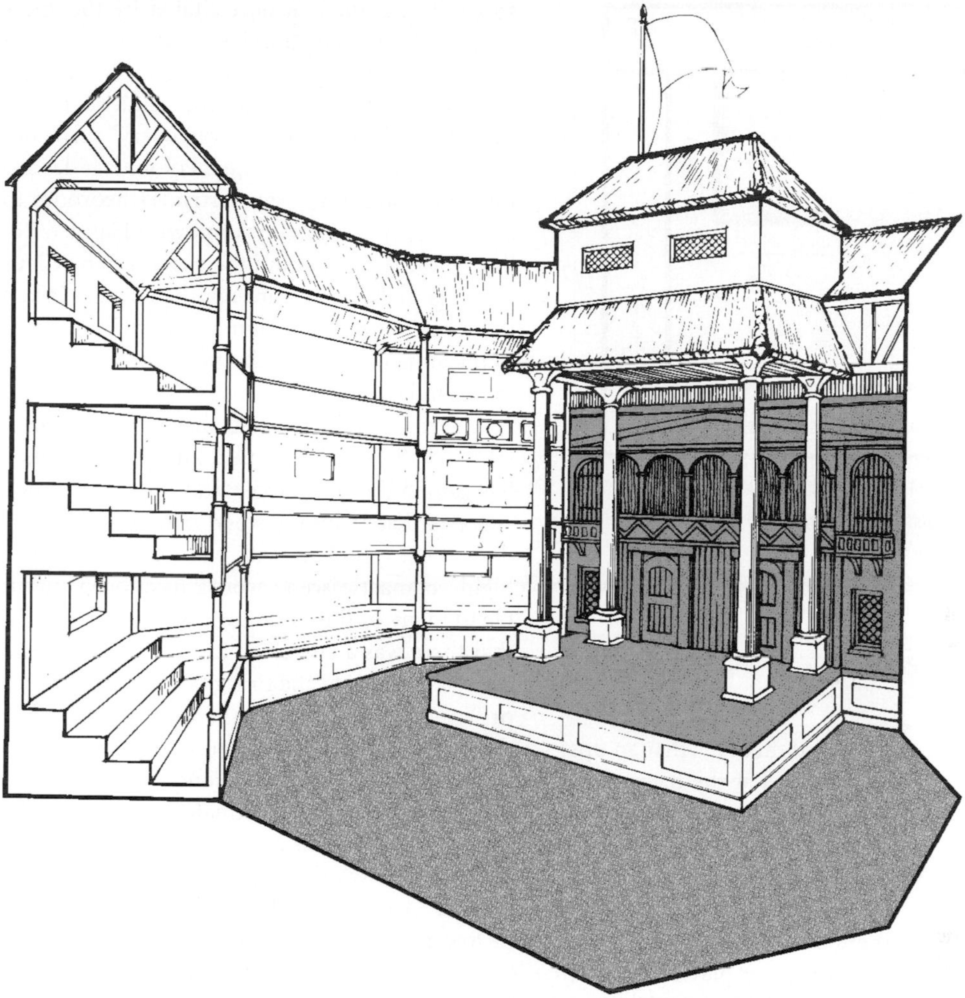

AN ELIZABETH PLAYHOUSE
This conjectural drawing shows the kind of stage on which the plays of Shakespeare and his contemporaries were first presented. A platform stage juts into an open courtyard, with spectators standing on three sides. Three levels of enclosed seats rise above the courtyard. There are doors at the rear of the stage for entrances and exits and an upper level for balcony scenes.

extending out from the rear wall. The excavation at the Rose suggests that the stage went right up to the rear wall. This back wall was made up of three sides of the polygonal playhouse and served as the facade of the tiring house, which would have been angled—not flat as shown in de Witt's drawing of the Swan Theatre.

The first level of the tiring house had doorways, but the number is debated; that there were at least two—one on each side—is shown by the drawing of the Swan. Many historians have maintained, though there is little pictorial evidence, that Elizabethan drama requires a "discovery space" or "reveal space" on the first level; this

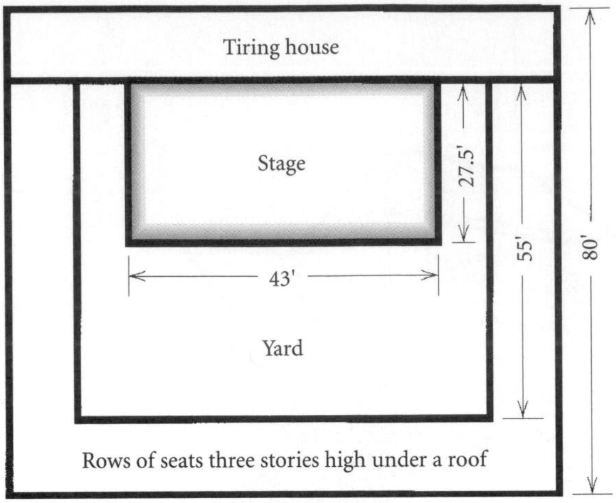

GROUND PLAN OF THE FORTUNE THEATRE
The only English Renaissance theatre for which we have a number of specific dimensions is the Fortune. From the builder's contract we know the size of the stage, the standing pit, the audience seating area, and the theatre building itself. The building was square; the backstage area ran along one side; the stage was rectangular; and the audience—both standing and sitting—was on three sides.

space, it is argued, is necessitated by the spectacular Elizabethan "discovery" scenes (in such a scene, for instance, a body might be suddenly discovered or revealed to the audience). The most famous example of a "discovery" scene occurs in Shakespeare's *Hamlet.* Polonius hides behind a curtain in Queen Gertrude's bedroom to eavesdrop on her conversation with Hamlet. Believing the figure behind the curtain to be Claudius, Hamlet stabs it through the curtain. When the curtain is drawn, Polonius's body is revealed to the audience. Where did the actor playing Polonius hide?

Three major theories have been formulated. The least complicated, and the one which has gained the most acceptance in recent times, suggests that Polonius stood behind one of the doors. The problem with this theory is that a highly climactic scene would have been invisible to many of the spectators. A second theory is that there was a curtained area between the two doors leading into the tiring house; this recessed or "inner" area would serve as a hiding space. The third theory is that an upstage "discovery" space would require a climactic scene to be staged at the back of the stage, away from the audience, and that this would have been highly unpopular, since Elizabethans expected intimate contact with the dramatic action. Instead, it is theorized, a pavilion-like structure, extending out from the tiring house, was erected between the two doors; this pavilion had a curtained lower level for staging "discoveries." A variation of this third theory is that there were also stairs leading up to the lower level of the pavilion.

An upper playing area—that is, a sort of second-story platform at the back of the stage—is also required in many Elizabethan dramas. This too has created controversy over the appearance of the tiring house. The best-known example of a scene requiring an upper playing area is the balcony scene in Shakespeare's *Romeo and Juliet.* Some scholars suggest that there were windows or a gallery above the doors. Historians who believe that there was an "inner below" for reveal scenes also believe that there was a similar "inner above" space between the two windows in the tiring house. Historians who think that a pavilion was used for "reveals" argue that the roof of this tentlike element would have provided an upper playing space.

The third level of the tiring house, called the *musicians' gallery,* probably housed the musicians who provided accompaniment for the plays.

A roof, extending out from the tiring house, protected the stage. This roof, called the *heavens* or the *shadows,* was supported by pillars in some theatres and was suspended from the back in others. The underside of the roof was often painted to represent the heavens literally. (In fact, some scholars believe that much of the interior of public playhouses was painted in a highly decorative way.) A flag was flown from the top of the tiring house to advertise that a performance was taking place.

(© Donald Cooper/Photostage, England)

ELIZABETHAN PRODUCTION: MINIMAL PROPS AND SETS
A contemporary production of *Cymbeline* at Shakespeare's Globe reminds us of the conditions under which Shakespeare's plays were presented in his own day. The bare-bones production shown here was originally produced at the reconstructed Globe in London. A small, all-male cast doubled in various roles. Their all-white costumes were minimalist, as were sets and props. Poles were used, as illustrated, as were gongs (seen in the background). The original productions were all-male, used few props, and also practiced doubling in the casts.

Influences on the Public Theatres

When we consider what influences shaped these outdoor public theatres, we again see how numerous elements came together in the English Renaissance. As noted earlier, the neutral platform stage came from medieval theatre, but the influence of the Roman theatre building can also be seen in the facade of the tiring house. Another influence is a tradition of earlier sixteenth-century English performers, who used a platform stage with a scenic structure erected as a background at one end of an inn yard. These early, temporary public theatres had standing room in the open courtyard and galleries in the walls of the surrounding building.

Possible influences on the tiring house of outdoor theatres, and the "heavens" (the ceiling covering part of the stage), were the hall screens and the roofs of indoor halls where performances were held. The surviving hall at Grey's Inn (where Shakespeare probably performed in *A Comedy of Errors*) or the surviving hall of the Middle Temple (where Shakespeare undoubtedly performed in *Twelfth Night* in 1602) may offer evidence of their influence.

(© Hulton-Deutsch Collection/Corbis)

POPULAR ARTS IN SHAKESPEARE'S TIME
Bearbaiting was a popular entertainment during Shakespeare's lifetime. Arenas were constructed for this form of entertainment, in which bears were attacked by trained dogs. Remarkably, this entertainment continued to attract audiences as recently as the early nineteenth century. Shown here is an illustration of bearbaiting in Westminster, London, in the 1820s.

Other likely influences on the appearance and configuration of the outdoor playhouses were the arenas for bullbaiting and bearbaiting, two extremely popular English entertainments. In bearbaiting, chained bears were attacked by trained dogs. A map of London, known as the Agas map, drawn in the latter part of the sixteenth century, shows both a bullbaiting and a bearbaiting arena. A temporary stage and tiring house could turn a bearbaiting arena into a public theatre. This is another example of something we see again and again in theatre history: the affinity between theatre and popular entertainment.

Private Theatres

The terms *private* and *public,* used to describe theatres in England, came into use about 1600. Elizabethan private theatres were indoor spaces, lit by candles and high windows. The word *private* in this context often causes confusion, because it seems to imply that certain classes of people would have been excluded. In England at this time, however, private theatres were open to the general populace, though they were more expensive to attend than the outdoor public theatres; in other words, poorer people would be excluded not because of policy, but because they could not afford the price of admission.

From the opening of the first private or indoor theatre, Blackfriars, in 1576 until about 1608, these theatres were used exclusively by the popular boys' companies. A second Blackfriars theatre was built by James Burbage in 1596 for his adult company; but complaints by wealthy neighbors, who were worried about what kind of people the playhouse would attract, prevented him from moving that company

DEBATES IN THEATRE HISTORY | The Campaign to Save the Rose

In January 1989, at an excavation site for a new high-rise office building in London, archaeologists from the Museum of London made a key discovery: the foundation of the Rose Theatre, one of the two most significant playhouses of the Elizabethan era (the other, of course, was the Globe). Analysis of the Rose's foundation has led historians to reevaluate much of what they once believed about the Rose. Earlier ideas had been based on all the sources then available, but those sources were insubstantial; the new discovery generated new scholarly debate over what the Elizabethan playhouse really looked like.

For example, the excavation suggests that the Rose was a thirteen- or fourteen-sided building, smaller than had previously been thought, and that its stage extended much less than halfway into the yard, even after the theatre was enlarged in 1592. In addition, the archaeologists suggest that the first Rose, built in 1587, did not have a "heavens" over the stage, but that the remodeled Rose included a "heavens" which extended to the front edge of the stage. The archaeologists also argue that the Rose's tiring house was not a separate unit like the one shown in de Witt's drawing of the Swan Theatre but was built into the theatre structure.

However, an even greater controversy arose over the excavation itself—a public debate over whether the site should be preserved or the new high-rise should be allowed to be built over it. Some people argued that the discovery was, historically, priceless and that covering the Rose over would be a desecration of a national treasure. The developers argued that forbidding construction would impede the modernization of London and that throughout English history each civilization had built on top of its predecessors. Christine Eccles, who chronicles the debate in *The Rose Theatre,* even suggests that "Philip Henslowe would have been taken considerably aback if told he could not have planning permission for the Rose Theatre because it might disturb some Roman revetments beneath."*

This debate was reminiscent of one that arose in New York City in the 1980s, when developers tore down two famous Broadway Theatres—the Helen Hayes and the Morosco—that had been the home of many historic productions. These developers argued that their project, a new hotel and theatre complex, was needed to revitalize the deteriorating Broadway district. People who wanted to save the theatres—including the founding director of the Public Theatre, Joseph Papp; and the American actress Colleen Dewhurst—argued that these theatres were cultural landmarks. Papp and Dewhurst actually chained themselves to buildings at the demolition site and were arrested.

For a few months, the Rose site in London was given a reprieve so that the archaeologists could study it. However, many people continued to maintain that the excavation should be preserved permanently. The Campaign to Save the Rose, as the preservationist movement was called, was supported by many noted performers, including Peggy Ashcroft, Ian McKellan, and Timothy Dalton. The developers, after proposing a revised version of their high-rise which they claimed would not damage the foundation of the Rose and would preserve it for future excavations, were victorious in court. The excavation was covered over with sand and concrete and the new office building, called Rose Court, was constructed over it. Ironically, the same debate immediately reappeared when a smaller section of Shakespeare's playhouse, the Globe, was unearthed in October 1989.

*New York, Routledge, 1990, p. 150.

into it. He, and later his sons, leased the space to boys' companies until 1608, when Richard Burbage's King's Men began to use it regularly in the winter while continuing to perform at the outdoor Globe in warmer seasons. But from then on, some private, indoor theatres were used for most of the year by London's adult companies and became popular.

Historians believe that the indoor theatres were similar to the outdoor public theatres, but there were some differences. Private theatres were usually smaller than public theatres, seating only about 600 to 750 spectators; it is for this reason that they were more expensive than the public theatres. The cheapest entrance fee at a private playhouse was sixpence; admission to the yard of a public theatre cost only

(Museum of London)

THE ROSE THEATRE

One of the earliest theatres built south of the Thames River in London was the Rose, a model of which is shown here. The first Rose was constructed in 1587 and enlarged in 1592. In 1989, the foundation of the Rose was unearthed in London, and much more was learned about the size and shape of the theatre. It was a building with thirteen or fourteen sides and was smaller than had originally been thought. The stage extended less than halfway into the yard, where groundlings stood on three sides.

a penny. The pit of a private theatre faced the stage in only one direction and had backless benches. The platform stage probably extended to the side walls. Galleries and boxes faced the stage on three sides. During the reigns of James I (1603–1625) and Charles I (1625–1642), known respectively as the *Jacobean* period and the *Caroline* period, wealthy audience members could sit on the stage itself. (A few historians believe that some stools may also have been set up on the stage of outdoor public theatres, but most surviving accounts of theatregoing suggest that stage seats were available only in indoor theatres.)

The price structure in private theatres also differed from that in public theatres. The benches and boxes closest to the stage were most expensive; those in the upper back wall, farther away from the stage, were cheapest. This system is closer to the way theatregoers are charged for seats today.

There are, again, many recent controversies regarding the configuration of Elizabethan private spaces. These controversies were set off by the discovery of drawings of two converted cockpits, one at Drury Lane and the other at court. *Cockpits* (as the term implies) were arenas for cockfighting—like bearbaiting, a popular entertainment. The drawings were most likely made by the renowned English designer Inigo Jones (who is discussed later in this chapter), and they seem to indicate that the stage in a private theatre did not extend very far into the pit area. They also suggest that the tiring house—at least in the cockpit at court—looked like the scaena of the Teatro Olimpico, with one large central doorway, smaller doors on each side, and one central window-like opening above the larger entrance.

Scenery and Costumes

Elizabethan scenery was quite distinct from that of the Italian Renaissance. The Elizabethans did not use painted-perspective scenery in public or private theatres, and the Elizabethan stage space did not represent a specific locale. The episodic nature of English drama required an ability to suggest rapid scene changes. This was accomplished in various ways. "Spoken decor" was used: characters in the plays would describe the settings, indicating that they were in a castle, a forest, or a bedroom. (This is a practical reason for the lengthy poetic descriptions of locales in Shakespeare's dramas.) The departure of all onstage characters and the entrance of a new group would also signal a scene change; and actors would sometimes bring out minimal properties to suggest a locale—for example, a throne could indicate the interior of a palace. The facade of the tiring house provided a constant scenic background.

The most striking element of an Elizabethan production was probably the costuming. Costuming followed the conventions and traditions of medieval English theatre. While Elizabethan dramas exhibit a great deal of historical and geographical variety, the Elizabethans were not overly concerned with accuracy; most costuming was in contemporary English fashion. Even though *Hamlet* takes place in medieval Denmark, for example, actors in the original production would have worn Elizabethan clothing. However, certain traditional costumes were worn to indicate antiquity, folk heroes, supernatural creatures, and racial groups. There is evidence, for instance, that ancient Greek and Roman characters wore a toga over Elizabethan clothing. Acting companies owned large stocks of costumes, either purchased or sometimes provided by their patrons.

Elizabethan Acting Companies

Throughout the English Renaissance, the monarchy increasingly tightened its legal control over theatre. By a decree of Queen Elizabeth in 1574, all plays and companies had to be licensed by the master of revels, a royal official. The number of acting companies was restricted by law, and according to an ordinance of 1572, all troupes had to be sponsored by a nobleman whose rank was no lower than baron. (Later, under James I, only members of the royal family were allowed to sponsor companies.)

An acting company needed a patron not only in order to receive permission to perform but also for financial backing, legal protection, and other types of support. In return for performing for their patrons, the companies received small financial subsidies and occasional allowances for costumes (and sometimes clothing from their patrons' wardrobes). The companies were named after their patrons; for instance, the company of which Shakespeare was a member was known as the Lord Chamberlain's Men.

The Lord Chamberlain's Men

"Hee addes grace to the Poet's labours: ... He entertaines us in the best leasure of our life," wrote one Elizabethan in praise of the actor. Elizabethan dramatists were matched by excellent actors and acting companies. The company that was most famous—for both its actors and its dramatist—was the Lord Chamberlain's Men (c. 1594–1642); Shakespeare acted in this company and wrote most of his plays for it.

The Lord Chamberlain's Men was founded in 1594. The theatres had been closed because of the plague; when they reopened, several actors who had been with other companies formed this new troupe under the protection of Henry Carey, Lord Hunsdon, who was the lord chamberlain. The group included Richard and Cuthbert Burbage, the clown Will Kempe, and the actor-playwright William Shakespeare. (The accomplishments of Richard Burbage as an actor will be discussed later.) At first the new troupe played at the Rose, but it soon moved to a playhouse called The Theatre, which was owned by the Burbages' father. It also performed at court and for special groups, like the lawyers of Grey's Inn.

When the government again closed the London theatres in 1597—this time because of an offensive satire—it is likely that the Lord Chamberlain's Men toured the provinces until the theatres reopened. When on tour, the company had to secure a license in each town, and this placed the troupe at the mercy of local magistrates. In spite of such problems, the group probably toured towns outside London for part of each season.

In 1599, when the lease on the land for The Theatre expired, some members of the company built the Globe Theatre as a permanent home. The ensemble had by then become the best in London. Its repertoire included plays by Shakespeare, Jonson, Dekker, Beaumont and Fletcher, and Tourneur. Kempe, who played clowns, left the company in 1599 to perform on the continent. At this time, many English actors and companies toured in Germany, the Netherlands, and Sweden. Kempe was replaced by Robert Armin, another noted clown.

In 1603, the troupe was taken under the protection of the new king, James I, and became the King's Men. Though the Blackfriars Theatre became its winter home in 1608, the company still played at the Globe during the summer, until the Globe burned in 1613. The Globe was rebuilt and was used by the company until 1642, when the theatres were closed by the Puritans and the group disbanded.

The Lord Admiral's Men

The only serious rival of the Lord Chamberlain's Men was the Lord Admiral's Men (1594–1621), under the management of Philip Henslowe and Edward Alleyn. The Lord Admiral's Men played at the Rose from 1594 to 1600 and at the Fortune from 1600 to 1621. Alleyn, their leading tragic actor, was considered nearly as fine a performer as Richard Burbage. A towering figure, Alleyn became well known for his portrayal of the leading characters in Christopher Marlowe's plays. He married Henslowe's stepdaughter and became the theatre owner's business partner.

Henslowe's detailed business diaries, preserved by Alleyn, provide one of the most significant sources of information about Elizabethan theatre.

Organization of Acting Companies

Most Elizabethan acting companies—each of which had no more than about twenty-five members—were organized on a sharing plan. Under this system, there were three categories of personnel in a company: shareholders, hired men or hirelings, and apprentices. Shareholders, the elite members of the company, bought a percentage ownership of the troupe and received a corresponding percentage of its profits as payment for their services. Their fortunes, therefore, would fluctuate with those of the company. Hirelings were actors contracted for a specific period of time and for a specific salary; they usually played minor roles. Apprentices—young performers training for the profession—were assigned to shareholders. Apprentices received room, board, training, and experience, and had hopes of eventually becoming shareholders. (Female roles were performed by boys—a fact which suggests that apprentices in a company may have been more significant than its hired men.) Since the King's Men owned the theatre in which they performed, star members were given part ownership in the theatre as an inducement to remain with the company; these actors were known as *householders,* a term which was also used for people who owned theatre buildings and rented them to acting companies. (Most acting companies leased their playhouses from such landlords.)

Acting companies needed a large number of plays; accordingly, they paid playwrights for each new work. Sometimes a writer was kept under contract to a company, and some authors also received all the profits after expenses of the second performance of a play. We need to keep in mind, however, that plays were not presented in long runs. A new play was usually performed once a week for a few weeks, and then performed several times later in the season if it proved to be popular. Acting five or six days a week, the Admiral's Men produced about sixteen new plays each season; the rest were revivals.

Acting Practices

The style of acting of Elizabethans continues to be debated. Some historians point to Hamlet's famous "advice to the players" as evidence of realistic acting. (For example, Hamlet says to the actors, "Nor not saw the air too much with your hand, thus, but use all gently.") Others suggest that the speech indicates a lack of realism in Elizabethan acting and that Shakespeare, speaking through Hamlet, is protesting its absence.

Most Elizabethan acting conventions seem to be evidence *against* realism. For one thing, there were no actresses; young boys performed the female roles. (Today, it may be difficult for us even to imagine that the sensuous Cleopatra and the romantic Juliet were first performed by males.) Second, since the plays required huge casts, doubling or tripling of roles was not uncommon. Third, to some extent typecasting was necessary, particularly for comic roles.

Fourth, the rigorous performance schedule also seems to argue against performances that could resemble behavior encountered in daily life. An acting company would rarely produce the same play on two consecutive days, and the company had

DEBATES IN THEATRE HISTORY | Elizabethan Acting Style

The debate over Elizabethan acting style illustrates how difficult it is to discuss the ephemeral art of performance. As we note in the text, scholars who argue that the acting style of the English Renaissance was realistic point to Hamlet's "advice to the players"—his coaching of the actors who are to perform the play-within-a-play. In this famous passage, Shakespeare seems to call for a natural performance style. However, there are many other references to acting in Shakespeare's plays, and many of these seem to indicate a highly conventional style. For example, in *A Midsummer Night's Dream,* a comic group of Athenian commoners, led by Peter Quince and Bottom the weaver, attempt to stage a play; Shakespeare uses them to poke fun at the bombastic style of the leading actor, the convention of doubling of roles, the lack of scenic reality, and the omnipresent prompter.

There are other inconsistencies as well. Most contemporary accounts of Richard Burbage's acting, for example, praise his natural approach; how are we to reconcile this with the highly theatrical qualities that are known to have been a part of Elizabethan performances?

Possibly, we need to realize that in any period of theatre history, audiences will perceive the acting of their contemporaries as "natural," because it is rooted in—and reflects—the concerns of their own society. Earlier audiences were more willing than we are today to accept theatrical conventions and suspend disbelief. Therefore, Shakespeare's audiences could readily believe in men playing women, actors playing more than one role, and characters conversing in verse: they simply accepted these and other highly theatrical conventions. J. L. Styan argues persuasively that in Shakespeare's theatre there was considerable intimacy between actors and audiences, and that the spectators were always aware of being in a playhouse and watching performers.* They were, then, able to see the honesty of performances and to view these performances as natural.

When we take all this into consideration, it is interesting to wonder whether the realistic acting we praise today will be considered "natural" by future scholars and students.

*"In Search of the Real Shakespeare; or, Shakespeare's Shows and Shadows," in *New Issues in the Reconstruction of Shakespeare's Theatre,* Lang, New York, 1990, pp. 185–206.

to be able to revive any play in its repertoire on very short notice. Thus, the primary concern would be, not a carefully realized production, but the effective delivery of lines; most actors seem to have learned their lines roughly and poorly. At the same time, the best actors must have had strong rhetorical skills, in view of the fact that the verse in plays by men like Marlowe and Shakespeare calls for expert delivery. Actors were provided with *sides,* which contained their own lines and cues rather than the full script. *Plots,* outlines of the dramatic action of the various plays, were posted backstage so that performers could refresh their memory about the sequence of scenes during a performance.

Fifth, rehearsals were run by playwrights or leading actors, and rehearsal time was minimal; the prompter, or bookholder, therefore became an integral figure during presentations. For all these reasons, gestures, movements, and speech were probably stylized. Also, improvisation must have been used frequently. (Hamlet's speech to the players suggests that comic actors, at least, often deviated from the script.)

Today, Elizabethan plays are sometimes considered too long to be produced unedited, and an uncut production seldom takes less than 4 hours. But performances during the English Renaissance lasted only 2 to 3 hours; a play would usually begin at 2 in the afternoon and would be presented with no intermissions (though in a public playhouse it was sometimes followed by a jig). We assume that the playing time was shorter not only because there were no intermissions but also because the performers spoke more quickly; and this too may be evidence against a realistic acting style.

Richard Burbage (c. 1567–1619), the leading actor in the Lord Chamberlain's Men, was probably the most famous Elizabethan performer. He first came into prominence in the role of Richard III, and he played the lead in many of Shakespeare's plays, including *Hamlet, King Lear,* and *Othello.* Shakespeare, as we have said, was also an actor with the company. Edward Alleyn (1566–1626), mentioned earlier, was Burbage's counterpart in the Lord Admiral's Men. He had played the leading role in several plays by Christopher Marlowe.

Will Kempe (?–1603), also of the Lord Chamberlain's Men, was a leading comic actor. Shakespeare's attack on comic improvisation, found in Hamlet's "advice to the players," was probably directed at Kempe; Hamlet says that actors should "speak no more than is set down for them. For there be of them that will themselves laugh, to set on some quantity of barren spectators to laugh too, though in the mean time some necessary question of the play be then to be considered. That's villainous and shows a most pitiful ambition in the fool that uses it."

(© Bettmann/Corbis)

RICHARD BURBAGE
Burbage—one of the Lord Chamberlain's Men and probably the most famous Elizabethan performer—played the lead in many of Shakespeare's plays.

Representation of Female Characters in Elizabethan Theatre

Historians continue to debate why women were not part of the Elizabethan acting companies. As we saw in Chapter 5, by this time in Renaissance Italy, women were significant members of the popular commedia dell'arte troupes. Most historians believe that the absence of female performers was a continuation of a medieval English tradition and also a result of the religious attitude toward actresses. It was contended that actresses were little better than whores.

The fact that women were not members of the Elizabethan companies has led to interesting discussions regarding the representation of female characters. Cross-dressing (that is, dressing as the opposite sex)—which in today's drama has become a popular way to point out sexual stereotyping—had many reverberations in Shakespeare's plays. For example, Rosalind, in the comedy *As You Like It,* dresses as a man in order to escape from her evil uncle. In modern theatre, this requires an actress to dress as a male; in Shakespeare's time, it would have meant that a young male actor would be playing a female character impersonating a male.

Feminist critics have considered the implications of this complex sexual impersonation, arguing that representation of females by males reinforced stereotypes of women found in many Elizabethan plays, such as Shakespeare's *Taming of the Shrew.* We should note that cross-dressing in Elizabethan drama usually did dramatize negative ideas about women; for example, the nurse in *Romeo and Juliet* would have been played by an older man who would have poked fun at her "masculine" qualities.

Some contemporary directors have used this complex subject to shed light on current feminist issues. Tracy C. Davis, in her essay "A Feminist Methodology in Theatre History," summarizes questions still to be answered about the absence of women from the Elizabethan stage and about the performance by women in today's modern theatre of female characters who were meant to be played by men:

> Therefore, feminist historians may wonder: when women were excluded from the public forum of the stage and males played female roles, was this necessarily an act of obliteration of women, usurpation of womanhood, misogyny, silencing or ridiculing? Were women's gestures, words, and gowns taken over by men to ridicule what the gowns, words, gestures, and women stood for? . . . What could it mean when women were subsequently permitted on the stage and performed the same texts that were written for males to play? . . . When do the words, gowns, gestures, and gender become those of the women characters and performers? Do they always remain male, even when spoken by women?"[1]

These same questions would also be relevant for classical Greek and medieval English drama and theatre.

It should be pointed out, on the other hand, that every society has customs which it takes for granted and which may or may not be fraught with meaningful and negative subtexts. Once something becomes part of a tradition, those participating in it do not consciously endorse the negative aspects pointed out by later generations. They may themselves be victims of history.

Jacobean and Caroline Drama

At the beginning of the chapter, we referred to various terms used to describe the period of English theatre we are examining. One was *early modern England;* another, the title of the chapter, is *English Renaissance;* another is *Elizabethan.* Any phrase has both advantages and disadvantages. One disadvantage of describing the entire period as Elizabethan is that Queen Elizabeth died in 1603, but the theatre that had begun to flourish during her reign continued well beyond that. Most scholars, for example, date some of Shakespeare's finest plays—*Othello, King Lear, Antony and Cleopatra,* and *The Tempest*—as coming after 1603.

The two monarchs who succeeded Elizabeth were James I and Charles I. James was the son of Mary, Queen of Scots, and ordinarily the English would never have allowed him on the throne, fearing that he would return the country to Catholicism. As a protestant king of Scotland, however, James had convinced the English that this would not be the case. Thus when Elizabeth died in 1603, he became king. When James died in 1625, his son Charles succeeded him. The two kings gave their names to the periods during which they ruled: Jacobean and Caroline.

The reigns of both James and Charles were marked by badly strained relations with Parliament; eventually, as a result of these disagreements, Charles I was challenged in a civil war. This war began in 1642 when the Puritans took control of Parliament. In 1649, when Charles was beheaded, a Commonwealth was created with Oliver Cromwell as "lord protector" of England.

[1]*Interpreting the Theatrical Past,* Thomas Postlewait and Bruce A. McConachie (eds.), University of Iowa Press, Iowa City, 1989, p. 74.

During the Jacobean period, many of the elements that had characterized Elizabethan drama continued. Gradually, however, over the next quarter century, heroism gave way to decadence and cynicism, and tragedy gave way to melodrama. One playwright who bridged the two eras was Ben Jonson (1572–1637). He had been active during the time of Shakespeare but continued until well past the latter's retirement.

BEN JONSON AND "COMEDY OF HUMOURS"

Jonson was particularly adept at comedy. A good example is his masterpiece, *Volpone,* which was staged in 1606. In this comedy, the schemer Volpone dupes old men out of their riches by pretending that he is at death's door. Volpone's servant, Mosca, promises each of these victims that when Volpone dies, the victim will inherit his fortune. Volpone's desire for the wife of one of the old men and Mosca's greed eventually lead to their undoing.

(National Portrait Gallery, London)

Ben Jonson.

As a playwright, literary critic, and poet, Jonson was one of the first writers in England to champion the neoclassical principles, and in his own work he wanted to prove that one could please the public by following these rules. Known for his sharp wit and imperious manner, he became an arbiter of literary taste, presiding over a group of younger poets who met regularly at the Mermaid Tavern in London.

In such plays as *Every Man in His Humour* (1598), *The Alchemist* (1610), and particularly *Volpone* (1606), Jonson developed a "comedy of humours" in which each principal character had an excess of one trait, or "humour." Unlike many of his contemporaries, who did not think of drama as literature, he considered his plays to be important works, and he personally supervised their printing in 1616. He was also unlike other English writers of his time in championing neoclassical structure for drama, though his own plays did not always adhere strictly to the neoclassical rules. His other writings include volumes of poetry, an English grammar, and—despite his preference for neoclassical form—a laudatory introduction to the collected plays of his friend William Shakespeare.

Jonson acquired his learning and social stature through his own efforts. Raised in a poor section of London, he was a scholarship student at the Westminster School; and though he wanted to attend college, his stepfather, a bricklayer, apprenticed him to another bricklayer. To escape that trade he joined the army and served in the Netherlands, where he killed a man in single combat. He married after his return to London in 1582, but he and his wife were incompatible and lived apart after 1603.

In the 1580s, Jonson continued his studies on his own and worked as a strolling player; at this time he also began writing for Henslowe's theatre. In collaboration with Thomas Nashe, he wrote *The Isle of Dogs,* a satire which proved so offensive that the authorities imprisoned everyone involved with the production, including Jonson, and closed all the London theatres. Jonson was imprisoned again the next year, this time for killing an actor in a duel.

When he was released, he became involved in the "war of the theatres," using his satiric comedies to ridicule his rivals. He had made many friends among the nobility, and when James I inherited the throne in 1603, Jonson became prominent at court. His collaboration on the satire *Eastward Ho!* landed him in prison again, but later he was restored to royal favor and became the court poet.

From 1605 to the early 1630s, he composed court masques, expanding the form to include an "anti-masque," a burlesque of the main theme. He often quarreled with the designer Inigo Jones over the use of spectacular settings; Jonson felt that such settings detracted from his poetic allegories. Eventually Jonson retired, though he wrote several plays for public theatres before his death in 1637. Two of his other well-known plays are *Sejanus: His Fall* (1603) and *Bartholomew Fair* (1614).

(© Carol Rosegg)

THE DUCHESS OF MALFI
The most important writer of the Jacobean period was John Webster. His drama *The Duchess of Malfi* is a passionate study of love, incest, and political intrigue in the Renaissance and contains violence, horror, grotesque comedy, and lyrical poetry. In this scene, from a production at the Shakespeare Theatre in Washington, D.C., we see Kelly McGillis as the Duchess, Robert Tyree as Antonio, and Caroline Clay as Cariola.

John Webster

As we pointed out, during the Jacobean period and then in the reign of Charles I from 1625 to 1649—the Caroline period—drama in England began to change. Plays became more sensational, more violent, and more contrived than the great Elizabethan dramas. One example is *The Duchess of Malfi* by John Webster (c. 1580–1630), probably the most renowned tragedy of the Jacobean era.

In his preface to his play *The White Devil,* Webster shows a thorough knowledge of Latin and a thorough understanding of drama. He also reviles most playgoers as "ignorant asses," makes frequent use of Latin proverbs and quotations, relates an anecdote about Euripides, and praises his fellow playwrights.

But aside from the fact that he was a man of wit and learning, little is known about John Webster's life. An actor of that name toured with an English company in Germany in 1596, and a man named John Webster was admitted to the Middle Temple to study law in 1598; it is possible that one of these was the playwright, or that both were.

Webster's early plays, written in collaboration with Thomas Dekker, included two popular comedies: *Westward Ho!* (1604) and *Northward Ho!* (1605). Two tragedies—*The White Devil* (l612) and *The Duchess of Malfi* (1613–1614)—are considered his masterpieces. Webster also wrote a tragicomedy, *The Devil's Law Case* (1623), and collaborated with several playwrights on other works. The playwright Thomas Heywood refers to Webster in the past tense in 1634, so it is assumed that Webster was dead by then.

Though his life is shrouded in uncertainty, and though his dramatic output was small in comparison with that of other Jacobean playwrights, Webster is considered a major playwright because of his two tragedies, which, after Shakespeare's, are regarded as the finest of the time. Both plays are passionate studies of love and political intrigue in Renaissance Italy. They contain violence and horror, grotesque comedy and satire, and lyrical poetry. Throughout these plays there is a brooding, ominous sense of pervasive evil and corruption. It is partly because of their spectacular elements and melodrama that Webster's plays are ranked below Shakespeare's.

The Duchess of Malfi is a terrifying study of the extent and destructiveness of human evil. After the death of her first husband, the duchess of Malfi is forbidden to remarry by her scheming brothers—one a duke and the other a cardinal—who want to acquire her duchy. She defies them by secretly marrying her steward, Antonio, but is betrayed to them by the servant Bosola. The evil brothers bide their time and then torment, torture, and finally murder the duchess and her children. Bosola, the main agent of these deeds, repents and warns Antonio that his life is in danger. In an effort to murder the cardinal, Bosola mistakenly kills Antonio. Bosola then attacks the cardinal, and the fight is joined by the duke, who by this point has been driven to insanity. In the struggle all three die.

Webster's pessimism, similar to the mood of some present-day dramas—"black comedies" and the like—is one reason why his tragedies are often revived.

Beaumont and Fletcher

Another significant development in English drama in the early 1600s was the mixing of serious and comic elements. Plays reflecting this development generally had many of the qualities of tragedy, but with a happy ending. Francis Beaumont (c. 1584–1616) and John Fletcher (1579–1625), two playwrights who often collaborated with each other, excelled at this form. We should note that coauthorship was not unusual in the English Renaissance. Since playwrights were paid by the script, they needed to produce dramas quickly; coauthorship could speed up the process. Some of Shakespeare's lesser-known plays, such as *Pericles* and *Two Noble Kinsmen,* are believed to have been written by Shakespeare with other playwrights.

(© Bettmann/Corbis)
Francis Beaumont.

During the English Renaissance, therefore, there were many well-known teams of writers; but the most famous of these collaborators were Beaumont and Fletcher. At one time, fifty-two plays were attributed to Beaumont and Fletcher jointly, but later scholarship has shown that they collaborated on no more than nine plays. The other plays were written by one or the other individually or with another playwright, but they are so similar in style and subject that the names of Beaumont and Fletcher are still linked to them.

In plays like *Philaster* (c. 1610) and *A King and No King* (c. 1611), Beaumont and Fletcher accelerated the development of tragicomedy—a genre that focused on serious themes but called for a happy ending. Jacobean theatre audiences were becoming increasingly aristocratic and demanded romance and witty satire. The two men wrote plays in an ornate, superficial, and somewhat artificial style that had become popular and was later to be influential, especially during the Restoration.

(© Bettmann/Corbis)
John Fletcher.

Beaumont and Fletcher came from similar upper-class backgrounds. Beaumont's father was a justice of common pleas; Fletcher's father was president of a college at Cambridge and later bishop of Bristol and of London. Both playwrights attended college, but neither completed his degree. Beaumont also entered the Inner Temple in 1600 to study law. The names of the two men are first linked in 1607, in the introductory remarks to Jonson's *Volpone.* During their partnership, they are said to have roomed together in Bankside, where they shared everything, including clothes and women.

Beaumont's marriage in 1613 ended the partnership. His most famous solo play is *The Knight of the Burning Pestle,* a comedy and literary burlesque. He died in 1616. Fletcher, after the partnership broke up, collaborated with several other playwrights, chiefly Philip Massinger. Shakespeare and Fletcher worked together on *Two Noble Kinsmen* (1613) and *Henry VIII* (1613). When Shakespeare retired, Fletcher became the chief dramatist for the King's Men until his death in 1625.

Court Entertainment: The Masque

A form of theatre not found in either public or private theatres was the *masque,* an elaborate entertainment presented at court. The masque flourished in the early seventeenth century during the reigns of James I and Charles I. It can be considered one of a long line of entertainments that have been favored by royalty and the nobility. Sometimes they are closely allied to theatre, with numerous theatrical elements. At other times they are more closely related to pageants or royal processions arranged for the visit of a monarch to a city. Queen Elizabeth I was especially fond of elaborate processions that greeted her when she visited towns throughout the kingdom.

The masques favored by James I and Charles I had many affinities with theatrical productions—especially productions in Italy, by which they were strongly influenced. A masque was generally created to honor the king or a member of the royal family or the nobility. There was an emphasis on music and dance, and even more on spectacle: elaborate, painted backdrops and side pieces, as well as moving equipment such as clouds that rose or fell. Frequently, the performers were amateurs who were members of the court.

Masques usually incorporated mythological and allegorical figures—gods, goddesses, nymphs, signs of the zodiac, and the like. Whatever the story, in the end the monarch proved to be the hero. Masques were colorful, ornate, and immensely expensive. James I spent more money on one masque in 1618 than he spent on all the standard theatrical productions presented at his court during the entire 22 years of his reign. The historical importance of the masque lies not in its elegance or ornateness, however, but in the fact that it introduced Italianate scenic practices to the London stage.

The major playwright of the masque form was Ben Jonson, but he stopped writing masques in the early 1630s because he believed that his literary contribution was being overshadowed by the elaborate scenic trappings. Many other dramatists continued to provide scripts for masques, but in this form the most important creative artist—as Jonson had correctly pointed out—was the designer. The most famous designer was Inigo Jones (1573–1652).

Inigo Jones

In the Elizabethan and Jacobean periods, English theatre followed scenic practices that had evolved from medieval theatre. It was Inigo Jones, court architect and designer for both James I and Charles I, who brought Italian innovations in scene design to England. These included temporary proscenium (picture-frame) arches, systems for changing scenery, and painted-perspective stage sets. In his settings for court masques, Jones introduced methods of staging that were to become standard after the Restoration.

Jones's designs were influenced by the work of Giuilo Parigi (c. 1570–1635) and Palladio, which he had studied on visits to Italy. Jones was the son of a London cloth worker and therefore not wealthy, but he had traveled to Italy by 1603 to learn painting and design. He became a portrait painter for Christian IV of Denmark before a commission from Christian's sister, Queen Anne of England, brought him to the court of James I. His first stage designs were the scenery and costumes for *The Masque of Blackness* (1605), which also began his long and stormy collaboration with the court poet Ben Jonson.

(© National Trust Photographic Library/ John Hammond/The Image Works)

Inigo Jones.

By 1610, Jones had become surveyor of works to Henry, prince of Wales; but Henry died in 1612, and Jones lost his job. He went back to Italy to study in 1613–1614 and on his return to England was appointed surveyor of works to James I, a position that involved building, rebuilding, and improving royal houses. In 1619–1622 Jones built the Banqueting House at Whitehall as a home for the court

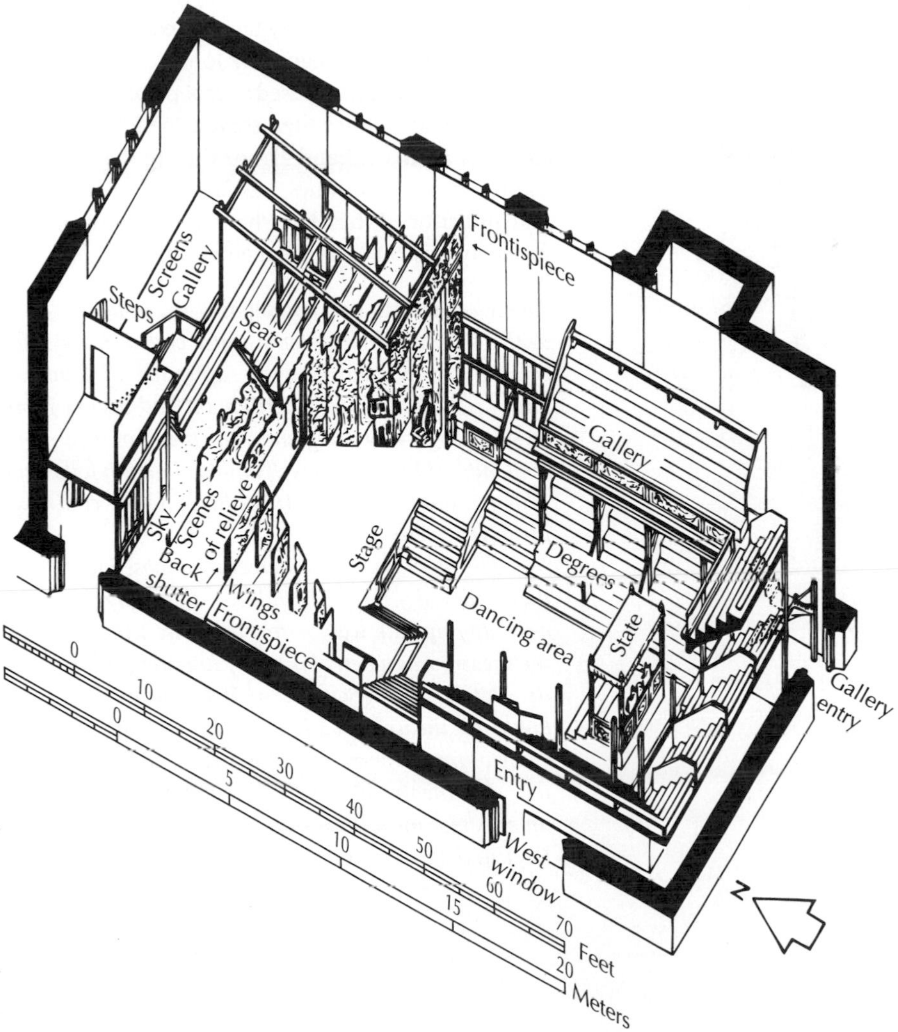

(Richard Leacroft, *The Development of the English Playhouse*, Cornell University Press, Ithaca, N.Y., 1973. By permission of Reed Book Services/Methuen London.)

A DESIGN BY INIGO JONES

This conjectural reconstruction of Jones's design for the pastoral *Florimene* (1635) shows a large hall in Whitehall palace arranged for a court masque. Italianate scenic devices were introduced into these spectacles: painted angled wings and back shutters shifted in grooves were used to give an illusion of depth.

(© Lebrecht Music and Arts/The Image Works)

DESIGN BY INIGO JONES FOR "A FIERY SPIRIT"
This was to appear in Thomas Campion's "Lord's Masque." Inigo Jones was the chief designer of court masques during the reigns of James I and Charles I. He designed theatre spaces, the scenery, and the costumes, such as the one shown here.

masques, but it was not used for this purpose because James's successor, Charles I, did not want its ceiling ruined by torch smoke. Jones's restoration of Saint Paul's Cathedral influenced the architect Christopher Wren and initiated the English classical school of architecture.

Jones was vain and dictatorial, though an able administrator. His famous quarrel with Jonson resulted in Jonson's loss of favor at court; thereafter, scenic splendor became the chief purpose of the masque, culminating in the wonders of *Salmacida Spolia* in 1640. Jones delighted his court audiences with new machinery, such as revolving platforms, that he used to make seemingly magical scene changes. All the elaborately fanciful costumes for the masques were also designed by Jones.

Political troubles caused a suspension of masques after 1640, and Jones then served the king as a designer of field arms and armor during the civil war. Captured in 1645, Jones was stripped of his estate and imprisoned, but later he was released and his property was restored. He died in 1652.

Though Charles I was not deposed—and beheaded—until 1649, the English Renaissance ended in 1642, for by then the civil war between supporters of Charles I and the Puritan-backed Parliament had begun. From 1649 through 1660, England was ruled not by a monarch but by Oliver Cromwell and his Puritan followers. When Cromwell died in 1658, his son took control of the government.

The Puritans were vehemently opposed to theatre; they believed—to put it mildly—that playgoing was an inappropriate way to spend leisure time and that the theatre was a den of iniquity and taught immorality. Not surprisingly, then, in 1642 the Puritans outlawed all theatrical activities. Although surreptitious entertainments were staged between 1642 and 1660, the vital theatre of the English Renaissance came to an end. Not until the restoration of the monarchy was English theatre to flourish again.

Summary

The English Renaissance was as theatrically rich as the Italian Renaissance. The greatness of this era was based on the development of brilliant drama: some critics believe that the plays of Christopher Marlowe, William Shakespeare, and Ben Jonson have been unequaled in the history of theatre. English drama did not follow neoclassical principles but refined the episodic structure which had originated in the Middle Ages.

The imaginative staging techniques of the English Renaissance were also a refinement of medieval conventions. The Elizabethan theatre, with its open platform stage and tiring house, allowed for rapid scenic transformations through the use of language, properties, entrances, and exits. There were two types of playhouses: larger outdoor public theatres; and smaller, more expensive indoor private theatres. Many of the performers—all of whom were male—were greatly renowned; they included Edward Alleyn of the Lord Admiral's Men and Richard Burbage of the Lord Chamberlain's Men.

English theatres open to the public did not use Italian staging practices such as the proscenium arch or painted-perspective wing-and-shutter scenery. These scenic innovations were introduced into court entertainments—masques—designed by Inigo Jones for James I and Charles I.

Early Tudor [1485–1558]

Theatre History

- *Interludes* written and staged by professionals at court
- English school drama (1500–1580): *Ralph Roister Doister* and *Gammer Gurton's Needle*

Cultural and Historical Developments

- 100 Years' War (1338–1453)
- War of Roses between rival houses of York and Lancaster (1455–1485)
- Henry VII begins reign (1485)
- Henry VIII reigns (1509) *(right)*
- Thomas More's *Utopia* (1516)
- Church of England established by Henry VIII (1534)

Elizabethan [1558–1603]

Theatre History

- Boys' acting companies established by Elizabeth I at court
- Thomas Sackville and Thomas Norton's *Gorboduc*
- Master of revels made licenser of plays and companies; James Burbage's Earl of Leicester's Men (1574)
- The Theatre, first permanent public playhouse; Blackfriars, first indoor private theatre, opened (1576)
- Thomas Kyd (1558–1594), *Spanish Tragedy*
- Christopher Marlowe (1564–1593), *The Tragical History of Doctor Faustus (below)*

- London theatres close during a plague (1593–1594)
- Leading actors in London: Edward Alleyn (1566–1626), Richard Burbage (c. 1567–1619), Will Kempe (d. 1603)
- Globe Theatre built (1599)
- William Shakespeare (1564–1616) *(right)*

Cultural and Historical Developments

- Elizabeth I, queen of England, rules (1558–1603) *(below)*

- Sir Walter Raleigh's expedition to Virginia (1584)
- Execution of Mary, queen of Scots (1587)
- England's naval defeat of Spanish armada (1588)

continued

Jacobean [1603–1625]

Theatre History

- Ben Jonson (1572–1637), *Every Man in His Humour*
- Inigo Jones (1573–1652), court architect and designer *(below)*

- John Webster (c. 1580–1630), *The White Devil*
- Francis Beaumont (c. 1584–1616) and John Fletcher (1579–1625), *Philaster*

Cultural and Historical Developments

- James I begins reign (1603)
- Jamestown, Virginia, founded (1607) *(below)*

- Hudson claims part of North America for United Provinces (1609)
- King James Bible (1611)
- Thirty Years' War begins (1618)
- Francis Bacon's *Novum Organum* (1620)

Caroline [1625–1649]

Theatre History

- John Ford (1586–c. 1637), *'Tis a Pity She's a Whore*
- Parliament closes British theatres; all theatrical activities outlawed (1642)

Cultural and Historical Developments

- Charles I begins reign (1625); dissolves Parliament (1629)
- English civil war (1642)
- Charles I beheaded (1649)

CHAPTER 7

The Theatre of the Spanish Golden Age

Corral of the Spanish Golden Age

The corrales were outdoor courtyard theatres used for secular drama during the Spanish golden age. These playhouses were similar in many ways to the public theatres in England during the Elizabethan era. Seen here is a corral that was uncovered accidentally in 1955, in Almagro, Spain. Note the platform stage, the balconies along the sides, and the openings at the rear of the stage.

(Courtesy Festival d'Almagro, Almagro, Spain)

Spain has had a unique and complex history. Located on the Iberian peninsula at the western end of the Mediterranean Sea, it is bounded on the east by the Mediterranean, on the west by Portugal and the Atlantic Ocean, and on the north by the Pyrenees—the mountains that separate it from France.

Background: The Spanish Golden Age

In the second century B.C.E., Spain (like many other regions) was conquered by the Romans and became part of the Roman empire. In 711 C.E., however, the Moors invaded from North Africa, and they soon controlled all of Spain except for certain areas in the extreme north. The Moors, with their Islamic culture and religion, were to rule Spain for the next 700 years. This Moorish domination had a lasting effect, even after Spain was retaken by Roman Catholic monarchies; Moorish influences appear later in architecture and the arts.

Attempts to reconquer Spain from the Moors began immediately after 711; and in the twelfth and thirteenth centuries, northern rulers in Spain began an earnest struggle to reconquer the south. It was not until the fifteenth century, though, that the entire peninsula was retaken from the Moors. This came during the reign of King Fernando and Queen Isabel. Fernando was king of Aragon; Isabel, after a struggle with other heirs, became the monarch of Castile and León. These two married in 1469 and thereafter consolidated their control of Spain.

For several reasons, 1492 was a significant year in their reign. The best-known event is Columbus's voyage to the western hemisphere. But 1492 was also the year when Fernando and Isabel drove the Jews out of Spain permanently. Spanish Jews were culturally and ethnically no different from Spanish Christians, but since they were not Catholics, they interfered with the goal of religious unanimity. A few years earlier, in 1478, Fernando and Isabel took control of the Spanish Inquisition, a religious tribunal which arbitrarily decided cases of heresy. Those found guilty had no court of appeal and were often banished, imprisoned, or burned at the stake. The Moors were expelled in 1609. Because of its expulsion of Moors and Jews, Spain lost some of its most notable doctors, philosophers, merchants, and scholars.

The Spain of Fernando and Isabel was, like other European countries, marked by religious intolerance; however, it was also rising to become a world power. Beginning with Columbus's discoveries and conquests in the Americas, Spain came to dominate Europe in the early part of the sixteenth century; it conquered other European lands and continued to control the seas. Spain was also successful in commerce and trade. By 1550, it was the leading power in Europe and was poised for what has come to be known as its "golden age," not only in conquest and commerce but also in the arts.

The year 1588, when its armada was defeated by England, marked the end of the unquestioned superiority of Spain as a sea power, but it continued to be a major factor in Europe for much of the sixteenth century. During this period, Spanish drama and theatre flourished.

Religious Theatre in Spain

After 711 many parts of Spain were occupied by the Moors, and because of this, the religious drama that thrived throughout much of Europe and England did not flourish in Spain until the country was united at the end of the fifteenth century. However, medieval Spain did produce examples of vernacular religious plays. Once religious drama established itself more fully, it became an important theatrical activity, and it remained important in Spain long after it had ended in other countries.

Spanish Golden Age
Year

1475 · 1500 · 1525 · 1550 · 1575 · 1600 · 1625 · 1650 · 1675 · 1750 · 1775

Theatre

- Juan del Encina's *The Eclogue of Placida and Victoriana* (1513)
- Bartolomé de Torres Naharro's *Propalladia* (1517)
- Lope de Rueda, Spain's first popular playwright (c. 1545)
- City councils assume responsibilities for the staging of autos (c. 1555)
- Corral de la Cruz; first permanent theatre in Spain (1579)
- Corral del Principe (1583)
- Women licensed to appear onstage (c. 1587)
- Strict censorship of plays (1608)
- Lope de Vega's *The Sheep Well* (1614)
- Felipe IV brings designer Cosme Lotti from Florence (1626)
- Cofradia de la Novena (actors' guild) established (1631)
- Calderón's *Life Is a Dream* (c. 1636)
- Coliseo, court theatre with proscenium arch, built (1640)
- Public theatres closed (1646–1651)
- Number of carros for autos increased from two to four (1647)
- First reference to Spanish designer José Caudi (1662)
- Autos sacramentales prohibited (1765)

Culture and Politics

- Spain united under Fernando and Isabel (1469)
- Inquisition established in Spain (1481)
- Jews expelled from Spain; Columbus discovers America, conquest of Granada (1492)
- Cortés conquers Aztecs (1519)
- Pizzaro takes Peru (1530)
- Opening of Potosí mines in Bolivia (1545)
- Jesuits begin missionary work in South America (1549)
- Felipe II (rules 1556–1598)
- Netherlands revolt against Spain (1567)
- Victory of Lepanto against Turks (1571)
- El Greco arrives from Greece (1575)
- Felipe II annexes Portugal (1580)
- Defeat of Spanish armada (1588)
- Felipe III (rules 1598–1621)
- Cervantes's *Don Quixote,* Part 1 (1605)
- Expulsion of Moors (1609)
- Felipe IV (rules 1621–1665)
- Velázquez completes painting *Vulcan's Forge* (1630)
- Revolt of Catalans and Portuguese (1640)
- Defeat of Spanish army by French at Rocroi (1643)
- Peace of the Pyrenees; Spain's power declines (1659)
- Charles II (rules 1665–1700)
- Murillo's *Immaculate Conception* (Murillo used this subject thirty times) (1678)
- Publication of Spanish Colonial Code (1680)
- Murillo dies (1617–1682)

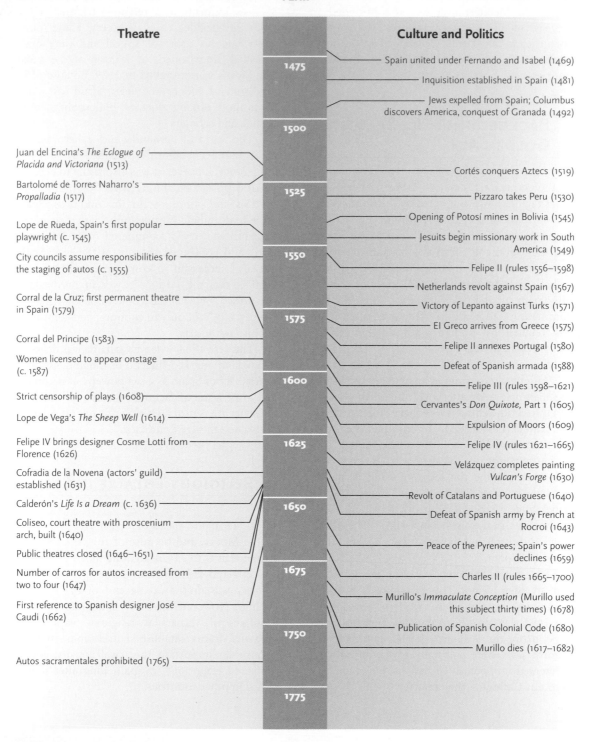

Religious Dramas: Autos Sacramentales

Religious dramas in Spain were originally produced inside churches and cathedrals as part of the services, just as they were elsewhere in Europe and England. In some parts of Spain, this practice—performing short religious dramas inside the sanctuary of a church—continued for many years. In fact, in Elche, a town in southern Spain, a mystery play telling the story of the death and assumption of the Virgin Mary, first performed in the fifteenth century, has since been presented continually and is still performed by the townspeople in the basilica of the cathedral during a festival each August.

Until roughly 1550, religious plays in Spain were similar to those produced elsewhere in medieval Europe; but after that time, in the last half of the sixteenth century, they took on distinctive characteristics that set them apart. These religious plays were written for Corpus Christi, a festival held in late May or early June—approximately 2 months after Easter—which celebrates the power of the sacraments. (Corpus Christi is also described in Chapter 4.) The plays presented at this festival came to be known as *autos sacramentales: auto* meaning a one-act play, and *sacramental* referring to the sacraments. In time, *auto sacramental* was the name given to any play presented at Corpus Christi, whether or not it was directly related to the sacraments.

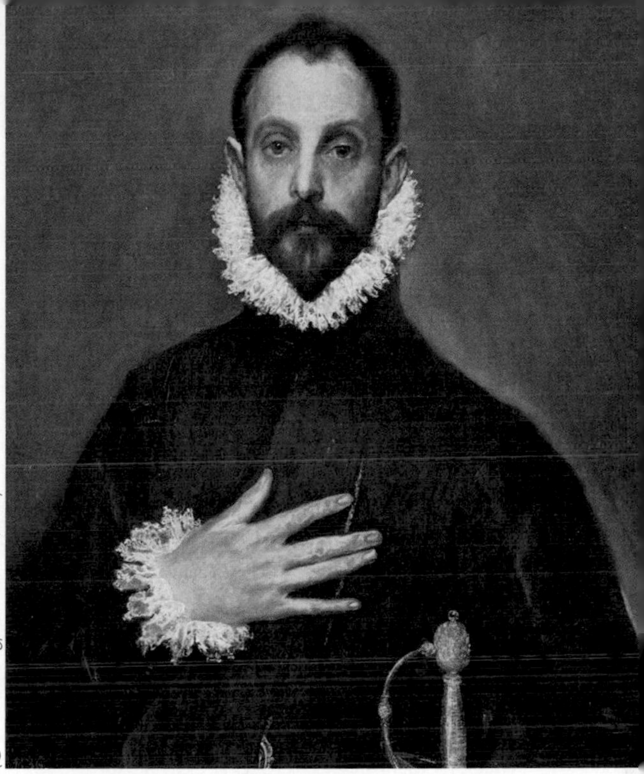

(© Erich Lessing/Art Resource, N.Y.)

EL GRECO: ARTIST OF THE GOLDEN AGE
El Greco (1541–1614) was a contemporary of the playwright Lope de Vega. The period at the end of the fifteenth century and the beginning of the sixteenth is referred to as the Spanish golden age because so many arts flourished then. The painting shown here, typical of El Greco's austere, magisterial, haunting work, is *Portrait of a Man with His Hand on His Breast* (c. 1585).

Autos sacramentales combined elements of medieval morality and mystery plays and could be based on secular as well as religious sources; they included supernatural, human, and allegorical characters. The one requirement was that they underscore the validity of the church's teachings.

The finest dramatists of the Spanish golden age, including Calderón, wrote autos—a fact that highlights the close relationship between religious and secular theatre in Spain. From 1647 until 1681, all the autos presented in Madrid were written by a single author—Calderón. After his death in 1681, there was a falling off in the quality of new autos; but they continued to be produced at Corpus Christi until 1765, when they were specifically prohibited. Autos were forbidden at that time because it was felt that they had become more secular and carnival-like and less religious; there had been a growing emphasis on the farces and dances that were interspersed between autos. For over 200 years, though, autos sacramentales, written by Spain's greatest dramatists, were an active, vital part of Spanish theatre.

(Courtesy Turisme d'Elx)

THE MYSTERY OF ELCHE
In the town of Elche in southern Spain, a medieval religious play has been produced continually since the fifteenth century. It is put on by the townspeople, who play all the parts, handing them down from one generation to the next. In this recent production, the Virgin Mary (on the left) is played by a young boy, as has been the custom for centuries.

Producing the Autos Sacramentales

In discussing the production of the autos sacramentales, we will focus on the city of Madrid, since its practices were similar to those of other localities.

In Madrid, religious plays were staged under the auspices of trade guilds until 1550. Sometime in the 1550s, however, the city council took over this responsibility and employed professional troupes to produce these plays. From about 1560 to 1592, a single professional company would present three autos at each festival. Beginning in 1592, four plays were produced in Madrid each year and two professional companies were employed. This continued until 1647, after which only two plays were given annually. Religious dramatic performances continued in Spain until 1765, when they were prohibited.

Before the Corpus Christi festival, the troupe employed to perform the autos would be required to give one preview performance for the king and another for the city council. The public performances would then be given at sites within Madrid specifically designated by the city government.

Troupes that performed at Corpus Christi would later tour neighboring villages and would also perform in public theatres. The companies chosen to present the autos were paid a handsome fee and, in addition, obtained funds from other public performances for which they were given exclusive rights.

Religious plays were mounted on wagons, called *carros,* which could be moved into place for the festival and moved elsewhere at other times. Before 1647, two carros were used for each play, to serve as a place for storing any scenic elements, changing costumes, and making entrances and exits. A third wagon was joined to these two carros to serve as a platform stage. After 1647, a fixed platform was used at each playing space and four carros were used: two drawn up at the rear of the platform stage and one at each side. By the 1690s, the platform stage was 36 feet deep and nearly 50 feet long. Each of the four carros was approximately 16 feet long and 36 feet high. Since the presentations were financed and administered by the local government, carros were built and stored in a city workshop.

Secular Theatre in Spain

An unusual feature of theatre in the Spanish golden age is that religious and secular professional theatre flourished side by side for quite a long time. We have already pointed out that Spanish playwrights created dramatic works for both theatres, and the two were equally professional with regard to other aspects, such as acting and production.

Secular theatre emerged in Spain at much the same time as professional religious theatre—during the sixteenth century. One way to trace this parallel development is through the career of Lope de Rueda.

LOPE DE RUEDA

During the sixteenth century, as we have noted, secular theatre emerged in Spain at much the same time as professional religious theatre. One important figure in this development was Lope de Rueda (c. 1510–1565), an actor, manager, and playwright, who was the most popular performer of the early Spanish theatre.

(Billy Rose Theatre Collection, New York Public Library at Lincoln Center, Astor, Lenox, and Tilden Foundations)

Lope de Rueda.

Rueda is first heard of in 1542, when he appeared as an actor in religious plays in Seville and was probably managing his own company. Nine years later, in 1551, he was summoned by the governors of Valladolid to perform before Felipe II. He continued to live and perform there and to write and direct autos sacramentales for the Corpus Christi festivals—receiving a large annual salary—until 1558. At the same time, he began writing popular secular plays, which became part of the lively theatrical activity that was growing throughout Spain.

A Spanish novelist of the golden age, Miguel de Cervantes, saw the young Rueda perform and praised him as an actor and writer of verse. Rueda wrote five full-length plays (secular plays came to be known as *comedias*) and about a dozen short comic pieces, called *pasos,* one of which is *The Olives.* Pasos were entertaining sketches drawn from events in daily life. Written in prose, the plots featured earthy humor and colloquial speech. They poked fun at the manners of the period and were used as humorous interludes between acts of longer works and sometimes were even incorporated into them. The characters depicted conventional figures such as simpletons and masters. Rueda excelled at playing fools and rascals. Several of Rueda's longer works survive, including *The Frauds, Medora, Armelina,* and *Eufemia.*

There were no permanent theatres during Rueda's lifetime. As *autor,* or author-manager, of his troupe, Rueda toured extensively throughout Spain with his company, building his reputation as a performer and manager. These first professional companies often traveled as strolling players, carting their own equipment along with them. In addition to performances at court, they sometimes performed in palace halls, but typically plays were presented in city squares or courtyards and were attended by the townspeople, demonstrating the adaptability and versatility of Spain's early secular theatre, which Rueda did much to popularize.

In the period just after Rueda, Miguel de Cervantes (1547–1616), best known for his novel *Don Quixote,* also wrote plays, though not of the quality of those that would come later from the playwrights of the golden age.

It is worth noting that as a theatrical tradition began to emerge in Spain, it was geographically dispersed. It developed not only in Madrid, which became the capital beginning in 1560, but also in Seville, Granada, Cordova, Barcelona, Valencia, and elsewhere.

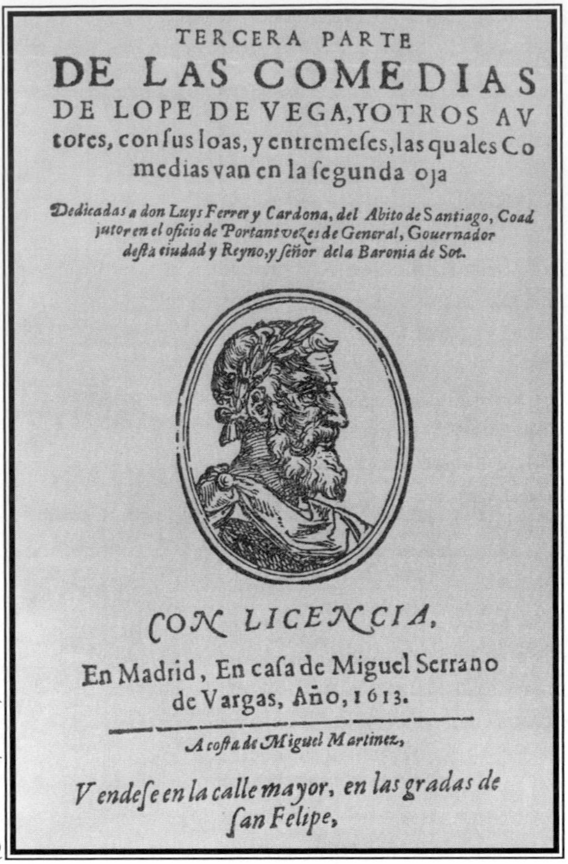

TERCERA PARTE
DE LAS COMEDIAS
DE LOPE DE VEGA, Y OTROS AV
tores, con ſus loas, y entremeſes, las quales Co
medias van en la ſegunda oja

Dedicadas a don Luys Ferrer y Cardona, del Abito de Santiago, Coad jutor en el oficio de Portant veзes de General, Gouernador deſta ciudad y Reyno, y ſeñor dela Baronia de Sot.

CON LICENCIA,
En Madrid, En caſa de Miguel Serrano de Vargas, Año, 1613.

A coſta de Miguel Martinez,

Vendeſe en la calle mayor, en las gradas de ſan Felipe,

(© Bettmann/Corbis)

LOPE DE VEGA'S COMEDIAS
One of the most prolific dramatists of all time was Lope de Vega, a Spanish contemporary of Shakespeare. He wrote plays of all kinds: history plays, religious plays, and dramas that mixed comedy and tragedy. Most of his full-length plays were referred to as *comedias*. Shown here is the title page of a volume of comedias by Lope de Vega, issued in 1613.

We should also note that touring Italian commedia dell'arte performers were extremely popular in Spain in the 1570s and 1580s and significantly influenced the dramatists of the later Spanish golden age.

Secular Dramas: Comedias

By the end of the sixteenth century, the different forms of Spanish secular drama that would flourish throughout the seventeenth century had taken shape. The full-length plays of the Spanish golden age were originally known as *comedias nuevas,* and then simply as *comedias.* They were given this name whether they were serious, comic, or some mixture of the two; in fact, there was great freedom and flexibility in mixing serious and comic elements. Comedias usually dealt with themes of love and honor, and the leading characters were often minor noblemen.

Like English plays of the same period, comedias were episodic in form and did not adhere to the neoclassical rules. The three unities of time, place, and action were for the most part ignored, though the unity of time was frequently observed within each act of a comedia; the supernatural was often an element, and comedias were written in three acts rather than five. A comedia was usually about 3,000 lines long.

We can get some idea of the episodic nature of comedias and the mixture of elements in them by looking at two plays by Lope de Vega, a playwright we will discuss shortly. The first, *The King, The Greatest Mayor,* was originally performed in 1620. Before the actual play, there is an amusing comic prologue. Then comes the play itself. *The King, The Greatest Mayor* is serious, but it also has comic elements. It concerns a farmer who promises his daughter Elvira to a peasant, Sancho. Sancho seeks approval for the marriage from his lord, Don Tello. Don Tello agrees, but when he sees Elvira, he wants her for himself. He postpones the wedding and later kidnaps Elvira. As the play unfolds, it seems to have all the ingredients of sparkling drama: a clash between peasants and the nobility, a wronged peasant, a kidnapping, a beautiful maiden in distress. The action moves rapidly from place to place, and there is a blend of comedy and suspense.

As the play continues, Sancho appeals to the king to help him regain Elvira from Don Tello; after several complications, the king arrives in disguise. When the king discovers that Don Tello has forcibly seduced Elvira, he orders Don Tello to marry her and then has him executed so that Elvira will be honorably widowed and can marry Sancho. *The King, the Greatest Mayor* has a total of thirteen scenes. Such a large number of scenes is typical of the episodic form and can also be seen in another play by Lope, *Fuente Ovejuna,* written earlier, about 1614.

Fuente Ovejuna—the title is often translated as *The Sheep Well*—is unusual in that its hero is not one person but an entire village. The commander of the area is a womanizer who is attempting to seduce a village maiden when he is thwarted by a peasant. Enraged, the commander beats the peasant and the girl's father and carries her off. The villagers are upset, but inclined to be cautious. However, when the young woman returns, nearly having been ravished by the commander, she shames them into killing him. They know they will not go unpunished by the authorities, but they decide to be steadfast in maintaining that the commander was slain not by any one person but by the whole village. Despite torture, they stick by their story. In the end the king and queen, after debating their difficult decision, choose to let the townspeople go.

In true episodic fashion, *Fuente Ovejuna* moves over a wide range of locations: from the commander's headquarters in the district to a public square in the village to a chamber in the offices of the rulers (Fernando and Isabel) to the open countryside to the town square to the house of the commander. The play also has a large cast of characters.

(© Donald Cooper/Photo*stage*, England)

FUENTE OVEJUNA

Most of the plays written by Lope de Vega and his contemporaries featured powerful individuals. Generally, the hero or heroine was a single person, who had allies and enemies. For this reason, a particularly unusual play of the period was Lope de Vega's *Fuente Ovejuna,* shown here in a production at the National Theatre in London. The hero of this play was not an individual but an entire village, which stands up against authority and eventually triumphs.

In form, therefore, plays of the Spanish golden age are very close to Elizabethan drama. There are differences in subject, however: conflicts of love and honor, daring adventures, melodramatic confrontations, and rescues are the essence of the Spanish plays. Also, there is a mixture of the serious and the comic, as mentioned above. Unlike a tragedy such as Shakespeare's *King Lear* or a comedy such as his *Twelfth Night,* a Spanish play of this period would seem closer to the popular melodramatic entertainments of our own day: swashbuckling films of the 1940s, romantic novels, and soap operas.

There were many types of comedias. One was known as *capa y espada,* "cape and sword." The name comes from the outfits usually worn by the minor nobility which the plays featured; it also suggests the daredevil, romantic quality of these plays. Another type of comedias featured saints, rulers, nobles, historical figures, legendary heroes, and mythological figures; this type was set in places and periods far removed from contemporary Spain. Dramas of the second type went by various names: *teatro, cuerpo* ("corpse"), and *ruido* ("noise"). Comedias written for court focused on scenes requiring elaborate stage machinery.

Before 1615, performances of comedias were preceded by a prologue, which was either a monologue or a short sketch; the intermissions between acts featured interludes, known as *entremeses,* some of which were spoken and others sung. Besides full-length plays, the Spaniards developed many popular, short, farcical forms which were presented on the same program with comedias.

Spanish Dramatists

The amount of dramatic activity during the Spanish golden age was remarkable. Although the two best-known dramatists are Lope de Vega and Calderón de la Borca, there were many others. One is Guillén de Castro (1569–1631), whose play about a Spanish hero, *The Cid,* was the source for a famous French play on the same subject by Corneille. Juan Ruiz de Alarcón y Mendoza (c. 1580–1639) was born in Mexico but wrote plays in Madrid between 1615 and 1625. Tirso de Molina (c. 1584–1648) is said to have written 400 plays; he wrote the first known play about Don Juan and is often compared to Lope and Calderón.

LOPE FÉLIX DE VEGA CARPIO

Lope de Vega (1562–1635), one of the most prolific dramatists of all time, was said to have written 1,500 plays (although scholars now suspect that 800 is a more realistic estimate; of these, 470 survive). Lope established a distinctive episodic structure for Spanish drama, and it is one of history's most fascinating coincidences that he lived at exactly the same time as Shakespeare and wrote in a similar form. Lope's plays, like Shakespeare's, have many scenes and large casts of characters, and they range widely over both time and space. Besides his plays, Lope wrote twenty-one volumes of prose and poetry.

(Bibliothèque Nationale de France)

Lope Félix de Vega Carpio.

As a dramatist, Lope had one aim: to please the audience. He made this point clear in a treatise, "The New Art of Playwriting" (c. 1609), in which he also defended his episodic style. Lope established the popularity of the three-act verse comedia in Spain, but he wrote plays in every genre, covering almost every possible topic and using characters from all parts of Spanish society. Several of his plays, including *The Sheep Well* (*Fuente Ovejuna,* c. 1614), deal with attempts by peasants to secure justice; others, like *The Dog in the Manger* (c. 1615), are "cape and sword" plays revolving around the intrigues of the minor nobility. Though Lope preferred happy endings, he wrote several tragedies, including *The Knight from Olmedo* (c. 1620–1625), one of his finest works. Lope's other well-known plays include *The Foolish Woman* (c. 1613); *The Flowers of Don Juan* (c. 1615); *The King, The Greatest Mayor* (c. 1620); and *Punishment without Revenge* (c. 1631), to name just a few.

Translations of his works were circulated throughout Europe and were influential in the development of French theatre.

It is difficult to imagine when Lope found time for writing, for he led a most active life. Born in 1562 to a working-class family in Madrid, he attended several Jesuit universities and at one point studied for the priesthood. Abandoning school, he joined the navy, took part in an expedition to the Azores, and became embroiled in the first of his many love affairs. He was banished from Madrid for 8 years because of one of his intrigues but immediately broke the ban to kidnap and marry a young noblewoman. He then sailed with the Spanish armada; on his return to Spain, he served several noblemen. After the death of his first wife, he had an affair with the actress Micaela de Luján that provided further stimulus to his writing career and also provided him with several children. However, when Lope was married again, it was not to Micaela but to a wealthy woman.

A growing interest in religion led Lope de Vega to join a lay confraternity; and in 1614, when he was widowed for the second time, he became a priest. Neither his playwriting nor his womanizing was affected by his priesthood. Felipe III appointed Lope director of the court theatre, a post he held until his death in 1635.

PEDRO CALDERÓN DE LA BARCA

After Lope de Vega died, Pedro Calderón de la Barca (1600–1681) became Spain's most popular playwright. Calderón's plays are written in a variety of styles. Many revolve around the favorite Spanish concerns—love and honor—and some examine violent family situations. In *Life Is a Dream* (c. 1636), he develops the idea that human beings are responsible for their own actions and must choose a path from a maze of possibilities.

(Bibliothèque Nationale de France)

Pedro Calderón de la Barca.

For court entertainments, Calderón wrote and produced poetic musical dramas like *Love, the Great Enchanter* (1637). His religious plays (autos sacramentales), like *Belshazzar's Feast* (1634) and *The Great Theatre of the World* (1649), combine image-filled poetry with philosophy. Among his popular secular plays, written for the public theatre, are *The Constant Prince* (1629), *A House with Two Doors Is Difficult to Guard* (1629), *The Physician of His Own Honor* (1635), *Secret Vengeance for Secret Insult* (1635), *The Mayor of Zalamea* (1642), and *Beware of Still Water* (1649). Many of his plays, translated first into French and then into English, influenced the playwrights of neoclassical France and Restoration England.

A year before his death, Calderón drew up a list of the plays he had written. It contained 111 secular plays and 70 autos sacramentales, a remarkable total for a man who had combined playwriting with several other careers.

As a young man, Calderón's first choice of a career was the priesthood. The son of a wealthy government official, he entered the Jesuit University of Alcala in 1614, the year he wrote his first play. After a few years of study, he left school in 1620 to enter government service. In 1623, he began to write plays for the court, becoming a leader among the court poets. His plays were also successful in the public theatres; and when Lope de Vega died in 1635, Calderón became director of the court theatre. The following year, Felipe IV knighted Calderón for his services.

Calderón changed careers again in 1640, joining the army to help suppress a Catalan rebellion. He proved to be a good soldier but was discharged 2 years later for medical reasons. With both the court theatres and the public theatres closed because of wars in Catalonia and Portugal and two deaths in the royal family (including the queen's), he was forced to find other work, and he became secretary to the duke of Alba. After the death of his brothers and his mistress, Calderón returned to religion and was ordained a priest in 1651. Though he stopped writing for the public stage, he continued to write autos for Corpus Christi. He was reappointed to his court post as director of theatre in 1663 and held that position until his death in 1681.

(Ros Ribas)

LIFE IS A DREAM
Two men were the major playwrights of the Spanish golden age: Calderón de la Barca and Lope de Vega. It was a period—partly coinciding with the Elizabethan era in England—in which theatre flourished in Spain. The actor here, Joaquín Notario, appears in *La Vida Es Sueño (Life Is a Dream)* by Calderón de la Barca, in a production of the Compañía Nactional de Teatro Clásico of Almagro, Spain.

Female Playwrights

There were a number of female playwrights in Spain during the seventeenth century. Most of their works were not produced during their lifetimes; however, recent scholarship has shown that these women wrote texts which subverted many of the traditions of the comedias and called into question the traditional views of gender roles, love and honor, and political authority. In addition, the female playwrights exhibited, within their dramas, great awareness of the theatrical traditions of the golden age; and in some instances male dramatists seem to have borrowed from their plays.

Six female playwrights of the Spanish golden age whose works have gained significant scholarly attention are Angela de Azevedo, Ana Caro Mallén de Soto, Leonor de la Cueva y Silva, Feliciana Enríquez de Guzmán, María de Zayas y Sotomayor, and Sor Juana Inés de la Cruz.

Except for Sor Juana, little is known about the lives of these playwrights, including their dates of birth or death. It is believed that Caro may have earned money for autos she wrote between 1641 and 1645. Zayas was a well-known literary figure who wrote prose and poetry. She was very much involved in the literary life of Madrid, receiving praise from many notable authors including Lope de Vega.

Sor Juana Inés de la Cruz (1651–1695), a nun, was born Juana de Asbaje y Ramirez, in San Miguel Nepantla, Mexico. Sor Juana, who spent her life in Mexico, wrote *The Trials of a Noble House* (1683) and *Love the Greater Labyrinth* (1689). These secular dramas were probably produced at the palaces of governmental officials. Her sacramental play *The Divine Narcissus* was published in Mexico in 1690. Sor Juana also wrote many other short dramatic works and poems, as well as prose.

Producing the Comedias

The Corrales

The nonreligious plays of writers like Lope de Vega and Calderón were staged in public theatres known as *corrales.* Corrales were constructed in existing courtyards; like Elizabethan public theatres, they were open-air spaces with galleries and boxes protected by a roof. These courtyard theatres were temporary at first but later became permanent spaces. The two most famous, both in Madrid, were the Corral de la Cruz (1579) and the Corral del Principe (1583).

The stage in a corral was a platform erected opposite the entrance to the courtyard. Access to the yard was usually through a street building; there were also several additional entranceways for other seating areas. The yard floor, or patio, was primarily an area for standing, like the pit of an Elizabethan public theatre; in Spanish corrales, the noisy groundlings were known as *mosqueteros* ("musketeers"). At the front of the patio, near the stage, a row of stools—later, a small number of benches called *taburetes*—were set up, separated from the rest of the yard by a railing. It is believed that in the later 1600s or early 1700s, the straight benches may have been replaced by semicircular benches called *lunetas*—literally, "small moons."

In the back wall opposite the stage, above the main entranceway in the yard, was a gallery known as the *cazuela,* or "stew pot." This was an area where women could sit; it had its own separate entrance and was carefully guarded to prevent men from entering. Above the cazuela, there was a row of boxes for local government officials; above these boxes was a larger gallery for the clergy, which may also have been divided to provide another section for unescorted women. At the back of the

(Museo Municipal de la Pacheca, Madrid)

COMBA'S VERSION OF THE CORRAL DEL PRINCIPE
This nineteenth-century drawing is speculative and incorrect in almost all details, but it has been used frequently by theatre historians and thus has misled scholars attempting to reconstruct the Corral del Principe. The differences between Comba's version and the reconstruction based on Allen's research are obvious.

A SPANISH CORRAL This drawing is based on John J. Allen's research on the Corral del Principe in Madrid. Note the various elements of the corral: the yard (patio), the seating areas (boxes and galleries), and the platform stage with the tiring house behind it.

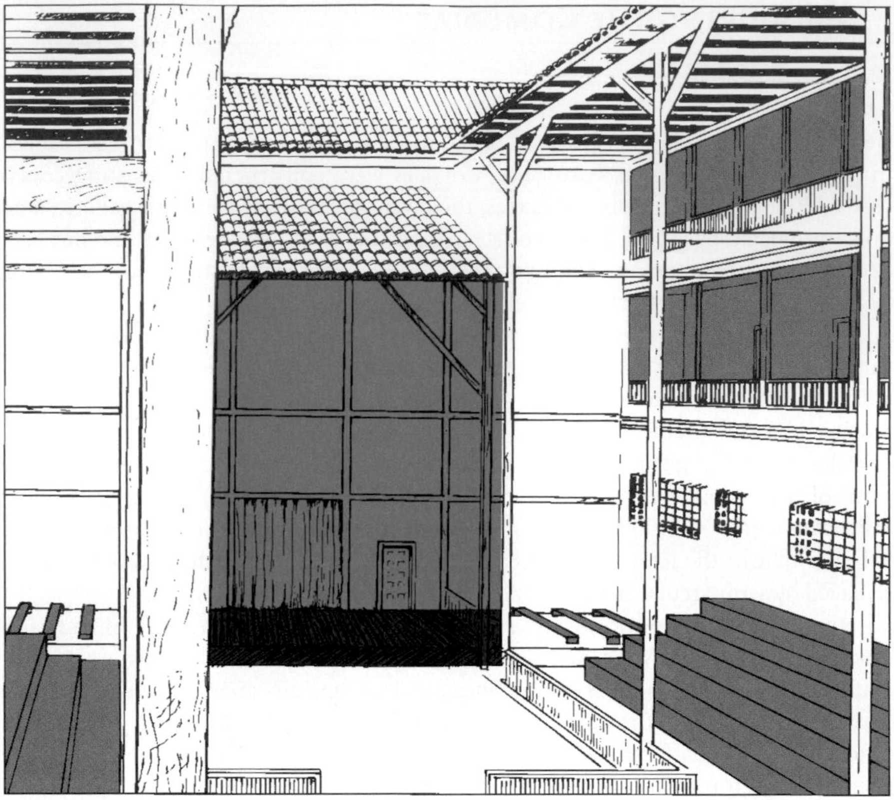

(Based on model, © 1983 by the Board of Regents of the State of Florida.)

patio, on one side of the main entrance, was a refreshments stand, the *alojero,* from which food and drinks were sold.

Along the side walls of the yard were *gradas*—raked, elevated benches. Above the gradas were *rejas*—windows, protected by grills, from which a play could be viewed. On the next level were boxes extended out from the buildings around the courtyard. A fourth floor contained *desvanes* ("attics"), which were cramped boxes with low ceilings.

A corral held about 2,000 spectators: 1,000 places for men, 350 for women, and the rest reserved boxes and other accommodations for government officials and the clergy. Special arrangements had to be made for renting boxes; individual agreements would be negotiated between the owners and inhabitants of the buildings and the people who were leasing the corral.

Corrales, clearly, were quite different from the proscenium-arch theatres that were developing in Italy; a corral was much closer to an Elizabethan public theatre.

Scenery, the Stage, and Costumes

Scenic conventions in Spain were also similar to those in England. In Spain, the basic scenic element was a two- or three-story stage house constructed behind the platform stage. A curtain, props, and flats might be used in conjunction with the facade of the stage house. There were three openings for entrances, exits, and "reveals" and

DEBATES IN THEATRE HISTORY — What Was the Appearance of the Corral del Principe?

The appearance of the Corral del Principe in Madrid, possibly the most famous theatre building of the Spanish golden age, continues to be debated, because there are so many questions about the few surviving contemporary illustrations.

A major problem has arisen in reconstructing the Corral del Principe because one frequently reprinted sketch was misidentified. This drawing, done for a historical study published in 1888, has often been wrongly described as dating from the seventeenth century. Actually, the sketch was made by a nineteenth-century artist, J. Comba, and it is loosely based on surviving visual sources from the Spanish golden age and on theories developed in the book for which he drew it. Moreover, a carefully detailed reconstruction of the Corral del Principe by John J. Allen clearly shows that little in Comba's sketch is accurate.*

It is, therefore, surprising and unfortunate that, as Ronald Vince points out in his *Renaissance Theatre: A Historiographical Handbook,* "the drawing continues to illustrate books on theatre history. In fact, of half a dozen popular and readily accessible introductory texts in the field, each one published or revised after 1967, only one notes that the sketch was done in 1888. This same volume also adds 'that it is inaccurate in many details.' "†

As we noted in Chapter 6 with regard to Elizabethan theatre, there are many controversies among historians over pictorial sources. What is particularly interesting about this one is that although Comba's drawing is unquestionably inaccurate, it continues to be used as a source for reconstructing the most famous public theatre of the Spanish golden age. We have reproduced Comba's sketch for the purposes of this discussion; but as far as historic reconstruction is concerned, the issue—as Vince notes—is, "Why print the picture at all?"‡

*John J. Allen, *The Reconstruction of the Spanish Golden Age Playhouse: El Corral del Principe, 1593–1744,* University of Florida Press, Gainesville, 1983.
†Greenwood, Westport, Conn., 1984, p. 68.
‡Ibid.

one or two upper playing houses. The facade, therefore, served the same function as the Elizabethan tiring house. "Spoken decor"—that is, dialogue indicating locale—was also used.

The stage in a corral was a platform raised above the patio. The separated dressing rooms were behind a central curtain that led into the stage house. There was also a doorway on each side of the curtain. There were trapdoors on the stage, which were used for special effects. At each side of the platform was a railed area that was used for additional bench seating unless a production required the entire stage.

As we have noted, this kind of stage was much closer to the stage of an English public theatre than it was to the proscenium-arch stage in use in Italy. During the Spanish Renaissance, the proscenium arch was introduced only at court; again, this parallels developments in English theatre. The first proscenium-arch theatre in Spain was probably the Coliseo, a court theatre at the king's palace, the Buen Retiro, in Madrid; it was designed by an Italian, Cosme Lotti (d. 1643), and completed in 1640. Throughout most of the seventeenth century, Spanish monarchs, like English monarchs, had lavish spectacles staged for them at court. A unique Spanish court entertainment, influenced by Italian opera and intermezzi, was the *zarzuela,* a stylized musical drama with a story based on mythology and ornate scenic effects. One of the most famous *zarzuelas* was *Celos Aun del Aire Matan* (1660).

Costuming in Spain was also similar to practices in Renaissance England. In most instances, contemporary clothes were worn. At times, historical or mythical figures would be dressed more elaborately; Moors were almost always portrayed as villains, and any Moorish character would be dressed in some distinctive way. Where the budget permitted, costumes were extremely lavish, and individual performers often owned expensive, elaborate outfits.

Acting Companies

In Spain during the golden age, acting troupes consisted of sixteen to twenty performers and included women. Acting companies were regulated by local government; all plays and troupes had to be licensed. Some Spanish troupes were *compañias de partes,* that is, "sharing companies" like those of Elizabethan England. Other Spanish companies, however, were organized by a manager, the *autor,* who contracted performers for a specific period of time and oversaw all artistic and business decisions. Plays were purchased from dramatists, who were paid a set fee.

As in Elizabethan companies, actors played multiple roles. Typecasting was common, since the comedias had stock characters such as *gracioso* (a witty fool) and *barba* (an old man).

The Status of Actresses

As we noted above, Spanish acting troupes, unlike Elizabethan companies, included women. During the Middle Ages, in many places on the European continent—in contrast to England—women had been allowed to act in religious dramas, and the inclusion of actresses in Spanish Renaissance companies was an outgrowth of this custom.

The status of the actress in theatres of the Spanish golden age theatre is an intriguing subject. It should be noted that the Catholic church in Spain was generally opposed to theatre and considered performers untrustworthy and licentious; because of this, local governments frequently intervened in theatrical matters and closely monitored the plays presented in public theatres. Given the church's opposition to acting in general, it should not be surprising that the clergy were particularly wary of women performers.

Numerous laws were passed during the late 1500s in an attempt to restrict the employment of women in theatre. In 1587, however, women were legally permitted to work as performers. (Before this, women had sometimes performed, but more often Spanish theatre had followed the Elizabethan convention of using young men for female roles.) The church's dissatisfaction with women performers in public theatres led to a ban in 1596, but this was ineffective. After a great deal of debate, a new law was passed in 1599, which allowed only actresses who were the wives or daughters of company members and banned cross-dressing (that is, dressing in the clothing of the opposite sex). Again, however, these restrictions were ineffective and the practices continued. In addition, throughout the late sixteenth century and early seventeenth century, numerous laws restricted the kinds of dances women were allowed to perform in theatres, since the church considered many of these dances too sexual.

What is extremely interesting about all these laws is the evident discomfort of Spanish society with women performers. This is understandable in light of the fact that the society was male-dominated and in general took the male perspective. But it is perhaps less easy to understand why at one point cross-dressing was considered more acceptable than the appearance of women onstage when later it was not. An attempt to control women and concern for clearly defining sexual identity are obvious motivations for the laws; thus these laws reflect gender issues that transcended theatre.

DEBATES IN THEATRE HISTORY | A Lost Spanish Popular Entertainment?

In the mid-1600s, during the Spanish golden age, King Felipe IV organized spectacular musical extravaganzas that mixed stories drawn from mythology, dance, and spoken text. These entertainments, which borrowed from the Italian Renaissance intermezzi and operatic traditions, were presented at the king's summer home and hunting lodge, known as "de la Zarzuela," and so it lent its name to this genre of musical performance.

For the next century and a half, the *zarzuela* was immensely popular in Spain; however, the Italian-born fourth wife of King Fernando VII, who reigned from 1808 to 1833, brought Italian opera to the Spanish court, ending the royal support of the popular Spanish musical form. Still, in 1857, four composers established El Teatro Zarzuela, which continues to operate today, and which succeeded in reestablishing the popularity of the genre with mass audiences throughout the Spanish-speaking world, including Latin America and the Philippines. Among the best-known *zarzuelas* of the eighteenth and nineteenth centuries are *Wind Is the Happiness of Love* (1752) by José de Nebra, *Play with Fire* (1851) and *The Merry Barber of Lavapiés* by Francisco Asenjo Barbieri, and *The Feast of the Dove* (1894) by Tomás Bretón. *Zarzuelas* continued to be composed into the twentieth century, until civil war and political chaos engulfed Spain in the 1930s.

The *zarzuela* is very similar to the English ballad opera (discussed in Chapter 10) and also has some similarities with American musical comedy, particularly because it mixes song and spoken dialogue. The subject matter of the *zarzuela* is quite diverse; it is sometimes tragic and sometimes comic, and it can range from Spanish folklore to mythology to historical drama.

Yet even with its popularity and longevity, the *zarzuela* is not well known outside Spanish-speaking countries. Why has less attention been paid to this form than to Italian opera or to American musical comedy? There is probably no single answer to this question. The form is often described as a popular amusement first created for royalty and then for popular audiences in the nineteenth and twentieth centuries, with little literary or musical substance. Furthermore, the subject matter of the *zarzuela* is seen as less universal and thus less accessible to international audiences. As with many popular theatrical forms, the *zarzuela* has been marginalized in chronicles of theatre history.

However, this popular Spanish musical entertainment may be going through an international renaissance. In 1996, a series of recordings of nineteenth-century *zarzuelas* with outstanding casts and musical accompanists were released to critical acclaim. Only time will tell whether the *zarzuela* will take its place among other popular musical forms of theatre in recordings and on stages throughout the world.

Between 1650 and 1700, Spain experienced a military, political, economic, and cultural decline, and its golden age came to an end. During the golden age, however, the theatre of Spain had been as vital as that of Elizabethan England.

SUMMARY

During their golden age, the Spaniards developed dramatic and theatrical practices quite similar to those of Elizabethan England: the structure of Spanish comedias was episodic; Spanish corrales were reminiscent of English public theatres; and staging practices in the two countries were almost identical. But Spanish drama had features that were characteristically its own. The plays of its two greatest playwrights, Lope de Vega and Calderón de la Barca, and their contemporaries dealt with Spanish heroes and heroines: both common people and the nobility. Also, during the golden age, Spain—unlike other European countries—continued to produce religious drama, and women were employed as performers.

MILESTONES CHAPTER 7 THE THEATRE OF THE SPANISH GOLDEN AGE [1550–1650]

Theatre History

- Religious plays staged in Madrid under trade guilds until 1550
- Lope de Rueda (c. 1510–1565) *(below)*, paso *The Olives* and comedia *Eufemia*

- Autos sacramentales presented at Corpus Christi (late sixteenth century)

Cultural and Historical Developments

- Moors rule Spain (711–1469)
- Marriage of Fernando V of Aragón and Isabel I of Castile (1469)
- Spanish Inquisition (1478)
- Jews expelled from Spain; Columbus reaches America *(below)*; conquest of Granada (1492)

Golden Age [1550–1650]

Theatre History

- *Capa y espada* ("cape and sword") plays (seventeenth century)
- Autos sacramentales staged by city councils with professional companies; *carros* (wagons) used in staging autos (c. 1555)
- Lope Félix de Vega Carpio (1562–1635) *(below), The Sheep Well*

- Guillén de Castro (1569–1631), *The Cid*
- Touring Italian commedia dell'arte performers popular (c. 1570–1580)

Cultural and Historical Developments

- Cortés conquers Aztecs (1519–1521)
- Pizzaro takes Peru (1531–1533)
- Opening of Potosí mines in Bolivia (1545)
- Miguel de Cervantes, *Don Quixote*, Part I (1605)
- Jesuits begin missionary work in South America (1549)
- Felipe II rules (1556–1598)
- Netherlands revolt against Spain (1567)
- Victory of Lepanto against Turks (1571)
- El Greco, *The Burial of Count Orgaz* (1586)
- Defeat of Spanish Armada by England (1588)
- Felipe III rules (1598–1621)
- Expulsion of Moors (1609)
- Felipe IV rules (1621–1665)
- Diego Velázquez, *Las Meninas* (1656) *(detail, right)*

continued

Photo Credits: Lope de Rueda. (Billy Rose Theatre Collection, New York Public Library at Lincoln Center, Astor, Lenox, and Tilden Foundations) / Lope de Vega. (Bibliothèque Nationale de France) / Isabella giving money to Christopher Colombus. (Julio Donoso/Corbis-Sygma) / Doña Maria Augustina de Sarniento; detail from *Las Meninas*, by Velázquez. (Scala/Art Resource, N.Y.)

MILESTONES CHAPTER 7 THE THEATRE OF THE SPANISH GOLDEN AGE [1550–1650] *continued*

Golden Age [1550–1650]

Theatre History

- Corral de la Cruz, considered first permanent theatre in Spain (1579)
- Juan Ruiz de Alarcón y Mendoza (c. 1580–1639)
- Corral del Principe built (1583)
- Tirso de Molina (c. 1584–1648) writes first known play about Don Juan
- Women licensed to appear onstage (c. 1587)
- Female golden age playwrights: Angela de Azevedo, Ana Caro Mallén de Soto, Leonor de la Cueva y Silva, Feliciana Enriquez de Guzmán, Maria de Zayas y Sotomayor
- Women banned from acting (1596)
- Felipe IV brings designer Cosme Lotti from Florence (1626)
- Pedro Calderón de la Barca (1600–1681) *(below), Life Is a Dream*

- Coliseo, count theater with proscenium arch, built (1640) designed by Cosme Lotti (d. 1643)
- Sor Juana Inés de la Cruz (1651–1695), *The Divine Narcissus*
- *Celos aun del Aire Matan*, court spectacle with Italian influences known as the *zarzuela* (1660)
- Autos sacramentales prohibited (1765)

Cultural and Historical Developments

- Revolt of Catalans and Portuguese (1640)
- Defeat of Spanish army by French at Rocroi (1643)
- Peace of the Pyrenees; Spain's power declines (1659)
- Charles II rules (1665–1700)
- Bartolomé Esteban Murillo, *Immaculate Conception* (1678) *(below)*

- Publication of Spanish Colonial Code (1680)

Photo Credits: Calderón de la Barca (Bibliothèque Nationale de France) / Murillo's *Immaculate Conception* (Scala/Art Resource, N.Y.)

CHAPTER 8
FRENCH NEOCLASSICAL THEATRE

LE BOURGEOIS GENTILHOMME

One of Molière's most popular works is *Le Bourgeois Gentilhomme (The Bourgeois Gentleman)* about a self-important man who puts on airs, attempting to move into the upper class. He takes lessons of all kinds—dancing, fencing, reading—but in each case makes a fool of himself without realizing it. The scene here shows the would-be gentleman, Jourdain, on the right, fencing with his maid, Nicole, as his wife looks on. The oil painting on canvas is by Charles Robert Leslie.

(Bridgeman Art Library/Victoria and Albert Museum, London)

France in the sixteenth century had a political history different from that of England or Spain. In Spain, the political situation began to stabilize in the late fifteenth century under Fernando and Isabel, and during the sixteenth century the country prospered. With the succession of Elizabeth I to the throne in 1558, England too achieved unity and stability. In France, however, the 1500s were a time of unrest.

Background: France in the Sixteenth and Seventeenth Centuries

The instability in France in the sixteenth century was partly due to a religious civil war between Catholics and Protestants, who were known as Huguenots. The civil war was finally brought to an end in 1594, when Henri IV—a Protestant who ascended to the throne in 1589—converted to Catholicism. Although Henry had renounced Protestantism, he resolved the religious strife by issuing the Edict of Nantes. This revolutionary proclamation offered non-Catholics, especially Huguenots, equality and tolerance under French law.

In the seventeenth century, therefore, French society could finally stabilize and flourish—particularly under Louis XIV, who reigned from 1643 to 1715. Like England, the Netherlands, Spain, and Portugal, France profited from exploration of the new world. Among the important areas the French explored and colonized were Canada and the Louisiana Territory.

A particularly strong influence on both politics and culture in France was Italy. Many reasons can be cited for the Italianization of French society. This development had begun in the sixteenth century when members of the Médicis family—the renowned merchant-princes and patrons of the arts who ruled the prosperous Italian city of Florence during the Renaissance—married into the French royal family. Henri II, who ruled France from 1547 to 1559, married Catherine de Médicis; after Henri's death, the three succeeding monarchs were all sons of Catherine, and she continued to wield a strong influence on the French court. In 1610, when Louis XIII inherited the throne, he was only 9 years old, and his mother—Marie de Médicis—controlled the French government.

Another major political force during the reign of Louis XIII was Cardinal Richelieu, who also advanced Italian culture in France. In 1643, the year after Richelieu's death, Louis XIII died. His son, Louis XIV, was also a child—only 5 years old when he ascended to the throne—and the Italian-born Cardinal Mazarin, who had replaced Richelieu, wielded the real power. Thus French government and in turn French culture were heavily influenced by the Italians.

Because of the civil and religious unrest in France during the sixteenth century, the Renaissance arrived there later than in other European countries. As noted above, when it did arrive in full force, the French Renaissance had a decidedly Italian flavor. This was especially true in theatre, both in the types of plays that were written and in theatre architecture, scenery, and production. In contrast to the English and Spanish theatres, which were characterized by episodic drama performed on platform stages, French theatre in the midseventeenth century adhered to neoclassical models and to Italian theatre architecture as well as scene design.

French Drama

Early Drama, Popular Theatre, and Pageantry

Although French theatre did not come into full flower until a third of the way into the seventeenth century, there were various kinds of theatrical activity for many years before then.

In 1402, a religious group, the Confrérie de la Passion (Confraternity of the Passion), was organized in Paris to present religious plays. For over a century it presented dramas sporadically. In the first part of the sixteenth century, the Confrérie used various locations in Paris for its presentations;

Neoclassical France

Year

1500 · 1525 · 1550 · 1575 · 1600 · 1625 · 1650 · 1675 · 1700 · 1725

Theatre

- Confrérie de la Passion (founded 1402) given monopoly of theater in Paris (1518)
- Religious plays prohibited; Hôtel de Bourgogne opens; perspective scenery used for first time at Lyon for performance celebrating marriage of Henri II and Catherine de Médicis (1548)
- Alexandre Hardy, first professional playwright, flourishes (1597)
- Valleran le Comte (King's Players), first important theatrical manager (1598)
- Farce players, Turlupin, Gaultier-Garguille Gros-Guillaume popular (1610–1625)
- Théâtre du Marais (1634)
- Corneille's *Le Cid* (1636)
- Richelieu's Palais Cardinel opens (later renamed Palais-Royal) (1641)
- New Marais with proscenium arch (1644)
- Torelli brings Italianate innovations to France (1645)
- Bourgogne remodeled (proscenium added) (1647)
- Vigarini comes to France (1659)
- Molière's troupe given Palais-Royal (1660)
- Molière's *The Miser* (1668)
- Jean-Baptiste Lully given monopoly of musical performances in Paris (1672)
- After Molière's death, Marais and his company amalgamated by Louis XIV (1673)
- Racine's *Phaedra* (1677)
- Comédie Française founded (1680)
- Comédie Française gets new theatre to be used until 1770 (1689)
- Parisian commedia troupe expelled (1697)

Culture and Politics

- Exploration of Gulf of St. Lawrence by Jacques Cartier (1534–1535)
- Henri II (rules 1547–1559)
- Outbreak of civil war between Protestants and royal troops (1562)
- St. Bartholomew's Day massacre; Protestants killed (1572)
- Montaigne's *Essays* (1580)
- Assassination of Henri III; Henri IV reigns (1589)
- Henri IV abjures Protestantism (1593)
- Edict of Nantes (1598)
- Permanent French outpost in Quebec (1608)
- Henri IV assassinated; Louis XIII (rules 1610–1643)
- Richelieu enters royal council (1624)
- Descartes's *Discourse on Method* (1637)
- Richelieu's death (Mazarin's takeover) (1642)
- Death of Louis XIII; Louis XIV (rules 1643–1715)
- Civil war (1648–1652)
- Louis XIV ("Sun King"), personal reign (1661)
- Founding of the French Academy of Science (1666)
- Revocation of Edict of Nantes (1685)
- Anglo-Dutch coalition wars against France (1689–1713)
- Louis XIV dies(1715)

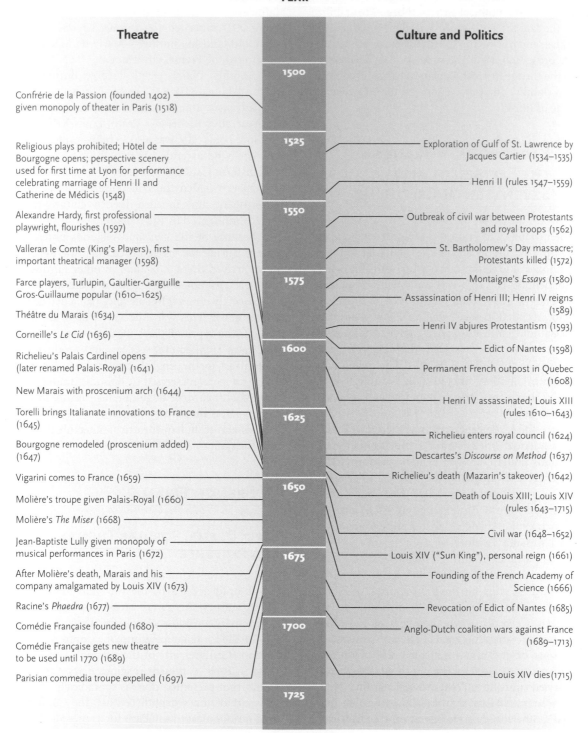

then, in 1548, it built a theatre—called the Hôtel de Bourgogne—which may well have been the first permanent theatre constructed in Europe since Roman times. (*Hôtel* is the French term for "town house," and the Bourgogne was called a *hôtel* because a duke's town house had once stood on its site and also because the neighboring buildings were town houses.) Before the Hôtel de Bourgogne was even completed, religious plays were banned in Paris, and so the Confrérie was never able to use the theatre for its own productions. However, because the Confrérie had been given a monopoly on theatre production in Paris, other groups were forced either to rent the Hôtel de Bourgogne or to pay a fee to the Confrérie.

During the sixteenth century, professional troupes began to spring up in other parts of France, and Italian commedia dell'arte companies performed in Paris and many other French cities. These commedia companies were another Italian influence on French theatre. Most of the drama offered by both the French and the Italian troupes was popular farce and often included song and dance as well as dramatic material.

In the middle 1500s in Paris, a literary group called the Pléiade was formed to further writing and culture; out of this group came French plays based on neoclassical models. The plays were derivative, not particularly original, and aimed almost exclusively at an upper-class, scholarly audience. In other words, in the latter part of the sixteenth century, when theatre was in full flower in Spain and England, its development in France did not really get under way until after the Edict of Nantes in 1598.

One other form of theatrical activity that did emerge in France in the last half of the sixteenth century is court entertainment. We have already mentioned Catherine de Médicis, whose husband and three sons ruled as kings of France from 1547 to 1589. Catherine enjoyed royal events: festivals, court spectacles, and triumphal entries into towns. In the 1560s, she made a 2-year tour of France, and each city she entered prepared an elaborate celebration in her honor. Out of such spectacles developed various kinds of court entertainments in France that were the equivalent of intermezzi in Italy and masques in England. The festivals and triumphal entries in France are an excellent example of the kinds of pageantry and visual spectacles that are closely akin to theatre. They lack the characters, the plot development, and the dialogue of conventional drama, but they contain a number of strongly theatrical elements.

It could be said that these royal entertainments—triumphal entries, pageants, masques—are at the opposite end of the theatrical spectrum from various popular entertainments that are also not dramatic in a traditional sense but have many theatrical components. One form appealed to the nobility and royalty; the other appealed to ordinary people.

In the public theatres, the person generally considered to be the first professional French playwright appeared at the end of the sixteenth century: Alexandre Hardy (c. 1572–1632). For 35 years, beginning in 1597, Hardy wrote several hundred plays, of which 34 survive. He was a popular dramatist: he used neoclassical devices such as messengers and the five-act structure—but he paid little or no attention to the unities of time, place, and action; he used supernatural characters; and he showed all the action, even the most violent, onstage. Most of Hardy's plays were probably produced at the Hôtel de Bourgogne, since that was the only permanent theatre in Paris at the time. Hardy not only achieved great success with the public; he also set the stage for the great era of French theatre that was soon to begin.

THE PALAIS ROYAL

During the reign of Louis XIII (1610–1643) the man behind the throne was Cardinal Richelieu, who ruled supreme not only in politics but also in cultural matters. In 1641 Richelieu had the architect LeMercier construct in his palace the first theatre in France with a fixed proscenium arch and a stage using flat wings. After the cardinal's death, the theatre was renamed the Palais Royal. Shown here at a performance in the theatre are, from left to right, the queen, Louis XIII, and Richelieu.

Most theatre in France in the first quarter of the seventeenth century probably consisted of popular farces; still, acting and production appear to have become more professional at the same time that writers like Hardy were making advances in playwriting.

Neoclassical Drama

Establishing the Neoclassical Ideals

At the beginning of the seventeenth century, French theatre was not notably Italian. Commedia dell'arte troupes traveled in France; but in both playwriting and production, the influence of native medieval theatre remained very much in evidence. There were no proscenium-arch theatres with an emphasis on scenic effects, and Hardy's plays did not observe the neoclassical unities of time, place, and action.

In other words, theatre in France in the early seventeenth century was as freewheeling as that in Spain and England in the same period, with little attention being paid to the strictures of neoclassical theory. An important thread in the story of French theatre is the conflict between this approach and adherence to Italian neoclassic ideals. The outcome of this struggle was the triumph of the neoclassic ideals. They dictated both dramaturgy, the way plays are written; and stagecraft, the way productions are designed and mounted.

In terms of dramaturgy, it will be recalled, from the discussion in Chapter 5, that the neoclassic rules call for strict unity of time, place, and action and forbid the mixing of tragedy and comedy. They also prohibit the use of such elements as the chorus, the soliloquy, and the deus ex machina.

We have observed how strong the Italian influence was on politics and society in France. In the seventeenth century, we can trace the emergence of a marked Italian influence on theatre as well. Beginning around 1620, during the reign of Louis XIII (which had begun in 1610), the most powerful man in France was Cardinal Richelieu, who ruled the country in the name of the king. After a series of new civil wars, Richelieu took power away from the nobles and the Protestants and consolidated it in the hands of the monarch.

Richelieu was particularly interested in establishing standards in French literature and the arts, and in giving them a strong Italian stamp. When he learned that some French intellectuals had organized a literary group, he urged them to form an academy along the lines of Italian academies. They did so in 1636, and the following year they were given a royal charter establishing the French Academy. The Academy—limited to 40 writers and other intellectuals—still exists today. It was to the French Academy that Richelieu turned when a serious question of dramatic rules arose. This came about because of *The Cid*, a play by Pierre Corneille.

PIERRE CORNEILLE

A native of Rouen, Pierre Corneille (1606–1684) was the son of a wealthy lawyer. Following his father's career, he obtained an appointment in the department of waterways and forests. He wrote a comedy, *Mélite*, in his spare time, and after an acting troupe played it successfully in Paris in 1629, he began to spend much of his leisure time writing plays. His early comedies attracted the attention of Cardinal Richelieu, who induced him to join the Society of the Five Authors, commissioned to write plays for the cardinal's entertainment. Corneille found it difficult to write to order and incurred the cardinal's wrath for altering a part of the plot assigned to him.

(Bibliothèque Nationale de France)

Pierre Corneille (1606–1684).

Though Corneille's first dramatic works were comedies, in 1636–1637 he wrote a serious play, *The Cid*, based on an earlier Spanish play by Guillén de Castro. Corneille's drama recounts the adventure of Rodrigue and Chimène, who are in love but are separated because of a quarrel between their fathers. The action takes place in Seville. Since Chimène's father has slapped Don Diegue, the father of Rodrigue, the latter must defend his father's honor. He challenges Chimène's father to a duel and kills him. Chimène must then seek revenge against the man she loves. That night Rodrigue sneaks into Chimène's room, and the two desperate young lovers agree that they must continue to follow the path of honor.

The next morning Rodrigue, having learned of an attack planned by the Moors on the city, gathers an army and successfully beats them off. The city heaps honors

(© Tony Frank/ Sygma/Corbis)

THE CID

One of the most famous and durable plays of the French renaissance was *The Cid* by Corneille. It was highly controversial because the French Academy said that it did not strictly follow the neoclassic rules for dramatic construction. But this story of a successful soldier who encounters and overcomes all manner of challenges, including a confrontation with the father of the woman he loves, became very popular with audiences. Here (right), in the role of the chief character, is Jean-Louis Barrault in a contemporary production of the play.

on him, including the title "the Cid," but Chimène still feels she must avenge her father's honor. A man fights a duel on her behalf. Because she thinks Rodrigue has been killed, Chimène declares her love for him, only to find he is still alive. She feels that all is lost, but the king steps in and urges her, after a suitable interval, to marry Rodrigue. Needless to say, Corneille's hero is an invincible superman who fights to uphold justice, morality, personal honor, and national honor.

The play was a huge success (in fact, it remains immensely popular in France to this day), but it was virulently attacked by critics who held that *The Cid* violated the neoclassical rules. They argued, for example, that though it observed the unity of time, it stretched credibility by cramming too much action into 24 hours. Also, Corneille had apparently mixed dramatic genres, because this serious play has a happy ending. In addition, Chimène's agreeing to marry her father's murderer was said to be inappropriate behavior for a character of her stature. Corneille vigorously defended the dramaturgy of *The Cid,* but the controversy continued. To settle the matter, Richelieu asked the newly formed French Academy for a judgment. (It should be noted that in England and Spain there was no equivalent to the French Academy—a group with royal blessing that could virtually dictate the rules of drama.)

When the French Academy published its opinion in 1638, it praised certain parts of the play but insisted that Corneille should have adhered more closely to the neoclassical ideals. Corneille was stung by the verdict and for several years refused to write any more dramas. In 1640, however, he began writing again, and from then on all his plays conformed to the unities of time, place, and action; to verisimilitude; and to the other restrictions of neoclassicism.

Corneille's famous tragedies *Horace* (1640), *Cinna* (1641), *Polyeucte* (1643), and *Rodogune* (1645) are models of adherence to neoclassical theory, and they established him as the most renowned playwright in France. His comedy *The Liar* (1643) was also extremely successful. He was elected to the French Academy in 1647 and continued to write until 1652, when a poorly received tragedy and uncertain political conditions led him to retire. The minister of finance was able to persuade him to return to playwriting in 1659, and he continued to write for another 25 years until his death in 1684.

As a dramatist, Corneille considered theatre a spectacular art. He wrote plays with heroic characters in suspenseful and surprising situations that force them to act. Long before his death in 1684, he was known as "the great Corneille," and *The Cid* had been translated and produced all over Europe, ensuring his lasting fame.

JEAN RACINE: THE TRIUMPH OF THE NEOCLASSICAL IDEALS

After the French Academy had spoken on *The Cid*, the neoclassical standards of the Italian Renaissance critics prevailed in French dramaturgy. No one was better able to create works incorporating these ideals than the tragic playwright who succeeded Corneille, Jean Racine (1639–1699).

In his tragedies—especially *Phaedra* (1677), *Berenice* (1670), and *Andromache* (1667)—Racine showed an extraordinary ability to create dramatic tension through concentration and characterization. By compressing dramatic action, Racine increases the pressure on the chief character, who is usually trying to reconcile some driving passion with honor and devotion to duty. The tension builds rapidly; the pressure becomes too much; and the character, tragically, begins to come apart.

(Bibliothèque Nationale de France)

Jean Racine.

The strictness of neoclassical form in Racine's plays matches the strictness of his own upbringing. Orphaned at the age of 4, he was raised first by his grandparents and then by his aunt, who was in a convent at Port-Royal. She enrolled the boy in the convent school, where he received an excellent but strict and austere education. In 1658 he went to Paris to continue his studies; he became a lawyer, but he spent much of his time with literary groups. In 1669 he published an ode on the marriage of Louis XIV, and he left school to concentrate on a literary career.

Racine was determined to succeed as a playwright and was constantly plotting and intriguing; not surprisingly, he made many enemies. Though Molière had given the first performances of Racine's works and had given him advice and

(© Robbie Jack/Corbis)

PHAEDRE

Racine's *Phaedre* is probably the best known neoclassic tragedy. It is the story of a queen who falls in love with her stepson, with the result that everyone involved—including these two, as well as Phaedre's husband—meets a tragic end. Shown here is Joanna Roth, in the title role, with Toby Stephens as Hippolytus in a production in London.

encouragement, Racine transferred one of his plays from Molière's troupe to a rival company. He also persuaded Madame du Parc—his own mistress—to leave Molière and join the rival group, an action for which he was severely criticized. Racine, however, had the support of several prominent writers, the court, and the king's mistress, and he did not hesitate to use their influence to thwart anyone who opposed him. In 1677, Racine's enemies brought about the failure of his play *Phaedra* by having another play open on the same night as its premiere. After this, Racine forsook theatre, married, and obtained an appointment as royal historiographer.

When Racine retired from playwriting, he returned to the strict religious beliefs of his youth. He remained in King Louis's favor for many years, and at the request of the king's second wife, wrote two pageants for her. Eventually, though, Racine's rigid religious ideas caused him to lose the king's favor. He returned to Port-Royal and died in 1699 after a long illness.

It is ironic that Racine's *Phaedra*, which was a failure when it opened, has become one of the most famous French tragedies of all time. *Phaedra* is based on a Greek play—Euripides' *Hippolytus*—and is a perfect example of neoclassicism. The heroine, Phaedra, who is the second wife of King Theseus, falls in love with her stepson, Hippolytus. The play is arranged so that all the events occur in one place—outside a room in Theseus's palace—and cover only a few hours. Its action is also unified, being confined to Phaedra's love for Hippolytus.

Having heard that Theseus is dead, Phaedra confesses her love for Hippolytus, first to her maid and then to Hippolytus himself. Hippolytus reacts with disgust when he hears her declaration; shortly thereafter, Phaedra discovers that Theseus is alive and will soon be returning to the palace. To avoid the shame of having openly declared her love for her stepson, Phaedra allows her maid to spread a false story—that it was Hippolytus who made advances to Phaedra, not vice versa. Theseus, believing this false report, invokes a god to punish Hippolytus, and the young man is slain. Phaedra is grief-stricken and confesses her guilt to Theseus; she then takes poison.

Because *Phaedra* begins near its final crisis and occurs in a short span of time, information about earlier events—the background that the audience needs to understand the play—must be reported in exposition. Racine manages this element well; he also masterfully articulates Phaedra's emotional conflict. Racine's language, especially his beautifully balanced phrases (in a line of poetry known as the *alexandrine*), established a model that was to be followed in France for the next three centuries. To this day, French playwrights put a premium on the verbal skills and intellectual arguments of their characters.

Among Racine's other works are *The Thebans* (1664), *Alexander the Great* (1665), *The Litigants* (1668), *Britannicus* (1669), *Bajazet* (1672), *Mithridates* (1673), *Iphegenia* (1674), *Esther* (1689), and *Athalie* (1690–1691).

MOLIÈRE: NEOCLASSICAL COMEDY

Corneille and Racine were masters of serious drama. Of all the French neoclassical playwrights, however, the one who exerts the most influence on modern theatre is one who specialized in comedy: Molière (Jean-Baptiste Poquelin, 1622–1673).

"If it be the aim of comedy to correct man's vices, then I do not see for what reason there should be a privileged class," wrote Molière in defense of his play *Tartuffe*. Several of his other comedies also shocked audiences, not because of their subject matter but because he insisted on depicting vices and follies truthfully. His plays nevertheless earned the respect and patronage of enlightened theatregoers, and he remains one of the most popular dramatists of all time.

(Bibliothèque Nationale de France)

Molière (Jean-Baptiste Poquelin).

Molière wrote in the same neoclassical form as Corneille and Racine; the dialogue in many of his plays consists of rhyming couplets. In plays such as *The School for Wives* (l662), *The Doctor in Spite of Himself* (1666), and *The Would-Be Gentleman* (1670), he combined farcical humor with a gift for witty dialogue and a keen eye for human foibles. The misers, misanthropes, and hypochondriacs in his plays are still recognizable to twenty-first-century audiences.

Many critics note the influence of commedia dell'arte on Molière: in particular, the characters in his plays resemble the stock types in commedia. In *The Miser*, for example, Harpagon is an avaricious old man reminiscent of Pantalone. He courts a young woman whom his son, Cléante, loves; and he betroths his daughter to an old man who does not require a dowry, even though she loves the younger Valère. His exaggerated miserliness is the basic obstacle to his children's happiness.

Molière's contrived plots, which adhere to the neoclassical rules, are frequently resolved by a deus ex machina. In *The Miser*, for example, Anselme, the old man to whom Harpagon's daughter is promised, coincidentally turns out to be the lost father of both Valère and the girl Cléante loves. Anselme allows his rediscovered son and daughter to marry Harpagon's children so that everyone can live happily ever after. Molière's plots, characters, and slapstick elements make his comedies especially popular with modern audiences.

Had he wanted financial stability, Jean-Baptiste Poquelin—Molière's original name—could have had either of two other careers. As the son of an upholsterer in the service of the king, he could have followed his father's profession; he could also have become a lawyer. In 1643, however, he left school, changed his name to Molière, and founded the Théâtre Illustre with the Béjart family of actors.

Molière's theatre went bankrupt in 1645, and he was imprisoned for debt. Forced out of Paris by poor economic conditions, the troupe played in the provinces for more than a decade, until 1658. During this time, Molière became an accomplished playwright and comic actor, noted for the subtlety of his performances. As a leader in the company, along with his mistress, Madeleine Béjart, Molière was able to coach the performers in his method, developing a disciplined ensemble.

In 1658, an influential patron secured a royal audience for the troupe. Louis XIV was much impressed by Molière's work, and the group was allowed to share

(Sara Krulwich/The New York Times)

TARTUFFE
One of the most famous comedies of all time is Molière's *Tartuffe*, about a religious hypocrite who completely hoodwinks Orgon, the bourgeois head of a French household. Everyone but Orgon sees through Tartuffe's false behavior. Almost too late, Orgon also understands the fraud. The scene here is from the Roundabout Theatre production with Kathryn Meisle and Henry Goodman.

a theatre in Paris with an Italian commedia troupe, a situation that left the two companies constantly competing for funds. Besides being the company manager and an actor, Molière wrote about one-third of his troupe's plays. Although many of his plays were successful with the public and at court, others, like *Tartuffe*, were banned.

In fact, *Tartuffe* was the cause of an enormous controversy. Molière first read it in 1664 to King Louis XIV at his palace at Versailles; the king liked it, but before it could be presented publicly, it had provoked an uproar because of its subject matter. The title character, Tartuffe, is a religious hypocrite who pretends to be very pious and wears clothing that looks like a religious habit, but he is actually interested in acquiring money and seducing women. He comes to live in the house of Orgon, a man who has been completely taken in by his false piety.

Orgon pays no attention to the members of his family when they tell him how dishonest and disreputable Tartuffe is. Only when Orgon learns for himself the awful truth about Tartuffe does he realize his error. This occurs in a scene in which Orgon, hiding under a table, hears Tartuffe try to seduce his wife. Orgon's discovery of Tartuffe's true nature seems to come too late: he has already handed his house and his fortune over to Tartuffe, disinheriting his own children. At the end of the play, however, the king intervenes.

Those who opposed having *Tartuffe* performed included a number of religious figures (one of them was the archbishop of Paris) who argued that the play was an attack on religion. Molière insisted that his play was an attack, not on religion, but on people who hide behind religion and exploit it. The play was presented once, in the summer of 1667, and then for only one night. The king was out of the country at that time, and in his absence the religious authorities had it closed down. In 1669, though, it finally had its official premiere, and it became a great success.

The king made Molière's troupe the King's Men in 1665, and Molière then wrote many court pageants and plays. By 1672, however, Louis's favor had gone to the composer Jean-Baptiste Lully, and Molière had to work harder for financial stability. Molière's home life was also unhappy. His wife, Armande Béjart, who was much younger, became notorious for her flirtations. Exhausted and suffering from a lung ailment, Molière collapsed during a performance of *The Imaginary Invalid*

(1673) and died a few hours later. Because he was an actor, and France at that time had laws preventing actors from receiving Christian burial, his funeral had to be held at night. Among his other frequently produced works are *Sganarelle* (1660), *The School for Husbands* (1661), and *The Misanthrope* (1666).

Ballet at Court

In the period between the plays of Corneille and those of Racine, particularly in the decade 1650–1660, a form of ballet became popular at the court of Louis XIV. It was a type of entertainment similar to the masques in England during the reigns of James I and Charles I. These ballets were not complicated pieces in terms of demands made on the dancers; in fact, they were so elementary that the king himself took part in many of them. They were called *ballets d'entrées,* a term referring to "entries" of which the pieces consisted. One ballet, *The Ballet of the Night,* produced in 1653, consisted of 43 entries, some featuring ordinary folk such as shepherds and Gypsies, others featuring the four elements and various gods. In the end, the sun appears. This, of course, was Louis XIV, the Sun King. Again, we have a royal entertainment that can be viewed as a first cousin, or distant relation, of the theatre of Corneille, Racine, and Molière.

Theatre Production in France

Architecture, Scenery, and Technology

We have already noted that in Europe, the French were the first after the Romans to construct a permanent theatre building. The Hôtel de Bourgogne, constructed by the Confraternity of the Passion, was completed in 1548 and for nearly a century was the sole permanent indoor theatre building in Paris. The Bourgogne was not a proscenium-arch theatre. It was a long, narrow building with a platform stage at one end. In front of the stage was a pit (the *parterre*) for standing spectators, and around the side and back walls were boxes (*loges*) and undivided galleries. The third tier of galleries along the side walls was known as the *paradis*, or "heavens." Until the seventeenth century, scenic practices at the Bourgogne were basically medieval.

When the Théâtre du Marais opened in 1634, the Hôtel de Bourgogne had its first competition. The Marais was a converted indoor tennis court. Court tennis (a game dating from the Middle Ages, played with a short-handled racket, usually in a roofed hall) was a popular Parisian diversion at the time; and before the Marais opened, if the Bourgogne was already leased to a theatrical company, other companies could perform in Paris in temporarily converted tennis courts. Since indoor tennis courts were long, narrow buildings like the Bourgogne and had galleries for spectators, they were easily transformed into theatres; erecting a platform stage at one end of the building and installing additional temporary galleries would produce a theatre space nearly identical to the Bourgogne. It is not surprising, then, that the second major Parisian theatre building, the Marais, was simply a permanently converted tennis court.

Italian influences on French theatre architecture became evident in 1641, when Cardinal Richelieu erected the Palais Cardinal, renamed the Palais-Royal after his

(Bibliothèque Nationale de France, Paris)

A FRENCH TENNIS COURT
This illustration, from the early seventeenth century, shows a French tennis court of the kind that was suitable for conversion to a theatre space. A platform stage would be set up at one end, and seating would be added on the floor; to create a permanent playhouse, additional galleries could be added. The Théâtre du Marais in Paris is a famous example of a playing space that was converted from such a tennis court.

death. The Palais Cardinal was the first proscenium-arch theatre in France; it also had Italianate scene-shifting machinery.

The theatre building was a rectangular space with a stage at one end and galleries on three sides around it. It accommodated almost 1,500 people: 300 standing in a "pit" in front of the stage, about 700 sitting in a raised amphitheatre behind the pit, about 330 sitting in the galleries, 70 standing at the very back, and 50 wealthy nobles sitting on the sides of the stage itself. Having spectators onstage was customary in French theatres but made performing difficult for the actors.

In the mid-1640s, the Italian scenic wizard Giacomo Torelli was brought to France to design scenery and install scene-changing equipment. Among his first undertakings was the transformation of a royal palace, the Petit Bourbon, into an Italian-style theatre. He built a platform stage 6 feet high, 49 feet wide, and 48 feet deep and installed his pole-and-chariot system for scene shifting. He also installed the same system in the Palais-Royal theatre. With the arrival of Torelli, Italian design and scene-shifting techniques became firmly established in France; thus by the 1640s, Italian models for both playwriting and production were completely accepted there.

To keep up to date, both the Théâtre du Marais and the Hôtel de Bourgogne were remodeled into proscenium-arch theatres in the 1640s. Painted-perspective, wing-and-shutter scenery—shifted by the pole-and-chariot system—was used in the two remodeled theatres.

French proscenium-arch theatre buildings differed slightly from those of the Italian Renaissance: in the back wall opposite the stage was an *amphithéâtre,* an undivided gallery that contained inexpensive bleacher-like seating. In both the Marais and the Bourgogne, there was probably a small upper stage, raised 13 feet above the main stage, which was used for special effects such as flying. Also, as we have noted, at the close of the seventeenth century members of the French upper class were frequently seated on the stage.

In the 1650s, Louis XIV's interest in ballet brought this form of entertainment back into prominence at court. Ballet productions were scenically quite spectacular. To satisfy the royal taste for elaborate effects, and to prepare for Louis's forthcoming marriage (which was to take place in 1660), Cardinal Mazarin, who had succeeded Richelieu, sent to Italy for another stage wizard, Gaspare Vigarani (1586–1663). To accommodate Vigarani's ambitious productions, the Petit Bourbon was torn down and a new theatre was built in a wing added to the Tuileries Palace. This theatre was known as the *Salle des Machines* ("Hall of Machines").

The Salle des Machines, completed in 1660, was the largest theatre in Europe; it was 52 feet wide and 232 feet long. The auditorium took up only 92 of the 232 feet, leaving 140 feet for the stage and its machinery. The backstage equipment included one piece of machinery on which the entire royal family and all their attendants—well over 100 people—could be "flown" into the space above the stage. Because of its unsatisfactory acoustics, its size—especially backstage—and the expense of producing spectacles, the Salle des Machines was rarely used after 1670.

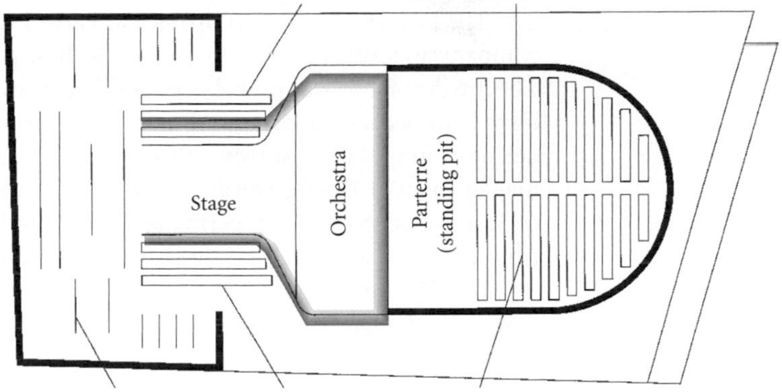

GROUND PLAN OF THE COMÉDIE FRANÇAISE
The French national theatre company performed in this playhouse for 81 years, beginning in 1689. The theatre had a proscenium-arch stage with machinery for scene shifts, and a horseshoe-shaped auditorium for improved sight lines. The parterre was where audience members stood; the amphitheatre contained bleacher-like seating.

A major theatre building of the French neoclassical period was the Comédie Française. This space housed the French national theatre, which had been founded by Louis XIV in 1680 and moved into its own building in 1689. This theatre was another converted tennis court; but its sight lines were significantly better than those of similar French spaces of the time because its interior had a horseshoe-shape construction. Such a horseshoe shape places spectators not in back corners but in a rounded area at the rear and sides with a better view of the stage.

Acting

Acting Companies

In seventeenth-century France, acting developed along with playwriting, stagecraft, and scenic effects.

The French acting companies of the seventeenth century were organized under a sharing plan, with *sociétaires* as shareholders and *pensionnaires* contracted to perform minor roles. Before 1650, there were generally eight to twelve performers in a company; after that, the number was larger: when the Comédie Française was formed in 1680, it had twenty-seven shareholders. Women were members of French theatre companies and could become sociétaires.

Troupes spent little time on rehearsals, which were supervised by the playwright, by a leading actor of the company, or by both. At any given time, a company would have a repertoire of up to seventy plays; and once a play had been introduced, the troupe was expected to be able to revive it on very short notice. The bill at a theatre was changed daily.

Shareholders provided their own costumes, which consisted of either contemporary clothing or conventional historical outfits. Since this was an expensive practice, actors often received a subsidy for the costumes they wore in court productions—which could then be reused in public performances.

The history of acting companies in Paris is complex. In about 1629, a permanent company was organized at the Hôtel de Bourgogne. A competing company at the Théâtre du Marais was probably established a year or so later, although it did not perform in its permanent playhouse until about 1635. Throughout the century, commedia dell'arte enjoyed great success in Paris; and in 1661, one commedia troupe, under the management of Tiberio Fiorillo (1608–1694)—who was renowned for playing the role of Scaramouche—took up permanent residence in the city. As noted earlier, Molière's troupe, housed at the Palais-Royal, was immensely popular between 1658 and 1673.

In 1673, then, there were five government-supported companies in Paris: the Opera, the Italian commedia dell'arte troupe, the Hôtel de Bourgogne company, the Théâtre du Marais company, and the troupe led by Molière. After Molière's death in 1673, Louis XIV ordered his troupe to merge with the Marais company, which thereafter performed as the Molière-Marais troupe.

In 1680, Louis consolidated the Bourgogne troupe with the Molière-Marais company. He gave the combined company a monopoly on the performance of spoken drama in French, making it the first national theatre in the world. (The term *national theatre* indicates a theatre that is supposed to represent an entire nation. Great Britain, for example, has a Royal National Theatre in London.) To distinguish it from the Comédie Italienne, which was also based in Paris, the new company was called the Comédie Française.

THE COMÉDIE FRANÇAISE

The establishment in 1680 of the Comédie Française, the government-supported French national theatre, was a milestone in theatre history.

(Giraudon/Art Resource, N.Y.)

THE COMÉDIE FRANÇAISE
The establishment of the French national theatre was a milestone in theatre history. Shown here is its present home, in Paris.

DEBATES IN THEATRE HISTORY | **Should We Envy Europe's National Theatres?**

Louis XIV's creation of the Comédie Française as the French national theatre in 1680 continues to have significant implications today. While theatre companies in the United States have received government support through the National Endowment for the Arts and state arts agencies, no theatre has been designated as our national theatre; and the concept of a government-supported theatre dedicated to a national drama is greatly envied by many American theatre artists. Should we envy nations with a national theatre?

People who say yes point to the long and illustrious history of the Comédie Française, and to the important playwrights whose works were produced there (the nineteenth-century romantic Victor Hugo is just one example). They argue that the Comédie Française keeps alive the classic plays of French theatre—it is, after all, called the "home" of Molière. They also ask where in our own country we could find a theatre dedicated to American drama and able to afford elaborate revivals of our great plays.

However, the issue is not that clear-cut. For one thing, the Comédie Française has frequently been criticized for being overly conservative. Many revolutionary and avant-garde playwrights, including the realists of the late nineteenth century, could not get their works produced there. In addition, its acting school—the Conservatoire, founded at the close of the eighteenth century—did not accept many of the performers who went on to significant careers and was often out of step with contemporary trends in performance. Often, the security represented by the Comédie Française has led to complacency and laziness among its tenured members. Critics of national theatres argue that rarely has the artistic director of the Comédie Française been innovative or daring. The historian Peter D. Arnott notes: "For the French, the Comédie Française has always been a mixed blessing. As a governmentally-supported institution, it has come to exemplify both the good and the ill of state intervention in the arts. . . . At times it has seemed that the main function of the Comédie Française has been to inspire experiment and creativity, out of sheer exasperation, in others."*

Furthermore, some commentators note that although government support is a financial boon to artists, it can also have insidious—even dangerous—implications. Governments can control content and political point of view through financial manipulation. Also, overreliance on government support can undermine a theatre company, and such support may suddenly decrease or vanish when there are changes in the economic or political climate.

Many other countries, of course, have established national theatres along the lines of the Comédie Française. In Britain, for instance, the Royal National Theatre and the Royal Shakespeare Company receive significant government subsidies. Both have been criticized for becoming too commercially oriented and for being more interested in the elaborate structures which house them than in presenting artistically innovative work. On the other hand, their defenders point out that many powerful and provocative productions have been mounted by these theatres in recent decades.

In the United States, many critics have argued that a national theatre is not possible because our large, diverse country does not have a natural artistic center. But even if a national theatre were to be created in the United States, the question remains: Can a government-supported theatre be innovative, revolutionary, and thought-provoking?

*Peter D. Arnott, *An Introduction to French Theatre,* Rowman and Littlefield, Totowa, N.J., 1977.

The new company—formed when Louis XIV merged two earlier troupes—had a number of distinguished players, and excellence in acting became one of its hallmarks. Through the years, its members have included many of France's leading actors: Adrienne Lecouvreur, Clairon (Claire Leyris de la Tudi), Henri Louis Lekain, François Joseph Talma, Élisa Félix (Rachel), Benoît Constant Coquelin, Sarah Bernhardt, and Jean-Louis Barrault.

To keep order among so many talented people, the Comédie Française was organized under the sharing plan of Molière's troupe; with some modifications, it still follows that plan today. Shares in the company were granted to its leading members

—the *sociétaires*—according to each actor's status; some received less than a full share. The sociétaires were responsible for all company policy, including the selection of plays. Vacancies caused by retirement, resignation, or death were filled from the *pensionnaires,* actors hired by the troupe on a fixed salary. To become a pensionnaire, a performer had to audition successfully in both comedy and tragedy. The head of the company—the *doyen*—was the actor with the longest service in the troupe.

For its first 9 years, the Comédie Française used the Théâtre de Guénégaud. In 1689, the company moved into its own building; like many other French theatres of the time, this was a converted tennis court, but it had a horseshoe-shaped interior which provided better sight lines. (Today, the Comédie Française is housed in a different, later building.)

The Comédie Française survived both the French Revolution and the problems created by its own organization. For one thing, a secure appointment as a sociétaire sometimes encouraged complacency and arrogance. Also, since the Comédie Française had been granted a monopoly, the lack of outlets for plays had a stifling effect on French drama; this problem was worsened by the sociétaires' preference for plays that were imitative rather than innovative. In the nineteenth century, with the popularity of melodrama and the boulevard theatres, the Comédie Française suffered financially. Throughout its long history, however, it has preserved the best of French classical drama—Corneille, Racine, and Molière—as well as a distinguished tradition of classical acting.

(Cliché Bibliothèque Nationale de France, Paris)

MLLE. CHAMPMESLÉ.
A portrait of Mlle. Champmeslé, a well-known French actress of the seventeenth century. It was a period when performers became famous and had large followings.

Performers

There were many popular performers in Parisian acting companies of the seventeenth century. From the 1620s until his retirement in 1647, the leading actor with the company at the Hôtel de Bourgogne—called the King's Players—was Bellerose (Pierre le Messier, c. 1592–1670), who excelled at both comedy and serious drama. (It was a common practice at this time for performers to use stage names, which were typically single names like Bellerose; another example, of course, is Molière.)

At the Théâtre du Marais, the outstanding actor was Montdory (Guillaume des Gilleberts, 1594–1654). Montdory was a favorite of Cardinal Richelieu, who granted him a subsidy. Among Montdory's roles was the title character in Corneille's *The Cid.* When Montdory retired from the Marais, he was replaced by Floridor (Josias de Soulas, 1608–1672). Because of Montdory and Floridor, the Marais troupe was regarded as the leading company in Paris until 1647; after that, the Hôtel de Bourgogne once more became the leading theatre.

In the last half of the seventeenth century, many of the leading performers were associated with Molière, who was a superb comic actor himself and performed in most of his own plays. A highly acclaimed actress in Molière's troupe was Madeleine Béjart (1618–1672), who played tragic heroines in the early stages of her career but later performed comic roles for Molière.

DuParc (Marquise-Thérèse de Gorla, 1633–1668), an outstanding tragic actress, began with Molière's company but was persuaded by Racine to act at the Hôtel de Bourgogne. Another leading tragic actress—near the end of the century—was Champmeslé (Marie-Desmares Champmeslé, 1642–1698), who created such roles as Phaedra; the most noted tragic actor of his day was Michel Baron (1653–1729).

MICHEL BARON

The finest French tragic actor of the late seventeenth century was Michel Baron (1653–1729). During a long and distinguished career, Baron worked with Molière and later became a member of France's first national theatre, the Comédie Française. From 1670 to his retirement in 1691, Baron, who was noted for his less stilted, more natural acting style, was recognized as the leading serious actor on the French stage.

(Billy Rose Theatre Collection, New York Public Library at Lincoln Center, Astor, Lenox, and Tilden Foundations)

Michel Baron.

The only surviving son of theatrical parents, Baron was a child performer, who was orphaned by the age of 10. Molière saw the young Baron perform as a member of the Troupe du Roi, a children's company, and was so impressed that in 1666 the master took him into his home, training him for his company. Though Molière was extremely fond of Baron, it appears that Armande Béjart, Molière's wife, did not share her husband's affection and once slapped Baron's face—with the result that Baron ran away and went back to his former troupe. Eventually persuaded to return, Baron worked with Molière at the Palais-Royal between 1670 and 1673, playing in Pierre Corneille's *Titus and Berenice,* as well as Molière's own *The Tricks of Scapin* and *The Learned Ladies.*

When Molière died, Baron left the troupe and joined the company at the Hôtel de Bourgogne, which was then the leading theatre in Paris. There, he starred in many of Jean Racine's tragedies, including *Phaedra* (1677). When the Comédie Française was formed in 1680, Baron was one of its founding shareholders.

As an actor, Baron—known as Boiron—was versatile and innovative. He prepared his roles carefully and introduced a more supple, natural style to the restricted postures and formal oratorical delivery of his day, especially for spoken verse, which other actors tended to deliver in singsong rhythms. He also wrote ten comedies; among the best are *The Philanderer* (1686), *The Flirt and the False Prude* (1687), and an amusing one-act play, *The Rendezvous at the Tuileries* (1685), in which several actors from the Comédie Française played themselves.

Though Baron retired in 1691, he occasionally performed in private theatres and at court. Then, almost 30 years later, at the age of 67, he returned to the Comédie Française. It is believed that his reemergence on the stage strengthened the trend toward more realistic acting in the eighteenth century. Like his mentor, Molière, he fell ill during a performance; he died several months later in 1729. Baron was survived by his wife, Charlotte, herself an actress—the daughter of the actor La

Thorillière—and their son, Étienne, who also became an actor and performed with the Comédie Française.

ARMANDE BÉJART

Armande Béjart (1642–1700)—who had been raised by Madeleine Béjart and eventually became Molière's wife—was the leading actress in his troupe in its later years. After its formation in 1680, she, Champmeslé, and Baron all joined the Comédie Française.

As the young wife of Molière, Armande Béjart created roles in many of his plays. She had been trained for the stage by Molière, and she also inspired some of his writing.

(© Bettmann/Corbis)

Armande Béjart (1642–1700).

The youngest child of Joseph Béjart and Marie Hervé, Armande Grésinde Claire Elisabeth Béjart was born in 1642, some months after the death of her father, into a large, poor Parisian family. Armande's oldest sister, Madeleine Béjart, gave birth to an illegitimate daughter at about the same time as Armande was born, and in later years Armande was widely believed to be Madeleine's daughter. There was even speculation that Molière was Armande's father.

By the time of Armande's birth, Madeleine and her brother Joseph had begun their acting careers; and in 1643 they joined with other actors, including Molière, to found the Théâtre Illustre. Madeleine Béjart was Molière's lover and a driving force in the company, holding many responsibilities such as overseeing its finances. By 1653, Armande Béjart was apparently traveling with the company, and her education was supervised by Molière.

Given her theatrical family and her prolonged exposure to the stage, it is not surprising that Armande Béjart became an actress. In addition to a lively and charming stage manner, which suited her to roles in comedy, Armande was a talented singer and dancer. Molière had directed Armande's theatrical training, and he married his pupil on February 20, 1662; but he did not let her make her debut until more than a year later, when he was convinced that she was thoroughly prepared.

Armande's first, small role was Élise in Molière's *Critique of the School for Wives.* In May of 1644, during entertainments held at Versailles for Louis XIV, Armande moved into major roles, creating the role of Elmire in the first presentation of *Tartuffe* and the Princess in the comedy ballet *Princess d'Elide.* Other roles in Molière's plays premiered by Armande include Lucinde in *The Doctor in Spite of Himself,* Angélique in *George Dandin,* Célimène in *The Misanthrope,* Lucille in *The Would-Be Gentleman,* Henriette in *The Learned Ladies,* and Angélique in *The Imaginary Invalid.*

Although they worked together successfully, Molière and Armande Béjart did not have a happy marriage. For one thing, Molière was 20 years older than his young wife; also, Armande was flirtatious and attracted many men, provoking the jealousy of her husband. In fact, the couple separated after the birth of their second child in 1665, though they were reconciled 5 years later. After Molière's death, Armande led his company in cooperation with the actor LaGrange. In 1677, she married another actor, Guerin d'Estriche. In 1680, along with the remainder of Molière's company, Armande became an original member of the Comédie Française. She acted with the Comédie Française until her retirement in 1694.

AUDIENCES

Before the founding of the Comédie Française, most French theatre companies performed only about three times a week for public audiences; in 1672–1673, for example, Molière's troupe gave only 131 performances. These public performances did not, apparently, attract very large audiences. In the year before his death, Molière's company averaged only 400 spectators per performance. Even the Comédie Française, which had a monopoly, played to only 425 to 450 spectators per performance during the last two decades of the century. These figures mean that the large public theatres were usually filled to only 20 to 25 percent of capacity. Some plays were popular enough to attract near-capacity audiences—and to run for 15 to 30 performances—but they were rare.

In Paris, performance time was early afternoon until 1680, when the Comédie Française began its plays at 5 P.M. Audiences at Parisian theatres included all strata of society. However, the theatre probably became less and less affordable for working-class people because admission to the parterre was priced significantly higher throughout the 1600s. The parterre was only for men; women sat in boxes or in the amphitheatre, depending on their social and economic status.

As in Shakespeare's time, there are some contemporary accounts of audience members as noisy and as misbehaving in other ways. However, scholars warn that these complaints must be taken with a grain of salt, since they were sometimes made by disgruntled playwrights or commentators who were unhappy with the state of French theatre.

By 1700, both the French nation and its theatre had settled into conservatism. In 1685, Louis XIV revoked the Edict of Nantes, which had ensured freedom of conscience. About 200,000 Huguenots were forced to leave the country, depriving France of wealth, intelligence, and talent—as had been the case in Spain 200 years earlier, when its Jews were expelled. Louis himself became more and more puritanical and no longer attended the theatre. As of 1697, when Louis expelled the Comédie Italienne after its performance of a political satire, the Comédie Française and the Opera monopolized theatre activity in Paris, and the popularity of opera put a premium on elaborate scenery. The days of new dramas by playwrights like Corneille, Racine, and Molière were over.

SUMMARY

French neoclassical theatre expanded and refined Italian Renaissance practices. Most French drama, including the tragedies of Corneille and Racine and the comedies of Molière, followed the neoclassical rules. The plays of seventeenth-century France, however, achieved a quality and distinction far exceeding those produced in the Italian Renaissance.

By the mid-seventeenth century, French theatres were proscenium-arch spaces with painted-perspective, wing-and-shutter scenery.

A milestone in theatre history was the establishment of the Comédie Française, the government-supported French national theatre, in 1680.

Theatre History

- Confrérie de la Passion organized in Paris to present religious plays (1402)
- Hôtel de Bourgogne opens (1548)
- Italian commedia dell'arte troupes performing in French cities (sixteenth century) *(below)*

- The Pléiade formed in Paris to further writing and culture; royal entertainments: pageants, masques, and triumphal entries sponsored by court (mid-sixteenth century)
- Alexandre Hardy (c. 1572–1632)

Cultural and Historical Developments

- Exploration of Gulf of St. Lawrence by Jacques Cartier (1534–1535)
- Henri II rules (1547–1559); marries Catherine de Médicis
- Outbreak of civil war between Catholics and Protestants (1567)
- St. Bartholomew's Day massacre (1572)
- Montaigne's *Essays* (1580; 1588)
- Assassination of Henri III; Henri IV reigns (1589); converts to Catholicism (1594)
- Edict of Nantes (1598)
- Permanent French outpost in Quebec (1608)

Neoclassical [1620–1700]

Theatre History

- King's Players organized at Hôtel de Bourgogne (1629)
- Bellerose (Pierre le Messier, c. 1592–1670)
- Pierre Corneille (1606–1684), *Le Cid*
- Madeleine Béjart (1618–1672), acclaimed actress in Molière's troupe
- Molière (Jean-Baptiste Poquelin, 1622–1673) *(below)*, *The Miser*

- DuParc (Marquise-Thérèse de Gorla, 1633–1668)
- Théâtre du Marais, converted tennis court, opens (1634); Montdory (Guillaume des Gilleberts, 1594–1654)

Cultural and Historical Developments

- Henri IV assassinated; Louis XIII rules (1610–1643)
- Cardinal Richelieu enters royal council (1624)
- French Academy established (1636)
- René Descartes's *Discourse on Method* (1637) *(below)*

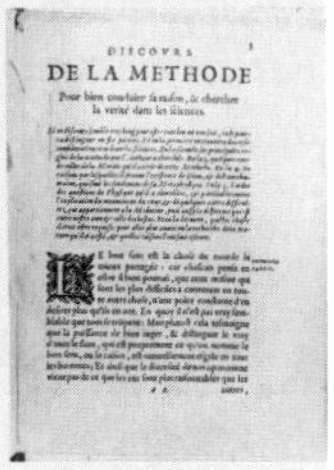

DISCOVRS
DE LA METHODE

- Richelieu's death; Cardinal Mazarin assumes post (1642)
- Death of Louis XIII; Louis XIV, the "Sun King," rules (1643–1715)

continued

PHOTO CREDITS: French and Italian actors at the Comédie Française, 1670; note Molière at the far left. (© Erich Lessing/Art Resource, N.Y.) / Molière. (Bibliothèque Nationale de France) / First page of *Discours de la methode* by Descartes. (Giraudon/Art Resource)

Neoclassical [1620–1700]

Theatre History

- Jean Racine (1639–1699), *Phaedra*
- Richelieu's Palais Cardinal opens (1641)
- Armande Béjart (1642–1700)
- Champmeslé (Marie-Desmares Champmeslé, 1642–1698) *(below)*

- Théâtre du Marais and Hôtel de Bourgogne remodeled with proscenium arch and Italian scenic devices (c. 1644–1647)
- Designer Giacomo Torelli brings Italianate innovations to France (c. 1645)
- *Ballets d'entrées* popular at court (1650–1660)
- Michel Baron (1653–1729)
- Court theater, Salle des Machines, completed (1660)
- Molière's troupe given Palais-Royal (1660)
- Tibero Fiorillo (1608–1694), manager of Italian commedia troupe, takes up permanent residence in Paris (1661)
- Comédie Française, French national theatre, founded (1680)

Cultural and Historical Developments

- Nicolas Poussin, *Landscape with the Burial of Phocion* (1648) *(below)*

- Civil war (1648–1652)
- Palace of Versailles (begun 1669) *(below)*

- Jean Baptiste Lully, *Le Bourgeois Gentilhomme* (1670)
- Louis XIV expels French Protestants (1683)
- Revocation of Edict of Nantes (1685)
- Anglo-Dutch coalition wars against France (1689–1713)
- Louis XIV dies (1715)

PHOTO CREDITS: Mlle. Champmeslé. (Cliché Bibliothèque Nationale de France, Paris) / *Landscape with the Burial of Phocion* by Poussin. (Scala/Art Resource, N.Y.) / The palace of Versailles. (Royalty-Free/Corbis)

Part Three
Theatres from 1660 to 1875

Between 1660 and 1875, people in Europe and America undertook to change the world—to transform politics, industry, and education.

In England, the monarchy was restored in 1660; but in the years to come, the power of kings and queens would be diminished and in many cases abolished. The end of the eighteenth century, saw the American and French revolutions. France returned to authoritarian rule in the early nineteenth century, with Napoleon, but the monarchy there was never to be the same again. Socially, during this period, there was a significant increase in the size and importance of the middle class.

The eighteenth century was known as the *age of enlightenment*. People at that time believed that the mind was all-powerful, and that all problems could be solved through the intellect. The nineteenth century was called the *century of progress*. It was the era of the industrial revolution—the development of machines for manufacturing and transportation. In the eighteenth century, ideas were supposed to solve problems; in the nineteenth century, industrialization was supposed to solve them. Workers in factories would get wages that would allow them to buy goods; the factories would supply goods for everyone. Things did not work out exactly as planned, but this expectation indicates the optimism of the time.

Social and political changes were reflected in the arts. Music moved from the baroque world of Bach and Handel to the classicism of Mozart and Beethoven, and then to the romanticism of Schubert, Chopin, and Liszt. Similarly, theatre during this era was in transition. The roots of modern theatre can be found in transformations that took place in drama of the English Restoration, the eighteenth century, and the early nineteenth century.

The theatrical innovations of this period are too numerous to list. A modern version of the proscenium-arch theatre—the version we still have on Broadway and across the country—was developed. Technology was introduced into scene design, and more realistic stage effects became popular. Primitive candle lighting gave way to more controllable gas lighting. (In 1881, electricity was to be introduced.) Historically accurate costumes became more commonplace, and costumes were designed in terms of characterization.

The business of theatre as we know it today took shape during these years, including the rise of the theatrical entrepreneur, the decline of the repertory company, the establishment of the long run, and the appearance of the star system. The art of acting gradually became more concerned with portraying everyday life, and the director became the controlling artist in theatre.

The dramatic forms of these two centuries—such as comedy of manners, romanticism, melodrama, and the well-made play—are still used by today's writers. Melodramatic films and television shows are direct descendants of nineteenth-century popular drama; the American dramatist Arthur Miller wrote well-made plays; and *Private Lives* (1930) and *Blithe Spirit* (1941) by the English playwright Noël Coward (1899–1973) are comedies of manners. If we look closely at our own theatre, we can see how indebted we are to the dramatic arts of these years of change.

(© T. Charles Erickson)

The Way of the World by William Congreve. Lee Mark Nelson (Waitwell) and Sandra Shipley (Lady Wishfort) at the Yale Repertory Theatre.

CHAPTER 9

The Theatre of the English Restoration

Aphra Behn: Female Dramatist

During the Restoration, women became an integral part of English theatre for the first time. Actresses appeared onstage, and female playwrights made an auspicious debut. One of the most prominent of the latter was Aphra Behn, whose play *The Rover* is shown here in a production at Illinois State University.

(© Peter Guither)

Charles I of England was removed from the throne by Oliver Cromwell and the Puritans after a bitter civil war lasting from 1642 to 1649. In 1649, Charles was beheaded. During the next 11 years, a period known as the *commonwealth,* England was governed by Cromwell, along with a Parliament that had been purged of his opponents. Cromwell died in 1658, however, and his son was unable to keep control of the English government; in 1660, Charles II, who had been living in France, was invited by a newly elected Parliament to return from exile to rule England. In other words, the monarchy was restored, and this gave the name *Restoration* to the period that followed.

Background: The Restoration

The reinstatement of the monarchy meant a restoration of other institutions. Parliament, the legislative body; the Anglican church (its counterpart in the United States is the Episcopal church), the official church formed by Henry VIII when he broke with Roman Catholicism; and the cavalier gentry, the nobles—lords, dukes, earls, etc.—who owned land and were next in rank to the royal family—all were restored.

Though Parliament was reinstated, Charles II refused to give it much power, and in the final years of his reign he ruled without it. When Charles died in 1685, he was succeeded by his brother, James II; who had been converted to Catholicism. James's reign was turbulent; when his wife gave birth to a son, it was feared that a Catholic line of succession threatened Protestant England. For this reason, Parliament, in 1688, invited James's Protestant daughter Mary and her husband William of Orange (from the royal house of the Netherlands) to rule England. William and Mary deposed James II in the bloodless, Glorious Revolution in 1688.

Many historians consider that England entered a new phase with the accession of William and Mary in 1688, and therefore that this date marks the end of the Restoration period. In theatre, though, the developments of the Restoration begun in 1660 continued until the turn of the century; that is, Restoration drama continued beyond 1688 to 1700. Mary died in 1694; when William died in 1702 and Mary's sister Anne became queen, both the political and the theatrical Restoration had come to an end.

During the Restoration, political thought in England was transformed by the philosophers Thomas Hobbes (1588–1679) and John Locke (1632–1704), who propounded the concept of natural law. According to both Hobbes and Locke, certain laws in the world are naturally right and should not be violated; any ruler who does violate them should be removed from power. Since human beings are rational, Hobbes and Locke believed that these natural rights could be discerned by reason. Hobbes and Locke, however, had different ideas about what form of government would best protect natural rights. Hobbes theorized, in *Leviathan,* that people give up freedom of action to absolute rulers in order to secure civil order and peace. Hobbes compared the structure of government to Leviathan, a biblical monster. Absolutism is meant to ensure individual welfare and uphold natural rights. (For this reason, Hobbes's ideal absolute ruler is the antithesis of such twentieth-century totalitarian dictators as Adolf Hitler and Joseph Stalin.)

Locke, on the other hand, preferred a representative government with a constitution, arguing that rulers are responsible to the people and serve as their representatives. Government is created to protect life, liberty, and property; rebellion against a government that violates these rights is more acceptable than allowing such violations to continue.

The views of Hobbes and Locke became highly influential in the eighteenth century. Enlightened despots—monarchs who believed that they ruled for the good of their people—modeled themselves after Hobbes's ideal absolutist. The leaders of the American and French revolutions were clearly influenced by the writings of Locke.

In England, transformations that took place during the reigns of Charles II, James II, and William and Mary were not only political or religious. Immediately after the Restoration, England expanded rapidly into the New World across the

English Restoration Year

Theatre

- Parliament closes theatres (1642)
- Davenant's *The First Day's Entertainment at Rutland House; Siege of Rhodes* (designer John Webb) (1656)
- Davenant's and Killigrew's companies granted patents (women in companies) (1660)
- Lincoln's Inn Fields Theatre (1661)
- Thomas Betterton foremost actor (c. 1662)
- Dorset Garden (1671)
- New Drury Lane opens (1674)
- Wycherley's *The Country Wife* (1675)
- Dryden's *All for Love* (1677)
- Aphra Behn's *The Rover* (1677)
- Otway's *Venice Preserved* (1682)
- Actress Nell Gwynn (1650–1687)
- Mary Pix's *The Innocent Mistress* (1697)
- Collier's *Short View of the Immorality and Profaneness of the English Stage* (1698)
- Congreve's *The Way of the World* (1700)

Year

1640 · 1645 · 1650 · 1655 · 1660 · 1665 · 1670 · 1675 · 1680 · 1685 · 1690 · 1695 · 1700

Culture and Politics

- English civil war (1642)
- Execution of Charles I (1649)
- Hobbes's *Leviathan* (1651)
- Anglo-Dutch wars (1652–1674)
- Protectorate under Oliver Cromwell (1653–1658)
- Cromwell dies (1658)
- Restoration of Charles II; Navigation Acts (1660)
- Royal Society founded (science) (1662)
- Milton's *Paradise Lost* (1667)
- Treaty of Dover between Charles II and Louis XIV (1670)
- Habeas Corpus Act (1679)
- Wren's Tom Tower, Christ Church, Oxford (1681)
- James II rules (1687)
- Newton's laws of gravity (1687)
- William and Mary; Glorious Revolution (1688)
- Locke's *Essay Concerning Human Understanding* (1690)
- Bank of England established (1694)

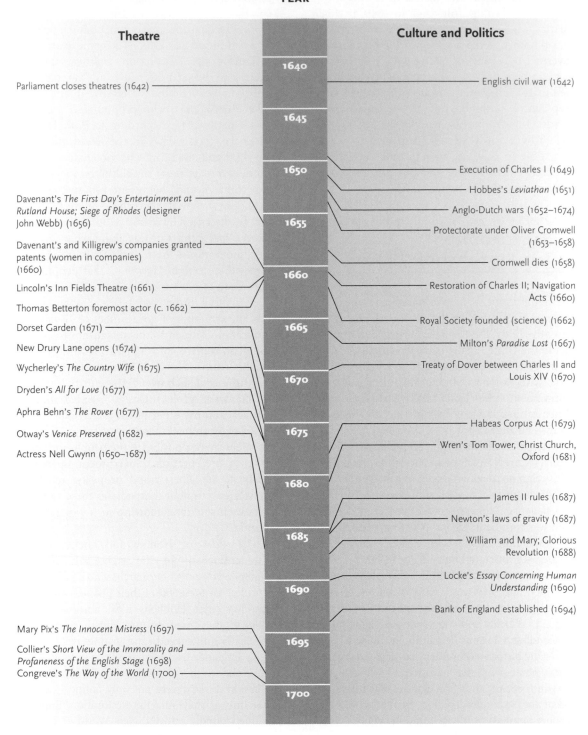

Atlantic; English colonies spread from New England to the Carolinas. The East India Company established trading posts in Surat, Madras, Calcutta, and Bombay. Cultural and scientific advances were also made. In 1662, the Royal Society of London for Improving Natural Knowledge was established; Isaac Newton, renowned for his experiments with gravity, was an original member. During the Restoration, the great architect Christopher Wren rebuilt Saint Paul's Cathedral, which had been destroyed by the fire of London in 1666. Thus, the restoration of the monarchy was followed by a restoration of trade, science, and culture.

Theatre during the Commonwealth

The Puritans closed the theatres in 1642, and from then until 1660 theatrical activity was severely curtailed. Elizabethan playhouses were dismantled, and actors were persecuted. Nevertheless, the laws forbidding theatre were not completely effective, and some entertainments were organized secretly. In the mid-1640s, for instance, performances were given at several theatres. Around 1650, when William Beeston (1606–1682) acquired the Salisbury Court Theatre, which had been closed, he rebuilt the theatre and began to train a company of boys to perform there. *Drolls*—short versions of full-length plays, usually comedies—were the form of drama most often staged.

A particularly important theatrical producer during the commonwealth period was William Davenant, who had been a court playwright before the closing of the theatres. Davenant was able to circumvent the ordinances against theatre by describing his presentations as musical entertainments and by staging them, at first, at his home. By the mid-1650s, however, opposition to the Puritans was increasing and subterfuge was not all that necessary. In 1656, Davenant presented *The First Day's Entertainment at Rutland House* and *The Siege of Rhodes.*

The Siege of Rhodes was particularly significant because the production had a proscenium arch and a wing-and-shutter setting—a stage arrangement that represented a clear departure from the platform stage of Shakespeare's day. Davenant's theatre was designed by John Webb (1611–1672), the son-in-law of Inigo Jones. Webb's use of Italianate devices was not surprising; his father-in-law had introduced such devices in court entertainments before Cromwell's abolition of the monarchy.

The Theatre of the Restoration Begins

At the beginning of the Restoration, when theatrical activity resumed, several trends became evident. One was a restriction on the number of theatres permitted to operate. Another was a change in several key aspects of theatre activity. These included new theatres, a new makeup in the audiences, and a new atmosphere that permeated attendance at theatres. This last had to do with the return of the monarchy in England and, along with royalty, the return of the nobility. Having been in France during their exile, the members of the court had been exposed to French and Italian theatrical influences; certain of these were expected by these audiences in the theatre they saw when they returned to England.

The most obvious change was the appearance of actresses onstage instead of the young boys who had previously portrayed female characters. Another change involved scenic practices. Equally important, however, was the fact that the nobility had for so long been denied the pleasure of attending theatre in their native land. Thus, in an almost defiant way, the upper classes claimed theatre as their own in the period immediately following the return of the monarchy.

In the beginning, several entrepreneurs attempted to initiate theatrical activity in England, but their efforts were beaten back by two figures who emerged to take control of the theatre: William Davenant (1606–1668) and Thomas Killigrew (1612–1683). Both men were familiar with English theatrical tradition, since they had been active in theatre before the commonwealth, but their leadership was to take English theatre in a new direction.

WILLIAM DAVENANT AND THOMAS KILLIGREW

William Davenant's theatrical experience went back to Shakespeare, who was said to have been a frequent visitor to his father's inn in Oxford and also to have been Davenant's godfather. After briefly attending Lincoln College at Oxford, Davenant began writing plays and collaborated with Inigo Jones on several court masques. In 1638, he succeeded Ben Jonson as poet laureate. He was knighted in 1643 for his service to the royalist cause, and he was imprisoned for a year by the Parliamentary forces.

(Harvard Theatre Collection, The Houghton Library, Fredric Woodbridge Wilson, Curator.)

William Davenant.

The other significant theatrical entrepreneur, Thomas Killigrew, was also a supporter of the royalist cause who had stayed with the royal family throughout its exile in France. Before the closing of the theatres, he had written a number of tragicomedies. According to the diarist Samuel Pepys, Killigrew was a "merry droll" and a favorite of Charles I.

Davenant's *The Siege of Rhodes* is considered the first English opera. It was also the first production in which actresses appeared on the English stage and the first public performance in which changeable scenery was used. In 1660, Davenant went to France to persuade Charles II to grant him a license for a theatre. That year, Charles granted Davenant and Killigrew a patent that gave them a monopoly on theatrical productions in London.

(National Portrait Gallery, London)

Thomas Killigrew.

After they had suppressed several unlicensed troupes, the two managers divided their own company. Killigrew formed the King's Company with the older, more experienced actors; Davenant's Duke's Company had several of the promising young actors, including Thomas Betterton, who was to become the finest actor of the Restoration. Davenant's company proved to be the stronger and better managed of the two, even after his death in 1668. Killigrew—who had been made master of the revels in 1673, with authority over all theatre in England—was often in financial difficulties. In 1682, a year before Killigrew's death, the two companies were reunited to prevent Killigrew's troupe from going bankrupt.

RESTORATION DRAMA

With the efforts of Davenant and Killigrew and the restoration of the monarchy, English theatre came to life again. During the English Renaissance, drama and theatre had not followed Italian Renaissance practices; but Italian practices had been introduced in Jacobean and Caroline court entertainments and in Davenant's presentations, and during the Restoration they truly took hold. This Italian influence was reinforced by England's contact with neoclassical France in the late seventeenth century. French culture was especially influential in Restoration society because Charles II had spent his exile in France and because James II had ties with Catholic Europe.

As we will see, the illusionistic—almost magical—devices of the proscenium-arch theatre, in which painted-perspective wing-and-shutter sets could be changed before the audience's eyes, would now become part of the English stage; however, much of the Elizabethan theatrical tradition would remain. In fact, the unique flavor of Restoration theatre is its fusion of Elizabethan stage conventions with those of the Italian and French theatres in drama, theatre architecture, and set design.

Serious Drama

Today the serious drama of the Restoration is rarely produced, or even read. One type of serious drama was *heroic tragedy,* popular between 1660 and 1675. Heroic tragedies dealt with extraordinary characters who undertook extraordinary deeds. These contrived plays, which deal with the themes of love and honor, are reminiscent of the dramas of the Spanish golden age and the French neoclassical era. Another type of serious drama, usually referred to as *Restoration tragedy,* became popular during the last quarter of the seventeenth century. The Italianate influence is immediately apparent in Restoration tragedies because of their adherence to the neoclassical rules.

John Dryden (1631–1700) is the most noted author of Restoration tragedy; his *All for Love* (1677) transformed Shakespeare's *Antony and Cleopatra* into a neoclassical tragedy. Among Dryden's other works were *The Indian Queen* (1664), *The Indian Emperor* (1665), and *The Conquest of Granada, Parts One and Two* (1669–1670).

It was not unusual for Restoration playwrights to rework Shakespeare into the neoclassical mold. *Romeo and Juliet,* for example, was provided with a happy ending by a writer named James Howard. Nahum Tate (1652–1715), who altered the ending of *King Lear* so that Lear is restored to his throne and Cordelia does not die, was among the best-known of the writers who adapted Shakespearean plays.

In the latter part of the seventeenth century, Thomas Otway (1652–1685) was another recognized author of Restoration tragedy. His two most notable dramas were *The Orphan* (1680) and *Venice Preserved* (1682).

Restoration Comedy

Comedies of Intrigue

The great plays of the English Restoration, however, were its comedies. Several types of comedy were popular. Comedies of "humour" followed the tradition of Ben Jonson, in which characters have one trait overshadowing all others. There were also farces; comedies of manners; and comedies of intrigue, which featured daring exploits of romance and adventure and had complicated plots. One of the most successful writers of comedies of intrigue was Aphra Behn (1640–1689).

APHRA BEHN

During the Restoration, when actresses were first appearing on the English stage, the first woman English playwright also appeared. Aphra Behn is not only the first known English woman dramatist; she is the first to have earned a living by writing. In addition to being a dramatist, she was also a poet and novelist.

(Billy Rose Theatre Collection, New York Public Library at Lincoln Center, Astor, Lenox, and Tilden Foundations)

Aphra Behn.

Her early life was both colorful and difficult. She was brought up in the West Indies, and her novel *Oroonoko* (1688) incorporates her early memories of life there. She returned to England in 1658, when she was 18, and married a Dutch merchant, but she was soon widowed. She went to the Netherlands as a spy during the war with the Dutch and was apparently successful in her work. She does not seem to have been paid, however, and she was briefly imprisoned for debt.

Friends helped her get out of prison, and she began writing. Beginning in 1670—when her first play, *The Forced Marriage,* was produced—she wrote at least twenty plays. Several of them proved successful, and some remained an active part of the theatre repertoire until well into the eighteenth century.

Behn wrote at the height of the Restoration, a time when licentiousness in drama was the rule rather than the exception, and her plays did not shy away from bawdiness. In such plays as *The Town Fop* and *The Rover,* both written in 1677, she even went so far as to show scenes in brothels. Defending her play *Sir Patient Fancy* (1678), she wrote, "It was bawdy, the least and most excusable fault in the men writers, to whose plays they all crowd, as if they came to no other end than to hear what they condemn in this, but from a woman it was unnatural."

Though there was some prejudice against her because of her gender, she overcame it with her successes. In fact, she and her friend John Dryden were the two most successful playwrights of the period. Dryden spoke of her as "writeing loosely, and giveing, if I may have leave to say so, some scandall to the modest of her sex. I confess, I am the last man who ought, in justice, to arraign her, who have been myself too much a libertine in most of my poems."

Behn is best-known for her plays of intrigue. (These are sometimes referred to as *comedies of intrigue* and at other times as *tragicomedies of intrigue.*) Behn's plays of intrigue, some of them influenced by Spanish theatre and Italian commedia dell'arte, are skillfully contrived. She also wrote tragedies, other types of comedies, and plays concerned with moral problems.

Her later work was primarily farce, which appealed to the taste of her audiences. Among her plays of intrigue are *The Dutch Lover* (1673), *Abdelazar* (1677), and *Sir Patient Fancy* (1678). Her popular comedies include *The Amorous Prince!* (1671), *The Feigned Courtesans* (1679), *The False Count* (1681), and *The City Heiress* (1682). One of her most successful farces was *The Emperor of the Moon* (1687). Thomas Betterton, one of the best-known actors of the time, performed in her first play, *The Forced Marriage,* and in her first success, *The Rover.* A lively, inventive writer, Behn was nicknamed the "divine Astrea" (Astrea was a goddess in classical mythology).

Following Behn, there were a significant number of other female playwrights in Restoration and eighteenth-century England.

Comedies of Manners

It is not, however, for tragedy, comedy, or plays of intrigue that Restoration drama is most remembered but rather for comedies of manners.

Comedy of manners, which was influenced by the French dramatist Molière, focuses on the fashions and foibles of the upper class gossip, adultery, sexual escapades. These comedies poke fun at the social conventions and norms of the time and satirize the preoccupation of the upper class with reputation: most of the upper-class characters in the plays are disreputable. Language—witty exchanges, repartee, and sexually suggestive references—is at a premium.

The dramatic structure of Restoration comedy of manners combines features of Elizabethan theatre with features of French and Italian neoclassical theatre. A good example is William Wycherley's *The Country Wife,* which has elements of both the crisis form and the episodic form. Its action is far more unified than the action in a Shakespearean play; it has only eight scene shifts and takes place in less than 36 hours. At the same time, unlike the plays of Racine or Molière, it moves from place to place, has a rather large number of characters, and includes a subplot. The characters in Restoration comedy are stock types; their names usually describe their distinctive personality traits. A common character is the fop who mistakenly believes himself to be witty and fashionable.

One of the first dramatists to perfect comedy of manners was George Etherege (c. 1633–1691), in plays such as *Love in a Tub* (1664), *She Would If She Could* (1668), and *The Man of Mode* (1676). The two most renowned playwrights of this type of Restoration comedy were William Wycherley and William Congreve.

WILLIAM WYCHERLEY

In his plays, William Wycherley (1640–1716) satirized the elegant, dissolute society of Restoration England. In his life, however, he was a member of that society, participating fully in all the vices and follies that he ridiculed as a dramatist.

Like many Restoration dramatists, Wycherley wrote only a few plays; playwriting for him was a way of proving his cleverness and wit rather than a serious profession. Unlike his contemporaries, he showed the faults of all members of his glittering society rather than just making fun of the usual fools. A well-read man, he borrowed characters and situations from several sources, especially Molière and Terence. He was a master of the sexual humor of his time (such as using words with double meanings); his works shocked the more prudish audiences of later centuries. Congreve wrote that Wycherley's purpose was "to lash this crying age" with his satire.

(National Portrait Gallery, London)

William Wycherley.

As the son of a landowner, Wycherley had the requisite family background for entrance into society. He was educated first in France and then, briefly, at Oxford. He began studying law at the Inner Temple in London but was soon practicing not law but pleasure. His first comedy, *Love in a Wood; or, St. James Park,* produced in 1671, brought him to the attention of the duchess of Cleveland, the king's mistress, who did not hesitate to share her favors.

Wycherley soon became one of London's leading wits and was sponsored at court by the duke of Buckingham, a favorite of Charles II. Three more of his comedies were successfully produced: *The Gentleman Dancing-Master* in 1672, *The Country Wife* in 1675, and *The Plain Dealer* in 1676.

THE COUNTRY WIFE
One of the most famous Restoration comedies is *The Country Wife* by William Wycherley. It epitomizes the wit, the satire, the gossip, and the depiction of sexual intrigue that characterize Restoration comedy of manners. In this play a man attempts to keep his wife away from the amorous advances of Horner, who specializes in seducing other men's wives. Shown here is a scene from a production by the New Jersey Shakespeare Festival, featuring Allison Daugherty and Howard Samuelsohn.

Wycherley's most famous play is *The Country Wife,* which concerns a man named Pinchwife, who has recently married Margery, a young girl from the country. Pinchwife tries to hide Margery away so that she will not be corrupted by the wicked ways of the fashionable set in London, but his precautions are undermined by a man named Horner. In the play, Horner spreads the rumor that he is impotent because of a venereal disease he contracted while abroad. Horner's doctor, Quack, substantiates the rumor, and Horner uses this "cover story" to gain access to his acquaintances' wives. The one he most desires is Margery Pinchwife, a naive woman whose husband usually keeps her locked away in the country and tries to disguise her as a boy when she is in town. Coming on Pinchwife and the disguised Margery in the street, Horner realizes that the "boy" is a woman in a man's clothing and takes advantage of the situation to make amorous advances, hugging and kissing her in front of her husband, who can do nothing.

As is typical of plays written in this period, the names of the characters indicate their desires and personalities. The chief character, Horner, wants to cuckold his acquaintances—that is, seduce their wives. His name, therefore, comes from a well-known image of the time: a husband with an adulterous wife was said to be wearing horns. Quack, obviously, is a disreputable doctor; Harcourt diligently courts a woman named Alithea. Two other characters, Fidget and Squeamish, are nervous about their reputations; Pinchwife does not want his wife pinched by other men. Sparkish, a fop, thinks he is a great wit, a social "spark"; in reality, he is dim-witted.

A good example of the licentious elements in Restoration comedies is a scene in *The Country Wife* known as the "china closet" scene. In this scene, Horner and Lady Fidget are in a room offstage while Lady Fidget's husband is onstage listening to their conversation. Horner and Lady Fidget are supposed to be examining Horner's collection of china, but the audience soon realizes that Horner is actually making love to Lady Fidget while her husband stands by in ignorance. Then another woman, Mrs. Squeamish, arrives, and she too asks to see Horner's china. When Horner tells Mrs. Squeamish he has no more, the audience knows that *china* has become a code word for *sex* and that Horner is unable at that moment to perform sexually.

At the conclusion of the play, Horner's scheme has been successful: he has made love not only to Margery but to the other wives as well. *The Country Wife* was revised by David Garrick in the eighteenth century as *The Country Girl;* stripped of some of the sexual innuendo of the original, this was a popular version.

After writing *The Plain Dealer,* Wycherley went to sea and fought in the Dutch wars. When he fell ill, the king, Charles II, gave him money to recuperate in France and promised to make him the tutor of one of the princes. Instead, Wycherley married a wealthy, jealous countess in 1681 and lost Charles's favor. Wycherley's wife died the following year; he became involved in litigation over her estate, lost the case, and spent 7 years in debtors' prison before James II paid his bills and gave him a small pension. Eleven days before his death in 1716, Wycherley married a young woman, apparently to provoke his nephew.

WILLIAM CONGREVE

Commenting on the fate of dramatists, William Congreve (1670–1729) wrote in a prologue to his play *The Way of the World:*

> Of those few fools who with ill stars are cursed,
> Sure scribbling fools called poets, fare the worst.

His words proved to be prophetic, for *The Way of the World* ended his own brief career as a playwright. With his four comedies, however, Congreve had established his reputation as one of the Restoration's finest dramatists.

(Victoria and Albert Museum, London)

William Congreve.

Congreve, the son of an English army officer, was raised and educated in Dublin, where the writer Jonathan Swift was one of his schoolmates. He returned to England to study law at the Middle Temple but instead became involved in the literary and social life of Restoration London. Congreve's first literary venture was an undistinguished novel; he turned next to playwriting with *The Old Bachelor,* produced in 1693 to great acclaim.

With his first success as a playwright came financial stability; this led to a series of government appointments secured for him by influential friends. Always careful with his money, Congreve acquired a reputation for miserliness in later life. His second comedy, *The Double Dealer* (1694), was less successful; but *Love for Love,* produced the following year by the actor Thomas Betterton, was Congreve's greatest stage triumph. A tragedy, *The Mourning Bride* (1697), was also well received. *The Way of the World,* however—which would later be considered the best Restoration comedy—was a failure when it was first produced in 1700, and Congreve stopped writing for the stage. One of the reasons for the failure of *The Way of the World* was a changed moral climate in England.

Congreve's *The Way of the World* (1700) is often considered a bridge between Restoration comedy and eighteenth-century English sentimental comedy, which stresses traditional morality, punishes the sinful, and rewards the virtuous. Like Restoration comedy, *The Way of the World* has a number of characters involved in adulterous affairs, and some traditional stock characters; it is also marked by brilliant wit and a dazzling prose style. But as in sentimental comedy, its two young lovers (Mirabell and Millamant) are united, while the wicked characters (Fainall and Mrs. Marwood) are punished. In one famous scene, Mirabell and Millamant "bargain" with each other over the prerogatives and conditions they will agree to once they are married.

His four comedies gave Congreve an assured place in the best literary and social circles of London—for the rest of his life he was a friend of Pope, Swift, Steele, and Gray. Congreve died in 1729 and was buried in Westminster Abbey.

With the exception of Aphra Behn, Wycherley and Congreve are the two Restoration playwrights most often discussed. But like Behn, other women had begun to write for the theatre in this period. The London season of 1695–1696, for instance, saw productions by seven female playwrights. Like actresses on the stage (whom we discuss shortly), this was a sharp departure in the English theatre from the days before the Commonwealth. Among the women writers, one particularly noteworthy group was known as the "female wits."

THE FEMALE WITS

The "female wits" included Catharine Trotter (1679–1749), Mary Pix (1666–1706), and Delariviere Manley (c. 1672–1724). The term was originally used in a negative sense; it was taken from the name of an anonymous satire on the trio. Later, however, "female wits" came to be used in a more positive light, to signify the importance of these figures to a feminist revision of late-seventeenth-century theatre history. Together the three female dramatists worked in the London theatre world in a highly collegial manner, publishing verses for each other's works.

(© T. Charles Erickson)

THE WAY OF THE WORLD

The Way of the World by William Congreve is often seen as a transitional play, combining elements of the Restoration comedies that it followed and the sentimental comedies that were to come. The characters are witty, clever, and from the upper class, concerned with infidelity and the like. But at the end of the play, the virtuous people are rewarded and the bad ones punished, in the manner of more moral plays later in the eighteenth century. Seen here in a production of *The Way of the World* at the Yale Repertory Theatre are Alicia Roper as Foible and Lee Mark Nelson as Waitwell.

Trotter's early life was marked by poverty, due to the death of her father, a naval commander. Known for her beauty and precocious intelligence, Trotter first published some verses at the age of 14—and the novel *Olinda's Adventures,* which had been published in half a dozen English editions by 1724. At age 16, Trotter wrote her first play, *Agnes de Castro,* based on a novel by Aphra Behn. Trotter's decision to write publicly for the stage may be in part explained by her family's financial plight. However, as her career continued she also wrote theological and philosophical works, producing an essay in defense of Locke as well as religious treatises.

When she was 29, she married a clergyman and gave up writing for 20 years to concentrate on her husband and children. After rearing four children, she returned to writing, producing a series of theological treatises. Trotter's dramatic output includes *Fatal Friendship,* produced at Lincoln's Inn Fields in 1689; *Love at a Loss* and *The Unhappy Penitent,* produced at Drury Lane around 1701; and *The Revolution of Sweden,* produced at Lincoln's Inn Fields in 1706.

Although Mary Pix was the most prolific of the female wits, she is the one about whom the least is known. What is known is that she married George Pix in 1684 at the age of 18, and the union produced a child who died in 1690. However, unlike Trotter,

Pix did not begin writing until the age of 30 and wrote many of her plays while married; historians attribute anywhere from seven to thirteen plays to Pix. Her first play—*Ibrahim, the Thirteenth Emperor of the Turks*—premiered in the 1695–1696 season and was soon followed by her comedy *The Spanish Wives,* as well as her novel *The Inhuman Cardinal.* Other works by Pix include *The Innocent Mistress* (1697), *The Deceiver Deceived* (1697), *Queen Catharine* (1698), *The False Friend* (1699), *The Beau Defeated* (1699–1700), *The Double Distress* (1700–1701), *The Czar of Muscovy* (1700–1701), *The Different Widows* (1703), *The Conquest of Spain* (1705), and *The Adventures in Madrid* (1706). The authorship of *Zelmane* (1704) is still in question, but some scholars attribute this play to Pix. Many contemporary historians believe that in addition to her own works, Pix possibly collaborated with Susanna Centlivre on her play *The Busy Body* (1709).

Delariviere Manley differed from her contemporaries in that she had a scandalous reputation; and of the three, she is most harshly treated in the satire *The Female Wits.* Born a gentlewoman, like Trotter, Manley also eventually turned to writing as a livelihood. After her father's death, Manley became a ward of her cousin John Manley, who claimed to be recovering from the death of his wife and eventually persuaded the young woman to marry him. However, some years and a son later, John Manley's wife was discovered to be alive and he left Delariviere, who was now marked by scandal and had borne an illegitimate child. In 1696 Manley published a collection of letters, as well as producing her comedy *The Lost Lover; or, The Jealous Husband,* followed by *The Royal Mischief,* which would become the subject of the anonymous satire. Manley's dramatic output is relatively small, with only *Alymyna: or, the Arabian Vow* (1706) and *Lucius, the First Christian King of Britain* (1717) surviving in addition to her two previous comedies. Much of Manley's literary reputation rests on her notorious narrative *The New Atlantis* (1709) and her autobiographical *The Adventures of Rivella* (1714). These narratives were perceived as pornographic, given their explicit emphasis on the sexual exploitation of women and reversed sexual roles. Manley also became involved in periodical writing, contributing to *The Female Tatler* as Mrs. Crackenthorpe.

Together, these three women worked to increase the involvement of female playwrights in English theatre—building on Aphra Behn's work. Although often beset with notoriety, scandal, and satire, the three marked the late seventeenth century and early eighteenth century with their writing both for and beyond the stage.

Restoration Audiences

Many Restoration comedies, including *The Country Wife,* indicate that audiences of that era, unlike modern-day spectators, were quite spirited in their behavior during performances. The fop Sparkish in *The Country Wife* describes how audience members purchased fruit from the "orange wenches" (many of these "wenches" were prostitutes), spoke back to the actors, arranged assignations with each other, and attended the theatre to be seen rather than to see the play. Activities like these provoked attacks by religious leaders who were opposed to theatre.

(Bettmann/Corbis)

AN UNUSUAL PROLOGUE
Seen here is a popular comedian of the Restoration period, Joe Haines, on horseback, delivering the prologue of a play to a Restoration audience. The place is the Theatre of the King's Company. Note the finery used or worn by the audience members: the fans, wigs, and tiaras.

Restoration audiences were primarily, but probably not exclusively, members of the upper class—the same group that was being satirized in the plays. Which social class attends theatre varies significantly in different periods and different places. Sometimes, audiences encompass everyone, rich and poor; at other times, audiences include only one social class. (For instance, in ancient Greece, in medieval theatre, and in Elizabethan public theatres, audiences included virtually all strata of society; by contrast, productions at European courts—such as masques—were seen only by the nobility and royalty.) It is usually assumed that in the first decades of the English Restoration, only a small portion of society—the upper class—attended the theatre. When theatre is aimed at a narrow group, this generally means that playwrights tailor their works specifically for the audience they know will be watching. As a result, the plays are not likely to have the universality of drama written for a wider audience. Restoration comedy, however, deals with subjects—social pretention and sex—that are familiar to sophisticated society in any age.

Performers

Actresses and Actors

One of the most obvious changes from English Renaissance theatre to Restoration theatre was the appearance of actresses on the English stage. In France and Spain, actresses had appeared on the stage for some time; but England forbade actresses until 1660, and so women onstage became a novelty that strongly appealed to the men in the audience. Moreover, once women were allowed to perform onstage in England, a favorite dramatic device was to have a woman dress as a man; parts that required this kind of cross-dressing were called *breeches roles.*

Seeing a woman's figure outlined in tight trousers, and getting a good idea of the shape of her legs—which were usually hidden under wide skirts—had a strong sexual fascination. A good example would be an attractive actress playing Margery disguised as a man in *The Country Wife.* Dressing actresses in tight breeches would not seem very provocative to modern audiences, but eighteenth-century religious leaders considered the practice highly licentious.

Many theatre historians have asked what the actual status of the actress was during this period. Financial success was possible for actresses, but they were often seen as no better than prostitutes and were frequently coerced into sexual liaisons with other company members or with wealthy audience members. In addition, their roles—particularly the breeches roles—focused on their sexuality. The question arises, therefore, whether the fact that women were admitted to the acting profession was in itself a sign of any kind of equality or equitable treatment; for many historians, the answer is that it was not. In many areas of society and life, women had an inferior status, and this may have carried through to the position of actresses.

(Bettmann/Corbis)

NELL GWYNN MEETS KING CHARLES II

Nell Gwynn, who began her career selling oranges in the theatre, went on to become a successful actress, especially in Restoration comedy at the Drury Lane Theatre. She later became the mistress of King Charles II. Shown here is a painting of Nell supposedly first meeting the king. His love for her is thought to have been partially responsible for his support of the theatre. Charles continued to be in love with Nell, who became the mother of at least one of his children.

Nevertheless, a number of actresses became extremely popular during the Restoration. Elizabeth Barry (1658–1713) was the leading actress with the famous tragedian Thomas Betterton (c. 1635 1710); Betterton was noted for his performances in Shakespeare's plays and Barry for her performances of the major female roles in these plays. Anne Bracegirdle, who had studied performing with Betterton, was a distinguished actress in Restoration comedies until her retirement in 1707. The best-known theatre personality of the era, however, was probably Nell Gwynn (1650–1687), famous for her comic performances, her dancing, and her liaison with Charles II.

ELEANOR (NELL) GWYNN

Nell Gwynn's remarkable career—which took her from the slums of London to the king's palace—can be attributed to her own beauty and high spirits and to the unique conditions of Restoration society. After over 20 years of Puritan rule, the main preoccupation of English society from 1660 on was the pursuit of pleasure. Theatre was a fashionable entertainment, and one of its attractions was the introduction of actresses to the English stage.

The daughter of the keeper of a bawdy house and an unknown father, Nell Gwynn grew up in the London slums. She was said to have begun her theatrical career as a girl selling oranges at the Theatre Royal in Drury Lane. There she attracted the attention of Charles Hart, the leading actor; she became his mistress and protégé and made her stage debut in December 1664. As an actress, she relied on her natural wit and charm; she excelled in singing and dancing but was a failure in tragedy. Her specialties were "breeches roles," in which she wore men's clothing, and the delivery of prologues and epilogues.

Nell Gwynn was not typical of Restoration actresses, but in some ways she is representative. Actresses were still a novelty, and many of them were assiduously pursued by Restoration gallants. It was no disgrace to have a mistress, or to be one; because the theatre was prestigious, actresses were favored as mistresses, and there were probably as many affairs within acting companies as with outsiders. Some actresses, however—such as Anne Bracegirdle—were as celebrated for their virtue as Nell Gwynn was for her impropriety.

When she delivered the epilogue to John Dryden's *Tyrannick Love* in 1669, Nell Gwynn drew the attention of Charles II. She became his mistress and left the stage, settling in a house in Pall Mall—though in 1670 she returned to the theatre to play in Dryden's *The Conquest of Granada.* She had two sons by Charles; the older one became the duke of Saint Albans, but the younger died in childhood.

It seems that Nell Gwynn's rise in social status did little to change her, except to make her more extravagant. She never denied her origins or claimed to be more than the king's mistress, and unlike his other favorites, she never meddled in politics. Her chief concerns were the king's amusement, her children, and entertaining his friends. Recognizing her faithfulness, Charles, on his deathbed, told his brother, "Let not poor Nelly starve." James II rescued her from her creditors and gave her a pension that enabled her to live comfortably until her death in 1687.

THOMAS BETTERTON

By all accounts the greatest actor of the Restoration stage was Thomas Betterton (1635–1710). A fellow actor, Barton Booth, once remarked, "Divinity hung round that man." Admired for his attention to detail, his self-discipline, and his majestic restraint, Betterton remained the model of English oratorical style until David Garrick took the stage in the middle of the eighteenth century. Betterton was noted for his dazzling characterizations of Shakespeare's tragic heroes, though he played an astonishing range of roles and was equally skillful in comedy or tragedy. In addition, he was heavily involved in playwriting, theatre management, and the training of actors as well as staging practices for most of his 50-year career.

(Billy Rose Theatre Collection, New York Public Library at Lincoln Center, Astor, Lenox, and Tilden Foundations)

Thomas Betterton.

Betterton was born and educated in London and is thought to have started his career under the guidance of William Davenant in the 1660s, when he joined the Duke's Company. He quickly became a shareholder and leading actor, receiving critical praise in roles such as Hamlet, Sir Toby Belch in *Twelfth Night,* and Bosola in John Webster's Jacobean tragedy *The Duchess of Malfi.* The diarist Samuel Pepys was especially impressed with Betterton as Macbeth and Hamlet. (He was still performing the latter role at 74!) He also created many Restoration tragic heroes, including Jaffier in Thomas Otway's *Venice Preserved* (1682). In 1662 he married Mary Saunderson (c. 1637–1712), a leading actress in the company, who shared his reputation for developing young talent.

After Davenant's death, Betterton assumed a position as comanager in the company, with responsibilities that included writing and adapting plays, overseeing rehearsals, and training young actors. He also traveled to Paris to learn about innovations in French theatre machinery and staging practices, pursuing a novel interest in mounting extravagant and costly operatic spectacles. The most successful of these—*The Prophetess* and *The Fairy-Queen*—were collaborations with the English composer Henry Purcell.

In 1682, the Duke's Company merged with Killigrew's faltering King's Company. The new United Company was headed by Betterton at Drury Lane, but it was financially controlled by a group of patentees, managed by the notoriously exploitative lawyer Christopher Rich (1660–1714). Following a series of disputes, largely due to financial mismanagement, Betterton led an actors' revolt against Rich and the management of Drury Lane in 1695. He was joined by the two leading actresses, Elizabeth Barry and Anne Bracegirdle, who both assisted in the organization of the new company. The rebels successfully petitioned the Lord Chamberlain with their grievances and were granted a license from the king. Under Betterton's direction, the rival company moved into Lincoln's Inn Fields Theatre.

Although the company of aging stars enjoyed initial success, the venture suffered from financial instability—for which Betterton was often criticized. With the rebel company's collapse in 1704, Betterton retired as manager. During his remaining years he played in the Haymarket Theatre, where he continued to perform many of his most popular roles. Sickened by gout, Betterton made his final appearance in 1710. The celebrated star was buried in the east cloister of Westminster Abbey.

ANNE BRACEGIRDLE

Among the first English actresses who captivated Restoration audiences was the extraordinarily talented Anne Bracegirdle (c. 1671–1748). Bracegirdle achieved resounding popularity for her portrayal of enticingly clever urban women in Restoration comedy and sympathetic heroines in tragedy, but perhaps her most famous attribute was her virtuous reputation; she was called the "celebrated virgin."

As a child Bracegirdle, who may have been the daughter of a coachman, coach maker, or coach renter, was placed in the care of the renowned actor Thomas Betterton and his wife Mary, when her own family—from Northamptonshire—fell on hard times. It is likely that under the guidance of the Bettertons, Bracegirdle was groomed for the stage. From her first appearance in 1688 until her retirement in 1707, Bracegirdle enjoyed success as one of the first great comediennes of the English theatre. As the leading comic actress at the United Company, she worked side by side with Betterton and Elizabeth Barry, the leading tragic actress, at Drury Lane. During the actor-led rebellion against Christopher Rich and the management of the theatre in 1695, Bracegirdle accompanied Betterton to Lincoln's Inn Fields Theatre and helped comanage the new company, gaining unprecedented stature for a woman at the time.

(Culver Pictures)
Anne Bracegirdle.

(Victoria and Albert Museum, London/Art Resource, N.Y.)

THEATRE BENEFITS One method by which Restoration actors were compensated was an annual "benefit." Once a year, the proceeds from a performance were given directly to the actor or actress. In the cartoon shown here a man is complaining about the misuse of a benefit performance, which had been double-booked. Learning of the situation, the man exclaims, "I wish I hadn't bought the tickets."

Bracegirdle was extremely popular in breeches roles (parts that featured cross-dressing); her shapely figure and legs were highly admired. She was a gifted singer, and her exceptional comic abilities were ideally suited to portraying the witty, sophisticated women in Restoration comedy of manners. Her bright, sparkling beauty and cheerful disposition inspired many a writer. Many of William Congreve's comic heroines were written especially for her, including perhaps her most famous role—Millamant in *The Way of the World* (1700). Congreve was not the only man in London intoxicated by Bracegirdle, but their relationship, in particular, fueled rumors—never proved—that they were secretly married.

The actor-manager Colley Cibber, in his memoirs, attributes Bracegirdle's popularity to her sexual discretion, which made her "the *Cara*, the Darling, of the Theatre." She retired at the height of her career amid speculation that she did not want to be overshadowed by a younger rival, Anne Oldfield (1683–1730). Her remaining years were spent comfortably out of the public eye. Both professionally and personally her legendary status was never overthrown. She was buried in Westminster Abbey.

Acting Companies

Restoration acting companies were larger than those of the English Renaissance; and the addition of women performers was, of course, a significant change. There were also less visible transformations, especially in organizational structure.

The sharing plan of companies like the Lord Chamberlain's Men—Shakespeare's company—almost disappeared in London during the course of the Restoration. Rather than sharing in the profits and losses of their companies, London actors during the Restoration were hired for a specific period of time at a set salary. The new practice was called the *contract system;* and the move from the sharing plan to the contract system marked a decline of actors' control over theatre in London. (Outside London, provincial companies—as well as companies established in the thirteen colonies of North America—continued to use the sharing plan, and their actors were still the controlling force.)

At the same time, the Restoration saw the emergence of theatrical entrepreneurs who were often part-owners of theatre buildings and companies. The most successful theatrical businessman of the late Restoration and early eighteenth century, the lawyer Christopher Rich, was also the most notorious. At the turn of the century, Rich controlled the patents Charles II had issued to both Davenant and Killigrew; his insufferable financial practices—he failed to provide reasonable salaries and did not always pay his performers—drove some actors in his group to rebel and establish their own company. (The rise of the entrepreneur as a powerful force in theatre was, of course, a step in the development of modern theatre business. A good example of an entrepreneur in today's commercial theatre is the British producer Cameron Mackintosh, who was responsible for such musicals as *Cats, Les Misérables, The Phantom of the Opera,* and *Miss Saigon.*)

In order to increase their set wages under the contract system, actors (and other company personnel) were provided with yearly "benefits." For each major performer in a company, one "benefit performance" was designated—a performance from which he or she would keep all the profits. Frequently, ticket prices for these benefit performances were increased so that the performer's earnings would be greater. A few minor performers might share the profits from one benefit performance. The benefit system was used in England from the Restoration through the nineteenth century.

Playwrights were rarely members of Restoration troupes. Instead, they were paid either a fee for their work or by a variation of the benefit system: a playwright would receive the profits from the third night of the premiere run of the play. By the turn of the century, the playwright might also receive the profits from the sixth consecutive night of the opening run. It should be remembered, however, that Restoration theatre was not like modern theatre, in which long runs are common; many Restoration plays never succeeded in running three nights in a row.

Actors learned their craft through apprenticeships and usually played a specific range of roles: for instance, one man would play serious heroes and another low-comedy types. Because (as in Elizabethan theatre) long runs were unusual, companies changed their bills frequently, and actors had to develop skills of quick study and retention.

Rehearsals for a new play would rarely extend past 2 weeks; a revival would merit little more than a run-through on the day of the performance. For a new play, the playwright would assist in the first rehearsal, but most of the rehearsal process was the responsibility of the company's manager, who was often one of its leading actors. The function of rehearsals was usually simply to ascertain whether or not the performers knew their lines; firsthand accounts tell us that on opening night they often did not. Given these rehearsal practices, Restoration actor-managers were never able to assume the functions of the modern director, telling performers where to move onstage or how to interpret their roles.

Many historians suggest that the acting style of the Restoration, particularly for tragedy, featured broad gestures and powerful declamatory delivery. Thomas Betterton, the leading actor of the Restoration—he was also a leader of the revolt against the entrepreneur Christopher Rich—was noted for his vocal prowess. The voice of his leading lady, Elizabeth Barry, was described as "full, clear, and strong so that no Violence of Passion could be too much for her." Because rehearsals were sketchy, out of necessity actors fell back on conventional patterns of stage movement; for example, much of the dialogue was delivered directly to the audience from the front of the stage. Some scholars argue, however, that the mechanical style of Restoration acting has been overstated; and some also believe that comic acting may have been less flamboyant than tragic acting.

Restoration Theatres

Government and the Theatres

Government regulations were an aspect of theatre production in the Restoration. When theatre was revived in 1660, the rules established during the reign of Elizabeth to oversee the theatres were reinstituted. The master of revels took control of theatre and issued licenses to three theatrical entrepreneurs. Charles II, however—as we noted earlier—issued patents to William Davenant and Thomas Killigrew that superseded those issued by the master of revels; as a result, Davenant and Killigrew had a monopoly on theatre in London.

By the early eighteenth century, this monopoly seemed unenforceable; the monarchs who succeeded Charles II had made exceptions to it, and some companies simply operated in defiance of it. In 1737, Parliament, questioning Charles's right to have issued patents without its approval, passed the Licensing Act—a new attempt to regulate London theatre. Under the Licensing Act, only two theatres were authorized to present "tragedy, comedy, opera, play, farce, or other entertainment for the stage for gain, hire, or reward," and the lord chamberlain became responsible for licensing plays; thus the tradition of governmental regulation established by Elizabeth I continued into the Restoration and, beyond that, into the eighteenth century. The two theatres authorized by the Licensing Act were Covent Garden and Drury Lane.

Theatre Architecture in the Restoration

During the Restoration, there were three theatre buildings of note in London: Lincoln's Inn Fields (1661), which was a converted tennis court; Dorset Garden (1671); and Drury Lane. Though each of them was distinct, all three had interiors that fused Italianate and Elizabethan features.

By the time of the Restoration, the Elizabethan tradition of open-air public theatres had ended; all theatres were now indoor proscenium-arch buildings. The area for the audience was divided into pit, boxes, and galleries. The pit in Restoration theatres had backless benches—unlike the pit in French neoclassical theatres, where the spectators stood. Also, the pit in the English houses was raked—slanted downward from back to front—for better sight lines. The total seating capacity was about 650. In size, then, as well as in many other respects, Restoration theatres were similar to Elizabethan private theatres.

The Restoration stage was highly unusual in that it was divided into two distinct, nearly equal halves: the apron—the forestage in front of the proscenium—was very deep, almost as deep as the area behind the proscenium. (In contrast, the apron in a twenty-first-century proscenium-arch theatre is usually small and inconsequential.) In the seventeenth century, only the English had theatre buildings with extended aprons; most historians believe that the extended apron was a vestige of the platform stage of the English Renaissance. The apron was the major area for performance in Restoration theatres; the area behind the proscenium housed the scenery. The entire stage was raked to improve sight lines.

The other unique elements of the Restoration stage were the proscenium doors with balconies above them. Most Restoration theatres had two proscenium doors on each side of the stage—a total of four doors—that led onto the forestage. These doors were used for exits and entrances, and for the concealment scenes—scenes in which one character listened out of sight of the others—popular in Restoration comedy. The balconies above these doorways could be used for balcony and window scenes.

Later, in the 1700s, the stage apron shrank, and the number of doors decreased from two on each side to one. Even so, the continued influence of Elizabethan theatre architecture kept the English playhouses from becoming exact duplicates of theatres on the European continent: English theatres continued to have a distinctly English quality.

(Bettmann/Corbis)

LOVE IN A TUB

Wit, urbanity, intrigue, infidelity, razor-sharp repartee: these are the hallmarks of Restoration comedy. One of the first dramatists to succeed with the form was George Etherege. Seen here is drawing of a scene from a production in 1664 at Lincoln's Inn Fields of his play *The Comical Revenge or Love in a Tub*.

Scenery, Scene-Shifting Technology, Costumes, and Lighting

Visual elements—scenery, lighting, and costumes—also illustrate the Italianization of the English stage during the Restoration. As noted in Chapter 6, Inigo Jones had designed and painted wing-and-shutter settings for court entertainments during the Caroline and Jacobean periods; and his son-in-law, John Webb, used these scenic devices at the close of the commonwealth in his design for *The Siege of Rhodes*. Not surprisingly, then, during the Restoration the basic scenic components were wings, shutters—in which two halves of a stiff backing at the rear of the stage opened or closed—and borders for masking. Sometimes the back shutters were replaced by a single backdrop that was rolled up or lowered. The sets, of course, were painted in perspective.

What made the scenic practices of Restoration England distinct from those of Italy and France was that the English rarely used Torelli's pole-and-chariot system for scene changes. Instead, flats were placed in grooves behind the proscenium and on the backstage floor; the flats were pulled off into the wings, revealing new scenery—other flats—directly behind them. With the groove system, each piece of scenery must be removed separately by individual stagehands; therefore, scene changes could not be synchronized as successfully in English theatres as in Italian theatres. In England, shifts were carried out by stagehands stationed at each groove position who moved scenery manually when a whistle was blown by the prompter. (This was a holdover from changes of sails on ships, which were coordinated by blowing a whistle.)

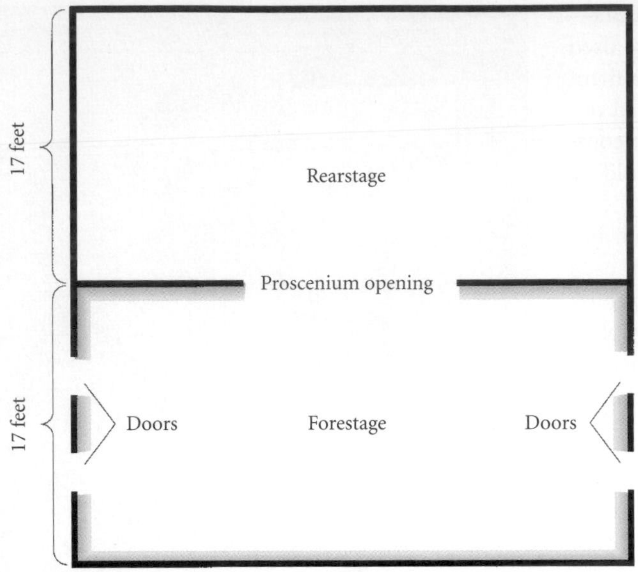

GROUND PLAN OF A RESTORATION STAGE
This stage was an unusual combination of English and Italian Renaissance stages. The Restoration saw the introduction of the Italianate proscenium arch into public playhouses in England. However, the extended apron, equal in depth to the rear stage area, and the two proscenium doors on each side of the stage were vestiges of the Elizabethan platform stage and tiring house.

Because the curtain was never closed during the course of a presentation, scene changes were carried out while the audience watched. Even musical entertainments—which were staged between the acts of full-length plays during the Restoration—were presented in front of the scenery already in view. As a result, the audience was always aware of the mechanical aspects of a theatre production. All through the nineteenth century, the English, except in their opera houses, used the primitive groove system for changing scenery.

Throughout the Restoration, companies kept collections of perspective settings that were reused frequently. Stock settings were the norm, primarily because of the expense entailed in having scenery painted. For this reason, most Restoration comedies have similar scenic requirements: the drawing room and the park.

Restoration costuming followed the traditions of the English Renaissance and the French neoclassical era: contemporary clothing was standard. Because they were set in the present day, everyday clothing was of course appropriate for Restoration comedies, but not for dramas set in the past. Though traditional costumes and accessories were sometimes worn to indicate historical figures or eras, there was no real attempt to be historically accurate. To take one example, until well into the eighteenth century an actor playing Shakespeare's Roman character Coriolanus would wear a kind of ballet skirt, breeches, laced boots reaching halfway to the knees, an embroidered jacket, a full wig, and a helmet with plumes—a costume unrelated to the historical setting of the play. This inappropriateness and lack of verisimilitude would make the conventions of Restoration costuming—like Restoration scenic practices—jarring to modern theatregoers.

Because Restoration theatres were indoors, lighting was a major concern. Theatre performances during the late seventeenth century normally took place in the afternoon, when windows could provide some natural lighting. Inside, candles were the predominant source of lighting, and chandeliers holding them were visible above the stage and the audience. Candles were also placed in brackets attached to the front of the boxes. The stage and the audience area were always lit, and footlights—lights on the floor running along the front of the stage—were also used. In today's theatre, footlights are rarely used because they cast unnatural shadows on the performers' faces. During the Restoration, however, theatre artists could not be choosy about the quality of lighting; their main concern was simple illumination.

The Dorset Garden Theatre

The scanty evidence available about the Dorset Garden Theatre has led to a great deal of debate over its appearance. For a number of years, two theatre historians—John R. Spring and Robert Hume—argued in scholarly journals about this. Their controversy was set off when Spring questioned an earlier reconstruction of the theatre by the historian Edward A. Langhans. According to Spring, Dorset Garden was essentially very similar to another important Restoration playhouse, Drury Lane: the size of the forestage and proscenium opening as well as the four proscenium doors and scenic machinery at Dorset Garden were almost identical to those at Drury Lane.

Hume's ideas, on the other hand, are closer to Langhans's reconstruction, which had suggested that the two theatres were quite different. Hume argues that the United Company of the Restoration, and later Christopher Rich's company, used Drury Lane for "everyday dramas" but used Dorset Garden for plays that required extensive scenic effects; and that there would have been no reason to use both spaces if they were nearly identical. He concludes: "One of the few things we can say about Dorset Garden is that it surpassed every English theatre of its time in its capacity for scenic splendor. To suggest that its scenic stage was all of 28 ft. 6 in. deep—far less than the space available at Drury Lane—is to suggest an absurdity."*

This debate shows how difficult it is to reconstruct a historic playhouse when few substantial sources survive. As Hume himself admits: "What we know with some certainty about the Dorset Garden theatre is derived from a few pieces of rather unsatisfactory evidence."† The well-known theatre historian Richard Leacroft, who has done some remarkable reconstructions of English playhouses—several of which are reproduced in this textbook—has said that he is unable to make an accurate reconstruction of Dorset Garden because the available information is so slight. Very probably, then, this debate will continue.

The first representation of an English Stage and Scenery,
from Settle's Empress of Morocco,
A Tragedy. London, 1673.
See Items Nos. 1499 and 1500.

(Culver Pictures)

STAGE SET AT DORSET GARDEN
A rare view of the stage in a Restoration theatre is this depiction of Settle's *Empress of Orocco* as presented at Dorset Garden. The engraving is dated 1673. The representation shown here does not settle the dispute as to the dimensions and other features of the Dorset Garden.

*"The Dorset Garden Theatre: A Review of Facts and Problems," *Theatre Notebook*, 1979, vol. 33, p. 16.
†P. 4.

The Decline of Restoration Comedy: The Transition to the Eighteenth Century

In the satirical universe of Restoration comedy, marital infidelity abounds yet goes unpunished. It is no wonder, then, that the Puritans attacked Restoration theatre. In 1698, Jeremy Collier, a minister, wrote *A Short View of the Immorality and Profaneness of the English Stage.* Some historians suggest that Collier's treatise marks the end of the theatrical Restoration: after his attack, the sexual content of plays was toned down; and in eighteenth-century English comedy, morality was stressed. Collier's attack may have been a symptom as much as a cause of the changes that took place. Near the end of the seventeenth century, as William and Mary ascended the throne, the temper of the times was already changing. The attitudes of society were less permissive and laissez-faire than they had been in the two or three decades immediately following the Restoration.

This change was reflected in theatre as in other aspects of society. We have noted that in some ways Congreve's *The Way of the World* was a transitional piece. Other plays that reflect this were written in the early years of the eighteenth century. Two good examples are *The Gamester* (1705) by Susannah Centlivre (1667–1723) and *The Beau's Strategem* (1707) by George Fahrquhar (1678–1707).

SUSANNA CENTLIVRE

(Billy Rose Theatre Collection, New York Public Library at Lincoln Center, Astor, Lenox, and Tilden Foundations)

Susanna Centlivre.

As noted earlier, there were many significant female dramatists in England during the Restoration and the early eighteenth century, including Aphra Behn and the "female wits." Susanna Centlivre (1670–1723) was the most commercially successful of these English female playwrights. She produced numerous letters and poems, sixteen full-length plays, and three short farces. Five of her plays became standard works in the eighteenth- and nineteenth-century repertoire: *The Gamester* (1705), *The Basset Table* (1705), *The Busy Body* (1709), *The Wonder: A Woman Keeps Her Secret* (1714), and *A Bold Stroke for a Wife* (1718).

The details of Centlivre's early life are unclear. Some biographers report that she was born to a Mr. Freeman of Holbeach, Lincolnshire, who died when she was 3. At 14, Centlivre supposedly ran away from home with a group of strolling players to escape a wicked stepmother. Other biographers suggest that Centlivre ran away with Anthony Hammond, who dressed her up as a man and took her with him to Cambridge. Shortly thereafter, she married a nobleman. She was widowed within a year and then married an army officer. Eighteen months later she was widowed again, when her second husband was killed in a duel.

After 1700, Centlivre's life is more accurately documented. Early in the century, she was actively involved in politics, working with the Whig party. She also returned to the stage, acting and writing plays. In 1707, she married Joseph Centlivre, a cook for Queen Anne, who had seen her playing a breeches role—that is, a role in which she was costumed as a man.

Centlivre wrote during a time when many audience members viewed female writers negatively. Like Aphra Behn, she was believed to be writing out of economic necessity, and she encountered so much hostility that she left the theatre for 2 years. She returned with a new play, *The Busy Body,* in 1709. This comedy premiered to a small audience, but by the third night (a performance for the benefit of the author) the theatre was filled.

After the success of *The Busy Body,* Centlivre, who had written a number of her earlier plays anonymously, never again hid her gender.

GEORGE FARQUHAR

Born in Londonderry, Ireland, George Farquhar (1678–1707) was often the target of criticism by his English contemporaries, who leveled heated charges against his language, plots, and characters, despite the stage success of many of his plays. Farquhar was educated at Trinity College in Dublin in 1694–1695. In 1696 he worked in Dublin as a press corrector for a bookseller, as well as beginning a career as an actor at the Smock Alley Theatre. Farquhar's acting career was brief, however, lasting only for the 1696–1697 season; he gave it up after accidentally wounding a fellow actor. Sometime around 1697, Farquhar moved to London, where his first play, *Love and a Bottle,* was produced in 1698. Farquhar married Margaret Pemell in 1703, and their union produced two daughters.

Many of Farquhar's plays are described in terms of their "realism," which has led to suggestions of autobiographical influence. Indeed, Farquhar's *Love and a Bottle* features an Irish gentleman who has just arrived in London. In 1700, shortly after the success of his first play, Farquhar traveled to the Netherlands. He served as a lieutenant in the Grenadiers in 1704, then as a recruiting officer in 1705. Farquhar wrote *The Recruiting Officer,* one of his most enduring plays, the following year—lending support to the idea that his works were partly autobiographical.

In addition to autobiographical influences, many of Farquhar's plays are marked by gentle treatment of the characters. His fools and rakes do not suffer harsh treatment, especially in plays such as his last, *The Beaux' Stratagem* (1707), and his first, *Love and a Bottle.* In addition to these plays, Farquhar also wrote *The Constant Couple: or, A Trip to the Jubilee* (1699); *Sir Harry Wildair, Being the Sequel of the Trip to the Jubilee* (1699); *The Stage Coach* (1701–1702); *The Inconstant: or, The Way to Win Him* (1702); and *The Twin Rivals* (1702); as well as two volumes of verse and the fictional novel *The Adventures of Covent Garden* (1698).

In recent years, theatre artists have frequently revived *The Beaux' Stratagem* and *The Recruiting Officer.* Farquhar's more realistic style and treatment of character seem to strike a responsive chord with contemporary audiences.

Threads in Theatre History

As we look at theatre history, we often see a thread running through several eras. For instance, the drama of Racine and Molière is a direct outgrowth of neoclassical theatre of the Italian Renaissance; and the plays of these two men in turn influenced French theatre for the next 300 years. Medieval Spanish theatre evolved into the secular dramas of Lope de Vega; traces of English medieval theatre appear in the plays of Shakespeare. The plays of Susanna Centlivre and George Farquhar look backward toward Restoration comedy, but forward to the sentimental comedy of the eighteenth century.

With the architecture of the Restoration stage, we also find such a process at work: the physical arrangement changes and develops, but elements of the earlier Elizabethan stage remain. Not only is the extended apron of Restoration theatres a vestige of the Elizabethan platform stage; the doors and balconies of the Restoration stage are remnants of the doorways and upper playing areas of the Elizabethan stage. The English were slow to give up familiar features of the Elizabethan stage, and even after the Restoration, eighteenth-century English and American proscenium-arch theatres retained some of these features.

Later, in the 1700s, the stage apron shrank, and the number of doors decreased from two on each side to one. Even so, the continued influence of Elizabethan theatre architecture kept the English playhouses from becoming exact duplicates of theatres on the European continent: English theatres continued to have a distinctly English quality.

An excellent example of a theatre that illustrates a thread in theatre history, beginning in the Restoration and running through to the present day, is the Drury Lane Theatre.

THE DRURY LANE THEATRE

The origins of the Drury Lane Theatre—a theatre in London that still exists today—go back to a patent that Charles II granted to Thomas Killigrew in 1662.

Killigrew built the first Drury Lane, known as the Theatre Royal, in Bridges Street in 1663. It was supposed to be handsome and well-equipped, but the diarist Samuel Pepys complained of catching cold there from a draft and from rain leaking from the glazed cupola over the pit.

In June 1672, the original building was partly destroyed by fire, and Killigrew housed his company in a deserted theatre while Christopher Wren built a new one. This new theatre opened in March 1674, with the king (Charles II) and queen in attendance. The theatre, a building 58 feet wide by 140 feet long, had a simple, classical, but elegant appearance. It seated 650 people, some in a pit facing the stage, others in boxes and galleries along the sides and back. Its stage was a platform about 34 feet deep; the front half of the stage was open, and the back half was framed by a proscenium that contained the scenic elements.

Killigrew's mismanagement so weakened the company that the theatre was closed in 1676. Thomas Betterton merged two London acting troupes—a troupe he managed for Davenant's heirs, and Killegrew's company—and reopened Drury Lane in 1682. The patent then passed to Christopher Rich, who was interested only in making money. Under his mismanagement the theatre again went bankrupt and closed in 1709.

Drury Lane reopened later that same year under new management and ran successfully until Charles Fleetwood got control of the patent. Under Fleetwood's regime, there was a riot in 1737 over the abolition of free admission for footmen in the gallery and another in 1741 at the first performance of Charles Macklin's realistic reinterpretation of Shylock.

When Fleetwood in his turn faced bankruptcy, David Garrick, the company's leading actor, became manager in 1747. Until this time, a few patrons had still been permitted to sit on the stage, but one of Garrick's reforms was to end this practice. Under his careful management, the theatre became both prosperous and respected.

Garrick was succeeded in 1776 by the playwright Richard Brinsley Sheridan and Sheridan's father-in-law. They enlarged the building between 1791 and 1794, supposedly making it fireproof. When the actor John Kemble and his sister, the actress

(© Historical Picture Archive/Corbis)

DRURY LANE THEATRE

A famous theatre of the Restoration period was the Drury Lane. It has an illustrious history: it began during the English Restoration and has continued to the present. This illustration is from 1808. By that time, the Drury Lane no longer had an extended forestage or proscenium doors; but it was still a "pit, box, and gallery" house. Through the years, the seating capacity continued to increase.

Sarah Siddons, left the company, the managers turned to melodrama and spectacle to avoid bankruptcy. Drury Lane burned to the ground in 1808, and for some time there was no money to rebuild it.

Samuel Whitbread, a brewer and a shareholder in the patent, finally raised the money, and the theatre was rebuilt in 1812. Drury Lane's history in the nineteenth century included a procession of managers who went into bankruptcy—though some of them had been successful at other houses—until August Harris took over in the 1880s. Harris's policy was to present spectacular shows and pantomimes, a formula that has worked successfully to this day; Drury Lane has now become the home of musicals.

Drury Lane is said to have a ghost: an eighteenth-century gentleman in cloak and riding boots who appears in the upper circle only at matinees when the house is full.

Italian and French influences were fused with English traditions to create the theatre of the Restoration. Restoration theatre, in turn, prepared the way for eighteenth-century theatre in England. In Chapter 10, we turn to the eighteenth century, in England and elsewhere.

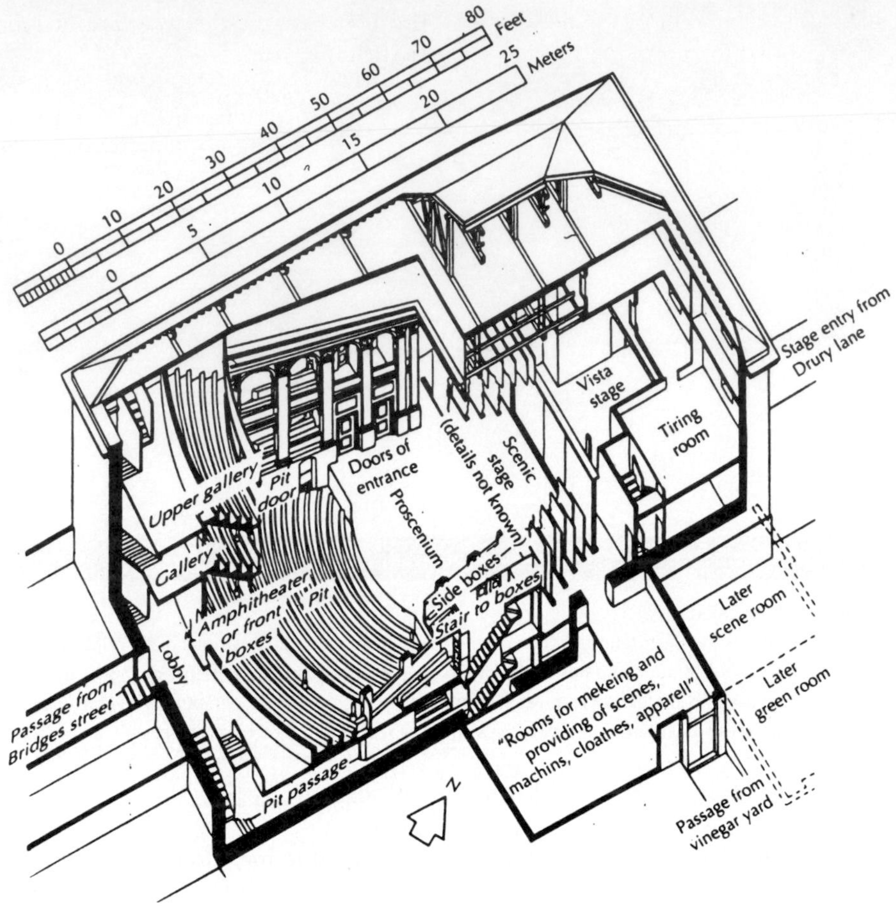

A RECONSTRUCTION OF DRURY LANE

This reconstruction, of the Restoration period, shows Christopher Wren's design for the Theatre Royal, Drury Lane, 1674. Note the pit for the audience and the two doors on each side of the stage.

SUMMARY

The Restoration brought a strong Italian influence to English stage practices. The proscenium arch, perspective painting, and wing-and-shutter (or backdrop) scenery became indispensable elements of the English stage. A French influence was also present; the neoclassical ideals were introduced into serious English drama.

Nonetheless, English theatre maintained its uniqueness. Proscenium-arch doors and balconies, and an extended apron, were significant vestiges of the Elizabethan stage. Comedy of manners, as exemplified in the works of Wycherley and Congreve, borrowed from the French neoclassical playwright Molière but was a unique reflection of English Restoration society. Also popular were the tragedies of John Dryden and the comedies of intrigue of Aphra Behn.

Women appeared on the English stage for the first time during the Restoration; women playwrights emerged on the scene for the first time; acting companies in London established a contract system; and theatrical entrepreneurs began to emerge.

MILESTONES CHAPTER 9 THE THEATRE OF THE ENGLISH RESTORATION [1649–1700]

Commonwealth [1642–1660]

Theatre History

- Parliament closes theatres; theatrical activity curtailed (1642)
- *Drolls* staged during commonwealth period
- William Davenant (1606–1668), *Siege of Rhodes*
- Thomas Killigrew (1612–1683) *(right)*

Cultural and Historical Developments

- English civil war (1642–1649)
- Execution of Charles I (1649); commonwealth established under Oliver Cromwell (1599–1658)
- Thomas Hobbes, *Leviathan* (1651) *(right)*

Restoration [1660–1700]

Theatre History

- Davenant's Duke's Company and Killigrew's King's Company granted patents; women perform on the English stage (1660)
- Theatre Royal (first Drury Lane Theatre), built by Killigrew (1663)
- John Dryden (1631–1700), *All for Love*
- George Etherege (c. 1633–1691), *She Would If She Could* (1668)
- Thomas Betterton (1635–1710)
- Aphra Behn (1640–1689), *The Rover*
- William Wycherley (1640–1716), *The Country Wife*
- Eleanor (Nell) Gwynn (1650–1687) *(right)*
- Thomas Otway (1652–1685), *Venice Preserved*
- Elizabeth Barry (1658–1713)
- Christopher Rich (1660–1714), theatrical entrepreneur
- Lincoln's Inn Fields, converted tennis court, opens (1661)
- William Congreve (1670–1729), *The Way of the World*
- Susanna Centlivre (c. 1670–1723), *The Busy Body*

Cultural and Historical Developments

- John Locke, *Essay Concerning Human Understanding* (1690) *(below)*

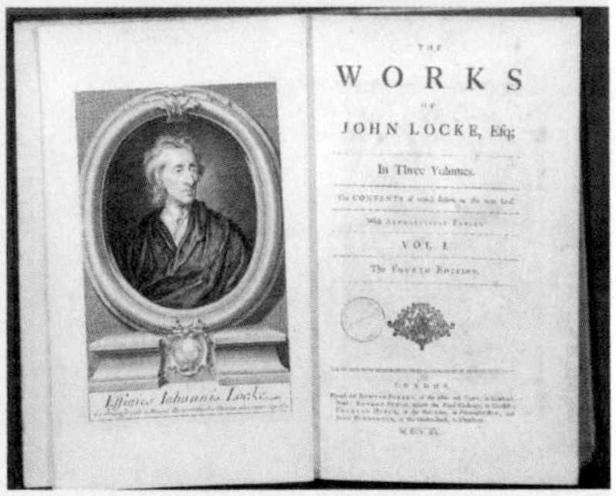

- Anglo-Dutch Wars (1652–1674)
- Restoration of monarchy; Charles II returns from exile; Navigation Acts (1660)
- Royal Society of London for Improving Natural Knowledge established (1662)
- Milton's *Paradise Lost* (1667)
- Treaty of Dover between Charles II and Louis XIV (1670)
- Habeas Corpus Act (1679)

continued

PHOTO CREDITS: Thomas Killigrew. (National Portrait Gallery, London) / Eleanor (Nell) Gwynn. (Bettmann/Corbis) / Title page from Hobbes's *Leviathan*, 1651. (Bettmann/Corbis) / John Locke's portrait as the frontispiece of his *Works*, 1740. (© Archivo Iconografico, S.A./Corbis)

Restoration [1660–1700]

Theatre History

- Dorset Garden opens (1671)
- Anne Bracegirdle (c. 1671–1748)
- New Drury Lane opens, built by the architect Christopher Wren (1674) *(below)*

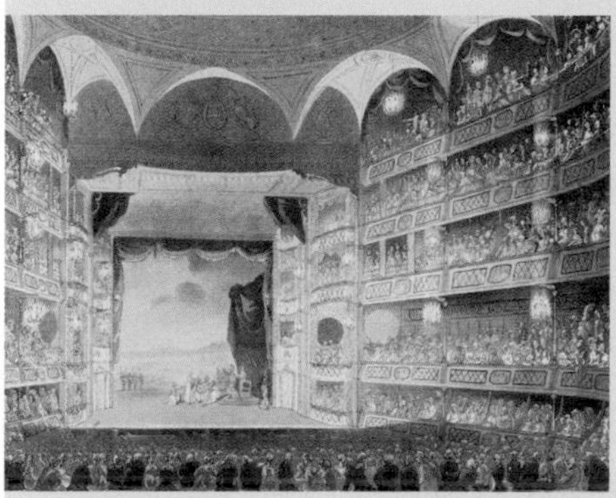

- George Farquhar (1678–1707), *The Recruiting Officer*
- "Female wits": Catharine Trotter (1679–1749), Mary Pix (1666–1706), Delariviere Manley (c. 1672–1724), Anne Oldfield (1683–1730)
- Jeremy Collier's *Short View of the Immortality and Profaneness of the English Stage* (1698)
- Licensing Act, strict regulation of London theatre (1737)

Cultural and Historical Developments

- Christopher Wren's Tom Tower, Christ Church, Oxford (1681)
- James II rules; Newton's laws of gravity (1687)
- William and Mary; Glorious Revolution (1688) *(below)*

- Bank of England established (1694)

PHOTO CREDITS: Drury Lane. (© Historical Picture Archive/Corbis) / Coronation of William and Mary. (HIP/Art Resource, N.Y.)

CHAPTER 10
Theatres in the Eighteenth Century

Eighteenth-Century Theatre

The eighteenth century was a time of transition and expansion in Europe and America. In the theatre, star actors came to the forefront; and elaborate scenic effects, strongly influenced by Italian designers, were increasingly adopted, as theatres also grew in size. Also, in Italy there was a rivalry between two playwrights: Carlo Goldoni and Carlo Gozzi. Goldoni wanted theatre to be more realistic; Gozzi wanted it to be more fanciful. Seen here is a scene from Gozzi's *King Stag* in a production at the American Repertory Theatre.

(© Richard Feldman)

Beginning with the eighteenth century, the study of history—including theatre history—becomes more complex. Homogeneous, self-contained so- cieties began to disappear as the world started to be transformed into a global community. An increase in mercantilism manufacturing and trade, particularly international trade—affected populations worldwide. Decisions made by the two major eighteenth-century mercantile powers, England and France, directly affected people in North America, India, and Africa. (One effect on Africa, for example, was a marked increase in the slave trade.)

This means that our study of theatre history becomes more complicated. We will not be able to discuss developments in a completely chronological manner or by national boundaries. Instead, we will try to focus on significant changes and innovations.

Background: The Eighteenth Century

The eighteenth century was a time of transition. In textiles, for example, there was a move away from wool, which had been the main fabric since the Middle Ages. There was also a remarkable shift in manufacturing. In the textile industry in Berlin, Germany, between 1750 and 1780, the number of looms for making cotton increased from 80 to over 1,000, and the number of silk looms jumped from less than 300 to more than 2,000. These changes are typical of what was happening, not only in Germany, but throughout Europe.

Transitions like those in manufacturing also affected other aspects of life, including theatre. Political, philosophical, economic, and cultural changes in the eighteenth century paved the way for even more revolutionary developments in the nineteenth and twentieth centuries.

Before the eighteenth century, wars had usually been fought for religious reasons; now they became territorial and economic. There were many wars in the eighteenth century, including the War of the Spanish Succession (1701–1714), the War of the Austrian Succession (1740–1748), and the Seven Years' War (1756–1763). In America, the French and Indian War (1754–1763), often considered part of the Seven Years' War, is a clear example of a struggle for mercantile dominance. The opposed powers were England and France, the leading colonists in North America; when France was defeated, England gained control of Canada and all the French territory in North America east of the Mississippi. Spain, which had sided with France, had to cede Florida to England, and in compensation was given the French lands west of the Mississippi (the Louisiana Territory).

Western Europe prospered more than ever before because of the growth in trade; ingenious and daring investors of capital became extremely wealthy. Profits from colonial trade filtered down to the emerging middle class, which included merchants and others involved in commerce; in the eighteenth century it became a social as well as a political force. However, the lives of those on the bottom rungs of the economic ladder—such as eastern European serfs, French peasants, and dispossessed English farmers—were not improved by the expansion of trade; some historians suggest that the disparity in wealth between the middle and lower classes became greater during this period.

Because there were many new developments in learning and philosophy, the eighteenth century is called the *age of enlightenment* or simply the *enlightenment*. Though France was its center, the enlightenment had international reverberations. The search for knowledge was supported by the educated middle class. Dictionaries and encyclopedias were in great demand; possibly the most famous was the seventeen-volume *Encyclopédie* edited by the French philosopher Denis Diderot between 1751 and 1772.

Besides Diderot, France produced many renowned philosophers in the eighteenth century,

Eighteenth Century Year

Theatre

- Ferdinando Bibiena introduces angle perspective (c. 1703)
- Susanna Centlivre's *The Busy Body* (1709)
- Gottsched and Neuber meet (1727)
- Gay's *The Beggar's Opera* (1728)
- Lillo's *The London Merchant* (1731)
- Voltaire's *Zaïre;* London's Covent Garden Theatre built (1732)
- English Licensing Act (1737)
- Voltaire's *Mahomet;* Macklin's Shylock—an attempt at costume reform (1741)
- Garrick becomes actor-manager at Drury Lane (1747)
- Goldoni's *The Comic Theatre* (1750)
- Hallams in Virginia (1752)
- Voltaire's *Orphan of China* (1755)
- Spectators banished from French stage (c. 1759)
- Boulevard theatres begin to develop in France (c. 1760)
- Piranesi continues to paint his "prison drawings" using chiaroscuro (1761)
- Gozzi's *Turandot* (1762)
- Drottningholm completed; Southwark Theatre in Philadelphia (1766)
- John Street Theatre in New York (1767) Lessing's *Hamburg Dramaturgy* (1767–1769) Hamburg National Theatre (1767–1769) "Storm and stress" movement (1767–1787)
- Goethe's *Goetz von Berlichingen;* Goldsmith's *She Stoops to Conquer* (1773)
- Sheridan's *The School for Scandal* (1777)
- Goethe "directs" Weimar court theatre; Schiller assists (1798)
- Schiller's *Mary Stuart* (1800)

Year

1700, 1710, 1720, 1730, 1740, 1750, 1760, 1770, 1780, 1790, 1800

Culture and Politics

- War of Spanish Succession in France (1701–1714)
- Peter the Great begins westernization of Russia (c. 1701)
- *The Spectator* begun by Addison and Steele (1711)
- Louis XIV dies (1715)
- Defoe's *Robinson Crusoe* (1719)
- Baroque music flourishes (Bach and Handel) (c. 1724)
- Swift's *Gulliver's Travels* (1726)
- John Key's "flying shuttle" loom patented (1733)
- Rococo style flourishes (1737)
- Frederick the Great of Prussia, "enlightened despot" (1740)
- *Encylopédie* begun (c. 1750)
- French and Indian War (1754)
- Seven Years' War begins (1756)
- Voltaire's *Candide* (1759)
- Rousseau's *Social Contract;* Catherine the Great of Russia begins reign (1762)
- James Watt patents a steam Engine (1769)
- Declaration of Independence (American Revolution 1775–1783); Adam Smith's *Wealth of Nations* (1776)
- Goya's *Don Manuel de Zuniga;* James Watt patents a locomotive (1784)
- Mozart's *Don Giovanni* (1787)
- French Revolution (1789)
- David's *Murder of Marat* (1793)
- Consulate of Napoleon (1799)

including Montesquieu (1689–1755), Voltaire (1694–1778), and Jean-Jacques Rousseau (1712–1778). Montesquieu, in *The Spirit of Laws* (1748), called for a separation and balance of powers in government to end absolute monarchy. Voltaire argued for religious tolerance. Among those who supported Voltaire was the German playwright Gotthold Ephraim Lessing (1729–1781), whose *Nathan the Wise* (1779) dramatized the ideal of religious unity.

In *The Social Contract* (1762), Rousseau argued that government exists because of an agreement among the people governed—not between a ruler and subjects—and that therefore government officials are representatives, responsible to their constituents. In earlier writings, Rousseau attacked organized society as such, arguing that humanity was better off in a "state of nature."

The political philosophies of Montesquieu, Voltaire, and Rousseau had noticeable effects on eighteenth-century Europe and America. While many rulers were absolutists, believing that their powers were God-given and therefore not to be questioned, some monarchs—known as *enlightened despots*—rejected this concept of "divine right." They believed in religious tolerance and wanted to reform their societies for the good of their subjects. Two major political and social upheavals, the American Revolution (1775–1783) and the French Revolution (1789–1799), were based on the ideals of the enlightenment. Thomas Jefferson's political philosophy, as expressed in the Declaration of Independence, was rooted in enlightenment thought; the American Constitution was a version of Rousseau's social contract. The French revolutionaries' cry for liberty, equality, and fraternity originated in the philosophies of Montesquieu, Voltaire, and Rousseau. Unfortunately, the ideals of the French Revolution were compromised by the Reign of Terror; and instead of liberty, equality, and fraternity, the French wound up with Napoleon in 1799.

The quest for new knowledge during this era had practical as well as political applications. Inventions of the late eighteenth century would facilitate the industrial revolution of the nineteenth century: the flying shuttle, the spinning jenny, and the cotton gin revolutionized the textile industry; James Watt's improved steam Engine revolutionized manufacturing and transportation.

In the arts, the seventeenth century and the early eighteenth century were characterized by the baroque style. In the seventeenth century, baroque painters, such as Peter Paul Rubens (1577–1640) and Rembrandt (1606–1669), emphasized detail, color, and ornamentation to create a total visual illusion. The emerging middle class frequently commissioned realistic baroque paintings. In the early eighteenth century, the most renowned baroque composers, George Frideric Handel (1685–1759) and Johann Sebastian Bach (1685–1750), achieved unity of mood and continuity of line; but, like baroque paintings, their music was filled with movement and action.

In the late eighteenth century, a new style of art emerged—*rococo*. Rococo art is typified by the paintings of Jean-Antoine Watteau (1684–1721); though less ornate and grandiose than baroque art, it was still characterized by careful attention to detail.

In the midst of all these transformations, theatre also changed. Although there were some major and many minor revolutions in eighteenth-century theatre, few of the theatrical experiments of the 1700s became generally accepted practices. Nevertheless, they served as the foundation for modern theatre.

Eighteenth-Century Drama

In theatre, the eighteenth century—as we will see—was most notably a time when star performers were glorified and people who began to function like the modern director emerged. Still, many first-rate plays were written; and the new dramatic forms that began to appear are evidence of the transitional nature of eighteenth-century drama.

Middle-Class Tragedy

During the early eighteenth century, much of the drama in Europe adhered to neoclassicism; but as the century progressed, there were numerous departures from the Renaissance rules. New forms that defied the neoclassical genres were introduced; there were also experiments with the episodic structure that had been used by William Shakespeare and other Elizabethans, and by dramatists of the Spanish golden age.

Many eighteenth-century dramatic forms deviated from traditional tragedy and comedy. Denis Diderot championed *drame*, a new form which was defined as any serious play that did not fit the neoclassical definition of tragedy. *Bourgeois*—or *middle-class*—*tragedy* and *domestic tragedy* were eighteenth-century examples of drame: they ignored the neoclassical requirement of royal protagonists and drew tragic heroes and heroines from the emerging middle class. Domestic tragedies focused on bourgeois family concerns. Bourgeois and domestic tragedies were often dramatizations of eighteenth-century middle-class morality—rewarding the virtuous and punishing the wicked—and they tended to be sentimental and melodramatic; that is, they openly appealed to the emotions as they pitted good against evil. The emergence of middle-class tragic heroes and heroines reflected the rise of the middle class as a political and social force: the new middle-class audiences expected dramas to reflect their problems and points of view.

The London Merchant (1731), by the English playwright George Lillo (1693–1739), is often cited as an early example of middle-class tragedy. In this play, an apprentice is seduced by an older woman; under her influence, he robs his good-hearted employer and murders his uncle, and he and the woman are eventually apprehended and sentenced to death. Later in the century, Diderot in France and Lessing in Germany wrote middle-class and domestic tragedies, as did many other minor writers. One, Louis Sebastian Mercier (1740–1814), loosely translated *The London Merchant* into French in 1769.

Today, most bourgeois tragedies seem trite and melodramatic, with their unconvincing last-minute reformation of drunken or evil characters. However, at the time they made the case that middle-class characters were appropriate subjects for serious drama. Many critics believe that modern realistic tragedy (such as Arthur Miller's *Death of a Salesman*), with its emphasis on family problems and social concerns, grew out of this earlier form. It is also clear that the theories of Denis Diderot were instrumental in changing the way people thought about serious drama and theatre in the eighteenth century.

DENIS DIDEROT

"We are slaves of custom," wrote Denis Diderot (1713–1784) in an essay on drama; but he hoped to bring about changes: he advocated a rationalist philosophy, based on nature and the intellect, to make things as they should be.

Diderot came from a conservative, middle-class provincial family in Langres, France. He was sent to Paris for his education and received a master of arts degree from the University of Paris in 1732. For a while he studied law, but he was much more interested in mathematics and languages. In 1734, after a quarrel with his family over their middle-class values, he began to lead a bohemian existence in Paris, living on the Left Bank and earning money as a hack writer. It was during this period that he met the philosopher Jean-Jacques Rousseau, who was to influence his theories. (He was reconciled with his family in 1744, after his marriage.)

(Culver Pictures)

Denis Diderot.

As his reputation as a writer grew, Diderot was approached by a publisher to plan an encyclopedia. Originally, it was to have been simply a translation of an English work, but Diderot saw it as an opportunity to expand knowledge and to expose reactionary forces in church and state. Work on the *Encyclopédie* began in 1750 and was not completed until 1772.

One of the subjects that Diderot explored in his writing was drama; he published his *Discourse on Dramatic Poetry* in 1758. To supplement the rigidly defined neoclassical genres of tragedy and comedy, he advocated the formation of a new genre: *drame bourgeois*. This new genre would examine the problems of ordinary middle-class people seriously and offer moral and philosophical conclusions. To accomplish this goal, he wanted greater realism on the stage, in both scenic elements and acting, and he wrote plays to illustrate his theories. The best-known of these plays are *The Illegitimate Son* (1748); *The Natural Son, or The Proofs of Virtue* (1757); and *The Father of the Family* (1758). None was a great success, but his ideas were influential, particularly in Germany and France, where a new realistic drama was to develop in the next century.

Diderot is also remembered for an important essay, "The Paradox of Acting," written in 1773. He argued in this essay that the best actors invoke strong emotions in an audience by using calculation and craft, not by experiencing these emotions themselves. Actors who rely on inspiration and "feeling the part" frequently give mediocre performances, he believed; a studied actor is more consistent. This idea has been debated for over two centuries by later theorists.

After the completion of the *Encyclopédie*, Diderot no longer had a regular salary. This meant that severe financial problems were added to the harassment he was undergoing because of his antigovernment and anticlerical ideas. To help him, Empress Catherine I of Russia bought his library, and then hired him as librarian and gave him the use of the books for his lifetime. For her, the philosopher drew up a plan on how to govern Russia. His books and manuscripts were sent to Russia after his death in 1784.

Diderot's theories about theatre were highly influential. His concept of a new genre focusing on the middle class and on domestic situations, and allowing for a combination of serious and comic elements, would influence many nineteenth-century playwrights. His theories of acting continued to be discussed throughout the 1800s; for example, in the late 1800s there was a public debate between the French actor Constant-Benoît Coquelin, who supported Diderot's views, and the English actor Henry Irving, who opposed them. Diderot's concept of the "fourth wall"—the idea that the audience views a play through an invisible wall and that audience and performer should not acknowledge each other's presence—would have a major effect on later realism.

New Popular Forms: Ballad Opera and Comic Opera

The English also originated new dramatic forms. *Ballad opera,* a parody of Italian opera, was popularized in the 1730s by the success of John Gay's *The Beggar's Opera*

(Tate Gallery, London/Art Resource, N.Y.)

THE BEGGAR'S OPERA

The eighteenth century was an eclectic period in theatre, as in other fields. In addition to tragedy, sentimental comedy, and other genres, popular forms such as ballad opera and comic opera also found favor. An immensely successful ballad opera was John Gay's *The Beggar's Opera,* which incorporated popular songs of the day in a story of scoundrels, thieves, and other low-lifes, who also proved to be appealing. This painting by William Hogarth shows a scene from Act III of *The Beggar's Opera.*

(1728). In ballad opera there was no sung dialogue—that is, no recitative. Instead, spoken dialogue alternated with songs set to popular contemporary melodies. Characters in ballad opera were drawn from the lower classes. Frequently, ballad operas were social and political satires poking fun at contemporary issues.

In France, a similar form, known as *comic opera (opéra comique)*, developed. It originated at the beginning of the century, when a pantomime-like entertainment was developed at fairground theatres in an attempt to get around the monopoly held by the Comédie Française and the Opera over drama and musical theatre. Actors dressed as cupids held signs onstage on which were printed the other characters' speeches (in rhymed couplets). The action was mimed by the performers, and spectators would often sing the dialogue, encouraged by performers planted in the audience. The characters were drawn from commedia dell'arte. As some of the legal restrictions were removed, comic opera became more like ballad opera, since it used popular music for its songs, satirized political and social issues or other forms of drama, and had no recitative. By midcentury, however, comic opera became less satirical, less comic in tone, and more sentimental, and it had recognizable French characters. Some historians suggest that French melodrama evolved from comic opera in the 1780s and 1790s.

Sentimental Comedy and Comédie Larmoyante

Another popular form was the sentimental comedy of eighteenth-century England; these comedies continue to be produced today. *Sentimental comedy* is like Restoration comedy except that it reaffirms middle-class morality: the virtuous are rewarded and the wicked punished. Sentimental comedies, which are comedies of manners, satirize social conventions and norms; they have many of the character types found in Restoration comedy. One of the best examples of sentimental comedy is *The Conscious Lovers* (1722) by Sir Richard Steele (1672–1729), which he based on *Andria* by the Roman playwright Terence. The play's protagonist is Young Bevil, who is promised in marriage by his father to Lucinda. Bevil, however, wishes to marry a poor orphan, Indiana, who eventually turns out to be the long-lost daughter of Lucinda's father. Indiana's changed circumstance allows the two young lovers to marry. The play also resolves happily for Lucinda, who is betrothed to Myrtle, Bevil's best friend.

In the early and middle eighteenth century, particularly in France, sentimental comedy featured saccharine, overwrought emotions and often dealt with virtuous characters who were threatened by serious misfortune but lived happily ever after. The French called this type of drama *comédie larmoyante*, "tearful comedy," because it was meant to bring sentimental tears to the audience's eyes.

Later in the century, however, some playwrights in England and France tried to strike a balance between upholding middle-class virtues and making fun of social pretensions. The major examples of this later form are *The Rivals* and *The School for Scandal* by Richard Brinsley Sheridan. In the emerging American theatre, Royall Tyler's *The Contrast* (1787)—the first play by a writer born in America—was patterned after Sheridan's sentimental comedies.

RICHARD BRINSLEY SHERIDAN

Richard Brinsley Sheridan (1751–1816) is the best-known writer of sentimental comedy, and he wrote a noted literary burlesque play, *The Critic.* He is remembered primarily as a playwright, but he was also a successful theatrical manager, and he himself would have preferred to be known as a politician. During his lifetime he combined all three careers, though they were sometimes in conflict.

(National Portrait Gallery, London)

Richard Brinsley Sheridan.

Because his father was an actor, novelist, and playwright, Sheridan was familiar with the stage from childhood. Though born in Ireland, he was raised in London, where his father's acting career had taken the family. His family hoped that he would study law, but at age 21 he eloped with the daughter of a prominent singer and composer and turned to the stage for a living. *The Rivals,* which was produced at Covent Garden in 1775, failed at its first performance; but Sheridan's revisions eventually made it a success. He followed this play with *The Duenna,* a ballad opera, which had an unusually long run of seventy-five performances.

These two works and a short farce made Sheridan the most promising new dramatist in London. David Garrick, who was planning to retire as manager of the Drury Lane Theatre, was impressed by Sheridan's talent and persuaded him and his father-in-law to become part-owners. Sheridan wrote several plays for Drury Lane, including *The School for Scandal* (1777), considered the best comedy of manners since the Restoration; and *The Critic* (1779), one of most famous literary burlesques.

As manager of Drury Lane, Sheridan appealed to the public taste for spectacle and pantomime and tried to enforce his monopoly by restricting unlicensed theatres. Politics, however, had become his chief interest after his election to Parliament in 1780. He held several cabinet posts and was an adviser to the Prince of Wales, who later became George III. Sheridan was also one of the best political orators of his day.

After 1808—the year Drury Lane burned—Sheridan's career took a downswing; he lost his seat in Parliament, drank heavily, and was constantly in debt until his death in 1816.

There is an important difference between plays like Sheridan's *The Rivals* and *The School for Scandal* and Wycherley's *The Country Wife,* written 100 years earlier. Though both are comedies of manners, Wycherley's work is far more amoral in its treatment of infidelity and other sexual matters. Sheridan's comedies, with their witty ridicule of the follies of society, can be seen as a link between the Restoration and the later comedies of Wilde and Shaw.

THE SCHOOL FOR SCANDAL

The School for Scandal is one of the most popular eighteenth-century comedies because of its recognizable character types and its comic love intrigues. Sheridan presents two brothers: Joseph Surface, a scheming hypocrite; and Charles, who is good-hearted but financially extravagant. Both brothers are courting Maria, the wealthy ward of Sir Peter Teazle. However, only Charles is truly in love with Maria. Joseph, on the other hand, is also trying to seduce Sir Peter's young wife, who socializes with such pretentious individuals as Sir Benjamin Backbite, Crabtree, Lady Sneerwell (who also loves Charles), and Mrs. Candour.

Sir Oliver Surface, the rich uncle of Joseph and Charles, returns from India and sets out to test his nephews to see who is deserving of his fortune. He convinces Charles that he is a moneylender who is willing to purchase Charles's family portraits. However, the only portrait Charles will not part with is that of Sir Oliver.

Meanwhile Joseph attempts to seduce Lady Teazle but is foiled when her husband arrives. Lady Teazle hides behind a screen and hears her husband speak of his great love for her and his suspicion that she is involved with Charles. When Charles also arrives, Sir Peter hides as well and, through the conversation he overhears, realizes that his jealousy of Charles is unwarranted. When Joseph is called out of the room, Charles and Peter decide to reveal the woman who is hiding behind the screen and who Joseph has said is a milliner. Both discover Lady Teazle, who begs her husband's forgiveness.

After the Teazles and Charles leave, Sir Oliver enters disguised as a poor relative, requesting financial assistance from Joseph. Joseph refuses, using as his excuse that his Uncle Oliver does not provide him with enough funds. Sir Oliver realizes that Charles is his honest and trustworthy nephew.

Even with additional conspiring by Lady Sneerwell, Maria and Charles are reunited, as are Sir Peter and Lady Teazle. Sheridan's comedy ends with the hypocritical punished and the good-hearted and honest rewarded.

(© T. Charles Erickson)

SENTIMENTAL COMEDY
A popular type of theatre in the eighteenth century was known as sentimental comedy. It satirized social pretensions but upheld middle-class values. A good example is *The School for Scandal* by Richard Brinsley Sheridan, which contains one of the most famous comic scenes of all time, the "screen scene." The false Joseph Surface's shenanigans with the ladies are exposed when a screen falls and reveals all. Here, Margaret Welsh is Lady Teazle and Robert Cuccioli is Joseph. The production is at the McCarter Theatre in Princeton, New Jersey.

Modifications of Sentimentality

Some playwrights modified sentimental comedy; the best-known of these was the English dramatist Oliver Goldsmith (c. 1730–1774), who wrote two plays: *The Good Natur'd Man* (1761) and *She Stoops to Conquer* (1773). In his "Essay on the Theatre," which appeared just before the premiere of *She Stoops to Conquer*, Goldsmith attacked sentimental comedy, calling instead for a "laughing comedy" which would force audiences to laugh at their own eccentricities and absurdities.

In France, the leading writer of this more subtle kind of comedy was Pierre Carlet de Chamblain de Marivaux (1688–1763). Marivaux's plays usually focus on the inner emotional conflicts of young lovers; this focus on characters' psychological makeup makes him seem more contemporary. Marivaux's best-known works are *The Surprise Love* (1722), *The Game of Love and Chance* (1730), and *The False*

Confessions (1737). Another French comic playwright who moved away from sentimentality and focused more on social and political satire was Beaumarchais (Pierre-Augustin Caron, 1732–1799). Beaumarchais's *The Barber of Seville* (1775) and *The Marriage of Figaro* (1783) have many of the same traditional comic characters as sentimental romantic works but also reflect the explosive political, economic, and social issues of the time.

The Marriage of Figaro, for example, caused more controversy in France than any play since Molière's *Tartuffe;* in fact, the king, Louis XVI, refused to give his permission for the production of *The Marriage of Figaro.* It is set in Spain, its main story line is an older man's attempt to seduce a servant girl, and its key character is a comic servant—but its real point is social and political satire.

The plot of *The Marriage of Figaro* is full of intrigue, unexpected twists, and moments of great comedy. Figaro, the servant, is Engaged to marry Suzanne, who is also a servant; but his master, Count Almaviva, wants to sleep with her himself. The count has been unfaithful to his wife, and we watch with great enjoyment the various complications that develop as he tries to conquer another young woman but is thwarted. At the end of the play, the count is caught in his plotting and is humiliated; he pledges fidelity to his wife, and Figaro and Suzanne are brought together.

Though the play is comic, the political implications are clear. It is the master who is ridiculed and frustrated; despite his social rank, his machinations are futile—his clever servants outwit him. Undoubtedly, Beaumarchais was questioning the social structure of France. Some people even charged that the play threatened French society with the kind of revolution seen at that time in the New World.

PIERRE-AUGUSTIN CARON DE BEAUMARCHAIS

Pierre-Augustin Caron (1732–1799) was born in Paris in January 1732. He is perhaps best-known for creating the character Figaro; however, this eighteenth-century dramatist was also a theorist, clockmaker, and harpist. Educated at L'École des Métiers d'Alfort until age 13, Pierre-Augustin then began an apprenticeship with his father, a clockmaker. This apprenticeship served him well, since he actually worked as a clockmaker; for that matter, his innovations in this profession were recognized by the Academy of Sciences in 1754.

(Réunion des Musées Nationaux/Art Resource, N.Y.)

Beaumarchais, in a portrait by Paul Constant Soyer (1823–1903) after Jean-Baptiste Greuze (1725–1805).

Pierre-Augustin was able to adopt the aristocratic name de Beaumarchais from his first wife, Madeleine-Catherine Franquet, who died a year after they married in 1756. In 1768 Beaumarchais married Geneviève-Madeleine Warebled, who died in 1770. The marriage produced one son, who also died—at age 3 in 1772. In 1786, Beaumarchais was married for a third time, to Marie-Thérèse Willermawlas. He divorced her in 1794 but then remarried her in 1797, two years before his own death.

Beaumarchais moved successfully in court circles, where he sometimes gave harp lessons and organized concerts. He was made a nobleman in 1761 after he purchased the title secrétaire du roi, and he was subsequently named lieutenant-general of hunting in the Varenne du Louvre. In addition to obtaining his titles, Beaumarchais worked as a government agent between 1774 and 1775, giving aid to American revolutionaries; he was later arrested on suspicion of arms profiteering. Seeking refuge in London, Beaumarchais was imprisoned for debt there in 1792 but was later released on payment of a ransom, after which he returned to France. Soon after his return, however—in 1793—he left for the Netherlands on a mission to buy arms, for which his family was imprisoned. Beaumarchais spent the year in exile in the Netherlands and Germany. In 1794 he returned to Paris, where he remained under close scrutiny.

Intrigue aside, Beaumarchais is best-known as a dramatist. His preface to his early work *Eugénie* (1767) reflects the influence of Diderot's drame bourgeois and offers a careful analysis of the genre. However, as noted above, Beaumarchais is also widely recognized for his character Figaro. The two plays that feature the cunning servant are *Le Barbier de Séville (The Barber of Seville;* 1775) and *Le Folle Journée; ou, Le Mariage de Figaro* (*The Follies of a Day; or, The Marriage of Figaro;* 1784). Both plays were produced at the Comédie Française, and both feature the quick repartee of comedy of intrigue and a battle of wits between master and servant. The comedies offer a look at class tension; characters of lower station possess sharp intellectual faculties and pride and are cognizant of the abuses of social class and pretension.

Beaumarchais's other dramatic works include *Les Deux Amis; ou, Le Négociant de Lyon* (*The Two Friends*, 1770); *Tarare,* with music by Antonio Salieri (first produced in 1787 and later revised in 1790, translated as *Axur, King of Ormus* in 1813); and *L'Autre Tartuffe; ou, la Mère Coupable* (1792), translated as *Frailty and Hypocrisy* in 1804, and later as *A Mother's Guilt* in 1984. In addition, Beaumarchais wrote essays espousing his philosophy of theatre, as well as collections of his memoirs and letters.

The emphasis on sentimentality and morality in serious and comic drama of the eighteenth century is understandable in light of eighteenth-century philosophy. Thinkers of the enlightenment, influenced by Locke and Hobbes, believed that human beings were rational and perfectible and that societies could learn from history. Sentimental comedies—like middle-class tragedies—expressed the moral optimism of the age.

Storm and Stress

In Germany, many playwrights of the late eighteenth century who rebelled against the neoclassical ideals also questioned the clear-cut morality of sentimental comedy and bourgeois tragedy. Lessing, in a critical treatise called *The Hamburg Dramaturgy* (1767–1769), challEnged the neoclassical interpretation of Aristotle. Lessing expressed admiration for Shakespeare's dramaturgy, and the Germans' admiration for Shakespeare and the Elizabethans culminated in a movement known as *Sturm und Drang*, or "storm and stress."

"Storm and stress" dramatists rejected dramatic rules. They were not uniform in their playwriting techniques; some of them patterned their works after Shakespeare, using episodic structure, mixing genres, and presenting violence onstage. The "storm and stress" movement included such plays as Johann Wolfgang von Goethe's *Goetz von Berlichingen* (1773) and Friedrich Schiller's *The Robbers* (1782).

The playwright Friedrich Schiller (1759–1805) was closely associated with Goethe, who will be discussed later in the chapter. Schiller's *The Robbers* is a remarkable first play, written out of his own disaffection as a recruit at a military academy. As a house dramatist at Mannheim he wrote two plays, and then a complex drama, *Don Carlos,* in 1787. After spending 10 years studying philosophy, history, and aesthetics, he returned to playwriting with a trilogy about a general of the Thirty Years' War, Wallenstein. Later he wrote two plays that are often revived: *Mary Stuart* (1800), about the conflict between Elizabeth I of England and Mary Queen of Scots; and the well-known *William Tell* (1804).

Because "storm and stress" plays, such as the early plays of Goethe and Schiller, were radical in subject matter and style, only a small number were staged; but the movement was the forerunner of nineteenth-century romanticism.

Realism and Antirealism in Commedia dell'Arte

In Italy during the middle of the eighteenth century, there was a struggle between two playwrights—Carlo Goldoni and Carlo Gozzi—over what direction commedia dell'arte should take. Goldoni wanted to make it less artificial; Gozzi wanted to make it more fantastic. For fifteen years, from 1748 to 1762, they carried on a fierce stylistic controversy, which foreshadowed the split between realists and antirealists in the nineteenth century.

CARLO GOLDONI AND CARLO GOZZI

(Bettmann/Corbis)

Carlo Goldoni.

(Bettmann/Corbis)

Carlo Gozzi.

As a former lawyer and the son of a doctor, Goldoni (1707–1793) belonged to the rising middle class of Venice, and many of his 212 plays reflect Venetian life. In 1734 Goldoni became the house dramatist for a theatre in Venice. He attempted to write comic interludes, tragedies, tragicomedies, and librettos for operas. Financial problems forced him to leave Venice in 1743, and for several years he practiced law in Pisa. He returned to Venice in 1748 as house dramatist for another theatre and began a particularly productive period as a playwright. In the season of 1750–1751 he produced sixteen comedies. It was in plays of this period that he began to move Italian commedia dell'arte from bare-bones scenarios to fully scripted literary works. He wanted theatre to be more realistic and less fanciful, and in his reform of commedia, he discouraged masks and improvisation in order to make the characters more lifelike. Two of his best-known works from this period were *The Venetian Twins* and *The Mistress of the Inn.*

In 1753 Goldoni moved to another theatre and continued his productive career. He also created plays with an oriental theme. He Engaged in several well-publicized rivalries with other playwrights; and in 1762, partially because he had grown tired of these quarrels, he accepted an invitation from the king of France to write for the Comédie Italienne in Paris. He remained there until his death in 1793. Goldoni was part of the eighteenth-century trend toward sentimentality; he softened the traits of the stock characters and made them less vulgar.

Goldoni's most celebrated rivalry was with Carlo Gozzi (1720–1806). Their lengthy, outspoken disagreements were carried out in correspondence and various published articles. Gozzi came from a noble but impoverished Venetian family. He began his literary career as a young man and spent much of his life defending Italian culture against what he considered corrupting influences. Gozzi felt that Goldoni's more realistic approach to commedia made it mundane, banal, and meaningless. Instead, he proposed a theatre of the fabulous, in which commedia would be transformed through a mixture of prose and poetry and a combination of improvised and planned actions. He benefited from a 25-year association with one of the best acting companies in Venice. His ten plays, performed between 1761 and 1765, are fantasies based on popular western and Asian myths. Two of his most popular were *The King Stag* (1762) and *The Green Bird* (1765).

Asian myths in particular suited Gozzi's idea of the exotic and the fantastic. He was unalterably opposed to the everyday, the realistic, the inclusion of contemporary situations. Instead he wanted in every aspect—scenery, costumes, language, story line—to emphasize the imaginative, the fanciful, the theatrical elements.

It is hard to say who won the argument between Goldoni and Gozzi. Goldoni left Venice, but his position at the French court was prestigious. Gozzi's plays were popular in Italy for a while, but they were appreciated more in Germany and France. As one of the first realistic playwrights, Goldoni heralded a movement that was to dominate the modern period. Many of his plays, including *The Fan* (c. 1763), *The Mistress of the Inn* (c. 1753), and *The Servant of Two Masters* (c. 1743), are still performed. Gozzi inspired the romantics of the early nineteenth century and nonrealistic theatre of the twentieth century. His *Turandot* (1762) was made into an opera by Puccini; and Prokofiev used his *Love of Three Oranges* (1761) as the basis for a ballet. *The King Stag* (1762), Gozzi's finest play, is still occasionally revived.

Melodrama: A Popular Genre Emerges

By the end of the eighteenth century, melodrama had begun to emerge at the boulevard theatres in Paris. (The theatrical genre of melodrama will be discussed more fully in Chapter 11.) Beginning in the 1790s, the French playwright René Charles Guilbert de Pixérécourt (1773–1844) was immensely popular; his plays presented spectacular effects, violent action, and moral lessons. The German playwright-actor August Wilhelm Iffland (1750–1814) created plays for his own performances; many of them were domestic middle-class melodramas. Another German author, Friedrich von Kotzebue (1761–1819), was—like Pixérécourt—very popular; and many of his plays, including *The Stranger, or Misanthropy and Repentance* (1787), were adapted for audiences in England and America. Kotzebue wrote plays in several different genres; the most successful were visually spectacular and dramatized the battle between good and evil.

Theatre Production in the Eighteenth Century

Government and Theatre

In certain countries—England, France, and the independent German states—the eighteenth century was marked by governmental attempts to regulate theatre production. There also continued to be religious attacks on theatre. Just before the start of the new century, as mentioned before, the clergyman Jeremy Collier wrote *A Short View of the Immorality and Profaneness of the English Stage Together with the Sense of*

(© Stephanie Berger)

REALISTIC ITALIAN COMEDY
Carlo Goldoni, in eighteenth-century Italy, was an advocate of comedy that incorporated features of commedia dell'arte but at the same time showed more realistic domestic situations. One of his most famous plays is *Arlecchino: The Servant of Two Masters*. Shown here is a production by Piccolo Teatro di Milano at the Lincoln Center Festivel, with (from the left) Paolo Calabresi as Dr. Lombardi, Enrico Bonavera as Brighella, and Giorgio Bongiovanni as Pantalone de'Bisognosi.

Antiquity upon This Argument (1698). In many cases, however, ingenious theatrical entrepreneurs found ways to outwit these restrictions and attacks.

Regulation of Theatres in England

As we have seen, government intervention in English theatre can be traced back to Elizabeth I, who issued proclamations limiting dramatic subject matter and also designated a master of revels as the licenser of theatrical companies and plays. When Charles II was restored to the throne in 1660, he issued the first of several licenses—called *patents*—to Davenant and Killigrew, which resulted in their monopolizing London theatre. When the legality of these patents was questioned, Parliament, in 1737, issued the Licensing Act, which restricted the presentation of drama to the

Drury Lane and Covent Garden theatres and made the lord chamberlain responsible for licensing plays.

Many theatrical figures tried to circumvent the Licensing Act. Some managers simply opened unlicensed houses, hoping that the act would not be vigorously enforced. Because—as we noted in Chapter 9—the act applied to performances of "tragedy, comedy, opera, play, farce, or other entertainment of the stage, for gain, hire or reward," some entrepreneurs argued that they were not profiting from their dramatic presentations. The manager of one unlicensed theatre, Henry Giffard, claimed that his audiences were paying to hear concerts and that his plays were presented as a free extra. (Musical entertainments were always part of the extended English theatrical bill of the eighteenth century.) Another manager, Samuel Foote (1720–1777), said that he was selling cups of hot chocolate, accompanied by theatrical presentations at no additional cost. Another way to circumvent the law was to argue that the type of entertainment presented was not covered by the Licensing Act, since many highly theatrical popular entertainments were not regulated by the statute. One such form was the burletta, which around 1800 was defined as any three-act play with five or more songs per act; clever theatre managers converted nonmusical dramas, such as Shakespeare's plays, into burlettas.

Despite all this, and although the Haymarket Theatre was licensed as a summer house in 1776, Drury Lane and Covent Garden dominated London theatre into the nineteenth century. The history of Covent Garden reveals a great deal about changes in London theatre practices in the 1700s and 1800s.

COVENT GARDEN

When John Rich, a holder of one of the patents for London theatres, ended the season of 1731, he began a subscription to raise funds for building a new theatre in Box Street, Covent Garden. Unlike his father, Christopher Rich—a lawyer who had bought the patent as a business investment and was a poor manager—John Rich was a very able manager; he was also an accomplished performer.

Covent Garden Theatre, a London playhouse that still exists today, opened on December 7, 1732, with a revival of *The Way of the World.* Under Rich, the theatre featured extravagant pantomimes with animals, tumblers, and contortionists, as well as revivals of older plays.

From 1737 to 1843, under the Licensing Act, Covent Garden and Drury Lane were the only two London theatres authorized to present legitimate drama. For a long time, therefore, their survival and management were particularly important: these two theatres provided the showcase for British drama.

When Rich died in 1761, his son-in-law managed Covent Garden, concentrating on opera. The Rich family sold the patent in 1767, and from then until 1803, Covent Garden had a series of managers, most notably George Coleman the elder from 1767 to 1774. To meet rising costs, the theatre was enlarged twice, in 1787 and in 1792; after the second enlargement, it held about 3,000 spectators.

John Philip Kemble, an actor, bought a share of the patent in 1803, and he and his sister, Sarah Siddons, performed at Covent Garden until they retired. In 1804, Covent Garden's sensation was Master Betty, a child actor so popular that Parliament

(Victoria and Albert Museum, London/Art Resource, N.Y.)

COVENT GARDEN
This famous theatre, which opened in 1732, is still in operation today. It was enlarged twice, in 1787 and 1792, in order to earn more revenue. The renovation of 1792 increased its seating capacity to 3,000. Fires destroyed the theatre in 1808 and again in 1856, but both times it was rebuilt.

adjourned to see him. The theatre burned down in 1808, and when it reopened in 1809 Kemble tried to recoup his losses by raising prices. This resulted in the Old Price Riots, which began on opening night and lasted for over sixty days until Kemble backed down.

Charles Kemble, who had succeeded his brother in 1817, presented Shakespeare's *King John* in 1824 with the first complete historically accurate scenery and costumes. When he found himself in financial difficulties in 1829, he was rescued by his daughter, Fanny Kemble, whose work as an actress helped him pay his debts. Although she had not intended to pursue an acting career, Fanny Kemble was a popular success as Juliet, Portia, Beatrice, and other heroines.

In the nineteenth century, several other people attempted to manage Covent Garden, with little success. The actor William Charles Macready had a fine company that performed excellent plays, but he refused to keep successes running. Madame Vestris staged several carefully researched Shakespearean revivals, but she also failed. A fire destroyed the theatre again in 1856, and it was rebuilt once more in 1858. The theatre was then turned over to opera; except for occasional dramatic performances, it has continued to be the home of opera and ballet ever since.

In the 1990s, the British government introduced a national lottery, many of the proceeds of which were intended to finance the improvement of the physical facilities of arts institutions. As a result, the Covent Garden Opera House was closed during 1998 and 1999 for a $400 million renovation and expansion.

Regulation of Theatres in France

In eighteenth-century France, there were government restrictions on what types of plays could be produced. Three major Parisian theatres were subsidized by the government: the Opéra; the Comédie Française, the home of nonmusical drama; and after 1716 the Comédie Italienne, the home of commedia dell'arte and later of comic opera.

For most of the eighteenth century, *boulevard theatres*—so called because they were located on Boulevard du Temple—catered to popular tastes. The boulevard theatres invented many types of musical entertainments in order to get around the monopolies granted by the government to other theatres. Boulevard theatres had developed from popular entertainers and companies performing at Parisian fairs; boulevard forms—such as comic opera, pantomime, and melodrama—were so popular that the government-supported houses eventually incorporated them into their own repertoire. All the boulevard theatres were eventually put under the control of the Opéra in 1784.

In 1791, during the French Revolution, the government restrictions and monopolies were abolished.

Government and Theatre in Germany

In Germany, government intervention in theatre was of a more positive nature. Eighteenth-century Germany was not unified; it consisted of several independent states. German theatre struggled to become established in the early eighteenth century and became an important artistic force during the last quarter of the century.

German theatre of the late 1600s and early 1700s consisted mostly of foreign performances, usually of opera and dance at court; educational presentations by the Jesuits; and an early form of popular theatre. This popular theatre was dominated by performers who had been influenced by English actors appearing in Germany during the first half of the seventeenth century—because of the language barrier, these English actors had emphasized physical action and slapstick in a style similar to commedia dell'arte. One of the German performers was Joseph Anton Stranitzky (1676–1726), who developed a comic peasant character, Hanswurst, and helped establish popular theatre in Vienna.

Between 1727 and the 1740s, Caroline Neuber and Johann Gottsched attempted to reform popular theatre: they introduced more traditional neoclassical dramatic forms; focused more on rehearsals and carefully staged performances; and, at first, eliminated some of the comic characters who had predominated. Neuber and Gottsched did not succeed in transforming German theatre, but they influenced many other significant German actor-managers, including Friederich Schönemann (1740–1782), Sophie Schroeder (1714–1793), Konrad Ekhof (1720–1778), Heinrich Koch (1703–1775), and Konrad Ackermann (1712–1771). Ackermann established Hamburg's first permanent theatre; it was there, in 1767, that Johann Friederich Löwen (1729–1771) established the Hamburg National Theatre, for which Lessing was a dramaturg, or literary manager. The Hamburg National Theatre was not government-subsidized; it was supported by leading businesspeople. Although it had many of Germany's most important actors, including Ekhof, it failed after only 2 years.

During the last quarter of the eighteenth century, state-subsidized theatres were organized in several German cities and states. Many of the rulers who established these theatres were trying to show off the cultural superiority of their courts; but some of the state theatres received only small subsidies and relied heavily on box-office receipts.

Government subsidization provided stability for German theatre artists and resulted in the organization of many excellent theatre companies; but it meant that the government could control theatrical presentations by withholding financial support. (Throughout history, this has been true of government support: it can be beneficial to artists, but it can also entail governmental control of dramatic content. The debate in the United States over whether the National Endowment for the Arts should support certain theatrical presentations with controversial subject matter is a recent example.)

Theatre Buildings

Theatres in Europe

Theatre buildings proliferated throughout Europe in the eighteenth century, in such countries as Germany, Russia, and Sweden. These theatres continued the architectural tradition established in the Italian Renaissance. Possibly the most significant theatre building surviving from this period is Drottningholm in Sweden, erected in 1766 as part of the royal summer palace outside Stockholm. Drottningholm was boarded up in the 1790s and for over 100 years remained closed until it was reopened in the early twentieth century. Today tourists can take a ferry from Stockholm to the palace grounds and see a perfect working example of an eighteenth-century Italianate proscenium-arch, pole-and-chariot theatre—even its wings and shutters, painted in perspective, remain intact.

Although theatres throughout Europe retained Italian Renaissance features, there were some important transformations in the eighteenth-century proscenium-arch theatres. For one thing, playhouses became larger to accommodate the new middle-class audiences, made up of the expanding mercantile class in the growing cities and towns. In London's Drury Lane, for example, the seating capacity increased from about 650 in 1700 to about 3,000 in 1800. Also, the interiors were ovoid (egg-shaped) to improve sight lines. And by the end of the century, the pit—even in France—had backless benches.

(© Massimo Listri/Corbis)

THE THEATRE AT DROTTNINGHOLM PALACE
This theatre in Sweden still has the same sets and stage machinery that were used when it was built as a court playhouse in the eighteenth century. It is an excellent example of an Italianate proscenium theatre with the pole-and-chariot system for changing scenery.

By the middle of the century, spectators had been removed from the stage in England and France. This change was in keeping with Denis Diderot's "fourth wall" convention. According to Diderot, an audience should not disturb a performance, nor should actors acknowledge the presence of spectators; in short, it should be as if there were an invisible glass wall between audience and actors. The "fourth wall" convention did not actually become an accepted theatrical practice until the nineteenth century, but the removal of spectators from the stage was a step in this direction.

(Drottningholms Teatermuseum)

STAGE MACHINERY AT DROTTNINGHOLM Drottningholm still has the machinery of an eighteenth-century Italianate proscenium theatre, and productions there today continue to use the same technology. Here, stagehands are using its pole-and-chariot system to execute a scene change.

An example of the developments in theatre spaces was the new building, opened in 1782, for the Comédie Française, the national theatre of France. In the new theatre building, there were seats for everyone. Before this building was constructed, the pit in front of the stage had no seats; in the company's earlier theatres, the spectators in the pit stood during performances. In fact, spectators in the old seatless pits would move about and socialize. Thus the new seats were controversial—Parisians had enjoyed the social ambience of the old pit, and a leading playwright of the day, Louis-Sebastian Mercier (1740–1814), publicly criticized the addition of benches. The audience area was egg-shaped, making it easier for everyone to see the action onstage. The stage was large and very deep. However, its apron was smaller than the aprons in the company's previous theatres—the actors all performed behind the proscenium arch. The scenery was painted and changed by wings and shutters.

Eighteenth-century English playhouses were significantly different from their counterparts on the continent, and from Restoration theatres. In the eighteenth century, the apron, or forestage, of English theatres shrank; it now extended out only about 12 feet from the proscenium arch, and the backstage area became much deeper. There were two proscenium doors—one on each side of the stage—leading out onto the apron; above each door was a proscenium box. On the European continent, by contrast, the basic configuration of eighteenth-century theatres followed the Italian Renaissance tradition more closely. A typical theatre would have a proscenium-arch stage—without doors or an extended apron—as well as pit, boxes, and galleries; it used pole-and-chariot scene-shifting machinery.

Theatres in America

Permanent theatres were also constructed in the New World in the eighteenth century. They had been preceded by touring players. The earliest examples of European theatre in America can be traced to the beginning of the 1600s, when there were amateur performances in French Canada and in Spanish Florida. The first English performance probably took place in 1665 in Virginia; presumably because of religious and governmental opposition, the actors were promptly arrested. Many popular entertainments are noted in early colonial America, such as tightrope walking and the exhibition of bears, but theatrical performances were rare until the early 1700s.

The first professional entertainer arrived in 1703 and performed in Charleston and New York; in 1714, the first play written in America was published. The first permanent theatre was built in Williamsburg, Virginia, in 1716 by William Levingston. Between 1749 and 1752, Walter Murray and Thomas Kean organized the Virginia Players Comedians, who performed in temporary spaces such as remodeled warehouses in Philadelphia and New York and throughout Virginia and Maryland. In 1752, a company led by Lewis Hallam (1714–1756) and his wife arrived in the British colonies and became quite successful.

After the American Revolution, theatre was revived in New York by Lewis Hallam Jr. (c. 1740–1808) and his company, and in Philadelphia by Thomas Wignell

(1753–1803), Hallam's leading comedian. The Philadelphia company had the Chestnut Street Theatre (1794) constructed along the lines of a small London theatre building. Philadelphia was the mercantile center of the new country and was to become its theatrical center in the early nineteenth century; the success of the Chestnut Street theatre building and its company was a factor in this development. When Hallam retired from the management of his New York company, William Dunlap (1766–1839), a popular actor and melodramatic playwright, took over, and the Park Theatre was opened in 1798 to replace the John Street (see page 310). The development of early American theatre buildings clearly reflected the influence of English theatre practice.

THE HALLAM FAMILY

In the eighteenth century, English actors and companies began arriving in colonial America. One of the earliest professional English companies on record is a family of performers: the Hallams (c. 1740–1800). Their history provides a glimpse into the beginning of professional theatre in the United States.

William Hallam (c. 1712–c. 1758) came from a line of English actors. For 10 years, he managed an unlicensed theatre in London, the New Wells Theatre in Goodman's Fields. By 1750 he was forced to close and was left bankrupt. Looking toward a new opportunity in the American colonies, Hallam hired an agent, Robert Upton, to investigate theatrical conditions in North America, but Upton disappeared once he had crossed the Atlantic. Hallam then hired a small troupe of ten performers organized on a sharing plan; outfitted them with costumes, scenery, and scripts; and sent them to America under the management of his brother Lewis (1714–1756). In 1752, the unknown company arrived in Williamsburg, Virginia, making their first appearance in Shakespeare's *Merchant of Venice.* With Lewis playing secondary roles, his wife as the leading actress, and their children—Lewis Jr., Adam, and Helen—in minor parts, the company secured brief Engagements in Charleston, New York, and Philadelphia with a repertoire that consisted of Shakespeare and popular Restoration and eighteenth-century English drama.

In 1755, the struggling troupe sailed to Jamaica, where a small community of English players had settled. There, they met the English actor David Douglass (d. 1786), who at the time was trying to recruit actors from England. The two companies decided to merge. When Lewis died in 1756, Douglass married Mrs. Hallam and took over the company, calling it the American Company.

(The Folger Shakespeare Library, Washington, D.C.)

ENGLISH ACTORS COME TO AMERICA
Among the most famous English families of actors who came to America in the eighteenth century were the Hallams. They were symbolic of the many English performers who moved to America to establish a tradition of English-style performances there. Shown here is Mrs. Hallam, wife of Lewis Hallam. She was a leading actress and also helped establish new theatre companies in America.

The American Company gained considerable success despite harsh public and religious opposition—obstacles players became adept at circumventing. When the company performed in Newport, Rhode Island, in 1761, they presented their repertoire as "moral dialogues" to bypass antitheatrical hostility. Constant touring helped establish audiences for professional theatre, and eventually Douglass built two permanent theatres: the Southwark Theatre (1766) in Philadelphia and the John Street Theatre (1767) in New York City—both modeled after provincial English theatres.

Mrs. Hallam (d. 1774) continued in leading roles for the American Company, where she was joined by her son, Lewis Jr. (c. 1740–1803). Described as a "woman of great beauty and elegance," Mrs. Hallam was popular for her sympathetic portrayals of Juliet, Desdemona, Cordelia, and Jane Shore. Lewis Jr. remained on the stage for fifty years. He developed a distinguished reputation in a broad range of roles and starred in the first professional production of an American play, Thomas Godfrey's *The Prince of Parthia* (1767).

The company toured the colonies until the Revolutionary War, when professional theatre ceased. After the American Revolution, and Douglass's death in 1786, Lewis Jr. revived the New York company with new partners. However, friction among his associates induced him to retire from management, though he continued to act until his death.

Scenery

In the eighteenth century, the pervasive influence on scene design was Italian. Most continental theatres used Italianate wing-and-shutter settings, painted in perspective, and shifted scenery by Torelli's pole-and-chariot system. (As we have noted, theatres in England, the Netherlands, and America used the groove system for shifting scenery.) Some additional elements were occasionally incorporated into the painted designs: these included borders at the top to mask the fly space; *ground rows,* which were silhouette cutouts along the stage floor; large scenic cutouts, such as painted trees, which could be shifted by the pole-and-chariot system; rolled backdrops, which replaced the shutters; and *act drops,* curtains at the front of the stage.

The major change in painted perspective, however, was the introduction of angle or multiple-point perspective. (In Italian, this innovation is referred to as *scena per angolo.*) Rather than having the perspective pull the viewer's eye to one vanishing point, there were now many vanishing points within a painted stage design. The multiple vanishing points also made the settings seem larger in scale and more grandiose, even though, in reality, they were not. The major innovators of angle perspective were members of the Bibiena family, discussed below.

The other major changes in scene design during this century had to do with creation of mood, depiction of recognizable locales, attempts at historical accuracy, and more frequent use of three-dimensional properties.

The Italian Giambattista Piranesi (1720–1778) heightened the atmospheric quality of designs by emphasizing the contrast between light and shadow in painting, a technique known as *chiaroscuro.*

Philippe Jacques de Loutherbourg (1740–1812)—who was hired by the English actor-manager David Garrick for the Drury Lane Theatre in 1771 and worked there for a decade—was among the designers who introduced local color into settings and strove to unify all the visual elements. *Local color* refers to the inclusion of places audience members will recognize from their own community; in eighteenth-century London, this would have meant such landmarks as the Tower of London and London Bridge. This interest in re-creating recognizable locales was in keeping with the popularity of eighteenth-century landscape painting, and it was a move away from the neoclassical tradition of stock sets. Still, eighteenth-century theatre companies (unlike theatres today) could not afford to construct a unique setting for each production.

In the middle of the century, a developing interest in ancient history also led some set designers to experiment—albeit usually unsuccessfully—with historical accuracy. But the real explosion in historically accurate designs would occur, as we shall see, in the nineteenth century.

As it had been in the Renaissance, Italy was the birthplace of many of these eighteenth-century scenic innovations. The most influential Italian designers and theatre architects of the period belonged to the Bibiena family.

THE BIBIENA FAMILY

For nearly 100 years, from 1690 to 1787, the name Bibiena was synonymous with scenic design throughout Europe. Spanning three generations, seven members of the Bibiena family were designers.

The Bibienas are noted for three innovations: their use of baroque art in scene designs; the vast scale and elaborate ornamentation of their settings; and their use of angle perspective. As we have noted, *angle perspective* is a convention that uses several vanishing points rather than the single vanishing point that had been used since the Renaissance; it gives a scene more complexity and depth than single-point perspective. Italian Renaissance painted sets pull the eye to a central vanishing point; in the Bibienas' designs, the eye is attracted to various vanishing points—the standard visual pattern is broken. The Bibienas' sets also seem to extend beyond the proscenium arch; Renaissance designs seem totally framed and enclosed by the arch.

The family originally came from a town near Florence, Italy, where Giovanni Maria Gialli Bibiena (1625–1665), an artist and the founder of the family, was born. His two sons, Ferdinando (1657–1743) and Francesco (1659–1739), studied painting in Bologna, Italy, and then studied scene design under an artist called Rivani, who had worked for Louis XIV at Versailles in France. Francesco became ducal architect at Mantua, Italy, and built theatres in Vienna, Rome, Verona, and Nancy. He also assisted his brother Ferdinando with spectacles at the court of Charles VI in Vienna. Before Ferdinando came to Vienna, he had worked in Parma and Barcelona and had published several books.

Ferdinando's sons also became designers. Alessandro (1687–1769) was court painter and architect to the elector of the Palatinate in Germany. Antonio (1700–1774) worked with his father in Vienna and also in Bologna and Mantua. Giovanni Maria (c. 1704–1769) built a theatre near Lisbon. Giuseppe (1696–1757) was the most noted of Ferdinando's sons. He succeeded his father as court designer in Vienna and also worked in Munich, Prague, Dresden, and Bayreuth. Before his death in Berlin, Giuseppe published his designs in three series of Engravings.

Giuseppe's son Carlo (1728–1787) was the last to follow the family profession. He also traveled most widely, working in Germany, France, the Netherlands, London,

A BIBIENA SET DESIGN
Scene design in eighteenth-century Europe was dominated by one family: the Bibiena family, whose second, third, and fourth generations carried on the tradition begun by Giovanni Bibiena. This Engraving shows a typical Bibiena design—vast in scale, ornate, and elegant, with its perspective vista disappearing in several directions.

Naples, Stockholm, and Saint Petersburg. The sets he designed for the court theatre at Drottningholm in Sweden are still in use today. Some of his designs were also published.

Together, the Bibienas established a style of scene design—on a grandiose scale—that dominated the stage throughout the eighteenth century.

Scenic and Technical Experiments

During the 1770s, more three-dimensional, practicable elements were introduced into painted stage settings. For example, the climactic scene in Richard Brinsley Sheridan's sentimental comedy *The School for Scandal* required a screen for concealment.

Increased use of such practicable elements began to transform painted wing-and-shutter settings and would eventually lead to the realism of the *box set*, an arrangement in which flats are cleated together at angles (rather than set up parallel to the audience) to form the three-dimensional walls of a room. Recent research suggests that some type of box set may have been used as early as the late Italian Renaissance. In the last decade of the eighteenth century, the Italian designer Paolo Landriani (1770–1838) used a box set at La Scala, Milan's opera house. The box set

DEBATES IN THEATRE HISTORY | When Was the Box Set Introduced?

The period when the box set was actually introduced into theatrical production has become more and more debatable with recent reevaluations of drawings and writings by scene painters from the seventeenth and eighteenth centuries. As recently as 30 years ago, the nineteenth century was often cited as the time when the box set was first used. However, recent analyses of drawings of operatic productions of the Italian Renaissance and of drawings from the eighteenth century seem to suggest that versions of the box set were used during those earlier periods.

In an article in *The Cambridge Guide to Theatre,* Arnold Aronson writes: "The introduction of the box set is frequently attributed to Mme. Vestris who worked with Planché at the Olympic Theatre in London from 1821 to 1838. However, something like a box set may have been achieved as early as 1642 in Venice by Torelli with the production of *Il Bellerofonte.* Painted perspective borders created an illusion of a ceiling and it is possible that he also placed panels between the wings to achieve continuous walls. And by the early 18th century, the free placement of flats and the enclosure of space downstage practiced by the Bibienas created at least the illusion, if not the fact, of a box set."*

In addition, there is a manuscript, *Construction of Theatres and Theatrical Machinery* (1688), by Frabrizio Carini Motta (1627–1699)—a designer who worked at Mantua—that contains a description of scenery which sounds like a box set; and the Italian designer Paolo Landriani is thought to have used a box set at La Scala, the opera house in Milan, at the end of the eighteenth century.

Earlier historians had probably overlooked times when sets with wings and shutters parallel to the audience had been enclosed on the sides by other flats to create the illusion of a room. These box-type sets were still part of the tradition of painted scenery and were therefore seen as closer to the wing-and-shutter system; their historical importance was not recognized. The nineteenth-century box set, on the other hand, began to incorporate more three-dimensional practical objects and so was more like today's settings; it is probably for this reason that theatre historians placed the origins of the box set in the nineteenth century. As historians continue to study even earlier drawings of Renaissance and baroque settings, there may be more discoveries regarding when the box set first appeared.

*"Theatre Design," in *The Cambridge Guide to Theatre,* Martin Barnham (ed.), Cambridge University Press, New York, 1992, pp. 972–987.

was to revolutionize scene design in the nineteenth century and would become an integral element in realistic staging.

There were also experiments with stage lighting in the late 1700s: attempts to mask lighting sources, to use silk screens for coloring, and to introduce oil lamps and other alternatives to candles. Loutherbourg was a key innovator in this area. But light sources were still not easily controlled, and the auditorium as well as the stage had to remain lit.

Costumes

Theatrical costuming remained a primitive art throughout most of the eighteenth century. Actors and actresses, who often provided their own wardrobes, believed that the chief criterion for a costume was showing the performers off to the best advantage. Traditional, conventional costumes for specific characters and eras were common. On the English stage, for example, the Italian Jew Shylock in adaptations of Shakespeare's *The Merchant of Venice* always had red hair and a large nose. Costumes were not unified within a production, nor was there much attempt to make costumes appropriate for characters or time periods. Eighteenth-century experiments with costuming did not make an immediate impact on these practices, though these experiments were seeds that would flower into a theatrical revolution in the nineteenth century.

Daring theatre artists throughout Europe experimented with historically accurate costumes. Their attempts were not often exact historical reconstructions, but the experimenters were not totally to blame: accurate historical information was limited, and audiences expected traditional costumes. (In addition, we should bear in mind that completely accurate historical costuming is rare even today: costuming as a production element is usually intended to create an illusion of time and place rather than an accurate reconstruction.) Another factor inhibiting the development of historically accurate costumes in the eighteenth century (and this is also true of settings) was their cost: it was simply too expensive to create new costumes for a show that would have only a short run in repertory. (Not until later, in the nineteenth century—with the extended run and larger audiences in urban centers—would it become economical to develop unique costumes and sets for individual productions.)

Artists who did veer from accepted costuming conventions were ridiculed by audiences. Nevertheless, in 1741 the English actor Charles Macklin (c. 1699–1797) attempted to present a truly Jewish Shylock; and in 1772 he performed Macbeth in Scottish garb. In France, three performers—Marie-Justine Favart (1727–1772), Clairon (1723–1803), and Henri-Louis Lekain (1729–1778)—experimented with costuming that was supposedly appropriate for the characters' social position, nationality, and historical era. The German actor-manager Friedrich Ludwig Schroeder (1744–1816) apparently used historically appropriate costumes in a production of Goethe's *Goetz von Berlichingen* in 1774. These first steps were important in setting the stage for greater historical accuracy in later periods.

Acting

The eighteenth century was an era of famous and enormously popular performers. All across Europe, successful actors and actresses developed a dedicated following. Some of these performers worked to improve the social status of the profession, but by and large actors remained suspect members of society.

CHARLES MACKLIN

As an actor, Charles Macklin (c. 1699–1797) is perhaps best-known for his revolutionary sympathetic portrayal of Shylock in Shakespeare's *The Merchant of Venice.* Macklin was born in Ireland and was educated near Dublin, at Island Bridge, studying under a Mr. Nicholson before running away to London sometime around 1717. In London, Macklin found work as a strolling player for several years, before he began acting at Lincoln's Inn Fields in 1725. By 1733, Macklin had become a member at the Drury Lane Theatre and was considered primarily a comic performer. In 1739 Macklin married the actress Ann Grace (d. 1758), who bore him both a son and a daughter; later, after Ann's death, he married Elizabeth Jones in 1759.

Macklin was notorious for his wild days as a youth; he had a green-room argument over a wig with Thomas Hallam in 1735, which resulted in Hallam's death. Brought to trial over the incident, Macklin ingeniously argued on his own behalf, so that he was simply branded on the hand as punishment and then released. Macklin's personality seemed argumentative, and he found himself in many lawsuits deriving from his perceived injustices. This propensity sometimes made him unpopular with fellow actors and managers.

His personality aside, Macklin is known for his more natural style of performing, rooted in his gift for observation and mimicry. Throughout his career, Macklin coached several other actors in his style of performance, including Samuel Foote and John Hill. Hill later published *The Actor* (1750), which described Macklin's method.

As noted above, Macklin is most famous for his success as Shylock in 1741. Previously, Shylock's character was presented as predominantly comical, almost clownish. However, Macklin presented Shylock as tragic and thus removed the comic representation from the English stage. To help shape his performance of Shylock, Macklin also observed Jewish life in England. He was acclaimed as the finest Shylock of his generation, but he was soon outstripped by David Garrick's increasing fame. The two actors had been friends before clashing over an actors' strike at Drury Lane in 1743, after which Macklin was dismissed from the company.

(The Folger Shakespeare Library, Washington, D.C.)

Charles Macklin as Shylock.

In 1746 Macklin turned to writing plays, and he eventually produced about forty plays in all. He first achieved success as a playwright in 1757 with his afterpiece *Love à la Mode,* and throughout the remainder of his life he continued to write plays as well as perform the role of Shylock. However, when he died in London in July 1797, he was penniless, primarily because of his constant clashes with theatre managers and other actors, which had diminished his employment opportunities. Although bankrupt, Macklin was honored by being buried in St. Paul's Cathedral.

Today, many historians credit Macklin with bringing a more lifelike style of performance to the eighteenth-century stage, and focusing on observation of daily life as a means of establishing character and costume.

Acting Styles

The predominant approach to acting in the eighteenth century is usually described as *bombastic* or *declamatory,* terms that suggest its emphasis on oratorical skills. Standardized patterns of stage movement were necessary because rehearsal time was brief and bills were changed frequently. More often than not, actors would address their lines to the audience, not to the character to whom they were supposed to be speaking. Among the performers who took this "bombastic" approach were the English actors Barton Booth (1681–1733) and James Quin (1693–1766).

In Europe and America, actors were often employed by "lines of business," that is, according to type. Normally, actors "possessed" their parts; once they performed a role, it would remain theirs until retirement or death. Performers often fell back on improvisation and relied on the prompter.

In the midst of these conventional practices, there were a few innovators. Some eighteenth-century performers tried to create natural, individualized characterizations, though they were not in the mainstream. Actors and actresses who rejected the bombastic style for a more natural approach include Charles Macklin and David Garrick (both English); Michel Baron (1653–1729), Adrienne Lecouvreur (1692–1730), Clairon, and Henri-Louis Lekain (French); and Friedrich Schroeder (German). They were opposed to the emphasis on declamation, stereotypical positioning of performers onstage, and singsong delivery of verse; they wanted to create individual characters, and they wanted to have more careful rehearsal procedures. These performers, however, worked in traditional eighteenth-century companies and were restricted by conventional stage practices; thus they could not attempt to reflect everyday life onstage. Nevertheless, they were the ancestors of modern realistic performers.

Differences in styles of acting in the eighteenth century can be illustrated by the conflicting approaches of two of France's most popular performers: Dumesnil and Clairon.

DUMESNIL AND CLAIRON

Two of the greatest actresses on the French stage during the eighteenth century, Dumesnil (1713–1803) and Clairon (1723–1803), were notorious rivals. Their rivalry was intensified by distinct contrasts in their acting technique and performance style.

(Giraudon/Art Resource, N.Y.)

DUMESNIL
An outstanding actress of the Comédie Française was Dumesnil (Marie-Françoise Marchand), shown here in the title role of *Athalie* by Racine. Sometimes erractic, Dumesnil was praised as an extraordinary natural talent.

Dumesnil (Marie-Françoise Marchand) began her acting career in the provinces and was invited to join the Comédie Française in 1737. A year later she was made a *sociétaire.* An actress of considerable natural ability, Dumesnil was considered excellent in passionate roles, such as Medea and Clytemnestra. She created characters in several of Voltaire's plays, most notably *Merope* (1743), although Voltaire later preferred the acting of Clairon.

Dumesnil's position as the leading tragic actress was challEnged in 1743 by Clairon (Claire-Josèph Hippolyte Léris de la Tude). Clairon had made her stage debut at age 13, playing small parts with the Comédie Italienne in Paris, and had then put in her time in the provinces. She returned to Paris to debut at the Opéra in March 1743; but because she was more talented as an actress than a singer, about 4 months later she applied for admission to the Comédie Française. Clairon was granted a debut with the Comédie Française during which she would be evaluated for membership in the prestigious company.

Although she had specialized in soubrette roles (a *soubrette* is a lady's maid), she chose to make her debut in tragedy; even more surprisingly, she insisted on playing Phaedra, a difficult role and one in which Dumesnil excelled. The company agreed, assuming that she would fail and learn a lesson in humility; but Clairon, who had not even rehearsed the play with the company, stunned both the actors and the audience with her wonderful performance.

While both Clairon and Dumesnil appeared successfully in leading roles at the Comédie Française for many years, their performance styles were quite dissimilar. Dumesnil was considered to have more natural talent; generally, she relied on the inspiration of the moment to suggest how to play a part. Clairon, on the other hand, became a great actress largely by the force of her own will; she relied on intelligent and industrious preparation—on craft rather than inspiration—and was a much more studied performer than Dumesnil. Clairon's style received praise in Diderot's treatise on acting, *The Paradox of Acting;* Dumesnil, on the other hand, was criticized for being erratic: sometimes brilliant with flashes of genius, and at other times ordinary. A studied performer like Clairon, Diderot said, would give more consistently excellent performances.

Another difference developed between Clairon and Dumesnil. Around 1752, Clairon began to adopt a less declamatory, more natural speaking style. Clairon also became interested in historical accuracy, using her costumes to reflect different periods and places. Dumesnil, in contrast, continued to wear her expensive contemporary fashions for every role.

This contrast between the spontaneous, intuitive style of Dumesnil and the more reliable, impressive style of Clairon was not an isolated example of differing performance styles separating performers who appeared in the same era. This is a recurring theme in the history of acting, appearing again, for example, in contrasting styles of Shakespearean performance in the nineteenth century and in the rivalry at the end of that century between Eleonora Duse and Sarah Bernhardt.

LA CLAIRON

French actresses often took a single name as a stage name. A famous actress of the eighteenth century was Mlle. Clairon (Claire-Josèphe-Hippolyte Léris de la Tude). Through determination and careful preparation she became one the finest actresses of the Comédie Française.

Acting Companies

Organization of acting companies varied from country to country (often, it varied even within a country). In English companies, for example, plays were rehearsed under the supervision of an actor-manager, who was usually the company's leading performer; rehearsals usually lasted about 3 hours a day for 2 weeks; and actors were contracted for a specific period of time. In France, the sharing plan remained in use in government-supported theatre companies in Paris, while the boulevard theatres were managed by business entrepreneurs. The Comédie Française was organized democratically; the company members voted on such issues as the bill.

The starting time of performances became later and later during the eighteenth century—usually, it was between 5 and 6 P.M. An evening's offering by an English company would be quite varied, with musical performances, a full-lEngth play, entertainments between acts, and an afterpiece. An evening's bill in France would not offer quite so much entertainment; but a French company would also frequently stage a full-length play accompanied by entertainments between acts and an afterpiece.

The complexity of the bill led to increases in the size of acting companies during the century.

Status of Performers

During the eighteenth century, there were attempts to treat the craft and profession of acting seriously. For example, Denis Diderot's *The Paradox of Acting* was a theoretical treatise. (In this work, as noted previously, he suggested that the more emotion a performer actually feels, the less emotion the audience will feel—a view that runs counter to most contemporary theories of realistic acting.) Attempts to establish acting schools in England and France were a further indication of a new, more serious attitude.

However, for the most part performers in the eighteenth century were not held in high esteem socially. (In Rome, to give just one example, women were still not allowed to perform, because of the opposition of the church.) Some performers tried to improve the social status of the profession; in the 1730s, for instance, the actress Caroline Neuber—who is well known for many innovations that she brought to the developing German theatre—attempted to accomplish this by policing the morality of her company.

CAROLINE NEUBER

Around 1720, as we noted earlier, German theatre consisted of traveling troupes who performed farces and improvised comedies at fairgrounds. The literary critic Johann Gottsched wanted to elevate the quality of German theatre by improving the repertoire with plays based on French models and by refining the acting style; but it was not until he saw the company headed by Caroline Neuber (1697–1760) that he found a troupe to carry out his reforms.

Neuber's name before she married was Caroline Weissenborn. In 1718, she eloped with Johann Neuber, a young clerk, to escape from her tyrannical father. After serving as apprentices in several companies, the Neubers formed their own troupe in about 1725 and secured a license to perform at the Leipzig Easter fair. Caroline insisted on memorization of lines and careful rehearsals instead of improvisation, and she was responsible for a number of important reforms in German theatrical practice. She attempted to upgrade performances by eliminating a popular clown character, Hanswurst, to improve the social standing of her actors, and to get better pay for her company. Because she shared Gottsched's desire to improve German theatre, she was quite willing to perform his model repertoire; she was also strong-willed and popular enough to impose her views on her company and her public.

The collaboration between Neuber and Gottsched began in 1727 and lasted 12 years, until friction between the independent actress and the dictatorial critic caused a break in 1739. In 1740 the Neubers took their troupe to Russia, introducing modern theatre to that country. When they returned to Germany the next year, Gottsched had allied himself with another troupe. The final break came when Caroline Neuber replaced the togas Gottsched had specified for one of his plays with flesh-colored tights. Gottsched attacked the actress in his reviews; she in turn described him as "bat-eared" in one of her prologues.

After the break with Gottsched, the Neubers' company began to decline; but they continued to struggle until they were impoverished by the outbreak of the Seven Years' War in 1756. Caroline died in 1760, a year after her husband. Her alliance with Gottsched—the first in Germany between the literary and performance sides of theatre—laid the foundation for late-eighteenth-century and nineteenth-century German theatre.

As an actress, Caroline Neuber was most acclaimed for her comic performances. Her staging practices influenced many young German actors—including Heinrich Gottfried Koch and Johann Griederich Schönemann—who worked with her and then went on to distinguished careers as actor-managers. She also produced one of Gotthold Ephraim Lessing's earliest plays, which he had written as a student.

The Emergence of the Director

Possibly the most significant development in the eighteenth century was the emergence of theatre practitioners who functioned, to some extent, like the modern director. Well into the eighteenth century, as we have noted, playwrights or leading actors normally doubled as directors of stage business. (The medieval pageant master was a distinct exception.) Since these playwrights and actors had more pressing primary concerns, their actual directing was minimal; furthermore, the time spent on preparing a production in rehearsal was limited. What was missing in theatre, then, was someone to oversee and unify productions, assist performers, and ensure the appropriateness of the visual elements.

Some of the innovative actor-managers and playwrights we have already mentioned attempted to oversee the quality of productions and thus established a foundation for the development of directing; among these were Voltaire, Neuber and Gottsched, Ekhof, Ackermann, Iffland, and Schroeder. However, the two figures who are said to be the founders of modern stage direction are the English actor David Garrick and the German playwright, poet, and novelist Johann Wolfgang von Goethe.

David Garrick

With his reforms in staging, David Garrick (1717–1779) revitalized eighteenth-century English theatre and won for it the respect of all Europe. Because he oversaw the entire production process, Garrick is often described as an early director.

Garrick's first stage success came in a school play when he was 11 years old. His father, an army officer, gave him a good education, including a term at Dr. Samuel Johnson's academy. A financial legacy enabled Garrick and his older brother to enter the wine trade; while working at the London branch of a wine company, he became acquainted with prominent actors and producers, including Charles Macklin, with whom he discussed theories of realistic acting.

(National Portrait Gallery, London)
David Garrick.

Resolved to try the stage as a career, Garrick played several roles in amateur productions. On October 18, 1741, he appeared as Richard III at Goodman's Fields, Henry Giffard's unlicensed theatre outside London, and his acting swept the city. Garrick was slender and of medium height, with expressive features and dark, piercing eyes. His style was surprisingly natural, compared with the declamatory speech and studied gestures typical of his time. He often based his characters on life, visiting

DAVID GARRICK: VERSATILE TRAGEDIAN

The most famous English actor of the eighteenth century was David Garrick, who was also a successful theatre manager. Known especially for his natural manner, even in roles where others gave way to histrionics, he excelled in every kind of drama. His versatility in Shakespearean roles is illustrated by this etching showing him portraying Lear, Macbeth, Richard III, and Hamlet.

DEBATES IN THEATRE HISTORY | Who Was the First Director?

The question of who was the first director in theatre history is complicated by a debate over the definition of the term *director*—that is, over the actual functions of the director. Clearly, during all periods of theatre history, there have been people who were responsible for overseeing the presentation of a production.

For example, in classical Greece, the playwright and the *chorididaskolos*—the trainer of the chorus—were responsible for rehearsing and staging productions. In the Roman era, the *dominus*—the manager of an acting company—oversaw rehearsals and the staging of plays for the festivals. During the Middle Ages, the pageant master organized the complicated details of presenting cycle plays. We know that the renowned Spanish pageant master Lope de Rueda managed extensive details for the presentation of complex religious dramas. In Shakespeare's time, the Elizabethan era, playwrights or leading actors in theatre companies were responsible for production details. During the French neoclassical era, the English Restoration, and the eighteenth century, leading actors managed the staging of productions.

However, we need to keep in mind that the concept of "overseeing a production" in these earlier eras was quite different from what we perceive as the duties of a contemporary director. For the most part, these early figures simply made sure that the actors knew their lines and that the production elements were readily available. They did not oversee extensive rehearsals or help the performers to develop characterizations. They did not consider themselves responsible for unifying the production, nor did they see a need to create unique visual elements for each production. In most cases, scenery and costumes were chosen from the stock owned by a company and were reused in production after production. In general, then, these individuals' managerial duties were regarded as an auxiliary function, and an actor or playwright who served in this capacity was probably closer to a stage manager than a director. This was also true of the medieval pageant masters, who were not actors or playwrights.

Therefore, many historians point to figures such as David Garrick and Johann Wolfgang von Goethe as the first directors in modern theatre. Garrick and Goethe both focused on unifying the stage productions they oversaw, and both were interested in providing appropriate scenery and costumes, arguing for historical accuracy. Also, they worked very closely with members of their acting companies regarding behavior during rehearsals and interpretation of characters. Many historians suggest that Goethe, at the Weimar court theatre, came closer to being a modern director, because he did not serve in a dual capacity—unlike Garrick, who was a leading actor.

Other historians cite nineteenth-century innovators who worked even more closely on unifying the stage production and made certain that acting, visual elements, and text came together seamlessly. In some cases, these individuals did not serve as leading actors but focused exclusively on staging productions. Adolphe Montigny in France and Richard Wagner and the duke of Saxe-Meiningen in Germany are often mentioned as early directors who focused on coordinating production elements. Some people argue that Stanislavski, with his focus on acting as well as visual elements, comes closest to our present-day concept of the director; however, Stanislavksi was also an actor, with the Moscow Art Theatre.

The argument over the "first director" is further complicated by an ongoing redefinition of the director's function. Is the director a coordinator or the author of a production? In modern theatre, such figures as Meyerhold, Artaud, and countless contemporary directors argue that the function of the director is to deconstruct texts and create unique readings and presentations. (Many of these directors will be discussed in later chapters.)

Given the lack of agreement over the function of the director, it is no wonder that a debate in the history of theatre continues to be, "Who was the first director?"

markets and law courts to study people. His repertoire included more than ninety roles, and he was equally good in comedy and tragedy.

In 1747, Garrick became one of the patent holders at the Drury Lane Theatre. He took an active part in the management of Drury Lane, where he assembled a distinguished acting company. The reforms he instituted made Drury Lane the dominant London theatre until his retirement in 1776.

(Victoria and Albert Museum, London/Art Resource, N.Y.)

A NEW APPROACH TO SCENE DESIGN
Philip James de Loutherbourg, a French artist and scene designer, was brought by the manager David Garrick to design sets for the Drury Lane Theatre. De Loutherbourg was well known for bringing local color to his scenery, including such sights as London Bridge and the Tower of London. The scene here shows his design for the play *The Chances*, featuring David Garrick as Don Juan. The painting, oil on canvas, is from the Dyce Collection, number 70.

Garrick was also a fairly accomplished writer. He adapted the works of many earlier playwrights, including Shakespeare, for presentation in his theatre. Frequently, he wrote new prologues and epilogues to plays, to be spoken by specific members of his company. *Miss in Her Teens* (1774) and *Bon-Ton; or, High Life Above Stairs* (1775) were two of the most successful of his original plays. He sometimes collaborated with other writers; for instance, he wrote *The Clandestine Marriage* (1766) with George Coleman the elder. *The Clandestine Marriage,* unfortunately, led to a dispute because Garrick would not agree to perform the part of Lord Ogleby; Coleman refused to let Garrick act in his later plays, and soon became Garrick's rival as manager of the Covent Garden Theatre.

Though his rivals considered him vain and snobbish, Garrick was a cultured man who enjoyed the company of literary and society figures. When he died in 1779, he was buried in the Poets' Corner of Westminster Abbey. His friend Samuel Johnson wrote, "I am disappointed by that stroke of death that has eclipsed the gaiety of nations, and impoverished the public stock of harmless pleasure."

It was between 1747 and 1776, when David Garrick was a partner in the management of the Drury Lane Theatre—and therefore responsible for artistic decisions—that he made his directorial innovations. As the company's leading performer, he championed a more natural style of acting; and he argued for careful development of characters' individual traits, based on meticulous preparation and research. His directorial policies were in keeping with his theories of acting. Garrick's rehearsals could last for weeks—much longer than the usual eighteenth-century practice. Garrick was also a strict disciplinarian: he required his actors to be on time, to know their lines, and to act—not simply recite—during rehearsals; and he established penalties for infractions of these rules. As part of his reformation of theatre practices, Garrick banished spectators from the stage.

Garrick was also concerned with the visual elements of his productions. Following the lead of Charles Macklin, Garrick experimented with historically accurate and appropriate costuming, and he is often credited with attempts to "mask," or hide, stage lighting. Garrick was also responsible for hiring the innovative stage designer de Loutherbourg for Drury Lane.

Thus Garrick was a complete theatre artist, undertaking many of the responsibilities that are now assigned to the director. However, he was still confined by tradition and by the commercial practices of eighteenth-century English theatre—unlike the German Johann Wolfgang von Goethe.

JOHANN WOLFGANG VON GOETHE

Johann Wolfgang von Goethe (1749–1832) was responsible for a number of important innovations in German theatre, comparable to those of David Garrick in England. Goethe was a man of many talents: in addition to being a theatrical director, he was a playwright, critic, and philosopher; he was also a minister of the court of Weimar, efficiently running everything from court theatricals to mining.

As the son of a wealthy Frankfurt merchant, Goethe had an excellent education. He studied at the University of Leipzig, the cultural capital of Germany, and in his enthusiasm wanted to learn everything. But the mental strain and a whirlwind love affair brought on a physical collapse that forced him to leave school. At home, he became interested in mysticism, alchemy, astrology, and the occult. It was at Strasbourg, where he finished his studies, that he became involved with the "storm and stress" movement in German literature and wrote his first important play, *Goetz von Berlichingen* (1773), in Shakespearean style. ("Storm and stress," which emphasized wide-ranging adventures of independent-minded heroes, was the forerunner of nineteenth-century romanticism.)

(Theater-Museum, Munich)

Johann Wolfgang von Goethe.

During a brief law practice, Goethe continued to write plays, poetry, and a novel; but in 1775 he accepted a post at the court of Weimar as director of theatre—a post soon expanded to the running of almost the entire duchy. Tired of the constant demands on his time, and seeking spiritual renewal, Goethe went to Italy in 1786 and stayed for 2 years. In Italy, he discovered the beauty of Greek and Roman ruins, which inspired a shift to classical themes and forms in his writing. When he returned to Weimar, he shed most of his court duties and devoted himself to writing and scientific research.

A friendship with the dramatist Friedrich Schiller led Goethe to take a renewed interest in the court theatre, which he had neglected for several years. Sharing a belief that drama should transcend ordinary experience and reveal ideal truths, the two writers transformed the Weimar theatre—Schiller with his plays and Goethe with his staging. After Schiller's death in 1805, Goethe again began to lose interest in the theatre and became an increasingly remote figure until his own death in 1832. Goethe's playwriting had culminated in his long dramatic poem *Faust* (Part I, 1808; Part II, 1832).

It was while he worked with Schiller at the Weimar court theatre that Goethe made most of the directorial innovations for which he is remembered. Goethe held intensive rehearsals and expected his actors to work as a unified ensemble company, and—like Garrick—he penalized those who broke his rehearsal rules. Goethe, however, was not an advocate of a more natural style of acting; he believed actors should address the audience rather than each other. He also followed routine blocking patterns, though he did emphasize careful stage composition, that is, the pictorial arrangement of performers onstage.

Goethe's approach to acting was reflected in his "Rules for Actors," a set of regulations for acting as well as personal behavior. How closely Goethe monitored his actors' personal behavior—to improve their social status—is apparent in the following rule: "The actor should show no pocket handkerchief onstage; even less should

(© Ruth Walz)

GOETHE'S FAUST
A man of great intellect and accomplishments was Johann Wolfgang von Goethe, a German writer who also ran a theatre in Germany. One of his crowning achievements was a play about Faust, who makes a pact with the devil. Shown here in a modern production, directed by Peter Stein, is Bruno Ganz in the title role.

he blow his nose, still less should he spit. It is frightful to be reminded of these natural occasions. One may have with him a small handkerchief, as indeed is now the fashion, as a help in case of need."[1] Not all his regulations were this trivial. Goethe forced his actors to take their craft and profession seriously; he included rules for stage movement and vocal technique as well as deportment in daily life. He also worked on establishing a uniform "stage German" so that his performers would not speak a variety of dialects.

Goethe carefully oversaw settings and costumes and believed in historical accuracy. He even trained his audiences by establishing rules for their conduct; the only appropriate reactions, he insisted, were applause and the withholding of applause. Our modern tradition of audience decorum was established by Goethe.

In short, the working methods Goethe used at the Weimar court theatre between 1794 and 1817 influenced many of the nineteenth-century directors who are among the founders of modern theatre.

The experimenters of the eighteenth century did not transform theatre overnight, but they helped set the stage for modern theatre—which would begin to develop in the nineteenth century. In Chapter 11, we turn to the first three-quarters of that century, the period from 1800 to 1875.

SUMMARY

The eighteenth century was a time of theatrical experimentation. In drama, many new forms were developed, including ballad opera, comic opera, middle-class tragedy, and sentimental comedy. Innovative playwrights moved away from the neoclassical rules; in Germany, the "storm and stress" movement, which included such authors as Goethe and Schiller, argued against strict dramatic rules. Many plays were episodic in structure.

In scene design, the Bibienas introduced multipoint perspective, and Piranesi used chiaroscuro. Also, local color and three-dimensional properties became

[1]Johann Wolfgang von Goethe, "Rules for Actors," Arthur Woehl (trans.), in *Actors on Acting,* Toby Cole and Helen Krich Chinoy (eds.), Crown, New York, 1970, p. 274.

more common in sets. Charles Macklin, Marie-Justine Favart, and Friedrich Schroeder were among those who experimented with historical accuracy in costuming. For much of the century, acting was bombastic; but performers such as Macklin and David Garrick attempted to make performing styles more like observed life. In the last half of the century, Garrick and Goethe established practices of modern directing.

MILESTONES CHAPTER 10 THEATRES IN THE EIGHTEENTH-CENTURY [1700–1800]

Theatre History

- Sir Richard Steele (1672–1729) *The Conscious Lovers*
- John Gay (1685–1732), *The Beggar's Opera*
- Bibiena family (1690–1787)
- George Lillo (1693–1739), *The London Merchant*
- Caroline Neuber (1697–1760)
- Charles Macklin (c. 1699–1797)
- Carlo Goldoni (1707–1793), *The Servant of Two Masters*
- Rival French actresses, Dumesnil (1713–1803) *(below)* and Clairon (1723–1803)

- David Garrick (1717–1779)
- Carlo Gozzi (1720–1806), *Turandot*
- Gotthold Ephraim Lessing (1729–1781), *Nathan the Wise*
- London's Covent Garden Theatre opens (1732)
- English Licensing Act (1737), restriction of theatre
- Pierre-Augustin Caron de Beaumarchais (1732–1799), *The Marriage of Figaro*
- Hallam family (c. 1740–1800), active in establishing professional theatre in America
- Friedrich Ludwig Schroeder (1744–1816)
- Richard Brinsley Sheridan (1751–1816), *The School for Scandal*

Cultural and Historical Developments

- Peter Paul Rubens's *The Judgment of Paris* (c. 1635)
- Rembrandt's *The Night Watch* (1642)
- Johann Sebastian Bach's *Brandenburg* Concertos (1721)
- George Frideric Handel's *Messiah* (1741)
- Montesquieu's *The Spirit of Laws* (1748)
- War of the Spanish Succession in France (1701–1714)
- Peter the Great begins westernization of Russia (c. 1701)
- *Encyclopédie* (1750–1772), edited by Diderot
- Louis XIV dies (1715)
- Daniel Defoe's *Robinson Crusoe* (1719) *(below)*

- Jonathan Swift's *Gulliver's Travels* (1726)
- John Key's "flying shuttle" loom patented (1733)
- Jean-Antoine Watteau's *The Embarkation for the Island of Cythera* (1717)
- Frederick the Great of Prussia, "enlightened despot" (1740)
- War of the Austrian Succession (1740–1748)
- French and Indian War (1754–1763)
- Seven Years' War (1756–1763)
- Voltaire's *Candide* (1759)
- Catherine the Great of Russia begins reign; Rousseau's *The Social Contract* (1762)
- James Watt's steam Engine patented (1769)
- American Revolution (1775–1783)

continued

PHOTO CREDITS: Dumesnil in *Athalie* by Racine. (Giraudon/Art Resource, N.Y.) / Cover of Defoe's *Adventures of Robinson Crusoe.* (Bettmann/Corbis)

- Johann Wolfgang von Goethe (1749–1832) *(below), Goetz von Berlichingen*

- Denis Diderot, *Discourse on Dramatic Poetry* (1758)
- Friedrich Schiller (1759–1805), *The Robbers*
- Drottningholm Theatre, Sweden, completed; Southwark Theatre, Philadelphia (1766)
- Hamburg National Theatre established; John Street Theatre, New York (1767)
- Comédie Française moves to new theatre with seating in the "pit" (1782)
- Government restrictions and monopolies on theatre abolished during French Revolution (1791)

- Declaration of Independence; Adam Smith's *Wealth of Nations* (1776) *(below)*

- Immanuel Kant's *Critique of Pure Reason* (1791)
- Francisco de Goya's *Don Manuel de Zuniga* (1784)
- Wolfgang Amadeus Mozart's *Don Giovanni* (1787) *(below)*

- French Revolution (1789–1799)
- Jacques-Louis David's *Murder of Marat* (1793) *(below)*

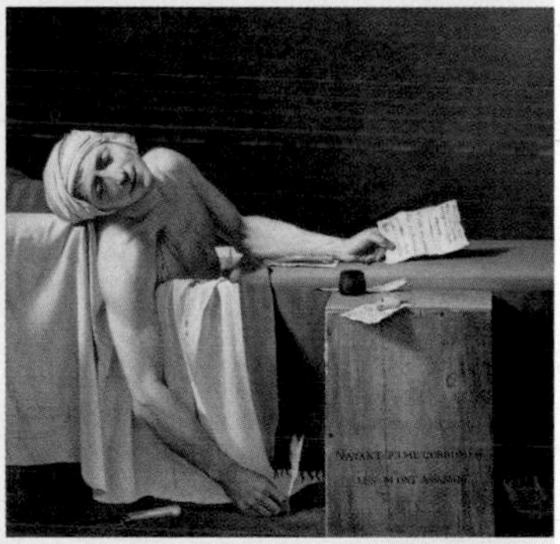

- Consulate of Napoleon (1799)

PHOTO CREDITS: Goethe. (Theater-Museum, Munich) / *The Declaration of Independence* by John Trumbull. (Architect of the Capitol) / Mozart's *Don Giovanni*, excerpt from the score. (Bettmann/Corbis) / Jacques-Louis David's *Murder of Marat*. (© Erich Lessing/Art Resource, N.Y.)

CHAPTER 11

THEATRES FROM 1800 TO 1875

THE COMÉDIE FRANÇAISE

A well-known theatre company that began in the seventeenth century and has continued up to the present day is the Comédie Française. The scene here shows the members of the company in 1840.

(photos12.com-Hachedé)

Major social changes—the industrial revolution, technological advances, and the rise of nationalism—took place between 1800 and 1875. We should note, however, that the period from 1800 to 1875, like most historical demarcations, is somewhat arbitrary. For example, Johann Wolfgang von Goethe was discussed in Chapter 10 as an eighteenth-century playwright and director; but he was still active in the early 1800s. Thus some of the figures we will discuss in the present chapter had careers that began before 1800, and some had careers that continued long after 1875; and we will make occasional references to events after 1875 that were closely related to preceding events. This should be borne in mind as we consider the changes of this period.

Background: The Nineteenth Century

Possibly the most important transformation during the early nineteenth century was the industrial revolution: the replacement of hand tools and human power by machinery, and the development of factories and the factory system. Many inventions were made—including an improved steam engine that transformed textile manufacturing, the leading industry of the time. The foremost textile manufacturing nation, and therefore the leader of the industrial revolution, was Great Britain.

The factory system, which required centralized labor forces, spurred urbanization and eroded traditional European agrarianism. The populations of European and American cities grew, but the way of life created by industrialization was far from pleasant for the working classes. Cities were polluted by coal, and housing was poorly constructed, cramped, and in short supply. Since the factory system required large numbers of unskilled laborers, whole families, including women and children (at first children as young as 6 years old), were employed at minimal wages; a workday was 14 hours long.

The industrial revolution, however, was a boon to the middle class, which was further strengthened financially. In acknowledgment of its new power, legislatures passed reforms beneficial to the middle class throughout the nineteenth century. Among other things, these reforms liberalized the qualifications for voting and for holding elected office. By 1884, three-quarters of all men in Britain could vote, as opposed to only one-eighth in 1832.

Eventually, the plight of the growing working class also began to improve. For example, in 1847 the British parliament passed the Ten Hours Act, which limited the working day for women and children to 10 hours. In the last half of the century, unionization began to develop, and the working class emerged as a social and political force to be reckoned with—as is evident from the numerous workers' uprisings in Europe between 1830 and 1871.

Technological innovations transformed not only industry but also transportation and communications. The improved steam engine led to the locomotive, and beginning in the 1840s extensive railroad construction was undertaken in Great Britain and the United States. By 1869, a transcontinental railroad linking the east and west coasts was completed in the United States. Nineteenth-century inventions—including Samuel F. B. Morse's telegraph (1837), Alexander Graham Bell's telephone (1876), and Thomas Edison's incandescent lamp (1879)—revolutionized daily life.

Nationalism, the desire of peoples to establish unified political states and their belief in the superiority of their own nations, was also a nineteenth-century phenomenon. Many historians suggest that nationalistic fervor was a reaction against Napoleon's attempt to conquer and consolidate most of Europe between 1800 and 1815. Nineteenth-century nationalism resulted in wars of independence in Latin America and Greece, and in the unification of Germany and Italy; but it also resulted in rampant colonialism, with developed countries exploiting the natural resources of underdeveloped areas such as Asia and Africa.

There was ferment on the intellectual front as well; nineteenth-century intellectuals questioned many traditional beliefs. Possibly the two most influential were Karl Marx (1818–1883) and Charles Darwin (1809–1882).

NINETEENTH CENTURY, 1800 TO 1875
YEAR

1800 · 1810 · 1820 · 1830 · 1840 · 1850 · 1860 · 1870 · 1880

Theatre

- Talma foremost actor in France (c. 1800)
- Goethe's *Faust,* Part I (1810)
- Kleist's *The Prince of Homburg* (1810)
- Pixérécourt and French melodrama flourish (1810)
- Edmund Kean's London debut (1814)
- Chestnut Street Theatre in Philadelphia becomes first totally gaslit theatre (1816)
- Daguerre exhibits diorama (1822)
- Charles Kemble's historically accurate *King John;* Shchepkin member of Moscow troupe (1823)
- Forrest's New York debut (1826)
- Hugo's *Hernani* (1830)
- Madame Vestris's management of Olympic Theatre begins (1831)
- Gogol's *Inspector General;* Büchner's *Woyzeck (1836)*
- Macready manages Covent Garden (1837)
- Scribe's *A Glass of Water* (1840)
- England's Theatre Regulation Act (1843)
- Astor Place Riot (1849)
- Dumas fils's *Camille;* first production of *Uncle Tom's Cabin;* Charles Kean's *King John* (1852)
- Adolphe Montigny innovates in directing at Gymnase (c. 1853)
- Sardou's *A Scrap of Paper* (1860)
- Edwin Booth's *Hamlet* runs 100 nights in New York (1864)
- Duke of Saxe-Meiningen begins reforms (1866)
- Booth Theatre (1869)
- Henry Irving at Lyceum (1871)
- Zola's *Thérèse Raquin;* preface discussed naturalism (1873)
- Paris Opéra building completed (1874)

Culture and Politics

- Louisiana Purchase (1803)
- Napoleon I, emperor of France (1804)
- Fulton's paddle steamer *Clermont* navigates on Hudson (1807)
- Latin American independence (1808–1826)
- Mme. de Staël's *Of Germany,* published in France (1810)
- Beethoven's Fifth Symphony (1810)
- Battle of Waterloo; Metternich system (1815)
- First Factory Act, England (1819)
- Greek war of independence (1821)
- Monroe Doctrine (1823)
- Decembrist uprising in Russia (1825)
- Comte's positivism (1830)
- Upper middle class enfranchised in England (1832)
- Davy Crockett killed at the Alamo (1836)
- Victoria of England (rules 1837–1901)
- Dickens's *Oliver Twist* (1838)
- Second French Empire; Napoleon III (1852)
- Crimean War (1853–1865)
- Perry in Japan (1854)
- Flaubert's *Madame Bovary* (c. 1857)
- Darwin's *On the Origin of Species* (1859)
- American Civil War (1861–1865); proclamation of the Kingdom of Italy
- Bismarck becomes Prussian prime minister (1862)
- Dostoyevsky's *Crime and Punishment* (1866)
- Marx's *Das Kapital;* extension of suffrage in Great Britain (1867)
- Tolstoy's *War and Peace* (c. 1869); American transcontinental railway (1869)
- German empire founded; Paris commune (1871)

Marx, a German newspaperman who spent most of his productive years in England, outlined a socialist philosophy in *The Communist Manifesto* (1848), which he wrote with Friedrich Engels, and *Das Kapital* (1867). Marxism was a reaction against evils he perceived in the industrial revolution. According to Marx, the working class (the proletariat) is exploited by the owners of private capital (the bourgeoisie); he believed that the workers would unite to overthrow their oppressors and create an egalitarian, classless society in which wealth would be shared. The state and religion—which he saw as bourgeois devices for exploiting workers—would disappear in this utopian socialist society. Thus Marxism questioned the dominant nineteenth-century economic, political, social, and religious beliefs.

Darwin's *On the Origin of Species* (1859) outlined his theory of evolution: that animal species evolve through natural selection. Species are always changing; these changes are transmitted by heredity; and the fittest individuals and species—those best adapted to the environment—survive and reproduce. Darwin's theory was revolutionary and controversial because it seemed to question traditional religious beliefs about creation, particularly the creation of humanity. Social Darwinism—a distortion of Darwin's theory which he himself never advanced—suggested that some races, nations, and religious groups are fitter than others, an idea that was insidiously exploited in the late nineteenth and early twentieth century.

Darwin and Marx presented a disturbing challenge to long-held beliefs in the supremacy of God and in a social hierarchy established by God. Their ideas and others—notably those of Sigmund Freud, the father of psychoanalysis—were to have a profound effect on the western world.

Theatre in the nineteenth century followed the innovations of the eighteenth century and paved the way for modern theatre, which began in the years immediately following 1875. As we noted in Chapter 4, there is sometimes a delay before written drama reflects social changes; and the ideas of Marx and Darwin did not surface noticeably in drama until the late nineteenth and early twentieth century. However, the theatre of the first 75 years of the nineteenth century directly reflected contemporary social and industrial developments. Urbanization and technology, for instance, brought about marked changes in theatre architecture and scene design. The concentration of people in cities made larger audiences available for longer runs of popular shows.

The changing tastes of a changing audience were mirrored in popular drama; and the increasing diversity of urban populations—particularly in the United States—led to splintered audiences who wanted a theatre that spoke to their own needs. For example, many foreign-language theatres for immigrant audiences developed in New York City in the middle and late 1800s. (The theatre of this era also reinforced biases and prejudices of its majority audiences by creating stereotypes of immigrants, African Americans, American Indians, Latinos, and women.) Because of its new complexity, theatre began to need an artistic overseer—a director.

Theatre in Nineteenth-Century Life

Before examining specific transformations in nineteenth-century drama and theatre production, we should consider the unique place theatre held during this era. The dramatic arts exploded during the 75 years between 1800 and 1875, as the masses who filled the fast-growing cities demanded theatre. For these new audiences, it was a fad, a passion, and also a seeming necessity. Nineteenth-century theatre, therefore, was a true popular entertainment. It attracted huge numbers of people, and its escapist dramas—though written quickly and often not particularly well—helped them forget the cares and drudgery of their lives.

Popular Entertainments

Popular entertainment, which often spotlighted performers and spectacle, also attracted the masses. Americans, for example, supported the minstrel show, burlesque, variety, vaudeville, and the circus.

In a *minstrel show,* white performers were made up as caricatured blacks. White men had performed in burnt cork with exaggerated lips and eyes before minstrelsy—one performer, Daddy Rice, captured the nation's fancy in the early 1830s with a grotesque jump-dance that he called "Jim Crow"—but minstrel shows made performances by whites in blackface commonplace, beginning in 1843 with a performance by the Virginia Minstrels, a company of four white men.

The recipe for a minstrel show was simple: a group of men, numbering from 6 to 100, dressed in colorful costumes with faces blackened and eyes and mouths enlarged by white and red lines, formed a semicircle on the stage. At one end of this arc sat Tambo, named for his tambourine; at the opposite end sat Bones, named for

(Library of Congress)

THE CIRCUS: A POPULAR ART

During the nineteenth century, a significant number of highly theatrical popular entertainments emerged. Among these was the circus, with trapeze artists, acrobats, clowns, and animal acts. The American entrepreneur P. T. Barnum was an innovator in developing the circus as we know it today. Seen here is a depiction of female trapeze artists.

DEBATES IN THEATRE HISTORY | Is Popular Entertainment Worthy of Serious Study?

The nineteenth century was an era of highly developed popular entertainments: the circus, minstrelsy, burlesque, melodrama, and variety entertainments presented in saloons and concert halls. Yet only recently have theatre historians begun to examine the historical development and impact of these popular forms.

Among historians of past generations, the debate was whether these popular presentations are truly theatre and whether they are worthy of serious study. Should the midget Tom Thumb and the plays written especially for him be studied in the same way that we examine the plays of Goethe and Hugo? (Thumb was immensely popular; he performed for Queen Victoria in the comedy *Hop o' My Thumb* while on tour in England, and by the 1860s he had amassed a fortune.) Should the careers of actors who performed in minstrel shows and music halls be as carefully recorded and examined as the careers of John Philip Kemble, Sarah Siddons, and Edwin Booth?

A number of contemporary historians argue that popular entertainments were unjustly overlooked by earlier scholars and are most definitely worthy of serious study. These entertainments were the most widely attended theatrical forms of the 1800s; they reflected the interests and concerns of the mass audience, and they frequently contained ideologies and political views that were accepted norms.

It is also argued that we will develop an elitist representation of theatre history if we focus only on works which we ourselves—with all our own biases—designate as historically significant; and we will never come to understand what types of presentations most people experienced or what theatregoing was most often like. If all we study in nineteenth-century theatre is Hugo and Goethe, then we are not getting a complete or accurate sense of this theatre or the society that created it. By the same token, future historians who studied only the works of David Mamet and Sam Shepard and ignored hit musical comedies or Neil Simon's popular plays would not be giving their readers an accurate representation of our theatre. Simon's better-known works include *The Odd Couple* (1965), *The Sunshine Boys* (1972), *Brighton Beach Memoirs* (1983), and *Lost in Yonkers* (1991).

The other side in this debate emphasizes the need for standards. If, for example, there is no measure of such things as quality, artistry, content, and substance, how does one differentiate between *King Oedipus, Hamlet,* and Eugene O'Neill's *Long Day's Journey into Night* on the one hand and a vaudeville skit or a superficial bedroom farce on the other? Is there not a need, those on this side argue, for some kind of distinction between enduring art of recognized quality and ephemeral, momentary amusement?

As for writing about contemporary popular entertainment, an excellent example is Alan Woods's "Consuming the Past: Commercial American Theatre in the Reagan Era."*

*In *The American Stage: Social and Economic Issues from the Colonial Period to the Present,* Ron Engle and Tice Miller (eds.), Cambridge University Press, New York, 1993, pp. 252–266.

sheep ribs that he played like castanets; in the center stood Mr. Interlocutor—the straight man and master of ceremonies, and the only performer not in blackface. Unburdened by plot or character development, the show was a combination of comic and sentimental songs, dramatic and farcical skits, and jigs and shuffle dances—all this seasoned with a peppering of dialect jokes.

The vast majority of minstrel shows featured white performers, yet by all accounts the greatest dancer of the period was a black man, William Henry Lane, known as Master Juba, who in 1845 received top billing with a white minstrel troupe. Charles Dickens, who wrote enthusiastically of Juba, called him the "greatest dancer known." It is also true that some blacks founded, operated, and performed in their own minstrel companies; most of these black troupes originated in the 1870s, after the Civil War, when they were able to capitalize on white spectators' interest in seeing "genuine Negroes." To prove that they were not whites in makeup, a few black performers did not use burnt cork; but audiences usually preferred minstrel performers, regardless of race, in blackface. Many talented black performers learned and practiced their art in minstrel shows. Among them was James Bland, the composer of "Carry Me Back to Old Virginny," now the state song of Virginia. W. C. Handy, who composed "The Saint Louis Blues," began in minstrelsy, as did Bert Williams and George Walker. This exploitation of black culture by whites changed the character of American music, dance, and theatre.

Another extremely popular theatrical form was the *burlesque.* Burlesques were usually parodies of serious plays, such as Shakespeare's works and popular melodramas. Today, takeoffs of popular films and television shows such as *Saturday Night Live* or *Mad TV,* as well as the Austin Powers spoofs of the James Bond films with Mike Myers (1963–), are examples of contemporary burlesques. Later in the nineteenth century, burlesques began to include women dancers; but it was not until the twentieth century that this form became a combination of comedians and strippers.

Throughout the nineteenth century, concert halls, saloons, and playhouses presented collections of entertainments—including songs, dances, acrobatics, and animal acts—on one bill; these developed into the popular *variety* and *vaudeville* presentations of the late nineteenth and early twentieth century. (Today, late-night television talk shows come closest to being the home of variety entertainment.)

The renowned popularizer of the *circus* was P. T. Barnum (1810–1891), who developed spectacular advertising to attract mass audiences. Barnum's earliest successes were at the American Museum in New York City from the 1840s through the 1860s; there he exhibited human curiosities and presented variety acts and plays in a theatre especially built for family audiences. Among Barnum's curiosities were Joyce Heth, who he said was 140 years old and had been George Washington's nurse; the "Fiji mermaid," which was actually the head of a monkey sewn onto the body of a fish; and the midget Tom Thumb. Between 1841 and 1865, Barnum sold 37,500,000 admissions to his American Museum. In the 1850s, he became involved with the circus, which was in many ways a touring version of his museum; he advertised the circus as the "greatest show on earth."

There were many other popular touring entertainments in the nineteenth-century United States. These included wild west shows and medicine shows. Buffalo Bill Cody (1846–1917) had a wild west show that was extremely popular in the 1880s, traveling with animals and recognizable western personalities. The medicine show consisted of a quack doctor touring with musical or comic performers (or both), who would stage presentations to help sell supposed remedies.

Audiences

The increase in numbers of spectators and types of entertainments resulted in the construction of more playhouses throughout the western world. With better rail transportation, dramatic arts were also brought to new areas and new audiences; the transcontinental railroad, for example, made it possible for touring theatre to reach people living in places like California.

The passion that audiences felt for theatre accounts for the immense popularity of the era's star performers; and this intense interest in theatre is also reflected in the desire of some of the century's most renowned literary figures to write dramas. Novelists, such as Charles Dickens and Henry James, saw how well drama could reach and affect mass audiences and attempted to write plays. Poets such as Byron, Keats, and Shelley also wrote dramas, though these—because of their unusual style—were rarely produced.

The popularity of theatre between 1800 and 1875 has not been equaled in modern times: today, theatre no longer holds the same central position. In some ways, movies and television are modern counterparts; they present similar kinds of entertainment, attract mass audiences, and have popular stars. But the intense passion of nineteenth-century audiences has rarely been found in other entertainments. The closest parallel today might be the emotional intensity of audiences at rock concerts.

THEATRE RIOTS

The nineteenth-century passion for theatre is clearly seen in—and helps to explain—several infamous riots. One of these episodes, the "Old Price Riots," took place when London's Covent Garden Theatre was remodeled in 1809 and prices for admission were raised by the actor-manager John Philip Kemble (1757–1823). When the lower-class audiences learned about the higher prices and also discovered that the third-tier gallery had been turned into expensive private boxes rented for the season, they disrupted performances for over sixty nights, chanting, sounding noisemakers, and throwing things. Eventually, the management gave in; the old prices for the pit were restored, and the number of boxes was reduced.

Another theatre riot took place in Paris in 1830, when *Hernani* by Victor Hugo (1802–1885) premiered at the Comédie Française, the home of French neoclassical drama. As we shall see, Hugo was a romantic and therefore opposed to neoclassicism, and *Hernani* broke all the neoclassical rules. For fifty-five nights, shouting, rioting, and fights broke out in the theatre between supporters of neoclassicism and advocates of romanticism. (At this time, French playwrights often paid certain audience members to applaud their works; a paid group like this was called a *claque,* and some of the uproar over *Hernani* may have been set off by rival claques.)

The most violent of the nineteenth-century riots occurred outside the Astor Place Theatre in New York City. This riot grew out of rivalry between an English star, William Charles Macready; and an American star, Edwin Forrest. Forrest, who was noted for his portrayal of melodramatic heroes, had made an unsuccessful English tour, and he blamed its failure on Macready, whose style was more subtle and realistic. When Macready appeared at the Astor Place Theatre on May 8, 1849, he was prevented from performing by Forrest's working-class fans. Macready's aristocratic admirers persuaded him to perform again on May 10, and a mob of 15,000 attacked the building. The infantry was called out to disperse the rioters, and when the violence finally ended, twenty-two people had been killed and many more wounded.

These events and other audience uprisings illustrate not only the passionate involvement of nineteenth-century audiences but also the social changes of the era.

(Painting by C. M. Jenkes. The Metropolitan Museum of Art, The Edward W. C. Arnold Collection of New York Prints, Maps, and Pictures, Bequest of Edward W. C. Arnold, 1954 [54.90.222].)

ASTOR PLACE RIOT

This riot, which erupted in New York City in 1849, was a result of nationalistic fervor and the passionate involvement of theatre audiences. It was set off when working-class fans of the American star Edwin Forrest attacked a theatre in which the English actor William Charles Macready, who had supposedly insulted Forrest, was performing.

The "Old Price" and Astor Place riots reflected a struggle between the working and upper classes, and the militancy of lower-class audiences foreshadowed later social revolutions. The Astor Place Riot also reflected a growing nationalistic fervor; the violence between Forrest's and Macready's fans was partially a result of anti-British sentiment in the United States.

Theatre and Nationalism

In fact, much popular drama itself reflected nationalism. For example, Anna Cora Mowatt, one of America's first significant female playwrights, wrote a comedy of manners, *Fashion* (1845), that depicted the values of hardworking America as more honest than the social pretensions of Europe. The character Adam Trueman in *Fashion* was a descendant of an earlier popular stock figure in American melodramas and comedies—the "stage Yankee," a representative of diligent, unpretentious, rural America.

ANNA CORA MOWATT

Anna Cora Mowatt (1819–1870) is most noted for her popular play *Fashion,* but she also had an active and distinguished career in other kinds of writing and as an actress. She was born in France to American parents, read widely as a child, and participated in her family's amateur theatricals. At age 15 she married James Mowatt, an older, wealthy attorney, and continued her study of literature and history; she also began to write for her own enjoyment. She turned to writing as a career around 1841 (when her husband lost his fortune, as well as his health and most of his eyesight), contributing articles to women's magazines. She also published novels and earned money by giving public recitations of poetry.

(Billy Rose Theatre Collection, New York Public Library at Lincoln Center, Astor, Lenox, and Tilden Foundations)

Anna Cora Mowatt.

Mowatt's first effort as a professional playwright was an astonishing success. *Fashion* premiered at an upscale theatre in New York—the Park Theatre—on March 24, 1845. It ran for at least eighteen performances, a remarkable achievement at a time when bills usually changed nightly.

One of the very first American social comedies, *Fashion* advocated American sensibility rather than slavish imitation of foreign fashions. It had several different character types—including a Yankee, a French maid, an African American servant, a French count, and an American hero—whose interaction created comic contrasts. The Yankee was an amusing, down-to-earth, homespun New Englander, related to the figure we know today as Uncle Sam; this was a popular, recurring character in American drama.

Fashion was especially important because American drama was not highly esteemed at that time. Many actors and managers in the United States were from England, and they tended to present English plays or adaptations of French or German plays. Because the United States was a young country, with no established dramatic literature, most theatregoers assumed that a play by an American could not be very good. Mowatt's status as a member of the social and literary elite ensured that *Fashion* would get more sympathetic attention than was usual for a new American play. (Appropriately, *Fashion* criticized the American tendency to prefer anything European.)

Her success as a playwright, combined with continuing financial pressure, encouraged Mowatt to become an actress: she made her debut on June 13, 1845, and was warmly received. This decision had important implications for the entire profession. Acting was still a low-status occupation, and the morals of actresses were suspect; Mowatt demonstrated that a woman of high social standing could appear onstage without destroying her reputation.

During the next 2 years, she toured the United States in starring roles. She also wrote a romantic drama, *Armand, or The Child of the People,* specifically for herself and E. L. Davenport, the leading man in her company. For the next few years, Mowatt also acted in England, to great acclaim. She then returned to the United States, making her last stage appearance in Boston in 1854.

NINETEENTH-CENTURY DRAMA

Three major forms of drama came to prominence between 1800 and 1875: romanticism, melodrama, and the well-made play. Romanticism and melodrama, however, were more than just types of plays. Romanticism was a philosophical and literary movement that had a significant impact on theatre production; melodrama was also a major style of theatre production and continues to exert a significant influence today.

ROMANTICISM

Romanticism, influenced by the German "storm and stress" movement, was a revolutionary philosophical and literary trend of the first half of the nineteenth century. Victor Hugo, the renowned poet, theorist, and novelist, outlined the characteristics of romantic drama in an introduction to his play *Cromwell* (1827). The romantics rejected the neoclassical rules; in fact, they rejected all artistic rules, suggesting that genius creates its own rules. Many of the romantics used Shakespeare's structural techniques: their plays were episodic and epic in scope. Unlike Shakespeare, however, the romantics were often more interested in creating mood and atmosphere than in developing believable plots or depth of character.

Romantic dramatists did not believe in purity of genre; they considered all subject matter—the grotesque as well as the ideal—appropriate for the stage; and they often used supernatural elements. The romantic hero was frequently a social outcast, such as a bandit, who quested for justice, knowledge, and truth. One of the most common romantic themes was the gulf between human beings' spiritual aspirations and their physical limitations.

Romantic drama was often imbued with the independent spirit of the time. This is another excellent example of drama as the mirror of an age: the American and French revolutions had occurred at the end of the eighteenth century, and concepts of freedom and liberty were in the air. Romantic playwrights created heroes who fiercely defended individuality and independence. In addition, these writers worked in many different literary forms—novels, poetry, and theoretical essays. Some were also interested in the other arts, including painting. Like later twentieth-century experimental artists, the romantics were stretching the boundaries of art forms and defying rigid artistic categorizations and aesthetic rules.

The most noted romantic dramas of the period were Victor Hugo's *Hernani* (1830) and Goethe's *Faust* (Part I, 1808; Part II, 1831). (*Hernani* relates the story of a noble outlaw—the title character—and his attempt to wed Dona Sol while facing the opposition of her guardian and the king, both of whom also love her. The Faust legend concerns a man who sells his soul to the devil in return for earthly powers of both intelligence and sensual pleasure.) Besides Goethe, other significant German dramatists of the nineteenth century were Ludwig Tieck (1773–1853), who experimented with Shakespearean staging as a director; Heinrich von Kleist (1771–1811); and Georg Büchner (1813–1837).

Kleist's work includes *The Broken Jug* (1808) and *The Prince of Homburg* (1811). The latter, considered Kleist's masterwork, concerns a youthful army officer who has disobeyed an order and as a result has won a military victory, but because of his disobedience he is sentenced to death. After admitting that he was led by ambition and confessing his error, he is pardoned.

Büchner's two best-known dramas are *Danton's Death* (1835) and *Woyzeck* (1836). The central figure in *Danton's Death* is an idealist whose high hopes are undermined by small-mindedness and sensuality. Set at the time of the "reign of terror" in the aftermath of the French Revolution, the drama is episodic in structure. *Woyzeck* shows a rather sad lower-class man caught in the forces of environment and heredity.

Both *Danton's Death* and *Woyzeck* were more radical and enigmatic than the dramas of Büchner's romantic contemporaries and became popular only in the twentieth century with the advent of naturalism, expressionism, and absurdism. *Woyzeck* (which was left unfinished when Büchner died at the age of 24) has often been staged in the twentieth century by avant-garde directors who are intrigued by its presentation of the physical and emotional destruction of a lowly soldier. In 1992, for example, a production by the American director Joanne Akalaitis drew parallels to the horrors of World War II.

(© Jack Vartoogian)

BÜCHNER'S WOYZECK

One of the most enigmatic plays of the nineteenth century was Georg Büchner's *Woyzeck*, which used romantic techniques but also foreshadowed elements of realism and expressionism that were to come much later. Written in 1836, it received almost no productions until the twentieth century. Shown here are Jens Jorn Spottag (Woyzeck) and Kaya Brüel (Marie) in Robert Wilson's adaptation, presented at Lincoln Center.

Melodrama

Melodrama means "song drama" or "music drama." The term originally comes from the Greek, but it usually refers to a theatrical form popularized by the French at the end of the eighteenth century and the beginning of the nineteenth. "Music" refers to the background music that accompanied these plays—similar to the music played with silent movies and the music used as a background in later films. In these melodramas, a premium was put on surface effects, especially effects evoking suspense, fear, nostalgia, and other strong emotions; the plays were written in a way that would arouse such feelings.

Heroes and heroines of melodrama were clearly delineated and stood in sharp contrast to the villains; the audience sympathized with the good characters and despised the bad ones. In addition to its heroes and villains, melodrama had other easily recognized stock characters: the threatened woman; the sidekick (a comic foil to the hero); and the "fallen woman" who, even after repenting, is punished for her wicked past. The fallen woman suggests the highly moral tone of traditional melodrama; a conflict between good and evil was clearly and firmly established, and virtue was always victorious.

A prime example of a nineteenth-century melodrama is *Uncle Tom's Cabin*, a stage adaptation of Harriet Beecher Stowe's novel. Adapting a popular story was a favorite way of developing plays in the mid-nineteenth century, and Stowe's abolitionist (antislavery) novel was a sensational best-seller. Like many popular melodramas of the day, *Uncle Tom's Cabin* reflected a significant social issue. It is the story of a slave—the title character—who is cruelly mistreated by an overseer, Simon Legree. Uncle Tom is devoted to his white owner's daughter, Little Eva, who dies during the course of the story. Another important figure is Eliza, a mulatto who attempts to escape from slavery.

There were several attempts to adapt the play to the stage, but the most successful one was by the playwright George L. Aiken (1830–1876). This production featured a series of spectacular, suspenseful scenes, especially one in which the slave Eliza, fleeing her captors, escapes across the frozen Ohio River. The play also appealed to the emotions of the audience by presenting the death of the angelic Little Eva, and the persecution and death of Uncle Tom at the hands of the evil Simon Legree. (The black characters were played by white actors and depicted stereotypically.)

An indication of the popularity of such melodramas is the fact that this version, which opened in New York in 1853, ran for 300 performances, sometimes being presented three times a day—an unprecedented event. By 1879, 49 traveling companies were touring the play, and in 1899 there were a total of 500 traveling companies. (In fact, *Uncle Tom's Cabin* remained a popular touring show until the 1930s, when its profitability was finally curtailed by the depression.)

Stock characters of nineteenth-century melodrama can be compared to those of commedia dell'arte in the Italian Renaissance, and to "lines of business"—the tradition in eighteenth-century theatre companies of having actors play specific types of roles. Today, many stock characters appear in situation comedies and soap operas on television, and many popular film and television actors (such as Clint Eastwood, Vin Diesel, Arnold Schwarzenegger, and Sylvester Stallone) play the same type of characters over and over again.

To hold the audience's interest, melodrama—past and present—has a suspenseful plot, with a climactic moment at the end of each act. In adventure shows on television, for instance—such as detective and cop shows—a climax like a car crash, a sudden confrontation, or the discovery of important evidence will occur just before a break for a commercial.

An example from nineteenth-century melodrama is the close of Act I of *The String of Pearls,* written in 1847 by George Dibdin Pitt (1799–1855). This is a play about Sweeney Todd, the "demon barber" of Fleet Street in London—the story on which the Broadway musical *Sweeney Todd* (1979) was based. In Pitt's play, Sweeney has been killing customers in his barbershop and turning the bodies over to Mrs. Lovett, who makes them into meat pies. At the end of Act I, Sweeney decides to get rid of those around him, including Mrs. Lovett; but she overhears his plans. In a few short lines, the action accelerates. She demands half of the profits; he insists that he will deduct money she owes him; she draws a knife and is about to attack him when he pulls out a pistol and shoots her; he then throws her body into a fiery furnace as the curtain falls.

When the aim of melodrama is pure escapism, it often stresses visual spectacle and special effects. Popular science-fiction films, such as the *Star Wars* and *The Lord of the Rings* series, are highly visual melodramas, with no expense spared to create technologically advanced special effects; and the omnipresent car chases in detective dramas on television and in films grew out of melodramatic spectacle. The nineteenth-century melodramatic playwright Dion Boucicault (1822–1890) used many special effects (though the available technology was less sophisticated); in *The Poor of New York* (1857), for example, a tenement burned onstage.

Most types of nineteenth-century melodramas have modern-day equivalents. Domestic melodrama became soap opera. Frontier melodrama became the western, and in the United States, for example, there were many plays which dealt with life in the west. Frontier melodrama depicted Native Americans in ways that would now be considered stereotyped and racist, though some plays of this era—such as *Metamora* by John Augustus Stone (1801–1834), which was written especially for Edwin Forrest—tried to present a more positive image. Crime melodrama became the popular mystery or detective show; one of the most famous nineteenth-century crime melodramas was *The Ticket of Leave Man* (1863), by the English playwright Tom Taylor (1817–1880), which dealt with a difficult issue: social acceptance of rehabilitated criminals.

Nautical melodrama, which dealt with sailors and pirates, was the forerunner of swashbuckler films; one of the most popular nautical melodramas was *Black-Eyed Susan* (1829) by the English dramatist Douglas William Jerrold (1803–1857). Equestrian melodrama—which featured horses performing spectacular tricks—and other popular melodramas which had animals as heroic stars were the predecessors of television and film melodramas featuring animals. A popular English equestrian, Andrew Ducrow (1793–1842), appeared in melodramas (and in Shakespearean productions that featured him on horseback); and Pixérécourt's *The Forest of Bondy, or The Dog of Montargis* (1814), which was translated into English for productions in London and New York, had a canine hero. (One of the twentieth century's great melodramatic filmmakers, Alfred Hitchcock, used birds as villains in *The Birds*.)

(© Paul Kolnik)

SWEENEY TODD: NINETEENTH-CENTURY MELODRAMA
The story of Sweeney Todd, a barber who cut the throats of his victims and gave the bodies to his colleague Mrs. Lovett to make into meat pies, was dramatized several times in London in the nineteenth century as a stage melodrama. In 1979 it was turned into a stage musical by Stephen Sondheim. Seen here, in a new version, shown recently on Broadway, are Michael Cerveris and Patti LuPone as Sweeney and Mrs. Lovett.

Today, however, there has been a major thematic change in much melodrama—a change that is most discernible in films of the 1960s and 1970s and beyond. Nineteenth-century audiences did not question social, religious, or moral norms; since the 1960s, by contrast—partly because of the war in Vietnam, the war in Iraq, and recurrent political scandals—audiences have questioned traditional values and no longer believe that good and evil are so easily delineated.

In films of the 1960s and 1970s like *The Wild Bunch, Bonnie and Clyde,* and *The Godfather,* as well as in later films like Clint Eastwood's Oscar-winning *Unforgiven,* characters who would once have been seen as villains are presented heroically; the forces of law are sometimes shown as evil. Also, traditional stereotypes, including racist portrayals of blacks and sexist portrayals of helpless women, have been rejected. These transformations in melodrama mirror our changing beliefs and values. On the other hand, many of today's melodramas—for example, the extraordinarily popular *Star Wars* and *Indiana Jones* films of the 1980s—continue to reflect traditional values.

THE WELL-MADE PLAY

Many popular melodramas of the nineteenth century had what is called a *well-made-play* structure. In the twentieth century, the term *well-made* came to describe a play that builds mechanically to its climactic moments and is intended mainly to arouse the audience's interest in these contrived climaxes—not to create truthful emotions or characterizations. When critics today describe a play as "well-made," they are usually being condescending. However, in the nineteenth century the term was complimentary: a "well-made" play was one that showed excellent craftsmanship, and the term itself implied admiration for all the well-crafted goods of the industrial revolution. It is also true that the well-made-play structure was sometimes used creatively by later dramatists.

A well-made play emphasizes careful cause-and-effect development; it is usually a tightly constructed crisis drama. The action often revolves around a secret known to the audience but not to the characters. The opening of the play carefully spells out the needed background information, or exposition. Throughout the play the dramatic action is clearly foreshadowed, and each act builds to a climactic moment. In the major scene, sometimes called the "obligatory scene," the characters in conflict confront each other in a showdown. The plot is carefully resolved so that there are no loose ends.

One example of a well-made play is *Let's Get a Divorce* (1880) by the French playwright Victorien Sardou (1831–1908). The exposition gives a picture of a bored young housewife and also mentions a liberal new divorce law that has been proposed in France. The restless wife flirts with her husband's young cousin. The cousin, hoping to make her his mistress, fakes a report that the proposed divorce law actually been passed and urges her to become his lover because under the new law she can soon become his wife. The husband encourages this scheme, on the assumption that if it succeeds, he will reverse positions with his cousin and become in his wife's eyes an exotic, out-of-reach lover. The "obligatory" scene takes place in a restaurant, where everything is sorted out and the wife returns to her husband.

Throughout a well-made play, devices such as letters and lost documents seem to motivate the dramatic action. Three of the most famous nineteenth-century well-made plays revolve around such specific dramatic devices: *A Glass of Water* (1840) by Eugène Scribe (1791–1861) as well as *A Scrap of Paper* (1860) and *Let's Get a Divorce* (1880) by Sardou. Scribe and Sardou—Scribe, like Sardou, was French—were the most renowned practitioners of the well-made play; other French playwrights who used this structure

(© Donald Cooper/Photostage, England)

THE WELL-MADE PLAY
A nineteenth-century specialty was the well-made play—a tightly constructed drama in which all parts fit neatly together. A number of playwrights perfected this form, and it was also used by their successors in later years. A good example is *The Heiress,* adapted by Ruth and Augustus Goetz from a novel by Henry James. The performers in this scene from the National Theatre production are Alan Howard (Dr. Austin Sloper) and Eve Best (Catherine Sloper), as his daughter, the title character.

were Alexandre Dumas the younger (Dumas fils, 1824–1895), best known for *The Lady of the Camellias,* or *Camille* (1825); Émile Augier (1820–1889); and Eugène Labiche (1815–1888).

A number of nineteenth-century playwrights who used the well-made-play structure focused on more realistic subject matter. For example, domestic melodrama dealt with everyday circumstances and issues, as did the plays of Dumas fils. The English playwright Thomas Williams Robertson (1829–1871) was noted for *Society* (1865) and *Caste* (1867), which were called "teacup and saucer" and "bread and butter" dramas because they emphasized realistic stage business and dealt with real social concerns—though all of Robertson's plays have contrived "happily ever after" endings. As we will see in Chapter 12, the logical causal structure of the well-made play—coupled with a developing interest in contemporary social issues—was to influence Henrik Ibsen, who has been described as the founder of modern dramatic realism.

NINETEENTH-CENTURY THEATRE PRODUCTION

We turn now to theatre production in the period from 1800 to 1875: to performers, managers, and directors; and to theatre architecture and the visual elements of productions—scenery, lighting, and costumes.

ACTING STYLES

Most historians agree that classical, romantic, and melodramatic performance styles dominated the nineteenth-century stage.

In the early nineteenth century, the most renowned classical actors were the English stars John Philip Kemble and his sister Sarah Siddons (1755–1831)—noted for their dignified, carefully planned, detailed performances.

The romantic stars, by contrast, were noted for emotional outbursts; they punctuated dramatic moments with strong physical gestures, made "vocal points" (that is, they emphasized specific speeches and lines), and relied on inspiration. Among the great British romantic actors was Edmund Kean (1789–1833), of whom the poet Samuel Taylor Coleridge wrote, "To see Kean was to read Shakespeare by flashes of lightning." The first native-born American star, Edwin Forrest (1806–1872), whose performances stressed his physical prowess, is often characterized as a romantic actor, as are the major French stars of the century, François Joseph Talma (1763–1826), Sarah Bernhardt, and Constant-Benoît Coquelin (1841–1909).

(© Hulton-Deutsch Collection/Corbis)

AN AGE OF STAR ACTORS
Though there were exceptions, the first 75 years of the nineteenth century were dominated by strong actors and actresses who favored classical, histrionic, romantic acting styles. A good example was Edmund Kean, shown here playing Hamlet. Kean was known for his explosive, turbulent portrayals of Shakespearean heroes and villains.

There were many popular melodramatic and comic performers, who portrayed specific character types and emphasized physical and emotional display. In American theatre, for example, many actors played a comic "Yankee," a country bumpkin with noble values who would eventually outwit a city slicker. Two actors who became successful playing this kind of character were James H. Hackett (1800–1871) and George Handel Hill (1809–1849).

Actors who specialized in specific types of roles throughout their careers were very popular in England and the United States. Some of these stars could never transcend their popular image and continued to play the same role over and over again. Two examples are the American actors Francis Chanfrau (1824–1884), who popularized "Mose the Bowery Fireboy"; and Frank Mayo (1839–1896), who made his debut in Shakespeare but became known for his portrayal of Davy Crockett—these two spent most of their careers acting in plays written especially for them and their characters.

Some actors, however, prepared the way for a style of performing which has become more the norm in modern theatre. They used stage movements, vocal patterns, and characterizations that were based on everyday life. Performers who worked in this new style included the English actor William Charles Macready; Marie Wilton Bancroft (1839–1921) and her husband, Squire Bancroft (1841–1926); the American Edwin Booth; the Italian Eleonora Duse; and the Russian Mikhail Shchepkin (1788–1863), a serf who began acting in a theatre established by his master and was released from his indenture through the efforts of Russia's leading literary figures.

EDMUND KEAN AND CHARLES KEAN

The Keans were one of the most renowned theatrical families in nineteenth-century England. Edmund Kean (c. 1789–1833) electrified audiences in England and America with his mercurial, romantic style. His son, Charles (1811–1868), followed him on the stage and also went on to become an important theatre manager and director.

The illegitimate son of a provincial actress, Edmund Kean was a rebellious youth, who struck off on his own by the age of 15; his origins would later take on legendary proportions. He spent 10 years performing on provincial tours and in minor London theatres. During these years of struggle, he married the actress Mary Chambers and they had two sons—the elder died in infancy. At age 27 Edmund Kean made a sensational debut at Drury Lane playing Shylock in Shakespeare's *The Merchant of Venice.* Discarding the traditional comic red beard and wig, Kean played the moneylender as a black-bearded demon armed with a butcher knife. He excelled in creating turbulent, energized portraits of Shakespearean villains and tragic heroes. Some of his most popular roles were Richard III, Macbeth, Hamlet, and Othello.

Small and agile, with fiery, expressive eyes, Kean relied on an exacting technique as well as his volatile personality. He rejected the sustained character development typical of the period's great actors. Instead, he constructed his roles to highlight emotional transitions with explosive highs and lows. However, a riotous lifestyle, and alcoholism, eventually diminished both his skill and his popularity. In 1833, while playing Othello to his son Charles's Iago, he collapsed in Charles's arms; he died a few weeks later.

As an actor, Charles Kean lacked his father's feverish intensity and expressive skill. His parents had sent him to Eton—partly to keep him off the stage—but he was forced to leave at age 16 when Edmund's career began to decline. Charles made his debut at Drury Lane in 1827 and had his first success in *Hamlet* (1838). He earned a respectable reputation in Britain and on American tours playing opposite his versatile wife, Ellen Tree (1805–1880)—one of the most accomplished actresses of her day.

From 1850 until his retirement in 1859, Charles managed the Princess Theatre, which became the most fashionable theatre in London. He made significant changes in the standard evening's format, dispensing with incidental entertainments between acts and replacing the afterpiece with a curtain-raiser to draw attention away from latecomers. As a director, he developed an artistic unity of scenery and lighting based on extensive historical research for each play. Productions such as *Macbeth* (1852), Lord Byron's *Sardanapalus* (1852), and a highly acclaimed version of *A Midsummer*

Night's Dream (1856) established him as an innovator in the trend toward pictorial realism and historical accuracy. He was elected a Fellow of the Society of Antiquaries in 1857.

THE KEMBLES

Two generations of the Kemble family dominated English theatre, beginning in the late eighteenth century when John Philip Kemble (1757–1823) and his sister Sarah Siddons (1755–1831), the eldest children of a provincial theatrical family, became major stars. Their "classical style" influenced English acting for decades.

John Philip Kemble trained for the priesthood but left to become an actor. He made his London debut in 1783 playing Hamlet. Tall and statuesque, he excelled as Roman heroes in Shakespeare's *Coriolanus* and Joseph Addison's *Cato.* Kemble's grandeur onstage was sometimes seen as self-conscious and overly intellectual, but his perceptive character studies and self-discipline made dignified grace the standard to meet—until the romantic actor Edmund Kean arrived in 1814.

In 1803, after a rocky engagement as manager of Drury Lane, Kemble became head of Covent Garden, where he and his sister enjoyed a triumphant reign until they retired. As a manager, Kemble is noted for making reforms in staging practices, but a decision to increase ticket prices at Covent Garden in 1809, after it was rebuilt following a devastating fire, resulted in riots—known as the Old Price Riots—that lasted over sixty nights and shook the financial state of the theatre.

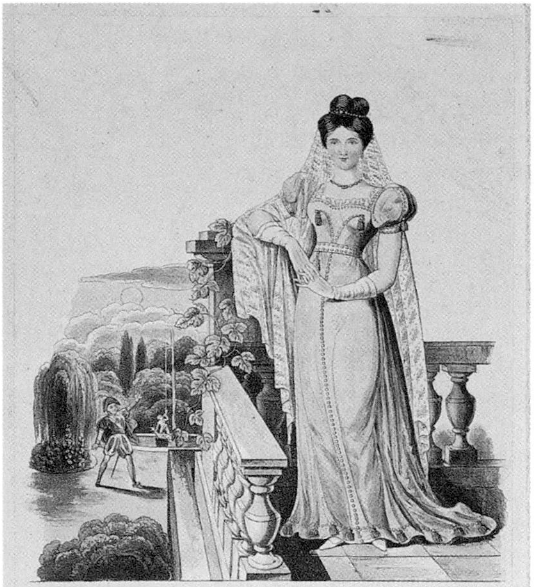

(Courtesy of the Trustees of the Victoria and Albert Museum, The Enthoven Collection)

THE ACTRESS FANNY KEMBLE

Frequently in nineteenth-century theatre there were famous acting families. An example was the Kemble family, one of whose members, Fanny Kemble, was well-known for her portrayal of Shakespearean heroines. Shown here is a painting of Fanny Kemble playing Juliet in Shakespeare's *Romeo and Juliet* at Covent Garden, London, in 1829.

The English artist Joshua Reynolds immortalized Sarah Siddons in his portrait of her as "The Tragic Muse." During her life she was heralded as the greatest tragic actress England had ever seen. One of her finest roles was Lady Macbeth, first performed at Drury Lane in 1785, in which she created a unified, deeply moving interpretation that she herself described as "fair, feminine, nay, even fragile."

Her early career was spent touring provincial theatres. At 18 she married an undistinguished actor, William Siddons, with whom she had five children and much unhappiness. After an unsuccessful engagement at Drury Lane in 1775, she returned 7 years later, appearing in Thomas Southerne's *Fatal Marriage* (1695) with extraordinary success. From then until her retirement in 1812 she was the undisputed "queen of tragedy."

The youngest Kemble, Charles (1775–1854), was an effective Shakespearean actor admired for his gentlemanly portrayals of Romeo, Hamlet, and Benedick. He succeeded his brother as manager of Covent Garden from 1817 to 1832. There, he pursued historically accurate staging, beginning with an innovative production of Shakespeare's *King John* (1823) using period costumes researched and designed by J. R. Planché (1796–1880)—a leader in the trend toward antiquarianism.

Charles Kemble's oldest daughter, Frances Anne, called Fanny (1809–1893), was a poet, dramatist, and diarist as well as an actress. She made her debut as Juliet in 1829 at Covent Garden. Her immediate popularity saved the theatre from impending financial ruin and started a craze for Fanny memorabilia among her fans in London. This fame followed her to the United States when she toured New York and Philadelphia with her father during 1832–1833.

At 25 Fanny Kemble married an American plantation owner and retired, but her marriage faltered over the issue of slavery—she was a fierce abolitionist. In 1845 she left her husband, who soon divorced her. Middle-aged and grown stout, she returned to the stage touring London's provinces. Over the next 26 years, she supported herself with popular public readings of Shakespeare on both sides of the Atlantic. She also wrote a multivolume autobiography and a novel, *Far Away and Long Ago* (1889).

WILLIAM CHARLES MACREADY

William Charles Macready (1793–1873) was an important figure in the nineteenth-century English theatre as both an actor and a director, and his career has been closely examined by scholars because of his innovations in many areas of production. A number of his innovations built on the foundation laid by David Garrick a century earlier.

As the son of an actor and provincial manager, Macready grew up with the theatre, but he entered Rugby School to prepare for a career in law. In 1810, after his father's death, he went onstage—temporarily, he thought—to support the family. After 6 years in the provinces, he made his London debut at Covent Garden as Orestes in *The Disturbed Mother.* He then played villains in several melodramas, winning acceptance as an actor but developing a growing loathing for the profession. He was finally allowed to play Richard III in 1819 and began to excel in tragic roles.

(Victoria and Albert Museum, London/Art Resource, N.Y.)

William Charles Macready as Macbeth, portrait by George Clint.

Macready was a dignified, studious actor who thoroughly researched and rehearsed each role. He was a pioneer in stage realism and introduced the "Macready pause"—he would pause momentarily during the delivery of his lines to give the impression that he was thinking.

Hoping to apply his principles to the acting of others, Macready directed the companies at Covent Garden and Drury Lane from 1837 to 1843. He was one of the first directors to impose blocking—planned stage movement—on his actors; he also made them act during rehearsals rather than go through the motions lifelessly. The scenic elements of his productions were united by an image or theme from the play and were carefully researched and elaborately executed.

(Author Unknown, *Pastimes at Home and School: A Practical Manual of Delsarte Exercises and Elocution* [Chicago: W. B. Conkey Co., 1897].)

THE DELSARTE ACTING METHOD
A nineteenth-century theorist of acting was François Delsarte, who was a forerunner of teachers of realistic acting. He believed there were external movements and poses that conveyed specific emotions. Shown here are three such positions: attack at the top; horror, lower left; and flight, lower right.

Besides his improvements in staging, Macready sought to improve the repertoire. He persuaded some leading literary figures to write for the stage and produced plays by Browning and Byron; Charles Dickens—his friend and a supporter of his efforts—tried several times to write a stageworthy comedy. Macready was also one of the first to begin restoring Shakespearean texts to something closer to the original versions.

Macready's management at Covent Garden and Drury Lane was not a financial success, partly because of his policy of presenting no drama more than four times a week. After he left management, he toured England and played twice in the United States. His rivalry with the American actor Edwin Forrest—sharpened by a quick temper on each side, and by anti-British sentiment—led to the Astor Place Riot described earlier in the chapter.

Macready retired from the stage in 1851, devoting the rest of his life to his family and his literary friends. His work had paved the way for the realistic acting and staging of the late nineteenth century.

Acting Theory: Delsarte

Much acting between 1800 and 1875 was based on stereotypical physical gestures and vocal patterns—as can be seen in the work of François Delsarte (1811–1871), the era's major acting theorist and teacher. Delsarte believed that actors could convey emotions and inner thoughts through specific, preestablished gestures and body movements, which were coordinated with vocal inflections. A sudden movement of the hand to the forehead, for instance, would convey surprise or awe. It was a scientific approach to acting, consistent with the scientific spirit of the age.

Delsarte began teaching his technique in 1839. Among those he influenced were Rachel, Macready, and Steele MacKaye, who brought his teachings to the United States. Delsarte's system was rejected by modern realists because it assumed that all human beings have the same physical reactions and thus did not allow for individual characterizations. Delsarte's method, however, did require that actors' physicalizations be based on observations of everyday life, and later realistic systems also stressed this as a source of artistic inspiration.

The Acting Profession

Touring

Touring—which developed because of the exploding populations in urban centers—allowed popular performers to bring their talents to people throughout the world and build international reputations. Early in the century, touring stars performed with local repertory companies. Later, as transportation improved, not only stars but also complete productions known as *combination companies* began to tour; these included supporting players, scenery, and costumes. (Combination companies were a factor in the decline of local repertory companies, discussed later.)

Star actors toured to make money, of course, but they sometimes had other reasons as well. For example, George Frederick Cooke (1756–1812), the first significant English actor to tour the United States (where he performed for the 2 years preceding his death), came to America because his alcoholism was destroying his reputation in England. On the other hand, in 1825 a significant American actor, Ira Aldridge, became a touring star in Europe because, as an African American, he could not gain acceptance in the United States. Before the 1960s, theatre historians paid little attention to early African American theatre artists. More recently, scholars have begun to redress this, and in particular they have focused on the career of Ira Aldridge.

IRA ALDRIDGE

One of the leading Shakespearean actors of the nineteenth century, Ira Aldridge (c. 1806–1867) performed for 40 years, mostly in Europe, where he won wide recognition. The son of a pastor of a Presbyterian chapel in New York City, he was born around 1806 or 1807 in either Manhattan or Bel-Air, Maryland. He attended the African Free School in New York until age 16, when he began acting with the African Grove Theatre in New York City.

The African Grove, the first formal black theatre company in America, was founded in the season of 1820–1821 by William Brown (an African American) and James Hewlett (a West Indian actor). On its stage, *King Shotaway* (1823)—believed to be the first play both written and performed by African Americans—was presented, and Hewlett became the first black man to play Othello. Its repertoire consisted mainly of Shakespearean drama and popular plays of the day.

When racial tension led the police to close the African Grove, Aldridge took a backstage job at the Chatham Theatre, but he continued to act in amateur productions, playing a few minor roles. His first lead was in Sheridan's *Pizarro.*

When, because of racial prejudice, he determined that he had poor prospects as an actor in the United States, he decided to try to further his career in Europe. At age 17, Aldridge found employment as a steward on a ship bound for England. After studying briefly at the University of Glasgow in Scotland, he went to London and appeared in many plays there, including the melodrama *Surinam, or A Slave's Revenge.* For the next 8 years he toured the British provinces, playing a number of roles and earning the reputation of one of the finest tragedians in England.

He returned to London in April 1833 as Othello at the Royal Theatre, Covent Garden. The critical praise was overwhelming; one account proclaimed the production the "greatest theatrical presentation London has ever witnessed." Aldridge also appeared as King Lear and Richard II and revived *Titus Andronicus,* which had not been staged in England for almost two centuries.

For the next three decades, Aldridge toured Europe, appearing before royalty and winning praise from such figures as the composer Richard Wagner and the tragedian Edmund Kean. He was sometimes billed as the "African Roscius." (Roscius, as noted in Chapter 2, was a famous actor in ancient Rome, and his name was often used to honor major performers.) The king of Sweden invited Aldridge to appear in

Stockholm. In 1852, Aldridge went to Germany; he stayed for 3 years and was awarded the Gold Medal of the First Class of Art and Science and the Medal of the Order of Chevalier.

Aldridge also visited Russia, where the czar granted him the Cross of Leopold, and the students of Moscow University accorded him their highest honor by unhitching the horses of his carriage and pulling it through the streets themselves. His performance as a slave in a farce delighted Russian audiences, though it offended some people because his pitifully comic portrayal aroused comparisons with the Russian serfs. When he performed in *The Merchant of Venice,* a procession of Jews came to thank him for his very human interpretation of Shylock.

Aldridge died on August 7, 1867, while on tour in Lodz, Poland. Today he is honored by a tablet in the New Memorial Theatre in Stratford-upon-Avon. In 1979 he was inducted posthumously into the New York Theatre Hall of Fame; this honor in his native land conferred on him the well-deserved recognition he could never achieve there during his lifetime.

(Billy Rose Theatre Collection, New York Public Library at Lincoln Center; Astor, Lenox, and Tilden Foundations)

IRA ALDRIDGE
Ira Aldridge, a gifted African American actor, had to go to Europe to practice his profession, because of racial prejudice at home. In Europe he had a celebrated career, and his talent was appreciated. One of the leading nineteenth-century Shakespearean actors, Aldridge is shown here as Othello.

The Long Run and the Decline of Repertory Companies

At about the same time that touring stars and combination companies were becoming prevalent, the long run became more common: a popular play might run for 100 consecutive performances (as the American Edwin Booth's *Hamlet* did in New York in 1864) or even more. This too was occurring because of expanding audiences in major cities, and also because of the proliferation of smaller theatres, which began to cater to specific segments of the larger audience.

During the nineteenth century, the traditional repertory company—a troupe of actors performing together for a set period of time in a number of plays—gradually disappeared, because the long run made hiring a repertory company impractical. By the close of the century—as in today's commercial Broadway theatre—a cast would be hired to perform a single play for the length of its run.

This movement away from repertory companies was a significant change for actors. Today, performers in commercial theatre are usually freelancers; they are hired for individual shows. If a production is unsuccessful, they must audition for something else. Many critics suggest that the demise of the repertory company made the lives of actors and actresses more unstable because they were no longer hired for a set time. Furthermore, in a repertory company young performers could be trained by actually performing, since beginners were hired to play minor roles. Today's performers have more difficulty finding opportunities to learn through actual stage experience.

The shortening of the typical evening's bill also diminished the need for repertory companies. The bill had previously included a full-length play, a curtain-raiser or afterpiece, and entr'acte entertainments. (A curtain-raiser preceded the main play; an afterpiece was a short play following the main play; entr'acte entertainments were variety acts—such as songs, dances, and acrobatics—presented during breaks in the main play.) As of 1900, however, the bill consisted only of the full-length drama.

By 1875, therefore, the number of repertory companies was diminishing. Not all repertory troupes disbanded, and in many countries such troupes still play a significant role; but in commercial theatre they became the exception rather than the rule.

The demise of the repertory company also led to the development of actor training schools and conservatories. In New York City, the first acting school was opened in the late nineteenth century.

The Rise of the Star

The nineteenth century was an era of star actors and actresses, performers who were idolized by the audiences that flocked to see them. Many of these actors were not simply national stars but became international figures; for instance, the Italian stars Adelaide Ristori (1822–1906) and Tomasso Salvini (1829–1915) toured Europe, the United States, and South America. Some of these performers amassed—and frequently lost—fortunes. Major changes in the art and business of acting were caused in part by the rise of the star.

Two of the most famous stars of the nineteenth century were Sarah Bernhardt and Eleonora Duse.

SARAH BERNHARDT AND ELEONORA DUSE

Two stars, Sarah Bernhardt (1845–1923) and Eleonora Duse (1858–1924), dominated the international stage in the latter part of the nineteenth century. They played many of the same roles, though they had different acting styles.

Bernhardt—"Madame Sarah"—was the more flamboyant of the two, and her eccentricities and temperament are legendary (among other things, she demanded her salary in gold and supposedly slept in a coffin). In 1862, she made her debut at the Comédie Française, and she continued an intermittent, stormy relationship with that company until 1880. Slim, with large dark eyes, Bernhardt was a master of stage technique, but her chief asset was her voice, which was often compared to a golden bell. Twice she managed theatres in Paris, and she was also a sculptor and a writer of poetry and plays. She toured the United States many times.

While Bernhardt looked backward to the "grand style" of the nineteenth century, Eleonora Duse foreshadowed the sincere realism of the twentieth century. Duse was as quiet and reclusive as Bernhardt was flamboyant. Her parents were both actors, and she made her own stage debut at age 4; at age 14, she was playing Juliet. After her parents died, she had to struggle for several years, until she appeared in Naples in 1879 as the title character in Émile Zola's *Thérèse Raquin* and astonished the critics with the anguish she conveyed. After touring as leading lady to the popular actor Cesare Rossi, she formed her own company.

Duse's repertoire included the poetic dramas of her lover Gabriele d'Annunzio, the melodramas of Dumas fils and Sardou, and the realistic plays of Ibsen. Her style was greatly admired by critics, such as George Bernard Shaw, who championed realism. Slender and attractive, she wore no makeup but used her expressive face, eyes, and gestures to convey the thoughts of a character. She was apparently the epitome of a natural, totally believable actress who projected sincerity and inner fire rather than outward

(Studio Umberto N. Serra)
Eleonora Duse.

(© Musée Citadelle Vauban/Corbis Sygma)

Sarah Bernhardt, portrait by Georges Clairin.

flamboyance. She retired in 1909 because of ill health, but financial reverses forced her to return to the stage after World War I, and she died while on tour, in Pittsburgh.

Steps toward Directing

The first steps toward the art of directing had been taken in the eighteenth century by David Garrick and Johann Wolfgang von Goethe. In the nineteenth century, further steps were taken by some actor-managers and playwright-managers. Two important figures in this evolution of the director are Richard Wagner and the duke of Saxe-Meiningen.

Actor-Managers and Playwright-Managers

The goal of innovative nineteenth-century actor-managers and playwright-managers was to create a unified stage picture, particularly through increased rehearsal time and more careful attention to production details. Many of them experimented with historical accuracy in scenery and costuming, and some expected a more realistic acting style.

Nineteenth-century actor-managers were responsible for choosing scripts, casting, overseeing rehearsals, working with scene painters, selecting costumes, and dealing with finances; in addition, an actor- or actress-manager was usually the company's star performer. Numerous actor-managers took greater interest and care in creating stage productions; almost all these innovators oversaw the visual elements, required careful rehearsals, and experimented with blocking patterns, and they are often credited with moving theatre toward greater realism. In England, they included Macready, who managed Covent Garden from 1837 to 1838 and Drury Lane from 1841 to 1843; and Madame Vestris, who managed the Olympic Theatre from 1831 to 1838. In the United States, they included Edwin Booth, who managed several theatres in New York.

Some innovators in directorial practices were not primarily actors; these included some playwrights. In France, Pixérécourt oversaw all the details of staging his spectacular and immensely popular melodramas; Adolphe Montigny (1805–1880) ran the Gymnase, a Parisian boulevard theatre, and strove for more realistic settings and acting in popular well-made plays; and the romantic novelist and playwright Victor Hugo staged his own dramas. In Germany, Ludwig Tieck and Karl Immermann (1796–1840) experimented with unlocalized staging for Shakespearean productions. The American playwright-manager Augustin Daly (1836–1899)—whose melodrama *Under the Gaslight* (1867) is often cited as the first play in which a character was tied to a railroad track—oversaw all elements of staging and wanted completely unified productions. Daly's acting company had many young stars whom he had discovered.

A number of the innovative theatrical managers were women—despite the fact that theatre management, like many other occupations in the nineteenth century, was unusual for a woman. In England, as we noted above, there was Madame Vestris (who will also be discussed later). In the United States, the major actress-managers were Anne Brunton Merry (1769–1808); Charlotte Cushman (1816–1876); Catherine Sinclair (1817–1891); Matilda Viney Wood (1821–1915), John Wood's wife; Louise Lane Drew (1820–1897), John Drew's wife; and Laura Keene, who was one of the most famous.

LAURA KEENE

The actress Laura Keene (c. 1826–1873) distinguished herself as a successful woman in the competitive business of theatre management during the nineteenth century in the United States.

Keene had been born in England, and—interestingly—she acted briefly in the company of Madame Vestris, the prominent London actress-manager. Little else is known of Keene's early life; even the year of her birth and her real name are uncertain. She was married at a young age to a man who was apparently exiled to Australia as a convict. When she arrived in America, her two small daughters from this marriage were introduced as her nieces.

(Billy Rose Theatre Collection, New York Public Library at Lincoln Center, Astor, Lenox, and Tilden Foundations)

Laura Keene.

James Wallack hired Keene as the leading lady at his new theatre, which opened in New York City in 1852. She was then relatively inexperienced, but, coached by Wallack, she added many new roles to her repertoire and quickly became a favorite with New York audiences.

Early in the 1853–1854 season, Keene surprised the theatrical world by suddenly leaving Wallack's company to accept an offer from several businessmen in Baltimore to manage her own theatre there. Keene's management of the Charles Street Theatre in Baltimore lasted only a few months. From there she traveled to California, where she acted and also had brief stints as a manager. These experiences helped prepare her to launch her management of a theatre in New York City.

When she opened Laura Keene's Varieties in December 1855, she became the first woman to run a large, first-class New York theatre. In the competitive world of commercial theatre, she was not welcomed by established male managers. In fact, Keene faced strong opposition during her first season, including libelous newspaper reports, the destruction of her scenery by a vandal on opening night, and the loss of her lease to a rival manager.

Still, she prevailed. She had a new theatre built, which she managed profitably until 1863. Laura Keene's Theatre gained a reputation for its scenic splendor; and she herself became known as a strict and resourceful manager who popularized such innovations as regular matinee performances and long runs of successful plays. One of the biggest hits of the nineteenth century, Tom Taylor's *Our American Cousin,* was first produced by Keene.

In 1863, Keene decided to give up her theatre and to tour as the head of a company. This gave her the variety of several roles in succession, in contrast to the monotony of a long run. She toured for the next several years and also briefly managed the Chestnut Street Theatre in Philadelphia.

Unfortunately, Keene is probably most often remembered as a footnote to a national tragedy: she was onstage performing in *Our American Cousin* at Ford's Theatre in Washington the night Abraham Lincoln was assassinated there.

Eventually forced into retirement by ill health, Keene died in 1873. By then, her prominence as a manager had already encouraged several other women to enter the field.

Two Early Directors

Possibly the most important directorial innovators at the close of this period were Richard Wagner and Georg II, the duke of Saxe-Meiningen. Neither of them was a performer in his company, and thus they are closer to our modern concept of the director.

RICHARD WAGNER

Wilhelm Richard Wagner (1813–1883), best-known as an opera composer, was also important as a stage and directing theorist. One of his theories was that a production, whether opera or theatre, should be a *Gesamtkunstwerk,* a "masterwork" in which all elements—music, words, action, scenery, lighting—are integrated as "total theatre." Wagner also argued that one person should serve as writer, composer, and director.

(Victoria and Albert Museum, London)

Richard Wagner.

Throughout the many reversals in his life, Richard Wagner held fast to his vision of opera. He was egocentric, forceful, and convinced of the superiority of his own ideas; and though his personality was sometimes his greatest hindrance, it eventually helped him achieve his goal of creating a new kind of opera.

Wagner's stepfather was a painter, singer, and actor; as a result, Wagner was acquainted with opera and theatre from his earliest years. Even as a child, growing up in Leipzig, Germany, he was impulsive and self-willed, neglecting all his studies except music. At age 17, he had an overture performed in the Leipzig Theatre. He spent a short (but wild) time at the University of Leipzig, and for the next several years he worked as the conductor of a series of third-rate provincial orchestras and composed his earliest operas. Shortly thereafter, he was forced to flee his creditors and went to Paris, hoping to dazzle its operatic establishment.

In 1842, after 3 poverty-stricken years in Paris, Wagner gladly returned to Dresden, where his opera *Rienzi* was a resounding success. He then received a post at the court opera. The works that followed—*The Flying Dutchman* (1843), *Tannhäuser,* (1845), and *Lohengrin* (1848)—were popular with audiences, though the critics disapproved of Wagner's "total theatre" and some of his other techniques. In 1849, Wagner was forced to flee again, this time to avoid arrest for having taken part in the revolution of 1848.

During his 12 years in exile, Wagner developed his theories and began composing the works that form his great operatic cycle, *The Ring of the Nibelung.* For these operas, he chose a national myth that he hoped would serve as a unifying force for Germany. (Because of Wagner's interest in Germanic myths, his belief in the superiority of the German people, and his anti-Semitism, he was Adolf Hitler's favorite composer. That, of course, took place long after his death; but his political and social ideas still make him controversial today.)

Wagner first tested his theories in 1876, when he staged the *Ring* cycle at his new theatre in Bayreuth, built with the help of his patron, Ludwig II of Bavaria. Several times during his years of struggle, he had nearly been ruined because of debts or adulterous affairs, but he persisted until he had overwhelmed his critics with his music. After his death in 1883, his second wife, Cosima Liszt Wagner—and then his sons and grandsons—carried on his work.

Wagner's concept of a totally unified artwork—the *Gesamtkunstwerk*—controlled by one person influenced twentieth-century theories of "total theatre" and has also been a major influence on modern directing theory. He believed that an opera, which is made up of many musical and theatrical elements, needs a controlling figure to unify it. He insisted that this figure must have dictatorial control; at his Bayreuth Festspielhaus, he put this theory into practice, becoming its *régisseur*—the French term for "director."

Wagner's innovations for increasing stage illusion are particularly important. Musicians were forbidden to tune their instruments in the orchestra pit, and audience members were not supposed to applaud during the course of a presentation. Wagner is also often credited with being the first director to extinguish the house lights in order to focus the audience's attention on the stage.

GEORG II, DUKE OF SAXE-MEININGEN

The other crucial late-nineteenth-century innovator in stage direction was Georg II (1826–1914) of Saxe-Meiningen a small German duchy. If he had been able to choose his own profession, he would have pursued a military career in Berlin, where he was a lieutenant in the Royal Guards. When the revolution of 1848 broke out in Germany, however, his father, Duke Bernhard II, ordered him to return to Saxe-Meiningen; once home, he became involved in theatre.

As the only son of Duke Bernhard, he was given an education which prepared him to rule the duchy. But two of his childhood tutors—one a theologian and the other an artist—instilled in him a love of nature and of art; and art remained a part of his education during his years at the University of Bonn and while he was in the Royal Guards. Though he painted in oils, his talent was mainly for drawing and sketching.

(Culver Pictures)
Georg II, duke of Saxe-Meiningen.

When he was called home in 1848, Georg became active at court, where he founded a competent but uninspired theatre company. In 1850 he married Princess Charlotte of Prussia, with whom he had three children. When she died 5 years later, he turned for consolation to art and music, traveling to Italy for a year of study. In 1858, he married a German princess, who died in 1872.

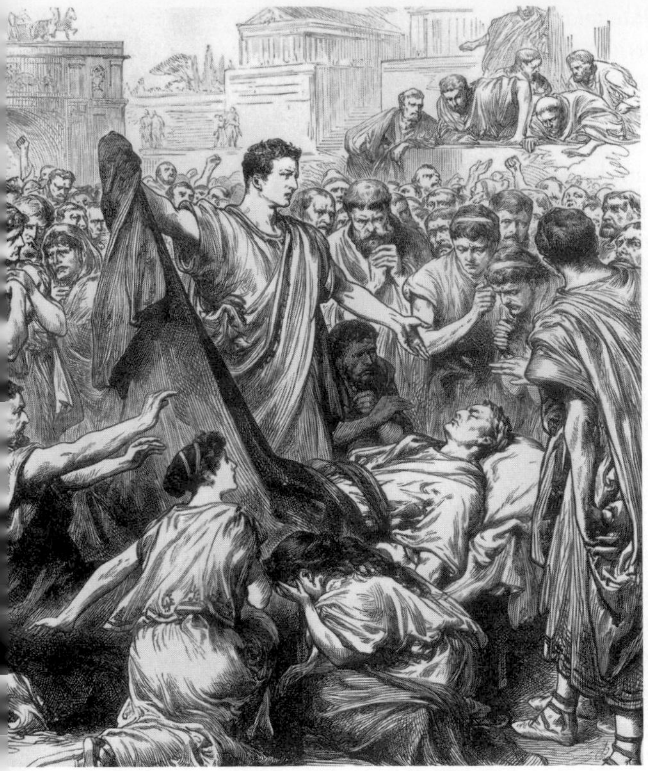

THE SAXE-MEININGEN TROUPE
The German duke of Saxe-Meiningen is considered one of the first modern directors. He drilled his company carefully and thoroughly and was famous for the crowd scenes he organized onstage. This drawing shows his company in a scene from his production of Shakespeare's *Julius Caesar* at Drury Lane in London in 1881.

During the 1850s and 1860s, Prussia was becoming the dominant force in Germany. Duke Bernhard opposed the Prussian influence; but Georg was in favor of Prussian–German unification, and in 1866 a Prussian army occupied Saxe-Meiningen and forced Bernhard to abdicate in favor of his son. As duke, Georg was an enlightened monarch, liberalizing land ownership, promoting trade agreements and tariff reforms, and providing health and welfare benefits for his subjects. He also served in the Franco-Prussian War of 1870.

In the evenings, he supervised the court theatre, planning and directing productions and providing sketches for scenery and costumes. By 1874 the duke had a team in place. Ludwig Chronegk, an actor in the company and its régisseur, was responsible for its daily operations. The third person involved in the company's artistic management was the duke's third wife, Ellen Franz, baroness von Heldburg, with whom he had eloped after the death of his second wife. She was responsible for the selection of plays and for the actors' stage diction.

The productions of the Meiningen players were quite stunning visually. To create appropriate scenic illusions, Georg insisted on historical accuracy and spent lavish sums on rich fabrics and authentic decor. He even extended his attention to the traditionally bare stage floor, decorating it with carpets, steps, shrubbery, and the like. The stage picture was further enhanced by carefully worked-out crowd scenes.

The Meiningen company astounded the world with its acting ensemble and its unified, historically accurate productions. Georg, Chronegk, and Ellen Franz continued to direct it until it was disbanded in 1890. The years before Georg's death in 1914 were tranquil, and his third marriage was happy.

The theatrical innovations that the duke supported made the Meiningen players the most renowned company in the world between 1874 and 1890; because of them, he is considered one of the first modern directors: as the director of many Shakespearean and romantic dramas, he revolutionized stage production. A major reason for his ability to organize such a successful theatrical venture was his enormous wealth. He rehearsed his actors with scenery and costumes for extensive periods of time, refusing to open a show until he believed that all the elements were completely unified. His intricately planned crowd scenes used company actors rather than amateurs or paid extras. (However, as an opponent of the star system, he employed mostly young performers.) His productions were admired for their historically accurate and practical settings; for their costumes, which helped to establish character; for their lighting; and for their sound effects. Moreover, all these theatrical innovations became well known throughout Europe because his company toured frequently, giving over 2,500 performances in thirty-eight European cities. Unquestionably, his work became an important influence on future directors of realistic drama.

Theatre Architecture

There were several developments in theatre architecture between 1800 and 1875 which led to the building of playhouses much like those in today's commercial centers.

Early in the nineteenth century, as we have already noted, playhouses were enlarged to accommodate expanding working-class urban audiences. (For a while in England, this influx of working-class audiences caused the social elite to abandon theatres for opera houses.) The Bowery Theatre in New York City—nicknamed "The Slaughterhouse" because it offered sentimental "blood and guts" melodrama—is an example of a huge nineteenth-century theatre for lower-class audiences. (The regular audience at the Bowery included the "Bowery boys," street toughs who drank, ate, and threw the remnants of their food into the pit from the gallery.) In its first year of operation, 1826, the Bowery held 2,500 spectators and was the largest playhouse in New York; 19 years later, it was enlarged to hold 4,000. Quite late in the century, large theatre spaces were still being built in Europe; one of these was the Paris Opera, which had a huge stage area and held over 2,000 spectators.

By the 1860s, however, there was generally a shift away from the construction of huge theatres. This shift can be explained by the proliferation of playhouses in European and American urban centers for specific segments of society. In London, for example, the number of theatres staging various types of dramas not covered by the Licensing Act of 1737 increased significantly during the early 1800s; in 1843, the Theatre Regulation Act finally abolished the unenforceable monopoly that was supposed to have been in effect.

The traditional proscenium arch and pit, box, and gallery dominated theatre buildings in the nineteenth century. English and American theatres became more like continental theatres: the proscenium doors began to disappear and the apron continued to diminish.

Many theatre buildings broke away from the traditional architectural pattern established during the Italian Renaissance, however. In London, the boxes in the Adelphi Theatre were raised so that the pit could be extended to the side walls, making the tiers more like balconies; late in the century, the English architect C. J. Phipps (1835–1897) popularized the balcony and orchestra configuration in many London theatres. By the late 1800s, advances in engineering and new materials, like structural steel, allowed balconies to be constructed without supporting columns; these technological advances also led to the construction of many new buildings because remodeling older playhouses became less cost-effective.

The comfort of the audience became a greater concern. The French architect Émile Trélat (1821–1907) recommended mechanical methods for improving ventilation in the galleries; and even early in the century a few innovative theatres had comfortable individual

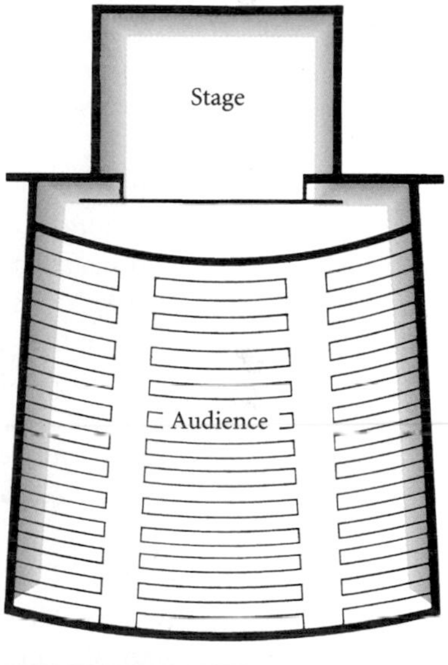

PROSCENIUM THEATRE
The audience faces in one direction, toward an enclosed stage encased by a picture-frame opening. Scene changes and performers' entrances and exits are made behind the proscenium opening, out of sight of the audience.

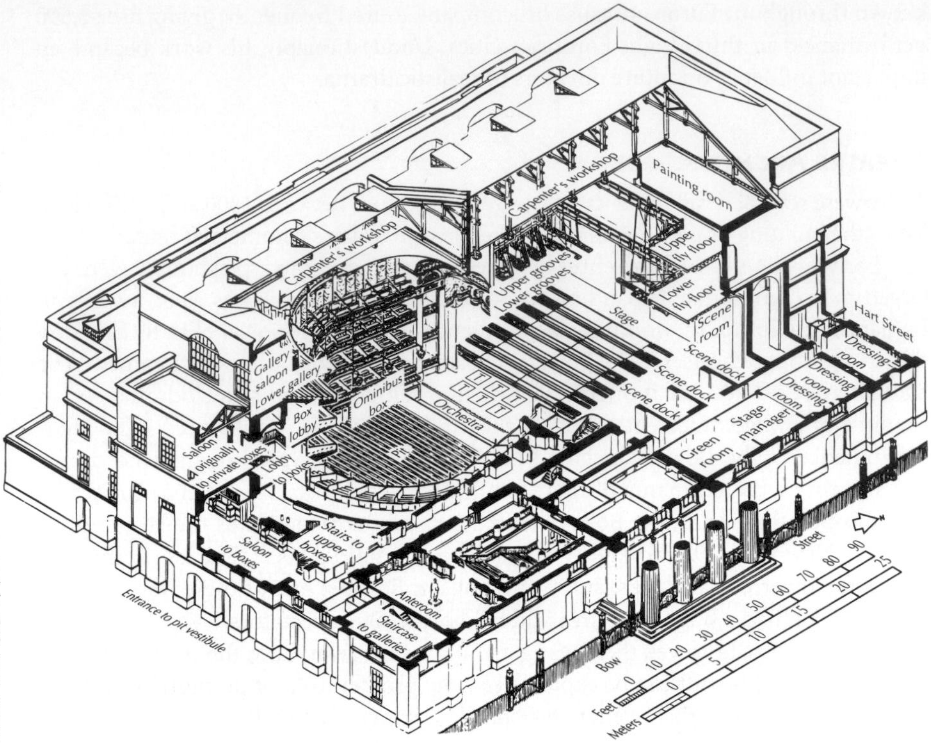

(Richard Leacroft, The Development of the English Playhouse, Cornell University Press, Ithaca, N.Y., 1973. By permission of Reed Book Services/Methuen London.)

COVENT GARDEN IN THE NINETEENTH CENTURY
This plan shows Covent Garden as it appeared in the 1800s. While it still had pit, boxes, and galleries, the proscenium doors and the large apron were disappearing. The theatre itself had also been enlarged.

seats instead of backless benches in the pit, so that this area became the equivalent of the modern orchestra. Marie and Squire Bancroft, for instance, removed the benches and installed individual seats in London's Haymarket Theatre. (The reforms of the Bancrofts also included changes intended to increase illusionism in all aspects of theatre: they used box sets, and they worked with the playwright Thomas William Robertson, whose dramas—as we have seen—dealt with real social concerns. Also, as we noted above, their acting style was more realistic.) Individual seats, of course, allowed for reserved seating, which had become more necessary with the advent of the long run and the need to know how much advance sale a show might have.

Booth's Theatre

Booth's Theatre, completed in 1869 for the renowned American Shakespearean actor Edwin Booth (1833–1893), is often said to have been the first modern theatre in New York City. Instead of a pit and galleries, it had a modern orchestra area and balconies. The seats were individual armchairs, although there were boxes in the proscenium arch. The stage in Booth's Theatre was also revolutionary: it was not raked and was not designed for traditional wing-and-shutter scenery. Scenery could be raised from the basement by elevators or lowered ("flown in") from above, and scenic pieces were often supported by braces. The fly space was high enough to accommodate scenic drops without their being rolled up. By 1875, with theatres like Booth's, the modern proscenium-arch theatre had been established.

EDWIN BOOTH

Edwin Booth's reputation as America's finest actor has survived for over 100 years, and his name will always be linked with Hamlet, his greatest role. His innovations in staging are not as well known, but they were also important in that he anticipated modern scenic developments.

Though Booth's father was a famous actor, Junius Brutus Booth, Edwin was not encouraged in his stage career; his family felt that it was his younger brother, John Wilkes Booth, who had inherited their father's fiery acting ability. However, Edwin began accompanying his father on tours at the age of 13, having proved adept at calming his father's mad moods and restraining his drinking. He made his own dramatic debut in 1849 in a bit role, to relieve an overworked prompter, and then continued to play small parts in his father's company. When the two toured the west, Edwin decided to remain there and played several seasons in repertory.

(New York Public Library Picture Collection)

Edwin Booth.

Edwin Booth's New York debut in 1857 established him as the most promising young actor in the United States. He was short and slight, with piercing eyes and a rich, melodious voice. His acting, particularly his portrayal of Hamlet, was remarkable for its depth of character, grace, and freedom from mannerisms. (As we noted earlier, in 1864 he played Hamlet for 100 consecutive nights in New York, a record that was not surpassed until 1923.)

Booth believed that art, including theatre, should inspire and ennoble. To carry out his ideas, in 1869 he built his own theatre, where for 5 years he presented a series of magnificent Shakespearean productions. He abandoned the wing-and-groove method of scene shifting and the raked stage, and he used heavy set pieces and freestanding scenery to create historically accurate settings. He also introduced an elevator stage for raising and lowering entire sets and installed flying equipment to raise scenery out of sight above the proscenium opening. He also used uncorrupted texts of Shakespeare's plays many years before the English theatre had returned to them.

Poor financial management forced Booth's theatre into bankruptcy in 1874, and for the rest of his life he was a touring star. His touring took him to England, where he alternated the roles of Iago and Othello with Henry Irving, and to Germany—he was one of the first American actors to achieve international fame.

In private life, Booth was quiet, almost melancholy. He experienced three personal tragedies: his beloved first wife died after 2 1/2 years of marriage; his second wife went mad after the loss of their infant son; and his brother assassinated Abraham Lincoln.

Edwin Booth had the respect and friendship of the leading literary and cultural figures of his day. He felt that acting was an honorable profession, and he endowed the Players Club in New York in 1888 as a place where actors and other gentlemen could meet. Booth presented the club with his house on Gramercy Park in New York City, where he lived until his death in 1893.

WAGNER'S FESTSPIELHAUS

A few years after Edwin Booth inaugurated his theatre in New York, another innovative nineteenth-century theatre building opened in Europe in 1876: the Bayreuth Festspielhaus, built for Richard Wagner.

(Victoria and Albert Museum, London)

WAGNER'S FESTSPIELHAUS
Richard Wagner's Festspielhaus at Bayreuth in Germany, completed in 1876 and designed to be the ideal home for his operas, was one of the first modern theatres. Its "continental" seating and balcony set the pattern for modern auditoriums, and its sunken orchestra pit became an integral part of the modern musical playhouse.

This theatre, which took four years to complete, also broke with the earlier tradition of pit, boxes, and gallery. Wagner wanted a theatre in which seating would not emphasize class distinctions. There were 1,300 individual seats in 30 raked rows, forming a fan-shaped auditorium; the rows became longer the farther away they were from the stage, and audiences entered and exited at the ends of rows: this type of arrangement is now known as *continental seating.* There was a single line of boxes at the rear of the house, and a 300-seat balcony above them. The price was the same for every seat in this opera house.

The stage of the Bayreuth Festspielhaus, modeled along traditional Italianate lines, was not as revolutionary as the auditorium, though it did have a few innovations. There was a double proscenium arch, and a sunken orchestra pit which separated the audience from the stage; Wagner referred to the orchestra pit as his "mystic gulf." For special effects, steam jets were built into the forestage.

Scenery, Costuming, and Lighting

Eighteenth-century experiments with realistic devices and conventions in scenery and costuming were carried farther in the nineteenth century.

Historical Accuracy

Historical accuracy in sets and costumes became more common with the increasing availability of works of historical research, such as J. R. Planché's *History of British Costume* (1843). This new knowledge about the past, combined with the nineteenth-century fascination with antiquity, led a number of theatre artists to mount historically accurate productions; they included the English actor-managers Charles Kemble, William Charles Macready, and Charles Kean (1811–1868), as well as the American actor-manager Edwin Booth and the duke of Saxe-Meiningen. In the Saxe-Meiningen presentations, as we have seen, costumes were carefully researched and authentic materials were used regardless of the cost or difficulty of obtaining them; moreover, performers were not allowed to alter their costumes. The same careful attention was given to the settings the duke designed.

The Box Set

In scene design, even more important than the trend toward historical accuracy was the gradual replacement of painted wing-and-shutter settings shifted by a pole-and-chariot or groove system. The wing-and-shutter arrangement did not suddenly disappear, however, and it continued to be used for some time. Nonetheless, alternatives were introduced throughout the first 75 years of the nineteenth century.

We have already mentioned experiments in Germany by Tieck and Immermann, who staged Shakespeare in a way they believed came closer to the Elizabethan playhouse. In the United States, as noted above, Edwin Booth broke with the traditional wing-and-shutter set by placing scenic pieces wherever he wished on the stage floor (in his theatre, the stage was not raked) and supporting them with braces. Also, many English and American theatre artists of the late 1800s began to stage all the action behind the proscenium; this reinforced the illusion of a "fourth wall."

Another significant alternative was the box set. A *box set* consists of flats hinged together to represent a room; it often has practicable elements, such as doors and windows, which can be used during the course of a presentation. Between 1800 and 1875, many theatre artists began to use box sets; Edwin Booth is credited with popularizing them in United States.

Madame Vestris, an English actress-manager, was often said to have introduced the box set, during her management of London's Olympic Theatre in the 1830s. We now know that Vestris was not the first to use the box set; as we noted in Chapter 10, some historians believe that it may have begun in the eighteenth century, or even as early as the Italian Renaissance. However, she was undoubtedly a key innovator, who popularized the box set and filled her settings with many realistic accouterments.

MADAME VESTRIS: LUCIA ELIZABETTA BARTOLOZZI

Theatre management—as we noted earlier—was an unusual profession for a woman in 1830 and, given the disorder and chaos of the London stage, a financially unstable profession for anyone. In spite of these difficulties, however, Madame Vestris (1797–1856) not only was able to make major innovations in staging but also made a profit as proprietor of the Olympic Theatre.

By the time she opened her theatre, Madame Vestris had 15 years of theatrical experience. The daughter of a London engraver, she married Auguste Armand Vestris—a dancer and one member of a famous family of ballet performers—when she was only 16. Two years later, she made her stage debut. After her husband left her in 1820, she continued acting, playing in Paris for several years and then at the Drury Lane and Covent Garden theatres in London. She had an excellent singing voice and might have made a career in opera but instead played in burlesques, extravaganzas, and comedies. She was much admired for her beautiful figure, sparkling eyes, and dark hair. Breeches roles—roles in which a woman played the part of a young man and thus had an opportunity to show off her legs—were one of her specialties.

(Bettmann/Corbis)

Madame Vestris (Lucia Elizabetta Bartolozzi, 1797–1856).

Madame Vestris opened her Olympic Theatre with *Olympic Revels,* an extravaganza written by J. R. Planché, the best writer of burlesques, extravaganzas, and farces in England at that time. Planché was to be her resident dramatist at the Olympic and later at the Lyceum Theatre. (Planché, as we mentioned earlier, also wrote a history of costumes.)

Though she presented only light entertainment at the Olympic, Madame Vestris produced it with a degree of care that was usually reserved for the classics, paying close attention to every aspect of a production and coordinating all the elements into a unified whole. She is credited with introducing the box set—complete with ceiling—to England around 1832. She dressed all her settings with real properties—doorknobs, dishes, rugs, tables, chairs, curtains—instead of painting them on the set as was usually done. Her care extended to costuming; she replaced the exaggerated costumes of extravaganza and burlesque with clothes from everyday life. To achieve the effects she wanted onstage, Madame Vestris also maintained strict control over her acting company.

In 1838, Madame Vestris married Charles Mathews (1803–1878), a light comedian in her company. After an American tour, they managed Covent Garden for 3 years. There they presented legitimate dramas, with the same staging practices she had used earlier at the Olympic. Though their production of *London Assurance,* Dion Boucicault's first play, was a success, this managerial venture ended in financial failure in 1842. They then took over the Lyceum Theatre in 1847, but their insistence on quality led to another failure. Madame Vestris died in 1856, in the midst of the Lyceum's bankruptcy proceedings.

New Technology

During the nineteenth century, the technology of the industrial revolution was applied to theatre. Many historians believe that the popularity of melodrama, with its emphasis on stage spectacle and special effects, accelerated these technological innovations. For example, Dion Boucicault was responsible for the introduction of fireproofing in the theatre when one of his melodramatic plays called for an onstage fire.

The *moving panorama*—painted settings on a long cloth which could be unrolled across the stage by turning spools—created an illusion of movement and changing locales. A popular American play, William Dunlap's *A Trip to Niagara* (1828), used this device to show a voyage from New York City to Niagara Falls. The emphasis on re-creating natural environments onstage was probably influenced by romanticism, which called for a "return to nature." (In film, a similar technique, known as *rear projection,* has been used to create an illusion of movement. Behind a stationary object—such as the interior of a car—a film of changing backgrounds and locales is projected; the stationary object and the projected material are then filmed.)

New means of scene shifting were needed for the new types of settings. In a book published in 1860, the French architect Trélat proposed hydraulic lifts for scene shifting. We have already noted that elevators and equipment for flying scenery were used at Booth's Theatre. By the close of the century, the elevator stage and the revolving stage were perfected. An *elevator stage* allows sections of a stage floor, or even the entire floor, to be raised or lowered. A *revolving stage* is a large turntable on which scenery is placed; as it moves, one set is brought into view as another turns out of sight. One innovative theatre technologist was Steele MacKaye (1842–1894). (MacKaye was a noted playwright whose melodramas focused on more realistic circumstances. He was also interested in the teaching of acting, particularly in Delsarte's methods; and he founded the American Academy of Dramatic Art, the first school of acting in New York City, which is still functioning today.) In 1880, at the Madison Square Theatre in New York, MacKaye used two stages, one above the other, which could be raised and lowered; while one stage was in view of the audience, the scenery on the other (which was either in the basement or in the fly area) could be changed.

Nineteenth-century technology revolutionized stage lighting, which until then had been primitive. The introduction of *gas lighting* was the first step. In 1816, Philadelphia's Chestnut Street Theatre was the earliest gaslit playhouse in the world. By the middle of the century, the *gas table*—the equivalent of a modern dimmer

(From *Scientific American*, April 5, 1884)

NEW THEATRE TECHNOLOGY

Toward the end of the period covered in this chapter, many advances were made in theatre technology. In 1880, Steele MacKaye opened his Madison Square Theatre, shown in this engraving. MacKaye had two stages built behind the stage, one of them invisible to the audience. These two stages could be lowered or raised by an elevator. While one stage was being used (here, the lower stage) the other was being set up for the next scene and could quickly be lowered into place when the previous scene concluded.

board—allowed a single stagehand to alter the intensity of lighting throughout a theatre. This new control of lighting allowed significant changes in architecture and staging. In the 1860s, two Parisian theatres were built without chandeliers hanging over the audience; gas lighting also allowed Richard Wagner to extinguish the lights in the auditorium of the Bayreuth Festspielhaus.

Thomas Edison's electric *incandescent lamp,* invented in 1879, was the next step. By 1881, the Savoy Theatre in London was using incandescent lighting, though some other playhouse may actually have been the first to introduce it. Electricity, of course, is the most flexible, most controllable, and safest form of lighting; in the twentieth century, it would make stage lighting design a true art.

Theatre in Russia

Most of the changes in theatre highlighted in this chapter were occurring worldwide: as an example we turn to Russia. As a background to Russian theatre in the nineteenth century, we will look briefly at developments in the 50 years before 1800. The first real signs of formal theatrical activity in Russia appeared in the middle of the eighteenth century. It was at this point that Fyodor Volkov (1729–1763), who had seen performances by traveling companies in Saint Petersburg, began presenting plays in his hometown, Yaroslavl. So successful were his early productions that he was asked to perform for Empress Elizabeth, and she in turn arranged for some of his actors to study at the Academy of the Nobility. At about the same time, Alexander Sumarokov (1717–1777) began writing plays in neoclassical form, but on Russian subjects.

In 1762, Empress Catherine II, known as Catherine the Great, began her reign, a reign that lasted until 1796. Catherine thought of the theatre as a "national school" and fancied herself as its premier teacher. Under her, theatrical activity increased: in 1771 she ordered that the Bolshoi Theatre should be built in Saint Petersburg, and in 1779 she established the Imperial Theatre School to train Russian actors, dancers, and singers.

The most successful playwright of this period was Denis Fonvizin (1745–1792). Two of his best-known dramas were *The Brigadier General* (1766), a satire on the Russian nouveau riche; and *The Minor,* satirizing the rural middle class.

In 1762, Catherine issued a charter freeing the nobles from many of their state obligations. One result was the creation of "serf theatres," in which wealthy landowners established theatres, using as performers and technicians the serfs who belonged to their estates. Eventually there were over 170 serf theatres throughout Russia, with more than a dozen in Moscow alone. One nobleman, Count Peter Sheremetyev, had a serf troupe in Moscow; it consisted of 230 members performing in three theatres he had established.

One other playwright of the late eighteenth century should be mentioned: Vasily Kapnist (1757–1823), whose play *Chicane* (1789) satirized judicial corruption and established more firmly than ever the social role of Russian comedy.

The early nineteenth century in Russia was marked by political crises. First, there were the Napoleonic wars, in which the French general Napoleon invaded

Russia and in 1812 got as far as Moscow before being turned back; second, shortly after Czar Nicholas I came to power in 1825 there was a rebellion—an outgrowth of previous unrest. The uprising was put down; but throughout this period, as in the century before, all creative activity, including theatre, was under the tight control of the state and censorship prevailed.

Even so, important playwrights and performers emerged. Alexander Griboyedov (1795–1829) was a successful playwright in the neoclassical form. In his best-known work, *Woe from Wit* (1824), he added refinement and complexity to both the plot and the characters, and he provided philosophical depth not evident in previous Russian plays. Romanticism began to take hold in Russia in the second and third decades of the nineteenth century, as it did elsewhere; and *Boris Godunov* (1825) by Alexander Pushkin (1799–1837) marked the arrival of the new form. This play, which is diverse, expansive, and poetic, concerns the interaction of a ruler and those under him. Because of censorship, the play was not printed until 6 years after it was written, and not produced for another 40 years after that.

Another play kept off the stage because of censorship was *Masquerade* by Mikhail Lermontov (1814–1841), which, though written in 1836, was not produced until 1852. A drama reminiscent of the work of England's Lord Byron, it is a romantic piece which blames society when a man murders his wife.

Realistic drama began to take its place beside romanticism in the work of Nikolai Gogol (1809–1852). Gogol's most famous play, *The Inspector General* (1836), continues to be widely produced today. The play exposes corruption in the government of a small town and features a gallery of exaggerated, comical characters whose fallibility and foibles are wittily exposed when a harmless visitor to the town is taken for a government inspector who has come to root out corruption.

All during the nineteenth century, the imperial theatres, under the control of the czar, enjoyed a monopoly on theatre production in the two most important cities: Moscow and the capital, Saint Petersburg. Actors at the theatres were hired, as they were in France, according to "lines of business."

Among recognized performers of the period, several stood apart. The actress Yekaterina Semyonova (1786–1839), who commanded a larger salary than her counterparts, was praised for her work in both tragedy and comedy. The actor Aleksey Yakovlev (1773–1817) was hailed for his spontaneous, energetic performances; and following him, Vasily Karatygin (1802–1853) made his mark as a more impressive classical actor.

These performers gained fame in Saint Petersburg, but as the middle of the century approached, leadership in theatrical activity began to pass to Moscow. On Moscow's stages, Pavel Mochalov (1800–1848) impressed audiences with his impulsive bravura, and Mikhail Shchepkin (1788–1863) came to be considered the finest Russian actor of his time. Shchepkin had been born a serf but obtained his freedom in 1821. Two years later he joined the Maly company in Moscow. As a performer he paid great attention to detail and insisted on ensemble playing with his fellow actors. Highly praised in later years by Konstantin Stanislavski, his work was a forerunner of later realism.

Playwrights, too, anticipated later realism. Ivan Turgenev (1818–1883) wrote a number of plays at mid-century, the most memorable being *A Month in the Country,* which was written in 1850 but not produced until 1872. In this play, the daily lives

(© Carol Rosegg)

NINETEENTH-CENTURY RUSSIAN THEATRE
Theatre in Russia in the first part of the nineteenth century anticipated the significant developments that occurred at the end of the century. A number of important playwrights emerged. One of them was Ivan Turgenev, whose play *A Month in the Country* was a precursor to the plays of Chekhov. Another play by Turgenev, given the title *Fortune's Fool* in a recent production, is shown here with the English actors Enid Graham and Alan Bates. Bates played the fool of the title—an engaging rascal who has lost his estate but is allowed to continue to live there.

of people on a country estate are carefully rendered at the same time that their inner lives are explored and exposed. This revealing approach to theatre would be perfected by Turgenev's successor, Anton Chekhov.

An important figure at mid-century was the playwright Alexander Ostrovsky (1823–1886), who wrote in a number of forms. His play *The Thunderstorm* (1859) is frequently referred to as Russia's first tragedy, but he also wrote historical dramas. And his work *Don't Get into Another's Sleigh,* produced by the Maly Theatre in 1853, was one of many plays that artfully depicted the life of Russian merchants. Often described as Russia's first full-time dramatist, Ostrovsky was a key figure in creating, in 1866, the Russian Society of Dramatic Authors and Composers, an organization which for the first time ensured that playwrights would have copyright protection for their work.

Two other playwrights are worth noting. Aleksei Pisemsky (1820–1881) wrote a strongly naturalistic play *A Bitter Fate* (1859), which predated, and in some ways surpassed, a similar work entitled *The Power of Darkness* (1886) by Leo Tolstoy

(1828–1910). Alexei K. Tolstoy (1817–1875) composed a trilogy, *The Death of Ivan the Terrible* (1866), *Tsar Fyodor Ivanovich* (1868), and *Tsar Boris* (1870), which featured psychologically detailed, powerfully opposed characters.

Along with developments in Russia, during the 125-year period from 1750 to 1875, theatre artists in Russia became increasingly aware of what was happening in western Europe and England in playwriting, acting, and theatre production. As the end of the nineteenth century approached, therefore, the way had been prepared in Russia for the advent of the landmark figures who were soon to appear—Konstantin Stanislavski and Vladimir Nemirovich-Danchenko, founders of the Moscow Art Theatre; and the playwright Anton Chekhov.

By 1875, the elements that would form the foundation for a realistic revolution were in place, including the emergence of the director, more realistic acting, and the box set. What was missing was serious realistic drama, and that began to emerge in the 1870s, as we will see in Chapter 12.

Summary

Transformations in theatre between 1800 and 1875 prepared the way for modern theatre. Live theatre reached its peak of popularity during this century and for the following 25 years. In drama, the romantics broke away from the neoclassical rules and argued that all subject matter—the grotesque as well as the ideal—was appropriate for the stage. Melodrama was the most popular nineteenth-century genre, and it is still popular in modern films and on television. The well-made play, refined by the French writers Scribe and Sardou, still exists in the early twenty-first century.

Acting was transformed in the nineteenth century by the star system, the long run, and the decline of the repertory company. While classical, romantic, and melodramatic acting styles were predominant, many performers—including William Charles Macready, the Bancrofts, Mikhail Shchepkin, and Eleonora Duse—based their acting more on observable life. Steps were taken toward the figure of the director as an overseer of the production process; Richard Wagner and the duke of Saxe-Meiningen were notable in this development.

The modern, comfortable proscenium-arch theatre became a reality. Two of the most innovative playhouses were Booth's Theatre in New York City and Richard Wagner's Festspielhaus in Bayreuth. Historical accuracy became more commonplace in scenery and costuming, and the box set began to replace painted scenery. Gas and then electricity provided a controllable source of light.

Theatre History

- Heinrich von Kleist (1771–1811), *The Prince of Homburg*
- The Kembles (c. 1783–1891)
- Mikhail Shchepkin (1788–1863)
- Edmund Kean (1789–1833) *(below)*

- Eugène Scribe (1791–1861), *A Glass of Water*
- William Charles Macready (1793–1873)
- Madame Vestris (1797–1856)
- Alexander Pushkin (1799–1837), *Boris Godunov*
- George Dibdin Pitt (1799–1855), *The String of Pearls*
- Victor Hugo (1802–1885), *Hernani*
- Johann Wolfgang Goethe's *Faust* (Part I, 1808)
- Ira Aldridge (c. 1806–1867)
- "Old Price Riots" at Covent Garden, London (1809)
- Nikolai Gogol (1809–1852), *The Inspector General*
- P.T. Barnum (1810–1891), popularized circus
- Charles Kean (1811–1868)
- François Delsarte (1811–1871) *(right)*

Cultural and Historical Developments

- Empress Catherine II of Russia begins reign (1762)
- Louisiana Purchase (1803)
- Napoleon I *(below)*, emperor of France (1804)

- Fulton's paddle steamer *Clermont* navigates on Hudson (1807)
- Latin America independence (1808–1826)
- Madame de Staël's *Of Germany* (1810)
- Beethoven's Fifth Symphony (1810)
- Battle of Waterloo; Metternich system (1815)
- Greek war of independence (1821)
- Monroe Doctrine (1823)
- Decembrist uprising in Russia (1825)
- Eugène Delacroix's *Liberty Leading the People* (1830)
- Samuel F. B. Morse's telegraph (1837)
- Victoria of England *(below)* rules (1837–1901)

continued

Photo Credits: Edmund Kean as Hamlet. (© Hulton-Deutsch Collection/Corbis) / Delsarte's "attack" pose. / Napoleon I, emperor of France (*Siege of Genoa*). (© Archivo Iconografico, S.A./Corbis) / Queen Victoria of England. (Adoc-photos/Art Resource, N.Y.)

MILESTONES CHAPTER 11 THEATRES FROM 1800 TO 1875 *continued*

- Georg Büchner (1813–1837), *Woyzeck*
- Chestnut Street Theatre, Philadelphia, earliest gaslit theatre (1816)
- Anna Cora Mowatt (1819–1870), *Fashion*
- African Grove Theater (1821–1823)
- Charles Kemble produces historically accurate *King John* at Covent Garden (1823)
- Bowery Theatre, largest theatre in New York, opens (1826)
- Georg II, duke of Saxe-Meiningen (1826–1914)
- Laura Keene (c. 1826–1873)
- Leo Tolstoy (1828–1910), *The Power of Darkness*
- Virginia Minstrels formed; England's Theatre Regulation Act (1843)
- Sarah Bernhardt (1845–1923) *(below)* and Eleonora Duse (1858–1924) dominate international stage

- Astor Place Riot (1849)
- Harriet Beecher Stowe's *Uncle Tom's Cabin* adapted successfully for the stage (1853)
- Booth's Theatre, New York, completed (1869)
- Richard Wagner's Bayreuth Festspielhaus (1876)
- Savoy Theatre, London, uses incandescent lighting (1881)

- Dickens's *Oliver Twist* (1838)
- Ten Hours Act, limited working day for women and children in England (1847)
- Karl Marx's *The Communist Manifesto,* written with Friedrich Engles (1848); *Das Kapital* (1867)
- Second French Empire; Napoleon III (1852)
- Crimean War (1853–1865)
- Gustave Flaubert's *Madame Bovary* (c. 1857)
- Charles Darwin's *On the Origin of Species* (1859)
- American Civil War (1861–1865); proclamation of the Kingdom of Italy
- Bismarck becomes Prussian prime minister (1862)
- Édouard Manet's *Le Déjeuner sur l'Herbe* (1863) *(below)*

- Fyodor Dostoyevsky's *Crime and Punishment* (1866)
- Extension of suffrage in Great Britain (1867)
- Meiji restoration; trade reopened between Japan and the west (1868)
- Tolstoy's *War and Peace* (c. 1869)
- American transcontinental railway completed (1869)
- German empire founded; Paris commune (1871)
- Alexander Graham Bell's telephone (1876)
- Thomas Edison's incandescent lamp (1879)

Part Four | Modern Theatres

The period beginning in 1875 and continuing to the present is called *modern,* not just because it is close to us in time but because it has characteristics and a shape all its own.

Forces that began to emerge in the nineteenth century had surfaced at its end. Charles Darwin's theory of evolution was a direct challenge to the centuries-old biblical concept that all living things, including human beings, are directly created by God; and the German philosopher Friedrich Nietzsche (1844–1900) went so far as to declare that God was dead. Just as Darwin's theory challenged traditional religious beliefs, so the theories of Karl Marx (1818–1883) challenged traditional economic and political beliefs, especially theories of capitalism. Sigmund Freud (1856–1939) declared that people are ruled as much by subconscious thoughts and desires as by conscious ones. In the early twentieth century, Albert Einstein (1879–1955) developed his theory of relativity, and certain aspects of the universe that had been considered fixed were now seen as changeable.

All this added up to a drastic shift in the way people regarded themselves and the world around them. This upheaval of long-held beliefs is one mark of the modern period. Another has to do with advances in technology and communications.

The past hundred years have seen the invention of radio, films, and television; of computers and telecommunications; and of propeller airplanes, jet planes, and space rockets. These inventions have brought the world closer together: news travels around the globe instantaneously, and people can travel from continent to continent in a matter of hours. This has brought advantages to people everywhere, but it has also increased the possibility of horror. Twentieth-century wars were often world wars, and mass murder—of Armenians in Turkey, of Jews by the Nazis, of political prisoners in Soviet Russia, of Muslims in Bosnia and Kosovo, and of one tribe by another in Africa—occurred on a scale never known before.

Turmoil in the modern world has included not only the two world wars but also the Russian Revolution, the great depression, the war in Vietnam, terrorism, the fall of communism in the former Soviet Union and eastern Europe, and wars in Africa and the middle east—including a war between Iraq and Kuwait in which the United Nations, and especially the United States, took part, and the invasion of Iraq by the United States in 2003. There was frequent unrest and continual tension between Israel and its neighbors; although 1993 brought the signing of a peace accord by Israel and the Palestine Liberation Organization, these agreements did not last.

Worldwide upheavals have been reflected in modern theatre, which has been fragmented by numerous movements and trends, particularly avant-garde movements. Some historians divide twentieth-century theatre into two camps: realists and antirealists. Realists include Henrik Ibsen, August Strindberg, George Bernard Shaw, Anton Chekhov, the Moscow Art Theatre, and the Group Theatre. Among the antirealists are symbolists, expressionists, futurists, dadaists, surrealists, and absurdists; included in this group are such figures as Vsevelod Meyerhold, Antonin Artaud, Bertolt Brecht, and Jerzy Grotowski. Other analysts make a sharp distinction between commercial artists—such as those who work in New York's Broadway theatre—and noncommercial artists who initiate idealistic ventures like "little theatres," off-Broadway, off-off-Broadway, and not-for-profit theatres nationwide.

Which twentieth-century and early twenty-first century theatrical trends will prove to be historically significant is still difficult to predict. What is certain is that modern theatre will be remembered for spawning a great many revolutionary movements.

(T. Charles Erickson)

John Earl Jelks (Citizen Barlow), Ruben Santiago-Hudson (Caesar, in the mask), and Phylicia Rashad (Aunt Ester) in August Wilson's *Gem of the Ocean*, directed by Kenny Leon at the Huntington Theatre. Costume design by Constanza Romero.

CHAPTER 12
THEATRES FROM 1875 TO 1915

MODERN THEATRE BEGINS

The seeds of modern theatre, still very much with us, were sown at the end of the nineteenth century and the beginning of the twentieth. Acting, production approaches, and playwriting all played a part in this important development. Among the important playwrights of the period was Henrik Ibsen. Shown here in Ibsen's *The Lady from the Sea* are Natasha Richardson as the title character and Tim McInnerny. The production at the Almeida Theatre, London, was directed by Trevor Nunn.

(© Geraint Lewis)

Many of the initiatives and innovations of the first part of the nineteenth century continued and even accelerated at the turn of the century. This was true of social and political changes such as technological advances and increased nationalism, in addition to improved communications and transportation.

Background: The Turn of the Century

Possibly the most significant social development of the late nineteenth century was the rise of the working class. As we saw in Chapter 11, industrialization resulted in urbanization; and throughout the nineteenth century the working class grew in size. It also grew in power: politicians, social scientists, and artists focused on its concerns. One indication of the increased political power of the working class was a trend, throughout Europe, to allow more people to vote. The growing suffragist movement, which sought voting rights for women, was tied to this political transformation. Workers also gained economic and political power by unionizing; some of the early American theatrical unions, for example, were founded during this era.

Scientific advances continued to alter western lifestyles radically. Advances in medicine increased life expectancy. The work of Freud, Einstein, and Nietzsche, following the writings of Darwin and Marx earlier in the century, were an assault on accepted religious, scientific, and political beliefs. In psychology, Sigmund Freud established a new approach: psychoanalysis. Psychological motivations, Freud maintained, could be discovered; and seemingly illogical subconscious processes, such as dreams, could be analyzed and explained. In physics, the work of people like Einstein altered our understanding of the universe. Many philosophers observe that the growth of modern scientific knowledge resulted in western society becoming more atheistic; God and religion became less important in daily life.

Einstein's term *relativity* is a key to these developments: things that were thought to be absolute or fixed became relative. Not only was religion questioned; the supposed "natural order" of the universe and even the workings of human beings—their conscious control of their actions—were challenged. It was a time of intellectual and moral upheaval.

There were also radical technological changes. Inventions—including Alexander Graham Bell's telephone, Thomas Edison's electric light, Wilbur and Orville Wright's flying machine, and the early automobile—made daily life easier. Some of the inventions of this period—such as recording devices, film, and radio—resulted in new electronic art forms. In addition, trends of the first part of the nineteenth century, such as nationalism, imperialism, and urbanization, continued to transform European and American society.

This radical transformation of western society between 1875 and the outbreak of World War I in 1914 was mirrored in theatre. To give one specific example, the further development of industrialization resulted in huge monopolies controlling certain businesses, and this had its counterpart in theatre. In 1896, for instance, American theatre became dominated by six producers who banded together to form the Theatrical Syndicate, which controlled the best playhouses throughout the nation and produced the most noteworthy touring shows.

More broadly, in theatre between 1875 and 1915 we can see the emergence of two artistic impulses that stood in sharp contrast throughout the twentieth century. On one hand, realistic artists attempted to create an illusion of everyday life onstage. On the other hand, many theatre artists continued to favor illusionistic and openly theatrical techniques and devices such as dream sequences, fantasy, poetry, music, and such otherworldly figures as ghosts and spirits. In addition, abstract theatre artists created seemingly illogical stage pictures rooted in the subconscious or in a dream world.

The Emergence of Realism

Here, we consider the first of the two contrasting twentieth-century approaches to theatre: *realism*, and a closely related movement called *naturalism*.

1875 to 1915
Year

Theatre

- Wagner's Bayreuth Festspielhaus opened (1876)
- Ibsen's *A Doll's House* (1879)
- Savoy Theatre in London uses electricity (1881)
- Antoine's Théâtre Libre (1887)
- Strindberg's *Miss Julie* (1888)
- Brahm's Freie Bühne (1889)
- Grein's Independent Theatre (1891)
- Lugné-Poë's Théâtre de l'Oeuvre (1893)
- Shaw's *Arms and the Man* (1894)
- Oscar Wilde's *The Importance of Being Earnest* (1895)
- Chekhov's *Sea Gull;* Jarry's *Ubu Roi;* revolving stage in Munich (1896)
- Moscow Art Theatre (1898)
- Appia's *Music and Stage Setting* (1899)
- Williams and Walker's *In Dahomey* (1902)
- Chekhov's *Cherry Orchard* (1904)
- Synge's *Riders to the Sea* (1904)
- Craig's *The Art of Theater;* Reinhardt succeeds Otto Brahm as director of Deutsches Theatre (1905)
- First modern Japanese drama presented by Osanai Kaoru (1909)
- Indian playwright, Rabindranath Tagore, receives Nobel Prize (1913)
- Théâtre du Vieux Colombier (1913)
- Anita Bush founds Lafayette Players (1914)
- Provincetown Playhouse (1915)

Year

1875
1880
1890
1895
1900
1905
1910
1915

Culture and Politics

- Telephone patented (1876)
- Edison's incandescent lamp (1879)
- Height of imperialism (1880–1914)
- Alexander II assassinated in Russia (1881)
- Trade unions in France legalized (1884)
- Dreyfus affair in France (1894)
- Boer War in South Africa (1899)
- Freud's *Interpretation of Dreams* (1900)
- Marconi's first transatlantic radiotelegraph message (1901)
- Boer War ends (1902)
- Wright brothers make successful airplane flight (1903)
- Einstein's theory of relativity (1905)
- Picasso's *Les Demoiselles d'Avignon* (1907)
- Stravinsky's *Le Sacre du Printemps* (1913)
- World War I (1914)

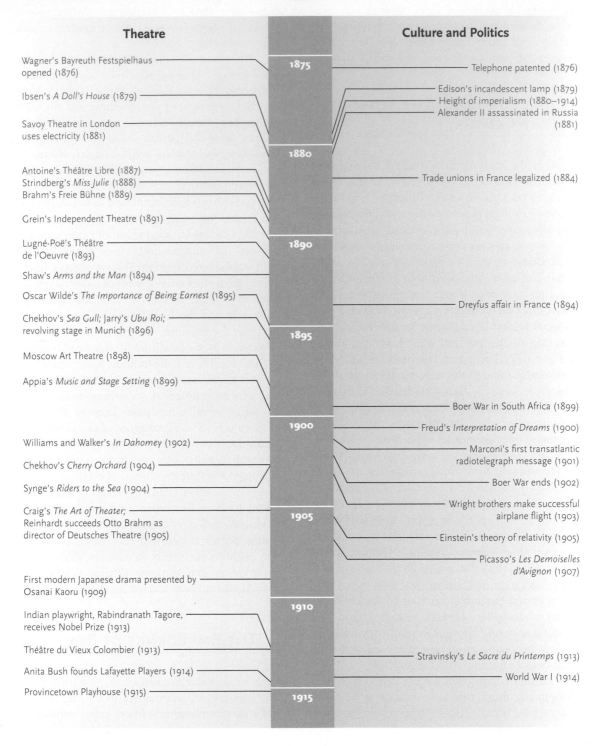

Later in this chapter, we will turn to the second approach; it took various forms which collectively can be called *departures from realism*.

Realistic Drama

What Is Realism?

Realism ushered in modern theatre. Realists sought to convince their audiences that stage action represented everyday life. Unlike drama that featured larger-than-life characters, was written in verse, and had supernatural figures such as witches and ghosts, realistic drama mirrored life. The action onstage resembled what people could observe around them: characters behaved, spoke, and dressed like ordinary people.

This is not, of course, a revolutionary concept for today's audiences, but in the late nineteenth century many theatregoers and critics were scandalized by realism in the theatre. One reason is that realism touched a raw nerve. In the attempt to portray daily life, realists argued, no subject matter should be excluded from the stage. Among the taboo subjects dramatized by realists were economic injustice, the sexual double standard, unhappy marriages, venereal disease, and religious hypocrisy. In fact, many realists believed that the purpose of drama was to call the audience's attention to social problems in order to bring about change.

Furthermore, realists refused to make simple moral judgments or to resolve dramatic action neatly. Unlike popular melodramas, realistic plays frequently implied that morality and immorality were relative—not easy to distinguish or define.

Instead of stock characters, realists created complicated personalities who would seem to have been molded—as real people are—by heredity and environment. The language of these characters was colloquial and conversational. Today's equivalent is the profanity, obscene language, explicit sex, and extreme violence sometimes seen in films, and in plays on television.

For all these reasons, it is not surprising that realists faced a great deal of opposition and were constantly plagued by censorship.

Henrik Ibsen: The Founder of Realism

The Norwegian playwright Henrik Ibsen is often said to be the founder of modern realism. As we will see later in this chapter, he was not a realistic dramatist throughout his career: as a young man, he wrote romantic dramas, and near the end of his career he experimented with abstract symbolist drama. (Another prominent realist, the Swedish dramatist August Strindberg, also later turned away from realism to highly surreal, dreamlike works.)

As a playwright, Henrik Ibsen (1828–1906) is known for his mastery of dramatic technique, his psychological insights into human nature, and his poetic symbolism.

(Norwegian Information Center)

Henrik Ibsen.

For much of his life, Ibsen was an outcast from the society that he dramatized. When he was born in Skien, Norway, in 1828, his father was a prosperous businessman; but in 1834 the business failed, and the family was forced to move outside of town. At 15, Ibsen left home to work as a pharmacist's apprentice; later he tried to qualify for the university. In 1852, at age 24, he became producer at the theatre in Bergen and was commissioned to write one play a year for the theatre's anniversary. While he was a producer at Bergen, he took a study tour of German and Danish theatres.

He moved to Christiania in 1857 to become artistic director of the Norwegian Theatre there. When it went bankrupt, he secured a small government grant and, in 1864, left Norway. For the next 27 years, he would live in Rome, Dresden, and Munich. He returned to Norway in 1891, continuing to work in his careful, methodical way (he allowed himself 2 years to write and polish a play).

Ibsen was incapacitated by a stroke in 1900; after another stroke the following year, he remained an invalid, nearly helpless, until his death in 1906.

Ibsen's earliest plays, based on Norwegian history and mythology, are romantic verse dramas examining the extremes of the Norwegian national character. They include *Lady of Ostraat* (1855), *The Vikings of Helgeland* (1858), *The Pretenders* (1863), *Brand* (1866), and *Peer Gynt* (1867). The plays of his middle period—the realistic social dramas for which he is best-known—explore the interaction of people with society, dealing with such problems as unhappy marriages, the sexual double standard, infidelity, and the position of women. Among these realistic plays are *The Pillars of Society* (1877), *A Doll's House* (1879), *Ghosts* (1881), *An Enemy of the People* (1882), and *Hedda Gabler* (1891). Because of their frank treatment of controversial subject matter, they often provoked angry debate when they were first presented.

While still working in a realistic Norwegian setting, Ibsen moved toward symbolism and mysticism in his last plays. The dramas in this group include *The Wild Duck* (1884), *Rosmersholm* (1886), *The Master Builder* (1892), *John Gabriel Borkman* (1896), *The Lady from the Sea* (1888), and *When We Dead Awaken* (1899). Regardless of their period or style, Ibsen's plays all have a common theme: the individual amid conflicting social pressures.

Ibsen's Realism: A Doll's House

As a realistic playwright, Henrik Ibsen sought to convince his audiences that the stage action in his dramas represented everyday life. But he went farther than that: He felt that drama should tackle subjects that had been taboo in theatre—economic injustice, the sexual double standard, and unhappy marriages, all of which are touched on in *A Doll's House.* (We should note that many contemporary critics and translators suggest that the title *A Doll House* is a more accurate translation and better reflects the thematic issues of the text.)

Ibsen and the realistic dramatists who followed him often insisted that the purpose of drama was to call attention to social problems in order to bring about change. *A Doll's House* uses many traditional elements of the nineteenth-century well-made play, including clearly developed exposition, withheld secrets, and theatrical devices such as a letter. Ibsen, however, subverts the traditional form by refusing to make simple moral judgments or resolve the dramatic action neatly—the norm in the well-made play of the era. Unlike popular well-made melodramas, realistic plays frequently implied that morality and immorality were relative and not clearly distinct or easily defined. Not surprisingly, Ibsen and other realists met a great deal of opposition in producing their plays and were constantly plagued by censorship.

A Doll's House was one of Ibsen's most controversial dramas. The play focuses on Nora, a wife who has saved her husband Torvald's life through an act of forgery. However, she discovers her unequal status in her home when her forgery is revealed in a letter sent to Torvald by a fired employee, Krogstad. Even when Krogstad rescinds

(© Joan Marcus)

MODERN REALISM

Henrik Ibsen addressed serious themes in the format of well-made plays. *A Doll's House* depicted a young woman trapped in a marriage in which she was treated by her husband as an object—a doll—as she had previously been treated by her father. When she innocently gets into trouble over a financial arrangement, her husband does not stand behind her. At the end of the play, to the husband's surprise, she walks out on him. Seen here are Janet McTeer as Nora, the wife; and Owen Teale as her husband, in the Broadway production.

the letter because he is to marry Nora's friend Mrs. Linde, Nora realizes that she can no longer live with Torvald in a relationship in which she is treated like a child. The play closes with Nora leaving her home, slamming the door behind her. Since Ibsen does not let us know what will happen to Nora or Torvald, the enigmatic ending implies an inability to dramatize a neat resolution to such a complex circumstance.

A Doll's House is still frequently produced because it focuses on issues that remain unresolved in the twenty-first century: the role of women in marriage as well as the unequal treatment of women inside and outside the home. Furthermore, the play also dramatizes how the middle-class values held by Torvald strangle Nora's independence. Her husband's concern over reputation, financial status, and appropriate social behavior, as well as his desire to control his wife physically and emotionally, imprison Nora within her home. Nora's sense of entrapment is heightened by her growing sense of self-determination. The "doll's house" becomes a metaphor for the constraints society places upon women. When Nora slams the door, her act signaled the call for the kinds of revolutionary changes that would be demanded at the end

THE LOWER DEPTHS BY MAKSIM GORKY
Shown here is a scene from the Moscow Art Theatre's original production of Gorky's famous naturalistic drama. In the center is Konstantin Stanislavski, the renowned actor, director, and theorist of realistic acting. *The Lower Depths,* set in a turn-of-the-century Russian flophouse, is an example of naturalism as defined by the French theorist Émile Zola.

(Sovfoto)

of the nineteenth century and throughout the twentieth.

Naturalistic Drama

Closely related to realism is naturalism, a movement that began in France in the nineteenth century and spread to other European countries. Naturalism can be seen as a subdivision of realism—an extreme form. As a pure movement it did not last long, but some of its ideas appeared frequently in later dramas as well as in films and on television.

The French writer Émile Zola (1840–1902) is probably the most famous proponent of naturalism. Zola espoused "scientific objectivity," the idea that an artist should present a picture of the real world without making his or her own presence felt. The best-known naturalistic dramas from this era are Zola's *Thérèse Raquin* (1881); two plays, *Before Sunrise* (1887) and *The Weavers* (Germany, 1892), by Gerhart Hauptmann (1862–1946); and *The Lower Depths* (Russia, 1902) by Maksim Gorky (1868–1936).

The naturalists argued that what should be presented onstage is a "slice of life": events should be shown as if they were sliced from a time continuum, without the selection, editing, and rearrangement that ordinarily occur in playwriting. Because the naturalists wanted the controlling hand of the artist to remain unseen, they argued against stage contrivances. Instead, the artist should function as an objective scientist; everything onstage—characters, language, properties, settings, costumes—should seem to have been lifted directly from everyday life. Authenticity was the basic requirement. (An analogous art form 100 years later was documentary film.)

Many naturalists believed that the most appropriate subject matter for drama was the lower class. The naturalists frequently focused on sordid and seamy aspects of society, to call attention to social problems and initiate reforms. Gorky's *The Lower Depths,* for example, presents characters who have sunk to the bottom of Russian society. Most naturalistic dramas present a series of episodes demonstrating the control that environment and our own animal desires have over us. For this reason, naturalistic works seem more loosely structured than realistic works.

Naturalism in theatre is a more stringent form than realism. One reason is its insistence on showing the stark side of life; the other is its attempt to be like a documentary, which means that its action cannot be shaped by the same kind of artistic techniques used in realism. Realism can use symbols and can structure events in a way that is often more aesthetically satisfying. In fact, the naturalists' extreme position ultimately prevented their movement from being more influential; realism was seen as a more viable theatrical form. Nonetheless, the naturalist movement helped to further the development of theatre dedicated to reproducing life onstage, and its influence can be seen in plays like Eugene O'Neill's *The Iceman Cometh* (United States, 1939) and David Storey's *The Changing Room* (England, 1971).

A modern parallel to this kind of naturalism is found in film documentaries, sometimes called *cinema verité,* of people who live wretched lives in squalid conditions: a film about a homeless man, for example, who sleeps in doorways and exists on scraps, or a film about people in a desert country suffering the effects of drought and famine. Other modern counterparts of naturalism would include "reality TV" in which television shows, such as *Survivor* and *Real World,* depict situations that are supposed to be "real" and unrehearsed—in other words, close to life. Still another example would be the use of webcam on the Internet to show people's daily lives.

Producers of Realism and Naturalism

There were both legal and commercial barriers to the production of realistic and naturalistic drama. In countries where theatre was censored, realists often could not get their dramas staged at all; in England, for example, the lord chamberlain refused to license many of these works. Even in countries with no official censorship, such as the United States, legal problems could still arise: in 1905, a production in Brooklyn of George Bernard Shaw's realistic play *Mrs. Warren's Profession* led to the arrest of the entire cast. Moreover, because realistic drama was so controversial, the theatre establishment did not consider it commercially viable.

In order to produce realistic and naturalistic drama, a number of independent theatres were established throughout Europe. These theatres were exempt from government censorship because they were organized as subscription companies, regarding their audiences almost like members of a private club. Also, the independent theatres were not striving for commercial success—rather, their objective was to present new dramatic forms to the small audiences who were interested in them. Some of these theatres also used realistic production techniques. In Europe, the four major independent theatres were the Théâtre Libre in France, Freie Bühne in Germany, Independent Theatre in England, and Moscow Art Theatre in Russia.

Théâtre Libre

The Théâtre Libre, or "Free Theatre," was founded in Paris in 1887 by André Antoine (1858–1943). At that time, Antoine was a clerk with a gas company and a member of an amateur theatre group. When he suggested that the group produce a one-act adaptation of a short story by Zola, the other members refused. Undaunted, Antoine rented a theatre and organized another company to present the work. From this modest beginning, the Théâtre Libre would go on to revolutionize French theatre, introducing Parisian audiences to major realistic and naturalistic playwrights like Zola, Ibsen, and Henri Becque (1837–1899).

By applying many of the illusionistic stage practices previously used by Madame Vestris and the duke of Saxe-Meiningen, Antoine popularized theatrical realism.

Antoine strove to create the illusion of a "fourth wall" so that audiences would seem to be peeking in on everyday life. His stage settings, individually designed for each production, were box sets filled with practicable elements. As part of his concern with illusionism, he used *motivated lighting*—illumination of the stage picture that seems to come from actual onstage sources, such as a table lamp. Like Richard Wagner in the Bayreuth Festspielhaus, Antoine extinguished the house lights to focus attention on the stage. (We should note, however, that Antoine also produced—though unsuccessfully—some plays which departed from realistic stage techniques.)

Antoine also transformed French stage acting. Arguing against the star system, as typified by Sarah Bernhardt and Constant-Benoît Coquelin (1841–1909), Antoine organized a company of amateur actors who worked to create ensemble performances. Ensemble acting requires balanced casting and integration of all performances, and it never allows a star to overshadow supporting players. In striving for an ensemble, he was following the example of the duke of Saxe-Meiningen. Antoine also believed that an actor should appear to be living—not acting—onstage, and accordingly he was opposed to conventional gestures, vocal patterns, and blocking.

Antoine transformed business practices by selling subscriptions to develop loyal audiences and financial support. His impact on modern French theatre can be seen in his later career. He left the financially troubled Théâtre Libre in 1894 and 3 years later founded the Théâtre Antoine. More significantly, in 1906 he was appointed head of the Odéon, France's second national theatre, an indication that by the first decade of the new century realism had become an accepted movement in France. Antoine's influence could also be seen in German and English independent theatres.

Freie Bühne

Two years after Antoine's Théâtre Libre was founded, the Freie Bühne, or "Free Stage," began in Berlin. Like Antoine's company, it was a subscription theatre dedicated to introducing realism and naturalism. The Freie Bühne was noted for its productions of the plays of Ibsen and the German naturalist Gerhart Hauptmann.

Though both were noncommercial, there were differences between the Théâtre Libre and the Freie Bühne. The Freie Bühne was operated by a board of directors, with Otto Brahm (1856–1912) as its chairman. Antoine, by contrast, was the dictatorial director of his company. Also, the Freie Bühne employed professional actors and therefore could perform only on Sundays, when its performers were not otherwise engaged; for this reason, it paid less attention to production details. In addition, the Théâtre Libre rented small, out-of-the-way Parisian theatres whereas the Freie Bühne rented professional houses.

The Freie Bühne ceased regular operations in 1891 but continued to produce occasional noteworthy dramas to which the German government had denied permission. For example, in 1892 the Freie Bühne was revived to produce Hauptmann's *The Weavers.* Brahm's success with the Freie Bühne was reflected in his appointment, in 1894, as director of Berlin's Deutsches Theatre.

The Independent Theatre

The English Independent Theatre, which was founded in 1891 by the Dutch-born critic Jacob Thomas Grein (1862–1935) and operated in London for 6 years, was organized as a subscription company to circumvent censorship by the lord chamberlain. The Independent Theatre was run much like the Freie Bühne: it hired professional actors, leased professional theatres, and performed on Sundays. Grein's goal was to introduce realists and naturalists, including Ibsen and Zola, to the English public. The company's first production was Ibsen's *Ghosts,* which received disparaging reviews.

In 1892, the Independent Theatre introduced the Irish-born George Bernard Shaw to the London public by producing his first play, *Widower's Houses.* As a theatre critic, Shaw defended the realists and naturalists, and he believed that drama should inspire social reform. Unlike the works of other realists, however, many of Shaw's socially conscious dramas are comedies. In Shaw's hands, subjects that most realists saw as gloomy and tragic became objects of satirical ridicule. When the Independent Theatre ceased operating in 1897, Shaw's works were staged by other independently organized English companies, including the Incorporated Stage Society and the Royal Court Theatre, which was run by John Vedrenne (1863–1930) and Harley Granville-Barker (1877–1945), himself an actor and playwright.

GEORGE BERNARD SHAW

If George Bernard Shaw (1856–1950) had died before his fortieth birthday, he would have been remembered—if at all—as a somewhat eccentric ne'er-do-well who let his mother support him, published five unsuccessful novels, and was a vegetarian and a Fabian socialist. It was only after a friend, the critic William Archer, got him jobs as a book reviewer and an art critic that Shaw was able to make effective use of his abilities as a writer.

(Theatre Collection, Museum of the City of New York)

George Bernard Shaw.

Shaw spent his years of unemployment developing his intellect and his writing style. He had been born in Dublin, Ireland, of English parents, and had been an indifferent student who wanted to pursue his own interests in art, music, and literature. At age 16, he was working as a clerk in a land agent's office. His mother had left his father—an alcoholic—and was living in London, teaching music. Shaw joined her in 1876. He read widely, wrote extensively on political issues for the Fabian Society (a socialist organization), and became a noted political speaker.

In 1895, Shaw became the theatre critic for the magazine *Saturday Review.* His commentaries, later published in book form as *Our Theatre in the Nineties,* set a new standard of excellence in dramatic criticism. He championed the new realistic theatre, particularly the plays of Ibsen, and condemned the stale commercial theatre of the time. Finding no English drama that reflected his views, he began writing his own plays to convey his ideas on political and social reform.

Shaw's first plays were produced privately for small, selected audiences to circumvent the censor, but in 1898 he published them as *Plays Pleasant and Unpleasant.* With this collection, Shaw began his practice of writing long prefaces discussing issues raised in his plays. He also provided stage directions to help readers visualize the plays.

Though most of Shaw's plays took up social problems and philosophical concepts, they were also witty, engaging comedies with lively dialogue and unusual, well-drawn characters. They could be characterized as realistic comedies of manners. Among the best-known are *Candida* (1895), *Caesar and Cleopatra* (1899), *Major Barbara* (1905), *Man and Superman* (1903), and *Saint Joan* (1923).

Shaw was awarded the Nobel Prize for literature in 1925. In his later years, his plays became more philosophical and less interesting dramatically. He was also

(© Austrian Archives/Corbis)

CHEKHOV AND THE MOSCOW ART THEATRE

A key figure at the beginning of the modern theatre was the Russian playwright Anton Chekhov. His plays, which depicted the Russian upper and middle class at a time of significant transition, were written with great subtlety and lyricism. His four major plays were all presented by the Moscow Art Theatre, directed by Konstantin Stanislavski. He is seen in this photograph from 1899 (at the center, holding the book) reading his play *The Sea Gull* to the cast of the production.

in disfavor socially and politically because of his attitude toward war in plays like *Heartbreak House* (1914–1919)—he considered war a useless enterprise—and his later occasional praise of Mussolini and Hitler. (However, he did write a play attacking all twentieth-century totalitarianism, the late play *Geneva.*) Greatly saddened by the death of his wife in 1943, he himself lived only 7 more years. On October 31, 1950, he announced, "I am going to die," and 3 days later he did.

Moscow Art Theatre

No doubt the most influential of the late-nineteenth-century theatres dedicated to realism was the Moscow Art Theatre, which was founded in 1898 by Konstantin Stanislavski and Vladimir Nemirovich-Danchenko (1858–1943) and continues to produce drama today. The production style of the Moscow Art Theatre was originally influenced by the duke of Saxe-Meiningen, but a turning point came as early as its first season, with the production of *The Sea Gull.*

This play premiered on December 17, 1898, and there was considerable trepidation among members of the Moscow Art Theatre as to how it might fare. The author, Anton Chekhov, was one of the best-known short-story writers in Russia; but when *The Sea Gull* was first performed 2 years previously in Saint Petersburg, it was a fiasco. The company in Saint Petersburg did not understand Chekhov's innovative dramatic techniques and had barely rehearsed the play. To make matters worse, the audience had come to the theatre that night hoping to see a favorite actress, a large woman who performed broad comic parts. When they discovered that she was not in the play, they began to hiss and yell, drowning out the dialogue. Chekhov had disappeared during the last act, and when the play was over he left the theatre in despair to walk the streets of Saint Petersburg most of the night. He was so devastated by the whole experience that he swore he would never again write for the theatre or let his plays be performed.

One reason why the production in Saint Petersburg failed so badly is that *The Sea Gull* was very different from any of the plays the actors were accustomed to performing. It takes place on a country estate in Russia and tells the story of two generations of actresses and writers. One of the main characters is Madame Arkadina, a vain, self-absorbed actress. Her son Treplev is an idealistic young writer in love with Nina, a young woman who aspires to be an actress. But Nina falls in love with Arkadina's lover, Trigorin, a successful writer dissatisfied with his life (Stanislavski played this role in Moscow).

A number of other people are involved with these four main characters, and one of the unusual features of the play is the way their lives are all closely intertwined. Another unusual feature is that the play has no melodramatic developments or confrontations. Sudden plot twists such as murders, suicides, and reversals of fortune were staples of nineteenth-century drama, but in Chekhov's play the action and the characters are understated and carefully modulated. This makes the characters much more lifelike, but it also calls for understanding and flexibility on the part of the actors—demands that are not made by traditional, stereotypical roles.

The same qualities that confused the Saint Petersburg company, however, attracted the playwright and producer Vladimir Nemirovich-Danchenko. He and Stanislavski wanted their theatre to be different from any other, and Nemirovich-Danchenko felt that *The Sea Gull* was just the kind of play to set it apart. At first, Chekhov refused to let the Moscow Art Theatre present *The Sea Gull* because of the debacle in Saint Petersburg; it took all of Nemirovich-Danchenko's powers of persuasion to win him over. Chekhov himself was so uneasy about the outcome on the first night in Moscow that he was not even present but far away in Yalta—partly because of ill health, but also because of his nervousness.

Halfway through Act I, the actors in Moscow could not tell how the audience was responding; when the act ended, they were greeted by a monumental silence. The actress Olga Knipper (who later became Chekhov's wife) fought desperately to keep from breaking into hysterical sobs. Then, all of a sudden, the silence was broken—there was thunderous, tumultuous applause. One member of the audience later wrote: "Like the bursting of a dam, like an exploding bomb, a sudden deafening eruption of applause broke out." The applause went on and on, and Stanislavski danced a jig.

The same reaction greeted the next three acts; both Chekhov and the Moscow Art Theatre had triumphed, and a new chapter in modern theatre had begun. The drama of Anton Chekhov, with Stanislavski's carefully realized realistic productions, would establish the company's reputation. So significant was the event that to this day the symbol on the curtain of the Moscow Art Theatre is a sea gull.

ANTON PAVLOVICH CHEKHOV

When he first arrived in Saint Petersburg in 1885 to finish his medical studies, Anton Chekhov (1860–1904) was astonished to discover that he was already a famous writer—the short stories that he had been writing casually to support his family and pay for his education had been highly acclaimed. As a result, he resolved to improve his work habits and concentrate on literature as a career.

(Bettmann/Corbis)
Anton Chekhov.

As a schoolboy in Taganrog, Russia, Chekhov had acted and written for the local theatre. During his last years in school, his father, a grocer, went bankrupt, and the family fled to Moscow to escape its creditors. Chekhov's literary sketches, written for magazines in Moscow and Saint Petersburg, helped him support the family and continue his medical studies. He did finish medical school, but because of his literary career he never entered active practice.

In 1887, Chekhov's first successful play, *Ivanov,* was produced in Moscow. (An earlier drama, *Platonov,* written while he was a student, had been rejected by the Moscow theatres.) Two one-act comedies—*The Bear* (1888) and *The Marriage Proposal* (1888)—were produced successfully; but his play *The Wood Demon,* influenced by Tolstoy's philosophy, was a failure in 1889. Chekhov also wrote several short farces—or "jokes," as he called them—in his late twenties. These early works are very different from his later dramas in structure and action, but they show his interest in ordinary incidents of middle-class provincial life and in the outside forces that change people's lives. Particularly in the farces, he was able to draw characters swiftly and insightfully and to intertwine comedy and tragedy.

It was 7 years before Chekhov's next play, *The Sea Gull,* was produced. During this time, he perfected his dramatic technique, relying on indirect action and character development to create tension. Like complex music, his plays have a variety of themes, and these themes are developed through many characters and images.

As we have seen, the first production of *The Sea Gull* was hardly a success, but the production by the Moscow Art Theatre was acclaimed. The Moscow Art Theatre also produced Chekhov's next three plays, *Uncle Vanya* (1899), *The Three Sisters* (1900), and *The Cherry Orchard* (1904). These too were successful, though Chekhov berated Stanislavski—who had directed all four—for neglecting the humor in them.

Chekhov's plays are significant not only as realism but also as perfect examples of modern tragicomedy. We have already seen that in some earlier periods of theatre history, such as Elizabethan England, comic scenes—like the grave diggers' scene in *Hamlet*—might occur in tragic plays, but they would be separated from the serious scenes. In modern tragicomedy, the tragic and the comic are blended; these plays are bittersweet. Comedy does not provide a contrast but rather increases our awareness of the tragic circumstances.

Sharpening the sense of tragedy in Chekhov's plays is the fact that his tragicomic characters are unable to fulfill their deepest desires. In *The Cherry Orchard,* Madame Ranevsky and her family lose their beloved country home, with its or-

(Sovfoto)

CHEKHOV'S UNCLE VANYA
The Moscow Art Theatre, famous for realism, is also known as the home of Chekhov's plays. *Uncle Vanya,* one of Chekhov's realistic tragicomedies, was first produced by the Moscow Art Theatre in 1899; it was directed by Konstantin Stanislavski. This production photo of *Uncle Vanya* was taken for the company's fiftieth anniversary in 1948.

chard, to Lopakhin, whose father was a serf—the play reflects the changing class structure of turn-of-the-century Russia. The members of the aristocratic family are often comic in their inability to save the orchard. For example, Varya—Madame Ranevsky's eldest daughter—and Lopakhin seem destined to marry, and their marriage would keep the orchard in the family. In the final act, Varya and Lopakhin are left alone so that he can propose. Instead, they are unable to discuss their feelings. The "nonproposal scene" is quite funny, because she is fumbling with luggage while he is discussing the weather, but after it is over we realize that the last chance to save the beloved orchard has been lost. Part of Chekhov's genius is his ability to make us see that underneath comedy there is often tragedy.

Chekhov had contracted tuberculosis when he was 23, and in the last years of his life was forced to leave his estate outside Moscow and move south to Yalta for the sake of his health. In 1901, he married Olga Knipper, an actress with the Moscow Art Theatre. He was elected to the Russian Academy of Science but resigned when his friend the writer Maksim Gorky was expelled. Chekhov died in 1904 at Badenweiler, Germany, where he had gone in another attempt to regain his health.

Realistic Acting

Konstantin Sergeivich Stanislavski: The Pioneer

The most famous system for training performers to act realistically—that is, to be believable—was developed by Konstantin Stanislavski (1863–1938), who was the cofounder of the Moscow Art Theatre and the director of Chekhov's major plays. Recollecting his early career, Stanislavski wrote: "Herein lies the problem, to bring life itself upon the stage."

(The New York Times)

Konstantin Sergeivich Stanislavski.

Konstantin Stanislavski's father was an industrialist, but his grandmother (who was French) had been an actress, and at 15 Stanislavski founded the Alekseev Circle, an amateur group consisting of many of members of his family. (Alekseev was his family's surname; Stanislavski was his stage name.) He attended a theatrical school and observed contemporary actors before studying with F. P. Komissarzhevsky, a dramatist and producer.

In 1888, he and Komissarzhevsky founded another amateur group, the Society of Art and Literature, which became noted for its productions of works by Tolstoy and Dostoyevsky. When the Meiningen players visited Russia, Stanislavski was fascinated by their realistic staging and modeled his own productions after theirs, but he sought to substitute realism in acting for their declamatory, or oratorical, style.

In 1898, the playwright V. I. Nemirovich-Danchenko, director of the drama school of the Moscow Philharmonic Society, invited Stanislavski to join him in forming a new theatre, which they called the Moscow Art Theatre. Nemirovich-Danchenko was responsible for literary and administrative duties while Stanislavski handled staging and production. With the Moscow Art Theatre, Stanislavski was able to refine his system of realistic acting.

The Moscow Art Theatre had early successes with productions of Tolstoy, but as we have seen, it became famous for its productions of Chekhov's plays. Stanislavski created many of the leading roles, including Trigorin in *The Sea Gull,* Doctor Astrov in *Uncle Vanya,* and Gaev in *The Cherry Orchard.*

Though most of his work was with realistic drama, Stanislavski also staged the symbolist plays of Maeterlinck and Andreyev and encouraged the work of other antirealist theatre artists. He worked with the designer Edward Gordon Craig (who will be discussed later in this chapter) on an experimental production of *Hamlet.* The leaders of Russian avant-garde theatre of the 1920s—Meyerhold, Vakhtangov, and Tairov—all worked with the Moscow Art Theatre early in their careers.

After the Russian Revolution, the Moscow Art Theatre confined itself to realism. Stanislavski himself was no longer acting, because of poor health, but he continued to develop his acting system until his death in 1938. Stanislavski's books explaining his system have been published in English as *An Actor Prepares, Building a Character,* and *Creating a Role.* He also wrote an informative memoir, *My Life in Art.*

The Stanislavskian Technique

Before the realistic drama of the late 1800s, no one had devised a method for achieving true-to-life believability onstage. Through their own talent and genius, individual actresses and actors had achieved it, but no one had developed a system whereby it could be taught to others and passed on to future generations. The person who eventually did this most successfully was Konstantin Stanislavski.

We might assume that believable acting is simply a matter of being natural; but Stanislavski discovered first of all that acting realistically onstage is extremely artificial and difficult. He wrote:

> All of our acts, even the simplest, which are so familiar to us in everyday life, become strained when we appear behind the footlights before a public of a thousand people. That is why it is necessary to correct ourselves and learn again how to walk, sit, or lie down. It is essential to reeducate ourselves to look and see, on the stage, to listen and to hear.[1]

To achieve this "reeducation," Stanislavski said, "the actor must first of all believe in everything that takes place onstage, and most of all, he must believe what he himself is doing. And one can believe only in the truth." To give substance to his ideas, Stanislavski studied how people acted in everyday life and how they communicated feelings and emotions; and then he found ways to accomplish the same things onstage. He developed a series of exercises and techniques for the actor which had the following broad aims:

1. To make the outward behavior of the performer—gestures, voice, and rhythm of movements—natural and convincing.
2. To have the actor or actress convey the goals and objectives—the inner needs—of a character. Even if all the visible manifestations of a character are mastered, a performance will appear superficial and mechanical without a deep sense of conviction and belief.
3. To make the life of the character onstage not only dynamic but also continuous. Some performers tend to emphasize only the high points of a part; in between, the life of the character stops. In real life, however, people do not stop living.
4. To develop a strong sense of ensemble playing with other performers in a scene.

Let us examine Stanislavski's techniques more closely.

RELAXATION When he observed the great actors and actresses of his day, Stanislavski noticed how fluid and lifelike their movements were. They seemed to be in a state of complete freedom and relaxation, letting the behavior of the character come through effortlessly. He concluded that unwanted tension has to be eliminated and that the performer must at all times attain a state of physical and vocal relaxation.

CONCENTRATION AND OBSERVATION Stanislavski also discovered that gifted performers always appeared fully concentrated on some object, person, or event while onstage. Stanislavski referred to the extent or range of concentration as a *circle of attention.* This circle of attention can be compared to a circle of light on a darkened stage. The performer should begin with the idea that it is a small, tight circle including only himself or herself and perhaps one other person or one piece of furniture.

IMPORTANCE OF SPECIFICS One of Stanislavski's techniques was an emphasis on concrete details. A performer should never try to act in general, he said, and should never try to convey a feeling such as fear or love in some vague, amorphous way. In life, Stanislavski said, we express emotions in terms of specifics: an anxious woman twists a handkerchief, an angry boy throws a rock at a trash can, a nervous businessman

[1] Konstantin Stanislavski, *An Actor Prepares,* Theatre Arts, New York, 1948, p. 73.

jangles his keys. Performers must find similar concrete activities. Stanislavski points out how Shakespeare has Lady Macbeth in her sleepwalking scene—at the height of her guilt and emotional upheaval—try to rub blood off her hands.

The performer must also conceive of the situation in which a character exists—what Stanislavski referred to as the *given circumstances*—in terms of specifics. In what kind of space does an event take place: formal, informal, public, domestic? How does it feel? What is the temperature? The lighting? What has gone on just before? What is expected in the moments ahead? Again, these questions must be answered in concrete terms.

INNER TRUTH An innovative aspect of Stanislavski's work has to do with inner truth, which deals with the internal or subjective world of characters—that is, their thoughts and emotions. The early phases of Stanislavski's research took place while he was also directing the major dramas of Anton Chekhov. Plays like *The Sea Gull* and *The Cherry Orchard* have less to do with external action or what the characters say than with what the characters are feeling and thinking but often do not verbalize.

Stanislavski had several ideas about how to achieve a sense of inner truth, one being the "magic if." *If* is a word which can transform our thoughts; through it we can imagine ourselves in virtually any situation. "*If* I suddenly became wealthy . . ." "*If* that person who insulted me comes near me again . . ." The word *if* becomes a lever for the mind; it can lift us out of ourselves and give us a sense of absolute certainty about imaginary circumstances.

WHAT? WHY? HOW? Another important principle of Stanislavski's system is that all action onstage must have a purpose. This means that the performer's attention must always be focused on a series of physical actions (also called *psychophysical actions*) linked together by the circumstances of the play. Stanislavski determined these actions by asking three essential questions: What? Why? How? An action is performed, such as opening a letter (the *what*). The letter is opened because someone has said that it contains extremely damaging information about the character (the *why*). The letter is opened anxiously, fearfully (the *how*), because of the calamitous effect it might have on the character. These physical actions, which occur from moment to moment, are in turn governed by the character's overall objective in the play.

THROUGH LINE OF A ROLE According to Stanislavski, in order to develop continuity in a part, the actor or actress should find the *superobjective* of a character. What is it, above all else, that the character wants during the course of the play? What is the character's driving force? If a goal can be established toward which the character strives, it will give the performer an overall objective. From this objective can be developed a through line. Another term for *through line* is *spine.*

To help develop the through line, Stanislavski urged performers to divide scenes into units (sometimes called *beats*). In each unit there is an objective, and the intermediate objectives running through a play lead ultimately to the overall objective.

ENSEMBLE PLAYING Except in one-person shows, performers do not act alone; they interact with other people. Stanislavski was aware that many performers tend to "stop acting," or lose their concentration, when they are not the main characters in a scene or when someone else is talking. Such performers make a great effort

(© T. Charles Erickson)

CHEKHOV AND ENSEMBLE PERFORMING

One feature of Anton Chekhov's plays is the emphasis on a group of characters that interact, not just on one or two leading characters. This requires ensemble performances from the actors. Shown here is a scene from Chekhov's *The Three Sisters* as produced at the Yale School of Drama.

when they are speaking but not when they are listening. This tendency destroys the through line and causes the performer to move into and out of a role. That, in turn, weakens the sense of ensemble—the playing together of all the performers.

Stanislavski and Psychophysical Action

Stanislavski began to develop his technique in the early twentieth century, and at first he emphasized the inner aspects of training: for example, various ways of getting in touch with the performer's unconscious. Beginning around 1917, however, he began to look more and more at purposeful action, or what he called *psychophysical action.* A student at one of his lectures that year took note of the change: "Whereas action previously had been taught as the expression of a previously-established 'emotional state,' it is now action itself which predominates and is the key to the psychological."[2]

Rather than seeing emotions as leading to action, Stanislavski came to believe that it was the other way around: he held that purposeful action undertaken to fulfill a character's goals was the most direct route to the emotions. When an action is performed as a result of the given circumstances in a play to bring about a change in the dramatic situation, emotion will follow. Because physical or purposeful action is the key, a well-trained body and vocal instrument are indispensable. This is borne out in Stanislavski's last two books to be translated in English, *Building a Character* and *Creating a Role,* in which he stressed the importance of an extremely well-developed

[2]Jean Benedetti, *Stanislavski,* Routledge, New York, 1988, p. 217.

and responsive instrument. This in turn is developed by means of techniques and exercises.

Stanislavski's influence on modern theatre cannot be overstated. Most actors in the United States today are trained with some variation of the Stanislavskian system. There have been alterations and adaptations of his system, but through it all his work remains pervasive.

Visual Elements in Realistic Theatre

For visual elements in realistic theatre, the goal was the same as for scripts and acting: to make every feature as much like everyday life as possible. To this end, costumes, lighting, and sets—the rooms the characters lived in—were to correspond to what audiences observed in their own lives. Characters' clothing duplicated that of real people from the same social station or occupation; and the lighting in a room would not seem to come from arbitrary spotlights or floodlights, but would be made to appear to come from a lamp on a table, say, or from sunshine coming through a window.

In his preface to *Miss Julie,* August Strindberg insisted that the pots and pans in the kitchen where the play takes place should be real, not painted on a piece of canvas as traditionally they would have been. Not surprisingly, the scenery in late-nineteenth-century realistic drama most often took the form of a box set, an arrangement that closely simulates a room in a home. This was closed in on three sides—sometimes with a ceiling—and was meant to be as lifelike as possible.

Early Departures from Realism

As we have noted, it can be said that the two basic theatrical trends of the past hundred years are realism and departures from realism. Between 1875 and 1915, there were many nonrealistic experimenters opposed to the concept of showing a "slice of life" onstage. Among dramatists, these included the symbolists and others—like Ibsen and Strindberg—who are not easily categorized. There were also nonrealist approaches to theatre production.

Symbolism

The leading antirealistic movement between 1880 and 1910 was symbolism. While its major proponents were French, symbolism influenced playwrights and other theatre artists throughout the world.

Symbolist drama was part of a deliberate reaction against the realistic theatre of the late nineteenth century. The well-made play, which had become predominant in so much theatre of the time, relied on suspenseful, often complex plots with recognizable actions and characters who strongly resembled those in everyday life. The symbolists turned away from literal realism and from dependence on events that mirrored observable life. They sought to replace these with the revelation and depiction of inner life.

Symbolist drama had almost no plot action; rather, it often took the form of lyric drama. It was static, indirect, evocative, and often ceremonial. It attempted to get at the inexpressible and the ineffable: those things that cannot be presented literally but must be suggested by symbols, metaphor, poetry, and music. There was a strong element of mysticism and spirituality in attempts at symbolist drama.

The chief influences on symbolist playwrights were the opera composer Richard Wagner, with his emphasis on myth; and the poet and critic Stéphane Mallarmé (1842–1898), who offered the dictum: "Depict, not the object, but the effect which it produces."

(© Corbis)

SYMBOLIST DRAMA A champion of symbolist theatre was the Belgian playwright Maurice Maeterlinck. He argued that theatre should depict not outward reality but inner feelings and moods—"shadows, reflections, projections of symbolic forms." Shown here is a poster for an early production of one of his most successful plays, *Pelléas et Mélisande.*

One of the leading symbolist playwrights was Villiers de L'Isle-Adam (1838–1889). His most important play was *Axel.* A loose, discursive, sprawling play, it tells the story of Axel, who leads a life of self-imposed exile in the Black Forest. Axel kills his worldly cousin Kaspar in a duel and later meets an ethereal creature, Sara, who is deeply committed to the occult. Axel and Sara are drawn to each other. In the end, at dawn on Easter day, these two confirm their love in a double suicide.

It is generally felt that the most successful symbolist dramatist was Maurice Maeterlinck (1862–1949). Maeterlinck argued that theatre should present not outward reality but "a shadow, a reflection, a projection of symbolic forms." He attempted to do this in such plays as *The Intruder* (1891), *The Blind* (1891), and *Pelléas and Mélisande* (1893). *The Intruder* particularly illustrates Maeterlinck's dramatic approach. The intruder of the title is death. Throughout the play there is a sense of foreboding and impending doom, which is heightened by a number of devices such as birds suddenly falling silent, the mysterious opening and closing of doors, and the arbitrary and unexpected dimming of lights. The play concentrates on atmosphere, and the characters are subjected to a feeling of suspense and eerie anticipation. At the same time, as in so much symbolist drama, there is little or no action.

The lack of action was one reason why the most successful symbolist plays were usually short works, and also why the movement never became widespread. One of the final plays bearing the stamp of symbolism was *The Tidings Brought to Mary* (1921) by Paul Claudel (1868–1955).

Departures from Realism: Wedekind, Ibsen, and Strindberg

It is difficult to categorize many of the authors who wrote dramas between 1880 and 1910. Even the symbolists tended to be highly individual in style, and some playwrights wrote both realistic and antirealistic drama or even mixed the two.

One turn-of-the-century German playwright who is not easy to classify was Benjamin Franklin Wedekind (1864–1918). Wedekind's plays, such as *Spring's Awakening*

(1891), combine symbolist and grotesque elements with realistic—sometimes controversial—subject matter. *Spring's Awakening,* for instance, deals with adolescent sexuality, and even today there have been protests when it is produced. Wedekind himself was a controversial figure who created and performed cabaret acts which were apparently sexually provocative and even obscene. Another German who broke from realism during this period was the playwright Hugo von Hofmannsthal (1874–1929). His initial dramatic work consisted of short plays, but around the turn of the century he began reworking classic pieces such as *Elektra* (1903) and *Everyman* (1912). In collaboration with the composer Richard Strauss, he also wrote librettos for the operas *Der Rosenkavalier* (1911) and *Ariadne auf Naxos* (1912).

Two important playwrights who were influenced by symbolism but whose works defy facile categorization are Henrik Ibsen and August Strindberg: both are remembered for their realistic plays, but late in their careers they moved away from realism. As we have seen, in *The Master Builder, Little Eyolf, John Gabriel Borkman,* and *When We Dead Awaken,* Ibsen followed many symbolist tenets. August Strindberg's later antirealistic dramas have been more influential than Ibsen's. The two best-known are *A Dream Play* (1902) and *The Ghost Sonata* (1907).

As its title indicates, *A Dream Play* evokes the world of a dream. We see a Christlike goddess, the Daughter of Indra, journeying through a variety of human situations and experiencing continual suffering. The scenes are not always causally related but rather are a series of stages or—to emphasize the Christian imagery—"stations" in the journey. Time, place, and characters are transformed suddenly and unexpectedly. Characters such as the Officer, the Attorney, the Poet, He, She, and the Dean of Philosophy are representatives, not individuals, and are referred to by titles or pronouns rather than names. Symbols abound: a castle grows out of a dunghill; a shawl holds all human suffering; two lands are referred to as Foulgut and Fairhaven; the Attorney's face has become hideously lined by the torment of those who have engaged him. In *A Dream Play,* Strindberg deals with many of the concerns found in his realistic dramas—the destructiveness of marriage, materialism, and the class struggle—but he dramatizes these concerns, as he says in the preface, in "the incoherent but outwardly logical form of dreams. Anything can occur; everything is possible; everything is probable."

AUGUST STRINDBERG

August Strindberg (1849–1912) was the son of a steamship agent and a former waitress and servant. He had an unhappy, insecure childhood, and his youthful unhappiness was a prelude to a troubled adulthood that included frequent episodes of mental illness; but he was able to use these experiences as a basis for his writings.

After some intermittent study at the University of Uppsala in Sweden, Strindberg returned to Stockholm and worked as a teacher, librarian, and journalist while revising *Master Olaf* (1872), his first play. In 1875, when he was 26, he met Siri von Essen, whom he married in 1877. Their stormy marriage, which lasted until 1891, provided many situations for his novels and plays, especially the dramas *The Father* (1887) and *Miss Julie* (1888). In 1884 Strindberg was prosecuted for blasphemy because of the publication of *Married,* a collection of his stories. This increased his paranoia and his dislike for Sweden, and as a result he spent much time abroad, particularly in Paris, until 1897.

(Theatre Collection, Museum of the City of New York)

August Strindberg.

When his second marriage failed in 1894, he went through a period of severe stress and mental instability—often referred to as his "inferno crisis," after *Inferno,* his autobiography of this time in his life. He then underwent a conversion to religious mysticism. His plays written after 1897—such as *To Damascus* (1898) and *A Dream Play* (1902)—were expressionistic, using symbolism and unrealistic shifts in action, and were steeped in his new beliefs. The plays from this period would influence the surrealist movement and, later, theatre of the absurd.

Several of Strindberg's late plays deal with events in Swedish history—a possible reflection of his return to Stockholm in 1899. In Stockholm, Strindberg, who was again embracing the radical ideas of his youth, wrote many social and political treatises for the press. In 1902 he married Harriet Bosse, a young actress, but the marriage failed in 1904.

Some of Strindberg's most experimental and influential plays were written for the Intimate Theatre in Stockholm, which he and August Falck ran for a time. His chamber plays, like *The Ghost Sonata* (1907), reflected his interest in music, particularly Beethoven, and showed a preoccupation with removing facades to reveal grotesque elements beneath the surface. (*Chamber plays* are analogous to chamber music: they are smaller-scaled and more intimate in terms of production and presentation.)

When Strindberg died in 1912, the Swedish Academy ignored him, as it always had, but the Swedish people mourned him as their greatest writer.

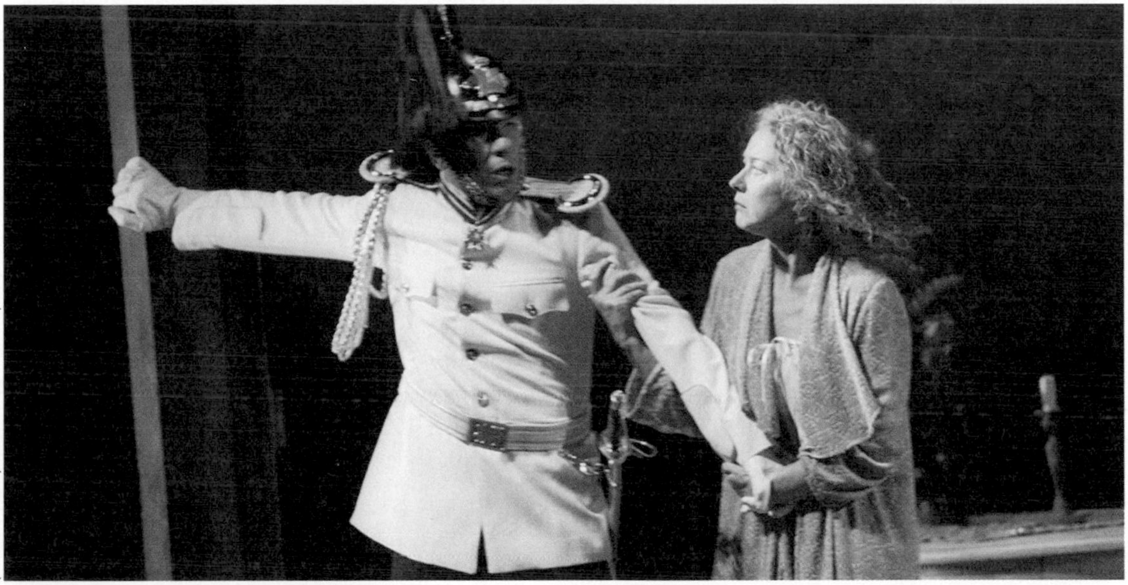

(Sara Krulwich/The New York Times)

STRINDBERG'S DANCE OF DEATH

A significant writer who heralded the arrival of realistic theatre was the Swedish playwright August Strindberg. He wrote fiercely intense dramas about real people, especially emphasizing the battle between the sexes. One of his plays portraying the conflicts between a husband and wife is *Dance of Death,* shown here in a production with Ian McKellen as the husband and Helen Mirren as the wife.

Producing Departures from Realism

Theatre Companies

Like the realists, the symbolists needed independently organized theatre companies. In France, two independent theatre companies were dedicated to antirealistic drama and production style. In 1890, Paul Fort (1872–1960) organized the Théâtre d'Art, which is remembered for producing Maeterlinck's one-act plays *The Intruder* and *The Blind.* When this theatre closed 3 years later, Aurélien-Marie Lugné-Poë (1869–1940)—who had acted for Fort, and for André Antoine at the Théâtre Libre—established the Théâtre de l'Oeuvre. Fort and Lugné-Poë both followed symbolist theories of stage production. They deemphasized scenery, experimented with stylized vocal and physical techniques, and presented avant-garde antirealistic drama.

Possibly the most notorious of Lugné-Poë's presentations was *Ubu the King* (*Ubu Roi,* 1896) by Alfred Jarry (1873–1907), a comic-book-style takeoff on Shakespeare's *Julius Caesar* and *Macbeth* and the history plays. Its farcical plot details how the bungling and gluttonous Ubu conspires to take over as ruler of Poland and is later dethroned by the assassinated king's only surviving son. The play's opening line, "Merdre"—from the French slang term for feces—created an immediate furor, as did its other scatological references. In light of twentieth-century history, Jarry's cynical and absurdist view of political leaders seems shockingly prophetic. Jarry's other Ubu works include *Ubu Bound* (1901) and *Ubu the Cuckold* (published posthumously in 1944).

An independent theatre in Ireland, the Abbey Theatre, is often associated with early symbolist drama. Its founders, in the first decade of the twentieth century, wanted to establish a company that would deal with the concerns and myths of the Irish people. The three playwrights initially associated with the Abbey were William Butler Yeats (1865–1939), Augusta Gregory (1852–1935), and John Millington Synge (1871–1909). Yeats, who was opposed to realism, created symbolist plays based on Irish myth and history in such plays as *Cathleen ni Houlihan* (1902) and *At the Hawk's Well* (1916). Later in his career, he experimented with the stylized conventions of Japanese nō drama.

The works of Gregory and Synge were more realistic; Synge, however—for instance, in *Riders to the Sea* (1904) and *The Playboy of the Western World* (1907)—created poetic drama in realistic form. Gregory's best-known dramas include *Spreading the News* (1904) and *The Gaol Gater* (1906). The Abbey Theatre also introduced the works of Sean O'Casey (1880–1964) in the 1920s, including *Juno and the Paycock* (1924) and *The Plough and the Stars* (1926). Today, it is the national theatre of Ireland.

Designers

There were also many individual artists whose style and theories of production departed from realism. Two of the most famous were the designers Appia and Craig.

ADOLPHE APPIA AND EDWARD GORDON CRAIG

Modern stage design begins with two men: Adolphe Appia (1862–1928), who was born in Switzerland; and Edward Gordon Craig (1872–1966), who was English. Among other innovations, they saw the tremendous possibilities of using light for scene changes and striking effects, and of moving away from the realistic box set.

Adolphe Appia was the first to develop a theory of antirealistic staging. Trained in music, he admired Wagner's operas but felt that realistic staging detracted from their effect. In 1891, he proposed simple, symbolic sets that would work with the actor. He also advocated multidirectional colored lighting to paint the stage and move in harmony with the production.

Appia had only a few opportunities to demonstrate his ideas. For some years he designed experimental and dance productions at a theatre school in Hellerau, Germany, run by Émile-Jaques Dalcroze (1865–1950). Appia also designed sets for Wagner's operas at La Scala and in Basel, Switzerland. He wrote two significant books: *Music and the Art of Theatre* (1892) and *The Work of Living Art* (1921). A simple, shy man, he shunned publicity, preferring to let his work speak for itself.

Edward Gordon Craig, by contrast, delighted in the limelight and sometimes was deliberately provocative in order to make his theories known. The son of the actress Ellen Terry and Edwin Godwin—an architect and scene designer—Craig had been an actor in Henry Irving's company before turning to design. Though he designed several productions for the Purcell Operatic Company and for his mother's theatre, he could not find financial support for his ideas in England.

In 1904, Craig was invited to go to Germany, and there he published his book *The Art of the Theatre.* Craig wanted to free theatre from dependence on realism, literature, and the actor, and to create a unified artwork—with light as a key element—under the control of one person. His magazine *The Mask* (1908–1928) was influential in avant-garde theatre. For a few years before World War I, Craig ran a theatre school in Italy. After the war, he lived in both Italy and France, writing

(Billy Rose Theatre Collection, New York Public Library at Lincoln Center; Astor, Lenox, and Tilden Foundations)

A DESIGN BY APPIA Adolphe Appia's ideas about lighting and scenery were revolutionary. He moved away from realistic settings to the use of shapes and levels that would serve as acting areas; one example is this design for *Iphigenia at Aulis.* Appia was also among the first to recognize the vast possibilities of modern lighting techniques.

(Billy Rose Theatre Collection, New York Public Library at Lincoln Center; Astor, Lenox, and Tilden Foundations)

A DESIGN BY CRAIG Edward Gordon Craig's ideas were ahead of his time, and most of them remained unrealized. Shown here is one of his designs, for a scene in *Electra*.

steadily, wittily, and sometimes acidly about his theories until his death in 1966.

Although these two designers worked independently of each other, they arrived at many similar conclusions. Both attacked realistic theatre, arguing against photographic reproduction as a basis for scene design. Appia disregarded the realistic "fourth wall" convention and designed a theatre building at Dalcroze's school which was the first in the modern era without a proscenium arch. Both men believed that settings should suggest, not reproduce, locale. Both used levels and platforms, designing spaces that were functional for performers. Moreover, both of them took full advantage of the introduction of electricity—which made it possible for stage lighting to develop as an art—and both used light as an integral visual element. Most of their designs are extremely atmospheric, stressing contrasts between light and dark.

However, Appia and Craig were not in total agreement. Craig believed that theatre needed a master artist who could create all the production elements. Appia believed that the régisseur, or "master" director, fused the theatrical elements and that the designer was an interpretive artist, bringing an author's work to life and providing a functional environment for the performers. Craig felt that the star system had made acting the weakest element of theatre and argued that the best performer would be an *Übermarionette,* a "superpuppet," who would allow the director to control the performance totally. Craig's designs were frequently conceived on a more grandiose scale than Appia's. Appia's designs usually required a set change for each locale; Craig, on the other hand, established the modern *unit setting*—one basic setting that can represent various locales through movement of its elements along with slight additions of properties. Craig was also especially noted for his experiments with movable screens.

Appia and Craig influenced many leading twentieth-century American designers, including Robert Edmond Jones (1887–1954), Lee Simonson (1888–1967), Norman Bel Geddes (1893–1958), Donald Oenslager (1902–1975), Boris Aronson (1900–1980), and Jo Mielziner (1901–1976). These designers, working between the world wars, proved the practicality of many of Appia's and Craig's theories.

Antirealist Directors: Meyerhold

The reaction against realism also influenced directors. In Russia, a number of artists rejected the artistic principles of Stanislavski and the Moscow Art Theatre. Possibly the most influential of these was Vsevelod Meyerhold.

VSEVELOD EMILIEVICH MEYERHOLD

If Konstantin Stanislavski was the most significant twentieth-century theorist of psychologically based realistic acting, Vsevelod Emilievich Meyerhold (1874–1940) was his counterpart in the external, antirealistic movement.

Meyerhold was born near Moscow in 1874. In the second year of his law studies, he was admitted to the drama school of the Moscow Philharmonic Society, where he studied with Nemirovich-Danchenko. As one of the original members of the Moscow Art Theatre, Meyerhold played the role of Treplev, the frustrated young writer, in its production of *The Sea Gull.* However, during the next 4 years Meyerhold's position in the Moscow Art Theatre became less prominent. In 1902, he left Stanislavski's company to work as a director.

Between 1902 and the outbreak of the Russian revolution in 1917, Meyerhold experimented with antirealism, staging a number of symbolist dramas. In 1905, he was invited to direct at an experimental studio in the Moscow Art Theatre, but this association did not last out the year. Meyerhold was then invited to direct the Russian actress Vera Komissarzhevskaya's company; again, however, after two seasons he was forced to leave because of his contention that the director, not the star performer, was the primary theatre artist. During the next 10 years, when he worked at the Imperial Theatre in Saint Petersburg, his productions became increasingly stylized and theatrical. He also staged studio productions using techniques of commedia dell'arte, vaudeville, and the circus.

Meyerhold's importance for Russian theatre became apparent after the Russian revolution. Between 1919 and the mid-1930s, as we will see, he would become the leading Russian "theatricalist." In 1920, he was appointed deputy commissar of the theatre department of the Commissariat for Education, and for 3 years he was involved in the government's organization of theatrical arts.

During the 1920s, Meyerhold undertook his renowned antirealistic experiments, in such productions as *The Magnificent Cuckold* (1922) and *The Inspector General* (1926). In the early 1930s, he was attacked by the Soviet government for failing to produce "socialist realism." Ironically, after his theatre was taken from him he was invited to work in the Opera Studio of the Moscow Art Theatre, where he staged *Rigoletto* in 1938. In June of 1939, he was invited to address the All-Union Conference of Stage Directors. It was expected that he would recant his stylistic experimentation, but instead he attacked Soviet-controlled theatre art and was arrested. Most historians believe that Meyerhold died in a Soviet labor camp in 1940. His wife, Zinaida Raikh, who was his leading actress, was found brutally murdered in their apartment.

MEYERHOLD'S THEATRICALIST EXPERIMENTS

Much of what would be called *avant-garde* in the theatre of the 1960s and later can be traced back to Meyerhold's experiments in the early twentieth century. Meyerhold's theatre was a director's theatre; as director, he was also literally the author of his productions, frequently restructuring or even rewriting classic works. He searched for suitable environments for his presentations, arguing for the use of found spaces—that is, spaces not originally meant for theatre, such as streets, factories, and schools. Meyerhold wanted to shatter the "fourth wall" convention. On occasion he would leave the house

(© The State Russian Museum/Corbis)

MEYERHOLD: REVOLUTIONARY DIRECTOR
One of the giants of twentieth-century theatre was the Russian director Vsevelod Meyerhold, who carried out many antirealistic experiments. Though he began his career with the realistic director Stanislavski, he soon broke away from Stanislavski's approach and created works in which his own vision prevailed, not that of the playwright. Shown here is an impressionistic portrait of Vsevelod Emilievich Meyerhold, painted by Boris Grigoriev, 1916.

lights on, extend the stage apron into the audience, or station performers in the house. He experimented with, and theorized about, multimedia in stage productions. He attempted to train his actors physically by using techniques from commedia dell'arte, the circus, and vaudeville. He frequently experimented with theatricalism. *Theatricalists* expose the devices of theatre, such as the way stage machinery works, to make audiences aware of watching a performance; they also borrow techniques from the circus, music halls, and similar popular entertainments.

Meyerhold's best-remembered experiments were undertaken in the 1920s, immediately after the Russian revolution. He devised an acting system known as *biomechanics,* which emphasized external physical training and performance style, and he suggested that the actor's body could be trained to operate like a machine. Furthermore, he argued that through physical actions performers could evoke desired internal responses in themselves and their audience. In his early biomechanical experiments, Meyerhold had his performers create outlandish physicalizations to represent emotional states, though later he moved to more natural physicalizations.

Meyerhold's settings, known as *constructivist* sets, provided machines for his performers to work on. These settings frequently looked like huge Tinkertoys, consisting of skeletal frames, ramps, stairways, and platforms. Constructivist sets were highly theatrical; they were not meant to indicate a specific locale, such as a room in a house, but were rather a practical apparatus for the actors.

Meyerhold used a constructivist design for his production of *The Magnificent Cuckold* in 1922. This setting, according to his biographer, Edward Braun,

> consisted of the frames of conventional theatre flats and platforms joined by steps, chutes, and catwalks; there were two wheels, a large disc bearing the letters "CR-ML-NCK," and vestigial windmill sails, which all revolved at varying speeds as a kinetic accompaniment to the fluctuating passions of the characters. Blank panels hinged to the framework served as doors and windows.[3]

A description of the opening scene indicates how the set worked:

> You heard an exultant voice ring out offstage, full of joyful strength and happiness; and then up the side ladder to the very top of the construction flew—and "flew" is the word—

[3]Edward Braun, *The Theatre of Meyerhold,* Eyre, Methuen, London, 1979, p. 170.

(Novosa/Sovfoto)

MEYERHOLD'S INSPECTOR GENERAL
Vsevelod Meyerhold incorporated a variety of approaches in his productions; he used commedia and circus techniques, created "constructivist" stage sets, and reinterpreted the classics. In this scene from his production of Gogol's *The Inspector General*, he crowds the stage with a wild assemblage of character types.

> [Igor] Ilinsky [Meyerhold's leading actor] as Bruno [the "magnificent cuckold"]. His wife Stella . . . ran to meet him and stood, indescribably youthful, lithe, and athletic, with her straight legs apart like a pair of compasses. Without pausing, Bruno hoisted her onto his shoulder, then slid down the highly-polished chute and gently lowered his weightless load to the ground.[4]

Meyerhold, as we have noted, was not the only Russian antirealist. Alexander Tairov, for example, also experimented with various nonrealistic techniques at his Kamerny (Chamber) Theatre between 1914 and 1950. After the revolution, he too was harassed by the Soviet regime.

Eclectics

Some early-twentieth-century theatre artists tried to bridge the gap between realism and antirealism. These *eclectics*, as they were known, were not doctrinaire in their

[4]Ibid., pp. 172–173.

(Billy Rose Theatre Collection, New York Public Library at Lincoln Center; Astor, Lenox, and Tilden Foundations)

MAX REINHARDT'S THE MIRACLE

A twentieth-century director who liked to present plays on a vast scale was the Austrian Max Reinhardt. Reinhardt used a circus building for some plays and the outside of a cathedral for an adaptation of *Everyman*. For *The Miracle,* shown here, he converted the inside of a theatre to look like a cathedral.

practices, arguing instead that each play should define its own form. Eclectic directors included the Austrian Max Reinhardt (1873–1943) and the Russian Yevgeny Vakhtangov (1883–1922).

Max Reinhardt began his career as an actor with the Freie Bühne. He was a major director in Austrian and German theatre from 1905 until 1933, when, as a Jew, he was forced to leave Hitler's Germany. Reinhardt's productions were particularly noteworthy because of his innovative use of theatre spaces. He staged *King Oedipus* and *Lysistrata* in a converted 3,000-seat circus building and directed a modern adaptation of the medieval morality play *Everyman* outside the cathedral at Salzburg. He experimented with adaptations of the Elizabethan stage for Shakespearean drama; and for his productions of a drama called *The Miracle* he had theatres remodeled to look like the interior of a cathedral. Reinhardt also experimented with Asian theatrical conventions and with conventions from earlier periods of western theatre history. Throughout his career, he was a total régisseur, or director-designer, overseeing all aspects of his productions. He produced a wide variety of plays; and during his career he staged over 500 productions and managed more than 30 playhouses and companies.

Another eclectic, Yevgeny Vakhtangov, staged most of his significant works for studios of the Moscow Art Theatre. Vakhtangov believed that every production had its own inherent style, derived from the text, the performers, and the intended audience. He directed his four best-known productions in 2 years: Maeterlinck's *The Miracle of Saint Anthony* (1921), Strindberg's *Erik XIV* (1921), S. Anski's *The Dybbuk* (1922), and Carlo Gozzi's *Turandot* (1922). Vakhtangov was able to synthesize Stanislavski's psychological realism with Meyerhold's theatricalism.

A leading performer with Vakhtangov was Mikhail Chekhov (1891–1955), Anton Chekhov's nephew, who developed a system of acting based on what he called the *psychological gesture*. He maintained that a performer could create a realistic stage portrayal by finding physical characteristics for a role that would then trigger internal responses. Again, one can see the influence of Stanislavski and Meyerhold. Mikhail Chekhov left Russia in the 1920s and taught acting in England and the United States.

Commercial and Popular Theatres

So far, we have been focusing on significant experimenters between 1875 and 1915. However, mainstream theatre of this period remained highly commercial in orientation, and popular dramas and theatrical entertainments predominated. This can be seen, for example, in both American and English theatre.

In the United States, melodrama remained extremely popular. Popular playwrights, such as Clyde Fitch (1865–1909), emphasized melodramatic plotlines and devices to excite their audiences. Many producers, such as David Belasco (c. 1853–1931), used highly realistic techniques to create sensational stagings of these melodramas, and many actors built successful careers performing in them. James O'Neill (1847–1920)—the father of playwright Eugene O'Neill—spent most of his career performing in a stage adaptation of *The Count of Monte Cristo.*

American theatre production was dominated by businesspeople who tried to monopolize it. One group of producers, nicknamed the "Syndicate," did exercise a monopoly over commercial American theatre by producing major shows with leading stars and allowing theatres across the country to book these shows only if the theatre owners did their booking exclusively with the Syndicate. In addition, Syndicate members controlled many of the major theatres throughout the United States and would not book other producers' shows. Star actors who would not work with the Syndicate found their opportunities severely limited. One actress who opposed the Syndicate was Minnie Maddern Fiske (1865–1932), who became well known for her performances in plays by Ibsen, Shaw, and Wilde. The Syndicate's stranglehold was broken by the Shubert brothers, whose organization then went on to monopolize American theatre until 1951, when it lost an antitrust suit and had to relinquish a number of its playhouses.

In England, there were many experimenters: the playwrights included Shaw and Oscar Wilde (1854–1900), the author of the popular comedies of manners *The*

DEBATES IN THEATRE HISTORY

Are Women's Contributions to Theatre History Overlooked?

As we have seen in several earlier chapters, feminist historians argue that significant female innovators in theatre history are frequently overlooked.

One case in point could be made with regard to the innovations in Russian theatre between 1875 and 1915. Only recently have the significant actresses in this period been discussed, in works such as *Women in Russian Theatre* (1996) by Catherine Schuler.

While the work of Stanislavski and Chekhov at the Moscow Art Theatre has received major attention, for instance, little notice has been paid to the acting career of Olga Knipper. Knipper was Chekhov's wife, but—more important—she was also the leading actress in this realistic theatre. What was her theory of acting? How did she further the realistic innovations made at the Moscow Art Theatre? Similarly, the leading actress in Meyerhold's company was his wife Zinaida Raikh, but her theoretical viewpoints and how they relate to Meyerhold's innovations are infrequently mentioned. Again, the dancer Alice Koonen, the wife of antirealistic director Alexander Tairov, must have been a major influence on his early theatricalism, yet there is little mention of her contributions to the work at the Kamerny Theatre.

As we examine the history of many of the major twentieth-century theatre companies, it is clear that the contributions of their women members receive less detailed examination than those of the men. (As a matter of fact, later in the present chapter, Henry Irving's contributions to the Lyceum Theatre are given more attention than those of Ellen Terry. Is our own representation of history unbalanced here?) Later examples might also be cited, including the Group Theatre in the United States: in discussions of the Group Theatre, the contributions of Cheryl Crawford and Stella Adler are almost always overshadowed by the directorial innovations of Lee Strasberg and Harold Clurman.

Are feminist historians right? Have women's contributions been excluded from theatre history by a male-dominated perspective? How can we address this issue? We tend to think that this question and the debate over it apply only to the remote past, but actually they cross all chronological boundaries. The issue will confront theatre historians as they consider how our historical perspective on all periods should be revised.

Importance of Being Earnest (1895) and *An Ideal Husband* (1895); and the directors included William Poel (1852–1914) of the Elizabethan Stage Society, who tried to revive unlocalized staging for Elizabethan plays. However, most productions in England during this period were staged in a conventional, illusionistic way; and most of the famous actor-managers chose plays by Shakespeare or by popular melodramatic authors. Among the best-known and most commercially successful actor-managers of the time were Herbert Beerbohm Tree (1853–1917) and Henry Irving.

HENRY IRVING

Henry Irving (1838–1905) was the most acclaimed actor on the English stage during the last part of the nineteenth century and one of the last great English actor-managers.

Irving was—like Edwin Booth, Richard Wagner, and the duke of Saxe-Meiningen—among the first modern theatre artists to insist on a total effect in his productions and was responsible for innovations in staging and lighting. He employed the best stage designers of the day, rehearsed his large corps of stagehands so that scene changes would be smooth and precise, and experimented with the control of stage lighting. In 1895, Irving became the first English actor to be knighted—in recognition of his work and his high professional standards.

Irving's real name was John Henry Brodribb; he spent 4 years as a clerk in London before changing it and becoming an actor. By 1871, when he had his first Lon-

(© Richard Feldman)

OSCAR WILDE AND COMEDY OF MANNERS
A playwright of the late nineteenth century who continued the tradition of English comedy of manners begun in the Restoration period was Oscar Wilde. With an emphasis on wit, clever phrases, satire, and amusing character types, his plays were amusing as well as provocative. A good example is *Lady Windermere's Fan*. Shown here is a production at the Williamstown Theatre Festival, featuring Isabel Keating and Adam Rothenberg.

don success as Mathias in Leopold Lewis's melodrama *The Bells,* Irving had spent 15 years on the stage, playing over 500 roles with provincial and London companies. He followed his success as Mathias with other leading roles in melodrama, and in 1874 he played Hamlet for a record-breaking 200 nights.

Though he was criticized for such physical flaws as an unmelodious voice and a shambling gait, as well as for unusual characterizations, Irving was a master at using gesture and pantomime to communicate a character's feelings and thoughts. He was not a romantic leading man but excelled in melodrama and in roles like Iago, in which he could portray scorn, malice, horror, and fear.

Irving became manager of the Lyceum Theatre in 1878 and for 21 years staged productions there that were known for scenic splendor and totality of effect. His leading lady, Ellen Terry (1847–1928), brought beauty, freshness, and vitality to her roles. They became one of the most renowned stage duos of the century.

Irving gave up management of the Lyceum in 1898, after several unprofitable seasons. His farewell London performance was at Drury Lane in 1905. Irving died while on tour and was buried in Westminster Abbey. Describing him, Ellen Terry wrote, "He was quiet, patient, tolerant, impersonal, gentle, close, crafty, incapable of caring for anything outside of his work."

(© ArenaPAL/The Image Works)

Henry Irving in 1892, as Cardinal Wolsey in Shakespeare's *Henry VIII*.

International Theatres 1875–1915

On the international scene in the period just before and after 1900, theatre in many areas was just beginning to develop an indigenous identity. In a number of places it remained derivative or heavily indebted to a country from which its citizens had immigrated or which had conquered or controlled it. Theaters were built, acting companies were formed, and playwrights began writing local dramas, but a truly independent native theatre had not been established.

In Canada and Australia, for example, theatre at this time was influenced by English models in its writing, its acting, and its theatre traditions, and in the touring companies from England. At the same time, around 1900 in Australia, there was the beginning of native playwriting, in which the characters spoke Australian English, not the British version.

In Latin America and Mexico, Spanish theatre was the dominant influence. In Argentina, between 1904 and 1914—a period known as the "glorious decade"—there was a flowering of local drama, when 200 plays, both short and long, were written and produced. It was an encouraging beginning to native drama. In Brazil, where Protuguese was the language spoken, not only Portugal but France set the tone for theatrical activities.

One exception on the international stage in terms of continuing activity was Asian theatre. In Asia, some theatrical traditions reached back hundreds of years and continued into the period before and after 1900.

Asian Theatres

In Chapter 3, we examined early Asian theatre: the development and the maturing of theatre in a variety of Asian countries, particularly India, China, and Japan. In some cases we brought theatre in those countries up to the seventeenth century. In this chapter, we will pick up Asian theatre once again, beginning with the nineteenth century and moving into the twentieth century.

During the nineteenth century, the western world came into closer contact with Asia. As western nations began to establish "spheres of influence," or imperialistic control, over Asian countries, there was a great deal of cross-cultural influence. Late in the 1800s and then in the twentieth century, western theatre would adopt many practices of traditional Asian theatres, and Asian theatre would be influenced by western practices.

Peking (Beijing) Opera: A Nineteenth-Century Development

The best-known Asian theatre to develop during the nineteenth century was Peking opera in China. (Peking is now known as Beijing, and thus this form might be called by the new name of the city; also, Peking opera has recently been called by other Chinese names, *jingju* and *xiqu* being two of them. Although mindful of the ration-

(© Robbie Jack/Corbis)

PEKING OPERA
Known sometimes as Beijing Opera (after the name of the Chinese city of Peking was changed to Beijing), this is a highly stylized form of theatre developed in China in the nineteenth century. Unlike western grand opera, it is much more a part of popular culture, combining song, dance, and acrobatics with traditional drama. It makes wide use of symbols—a table, for instance, may stand for a mountain. Here we see a performance of *The White Snake* at the Sadler's Wells Theatre in London.

ale for each of these, we will use the traditional term *Peking opera.*) In Peking opera, elements of folk drama and other genres close to ordinary people form the basis of what is truly a popular theatre—one of the most colorful and striking theatrical forms now practiced in Asia.

Though it is called *opera,* Peking opera combines music, theatre, and dance in its own unique way. Because of its origins in popular entertainment, it has little to offer in terms of high literary merit or philosophical speculation. But it preserves long traditions of popular singing, acrobatics, and acting and thus provides insights into the high development of performance techniques in traditional Chinese theatre. Its plays or skits involve elaborate and colorful conventions of makeup, movement, and voice production.

In staging, Peking opera stresses symbolism. The furniture onstage usually consists only of a table and several chairs, but these few items are used with imagination. Depending on how they are arranged or referred to, they may represent a dining hall, a court of justice, or a throne room. The table may stand for a cloud, a mountain, or any other high place. A tripod on a table, holding incense, indicates a palace. When the script calls for a long journey, the performers walk in a circle about the stage. Later, this creative use of the stage impressed many western dramatists, among them the

German playwright Bertolt Brecht and the American playwright Thornton Wilder, author of *Our Town.*

Well before the turn of the twentieth century, the vitality of Peking opera had made it the most popular form of traditional theatre in China; and later its stars—including the great twentieth-century actor Mei Lanfang—became performers of enormous reputation not only in China but also in the west.

We turn now to Asian theatres of the early twentieth century.

THEATRE IN INDIA

By the turn of the twentieth century, Ibsen and Chekhov began to influence intellectuals in India (as they also would in China and Japan). Perhaps the greatest of the Indian writers influenced by both modern European theatre and traditional Indian theatre was Rabindranath Tagore, whose fifty plays, some in modern style and some in a more traditional mode, formed the basis and inspiration for much of the best work that has followed. Tagore is regarded as a classic writer in India, where his plays are frequently produced. However, attempts to stage his elusive, poetic dramas have met with great difficulty in the west.

RABINDRANATH TAGORE

Rabindranath Tagore (1861–1941) was the youngest of fourteen children of Debendranath Tagore, a prominent philosopher and social reformer. He received an excellent education, particularly in Hindu philosophy, and began writing verses while still at home; his first important collection of poetry, *Manasi,* was published in 1890. In 1891, Tagore became the manager of his father's estates in Shileida and Sayadupur. Through close contact with the villagers, he learned about their lives and problems and also became familiar with traditional Bengali folk drama.

(© D.P.A./The Image Works)

Rabindranath Tagore.

Tagore's plays, written in Bengali, cover a wide variety of styles and subjects. *Nature's Revenge* (1884) uses the nature imagery of Sanskrit poetry. *The King of the Dark Chamber* and *Rakta Karaui* (1924) are allegories. In *Vis Barjan* (1890), Tagore invents a myth to focus on the issue of nonviolence. In *Last Cause* (1904) and *The Bachelor's Club* (1904), he writes realistic comedy and satire. Many of Tagore's later works, such as *Chitrangada* (1936), are dance dramas, a form he came to favor late in life. His works include song, mime, dance, and lyrical verse and are tinged with mysticism. Because of these elements, English translations of this plays, even those Tagore did himself, seem stilted and unnatural.

Tagore received the Nobel Prize for literature in 1913 and was knighted in 1915, but he relinquished his title in 1919 to protest the Amritsar massacre, in which British troops had killed nearly 400 Indians during an outbreak of rioting and mass demonstrations. In 1924, he founded Visva-Bharati University in Santiniketan as a center for Indian and international culture. At his school in Santiniketan, he directed and acted in his own plays. Since his death in 1941, Tagore's reputation in India as a dramatist has grown. Much of his international reputation comes from his numerous collections of poetry and short stories and his lectures in Europe, America, and Asia.

In the last part of the nineteenth century and the early years of the twentieth century, the theatre that had been influenced by the English and other Europeans throve in India. In several major centers—Calcutta, Bombay, Madras—there was a proliferation of proscenium-arch theatres with the accoutrements of such theatres in the way of audience seating, backstage equipment, and the like. The plays written for these theatres were often in the local regional languages.

Theatre in China

At the turn of the century, increased contact with the west by Chinese scholars and intellectuals led to great curiosity concerning western drama. Students in urban centers were excited to realize that theatre could deal with ideas as well as sentiment, and they began to translate and stage plays by Ibsen, Chekhov, and Shaw as a way of educating the public about social and political problems. Many of the writers and actors who became interested in this *spoken drama,* as they called it, had been impressed by its possibilities while living in Japan, where interest in European theatre had developed even earlier. With the help of Japanese colleagues, Chinese students living in Tokyo staged versions in modern Chinese of *La Dame aux Camelias* and *Uncle Tom's Cabin.*

Theatre in Japan

In 1868 the Japanese ruling family—the house of Tokugawa—was overthrown, and this led to contact with the west, which had long been forbidden. When young Japanese intellectuals began to travel abroad, western influence spread in Japan. Among the Japanese intellectuals drawn to the west were a number of gifted men who developed a strong interest in theatre and saw it as a way to express social concerns. The work of Ibsen became a particularly strong force for these men. Feeling that traditional kabuki had nothing to contribute to such a movement, they decided to create a means of performing spoken drama in the western manner.

In 1909, Osanai Kaoru (1881–1928) presented the first professional production in Japan of a modern play, with specially trained actors. A remarkable pioneer in the development of western-style theatre, Osanai continued his experiments until 1923. Then, with the help of a wealthy colleague, Hijikata Yoshi, he was able to build the Tsukiji Little Theatre, which served as the center for the development of modern Japanese drama until its destruction in the bombing of Tokyo during World War II.

The Emerging American Theatre

For a good part of the eighteenth and nineteenth centuries, theatre in America was heavily influenced by English theatre. Actors and managers came to the United States from England; the permanent theatres on the east coast (from Boston to Charleston) were modeled on their English counterparts; and other resident or touring companies often bore the stamp of similar operations in England.

There were, however, important native developments. Actors, managers, and playwrights began to assert their independence, just as the United States had announced its independence in 1776. We have previously mentioned American playwrights who emerged: Royall Tyler (*The Contrast,* 1787), Anna Cora Mowatt (*Fashion,* 1845), George L. Aiken (*Uncle Tom's Cabin,* 1852), and Augustin Daly (*Under the Gaslight,* 1867).

American Playwrights after 1875

In the latter nineteenth century, more American playwrights appeared. Steele MacKaye (mentioned in Chapter 11 for his advances in theatre technology) adapted or wrote nineteen plays. Prominent among them were *Won at Last* (1877) and *Hazel Kirke* (1878–1880). *Hazel Kirke,* though a melodrama, included strong realistic elements. MacKaye's contemporary Bronson Howard (1842–1908) was America's first full-time professional playwright. His *Saratoga* (1870), when first produced, played for a remarkable 101 performances. Howard's eighteen plays, which also included *The Banker's Daughter* (1878) and *Shenandoah* (1888), like those of MacKaye, were noted for their realism.

Others also followed this trend toward realism in drama (away from fantasy and melodrama). *My Partner* (1879) by Bartley Campbell (1843–1888) emphasized frontier life, and *Alabama* (1891) and *Arizona* (1897) by Augustus Thomas (1857–1934) stressed the local color of the states involved.

Two other playwrights of the period continued the movement toward greater realism. One was William Gillette (1855–1937), an actor as well as a playwright. Gillette used the Civil War as the background for two of his successful plays: *Held by the Enemy* (1886) and *Secret Service* (1895). A scene in the latter play featured an exact onstage reproduction of a telegraph office. The second playwright was James A. Herne (1839–1901), whose play *Drifting Apart* (1888) offered a realistic portrayal of the adverse effects of alcohol on a fishing village in Massachusetts. Herne's *Margaret Fleming* (1890), of all the American dramas of the nineteenth century, is considered the most realistic.

David Belasco won attention as a dramatist with such plays as *The Heart of Maryland* (1895), *Madame Butterfly* (1900), and *The Girl of the Golden West* (1905). It was as a producer, however, that Belasco became closely identified with literal realism. *The Governor's Lady* (1912) featured an onstage reproduction of Child's, a well-known restaurant chain of the time, and real food from the chain was consumed onstage at each performance. For another play, *The Easiest Way* (1912), Belasco had the wallpaper and all other details from an actual room in a boardinghouse transferred to the stage. (To add further authenticity to his productions, Belasco abandoned unnatural footlights and substituted overhead spotlights.)

Other American playwrights of the period included Clyde Fitch (1865–1909), who is credited with writing sixty plays, including *Captain Jinks of the Horse Marines* (1901) and *The Girl with the Green Eyes* (1902). Fitch, who emphasized suspenseful melodrama in his plays, is noted for another first for an American dramatist: he had his plays published, a practice that dramatists have continued up to the present. Another playwright of the early twentieth century, William Vaughn Moody (1869–1910), is recognized chiefly as the person who, in his play *The Great Divide* (1906), first combined serious literary elements with dramatic features.

The early nineteenth century also saw the appearance of several noteworthy female playwrights, one being Martha Morton (1865–1925), who is considered the first female professional playwright. Among her thirty-five plays are *His Lord and Master* (1903) and *The Movers* (1907). Another important female playwright was Josephine Preston Peabody (1874–1922), who won acclaim for her play *The Piper* (1910), a poetic drama about the Pied Piper of Hamelin.

When we add the acting achievements of Edwin Booth and the technical accomplishments of Steele MacKaye and David Belasco to the many successes of American playwrights, it is clear that from 1875 to 1915 American theatre began to establish a character very much its own. As a part of this scene, there were several noteworthy developments in African American theatre.

African American Theatre

The 1890s, called the "gay nineties" (at that time, the word *gay* meant simply "lighthearted" or "blithe"), was ironically also a decade which saw widespread lynchings, and in which the Supreme Court—in *Plessy* v. *Ferguson*—made Jim Crow principles the law of the land by permitting "separate but equal" schools for white and black children. In this decade, too, the Reverend Thomas Dixon adapted his novel in praise of the Ku Klux Klan for the stage, and later into the film *Birth of a Nation.* In theatre, though, the same period encompassed a series of vibrant musical shows written, acted, and produced by African Americans.

Rising prices, worn-out jokes, the incipient motion picture industry, and the introduction of women into revues all contributed to the decline of the minstrel show. By 1895, musical theatre had developed a new form, *the revue,* which had more plot than vaudeville and a new kind of music—the vigorous, infectious ragtime.

The syncopated rhythms of ragtime had originated in saloons, sawmill camps, and houses of prostitution from the spontaneous talent of unknown African American composers and piano players. American youngsters, who had been plunked down on piano stools to practice "Whispering Hope," discovered suddenly that it was more fun to play "Maple Leaf Rag" by Scott Joplin (1868–1917). (Sixty years later, Joplin's music would become a hit again in the musical *Pippin* and the movie *The Sting.* Joplin, who died in poverty, was buried in an unmarked grave, and his ragtime opera *Treemonisha,* published at his own expense, remained unproduced until 1972.)

As ragtime spread across the nation, it served as a bridge to legitimate musical comedy for a number of talented African Americans. In 1891, *The Creole Show* introduced sixteen beautiful "colored" women into minstrelsy. Bob Cole (1864–1912) and William Johnson (1873–1954) conceived, wrote, produced, and directed the first black musical comedy, *A Trip to Coontown,* in 1898.

In the same year, William Marion Cook (1869–1944) and Paul Laurence Dunbar (1872–1906) wrote "Clorind: The Origin of the Cakewalk." This high-stepping ragtime dance was an instantaneous success and the first of many black dances—such as the turkey trot, the Charleston, the lindy hop, the jitterbug, and the twist—to become popular in the United States.

Among the great cakewalkers, the comedians Bert Williams (1874–1922) and George Walker (1873–1911) as well as their wives joined composers and writers to produce musicals and operettas that put black performers on Broadway. Their most successful shows, *In Dahomey* (1902) and *Abyssinia* (1906), reflect two different but important interests of the time: operetta, with its aristocratic characters involved in

ABYSSINIA: AN EARLY AFRICAN AMERICAN MUSICAL
Bert Williams and his partner George Walker were among the early twentieth-century African American artists who helped create Broadway musicals and operettas that starred black performers. Shown here is a scene from a revival of their musical *Abyssinia*, featuring Williams and his wife, Lottie Thompson (Cole) Williams.

romantic plots; and Africa and things African. For the first time Americans saw blacks onstage without burnt cork, without dialect, and costumed in high fashion.

African American Stock Companies: The Lafayette Players

The success of black writers and producers encouraged the formation of African American stock companies. The first of these was founded in 1904 by Robert Motts (died 1911) on Chicago's South Side. At his Pekin Theatre, a new show opened every 2 weeks. In 1914, a second important stock company was founded in New York by Anita Bush (1883–1974), who had played in Williams's and Walker's shows. Her stock company opened at the Lincoln Theatre in Harlem, but a year later she moved the troupe to the Lafayette Theatre and dubbed it the Lafayette Players.

The Lafayette Players produced a new play every week. By 1932, when the company finally closed in the face of the depression, it had presented over 250 productions and employed a host of black stars, including Charles Gilpin (1878–1930), Evelyn Preer, and Clarence Muse.

The company's repertoire consisted entirely of "white" plays—that is, it brought Broadway to African American audiences. One of the great delights for these audiences was to watch Clarence Muse, a very dark-skinned man, play *Doctor Jekyll and Mister Hyde* in white makeup and wig. Muse later moved to Hollywood and starred in *Hearts in Dixie* (1929), the second talking picture with an all-black cast.

The Lafayette Players proved to white audiences that black actors were capable of serious drama and that a black company could sustain itself financially over a long period. Certainly the African American dramatic groups that followed—the Negro Art Theatre, the Gilpin Players, and the Ethiopian Players—owed their inspiration to Anita Bush's pioneer work.

African Americans in Popular Theatre

Most African American performers in this era, and later, made a living not on the legitimate stage but in vaudeville. While a few white circuits like Keith-Albee and Columbia would book blacks, most black vaudeville acts depended on the Negro circuit, which extended from New York to Texas and from Chicago to Birmingham. Bookings were handled by the Theatre Owners Booking Association, TOBA—an acronym which the performers translated as "Tough on Black Actors." The Negro circuit, founded by blacks in 1920, was eventually able to book acts in over eighty theatres, however, and according to the theatre historian Henry T. Sampson, between the years 1910 and 1930 blacks owned and operated seventeen theatres.

Black vaudeville acts, like white acts, included song-and-dance teams, stunt dancing, cakewalk artists, blues singers, comics, specialty acts, and even dramatic skits. Among the hundreds of black vaudeville performers were Pigmeat Markham, the Nicholas Brothers, Nipsey Russell, Bessie Smith, Butterbeans and Susie, and Sweet Mama Stringbean (Ethel Waters). This lucrative circuit collapsed with the great depression of the 1930s.

As we turn, in Chapter 13, to the revolutionary theatrical developments from 1915 to 1945, the strong influence of trends and innovators of the turn of the century will be apparent.

Summary

The beginning of modern theatre was marked by the advent of realism and naturalism. The most noted realistic playwrights were Henrik Ibsen, August Strindberg, George Bernard Shaw, and Anton Chekhov; among the naturalists were Émile Zola, Gerhart Hauptmann, and Maksim Gorky. The controversial works of these playwrights were produced by independent theatres, which included André Antoine's Théâtre Libre, Otto Brahm's Freie Bühne, J. T. Grein's Independent Theatre, and Konstantin Stanislavski's Moscow Art Theatre.

One of the earliest reactions against realism was symbolism, and theatres like the Théâtre d'Art and the Théâtre de l'Oeuvre were independent producers of symbolist plays. Among designers who broke with the conventions of realistic theatre were Adolphe Appia and Edward Gordon Craig; directors who experimented with antirealistic staging included Vsevelod Meyerhold and Alexander Tairov.

Eclectics, such as Yevgeny Vakhtangov and Max Reinhardt, strove to reconcile the contrasting styles which were emerging in early modern theatre. Some writers, like Ibsen and Strindberg, created both realistic and nonrealistic drama.

American and English theatre, though primarily commercial in orientation, did have some experimenters. The work of American playwrights during this period demonstrated that American theatre was beginning to take shape. African Americans had a significant impact in the United States as members of stock companies and in popular theatre.

Various theatres in Asia—in India, China, Japan, and elsewhere—in addition to continuing their ancient traditions, began to be influenced by theatre trends in the west, especially realism.

Theatre History

- Henrik Ibsen (1828–1906) *(below)*, *A Doll's House*

- Henry Irving (1838–1905)
- Émile Zola (1840–1902), *Thérèse Raquin*
- Gerhart Hauptmann (1862–1946), *The Weavers*
- Maksim Gorky (1868–1936), *The Lower Depths*
- August Strindberg (1849–1912), *Miss Julie*
- Augusta Gregory (1852–1935), *Spreading the News*
- David Belasco (c. 1853–1931)
- Oscar Wilde (1854–1900), *The Importance of Being Earnest*
- George Bernard Shaw (1856–1950), *Major Barbara*
- Anton Pavlovich Chekhov (1860–1904), *The Sea Gull*
- Rabindranath Tagore (1861–1941) *(below)*, *Nature's Revenge*

Cultural and Historical Developments

- Scott Joplin (1868–1917), ragtime
- Mark Twain's *The Adventures of Tom Sawyer* (1875)
- Alexander Graham Bell's telephone (1876)
- Thomas Edison's incandescent lamp (1879)
- Auguste Rodin's *The Thinker* (1880)
- Height of imperialism (1880–1914)
- Alexander II assassinated in Russia; Henry James's *Washington Square* (1881)
- Friedrich Nietzsche's *Thus Spake Zarathustra* (1883–1885)
- Trade unions in France legalized (1884)
- Robert Louis Stevenson's *Dr. Jekyll and Mr. Hyde* (1886)
- Eiffel Tower *(below)* completed (1887–1889)

- Vincent Van Gogh's *The Starry Night* (1889)
- Dreyfus affair in France; cinematograph invented (1894)
- Giacomo Puccini's *La Bohème* (1896)
- Sigmund Freud's *The Interpretation of Dreams* (1899)
- Boer War in South Africa (1899–1902)
- Theodore Dreiser's *Sister Carrie* (1900)
- Marconi's first transatlantic radio telegraph message (1901)

PHOTO CREDITS: Ibsen. (Norwegian Information Center) / Rabindranath Tagore. (© D.P.A./The ImageWorks) / Eiffel Tower. (Library of Congress)

continued

- Stage designers: Adolphe Appia (1862–1928) *(below, left)*; Edward Gordon Craig (1872–1966) *(below, right)*

- Maurice Maeterlinck (1862–1949), *The Intruder*
- Konstantin Sergeivich Stanislavski (1863–1938)
- William Butler Yeats (1865–1939), *Cathleen ni Houlihan*
- John Millington Synge (1871–1909), *The Playboy of the Western World*
- Max Reinhardt (1873–1943)
- George Walker (1873–1911)
- Bert Williams (1874–1922)
- Vsevelod Emilievich Meyerhold (1874–1940) *(below)*

- Sean O'Casey (1880–1964), *Juno and the Paycock*
- Théâtre Libre, Paris (1887); Freie Bühne, Berlin (1889); Independent Theater, London (1891); Moscow Art Theatre, Russia (1898); Abbey Theatre, Ireland (1904)
- Théâtre d'Art (1890) and Théâtre de l'Oeuvre, Paris (1893)
- Theatrical Syndicate formed in United States (1896)
- Anita Bush's Lafayette Players (1914)

- Wilbur and Orville Wright make successful airplane flight (1903) *(below)*

- Claude Monet's *Water Lily Pond* (1904)
- Einstein's theory of relativity (1905)
- Suffragette movement launched (1906)
- Picasso's *Les Demoiselles d'Avignon* (1907)
- Model T car introduced by Ford Motor Company (1908)
- NAACP founded (1909)
- Henri Matisse's *The Red Studio* (1911) *(below)*

- *Titanic* sinks on maiden voyage; C. G. Jung's *The Theory of Psychoanalysis* (1912)
- Stravinsky's *Le Sacre du Printemps* (1913)
- World War I (1914)

PHOTO CREDITS: Adolphe Appia. (New York Public Library, Picture Collection) / Edward Gordon Craig. (Windown and Grove, Enthoven Collection, Victoria and Albert Museum, London) / Vsevelod Meyerhold, portrait. (New York Public Library/Art Resource) / The Wright brothers' glider. (Library of Congress) / Matisse, *The Red Studio*. (© 2006 Succession H. Matisse, Paris/Artists Rights Society (ARS), New York; Digital Image © The Museum of Modern Art/Licensed by SCALA/Art Resource, N.Y.)

CHAPTER 13

Theatres from 1915 to 1945

Bertolt Brecht: Theatrical Iconoclast

An important theatrical figure who emerged between the two world wars was the playwright Bertolt Brecht. Using epic structure and setting many plays in the past or a mythical country, Brecht tackled important moral and political issues. After World War II, he founded the Berliner Ensemble, which presented many of his plays written earlier. Shown here is one of his earlier works, *The Threepenny Opera,* with music by Kurt Weill. The scene here is from a recent production of the musical at the Jean Cocteau Repertory Theatre.

(© Gerry Goodstein)

The period from 1915 to 1945—from the year after the start of World War I to the end of World War II—was a time of unusual unrest for the western world. On the one hand, the world was being brought closer together by radio, telephone, and motion pictures. On the other hand, some nations were jealously guarding their independence and sovereignty as other nations tried to take them over. Drastic political and economic changes led to instability.

Background: A Time of Unrest—The World Wars

The era of unrest after 1915 was ushered in by World War I, which resulted in nearly 8.5 million deaths. The ultimate cost of the conflict—which the American president Woodrow Wilson had called the "war to make the world safe for democracy"—was not, however, immediately apparent. When the war ended in 1918, most people believed President Wilson's idealistic pronouncements, and attempts were made to organize a workable League of Nations and World Court. Unfortunately, a policy of isolationism—that is, a determination to stay out of foreign affairs—prevented the United States from becoming a member of the League, and thus the organization could never become a viable international force. Furthermore, because of fervent nationalism, many countries refused to give the League of Nations any real power.

Unrest in Europe also contributed to the Russian revolution, which began in 1917 and led to the establishment of the Soviet government. Before it took control, the new communist regime had to fight a costly civil war.

Throughout Europe and America, economic problems developed. In the 1920s, rampant inflation was followed by a depression—another cost of the previous political turmoil. The economies of many nations were destroyed, and monetary systems were devalued. A famous photograph of the period shows a German citizen pushing a wheelbarrow full of paper money to buy a loaf of bread.

Many historians believe that this political and economic unrest set the stage for the rise of totalitarianism in Europe. Totalitarianism is a form of government under which the individual is totally subservient to the state; most totalitarian states are controlled by dictators. Between the world wars, there were fascist totalitarian dictatorships in Italy and Germany, nationalist dictatorships in several other countries, and a communist totalitarian dictatorship in the Soviet Union. The fascists believed in dictatorial government and forcible suppression of opposition; they argued that nation and race were more important than the individual, and they established extreme economic and social regimentation. The leading fascist dictators were Adolf Hitler, whose Nazis dominated Germany beginning in 1933; Benito Mussolini, who took control of Italy in 1922; and Francisco Franco, who ruled Spain from 1939 until his death in 1975.

The extremes of fascism were horribly illustrated in Nazi Germany, known as the Third Reich. Political opposition and individual liberties were totally suppressed, and dissenters were imprisoned in concentration camps. The Nazis also imprisoned Jews, Gypsies, homosexuals, and pacifist Jehovah's Witnesses. The "Aryan race"—an unscientific concept grouping non-Jewish, Nordic Europeans—was exalted, and "non-Aryans" were persecuted as racially inferior.

Hitler used nationalistic arguments as a pretext for the takeover of Austria and the dismemberment of Czechoslovakia; his invasion of Poland on September 1, 1939, began World War II. During the war, the Nazis turned some of their concentration camps, such as Auschwitz in Poland, into extermination centers. All together, the Third Reich murdered 6 million Jews and 1 million Gypsies.

Similar atrocities took place in the other fascist regimes, and in the Soviet Union under the communist dictatorship of Joseph Stalin, who was in power from 1928 until his death in 1951. Stalin suppressed individual freedom and imprisoned his political opponents, dispatching several million people to slave-labor camps in Siberia—the infamous "gulag archipelago"—where many of them died. (As we saw in Chapter 12, one of Stalin's victims was the director Vsevelod Meyerhold, who was executed in a prison camp.)

1915 TO 1945

Theatre	Year	Culture and Politics
Major futurist productions at Piccolo Teatro in Rome (1918)	1915	Easter Rebellion in Ireland (1916)
Soviet renaissance: Meyerhold, Vakhtangov, Tairov, Erveinov		Bolshevik revolution (1917)
Toller's *Man and the Masses;* Pirandello's *Six Characters* (1921)		Prohibition in United States; peace of Versailles (1919); women's suffrage in United States (1920)
O'Neill's *The Hairy Ape* (1922); Dullin's *Atelier* (1922)	1920	Joyce's *Ulysses;* Mussolini's march on Rome (1922)
Jouvet in *Doctor Knock* (1923)		Hitler's beer hall putsch in Munich (1923)
Stanislavski's *My Life in Art;* Breton's *First Manifesto;* O'Neill's *Desire Under the Elms* (1924)		Ortega y Gassett's *The Dehumanization of Art;* Kafka's *The Trial;* Thomas Mann's *The Magic Mountain* (1924)
Meyerhold's *Inspector General* (1926)	1925	Schoenberg's twelve-tone music (1926)
Brecht's *Threepenny Opera* (1928)		Depression begins; Wolfe's *Look Homeward, Angel;* Faulkner's *The Sound and the Fury* (1929)
O'Neill's *Mourning Becomes Electra* (1931)		
Group Theatre, United States (1931)		
Socialist realism declared proper style in Soviet Union; Brecht and other German artists emigrate (c. 1934); Gielgud's *Hamlet* (1934)	1930	Spain's monarchy collapses (1931)
Lorca's *House of Bernarda Alba;* Giraudoux's *The Trojan War Will Not Take Place;* Federal Theatre Project in United States (1935)		Hitler takes power in Germany; New Deal in United States (1933)
		Italy attacks Ethiopia; purges in Soviet Union; Nuremberg laws against Jews in Nazi Germany (1935)
Tyrone Guthrie appointed administrator at the Old Vic (1937)	1935	Spanish Civil War; first television broadcast (1936)
Artaud's *Theater and Its Double* (1938)		World War II (1939–1945)
Thornton Wilder's *Skin of Our Teeth* (1942)		
Othello with Paul Robeson (1943)		
Sartre's *No Exit* (1944)		
	1940	Hemingway's *For Whom the Bell Tolls* (1940)
		Camus's *Myth of Sisyphus* (1943)
	1945	United States drops atomic bomb on Japan; United Nations formed (1945)

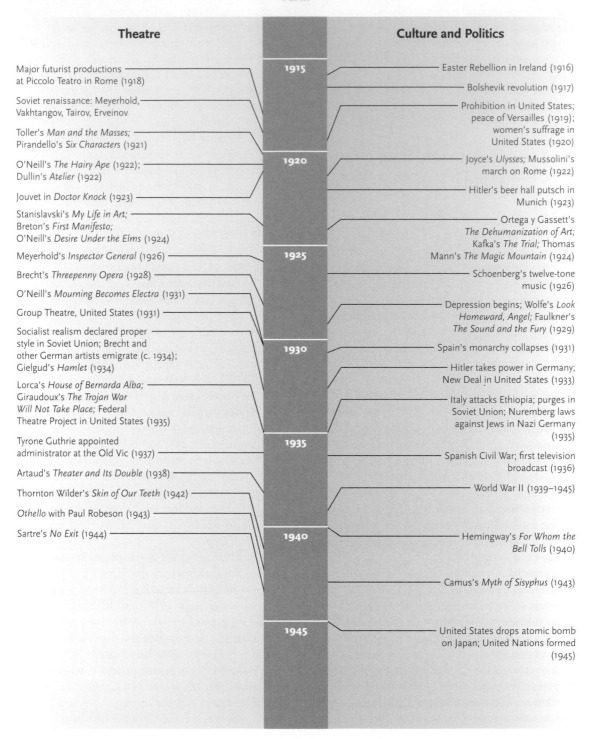

In 1940, the prime minister of Japan, General Hideki Tojo, allied himself with the fascist dictators in Europe. A Japanese attack on Pearl Harbor on December 7, 1941, brought the United States into World War II, which was then fought in the Pacific as well as in Europe.

Given the nationalistic fervor of the totalitarian dictators, the chaotic economic situation, and the widespread political instability, many historians believe that World War II was inevitable. It lasted 6 years and was even more horrible than any of its predecessors: over 35 million people died. The Nazi concentration camps became mechanized death factories, where innocent victims of anti-Semitism and of the war were exterminated. The atomic bomb, which finally ended the war, proved that humanity was now capable of annihilating itself.

World War II confronted us with unanswerable questions: How could civilized, rational societies wreak such irrational destruction? Were individuals responsible for societal actions? How could genocide be explained?

Theatre of Unrest: Dramatic Movements

Not surprisingly, the years from 1915 to 1945 were also turbulent ones for theatre. There were conflicts of several kinds: some were reactions to the outside world, others were conflicts within theatre. During the era of the world wars, theatre mirrored the general unrest, and many of the theatrical movements we will examine were defined by their relationship to emerging political, social, or economic ideologies.

Some innovators were reacting to popular commercial theatre as well as to the tumultuous world situation. Artists who rebelled against commercial theatre—particularly in France, Great Britain, and the United States—did not equate artistic accomplishment with financial success. As the cost of productions increased because of inflation, depression, unionization, and other factors, innovative artists searched for noncommercial outlets.

Many theatrical innovators between the wars also rebelled against realism. Realism had by then become the most popular form of theatre, but for a number of avant-garde artists and theorists, it seemed simplistic and too limited. Several antirealist practitioners discussed in Chapter 12, like the Russians Meyerhold and Tairov, continued to be productive; and the eclectics—people like Vakhtangov in Russia and Reinhardt in Germany, who worked in more than one form of theatre—introduced new production techniques. In the early twentieth century, many new departures from realism developed in continental Europe: they included expressionism, futurism, dada, and surrealism. Several of them began primarily as movements in the visual arts and subsequently became important in avant-garde theatre.

Still, most of the movements and artists we will consider were reacting not so much to each other as to the chaotic world scene. Some movements, such as expressionism and epic theatre, supported socialism. Others, such as futurism, supported fascism. Many playwrights—including Ernst Toller (Germany, 1893–1939), Stanislaw Ignacy Witkiewicz (Poland, 1885–1939), Karel Čapek (Czechoslovakia, 1890–1938), Jean Giraudoux (France, 1882–1944), and Bertolt Brecht (1898–1956)—dealt with specific political concerns.

Expressionism

The term *expressionism* was first used in France just after the turn of the twentieth century to describe a style of painting. Expressionism developed in Germany around 1905 as a movement in art and literature in which the representation of reality is distorted to communicate inner feelings. In a painting of a man, for example, the lines in his face might be twisted to indicate his inner turmoil.

Expressionist Drama

Expressionism in drama was a first cousin to symbolism (which we discussed in Chapter 12), and it had well-defined characteristics. Expressionist plays are often highly subjective: the dramatic action is seen through the eyes of the protagonist and

(Billy Rose Theatre Collection, New York Public Library at Lincoln Center; Astor, Lenox, and Tilden Foundations)

EXPRESSIONISM IN THEATRE
One major departure from realism in the years between the world wars was expressionism. The expressionists presented dramatic action as seen through the eyes of the protagonist, and thus it is often distorted or dreamlike. Among the significant expressionist playwrights was the German Ernst Toller. Shown here is a scene from a production in New York of Toller's *Man and the Masses* in the 1920s.

therefore frequently seems distorted or dreamlike. Expressionist drama is often opposed to society and the family. The protagonist in a typical expressionist play journeys through a series of incidents that are often not causally related. These dramas are therefore said to be structured as *station plays,* a term that refers to the stations of the cross and thus emphasizes parallels between the protagonist and Christ. The characters are representative types who are often given titles (such as Man, Woman, or Clerk) rather than names. The language is telegraphic, with most speeches consisting of one or two lines, though these sections of short speeches alternate with long lyrical passages. Many of the expressionist playwrights were politically motivated, supporting socialist and pacifist causes, though some were apolitical.

One of the first German expressionist playwrights was Walter Hasenclever (1890–1940). Hasenclever's play *The Son* (1914) depicts an angry young man who threatens to kill his father, feeling that his parents' rigidly restrictive, hypocritical attitude has inhibited his own ability to experience life to the fullest. During World War I, expressionistic writers began to move from such highly personal issues to a concern with social oppression. For example, Hasenclever's *Antigone* (1916)—written 2 years after *The Son*—put forward the idea that love offers the only way to achieve happiness but cannot flourish until immoral, authoritarian rulers are deposed. World War I presented a stark example of evils abroad in the modern world—evils which the expressionists and other serious dramatists had been proclaiming.

Two other German expressionists were Georg Kaiser (1878–1945) and Ernst Toller. Kaiser's *From Morn to Midnight* (1916) is a typical expressionist play: in a single day, an Everyman character moves through a series of episodes, seeking the meaning of life but finding only cruelty and greed; he ends as a defeated martyr. In a trilogy of plays by Kaiser—*Corral* (1917), *Gas I* (1918), and *Gas II* (1920)—the main characters, successive generations of a wealthy industrialist family, move from optimism to pessimism. *Gas II* suggests that because of the cataclysmic disruptions the world is undergoing, there is little hope of salvation.

Toller also depicted the descent from optimism to disillusionment. His play *Transfiguration* (1918) has a protagonist who begins as an innocent, patriotic soldier and ends as a militant antiwar activist. Toller's most important work, *Man and the Masses* (1921), is noteworthy—among other reasons—because its main character is a woman. Toller's heroine struggles to aid oppressed workers but is caught in the cross fire between those who uphold humanitarian ideals and zealous idealogues who believe that any means, including violence, is justified in attaining the workers' aims. Again, *Man and the Masses* ends on a note of despair.

Expressionistic Directors

Several directors developed expressionistic production techniques. Jürgen Fehling (1890–1968), for example, directed *Man and the Masses* at Berlin's Volksbühne Theatre, using devices that underscored the play's expressionistic style: for a scene in a stock exchange, the furniture was extremely exaggerated and distorted; for an episode in a prison, the protagonist was in a small, cramped birdcage.

Another expressionist director, Leopold Jessner (1878–1945), worked on both classic and contemporary plays. He became well known for using platforms and flights of stairs, and for changing the lighting and costumes to reflect emotions. In his 1919 version of Shakespeare's *Richard III,* for instance, he used blood-red costumes for the scene of Richard's coronation and white costumes for the army of Richard's opponent Richmond, and Richard dies under an intense red spotlight.

In its pure form, expressionism was short-lived, lasting only about 15 years. Many expressionistic techniques, however, found their way into later experimental and traditional theatre, and today's dramatists still use nonrealistic devices that can be called expressionistic.

Futurism and Dada

Two other movements that emerged around the time of Word War I, futurism and dada, had less impact on theatre than expressionism. Later, however, the aesthetic principles of these movements influenced avant-garde theatre artists in the 1960s and beyond.

Futurism originated in Italy in 1909; its leading exponent was Filippo Marinetti (1876–1944). The futurists, unlike the expressionists, idealized war and the developing machine age. In the first decade of the twentieth century, Italy was the least industrialized nation in western Europe, and this may explain the futurists' fascination with machinery and war. The futurists attacked artistic ideals of the past, ridiculing "museum art" and arguing that new forms had to be created for this new era. They advocated a "synthetic" theatre of short, seemingly illogical dramatic pieces: one example is Marinetti's *They're Coming* (1915), in which actors playing servants do nothing more than rearrange furniture onstage. They also believed that audiences should be confronted and antagonized, and they argued against the separation of performers and audience. The futurists also wanted to incorporate new electronic media, puppetry, and visual arts into theatre.

Dada, which originated in Switzerland in 1916 with a series of manifestos written by Tristan Tzara (1896–1963), was a short-lived movement that never really caught on, though (like futurism) it did influence other, later avant-garde movements. Dada was a reaction to the insanity of World War I, and its proponents argued that it mirrored the madness of the world. Like the futurists, the dadaists railed against traditional "museum" art and tried to confuse and antagonize their audiences. Unlike the futurists, however, the dadaists did not glorify war—on the contrary, they were pacifists. They concentrated on nonsense and the irrational, and questioned conventional definitions of art, suggesting that almost anything could be art. Along with other types of radical artistic expression, they presented short plays that defied rational explanation—reflecting in this way the irrationality of the world they saw around them.

Both futurism and dada emphasized a mixture of arts and the use of techniques of popular entertainment; in this, they foreshadowed today's performance art (discussed in Chapter 15).

Surrealism

In 1924, *surrealism* developed out of the dada movement. The major exponent of surrealism was the French writer André Breton (1896–1966), but the term itself had been used earlier: in 1917, the French playwright Guillaume Apollinaire (1880–1918) described his play *The Breasts of Tiresias* (1917) and the ballet *Parade* (1917) as surrealistic. The surrealists argued that the subconscious was the highest plane of reality and attempted to re-create its workings dramatically. Many of their plays seem to be set in a dreamworld, mixing recognizable events with fantastic happenings.

(© Hulton-Deutsch Collection/Corbis)

JEAN COCTEAU'S SURREALISM
Surrealism was a nonrealistic theatre movement that began in France. The name means beyond realism, and the movement emphasized symbols, the subconscious, and dreams. The scene here—an elderly woman in a Victorian dress with a whip in her hand, a child wrapped with ropes made of bells standing on a mantel, and a ladder against a wall—is typical of the tableaux the surrealists favored. It is from Jean Cocteau's *Le Sang d'un Poète,* c. 1925.

France was the center of surrealism, and one French playwright influenced by surrealism was Jean Cocteau (1889–1963), who worked on the ballet *Parade.* Cocteau's best plays—*Antigone* (1922), *Orpheus* (1926), and *The Infernal Machine* (1934), a reworking of the Oedipus story—were based on Greek myths and contrasted modern ideas with these traditional stories.

The surrealist movement also had an international impact. Stanislaw Ignacy Witkiewicz, for example, was a noted Polish surrealist; his dramas include *The Water Hen* (1921), *The Cuttlefish* (1922), and *Gyubal Wahazar* (1921).

Theatre of Cruelty

Antonin Artaud, who had originally been associated with the surrealists, theorized about a *theatre of cruelty* in a series of essays and manifestos written in the 1930s. He believed that western theatre needed to be totally transformed, that its literary tradition—which emphasized language—was antithetical to its ritualistic origins, and that western theatre artists should study the stylized Asian theatres. Renouncing literary tradition, Artaud asserted that there were "no more masterpieces." By this he meant that classics should be produced not for the sake of their historical significance but only if they were still relevant to contemporary audiences. Furthermore, he did not believe that the text was sacred; he felt that a script could and should be reworked in order to point up its relevance.

Theatre, for Artaud, was not a literary event but a sensory experience. His emphasis on the sensory is what characterizes theatre of cruelty. Artaud did not use the term *cruelty* to mean that theatre artists should literally assault or maul their audiences—although some later avant-garde theatre artists did think of cruelty as actual physical confrontation with spectators. Rather, he meant that the viewers' senses should be bombarded. Today's multimedia presentations are designed to create such sensory involvement.

Artaud, like many of the antirealists who preceded him, called for a restructuring of the theatrical event. He wanted, for example, to reorganize the theatre space to make the audience the center of attention. He argued that productions could be staged in "found spaces"—spaces such as warehouses or airplane hangars that had not originally been intended for theatre. He also attacked Stanislavski's acting technique, arguing instead for stylized, ritualized, Asian-like performances.

Artaud believed that humanity's natural inclination toward violence and aggression—manifested in Europe in the mid-1930s by the rise of fascism and Stalinism—could be purged in theatre of cruelty. For Artaud, theatre could act (as he put it) like a "plague," cleansing modern society of all that was ugly.

Artaud was the most radical and innovative theorist in France during this period. Like the designers Adolphe Appia and Edward Gordon Craig (discussed in Chapter 12), he had few opportunities during his lifetime to put his theories into practice, but his ideas were extremely influential in the decades that followed. Artaud's own life reflected much of the anguish and pain with which his theories dealt.

ANTONIN ARTAUD

Antonin Artaud (1896–1948) was born in Marseille, France. He went to Paris in 1920 and became an actor, working with several important directors: Lugné-Poë, Charles Dullin, George Pitoëff, and Louis Jouvet. He also acted in films, where his most notable role was the monk in Carl Dreyer's *The Passion of Joan of Arc*. For Dullin, he directed and designed Calderón's *Life Is a Dream*. Some of his poems were also published.

(Martinie/Roger-Viollet Collection/Getty Images)
Antonin Artaud.

From 1924 to 1926, Artaud was intensely involved with the surrealist movement in theatre and wrote the play *Spurt of Blood* (1924). Later, however, because of his interest in the occult, Asian religions, and mysticism, he was expelled from the movement by its leader, André Breton. Artaud, who suffered from physical as well as mental disorders all his life, also experimented with drugs, chiefly morphine. In 1926, together with Roger Vitrac and Robert Aran, Artaud founded the Théâtre Alfred Jarry, which produced four programs between 1927 and 1929, including Strindberg's *A Dream Play*.

Artaud was greatly influenced by a group of Balinese dancers he saw in Paris in 1931; he was impressed by their use of song, dance, and pantomime in a physical, nonverbal form. Artaud went to Mexico in 1936 to search for an authentic primitive culture. He lived among the Tarahumara Indians and experimented with peyote. Convinced that unidentified forces were seeking to destroy him, he returned to France the following year and then spent the next 9 years in mental institutions.

He was released in 1945, through the efforts of his theatrical associates, but died of cancer 2 years later.

Most of Artaud's books and theories were written in the 1930s but not published until later. Though overlooked in his time, they became a major influence on the experimental theatre of the 1960s. Jerzy Grotowski, Peter Brook, and the Living Theatre were, in part, inspired by Artaud's theatre of cruelty.

Epic Theatre

Germany was the birthplace not only of expressionism but also of *epic theatre.* Though epic theatre is often associated with Bertolt Brecht, who appropriated the term in his writings, the director Erwin Piscator (1893–1960) could more justifiably claim to have developed the concept.

Piscator and *The Good Soldier Schweik*

Piscator was greatly influenced by the communist revolution in Russia and wanted to develop what he called "proletarian theatre." After working in other theatres in the early 1920s, Piscator became director of the Volksbühne Theatre in Berlin from 1924 to 1927. In his productions there, and in later productions, he introduced a number of elements that would become hallmarks of epic theatre.

Piscator's epic theatre was first and foremost political and was meant to instigate social change. To underline his political concerns, Piscator often used documentary materials—that is, dramatizations of or interpolations from current events—and he believed that a director could make whatever changes seemed necessary in a text. His productions had heightened theatrical and staging effects, such as multimedia. He also explored ways of changing the traditional actor–audience relationship, and the architect Walter Gropius (1883–1969) designed a playhouse for him which could change from proscenium to thrust to arena, though it was never actually built.

In 1919, Gropius had established schools of arts and crafts and of fine arts in Weimar, Germany, known as the Bauhaus. The aim was to break down the barriers between craftspeople and artists, particularly in architecture and design. The Bauhaus experimenters were interested in a total concept: a unified approach to houses, furniture, interior decoration, and all aspects of design. Though the Bauhaus was forced to close in 1932, it was to have considerable influence in architecture and related fields in later years. Its influence in theatre was not particularly strong; however, the theatre design which Gropius developed for Piscator no doubt influenced later theatre architects because of its flexibility and its ability to incorporate projections and other visual elements.

Piscator's most famous production was probably *The Good Soldier Schweik* (1928), a dramatic adaptation of a novel by the Czechoslovakian writer Jaroslav Hasek in which a lowly soldier in World War I, Schweik, continually exposes the foolishness and cruelty of people in authority—often unintentionally. Piscator used a conveyer belt or treadmill (reminiscent of an impersonal, mechanized factory) on which the "antihero" Schweik walked through the many phases of his life. The production also included film sequences, caricatures, marionettes, and other theatrical devices. He described the play as *epic* because of its epic sweep, because Schweik's journey is a kind of modern epic, and because the audience—like people reading an epic—saw many dimensions of Schweik's saga.

Brecht's Epic Theatre

Bertolt Brecht is one of the few dramatists who are as well known for their theories as for their plays. Brecht's theories—most of which were formulated in the 1930s but were frequently revised—have influenced many later playwrights and directors. Brecht had worked with Piscator during the 1920s and used many of Piscator's techniques in his own plays. Because Brecht was also a dramatist, however, his epic theatre was more text-centered than Piscator's.

Developing his own form of epic theatre, Brecht wrote plays that are episodic in structure. They usually deal with history or foreign lands, cover a long period of time, shift locale frequently, have intricate plots, and include many characters. The goal of epic theatre, according to Brecht, is to instruct. An ardent socialist, he believed that theatre could create an intellectual climate for social change. In the early 1930s he wrote short dramas he called *Lehrstücke*—"learning pieces"—and he attacked theatrical works created purely for mass consumption and entertainment, referring to them as "culinary art."

(Percy Paukschta/Berliner Ensemble)

A BRECHTIAN CHINESE FABLE

Since Brecht believed that theatre should be highly theatrical, he was greatly influenced by Chinese theatre, and his work *The Caucasian Chalk Circle* is based on a Chinese play. Brecht used this fable to create a modern play which attacked capitalism. In the play, a child is placed in a circle, and the two women who each claim to be his real mother vie for him. The one who truly loves him will not reach into the circle and tear him apart. The scene shown here is from a production by the Berliner Ensemble.

Brecht felt that if theatre was to succeed at teaching, the audience should be involved not emotionally but intellectually. (Here too he differed from Piscator, who believed in emotional engagement.) He argued that a production should actually force the audience to remain emotionally detached—or "alienated," as he put it—from the dramatic action. (The German term he used, *Verfremdung,* means "to make strange" or "distancing.") To achieve this effect, he held, epic theatre had to abandon Wagner's goal of a *Gesamtkunstwerk,* a unified work of art. Instead, each production element should independently convey the political message.

To prevent emotional involvement, Brecht's works are highly theatrical. Narrators are frequently used to comment on the dramatic action, and audiences are always made aware that they are in a theatre. Lighting instruments, for example, are not hidden but are clearly visible to the audience, and multimedia are often used. Brecht also warned actors against Stanislavski's techniques; he believed that the audience should be aware of watching an actor play a character.

To alienate or distance the audience, Brecht also used a technique he called "historification." Though many of his plays, such as *Galileo* (1938–1939), are set in the past, it is apparent that he is really concerned with contemporary events paralleling the historic ones. Placing the events of the play in the past is simply a way of distancing the audience from the dramatic action. Similarly, Brecht often set his plays in fictitious foreign lands.

Brecht used many other epic techniques in his plays and productions. As another way of preventing the audience from becoming too involved in the dramatic action, scenes in his plays sometimes have opening titles which indicate what is to happen. Another device for commenting on the action was music. The songs in his plays, rather than revealing more about plot or character, usually underline the political message.

Brecht's life was as dramatic as many of his plays and was greatly affected by the political unrest of his time.

BERTOLT BRECHT

Bertolt Brecht (1898–1956), who was educated in his native Bavaria, was bored by regular schooling but loved to write. When he graduated from high school in 1917, he began to study medicine in Munich, but he was drafted as an orderly in 1918.

Brecht's father offered to publish his first play, *Baal* (1918), but only if the Brecht family name was not mentioned—a condition the playwright refused. In 1922, Brecht's *Drums in the Night* was awarded the Kleist Prize, one of Germany's highest literary honors. Both of these early plays were expressionistic.

(Internationes/German Information Center)

Bertolt Brecht.

In 1924, Brecht settled in Berlin, where he worked for a time with the directors Max Reinhardt and Erwin Piscator, but mostly with smaller experimental groups. While in Berlin, Brecht wrote *Man Is Man* (1926). One of Brecht's friends was the composer Kurt Weill, with whom he wrote *The Threepenny Opera,* the modern version of *The Beggar's Opera.* The plot of *The Threepenny Opera* has to do with a group of lowlife figures in Victorian England. One of them is Peachum, the boss of a gang of underworld beggars who pose as disabled people; another major figure is Macheath, a swashbuckling burglar who marries Peachum's daughter Polly; another is Tiger Brown, the chief of police. Several songs became well known: "Mack the Knife," a song by Polly Peachum about "Pirate Jenny," and a duet by Macheath and Tiger Brown about their army days in India.

While he was in Berlin, Brecht became a Marxist and at this same time began to develop his theories of theatre. Forced by the Nazis to flee Germany in 1933, he lived in Denmark, Sweden, and the United States, where he did some filmwriting in Hollywood.

During his years in exile, Brecht had time to refine his ideas on epic theatre and wrote several important plays, including *Mother Courage and Her Children* (1938), *Galileo* (1938–1939), *The Good Person of Setzuan* (1938–1940), *The Resistible Rise of Arturo Ui* (1941), and *The Caucasian Chalk Circle* (1944–1945). In 1947, Brecht was called before the House Committee on Un-American Activities because of his Marxist ideas, and he left the United States shortly thereafter.

He settled in East Berlin, where the government gave him his own theatre, the Berliner Ensemble, which opened in 1949 with *Mother Courage*. For the next 7 years, he and his wife, the actress Helene Weigel (1900–1971), worked to develop epic theatre. When Brecht died in 1956, his wife took over the company, which had developed into one of the foremost acting troupes in the world; it continues to produce today.

During his lifetime, Brecht was a controversial figure, and he has been equally controversial in the years since his death. Many have judged him to be one of the most innovative dramatists and theoreticians of twentieth-century theatre. But he has also been criticized for his habit of frequently appropriating the work of others—particularly female collaborators—without acknowledging their contributions when his plays were produced and published. John Fuegi made a persuasive argument for this point of view in the book *Brecht and Co.*[1] Also, though Brecht was an avowed Marxist, he managed his financial affairs with the self-interest of a full-fledged capitalist and was unwilling to confront the totalitarian government of East Germany.

Mother Courage and Her Children

The play with which Brecht opened the Berliner Ensemble, *Mother Courage and Her Children,* is probably his most famous work, and it reflects many of his ideas about epic theatre.

Mother Courage is set in Europe between 1624 and 1636, during the Thirty Years' War. An episodic play, consisting of twelve scenes with many shifts in locale, it chronicles the losses of Anna Fierling, known as Mother Courage, who operates a traveling canteen from which she sells supplies to soldiers. During the course of the dramatic action—sometimes because of her own greed and opportunism—Mother Courage loses her two sons and her deaf-mute daughter.

Mother Courage teaches a political lesson. "Courage" is an ironic name for the protagonist. As is noted by Eric Bentley, a leading critic and translator of Brecht,

> Valor is conspicuously absent at those times when Mother Courage however unwittingly seals the fate of her children. At moments when, in heroic melodrama, the protagonist would be riding to the rescue, come hell or high water, Mother Courage is in the back room concluding a little deal.[2]

Ultimately, Brecht shows a protagonist and a war which are both created and controlled by the profit motive, and he is arguing for a change in the capitalist economic system.

---

[1]Grove, New York, 1994.

[2]Bertolt Brecht, *Mother Courage and Her Children,* Eric Bentley (trans.), Grove, New York, 1966, p. 10.

Many techniques of epic theatre are used in *Mother Courage and Her Children.* One, obviously, is historification. Though the play is set during the Thirty Years' War—which has been described as a seventeenth-century world war—contemporary parallels can be drawn; the play was written in 1938 and revised by Brecht in the early 1940s, and its premiere took place in 1941; the reverberations of World War II are apparent.

Another epic technique is Brecht's use of titles preceding each scene, revealing the coming action and forcing the audience to think about its political and economic implications. Scene 1, for example, opens with a title that reads: "Spring 1624. In Dalarna, the Swedish Commander Oxenstierna is recruiting for the campaign in Poland. The canteen woman Anna Fierling, commonly known as Mother Courage, loses a son."[3] A number of songs comment on the thematic implications of the dramatic action. The most famous is "The Song of the Great Capitulation," in Scene 4, which describes a person who begins life with high ideals but quickly learns to compromise. The representative nature of Brecht's characters is also clear, since they are frequently referred to by titles rather than names (e.g., Chaplain, Cook, Recruiting Officer).

European Theatres During the War Years

We turn now to some other developments in theatre from 1915 to 1945, on the European continent and in England. We will also note briefly what became of theatre under the totalitarian regimes.

France

Copeau and Text-Oriented Theatre

One person who promoted text-oriented theatre in France after World War I was Jacques Copeau. He insisted on high standards in production, and his theoretical concepts were to influence a generation of French theatre directors.

Jacques Copeau

Working as a theatre critic in Paris in the early twentieth century, Jacques Copeau (1879–1949) became convinced that drama as an art had reached a low point, and that the time had come for new, practical research into European theatrical methods. While he applauded French directors such as André Antoine for bringing the works of Ibsen, Hauptmann, and others of the new "naturalist" school to the attention of the public, Copeau felt that naturalism denied the "essential theatricality" of theatre. He was appalled by the growing reliance on stage "tricks" like moving walls and excessively detailed and realistic sets, and he argued that theatre ought to focus on the play rather than on its trappings.

(LAPI/Roger-Viollet Collection/Getty Images)

Jacques Copeau.

With this end in mind, Copeau, at the age of 34, founded a new theatre company, the Théâtre du Vieux Colombier. The new company made a somewhat hesitant start but soon had a tremendous success with Copeau's production of Shakespeare's *Twelfth Night.*

The outbreak of World War I closed Copeau's theatre, Copeau joined the army, and the company dispersed. However, Copeau was discharged from military service

[3]Ibid., p. 23.

in 1915 because of injuries and then spent his time preparing for the rebirth of the Vieux Colombier. He studied constantly, corresponded with members of the company who were at the front, and managed to visit Edward Gordon Craig in Italy and Adolphe Appia in Switzerland. Georges Clemenceau, the head of the French government, had been a great fan of the Vieux Colombier in its first season, and it may have been his influence that allowed Copeau to take a company to New York in 1917. The company mounted two seasons of performances there, and Copeau gave many lectures on his theories of drama, which were influential in the development of postwar American theatre.

Copeau's work focused strongly on training the actor. His contributions to modern training include emphasis on the text, improvisation as a tool for exploring a text, drama games, ensemble acting, mask work, and theatre as communion. Copeau rejected the naturalists' idea of theatre as presenting a scientifically objective view of the world, and he sought ways to break down the barrier between audience and actor. He designed his theatre as a bare stage with no proscenium arch, and he used simple screens and lighting effects to establish locale.

In his later years, Copeau distanced himself from the company he had founded and left Paris for nearly 15 years before returning to head the Comédie Française from 1939 until he was forced to leave during World War II.

As was true of many of his contemporaries, some of Copeau's fondest aspirations for a new theatre were never realized. His greatest contribution to modern drama may be his belief that theatre is an ongoing process rather than a finished work. Two important directors influenced by Copeau were Louis Jouvet (1887–1951) and Charles Dullin (1885–1949). He also influenced his nephew Michel Saint-Denis (1897–1971), who worked with leading companies and theatre schools in France, Great Britain, and the United States.

Giraudoux and Anouilh

Two significant French playwrights of the period between World War I and World War II were Jean Giraudoux (1882–1944) and Jean Anouilh (1910–1987). Giraudoux, whose plays were frequently directed by Jouvet, believed in the primacy of the word, and his language was usually eloquent as well as witty. He also stressed contradictions, ironies, and antitheses in working out the themes of his plays. Among his better-known works are *Amphitryon 38* (1929), *Judith* (1931), *The Trojan War Will Not Take Place* (1935), and *Ondine* (1939). As can be seen from their titles, many of his plays were based on classic themes or plots. Jean Anouilh also used a classic source for his best-known play, *Antigone* (1943), a reworking of the Greek classic which spoke to the situation in Nazi-occupied France.

Spain

In 1913, one of Spain's most esteemed philosophers, Miguel de Unamuno (1864–1936), wrote a treatise about theatre—*The Tragic Sense of Life*—which was to have considerable influence, especially on the existential playwrights who emerged just after World War II. In this work, Unamuno juxtaposes the human desire for immortality and the serious doubt that it can be achieved. From the conflict of these two notions arises tragedy.

(© Robbie Jack/Corbis)

GARCÍA LORCA'S DOÑA ROSITA

A major writer of the early twentieth century was the Spanish playwright Federico García Lorca. He wrote some realistic plays and some plays filled with fantasy, but almost all of them centered on the passions aroused by family and personal situations. The scene here is from his play of 1935, *Doña Rosita, the Spinster* in a London production.

Because of the political climate in Spain, Unamuno's plays—such as *Fedra* (1917) and *Dream Shadows* (1931)—were given few productions before the end of World War II. The same was true of the plays of another Spanish dramatist, Ramon del Valle-Inclán (1866–1936). Inclán's works had grotesque elements, and he sometimes used traditional devices such as puppets.

Perhaps the most significant Spanish dramatist of this period was Federico García Lorca, a poet as well as a playwright. García Lorcas's plays, in language of exquisite lyricism, dealt with the unfortunate effects of the strictures of Spanish society, and with the dark side of the Spanish character.

FEDERICO GARCÍA LORCA

Spain's best-known twentieth-century poet and playwright, Federico García Lorca (1898–1936), was killed in the Spanish civil war. His death at the hands of the fascists ended a productive career but enhanced his reputation. His plays, which were banned in Spain until the death of Franco in 1975, were seen as a protest against the oppression of the Spanish people.

(© Archivo Iconografico, S.A./Corbis)

Federico García Lorca.

Born into a wealthy family, García Lorca was presenting elaborate theatricals at home by the age of 8. When he was 16, his family moved to Granada, and he began to study philosophy, literature, and law at the university there. His first book of prose was published in 1918.

Later, García Lorca studied in Madrid, where his first play, *The Butterfly's Crime,* was produced in 1920. Three books of poems followed, along with other plays—*Mariana Pineda* (1927), based on a historical character from the nineteenth century; and *The Love of Don Perlimplin and Belisa in the Garden* (not published until 1931). In June 1929 García Lorca left Spain to spend a year in North America. His many writing projects from that year included *Poet in New York* (a collection of poems published in 1940) and the completion of his comic play *The Shoemaker's Prodigious Wife.*

On his return to Spain, García Lorca was appointed director of La Barraca, a traveling theatre company—sponsored by the government and composed mainly of university students—that performed classic Spanish plays for remote, rural audiences. This experience inspired García Lorca to develop his own plays based on traditional Spanish stories, themes, and characters and intended for a popular audience. Of these folk plays, his most successful were a tragic trilogy: *Blood Wedding* (1933), *Yerma* (1934), and *The House of Bernarda Alba* (1936).

All three folk tragedies have strong female protagonists whose desires are thwarted by the oppressive circumstances of their lives. In *The House of Bernarda Alba* (completed shortly before Lorca's death and produced posthumously), a recently widowed woman, Bernarda Alba, determines to keep her five unmarried grown daughters locked in her house and away from all men. Imprisoned, the daughters oppose their mother and jealously compete with each other for the chance to marry Pepe el Romano (an offstage character). The play ends tragically when the youngest daughter hangs herself. Bernarda is not moved to repent—in fact, she believes, probably falsely, that her daughter died a virgin; and she takes pride in this. The play is often interpreted as a criticism of the self-destructive course of Spain under Franco in oppressing its own people.

Italy

In Italy, by far the most original dramatist between the two world wars was Luigi Pirandello. The characters in Pirandello's plays often engaged in philosophical debates questioning, for example, the relationship between appearance and reality. Also, in his plays he used highly theatrical devices. In an unusually imaginative way, Pirandello broke the bounds of traditional dramatic construction to call attention to the work itself. In his *Six Characters in Search of an Author* (1921), for instance, six fictional characters, created and then abandoned by a writer, appear at the rehearsal of a play and demand that their story be presented. The juxtaposition of real actors and imaginary characters gives rise to many philosophical and aesthetic issues, including appearance versus reality, the relativity of truth, and the role of fiction.

Pirandello's life and career, like his plays, reflected theoretical, social, and political upheavals in Italy and Europe.

LUIGI PIRANDELLO

The Italian dramatist Luigi Pirandello (1867–1936) experimented boldly with theatrical techniques to dramatize ideas that fascinated him. "My art is full of bitter compassion for all those who deceive themselves," he wrote, "but this compassion cannot fail to be followed by the ferocious decision of destiny which condemns man to deception." Deception, illusion, and the subjectivity of truth were concepts Pirandello explored in his plays, novels, and short stories.

As the son of a sulfur merchant, Pirandello received private tutoring at home in Agrigento, Sicily, before attending universities in Palermo, Rome, and Bonn. He received his doctorate in Bonn in 1888. His father had wanted him to become a businessman, but Pirandello chose literature as a career and by 1893, when he was 26, he had settled in Rome. He was married the following year to a woman he barely knew—an arranged marriage to unite two families of sulfur merchants. When the sulfur mines were flooded in 1904, the family fortune was lost, and his wife became mentally ill for the rest of her life. This economic and personal disaster forced Pirandello to supplement his earnings from writing by teaching at a girls' school.

(Photo by Edward Steichen, 1935 © Condé Nast Archive/Corbis)

Luigi Pirandello.

By the beginning of World War I, Pirandello had become a respected novelist and short-story writer but had done little playwriting. After the success of his play *Right You Are If You Think You Are* in 1916, he began to concentrate on drama. In *Right You Are,* as in his other famous plays—*Six Characters in Search of an Author* (1921) and *Henry IV* (1922)—Pirandello explores illusion versus reality, truth versus fiction, and madness versus sanity. Other well-known dramas by Pirandello are *Each in His Own Way* (1924) and *Tonight We Improvise* (1930).

Pirandello ran his own theatre, the Teatro d'Arte, from 1925 to 1928, touring its productions in Europe and America. In 1924 he had joined the fascist party, possibly partly because his theatre needed state subsidies. But it is also true that Pirandello's political views were conservative, and he often praised Mussolini in his newspaper articles; he even donated his Nobel Prize for literature (which he won in 1934) to the Italian government during its invasion of Ethiopia.

Pirandello's private life was brightened by his love for Marta Alba (1906–1988), the leading actress in the Teatro d'Arte, to whom he willed nine of his plays. He died in Rome in 1936, requesting that his death be ignored and his body burned.

Great Britain

British theatre between the world wars was, unlike much of the theatre on the continent, highly commercial. However, in reaction to this growing commercialization, several small, independent theatres arose. There were also individual actors and directors, most of them renowned for their work with Shakespeare, whose focus was on the artistic rather than the business side of theatre.

Britain's most noteworthy directors during this era were Harley Granville-Barker (1877–1946) and Tyrone Guthrie (1901–1971). Granville-Barker, who was also a playwright and critic, is best remembered for his approach to staging Shakespeare. He focused on remaining faithful to the spirit of the plays and making their poetry come alive. He considered acting the central element in his productions, and so his settings were simple and suggestive and his costumes not lavishly detailed.

Tyrone Guthrie is remembered in North America for founding two theatres: the Stratford Theatre in Ontario, Canada, in 1953; and the Guthrie Theatre in Minneapolis in 1963. However, he had made his reputation at the Old Vic in London between the wars. The Old Vic was the home of Shakespearean productions, and Guthrie broke with traditional staging by interpreting classic dramas imaginatively and developing unique production concepts. He often presented Shakespeare in modern dress. Guthrie's influence is still felt by directors who attempt to direct Shakespeare's works in ways that will make them more accessible to today's audiences. Many of the productions staged for the summer Shakespeare festival in New York's Central Park—such as the musical version of *Two Gentlemen of Verona* and A. J. Antoon's *Much Ado about Nothing,* with its use of Mack Sennett's comic silent-film techniques—are descendants of Guthrie's experiments.

Most of the British playwrights who were considered significant during this era are no longer as popular as they once were. Noël Coward (1899–1973), in such witty works as *Hay Fever* (1925), *Private Lives* (1930), and *Blithe Spirit* (1941), continued the tradition of comedy of manners, satirizing the social pretensions of theatre people and the English upper class. The poet T. S. Eliot (1888–1965)—an American by birth who spent most of his life in England—attempted to revive verse drama in such works as *Murder in the Cathedral* (1935) and *The Family Reunion* (1939). While British drama between the wars was less avant-garde than continental drama, British experimentation with traditional forms and classic plays foreshadowed similar undertakings in the decades that followed.

British theatre between the wars introduced many performers who developed international reputations. Most were noted for their Shakespearean work, but they were amazingly versatile; many of them, for example, also had successful careers in film. Their technique is often contrasted with that of American realistic performers. Among the most important are Edith Evans (1888–1976), Peggy Ashcroft (1907–1993), Michael Redgrave (1908–1985), Alec Guinness (1914– 2000), Laurence Olivier (1907–1989), Ralph Richardson (1902–1983), and John Gielgud (1904–2000).

LAURENCE OLIVIER, RALPH RICHARDSON, AND JOHN GIELGUD

Considered by many to be the greatest English-speaking actor of recent times, Laurence Olivier was equally acclaimed in Shakespearean and modern roles. A handsome man, able to effect dramatic changes in his appearance, Olivier had tremendous range as an actor, from deep passion to comedy. Besides his versatility, he was noted for his intelligence and discipline.

(Bettmann/Corbis)

Laurence Olivier.

Born in 1907, Laurence Kerr Olivier first attracted attention in 1922, as Katherine in a school production of *The Taming of the Shrew*. During his first years as a professional, he was a member of the Birmingham Repertory Theatre. By 1935, he was appearing at the New Theatre in London, alternating the roles of Romeo and Mercutio with John Gielgud.

Olivier rose to real fame after joining the Old Vic company in 1937. His uncut production of *Hamlet* was especially notable. In 1944, Olivier became codirector of the Old Vic with Ralph Richardson; later, he was director of the Chichester Festival Theatre. While continuing his acting career, he also made a name as a stage and film director. His film versions of *Hamlet, Henry V,* and *Richard III,* starring himself, brought Shakespeare to a wide audience. Olivier was head of the National Theatre from 1963 to 1973. He was knighted in 1947, and in 1970 he became the first actor to be made a life peer.

(© Hulton-Deutsch Collection/Corbis)

Ralph Richardson.

In 1974, ill health forced Olivier to retire from the physical demands of the stage, but he continued to appear in movie roles. He published an autobiography, *Confessions of an Actor,* in 1982; and another book, *On Acting,* in 1986. Olivier was married three times, to the actresses Jill Esmon, Vivien Leigh, and Joan Plowright.

Though Olivier may have been England's greatest twentieth-century actor, he was closely rivaled by John Gielgud and Ralph Richardson. Richardson began his career in 1921 and first became known to audiences in the United States during a tour in 1935. His ability to reveal the strong, somewhat hidden passions of rather ordinary men—especially the frightening or baffling emotions that can suddenly surface—was one of his trademarks. He was knighted in 1941.

John Gielgud—the grandnephew of Ellen Terry—made his debut at the Old Vic in 1921, achieved popular success as an actor in the 1930s, and was knighted in 1953. Especially noted for his excellent speaking voice, Gielgud also directed plays, managed theatre companies—including the Queen's Theatre (1937–1938) and the Haymarket (1944–1945)—and acted in many films. He continued to perform both onstage and in films through the 1990s. He wrote several volumes of autobiography, including *Early Stages* and *Stage Directions.*

(AP Images)
John Gielgud.

Theatres under Totalitarianism

As might be expected, totalitarianism curtailed the development of European theatre and drama. This is not to suggest, however, that theatrical activity ceased under totalitarianism. In the totalitarian societies, particularly the Soviet Union under Stalin and Germany under Hitler, there were government-supported theatres, used as instruments of propaganda. There were also some daring theatre artists who attempted to attack these regimes, though for the most part expression and experimentation were suppressed.

The Soviet government immediately recognized the value of theatre as propaganda. After the revolution, mass spectacles—usually elaborate outdoor events with casts made up partly of amateurs—were organized. In the 1930s, the Soviet Union established "socialist realism" as the only acceptable theatrical form: plays were to be written in realistic style and were to convey a clear socialist message. In Nazi Germany, analogous theatrical forms were supported, and numerous melodramas exalting Nazism were staged. Early in Hitler's regime, mass spectacles called *Thingspielen* were presented. One example of this form was Richard Euringer's *Deutsche Passion: 1933,* which presented Hitler as a Christ figure, wearing a "crown of thorns" made of barbed wire, and gathering apostles and converts to save Germany from the evil Weimar Republic; after rescuing the fatherland, the Nazi dictator is crucified and ascends to heaven amid organ music and a chorus of angels.

Obviously, theatre artists who opposed totalitarian regimes were suppressed. In Spain, as we have seen, the playwright Federico García Lorca was killed by Franco's forces during the Spanish civil war, and productions of Lorca's works—which dramatized the oppression of Spanish women—were prohibited (this ban remained in effect until Franco's death in 1975).

In the Soviet Union, the works of playwrights considered politically dangerous were censored and were not allowed to be staged. About 50 years after it was written, one of these dramas—Nikolai Erdman's *The Suicide* (1928), which presents suicide as an act of political resistance—was produced in London, Chicago, and New York. We have already noted that the director Vsevelod Meyerhold, who attempted unsuccessfully to stage *The Suicide* in 1929, was imprisoned and later executed for his opposition to "socialist realism."

Numerous German theatre artists, because of their religion or their politics, were forced to flee Germany after Hitler came to power in 1933. They included the directors Max Reinhardt and Erwin Piscator as well as the playwrights Bertolt Brecht and Ernst Toller. Many artists who opposed the Third Reich but did not leave were interned in Nazi concentration camps.

DEBATES IN THEATRE HISTORY | **Evaluating Totalitarian Art**

How can we evaluate works created by artists who support dictatorial regimes? We have noted that there were many playwrights who wrote "socialist realism" during the Stalin era. There were also many actors, directors, and designers who served Hitler by creating theatrical propaganda. How can we assess such works aesthetically? Can anything be classified as great art if it is politically horrendous? Can we distinguish between an artist's politics and the aesthetic qualities of his or her works?

One debate of this nature is over the films of Leni Riefenstahl (1902–2003), a German director greatly admired by Adolf Hitler. Riefenstahl's films are documentaries which are formally beautiful and were significant advances in the art of documentary filmmaking. However, her films *The Triumph of the Will* (1935) and *Olympia* (1936–1938) glorify Nazism and paint a glowing picture of Hitler's Germany in the mid-1930s. Can we divorce the aesthetic qualities of these works from their politics? How should we discuss Riefenstahl's contributions to filmmaking?

Similar questions can be asked about the theatre artists who wrote and produced plays in Hitler's Germany, Mussolini's Italy, Franco's Spain, and Stalin's Soviet Union. For example, the playwright Maksim Gorky became a proponent of socialist realism. How can we evaluate his later works, in light of the terror that was inflicted on artists who resisted the aesthetic control imposed in the name of socialist realism? How can we deal with Luigi Pirandello, who was an avid supporter of fascism and Mussolini and donated his Nobel Prize to the fascist Italian government? Does Pirandello's support of a fascist regime decrease the significance of his plays? How can we reconcile his politics with his aesthetics?

Such questions do not seem difficult when an artist's work is, aesthetically, simply not very good; but they become extremely difficult when the work is aesthetically accomplished.

Nonetheless, some theatre artists did resist the rise of totalitarianism. During the 1940s, for example, the exiled Bertolt Brecht wrote *The Resistible Rise of Arturo Ui,* which characterized Hitler as a Chicago gangster.

Theatre as a form of resistance to totalitarianism—and to the horrors of World War II—is most vividly illustrated by the theatrical activities organized by inmates of the Nazi concentration camps. In the mid-1930s, the Nazi guards for their own amusement at Oranienburg and Dachau forced internees to stage productions. Surviving accounts reveal that these presentations satirized the camps, yet the artists were not punished. During the war, in the concentration camps in Nazi-occupied territories such as Auschwitz, there were surreptitious, improvised entertainments in the barracks. These presentations consisted of literature and drama recited from memory, satirical skits, and traditional songs. In the camp at Theresienstadt, in Czechoslovakia, satirical plays, operas, and cabaret entertainments were written and staged. Such entertainments were possible there because the Nazis were using Theresienstadt as a "model" camp: they showed it to Red Cross officials and foreign visitors to discredit rumors of atrocities. Most of the artists at Theresienstadt were later sent to extermination centers.

International Theatres, 1915–1945

In the period between the two world wars, theatre continued to emerge in many parts of the world. In Mexico, for instance, during the 1920s and the 1930s, playwrights and theatre groups emerged. Some were traditional; but, interestingly, several

(Eastfoto/Sovfoto)

Mei Lanfang.

took up the cause of the avant-garde theatre that had taken root in Europe. This movement was headed by Xavier Villaurruita (1903–1950) and Rodolfo Usigli (1905–1979).

In Australia, where a native drama had begun at the turn of the century, a play in this form called *On Our Selection* was the most frequently performed drama between 1912 and 1920. A commercial theatrical syndicate controlled professional productions in Australia and New Zealand at this time, but also developing were a large number of "little theatres"—amateur and semiprofessional groups—which added to the theatrical vitality of the two countries.

Asian Theatres

In Chapter 12 we described Peking opera as a theatrical form that emerged in China in the nineteenth century. One performer in Peking opera who achieved international fame in the years between the two world wars was Mei Lanfang.

MEI LANFANG

Mei Lanfang (1894–1961), the most renowned modern performer of Peking opera, preserved and expanded its traditions. He was acclaimed throughout the world for his portrayal of female characters and was one of the first Asian theatre artists to influence the development of western theatre.

Like most actors in Peking opera, Mei came from a family of performers; both his father and his grandfather had specialized in *tan,* or female roles. Mei began his training at age 8 and made his stage debut when he was 10. Through his technical perfection and precise characterizations, he enhanced the importance of the female roles, which had been considered secondary. Mei worked with the playwright and theatre scholar Qi Rushan to expand and revise the traditional repertoire and to introduce historical accuracy in costumes and dances.

In 1919 and 1925, Mei toured Japan, where his performances and innovations were greatly admired. When he performed in the United States in 1930, he was the guest of Douglas Fairbanks and Mary Pickford in Hollywood. He also met Charlie Chaplin, whom he enthusiastically admired. During his tour of Russia in 1935, Mei met both Konstantin Stanislavski and Bertolt Brecht; Mei's work was one of the most important influences on Brecht's theories of acting.

After the Japanese invasion of China in 1937, Mei refused to act; he grew a mustache so that it would be impossible for him to play female roles. Though it meant financial hardship, he continued his retirement until the Japanese surrendered in 1945. After the war, when he returned to performing, he made several films, including *Bitter Life and Death* (1947). Throughout his career, he trained many performers, including some of the first actresses to appear in Peking opera. Mei continued to perform until 1959, 2 years before he died.

Kathakali in India

An interesting form of dance drama prominent in southwestern India during the past three centuries is kathakali. It is presented at night, by torchlight, on a stage approximately 16 feet square covered with a canopy of flowers. It heightens elements of Sanskrit drama: violence and death are shown on stage in dance and pantomime. The stories revolve around clashes between good and evil, with good always winning. The passions of demons and gods, as well as extraordinary human beings, are featured.

Theatre in China

After the revolution of 1911, when the Qing dynasty was overthrown, Shanghai—the most westernized of the large cities in China—became the focal point for a growing interest in modern spoken Chinese drama. Many of the Chinese playwrights were politically leftist and wrote on social themes. The greatest playwright of this period was Cao Yu (1910–1996), whose works were written before World War II. His *Thunderstorm* (1934) and *Peking Man* (1938) show both a grasp of modern dramaturgy and a burning sense of social injustice. Novelists and other writers, among them Mao Dun and Lao She (1899–1966), also began to create plays.

Theatre in Japan

By the 1930s, two kinds of modern drama were important in Japan. One was leftist political drama, usually based on German and Russian models; the other was a drama, strongly literary in flavor, that took French plays and Chekhov as models. Probably the finest literary dramatist of the period was Kishida Kunio (1890–1954), who had studied with Jacques Copeau in Paris and whose work as a critic, playwright, and producer did much to incorporate western influences in the theatre of his time.

American Theatre

In the period between the two world wars, theatre in the United States finally began turning to the experiments in realism and nonrealism that had started in Europe several decades earlier. This kind of experimentation still did not develop rapidly, however, because the grip of commercial theatre was very strong.

(Billy Rose Theatre Collection/The New York Public Library for the Performing Arts, Astor, Lenox and Tilden Foundations)

SHOW BOAT: A LANDMARK MUSICAL

When *Show Boat* opened in 1927, it began a new chapter in the history of the American musical. The chorus line was eliminated; a romance between a white man and a black woman was treated onstage for the first time; and some of the problems facing African Americans were touched on. Also, it had a glorious musical score by Jerome Kern and Oscar Hammerstein II. Shown here is a scene from the original production.

Commercial Theatre in the United States

At the beginning of the twentieth century, realistic production techniques had been appropriated by American commercial theatre and had become so popular and so commonplace that audiences expected detailed, authentic settings for even the most banal melodrama. The turn-of-the-century American producer David Belasco was one popularizer of authentic settings and lighting; as pointed out before, in a melodrama of 1912 he re-created a Child's restaurant onstage.

Still holding onto the past, American theatre between the world wars remained probably the most commercially oriented in the world. The Theatrical Syndicate, a group of businesspeople who had controlled theatre in the United States, was toppled in 1915 by Lee Shubert (1875–1954) and his brother Jacob J. Shubert (1880–1963);

but the Shuberts developed their own monopoly, owning or controlling almost 75 percent of all theatre buildings in the country. The Shubert organization, now organized as a foundation, still controls 50 percent of the Broadway theatres in New York.

Possibly the most commercially successful form of this period was the musical. In the 1920s and 1930s, *revues*—productions consisting of dramatic sketches and musical numbers—were extremely popular. The Broadway producer Florenz Ziegfeld (1869–1932) made his reputation with annual productions of the spectacular *Ziegfeld Follies.* More important, the modern American musical comedy was born during this era. In the 1920s and 1930s, a generation of composers and lyricists created for Broadway musicals songs that are still performed around the world. Outstanding composers included Jerome Kern (1885–1945), Irving Berlin (1888–1989), George Gershwin (1898–1937), Cole Porter (1891–1964), and Richard Rodgers (1902–1979). Among the important lyricists were Ira Gershwin (1896–1983), who teamed with his brother George; and Lorenz Hart (1895–1943), who collaborated with Richard Rodgers.

The stories of musical comedies were usually inconsequential. However, beginning with *Show Boat* (1927)—by Oscar Hammerstein II (1895–1960) and Jerome Kern—music, song, and dance were more carefully integrated with plot and character development. *Oklahoma!* (1943)—by Richard Rodgers and Oscar Hammerstein, with choreography by Agnes DeMille—is often considered a landmark in this integration of story, songs, and dance.

During this period, there were also notable comedies by Philip Barry (1896–1949), George S. Kaufman (1889–1961), and Moss Hart (1904–1961).

Despite its successes, American commercial theatre was facing troubles. Economic unrest in the 1920s, as well as higher production costs, decreased the number of commercial shows produced annually. Another factor hurting commercial theatre was the growing popularity of movies, especially after the introduction of sound in 1929.

Noncommercial Drama and Theatre in the United States

Commercial theatre held sway in the United States through the 1920s and 1930s; but beginning at the time of World War I, playwrights, actors, directors, and producers began to develop the kind of serious theatre that had become established in Europe, including both realism and nonrealism. One example of an actress-director committed to producing serious drama in repertory was Eva Le Gallienne, who ran the Civic Repertory Theatre in New York from 1926 to 1933.

EVA LE GALLIENNE

The British-born actress-director Eva Le Gallienne (1899–1991) made many significant contributions to American theatre. In addition to an illustrious acting career, for which she was named Woman of the Year (1947) and won a special Tony (1964), an ANTA award (1964), and an Emmy (1978), Le Gallienne was an early pioneer in and a lifelong supporter of noncommercial theatre in America, dedicated to making serious drama available to American audiences.

Born at the turn of the twentieth century, Le Gallienne liked to say she was a "step ahead of the century." She was the daughter of estranged parents: her father was the novelist and poet Richard Le Gallienne, and her Danish mother, Julie Nørregaard, was a feminist and journalist. Le Gallienne spent her childhood in London and Paris. She found her muse at a young age, 7; her inspiration was watching the ageless Sarah Bernhardt perform. Later, she came under the influence of Eleonora Duse. Le Gallienne trained at London's Royal Academy of Dramatic Arts and began her professional career playing character roles. At the age of 17, she moved to America and made her debut as a black maid in *Mrs. Boltay's Daughters* (1915); she went on to work with Ethel Barrymore for 2 years before her own first major success on Broadway, playing opposite Joseph Schildkraut in Ferenc Molnár's *Liliom* (1921). Throughout more than 60 years on the stage, Le Gallienne was a dedicated artist, known for her piercing intelligence and her studiously prepared roles, which she developed from the inner life of each character.

(UPI/Corbis)

Eva Le Gallienne.

From 1926 to 1933, La Gallienne left Broadway to run the Civic Repertory Theatre on West Fourteenth Street in Manhattan, which offered classic as well as modern plays at low ticket prices. There, she produced, directed, and acted in an expansive range of drama, including *The Three Sisters, The Cherry Orchard, The Master Builder, Hedda Gabler,* and *Romeo and Juliet,* as well as a popular adaptation of *Alice in Wonderland.* Le Gallienne also presented *Peter Pan,* in which she was the first actress to "fly." With the depression, Le Gallienne lost much of her financial backing and the theatre was forced to close. Another attempt at forming a permanent ensemble company occurred in 1946, when Le Gallienne, Cheryl Crawford, and Margaret Webster founded the short-lived American Repertory Company.

Le Gallienne published two autobiographies: *At 33* (1934) and *With a Quiet Heart* (1953), as well as a biography of Eleonora Duse. Her numerous translations, including works by Ibsen and Chekhov, attest to her broad knowledge of languages and her commitment to learning. Le Gallienne's last appearances were in *To Grandmother's House We Go* (1981) and the film *Resurrection* (1980). The acclaimed actress died at the age of 92. Recent scholarship by the historian Robert Shanke, including his book *Shattered Applause: The Lives of Eva Le Gallienne,* focuses on the relationship between the performer's lesbianism and her career.

Playwrights in the United States

There were many important dramatists in the United States between the world wars. In *The Adding Machine* (1923), Elmer Rice (1892–1967) used expressionism to explore the depersonalization and mechanization of American life. In *Our Town* (1938), Thornton Wilder (1897–1975) used a narrator to paint a picture of small-town life and set it against larger issues. Maxwell Anderson (1888–1959) attempted a return to dramatic poetry in *Winterset* (1935). A new, vigorous realism emerged in the plays of Clifford Odets (1906–1963) and in such works as *The Little Foxes* (1938) by Lillian Hellman (1905–1984).

One playwright, Eugene O'Neill, is frequently cited as having paved the way for meaningful drama in the United States. O'Neill saw theatre not just as entertainment or a way to make money, but as a high calling. He considered theatre not a commercial enterprise but art. Like many European experimental theatre artists, O'Neill had much pain and sorrow in his own life, and his later drama was often autobiographical.

(Vandamm Photo © Museum of the City of New York, Theatre Collection)

THORNTON WILDER'S OUR TOWN

An important American playwright of the mid-twentieth century was Thornton Wilder. In his play *Our Town* he applied techniques from Chinese theatre and other nonrealistic sources to tell a quintessential American story about the life of average New Englanders. Two important features were a narrator, who also played small parts, and a bare stage on which scenes were created by the imaginative use of just a few essentials. The scene here is from the original Broadway production in 1938, with Martha Scott and John Craven (left) as a young couple, and Frank Craven (center) as the narrator.

EUGENE O'NEILL

The reputation of Eugene Gladstone O'Neill (1888–1953) as a leading American playwright rests in part on his ambition and persistence. He wrote almost every form of drama—realism, expressionism, modern versions of Greek tragedy—in an attempt to bring American theatre to maturity. In large measure, he succeeded.

(Carl Van Vechten/Theatre Collection, Museum of the City of New York)

Eugene O'Neill.

As the son of James O'Neill—an actor famous for playing the role of the Count of Monte Cristo throughout the United States—Eugene O'Neill spent his childhood in hotels and on trains before being sent to a series of boarding schools. His mother, Ella, was recurrently addicted to drugs, and his older brother James was an alcoholic who introduced the young Eugene to a loose, bohemian lifestyle.

After being expelled from Princeton for a prank, O'Neill spent 6 years leading a haphazard, alcoholic existence, often working as a sailor. After a suicide attempt, he pulled himself together and worked as a newspaper reporter for 6 months. He had to leave the newspaper when he contracted tuberculosis; confined to a sanitarium, he became an avid reader and began to work seriously on his writing.

He spent a year at Harvard in George Pierce Baker's playwriting course. In 1916, an experimental theatre group in Provincetown, Massachusetts, produced his one-act play, *Bound East for Cardiff*. The Provincetown Players reappeared that fall in Greenwich Village, New York, where O'Neill then lived. Several of his early plays were produced there before moving to Broadway. In 1920 he won his first Pulitzer Prize for *Beyond the Horizon*.

(© Donald Cooper/Photostage)

O'NEILL'S LONG DAY'S JOURNEY

The playwright generally credited with being the first important serious dramatist in America is Eugene O'Neill. Always serious and dedicated in his approach to theatre, he experimented with a variety of styles through the 1920s and 1930s. The play many consider his masterpiece is an autobiographical work, *Long Day's Journey into Night.* The scene here features Jessica Lange as the mother, Charles Dance as the father, and Paul Nicholls as the younger son in a production in London.

O'Neill experimented with a variety of forms and styles throughout his career. His early plays, like *Anna Christie* (1921), are realistic, and many of them deal in some way with the sea. He experimented with expressionism in *The Hairy Ape* (1922), with characters who speak their subconscious thoughts in *Strange Interlude* (1928), and with masks in *The Great God Brown* (1926).

The Hairy Ape, which has many expressionistic elements, is an excellent example of how O'Neill experimented with avant-garde dramaturgical techniques. The protagonist, Yank, a stoker on a ship, is ridiculed by a wealthy woman and begins to see himself as an impotent, hairy ape. Later, Yank punches a wealthy man who is strolling on Fifth Avenue, but the man shows no effect: he is unharmed. When Yank is imprisoned for this attack, he acts like a caged animal. The play has eight scenes, which present the action from the highly personal viewpoint of the protagonist. Most of the characters are representative types, and the play is an attack on the depersonalization of twentieth-century society.

A later three-part drama, *Mourning Becomes Electra* (1931), combines Greek myth (the *Oresteia* of Aeschylus) with Freudian psychology. Though O'Neill planned an eleven-part saga covering one family's life in America, he finished only a portion of it. A significant later play is *The Iceman Cometh* (1939), revived successfully in London and New York in 1999 as well as on Broadway in 2003. His last plays are tied closely to his own experiences, especially the powerful realistic drama *Long Day's Journey into Night* (1957), in which he finally comes to an understanding of his family. The play covers one day in the life of a family similar to O'Neill's own family:

a mother, a father, and two sons. O'Neill is represented by the younger son. In a series of confrontations and revelations, we learn of the mother's drug addiction; the father's regrets over having wasted his acting ability; and the self-destructiveness of the older son, who threatens to carry the younger son down with him.

In 1936, O'Neill became the first American dramatist to win the Nobel Prize for literature. After that, however, he wrote less, though the plays he did write are among his finest. In his final years, he became depressed and was hampered by a nerve disorder that eventually made him an invalid. His first two marriages ended in divorce, and his third, to Carlotta Monteray, was often stormy. At the time of his death—in a hotel in Boston in 1953—his plays were considered outmoded, but he is now recognized as the finest dramatist the United States has produced.

Women Playwrights in the United States

In addition to Lillian Hellman, mentioned above, a number of other women dramatists were active during the 1920s and 1930s. Rachel Crothers (1876–1958) was one of the most successful, with such plays as *He and She* (1920) and *Susan and God* (1937). *Miss Lulu Bett* (1920) by Zona Gale (1874–1938) was the first play by a woman to win the Pulitzer Prize. Another winner of a Pulitzer Prize was *The Old Maid* (1934) by Zoe Akins (1886–1958). A particularly important drama of the period was *Machinal* (1928), which is still performed today. Written by Sophie Treadwell (1885–1970), this play tells the story of a woman trapped in a world that operates like a machine; eventually, her mechanistic surroundings drive her to murder.

The "Little Theatre" Movement

In a development paralleling the emergence of serious playwrights, a number of small independent producing theatres also appeared at the time of World War I. In one sense, these noncommercial "little theatres" were the spiritual heirs of independent theatres of the late nineteenth century in Europe and Great Britain. Many historians believe that "little theatres" inspired the off-Broadway movement that began after World War II.

The "little theatre" movement flourished in the second decade of the twentieth century. Among the "little theatres" were the Provincetown Playhouse and the Washington Square Players, both founded in 1915 as an alternative to commercial theatre.

The Provincetown Playhouse provides a good example of the development of the "little theatre" movement. The company was organized in 1915 in Provincetown, Massachusetts, by vacationing artists. Its two founding members were George Cram Cook (1873–1924) and his wife, the playwright Susan Glaspell (1882–1948). Glaspell was the author of such works as *Trifles* (1916), *The Verge* (1921), and *Alison's House* (1931), which won the Pulitzer Prize. After presenting a series of plays in Massachusetts, the playhouse moved, the following year, to a small Greenwich Village theatre in New York City, outside the Broadway district. In 1923, the company split into two separate producing agencies, and in 1929 the depression brought the venture to an end.

The Provincetown was an extremely influential theatre. In its earlier years, it was dedicated to new American drama; and as the first theatre to produce the works of Eugene O'Neill, it helped establish him as an important playwright. The Provincetown also introduced new production styles, particularly the designs of Robert Edmond Jones (1887–1954), a leading figure in the "new stagecraft" movement in the United States. This design movement put into practice many of the theories of Adolphe Appia and Edward Gordon Craig, especially their emphasis on lighting. The "new stagecraft" designers also strove for "simplified realism," using detail only to suggest specific locales and to reinforce characterization and dramatic action.

Another "little theatre," the Washington Square Players, operated in Greenwich Village from 1915 through 1918 and later evolved into the Theatre Guild. The Guild, a subscription-based professional organization—which eventually built its own theatre in the Broadway district—introduced in the 1920s many leading experimental European and American playwrights, including O'Neill, as well as new production techniques. The Guild also attempted to establish a permanent acting company. The Guild was so badly hurt by the depression—and by its own attempts to expand into other American cities—that it eventually became simply another commercial producing entity. During its most active period, the Theatre Guild supported the early efforts of the Group Theatre.

(Billy Rose Theatre Collection, New York Public Library at Lincoln Center; Astor, Lenox, and Tilden Foundations)

THE GROUP THEATRE'S AWAKE AND SING

Clifford Odets's *Awake and Sing,* first produced in 1935, is an example of a realistic social drama: it deals with American concerns of the 1930s. The play—an intense family drama set in a Bronx apartment during the depression—required the realistic ensemble acting for which the Group Theatre was noted. This scene shows Stella Adler, Art Smith, and Sanford Meisner in the original Broadway production directed by Harold Clurman.

The Group Theatre

The Group Theatre—often referred to as America's Moscow Art Theatre—was a noncommercial company which produced plays in the Broadway district. It was dedicated to introducing Stanislavski's system to the United States and to producing socially relevant drama. Politically, the company leaned toward the left wing, and its members hoped to motivate political and social action through theatre.

The founding members of the Group Theatre were Lee Strasberg (1901–1982), Cheryl Crawford (1902–1986), and Harold Clurman (1901–1980), and its actors included Franchot Tone, Morris Carnovsky, Stella Adler, Luther Adler, and John Garfield. The company's resident playwright was Clifford Odets. Its productions of Odets's *Waiting for Lefty* (1935), *Awake and Sing* (1935), and *Golden Boy* (1937) set a standard for realistic writing and performance that was to last for several decades.

Dissension over the correct interpretation of Stanislavski's system developed in the Group Theatre in the mid-1930s, and Lee Strasberg left the Group after Harold Clurman and Stella Adler had criticized him for overemphasizing emotional recall—the technique of calling on past experiences to create present emotions. (Adler called for greater emphasis on analysis of a script's "given circumstances.")

The Group Theatre disbanded in 1941, but its influence on American theatre continued to be strong. Harold Clurman was a leading director and critic until his death in 1980; and Lee Strasberg, beginning in the late 1940s at the Actors Studio, trained many well-known actors, including Marlon Brando (1924–2004). Two other members of the Group Theatre, Elia Kazan (1909–2003) and Robert Lewis (1909–1998), became leading directors. Stella Adler (1902–1992) remained a prominent acting teacher until her death.

STELLA ADLER

Konstantin Stanislavski's theory of acting did not reach the United States until the 1920s, when some members of the Moscow Art Theatre emigrated to New York and began teaching it. In 1931, however, the Group Theatre was founded, in part to explore the Stanislavskian system. One of its founding members was Stella Adler, an actress with 25 years of stage experience.

(Museum of The City of New York/Getty Images)

Stella Adler.

In Yiddish theatre, an important part of theatre in New York City at the turn of the twentieth century, the name Adler was synonymous with excellence in acting. Stella's father, Jacob Adler, was the premier actor of the Yiddish stage, famous for his portrayal of King Lear. Stella Adler made her own stage debut in 1906 as a member of her father's Yiddish company, in which she performed for several years. In 1919, she made her London debut; and in 1922, her Broadway debut. Her three sisters and two brothers were also actors.

Stella Adler and her brother Luther studied Stanislavski's system under Maria Ouspenskaya and Richard Boleslavsky, who had come to the United States after distinguished theatrical careers in Europe. Stella and Luther Adler became original members of the Group Theatre, and in 1934, Stella and Harold Clurman—one of the Group's principal directors—went to France to study with Stanislavski himself. When they returned, they reported that Stanislavski placed more emphasis on the study of text and character than on the actor's emotional memory. As we have seen, this led to dissension with Lee Strasberg, who left the company.

Though Stella Adler had an active career as an actress and director, she was primarily interested in teaching acting. After teaching in the Dramatic Workshop of the New School for Social Research, she opened the Stella Adler Theatre Studio in New York City in 1949. Following her own interpretation of Stanislavski's method, she emphasized the text of the play and encouraged students to explore the possibilities of their characters. Many leading American film actors studied with her throughout her illustrious career.

THE FEDERAL THEATRE PROJECT

One additional experiment in noncommercial American theatre between the wars should be noted. During the depression, President Franklin Delano Roosevelt established the Works Progress Administration (WPA), which organized government-subsidized agencies to put the unemployed back to work. The Federal Theatre Project, headed by Hallie Flanagan Davis (1890–1969), a college professor, was one of these agencies. For 4 years, the Federal Theatre Project supported theatrical ventures throughout the United States and helped to revitalize interest in theatre outside New York City. One of the most popular forms developed by the project was the *living newspaper*—dramatizations of current events, such as bread lines and rising unemployment.

(Billy Rose Theatre Collection, New York Public Library at Lincoln Center; Astor, Lenox, and Tilden Foundations)

THE FEDERAL THEATRE PROJECT A theatre funded by Congress during the depression to give work to theatre professionals, the Federal Theatre Project nurtured a great deal of talent and achieved some important productions. One was the all-black version of *Macbeth* shown here. Set in Haiti, it was conceived and directed by Orson Welles.

For political reasons, the government discontinued funding the Federal Theatre Project in 1939—many legislators had said that the project was sympathetic to communism. Today, federal, state, and local governments provide some support to theatre companies, but the Federal Theatre Project is the closest the United States has come to establishing a national theatre.

College and University Theatres

Another noteworthy development in the United States at this time was the emergence of theatre departments in colleges and universities across the country. George Pierce Baker (1866–1935) at Harvard and Yale, Thomas Wood Stevens (1880–1942) at the Carnegie Institute of Technology (now Carnegie Mellon) in Pittsburgh, and Frederick Koch (1877–1944) at the University of North Carolina inaugurated the study of theatre at academic institutions. This unprecedented movement was to become important in preparing playwrights, performers, directors, designers, and technicians for both professional and nonprofessional theatre.

African American Theatre

During World War I, thousands upon thousands of rural southern blacks in the United States went north to find work in the war industries. With them, they brought their folk customs, music, religion, and dreams of a better life. When the war ended in 1918, a spirit of unity and hope prevailed.

African American Theatre in the 1920s

The early twentieth century saw the formation of African American stock companies. The most significant of these was the Lafayette Players, discussed in Chapter 12: by the time it closed in 1932, it had employed many black stars and presented over 250 productions. African American performers and writers were also making inroads in commercial theatre during the 1920s. Twenty plays with black themes were presented on Broadway in this decade, five of them written by African Americans. These included *Shuffle Along* (1921), with lyrics by Noble Sissle (1889–1975) and music by Eubie Blake (1883–1983). The decade also saw some black performers achieve recognition in serious drama, including Charles Gilpin (1878–1930) and Ethel Waters.

ETHEL WATERS

The Broadway and motion picture actress and singer Ethel Waters (1896–1977) made famous such songs as "Taking a Chance on Love," "Cabin in the Sky," and "Am I Blue." At the height of her popularity she was reported to be worth several million dollars, but when she died in 1977 she was close to poverty.

(Bettmann/Corbis)

Ethel Waters.

Ethel Waters was born on October 13, 1896, in Chester, Pennsylvania. Her early years were hard. As she revealed in her autobiography, *His Eye Is on the Sparrow* (1951), her first job was as a chambermaid at a small hotel in Philadelphia, earning $4.75 a week. She sometimes stole food to keep from going hungry.

Her luck began to change when, at the age of 17, she won a talent contest at a local theatre. This led to a job singing and dancing at the Lincoln Theatre in Baltimore, Maryland. From there Waters began working the TOBA circuit (the booking organization mentioned in Chapter 12), playing mainly to black audiences in the south. She was known to her fans as "Sweet Mama Stringbean."

Waters began to taste real success with her rendition of W. C. Handy's classic "Saint Louis Blues." By the time she moved to New York in the early 1920s, she was already a star in the south, known for the class and innocence she brought to her repertoire of mostly "blue" material.

In 1924, she substituted for the singing sensation Florence Mills in *The Plantation Revue of 1924.* From that point on, Waters became one of New York's brightest stars. Irving Berlin, after hearing her rendition of "Cabin in the Sky," wrote several songs for her, such as "Harlem on My Mind," "Heat Wave," and the poignant lament "Supper Time." Waters introduced these songs in the Broadway revue *As Thousands Cheer* (1933). She also appeared in several other revues on Broadway: *Africana* (1929), *Blackbirds* (1930), *Rhapsody in Black* (1933), and *At Home Abroad* (1935).

In 1938, Waters received critical acclaim for her first dramatic performance on Broadway, in Dorothy and DuBose Heyward's play *Mamba's Daughter.* She returned to the musical stage in 1940 in *Cabin in the Sky*. For this performance, the *Herald Tribune* praised Waters as "one of the great musical comedy stars of her time." In 1943, Waters appeared in a movie version of *Cabin in the Sky,* which also featured such notables as Lena Horne, Louis Armstrong, Eddie "Rochester" Anderson, Rex Ingram, and Butterfly McQueen.

Waters appeared in nine motion pictures, starred in several radio and television shows, and performed all over Europe, but her most remarkable performance was in Carson McCullers's *A Member of the Wedding,* at first on Broadway in 1950, and then in a film version in 1952. McCullers's play was directed by Harold Clurman and featured Julie Harris as an adolescent girl on the threshhold of womanhood and Waters as the family maid who is her main support.

Waters died in Chatsworth, California, of kidney and heart failure. In her final years, she had devoted her life to religion, singing in revivals all over the world.

AFRICAN AMERICAN THEATRE IN THE 1930s AND 1940s

The depression curtailed the advances that were being made by African American theatre and theatre artists, forcing performers to turn to other careers or to devise ingenious ways of creating their own theatre. The 1930s did see two popular shows written by whites for black performers: *The Green Pastures* (1930) and *Porgy and Bess.* There were also a few Broadway productions of plays by African Americans: the folk musical *Run Little Children* (1933) was one, and another was *Mulatto* (1935) by Langston Hughes (1902–1967).

Possibly the most significant development of the 1930s for African American theatre was the Federal Theatre Project, discussed above, which was meant to help theatre artists through the depression. The project formed separate black units in twenty-two cities. These units mounted plays by African American and white authors and employed thousands of African American actors, dancers, vaudevillians, technicians, writers, and scholars. The Federal Theatre Project created a new generation of African American theatre artists who would develop the theatre of the 1940s and 1950s.

The 1940s saw, in 1941, a stage adaptation of the controversial novel *Native Son* by Richard Wright (1908–1960). Directed by Orson Welles (1915–1985) and presented by Welles's Mercury Theatre, it featured Canada Lee (1907–1952) in the lead role and was unanimously praised. Other important Broadway ventures included *Tropical Revue* (1943) by the choreographer Katherine Dunham (1910–), which consolidated her dance company and her influence on American dance; and *Our Lan'* (1946), a historical drama about the struggle of freed slaves to hold property. The longest-running venture was *Anna Lucasta* (1944), adapted by Abram Hill (1911–1986), which played for 3 years. *Anna Lucasta* originated with the American Negro Theatre (ANT), which was founded in 1940 and created training workshops for actors, playwrights, and technicians.

The 1940s introduced many new African American stars, but the leading actor of the 1940s was a man who had been struggling for almost two decades to earn his rightful place on the American stage—Paul Robeson.

PAUL ROBESON

Internationally known as an actor, singer, athlete, scholar, and political activist, Paul Robeson (1898–1976) had a luminous but controversial career that spanned 50 years.

Born on April 9, 1898, in Princeton, New Jersey, Robeson was the son of a runaway slave who had become a Presbyterian minister. He attended Rutgers University on an academic scholarship but rose to national prominence as a college athlete, winning a total of twelve athletic letters in four different sports and being named an All-American in football in 1917 and 1918. After graduating (having been elected to Phi Beta Kappa), Robeson attended Columbia University and earned a law degree in 1923.

Eugene O'Neill saw Robeson perform in an amateur production and offered him the lead in *The Emperor Jones.* Robeson initially turned it down because of other commitments, but later he played Brutus Jones onstage in 1924 and in the film version in 1933. Robeson also appeared in O'Neill's controversial *All God's Chillun Got Wings.*

It was in *The Emperor Jones* that Robeson launched his career as a concert singer. Asked by the director to whistle in one scene, Robeson sang instead, and the response was overwhelming. In 1926, following a series of successful performances the year before at the Greenwich Theatre, Robeson presented a program of spirituals and work songs at Town Hall in New York City. This was the first program of all-black music ever sung on the New York stage by a solo artist.

From 1927 to 1939, while living in England, Robeson appeared in many productions, including *The Hairy Ape, Stevedore,* and *Show Boat,* in which he introduced "Ol' Man River," the song that was to become his trademark. But his greatest achievement in England was *Othello,* in which he headed a cast that included Peggy Ashcroft, Sybil Thorndike, and Ralph Richardson. Robeson repeated this success on Broadway in 1945 with Uta Hagen as Desdemona and Jose Ferrer as Iago. The play ran for 296 performances, a record for any Shakespearean play on Broadway.

In Europe, Robeson had become very outspoken about the racial situation in the United States. Because of this, and because of his strong affection for the Soviet Union, the State Department took away his passport in 1950, effectively denying him the right to leave the country. He was blacklisted and denied the use of recording studios and concert halls, and his annual income fell from $104,000 to $16,000.

In 1958, after an 8-year worldwide campaign by his supporters, Robeson regained his passport. He gave a triumphant concert at Carnegie Hall and then left the country. In 1959, he appeared as Othello in Stratford-upon-Avon and went to the Soviet Union to receive the Stalin Peace Prize. In 1963, Robeson returned to the United States. He spent the remainder of his life in seclusion, making only a few public appearances, and died on January 26, 1976.

(Library of Congress)

PAUL ROBESON AS OTHELLO
An important African American actor of the twentieth century was Paul Robeson. In addition to his acting skills, he had a powerful, melodic singing voice. He was denied freedom of movement into and out of the United States for political reasons, but when he was allowed to perform, his work was highly lauded. When he appeared as Othello, the production set a record for consecutive performances of a Shakespearean play. He is seen here in the title role in that production, with Uta Hagen as Desdemona. It was produced by the Theatre Guild during the 1943–1944 season.

Theatre during the era of the world wars illustrates the significance of drama in western culture. Drama and theatre of this period offered an escape from harsh realities, reflected social upheavals, and were used for both propaganda and political resistance. Theatre between 1915 and 1945, in many ways, suggests why the dramatic arts survive the transformations and ravages of history. In Chapter 14, we turn to theatre in the post-World War II period from 1945 to 1975.

Summary

Theatre between 1915 and 1945—the era of the world wars—mirrored the social upheavals of these three decades.

In Europe, many antirealistic movements developed, including expressionism, futurism, dada, and surrealism. Possibly the two most influential European theorists were Antonin Artaud and Bertolt Brecht. Artaud had few opportunities to realize his theatre of cruelty, but Brecht developed his epic style in his own plays and later in plays he directed at the Berliner Ensemble after World War II.

The rise of totalitarianism affected theatre in the Soviet Union, Germany, Spain, and elsewhere. Theatre was used for propaganda by totalitarian regimes, and courageous artists also used it as a means of resistance.

In the United States, "little theatres," such as the Provincetown Playhouse and the Washington Square Players, reacted against commercial Broadway fare and introduced new playwrights. The Theatre Guild and the Group Theatre also produced new dramas using innovative production styles. During the depression, the Federal Theatre Project was an experiment with government-subsidized theatre, and African American theatre made inroads in commercial theatre.

Theatre in Asia—in India, China, Japan, and other parts of the continent—continued to modernize and be influenced by theatre in the west while also continuing traditions from the past. Mei Lanfang, a performer in Peking opera, became an actor of international renown.

Theatre History

- Luigi Pirandello (1867–1936), *Six Characters in Search of an Author*
- Harley Granville-Barker (1877–1946)
- Charles Gilpin (1878–1930)
- Georg Kaiser (1878–1945), *From Morn to Midnight*
- Leopold Jessner (1878–1945)
- Jacques Copeau (1879–1949)
- Jean Giraudoux (1882–1994), *Amphitryon 38*
- Stanislaw Ignacy Witkiewicz (1885–1939), *The Water Hen*
- Eugene O'Neill (1888–1953) *(below), The Great God Brown*

- Jean Cocteau (1889–1963), *Antigone*
- Walter Hasenclever (1890–1940), *The Son*
- Jürgen Fehling (1890–1968)
- Ernst Toller (1893–1939), *Man and the Masses*
- Erwin Piscator (1893–1960)
- Antonin Artaud (1896–1948), theatre of cruelty
- Ethel Waters (1896–1977)
- Federico García Lorca (1898–1936), *The House of Bernarda Alba*
- Bertolt Brecht (1898–1956), *Mother Courage and Her Children*
- Paul Robeson (1898–1976)
- Eva Le Gallienne (1899–1991)

Cultural and Historical Developments

- Easter Rebellion in Ireland (1916)
- Russian Revolution (1917)
- End of World War I (1918)
- Flu epidemic kills 22 million people worldwide (1918–1920)
- Versailles Peace Conference; prohibition in United States (1919)
- Harlem Renaissance (1920s)
- Women's suffrage in United States; League of Nations established (1920)
- British Broadcasting Corporation founded (1921)
- Benito Mussolini rises to power in Italy; James Joyce's *Ulysses* (1922)
- Alfred Stieglitz's *Equivalent* (1923)
- Franz Kafka's *The Trail;* Thomas Mann's *The Magic Mountain* (1924)
- Scopes trial in United States over teaching of evolution theory; F. Scott Fitzgerald's *The Great Gatsby* (1925)
- Arnold Schoenberg's twelve-tone music (1926)
- Joseph Stalin *(below)* assumes control in Soviet Russia (1928–1951)

- Stock market crash on Wall Street; economic depression; William Faulkner's *The Sound and the Fury* (1929)
- Grant Wood's *American Gothic* (1930)

continued

Photo Credits: Eugene O'Neill. (Carl Van Vechten/Theatre Collection, Museum of the City of New York) / Joseph Stalin. (Library of Congress)

- Tyrone Guthrie (1901–1971)
- Ralph Richardson (1902–1983)
- Stella Adler (1902–1992) *(below)*

- John Gielgud (1904–2000)
- Laurence Olivier (1907–1989)
- Futurism appears in Italy (1909)
- Jean Anouilh (1910–1987), *Antigone*
- "Little theater" movement in the United States (1910s)
- Dada introduced in Switzerland (1916)
- Walter Gropius establishes Bauhaus (1919–1932)
- Surrealism develops in France (1924)
- Soviet Union establishes socialist realism as official theatre form; *Thingspielen,* mass spectacles, staged in Nazi Germany (1930s)
- Group Theatre (1934)
- Federal Theatre Project (1935–1939) *(below)*

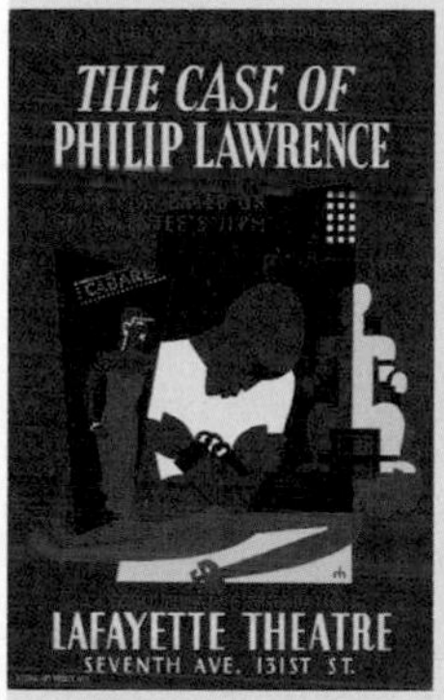

- Spain's monarchy collapses (1931)
- Aldous Huxley's *Brave New World* (1932)
- Adolf Hitler rises to power in Germany; Franklin Roosevelt introduces New Deal (1933)
- Italy attacks Ethiopia; purges in Soviet Union; Nuremburg laws against Jews in Germany (1935)
- First television broadcast (1936) *(below)*

- Spanish civil war (1936–1939)
- Jacob Lawrence's *Harriet Tubman Series* (1939–1940) *(below)*

- World War II (1939–1945)
- Ernest Hemingway's *For Whom the Bell Tolls* (1940)
- Japanese attack Pearl Harbor (1941)
- Langston Hughes's *Shakespeare in Harlem* (1942)
- United States drops atomic bomb on Japan (1945)

Photo Credits: Stella Adler. (Museum of The City of New York/Getty Images) / Poster for the Federal Theatre Project. (Library of Congress) / Family watching television, 1940s. (© H. Armstrong Roberts/Corbis) / Jacob Lawrence, *The Life of Harriet Tubman, #7,* 1940. (Photo: © 2008 The Jacob and Gwendolyn Lawrence Foundation, Seattle/Artists Rights Society (ARS) New York; Photo supplied by Art Resource, NY.)

CHAPTER 14

THEATRES FROM 1945 TO 1975

THEATRE AFTER WORLD WAR II

The period following World War II was a particularly fertile one for theatre. Realism continued strongly, but a number of nonrealistic forms of theatre also thrived. Among the latter was a movement called absurdism, which stressed illogical, random, inexplicable events and characters. An important playwright of absurdism was Eugène Ionesco, whose play *The Bald Soprano,* in an English version by Tina Howe, is shown here. The production was at the Atlantic Theater.

(© Carol Rosegg)

World War II, as we noted in Chapter 13, left many haunting questions. How could the civilized world have engaged in a war that resulted in over 35 million deaths? How could rational societies undertake genocide? Would the atomic bomb result in annihilation of the human race? Questions like these led to other questions, forcing western society to reevaluate its most cherished beliefs. Is humanity as rational and civilized as the eighteenth- and nineteenth-century philosophers proclaimed? Could God exist and allow the destruction of so many innocent human beings? Are individuals responsible for group actions? This questioning formed the basis of new philosophies, such as existentialism, which rejected traditional beliefs.

Background: The Postwar World—A Time of Social Upheaval

The end of World War II did not mean the end of conflict. Possibly, the most destructive struggle was psychological. In the 1950s, the superpowers—the United States and the Soviet Union—began a "cold war," each trying to establish military superiority and extend its sphere of influence. The toll of this cold war was high, and both sides feared a nuclear holocaust. A climax was reached in 1962, when the American president, John F. Kennedy, threatened to blockade communist Cuba if the Soviet Union did not remove nuclear missiles it had set up there. The situation was defused, and later—in the 1970s, during the administration of Richard Nixon—a policy of détente and disarmament was undertaken; but détente was threatened by events like the Soviet Union's intervention in Afghanistan in 1980 and the suppression of the Polish labor union Solidarity at the close of 1981.

The United States was also involved in several military conflicts during the 30 years from 1945 to 1975. In the early 1950s, the Korean war was an attempt to prevent communist North Korea from invading South Korea; and in the late 1960s and early 1970s, the United States fought a controversial war in Vietnam. This war in Vietnam aroused enormous opposition: antiwar activities included draft resistance and sit-ins that were often violent. Many Americans felt that the United States was protecting a corrupt regime in South Vietnam and should not have become involved in a civil war. In 1972, the United States pulled out of Vietnam, which eventually became entirely communist. Reverberations of this war are still apparent, and the ambivalence of the American conscience is reflected in such plays as *Streamers* (1976) by David Rabe (1940–), *Still Life* (1983) by Emily Mann (1952–), and *Redwood Curtain* (1993) by Lanford Wilson (1934–). Today, continued political turmoil throughout southeast Asia precludes any final analysis of American involvement in Vietnam.

During this period there were also a series of wars in the Middle East, following the founding of the state of Israel. These wars were a product of Israeli and Arab nationalism, complicated by geography, oil resources, and competition between the superpowers.

The desire for worldwide peace was strong, however. The institution that represented this idealistic goal was the United Nations, founded immediately after World War II; but peace proved elusive, and nationalistic fervor often prevented the United Nations from resolving international conflicts.

Nationalism was a factor in the rise of third world nations. African nations, for example, broke from colonial rule and asserted their independence. While many of the third world nations in Africa and Asia have valuable natural resources, they are still struggling to develop self-sustaining economies. The third world nations that prospered most were the oil-rich Middle Eastern countries. Unfortunately, many third world nations were racked by political turmoil: two examples are Uganda, which deposed its dictator Idi Amin but was then unable to establish a stable government; and Iran, which deposed its shah but was then controlled by the unstable Islamic regime of Ayatollah Khomeini.

1945 to Present
Year

Theatre

- Barrault's Compagnie Madeleine Renaud-Jean-Louis Barrault established (1946)
- Genet's *The Maids;* Williams's *A Streetcar Named Desire* (1947)
- Ionesco's *The Bald Soprano;* Berliner Ensemble; Miller's *Death of a Salesman;* Arena Stage in Washington (1949)
- Vilar at Théâtre National Populaire (1951)
- Beckett's *Waiting for Godot* (1953)
- Thornton Wilder's *The Matchmaker* (1954)
- Osborne's *Look Back in Anger;* Dürrenmatt's *The Visit* (1956)
- Pinter's *Birthday Party;* Laterna Magika (1958)
- Hansberry's *A Raisin in the Sun;* Grotowski founds Polish Laboratory Theater (1959)
- Café La Mama founded; Albee's *Who's Afraid of Virginia Woolf?* (1962)
- National Theater under Laurence Olivier (1963)
- Lonne Elder's *Ceremonies in Dark Old Men* (1969)
- Sam Shepard's *Buried Child* wins Pulitzer Prize (1979)
- August Wilson's *Fences* wins Pulitzer Prize (1987)
- *Lost in Yonkers,* Neil Simon wins Pulitzer Prize (1991)
- *Angels in America,* Tony Kushner wins Pulitzer Prize (1993)
- Eugène Ionesco dies (1994)
- Heiner Müller dies (1995)
- *Wit* by Margaret Edson wins Pulitzer Prize (1999)
- Peter Stein directs *Faust,* Berlin, Germany (2000)
- *Topdog/Underdog* by Suzan-Lori Parks wins Pulitzer Prize (2002)
- Kevin Spacey assumes artistic direction of London's Old Vic (2004)
- Guthrie Theatre moves into new facility (2006)

Year markers

1945 · 1950 · 1955 · 1960 · 1965 · 1975 · 1985 · 1990 · 1995 · 2000

Culture and Politics

- Nuremberg trials (1946)
- Orwell's *1984;* Germany divided (1949)
- Korean War (1950–1953)
- Stalin dies (1953)
- McCarthy-Army hearings; hydrogen bomb tested (1954)
- Russia crushes Hungarian revolt; Suez crisis (1956)
- Sputnik I and II (1957)
- Belgian Congo granted independence (1960)
- Berlin Wall (1961)
- Cuban missile crisis (1962)
- Warfare escalates between North and South Vietnam; Martin Luther King arrested in Birmingham; John F. Kennedy, president of the United States, assassinated (1963)
- Khrushchev resigns (1964)
- American astronauts walk on moon (1969)
- Camp David accord reached between Israel and Egypt (1977)
- Muslim revolution in Iran (1979)
- Ronald Reagan elected president (1980)
- Chinese government crushes pro-democracy demonstration (1989)
- Berlin Wall taken down; eastern Europe democratized (1990)
- Soviet Union dissolves (1991)
- Bill Clinton elected president of the United States (1992)
- Bill Clinton reelected president (1996)
- George W. Bush elected president of the United States (2000)
- Terrorist attack on World Trade Center in NYC (9/11/2001)
- War in Iraq (2003)
- George W. Bush wins reelection as president of the United States (2004)
- Hamas wins Palestinian election (2006)

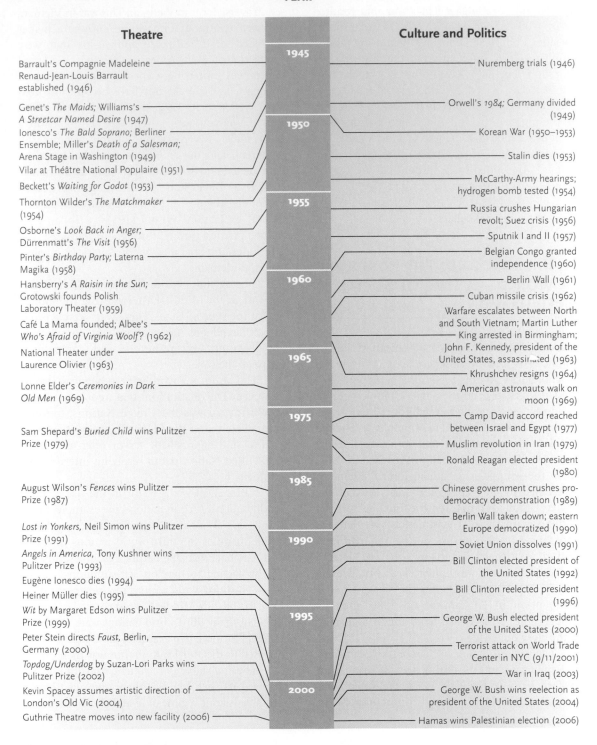

This 30-year period was a time of general social unrest. In the United States, a series of assassinations claimed the lives of John F. Kennedy, Robert Kennedy, Martin Luther King, Jr., and—12 years later—John Lennon. Throughout the western world, terrorist organizations used violence as a means of publicizing political discontent.

In addition to political unrest, there were significant cultural changes during the period between 1945 and 1975. This was particularly true in the United States and western Europe. Symbolic of this cultural upheaval was the emergence in the late 1950s and early 1960s of the singer Elvis Presley (1935–1977), and in Britain of the musical groups the Beatles and the Rolling Stones. Rock 'n' roll music signaled an era of more provocative sexual movements by performers, of informality in dress, of permissiveness in profanity—in fact, of a social revolution in behavior and attitudes which often pitted young people against their parents. The repercussions of these changes were to be felt through the rest of the twentieth century.

Other movements were part of this era of unrest. The civil rights, gay rights, and feminist movements forced people to reevaluate their perceptions of minorities and oppressed groups. The sexual revolution brought a reevaluation of traditional morality, including such institutions as marriage and the family. Twentieth-century society continued to be technologically innovative: television joined film as a major competitor of theatre; medical advances resulted in the eradication of polio and in genetic experimentation; nuclear energy became a controversial source of power; and space exploration culminated in Americans' walking on the moon.

Theatre reflected the social upheaval of these tumultuous decades. Though it is still difficult to assess the relative importance of the theatrical innovations of this era, there is no question that many theatre artists forced us to question long-held beliefs about life and about theatre itself.

Postwar Experimental Theatres

The 30 years from 1945 to 1975 were turbulent for theatre. There was an explosion of experimentation, with new avant-garde trends springing up one after another. These movements are so close to our own time that we cannot evaluate their historical significance conclusively. It is clear, however, that established theatrical and dramatic forms were questioned and restructured, and that movements such as absurdism and environmental theatre led to new perceptions and new definitions of drama and theatre.

Existentialism

Existentialism is a philosophy most clearly articulated by two Frenchmen: Jean-Paul Sartre (1905–1980) and Albert Camus (1913–1960). Existentialists believe that there is little meaning to existence, that God does not exist, and that humanity is therefore alone in an irrational universe. The only significant action an individual can take is to accept responsibility for his or her own deeds. Most historians see an obvious impact of World War II on the existentialists.

Camus and Sartre both wrote existentialist plays. The best-known are Sartre's *The Flies* (1943), an adaptation of the Greek *Oresteia;* and *No Exit* (1944), in which hell is represented as other people. In *No Exit,* three people who have died—a man

(© T. Charles Erickson)

EXISTENTIALISM IN THE THEATRE
A notable philosophical movement in the period after World War II was existentialism, which holds that the universe is random, that God does not exist, and that human beings must create their own "existence." Two proponents of this philosophy were Albert Camus and Jean-Paul Sartre. The latter, particularly, put his ideas in the form of drama, one example being *No Exit,* in which three people are trapped in an eternal hell. The scene here is from a production at A.R.T. directed by Jerry Mouawad, who also designed the set. The costumes are by Rafael Jaen, and the lighting is by Jeff Forbes.

and two women—are locked in a room from which they cannot escape. The man loves one of the women but she does not love him; she loves the other woman, who does not return her love but loves the man. Thus, each one loves a person who does not return the love. Other existential dramas by Sartre include *The Respectful Prostitute* (1951) and *The Condemned of Altona* (1959).

While the philosophy of these dramas by Camus and Sartre is revolutionary, their dramatic form is fairly conventional: the plots are based on traditional cause-and-effect logic, and the characters are recognizable, fully developed human beings.

Theatre of the Absurd

After World War II, a theatrical approach emerged that combined existential philosophy with revolutionary, avant-garde dramatic form. Although it was not an organized movement, it was called *theatre of the absurd* by the English critic Martin Esslin (1918–2002) in a book of the same title, written in 1961.

Absurdist Drama

Absurdist playwrights differ markedly from one another, but they have certain qualities in common. One is their belief that much of what happens in life cannot be explained logically; it is ridiculous or absurd. Another is their attempt to reflect this ridiculousness or absurdity in the dramatic action of their plays.

(Joseph Abeles Collection)

ABSURDIST DRAMA ASSERTS ITSELF Among the playwrights characterized as writing in the style of theatre of the absurd was Eugène Ionesco. In his play *Rhinoceros,* about people giving way to the herd instinct, a man changes into a rhinoceros. Seen here in the midst of his transformation in the original New York production is the actor Zero Mostel.

Absurdist drama presents human existence, including relationships and language, as futile or absurd. In order to reinforce this thematic statement, it also uses seemingly illogical dramatic techniques. Plots do not have either traditional climactic structure or episodic structure. Frequently, nothing seems to happen, because the plot moves in a circle, concluding the same way it began. The characters are not realistic, and little expository information is provided about them. The setting is frequently a strange, unrecognizable locale or an ostensibly realistic world that suddenly becomes topsy-turvy. The language is often telegraphic and sparse; the dialogue seems to make little sense, and the characters fail to communicate. An example of absurdist dialogue is the following exchange from Ionesco's play *The Bald Soprano:*

Mr. Smith: Take a circle, caress it, and it will turn vicious.

Mrs. Smith: A schoolmaster teaches his pupils to read, but the cat suckles her young when they are small.

Mrs. Martin: Nevertheless, it was the cow that gave us tails.[1]

Some critics have argued that not all presumably absurdist playwrights fit neatly into a category that can be labeled *theatre of the absurd,* since their work is highly individualistic and not all the characteristics we have just mentioned appear in all of it. The playwrights who are most often categorized as absurdists are Samuel Beckett, Eugène Ionesco, and Harold Pinter. These three are also among the most influential dramatists of their generation.

SAMUEL BECKETT

Samuel Beckett (1906–1989) was the most renowned of the absurdist playwrights. His dramas deal with the dullness of routine, the futility of human action, and the inability of humans to communicate; and the plots, language, and characters themselves seem absurd. Thus his dramatic style underlines his thematic statements: he captures the ridiculous aspects of life in dramatic form.

(Louis Monier/AP Images)

Samuel Beckett.

Beckett was born on April 13, 1906. The day of his birth happened to be not only Friday the thirteenth but Good Friday, and the sense of sorrow, isolation, and ill luck associated with these dates was an important concept to him. However, for someone so obsessed with the futility of existence, Beckett had a very normal childhood in a cultured, affectionate, upper-middle-class Irish family. At prep school, he was not only a brilliant scholar but an extremely popular student and an excellent athlete, particularly at cricket. He received his M.A. in modern languages from the University of Dublin in Ireland. He then taught at schools in Paris and Dublin, wandered around Europe for a while, and finally settled in Paris in 1937.

It was during his first visit to Paris, in 1929, that Beckett became acquainted with the writer James Joyce. Joyce encouraged Beckett to write and arranged to have some of his early essays published; in turn, Beckett sometimes assisted Joyce with *Finnegan's Wake.* They were drawn together by their shared Irish background, literary tastes, and tendency to depression. According to one account, they conversed mainly in silences.

Beckett wrote and published essays, short stories, poetry, and novels during the 1930s and the 1940s, but his work was known only to a very small part of the avant-garde. A French translation of his novel *Murphy* sold ninety-five copies in 4 years. It was not until the early 1950s, with the publication of three novels and the play *Waiting for Godot* (1953), that he came to be considered one of the major writers of the postwar generation.

In *Waiting for Godot,* Beckett used many themes and dramatic techniques that would recur in his later plays. The futility of action reappears as a theme in *Act without Words* I (1957) and II (1960). Two people who need each other but cannot

[1]Eugène Ionesco, *Four Plays,* Donald M. Allen (trans.), Grove, New York, 1958, p. 38.

get along are seen again in *Endgame* (1957). *Happy Days* (1961) and *Krapp's Last Tape* (1958) dramatize failure to communicate. One of Beckett's last short plays, *Catastrophe* (1982), uses the setting of theatre to reflect on totalitarian control of the artist and ideas. He dedicated this drama to the Czech playwright Václav Havel (1936–), who at the time was under attack by the communist regime of Czechoslovakia. (After the fall of communism, Havel became president of his country.)

Besides writing for the theatre, Beckett wrote for television and radio and also wrote a short film that starred Buster Keaton. After a spurt of writing in the late 1950s and early 1960s, his output diminished, but his short plays of the 1960s, 1970s, and 1980s—including *Play* (1963), *Come and Go* (1966), *Not I* (1971), and *Rockaby* (1981)—showed that neither his concerns nor his dramatic powers had changed. Beckett received the Nobel Prize in 1969 but did not attend the ceremony.

WAITING FOR GODOT

Samuel Beckett's *Waiting for Godot* is probably the most famous of the enigmatic, nontraditional absurdist dramas.

It is about two tramps who meet each day on a barren plain, hoping that an unknown figure named Godot will come. They have a vague expectation that somehow Godot—if he ever comes—will be able to help them; and while they wait for him, they try to break up the painful monotony of their lives with bickering and occasional vaudeville routines. The play is filled with literary and religious references.

The setting is "A country road. A tree." The tree is leafless in Act I, but in Act II four or five leaves appear on it. The two central characters, Vladimir and Estragon—also known as Didi and Gogo—are tramplike clowns. They are waiting for Godot, but Godot's identity is never revealed, nor does he ever appear. Instead, a young messenger appears toward the end of each act and promises that Godot will arrive tomorrow. Godot may be God, or he may not even exist. Two additional characters, Lucky and Pozzo, switch roles as master and slave in their two appearances.

Waiting for Godot epitomizes the absurdist form. The characters are absurd, clownlike figures who have problems communicating and dealing with their environment. They contemplate suicide, for example, as a means of relieving their perpetual boredom. The setting represents everywhere and nowhere. Some critics have remarked that this barren, sterile world conjures up an image of the aftermath of a nuclear holocaust. The language is stichomythic—that is, written in brief, alternating lines—and frequently ludicrous. Lucky, in Act II, gives a three-page speech of seemingly unrelated ideas. As in many absurdist dramas, the plot is cyclical: the action appears to start over with nothing having changed. The closing lines and stage direction suggest the absurdity of the universe:

Vladimir: Well? Shall we go?

Estragon: Yes, let's go. *(They do not move.)*[2]

[2]Samuel Beckett, *Waiting for Godot*, Grove, New York, 1954, p. 61.

(Agence de Presse Bernand)

BECKETT'S WAITING FOR GODOT

A landmark play of the post–World War II period was the absurdist drama *Waiting for Godot,* in which two tramps on a barren plain wait for a figure called Godot, who never comes. The play, which has little overt action, combines beautiful language with a bleak view of the human condition. The scene here is from the original production in 1953, directed by Roger Blin of France.

This final moment of *Waiting for Godot* underlines its absurdist philosophy of futility. Vladimir and Estragon have spent their time waiting; they accomplish nothing, showing only their inability to take control of their existence. Lucky and Pozzo have no control over their destiny; fate reverses their roles, transforming one from master into servant and the other from servant into master.

Some critics suggest that *Waiting for Godot* is a modern allegory, much like the medieval *Everyman.* The playwright suggests that we spend our lives waiting for the unknowable. Godot may represent God; more generally, though, Godot is anything and everything that human beings wait for during their lives—and our lives are thus defined by absurd waiting rather than by our actions. Beckett himself described *Waiting for Godot* as a "tragicomedy in two acts," revealing his own view of the human condition: human inaction is comical but has tragic consequences.

EUGÈNE IONESCO

Eugène Ionesco (1912–1994) was one of the most productive of the playwrights who have been grouped together as absurdists. He often turned his characters into caricatures and pushed dramatic action to the point of the ridiculous. Since he was particularly concerned with the futility of communication, the language of his plays frequently seems nonsensical. He dramatized the absurdity of the human condition by presenting comic characters who lose control of their own existence.

As a child, Ionesco was enchanted by Punch and Judy puppet shows and enjoyed performing in plays. He was born in Romania, but as a boy he lived with his mother in Paris for 13 years; when he returned to Romania, he had to learn his native language. At the University of Bucharest, he studied French and occasionally wrote poetry. When he graduated, he taught French in high school. He married in 1936, and in 1938 he returned to France on a government grant, supposedly to write a thesis on Baudelaire. He apparently never wrote a word of the thesis.

(Billy Rose Theatre Collection, New York Public Library at Lincoln Center, Astor, Lenox, and Tilden Foundations)

Eugène Ionesco.

(© Michal Daniel)

THE CHAIRS BY EUGÈNE IONESCO

In Ionesco's absurdist play *The Chairs,* two old people, living in a lighthouse, imagine that a huge crowd is coming to hear a final, monumental speech by the husband. Fantasizing that the people are assembling, the two bring a great quantity of chairs onstage for the presumed audience. In this production at the Guthrie Theater the husband is played by Christopher McCann and the wife by Barbara Byrne.

Ionesco became a playwright by accident. As a reader in a legal publishing firm, he decided to learn English and began by using a simple primer. He took the empty and illogical phrases he was learning in the primer and turned them into dialogue for his first play, the one-act drama *The Bald Soprano* (1949). That he wrote a play at all is somewhat ironic, because at the time he claimed to dislike theatre—he felt that the reality of living performers clashed with the fictionalized world of the stage.

Ionesco followed his first play with several other dramas, including *The Lesson* (1951), *The Chairs* (1952), *Amedée* (1954), *The New Tenant* (1957), *The Killer* (1959), *Rhinoceros* (1959), *Exit the King* (1962), *Hunger and Thirst* (1966), and *The Homes of the Dead* (1981). He also wrote several volumes of sharp, sometimes argumentative criticism and some political works. Throughout his career he remained adamantly opposed to the concept of didactic drama, feeling that the purpose of theatre is not to teach a lesson but to present a vision of life that is enlightening, entertaining, or both. Ionesco's election to the French Academy in 1970 was a clear indication that absurdism had been accepted by the mainstream.

HAROLD PINTER

Harold Pinter (1930–) became the leading English-language absurdist playwright. In his dramas, he feels no need to explain why something happens or who a character is; existence within the world of the play is sufficient. Characteristics of Pinter's works include a lack of explanation of backgrounds or motives; introduction of menacing outside forces (which upset a seemingly stable environment); and dialogue that captures the pauses, evasions, and incoherence of modern speech. Pinter acknowledges Franz Kafka, Samuel Beckett, and American gangster films as the strongest influences on his work. Unlike Beckett and Ionesco, he creates a dramatic world that seems to be somewhat realistic.

(AP Images)

Harold Pinter.

Though Pinter began writing poetry while still at school in London's East End, his first choice of a career was acting. He attended the Royal Academy of Dramatic Art for a time, completed his studies at the Central School of Speech and Drama, and acted professionally under the name David Baron.

Pinter's debut as a playwright was accidental. He had mentioned an idea for a play to a friend in the drama department of Bristol University. The friend wrote that he was interested in the play but needed the script within a week if the school was to produce it. Pinter wrote back "no," but he finished the play anyway—in 4 days. It was called *The Room* and was performed in May 1957. Two of his other plays, *The Dumbwaiter* and *The Birthday Party,* were also produced in 1957.

The term *comedy of menace* is sometimes applied to such plays as *The Birthday Party, A Slight Ache* (1958), and *The Homecoming* (1965) because they frighten and entertain at the same time. The term is not as applicable to Pinter's later plays, such as *Old Times* (1971), which, though uncomfortably funny, deal more realistically with failed human relationships and do not have as many unexplained, menacing forces. In a later work, *Betrayal* (1978), Pinter experiments with form, reversing time in order to trace a relationship from its end back to its beginning. For some time, Pinter did not do much playwriting, except for some short plays, including *A Kind of Alaska* (1982), *One for the Road* (1984), and *Mountain Language* (1988); but a new full-length play, *Moonlight,* was well received in 1993, as were more recent plays, *Ashes to Ashes* (1996), *Celebration* (1999), and *Remembrance of Things Past* (2000).

Pinter also writes for television, radio, and film, adapting his own plays and the works of others as well as writing original scripts. He also directs for the theatre, and he is noted especially for staging plays of the British dramatist Simon Gray (1936–). In late 1992 and early 1993, Pinter returned to acting, appearing in a revival of his own play *No Man's Land.*

Pinter's creativity and adaptability in several media make him one of the most vital forces in English theatre. In 2002, Pinter was named a Companion of Honor by the queen for his literary contributions. Pinter, suffering from ill health, received the Nobel Prize for literature in 2005. In making the award, the committee stated that Pinter is a dramatist "who in his plays uncovers the precipice under everyday prattle and forces entry into oppression's closed rooms." His prerecorded acceptance speech was controversial because of his attack on the United States' engagement in Iraq.

(© Dennis Stock/Magnum Photos)

GENET'S THE BLACKS

A playwright who applied highly theatrical techniques was the Frenchman Jean Genet. His play *The Blacks,* for example, was part ritual, part minstrel show, part court trial. Set in Africa, it featured black actors wearing white masks, the reverse of early minstrel shows. The production was off-Broadway.

In addition to Beckett, Ionesco, and Pinter, others who were described as absurdist dramatists included the Frenchman Jean Genet (1910–1986) and the American Edward Albee (1928–). Genet, who spent a number of years in prison, saw himself for most of his life as an outsider. He viewed life as both arbitrary and absurd, and in his plays he attempted to find some order in the chaos he saw around him. The means he chose most often consisted of ritual, ceremony, and role playing. In an early play, *The Maids* (1947), he had servants playing the part of their masters in an elaborate ritual. His play *The Balcony* (1956) was set in a brothel, in which customers assumed the roles of persons of authority: a bishop, a general, a judge, and so forth. The men dressed in elaborate, outsize outfits to impersonate these characters, and the women wore costumes to complement them. For example, the woman who was with the man portraying a general impersonated a horse which he could ride. Other plays by Genet include *The Blacks* (1959) and *The Screens* (1961).

Several of Albee's early works, such as *The American Dream* (1960), had decidedly absurdist elements. In *The American Dream,* the main character, a young man, is really one person split in two, and at times unrealistic things occur, such as rooms disappearing. A later, full-length play, *Tiny Alice* (1964), has unrealistic elements which veer strongly toward absurdism. Even Albee's most realistic work often has a symbolic component. In *Three Tall Women* (1991) there is a device of having three actresses play one woman at different points in her life.

Directors of Absurdist Drama

While many absurdist dramatists—including Beckett, Pinter, and Albee—have directed their own plays, some directors who are not playwrights have become renowned for their staging of dramas that reflect absurdity, ridiculousness, or the enigmatic. In France, for instance, Roger Blin (1907–1984) was noted for his productions of Samuel Beckett's dramas in the early 1950s.

The reputation of the American director Alan Schneider (1917–1984) was based on his productions of plays by Beckett, Albee, and Pinter. Schneider was especially known for productions that carefully illuminated these enigmatic texts. When he was directing *Waiting for Godot,* he wrote to Beckett and asked point-blank, "Who is Godot?" Beckett answered that if he had wanted anyone to know, he would have revealed the answer in the text.

The English director Peter Hall (1930–), who served as the artistic director of the Royal Shakespeare Company in the 1960s and the Royal National Theatre in the 1970s and 1980s, established his early reputation with productions of Beckett's and Pinter's works. (The Royal Shakespeare Company, which grew out of the Stratford Memorial Theatre in 1961, is noted for significant productions of new plays and revivals by important directors. The Royal National Theatre is known best for revivals with major British and international directors and significant actors. It was founded as a government-subsidized theatre in 1963, after the Old Vic had closed; Laurence Olivier was its first artistic director, followed by Hall in 1973.)

Hall, who is a truly eclectic director, left the National Theatre in the late 1980s and established his own production company, dedicated to reviving difficult texts by historically significant authors as well as producing new plays and touring them in the United States and throughout Europe. His productions of Tennessee Williams's *Orpheus Descending* featuring Vanessa Redgrave in 1988, *The Merchant of Venice* with Dustin Hoffman in 1989, and Oscar Wilde's *An Ideal Husband* in 1992 were all well received. (The first two were transferred from London to New York.)

During the 1960s and into the 1970s there were further attempts to break away from traditional theatre practices. Some of these experiments built on the work of Artaud and Brecht, and they went in many directions—a reflection, no doubt, of the fragmentation of modern life. This experimentation included happenings, multimedia, and environmental theatre.

Happenings and Multimedia

Two developments of the 1960s and 1970s were happenings and experiments with multimedia. *Happenings* were what the term suggests: nonstructured events that occurred with a minimum of planning and organization. The idea, which was quite popular in the 1960s, was that art should not be restricted to museums, galleries, or concert halls but can happen anywhere—on a street corner, in a grocery store, at a bus stop. Happenings were closely analogous to the work of abstract painters, and a happening usually took place only once. The originator, with a few colleagues, would set up a situation and then act it out in an improvisatory fashion.

Multimedia joins theatre with other arts, especially dance, film, and television. Work of this sort, in which live performers interact with sequences on film or television, still goes on. The idea is to fuse the art forms or to incorporate new technology into a theatrical event.

Environmental Theatre

The term *environmental theatre* was coined in the 1960s by the American director and teacher Richard Schechner (1934–), but many characteristics of environmental theatre had developed out of the work and theories of earlier twentieth-century avant-garde artists, including Vsevelod Meyerhold and Antonin Artaud. Environmental theatre is based on the idea that the entire theatre space is performance space—a concept which implies that the division between performers and spectators is artificial. For every production, the spatial arrangements are transformed. Schechner does not consider the script sacred, or even essential, and he allows both improvisation and reworking of the text. The major influence on Schechner's theories was the Polish director Jerzy Grotowski.

Jerzy Grotowski

The son of a painter-sculptor and a schoolteacher, Jerzy Grotowski (1933–1999) was born in Rzeszow, Poland. His family was well educated, and both of his parents were interested in Asia, an interest that he shared. Grotowski became gravely ill at the age of 16 and spent an entire year in the hospital, much of it in a ward for terminal patients; but instead of following his doctor's advice and remaining indefinitely under care, he returned home and began to lead a normal life. He also began to meditate and to read extensively.

(AP Images)

Jerzy Grotowski.

Despite his family's opposition, Grotowski entered the Advanced School of Dramatic Art in Cracow in 1951, first to study acting and then to study directing. He became interested in Stanislavski's work, which he admired because he felt that Stanislavski had asked the right questions about acting. The work of another Russian, Meyerhold, was also an important influence on him. During a trip abroad, Grotowski was impressed by the Berliner Ensemble's production of Brecht's *Mother Courage.* In 1959, he became director of a theatre in Opole in Poland, where he began his Polish Laboratory Theatre. In 1965, the Laboratory Theatre—later, the Institute for Research in Acting—moved to Wroclaw.

Grotowski's productions for the Polish Laboratory Theatre, particularly *Akropolis* (1962–1967), *The Constant Prince* (1965–1968), and *Apocalypsis cum Figuris* (1968), attracted worldwide attention. The group performed in New York in 1969 to small, select audiences and transformed the way many theatre artists thought about theatre. In the 1970s, the Polish Laboratory Theatre undertook a series of paratheatrical experiments, including *Holiday* (also known as *Special Projects,* c. 1970–1973) and *Mountain Project* (c. 1975–1978), in which the company and outside participants organized communal events lasting for extended periods of time.

As is true of Artaud and Brecht, many historians believe that Grotowski's theories, rather than his practical work, have exerted the most influence on modern theatre. However, Grotowski—unlike Artaud or Brecht—was sometimes criticized for being more interested in the nature and form of theatre as an art than in theatre as a social or political instrument.

In the 1980s, Grotowski came to the United States and worked at the University of California at Irvine. The Polish Laboratory Theatre ceased to function in 1984. From the late 1980s through most of the 1990s, Grotowski worked in Italy with a group of artists on further paratheatrical experiments. He died of leukemia, a disease he had been fighting for some time, in 1999 at the age of 65 in Italy.

Grotowski's Poor Theatre and Paratheatrical Experiments

Jerzy Grotowski's concept of *poor theatre,* which he developed while working with his Polish Laboratory Theatre, was an attempt to answer the endlessly debated question, "What is theatre?" It stemmed from his belief that there are only two essentials for theatre: the actor and the audience. Script, scenery, and other elements were considered less important—hence the term *poor.* To intensify the actor–audience relationship, Grotowski experimented with various spatial arrangements that would intertwine performers and spectators, though he did not advocate eliminating the barrier that separates them. The plays he produced were reduced to their essential ideas, and they were cut, rearranged, or rewritten to serve his purposes. The actor—the core of his productions—was trained so that nearly every muscle of the body would be under complete control and could be moved at will.

Grotowski's theories and the works he staged with the Polish Laboratory Theatre from its founding in 1959 until 1970 presented the guiding principles of environmental theatre. For each production, the theatre space and the actor-audience relationship were arranged to conform to the play. In his production of *Kordian* (1962), the space resembled a mental institution, with audience members scattered among beds and patients (the actors). In his version of *Doctor Faustus* (1963), the theatre space was filled with two large dining tables at which audience members sat as if attending a banquet given by Faustus. And in *The Constant Prince,* a small fence was built around the playing area and the audience sat around it as if watching a bullfight.

For most of Grotowski's productions, existing scripts were radically modified by the actors and director; the classic turn-of-the-century Polish play *Akropolis,* for example, was placed in a Nazi concentration camp, and Grotowski turned the script into a scenario. The acting style for this production—as for all his works—was externally based, with the emphasis on control of body and voice rather than on inner emotions; and there was no attempt to create a realistic representation of a concentration camp. Grotowski was attempting, through such productions, to identify the essential elements of theatre. He concluded, as we have noted, that the essence of theatre is interaction between performers and audiences, and his emphasis on reorganizing the spatial arrangements followed from this. (His stress on the theatrical environment and on nonverbal aspects of performance had a strong affinity with the ideas of Antonin Artaud.)

After about 1970, Grotowski stopped producing and became involved in *paratheatrical* experiments. In these experiments, the members of his company, and some other people, took part together in rituals of daily life to rediscover the origins of theatre. Many critics felt that this was closer to a form of religion or to therapy—sociodrama or psychodrama—than to theatre.

Postwar Realistic Drama

Although realism was constantly questioned in the years from 1945 to 1975, its hold on theatre remained apparent. One good indication is the fact that most of the plays which won the Pulitzer Prize in the United States in those years were realistic. These included *The Subject Was Roses* (1965) by Frank D. Gilroy (1925–), *That Championship Season* (1973) by Jason Miller (1939–2001), and *The Gin Game* (1978) by D. L. Coburn (1938–).

Selective Realism

The leading postwar American playwrights, Arthur Miller and Tennessee Williams, wrote realistic works but were also successful with *selective realism,* a type of realism that heightens certain details of action, scenery, and dialogue while omitting others. For example, in *Death of a Salesman* Miller highlights selected physical elements of the world of Willy Loman—the salesman of the title—which symbolize his downfall: a refrigerator in need of repair, a tape-recorder in his boss's office. Rarely is the setting completely naturalistic; frequently, scenes from the past are presented from Willy's point of view. However, the play is set in a recognizable, realistic world. Williams uses a similar stylistic technique in such plays as *The Glass Menagerie* (which has a narrator) and *A Streetcar Named Desire:* elements of a realistic world are carefully selected to underline thematic concerns.

Miller and Williams have had a strong impact on the development of American drama; along with Eugene O'Neill, they are considered perhaps the most important playwrights in the history of American theatre. Another American mentioned earlier, Edward Albee, is also among the most significant playwrights of the postwar period.

ARTHUR MILLER

Focusing on failure, guilt, responsibility for one's own actions, and the effects of society on the individual, Arthur Miller (1915–2005) repeatedly tried to make us examine our own lives. His most successful dramas are reminiscent of Ibsen's well-made problem plays, and in fact he wrote an adaptation of Ibsen's *An Enemy of the People* in the early 1950s.

As the son of a garment manufacturer who lost his business in the depression, Miller understood failure. After high school, Miller worked as a shipping clerk in a warehouse before attending the University of Michigan. There he won a Hopwood Award for playwriting. Until he became a successful dramatist, he worked for 10 years at a variety of jobs, including one at the Brooklyn Navy Yard, and wrote at night.

(AP Images)

Arthur Miller.

Though his first Broadway play, *The Man Who Had All the Luck* (1944), was a failure, *All My Sons* (1947), the story of a wartime manufacturer, established Miller as a promising new dramatist. With the Pulitzer Prize–winning *Death of a Salesman* (1949)—often characterized as a modern "tragedy of the common man"—he became one of the most renowned American playwrights. His next play, *The Crucible* (1953), was about witch-hunting in seventeenth-century Massachusetts and was also a commentary on the investigations of the McCarthy era. Miller returned to contemporary America in his next two plays, *A View from the Bridge* (1955) and *A Memory of Two Mondays* (1955). In *After the Fall* (1964), he gives a thinly disguised account of his marriage to Marilyn Monroe. Miller's last produced play, *Finishing the Picture* (2004), also focused on the actress. *Incident at Vichy* (1964) deals with the issue of guilt during the Nazi Holocaust.

Except for *The Price* (1968), Miller's later dramas were not as well received by American critics as his earlier works. His two plays of the 1970s—*The Creation of the World and Other Business* (1972) and *The Archbishop's Ceiling* (1979)—were failures, though *The American Clock,* which opened in 1980, and the New York productions of *The Last Yankee* (1993) and *Broken Glass* (1994) did better. Several of his early plays have recently been revived successfully, particularly in England; and *The Ride Down Mount Morgan* premiered successfully in London in 1991 and in New York in 1998. In 1999 a successful fiftieth-anniversary production of *Death of a Salesman* played on Broadway, and in 2002 there was a revival of *The Crucible.* That same year, Miller's *Resurrection Blues* premiered at the Guthrie Theatre in Minneapolis.

Miller's television adaptation of a musician's account of life in a concentration camp, *Playing for Time* (1980), was critically acclaimed. He also wrote short stories and screenplays, as well as his memoir *Timebends* (1988). Miller died of heart failure on February 10, 2005.

TENNESSEE WILLIAMS

Tennessee Williams (Thomas Lanier Williams, 1911–1983) was one of the foremost twentieth-century playwrights in the United States. He had a series of critical and popular successes from the 1940s through the 1960s, including *The Glass Menagerie* (1945), *A Streetcar Named Desire* (1947), *Summer and Smoke* (1948), *The Rose Tattoo* (1950), *Cat on a Hot Tin Roof* (1954), *Sweet Bird of Youth* (1959), and *The Night of the Iguana* (1961). Both *A Streetcar Named Desire* and *Cat on a Hot Tin Roof* won the Pulitzer Prize.

(Theatre Collection, Museum of the City of New York)

Tennessee Williams.

A common theme running through these works is the plight of society's outcasts, outsiders trapped in a hostile environment. These characters are usually victims who are unable to comprehend their world, and Williams evokes compassion for them through the use of lyrical and poetic language as well as symbolism. In the eyes of many critics, no other American playwright has achieved the same degree of lyricism as Williams did in the dialogue of his plays. His most popular plays are fairly realistic, but he also experimented with symbolism and other nonrealistic devices in his later dramas—such as *The Milk Train Doesn't Stop Here Anymore* (1962) and *The Seven Descents of Myrtle* (1968).

Williams had a long wait for his critical and commercial success. The son of a traveling shoe salesman, he was born in Columbus, Mississippi, and grew up in Saint Louis. He entered the University of Missouri in 1929, but financial difficulties forced him to leave school. After several years and many jobs, he received his B.A. from the University of Iowa in 1938.

In 1939, Williams received a citation from the Group Theatre for his collection of one-act plays, *American Blues.* The Theatre Guild production of his full-length drama *Battle of Angels* closed in Boston in 1940 after a brief run. He spent 6 months as a contract writer for Metro-Goldwyn-Mayer in 1943, and it was while he was in Hollywood that he wrote the first draft of *The Glass Menagerie.*

(Theatre Collection/Museum of the City of New York)

A STREETCAR NAMED DESIRE
A major American playwright of the post–World War II period was Tennessee Williams, who combined lyrical language with strong dramatic characters, locked in revealing relationships. Often a victim is in an environment in which the person must fight for his or her life. Such is the case in the play *A Streetcar Named Desire*. Blanche Dubois, a woman at the end of her rope, is forced to live with her sister and brutish brother-in-law, Stanley. Seen here are Marlon Brando as Stanley and Jessica Tandy as Blanche in the original Broadway production.

In his later years, Williams himself became somewhat of an outsider, at least to theatre. His late full-length plays were failures, though some of his shorter plays like *Small Craft Warnings* (1973) had extended runs off-Broadway. Among his last works were *A Lovely Sunday for Creve Coeur* (1979), *Clothes for a Summer Hotel* (1980), and *Something Cloudy, Something Clear* (1981). His work continues to be performed very frequently and to influence other American playwrights. In 1998, the English director Trevor Nunn staged a newly discovered early play by Williams: *Not about Nightingales* (1938).

EDWARD ALBEE

Edward Albee (1928–) was mentioned previously as an American whose early work had an affinity with the absurdist writers of Europe, but Albee has also practiced his own brand of selective realism and has often ventured into symbolism.

(© Gino Domenico/Getty Images)

Edward Albee.

An orphan, Albee was adopted by Reed Albee and his wife Frances. The elder Albee was a member of a famous theatrical producing family which at one time controlled 700 vaudeville theatres across the United States. Edward Albee's family sent him to expensive private schools, but he rebelled against formal education and left several schools, including Trinity College, before completing his courses. He was interested in music and the visual arts as well as theatre, and in his late twenties he turned to playwriting. When a one-act play, *The Zoo Story* (1958), was successfully presented in Europe and then in the United States, he began to devote himself to theatre. Several one-acts followed: *The Death of Bessie Smith* and *The Sandbox* in 1959, and *The American Dream* in 1960. Mixing absurdism with sharp wit, Albee took aim at American family life and other institutions.

In 1962, with *Who's Afraid of Virginia Woolf?*—which played on Broadway—Albee entered the mainstream of American theatre. But he retained a degree of symbolism in this work, because the "child" in the play proved to be imaginary. Albee developed several adaptations of other works but also continued to write original dramas: *Tiny Alice* (1964), *A Delicate Balance* (1966), *All Over* (1966), and *Seascape* (1975). These plays mixed realism with mysticism and symbolism, creating a certain obliqueness and obscurity that puzzled some critics and audience members and pleased others. All his plays are marked by wit, intelligence, and a concern for language.

For a time Albee seemed to be in eclipse as a writer, but he reemerged in the 1990s and afterward with several strong works: *Three Tall Women* (1991)—on one level a play about Albee's mother and his difficult relationship with her—*The Play About the Baby,* which premiered in London in 1998, and *The Goat, or Who Is Sylvia*? which won the Tony Award in 2002. Three of Albee's plays have won the Pulitzer Prize for drama, and he has been awarded numerous other honors, including the National Medal of Arts in 1996 and a Tony Award for Lifetime Achievement in 2005. *Who's Afraid of Virginia Woolf?* and *Seascape* were successfully revived on Broadway in 2005.

Albee has encouraged other writers. For a number of years, for example, he has taught a course in playwriting at the University of Houston.

(Henry Grossman/Time Life Pictures/Getty Images)

A NEW PLAYWRIGHT EMERGES: EDWARD ALBEE
Following in the footsteps of O'Neill, Williams, and Miller, Edward Albee became a major American playwright who has continued to produce plays for nearly half a century. His first plays were successful off-Broadway, but in 1962 he moved from off-Broadway to Broadway with *Who's Afraid of Virginia Woolf?*—a play about a voracious woman, the daughter of a college president, who is married to a man with whom she is almost constantly sparring verbally. Shown here in the original production are, left to right, George Grizzard, Uta Hagen, Arthur Hill, and Melinda Dillon.

Angry Young Playwrights

In England in the 1950s, a group of antiestablishment playwrights known collectively as the *angry young men* dealt with the dissolving British empire, class conflict, and political disillusionment. Most of the dramas by the "angry young men" are in traditional realistic form, slightly modified. The most famous of these plays was *Look Back in Anger* (1956) by John Osborne (1929–1994).

Two theatre companies in the 1950s were extremely well known for introducing "angry young" playwrights to English audiences: the English Stage Company and the Theatre Workshop. At the time of its founding in 1956, the artistic director of the English Stage Company was George Devine (1910–1966); the company performed at the Royal Court Theatre and became best-known for giving the first performances of Osborne's *Look Back in Anger* and *Saved* (1963) by Edward

Bond (1935–). Under succeeding artistic directors, the Royal Court has continued to introduce new playwrights whose works are often controversial in style and content.

The other company that developed a reputation for staging the works of angry young playwrights was the Theatre Workshop, particularly under the direction of Joan Littlewood (1914–2002). Two important playwrights—Brendan Behan (1923–1964), author of *The Hostage* (1958); and Shelagh Delaney (1939–), author of *A Taste of Honey* (1958)—were nurtured at this theatre.

Some critics say that the commercially successful English playwright Peter Shaffer (1926–) is continuing the "angry young men" movement in such works as *The Royal Hunt of the Sun* (1964), *Equus* (1973), *Amadeus* (1980), and *The Gift of the Gorgon* (1992). Shaffer's plays, particularly *Equus,* combine realistic characteristics and causally related plots with highly theatrical devices. In *Equus,* for example, actors wear metallic kothornoi (platform shoes) and head coverings to represent horses.

Documentary Drama

A German movement of the 1960s called *documentary drama* has also proved to be influential. Documentary dramas, by such playwrights as Peter Weiss (1916–1982), Rolf Hochhuth (1931–), and Heinar Kipphardt (1922–1982), are based on historical documents, which give them an air of authenticity. Such dramas include Hochhuth's *The Deputy* (1963) and *Joel Brand* (1965) and Kipphardt's *In the Case of J. Robert Oppenheimer* (1964). The basic goal of documentary drama was to convince audiences that they were actually watching history unfold. These dramatists, however, did modify documents for dramatic effect.

Peter Weiss's *The Investigation* (1965) dramatizes the Frankfurt war-crimes tribunal, which tried people who had been guards at the Nazi extermination camps. While Weiss's play is based on transcripts of the proceedings, he has made specific changes and has used Brechtian epic techniques. His witnesses are given numbers, not names; this symbolizes the way camp inmates were stripped of their identity. His stage directions require the actors to delivery testimony unemotionally so that the audience will focus on the facts. The victims are not referred to as Jews, nor is the camp specifically identified, since Weiss's intention is to universalize the Holocaust so that it will represent all kinds of barbarity. Weiss also wrote *The Persecution and Assassination of Jean-Paul Marat as Performed by the Inmates of the Asylum of Charenton under the Direction of the Marquis de Sade* (1964), which was directed by Peter Brook.

We should note that during the 1950s and 1960s a number of other important German-language playwrights dealt with themes similar to those of Hochhuth and Weiss, but not in documentary form. These playwrights focused on the issue of responsibility in a society that asks people to act inhumanely. Two of the most famous examples of fictional drama dealing with this issue are *Biedermann and the Firebugs* (1958) by Max Frisch (1911–1992) and *The Visit* (1956) by the Swiss playwright Friedrich Dürrenmatt (1921–1992).

Documentary dramas were also written in the United States during the 1960s. Many of them reflected social upheavals, including the civil rights movement and

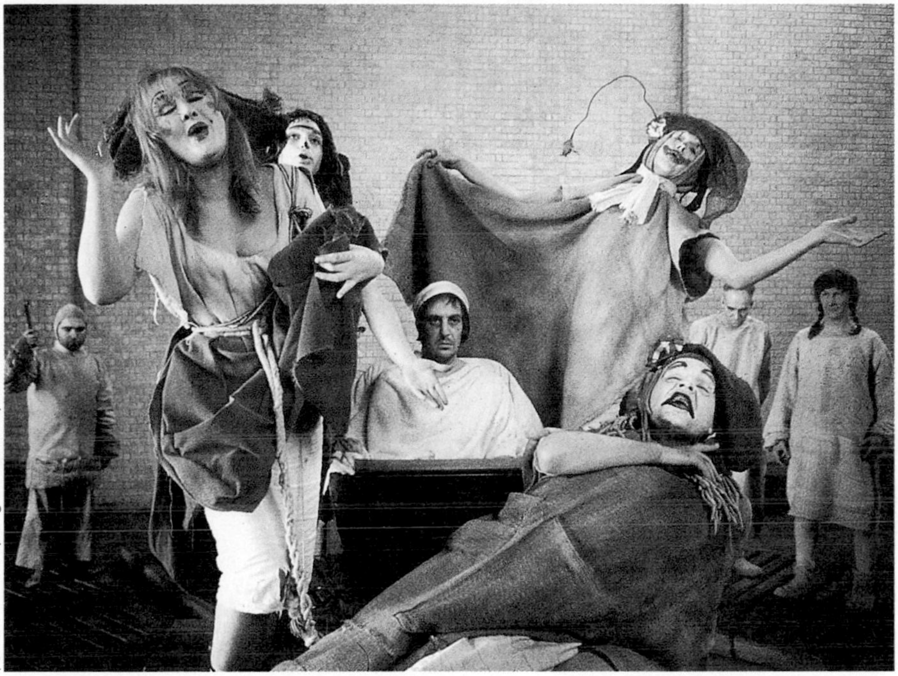

(© Dennis Stock/Magnum Photos)

DIRECTORS FRONT AND CENTER
The period after World War II saw a number of important theatre directors make a mark. One of them was Peter Brook, who distinguished himself first with Shakespeare and traditional material, but then became increasingly experimental. One of his bold productions, influenced by the theories of Artaud and others, was *Marat/Sade* by Peter Weiss, which was set in an insane asylum at the time of the French Revolution. Shown here is a scene from the original production.

the war in Vietnam. Among these plays were *The Trial of the Catonsville Nine* (1970) by Daniel J. Berrigan (1921–) and *Are You Now or Have You Ever Been* (1972), a play about the McCarthy era by Eric Bentley (1916–). Documentary dramas continued to be written after the 1970s. One example is Emily Mann's *Execution of Justice* (1984). Another, more recent example is *Exonerated* (2002), a documentary about former death-row inmates who turned out to be innocent. Today, docudramas—as they are sometimes referred to—are also popular as movies made for television.

Postwar Eclectics

In the period from 1945 to 1975, there were many theatre artists around the world who experimented with a wide variety of techniques and whose artistic output defies easy categorization. These artists can be described as *eclectics.*

Among the postwar European theatrical innovators were numerous directors whose productions borrowed from the theatrical experiments discussed above—eclectics who used varied avant-garde techniques. It would be impossible to cite all of them, but we can mention a few.

The French director Jean-Louis Barrault (1910–1994), who worked with the director Charles Dullin (1885–1949) and Antonin Artaud between the wars, used many Artaudian and environmental staging techniques. These techniques were particularly prominent in Barrault's production of *Rabelais* in 1968. Barrault was noted for his productions of Ionesco's plays, and also for his outstanding abilities as an actor.

Two Italian directors had an impact on the international theatre scene: Giorgio Strehler (1921–1997) and Franco Zeffirelli (1923–). Strehler did important productions of classical and contemporary plays at the Piccolo Teatro, which he founded in Milan in 1947; and at the Théâtre de l'Europe, which was founded in 1983 as a showcase for major productions from the countries of the European Union. (The European Union is an ongoing attempt to unify Europe economically; one of its accomplishments is the single currency, the euro. In 2002, the European Union voted to add ten new members.) Strehler was director of the Théâtre de l'Europe until 1990 and directed many historically important plays for it. All together, he directed over 200 productions, including dramas, comedies, and operas; but his most famous was *The Tempest* in 1983, which he brought to the United States.

Zeffirelli, who first worked in theatre as an actor and designer, is best-known for his Shakespearean productions—*Romeo and Juliet* (1960), *Othello* (1961), and *Hamlet* (1964)—and his opera productions. He has also done film versions of *Romeo and Juliet* (1965) and *Hamlet* (1991), the latter starring Mel Gibson.

The English director Peter Brook is, however, possibly the most renowned of the contemporary eclectics.

PETER BROOK

Peter Brook (1925–) is an English producer-director whose daring work contributed significantly to the development of twentieth-century theatre. He was born in London and educated at Oxford, where he founded the Oxford University Film Society. As a young man, he had already attained the status of one of the foremost British directors. He introduced the plays of Jean Cocteau and Jean-Paul Sartre to England. In the 1950s and early 1960s, he directed productions of Shakespeare's *Titus Andronicus, The Winter's Tale,* and *King Lear* and worked with some of England's leading actors, including Laurence Olivier. Influenced by Artaud's theatre of cruelty, he produced Jean Genet's *The Screens* and, in 1964, Peter Weiss's sensational play *The Persecution and Assassination of Jean-Paul Marat as Performed by the Inmates of the Asylum of Charenton under the Direction of the Marquis de Sade* (usually referred to as *Marat/Sade*). The unconventional style and staging of *Marat/Sade* shocked the theatre world and won Brook international fame. Brook's production of Shakespeare's *A Midsummer Night's Dream* (1970) was clearly influenced by Meyerhold's experiments with biomechanics and circus arts; for example, the fairies appeared on trapezes.

(AP Images)
Peter Brook.

Brook has staged plays at the Birmingham Repertory Theatre, at Stratford-upon-Avon, and at many theatres in London, in New York, and on the European continent. In the early 1960s, he was part of the artistic team that managed the Royal Shakespeare Company. In 1971, he founded the International Theatre Research Center in Paris, where he continued to create experimental productions. Brook's eclecticism is also illustrated by several productions of the 1980s: a stripped-down version of the opera *Carmen,* an adaptation of the Indian epic *Mahabharata,* and a production of *The Cherry Orchard* played without intermissions. His films include *Lord of the Flies, Marat/Sade,* and *King Lear.* In 1993, he staged *L'Homme Qui,* an adaptation of a book about thirteen hospital patients with serious neurological disorders.

Brook's work reflects the influence of Grotowski's innovations. Like Grotowski, Brook became more concerned with the *process* of theatre—that is, how things are done—than with the product or end result. As he indicates in his theoretical work *The Empty Space* (1968), he tries to avoid "deadly" commercial theatre, which does not allow for experimentation. In 1988, Brook published his autobiography, *The Shifting Point: Forty Years of Theatrical Exploration, 1946–1987.* In 1998 he published a memoir, *Threads of Time.*

New Technology

Any discussion of postwar theatre must take into account the introduction of new technology into scene and lighting design. Computer technology, for example, has been incorporated into many modern theatre buildings, and lighting can now be controlled by computer. Some critics, however, argue that the human factor—the performer—is the basic element of theatre and that this fact will limit computerization.

The Czechoslovakian designer Josef Svoboda experimented with such technological elements as projections, multimedia, movable platforms, and new materials, including plastics.

JOSEF SVOBODA

Josef Svoboda (1920–2002) was born in Caslav, Czechoslovakia, a small city some 50 miles east of Prague. Even in his early years, Svoboda demonstrated the multiplicity of talents and interests that would mark his work throughout his life. His father was a cabinetmaker and carpenter who taught Svoboda the fundamentals of these trades at an early age. He attended a local gymnasium—an academically oriented high school—where he showed talent as a painter and scene designer. In 1939, he was admitted to Prague's Charles University, apparently destined for an academic career in the fine arts and classical studies. The German occupation of Bohemia closed down the universities, however, and Svoboda entered a 2-year advanced vocational school for master carpentry.

During the war years, Svoboda continued his technical training, but he also pursued his interest in painting and—more important—an active participation in theatre. He established ties with the intensely dedicated young theatre artists in Prague and was a principal organizer of the semiprofessional New Group theatre housed in Prague's Smetena Museum.

After the war, several members of the New Group became the principal organizers of a new major theatre ensemble, the Grand Opera of the Fifth of May, which moved into Prague's largest theatre. While working for a university degree in architecture, Svoboda became its chief designer and technical director.

(Czechoslovak News Agency/Sovfoto/Eastfoto)

JOSEF SVOBODA: SCENIC INNOVATOR
Many technical wonders of today's theatre are offshoots of Svoboda's innovations. This scene with screens and projections is from his production of *The Snow Queen.*

Svoboda's work was greatly influenced by the multimedia experiments of Czechoslovakian theatre artists before World War II. He became internationally known when his designs, which combined live performers with images projected on multiple screens, were presented at the Brussels World's Fair in 1958. In spite of varying degrees of government censorship during the 1950s and 1960s, when Czechoslovakia was under the domination of the Soviet Union, Svoboda became one of the leading influences on design worldwide.

Svoboda's work centers on the concept of *kinetics.* He believed that because a play exists only in performance, its setting must be dynamic, changing throughout the performance according to the demands of the text. Toward this end, he experimented with complex integrations of performers and projected images, a technique he called *laterna magika.* Svoboda was also interested in finding ways to change settings easily and fluidly, and (as we have noted) he experimented with a wide variety of new materials, such as plastics.

In the past three decades, Svoboda designed in many of the major cities in Europe and the United States, and he is credited with having worked on over 500 productions. From 1969 to 1990 he was a professor of architecture at the School of Applied and Industrial Arts in Prague. Beginning in 1970, he was the chief scenographer at the National Theatre in Prague; and from 1973 until his death in 2002, he was the artistic head of a branch of the National Theatre in Prague dedicated to experiments with the media techniques for which he is famous—this branch is called, appropriately, Laterna Magika. He received many awards, including one for outstanding achievement from the United States Institute for Theatre Technology (USITT) in 1986 and the Gold Medal for Scenography in Czechoslovakia in 1988. In 1992, an English-language edition of Svoboda's writings, *The Secret of Theatrical Space,* was published.

It is clear that many of the technical wonders which fascinate audiences in today's theatre are offshoots of experiments undertaken by Svoboda since the 1950s.

Postwar Developments in American Theatre

We will now look specifically at the United States in the period 1945–1975, since many of the international developments we have been examining can also be found in American theatre. This is true despite the fact that at the close of World War II, there were limited outlets for experimentation in the United States.

One reason for this limitation was (and still is) the high cost of commercial productions. Commercial Broadway theatre, located on the west side of midtown Manhattan in New York City, has always been traditionally oriented, with large proscenium-arch playhouses and plays that usually appeal to popular tastes. For example, among the most popular productions since World War II have been musicals and the comedies of Neil Simon (1927–   ), including *The Odd Couple* (1965), *The Sunshine Boys* (1972), *California Suite* (1976), *Brighton Beach Memoirs* (1982), *Biloxi Blues* (1984), and *Lost in Yonkers* (1991). Though significant serious drama has also been produced on Broadway—including Arthur Miller's and Tennessee Williams's major works as well as more recent plays—the commercial nature of Broadway theatre leads primarily to popular entertainments.

Musical Theatre

A number of commentators have pointed out that the popular musical is the one original theatrical form America has contributed to world theatre. By 1945, two important Broadway composers had died: George Gershwin and Jerome Kern. But their contemporaries were still in top form, and soon others would join them to create an astounding outpouring of musical theatre.

These were productions with memorable music as well as witty and often poignant lyrics. Moreover, the songs were directly related to the plot. Not only was there usually a strong story line; there was often a subplot as well. The subject matter ranged widely, from adaptations of classic plays, novels, and short stories to original work.

As we saw in Chapter 13, *Oklahoma!*—which brought the team of Rodgers and Hammerstein together for the first time—was produced in 1943. It heralded a golden age of the American book musical. *Oklahoma!* seamlessly brought together story, music, lyrics, and dances so that the production combined tone, mood, and

(Billy Rose Theatre Collection, New York Public Library at Lincoln Center; Astor, Lenox, and Tilden Foundations)

MUSICAL THEATRE FLOURISHES
One of the great American "golden age" musicals is *Oklahoma!* by Richard Rodgers and Oscar Hammerstein. It is credited with being the first American musical that mixed serious and comic elements in a seamless manner and also the first that introduced ballet as an integral part of the production. Shown here is the party scene from the original Broadway production in 1943.

intention in a unified whole. Its choreography, by Agnes DeMille (1909–1993), included a famous ballet sequence and influenced many later choreographers in musical theatre, including Jerome Robbins (1918–1998) and Bob Fosse (1927–1987). Rodgers and Hammerstein went on to create other significant musicals, such as *Carousel* (1945), *South Pacific* (1949), *The King and I* (1951), and *The Sound of Music* (1959).

Other notable musicals during the 1940s and 1950s included Irving Berlin's *Annie Get Your Gun* (1946), based on the life of Annie Oakley; Cole Porter's musical version of *The Taming of the Shrew,* called *Kiss Me, Kate* (1948); *Guys and Dolls* (1950) by Frank Loesser (1910–1969), successfully revived on Broadway in 1992; *My Fair Lady* (1956) by the librettist and lyricist Alan Jay Lerner (1918–1986) and the composer Frederick Loewe (1901–1988), based on George Bernard Shaw's *Pygmalion;* and *West Side Story* (1957), a modernization of *Romeo and Juliet* which was created by the composer Leonard Bernstein (1918–1990), the lyricist Stephen Sondheim (1930–), and the librettist Arthur Laurents (1918–).

Musical theatre continued to be vibrant in the 1960s. Typical of the work in this period were two musicals intended purely for entertainment and one with a more serious purpose. The two lighter pieces were *Hello, Dolly* (1964), with music and lyrics by Jerry Herman (1932–) and book by Michael Stewart (1924–1987); and *Sweet Charity* (1966), with music by Cy Coleman (1929–), lyrics by Dorothy Fields (1904–1974), and book by Neil Simon. *Hello, Dolly* is a period piece about a woman from Yonkers who entraps a wealthy merchant; *Sweet Charity* is the story of a dance hall girl who has a brief moment of happiness away from her former life.

The more serious piece was *Fiddler on the Roof* (1964)—with music by Jerry Bock (1928–), lyrics by Sheldon Harnick (1924–), and book by Joseph Stein (1912–). *Fiddler on the Roof,* which tells of a Jewish family whose father attempts to uphold tradition in a Russian village where the Jewish community faces persecution, was directed and choreographed by Jerome Robbins.

Three musicals at the end of the period 1945–1975 signaled a move away from an emphasis on story and plot. Significantly, two of the three, *Hair* and *A Chorus Line,* began off-Broadway, at the Public Theatre, before moving to Broadway. *Hair* (1967), which many consider the first true rock musical, had music by Galt MacDermot (1928–) and book and lyrics by Gerome Ragni (1935–1991). It celebrated the free and easy lifestyle of hippies in the East Village of Manhattan.

Company (1970), with music and lyrics by Stephen Sondheim and book by George Furth (1932–), consisted of a series of vignettes depicting various aspects of marriage. The focus was a bachelor, Robert, and five couples with whom he interacted. *A Chorus Line* (1975) had music by Marvin Hamlisch (1944–), lyrics by Edward Kleban (1939–1987), and a book by James Kirkwood (1924–1983) and Nicholas Dante (1942–1991). Once again, there was no overarching plot, but rather a series of scenes in song and dance illuminating the lives of individual dancers in a chorus. The entire show was held together by the direction and choreography of Michael Bennett (1943–1987). *A Chorus Line* was revived on Broadway in 2006.

Off-Broadway and Off-Off-Broadway

The off-Broadway movement developed in the late 1940s as a reaction to Broadway commercialism. Its primary goal was to provide an outlet for experimental and innovative works, unhindered by commercial concerns. Off-Broadway was dedicated to introducing new playwrights and reviving significant plays that had initially been unsuccessful on Broadway. For example, one noted off-Broadway playhouse, the Circle in the Square, revived Tennessee Williams's *Summer and Smoke* in 1952 and Eugene O'Neill's *The Iceman Cometh* in 1956; both plays had failed in their original runs on Broadway. In the 1960s, plays of several young Americans, including Israel Horowitz (1939–), John Guare (1938–), and Lanford Wilson (1934–), were produced off-Broadway.

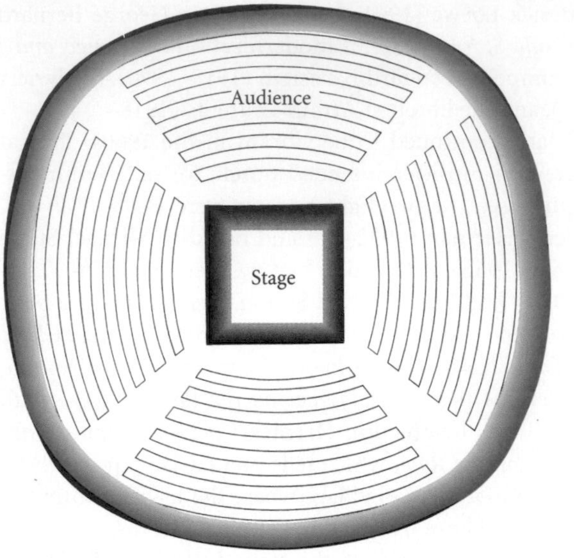

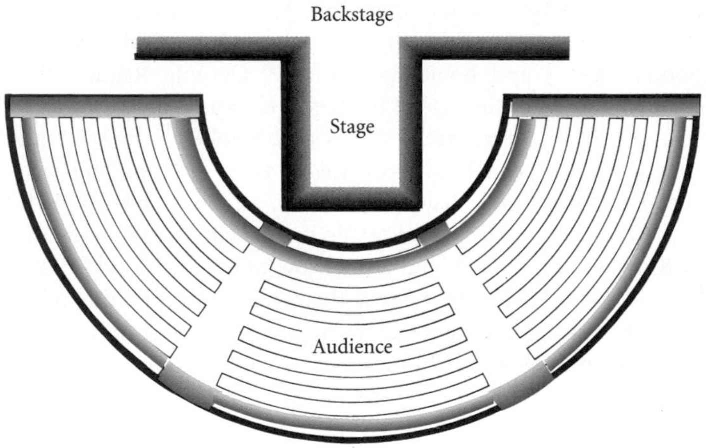

Two theater configurations—both with antecedents in the past—employed by off-Broadway and regional theaters.

PLAN OF AN ARENA STAGE (TOP)
The audience sits on four sides or in a circle surrounding the stage. Entrances and exits are made through the aisles or through tunnels underneath the aisles. A feeling of intimacy is achieved because the audience is close to the action and encloses it.

THRUST STAGE WITH THREE-QUARTERS SEATING (BOTTOM)
The stage is surrounded on three sides by the audience. Sometimes seating is a semicircle. Entrances and exits are made from the sides and backstage. Spectators surround the action, but scene changes and other stage effects are still possible.

This movement also introduced new actors, directors, and designers. Among the performers who made debuts off-Broadway were Jason Robards, Colleen Dewhurst, Dustin Hoffman, and Al Pacino—all later recognized as significant professionals. The director José Quintero (1924–1999) established his reputation as the leading interpreter of Eugene O'Neill at the Circle in the Square.

Off-Broadway also popularized intimate playhouses that did not take the traditional proscenium-arch form. Off-Broadway theatres typically seat only about 200 spectators, and many of these theatres have thrust or arena stages. Even those with proscenium-arch stages are much more intimate than their Broadway counterparts, because of their smaller size. Such theatres had been found earlier in the United States, but off-Broadway playhouses—along with many regional theatres—proved the viability of alternative spaces.

In the 1960s and 1970s, off-Broadway itself became more commercial and therefore less experimental. As production costs rose, more conventional productions were staged. In the past two or three decades, many off-Broadway productions—such as the enormously popular musical *Grease*—have later moved to Broadway, indicating that the distinction between the two has been blurred.

Beginning in the 1960s, and increasingly in recent years, off-off-Broadway has replaced off-Broadway as the center for experimentation in New York. Off-off-Broadway is—as off-Broadway originally was—dedicated to introducing and showcasing new talent, experimenting with new styles of production, and avoiding the limitations of commercialism. Many off-off-Broadway groups perform in *found spaces,* that is, spaces (such as factory lofts, churches, and warehouses) not originally intended for theatre. American experiments with environmental theatre have frequently been undertaken off-off-Broadway, as have some of the experiments with participatory theatre—theatre in which audience members are asked to take an active part.

The number of experimental off-Broadway and off-off-Broadway groups that tried to transform accepted theatrical conventions is impressive. Many of these companies flourished in the turbulent 1960s and were highly political, attacking capitalism, traditional values, and American involvement in Vietnam. Three such groups that deserve mention are the Living Theatre, founded in 1946 by Julian Beck and Judith Malina; the Open Theatre, founded in 1963 by Joseph Chaikin (1935–2003); and the Performance Group, founded by Richard Schechner in 1968. Each of these groups went through several phases, and the three were distinct in style, but they all experimented with improvisation, restructuring of texts, environmental staging, and acting based on externals.

The turbulent career of the Living Theatre is in many ways representative of the many political companies that developed in the 1960s. Two significant individuals are Ellen Stewart and Joseph Papp.

THE LIVING THEATRE

The Living Theatre, founded in 1946 by Julian Beck (1925–1985) and Judith Malina (1926–   ), was a particularly influential avant-garde company of the late 1950s and the 1960s. Its transformations reflected changes in American society and experimental theatre.

JULIAN BECK AND JUDITH MALINA Beck and Malina founded the Living Theatre in 1946. The group featured experimental, politically charged work, often created by the ensemble itself. It sometimes included confrontations and interaction with audience members, and was frequently presented in site-specific spaces such as streets and town squares. It came to symbolize the revolutionary spirit of much of post World War II theatre.

(AP Images)

Initially, the Living Theatre performed poetic dramas and plays by earlier avant-garde dramatists. Among the authors whose work it staged were Bertolt Brecht, Federico García Lorca, Gertrude Stein (1874–1946), W. H. Auden (1907–1973), August Strindberg, Jean Cocteau, and Jean Racine. The group also experimented with production styles, using masks, stylized gestures and vocalizations, and theatrical conventions from the past. In the late 1950s, the Living Theatre also became interested in the theories of Antonin Artaud.

The two productions that established the Living Theatre's reputation were *The Connection* (1959) by Jack Gelber (1932–2003) and Kenneth Brown's *The Brig* (1963). *The Connection* presents dope addicts waiting to make a connection for a fix. *The Brig* dramatizes the daily routine in a Marine Corps prison. Both productions tried to make the spectators feel as if they were watching actual occurrences.

In the 1960s, because of tax problems, the Living Theatre became nomadic, presenting many of its productions in Europe. (These problems were related to the political activism of its members, particularly their opposition to the war in Vietnam and to capitalism, and their anarchism. In 1971, members of the company were arrested in Brazil for political activities.) During this period, the group also developed the production style for which it became noted. Many of the works it staged were created by improvisation. Rather than play characters, the members portrayed themselves confronting social institutions and norms. Their best-known work of this period, *Paradise Now* (1968), included audience participation and confrontation in order to arouse spectators to the call for social revolution. Two other noteworthy works by the Living Theatre in the mid-1960s were *Frankenstein* and *Mysteries and Smaller Pieces.*

The Living Theatre has undergone numerous personnel changes. One early member, Joseph Chaikin, left the group and organized the Open Theatre. Before the Brazilian tour, the company broke up into three groups.

Beck, Malina, and the Living Theatre were not highly visible in the 1970s, but they continued to produce. In their production of *Prometheus* in London in 1979, audience members were invited to help enact the communist revolution and, after the performance, to join the company in a march outside a nearby prison. This production was a continuation of the Living Theatre's experiments of the 1960s.

A revival of the 1960s productions in 1984 at New York's James Joyce Theatre was unsuccessful. In the late 1980s, after Julian Beck's death, Judith Malina, along with a new codirector, Hanon Reznikov, reorganized the Living Theatre in a small storefront space on the lower east side of New York. The company dedicated itself to contemporary political and social issues; for example, it created a production employing homeless people who lived in the neighborhood. In 1993, the Living Theatre once again had problems with the authorities: the city condemned the space in which it was working.

Since being evicted from its lower east side space, the Living Theatre has been in residence in Italy and touring throughout the world. Its recent productions include *Not in My Name* (2002), an anti-capital punishment piece performed on nights of executions, and *Resistance* (2002). The Living Theatre has an active website at http://www.livingtheatre.org/

ELLEN STEWART AND JOSEPH PAPP

Another influential off-off-Broadway figure, Ellen Stewart (c. 1920–)—who is of Cajun extraction—began as a fashion and millinery designer. Stewart founded Cafe La Mama in 1961 and has been instrumental in introducing new playwrights and directors. She helped establish the careers of such authors as Lanford Wilson, Sam Shepard, Rochelle Owens (1936–), and Megan Terry (1932–). Stewart continues to work in New York at an East Village space she moved into in 1969; however, she almost lost her theatre in 1992 for lack of funding.

(D. E. Matlack/Courtesy of La MaMa E.T.C.)

Ellen Stewart.

Joseph Papp (1921–1991; his name was originally Papirofsky) was an off-off-Broadway producer who had a strong impact on American theatre. (He was also a director, but he was more successful as a producer.) In 1954, he opened the New York Shakespeare Festival, which gives free Shakespearean productions every summer in New York's Central Park. Beginning in 1967, he also operated the Public Theatre—known simply as the Public—a series of theatre spaces in a converted library. The Public is noted (among other things) for casting roles without regard to race.

At the Public and for the Shakespeare festival, Papp produced a number of successful shows which he moved to Broadway to help underwrite the production costs of his off-off-Broadway spaces. These included *Hair* (1968), *Two Gentlemen of Verona* (1971), *That Championship Season* (1973), and *A Chorus Line* (1975). Papp introduced a number of significant young playwrights, among them David Rabe, the author of three dramas on the war in Vietnam: *The Basic Training of Pavlo Hummel* (1971), *Sticks and Bones* (1971), and *Streamers* (1976). In the summer of 1980, he presented Gilbert and Sullivan's operetta *The Pirates of Penzance* in Central Park, with the pop star Linda Ronstadt—another show that moved successfully to Broadway.

Because Papp was so effective at the Public, he was asked in 1973 to run the theatre at Lincoln Center, the major performing arts complex in New York City; but despite some artistically interesting productions, he was not successful there.

In the 1980s, Papp began staging Shakespeare's plays at the Public and the summer festival with famous film stars. As his health deteriorated, he appointed associate artistic directors at the Public, among them Joanne Akalaitis (1930–) and the African American director-playwright George C. Wolfe (1955–). When Papp died, Akalaitis was appointed to head the Public, but after a tumultuous 18 months she was replaced by Wolfe. (Akalaitis and Wolfe will also be discussed in Chapter 15.)

(© Jacques M. Chenet/Corbis)
Joseph Papp.

Regional Theatre

American theatre was transformed by the professional regional theatre movement, which began in the late 1940s. A regional theatre company is a permanent company operating in one community; among the most notable regional companies are the Alley Theatre in Houston (founded in 1949); the Arena Stage in Washington, D.C. (1949); the Tyrone Guthrie Theatre in Minneapolis (1963); the Actors Theatre of Louisville (1964); the Long Wharf in New Haven (1965); and the Mark Taper Forum in Los Angeles (1967).

These regional companies presented theatre relevant to their communities. They offered classics and also discovered new talent. A few were resident companies, that is, acting troupes which remained together for an extended period of time. Their playhouses were often architecturally innovative; many of them were thrust or arena spaces. Many regional theatres continue this architectural trend. The Guthrie, for example, opened a facility with three playhouses—including one that retains its signature thrust configuration—in 2006. The new Guthrie, situated on the Mississippi River in Minneapolis, was designed by the world-renowned architect Jean Nouvel.

One indication of the success of the regional movement is the number of dramas that originated in regional theatre and were then transferred to Broadway in the 1960s and 1970s; they included Howard Sackler's *The Great White Hope,* Preston Jones's *The Texas Trilogy,* Michael Cristofer's *The Shadow Box,* G. L. Coburn's *The Gin Game,* and Mark Medoff's *Children of a Lesser God.*

The impact of large regional theatres remains strong today. The Mark Taper Forum, for example, was an early producer of *Angels in America: The Millennium*

Approaches (1993) by Tony Kushner, which won both a Pulitzer Prize and a Tony Award. However, as we shall see in Chapter 15, regional theatres became financially pressed in the 1970s, 1980s, and 1990s. Also, to keep afloat financially, in many instances regional theatres, which in former years were more adventuresome, became less experimental and innovative. As a result, a new generation of alternative theatres would be established outside New York City.

African American Theatre

As we mentioned at the opening of this chapter, the era from 1945 to 1975 saw many major social changes in the United States. One of the most significant was the civil rights movement, which included the Supreme Court decision ordering integration of public schools; the ascendancy of the African American leaders Martin Luther King, Jr., and Malcolm X; and both violent and nonviolent activism. African American theatre reflected this struggle.

African American Theatre in the 1950s

The 1950s saw the first phases of an explosion of African American theatre that would occur over the next three decades. *Take a Giant Step* by Louis Paterson (1922–), a play about growing up in an integrated neighborhood, premiered in 1953. In 1954, the playwright-director Owen Dodson (1914–1983)—a significant figure in black theatre since the 1930s—staged *Amen Corner* by James Baldwin (1924–1987) at Howard University.

At this time, too, the Greenwich Mews Theatre, an off-Broadway house, began casting plays without regard to race. Two history dramas were staged there: *In Splendid Error* (1954) by William Branch (1927–), about the conflict between John Brown and Frederick Douglass; and *Land Beyond the River* (1957) by Loften Mitchell (1919–2001), about a black minister's efforts to end school segregation. The Greenwich Mews also produced *Trouble in Mind* by Alice Childress (1920–1994). Although by this time there had been approximately 125 plays written by African American women, *Trouble in Mind* was the first to receive a professional staging. Three years later, Lorraine Hansberry became the first black woman to have a play on Broadway.

LORRAINE HANSBERRY

The first play by Lorraine Hansberry (1930–1965), *A Raisin in the Sun,* is considered by many critics to have been a turning point in American theatre. To quote James Baldwin: "Never before in the entire history of the American theatre has so much of the truth of black people's lives been seen on the stage."

Hansberry was born into an upper-middle-class family in Chicago. She first wanted to be a painter and studied at the Chicago Art Institute, at the University of Wisconsin, and in Guadalajara, Mexico. At Wisconsin, however, she saw a production of Sean O'Casey's *Juno and the Paycock.* Inspired by O'Casey's ability to universalize a specific people and their culture—in this case, the Irish—she decided to become a playwright.

In 1952, Hansberry went to New York and joined the staff of *Freedom,* a Harlem-based journal founded by Paul Robeson. Reacting against what she called a "whole body of material about Negroes. Cardboard characters. Cute dialect bits.

(UPI/Corbis)

Lorraine Hansberry.

Or hip-swinging musicals from exotic scores," Hansberry set out to write a "social drama about Negroes that will be good art." That play was *A Raisin in the Sun.*

A Raisin in the Sun takes its title from a poem by Langston Hughes which asks, "What happens to a dream deferred?" It is set in the apartment of the Younger family on Chicago's South Side, and by including several generations within this one household, Hansberry was able to present an across-the-board picture of the changing and conflicting ideologies, dreams, and frustrations of black Americans in the 1950s.

When *A Raisin in the Sun* opened on Broadway on March 11, 1959, it marked several firsts: Hansberry was the first black female writer—as well as the youngest American playwright to that date and only the fifth woman—to win the New York Drama Critics Circle Award for Best Play of the Year; and Lloyd Richards (1922–2006) was the first African American director on Broadway. (Richards later became head of the Yale School of Drama, a post he held until his retirement in 1992; at Yale, he nurtured the talents of the African American playwright August Wilson in the 1980s.)

A Raisin in the Sun also began an explosion of black theatre in New York in the 1960s and 1970s. Hansberry's second play to be produced, *The Sign in Sidney Brustein's Window* (1964), was—in her words—about "the Western intellectual poised in hesitation before the flames of involvement." It had the passionate support of the artistic community, but it ran for only 101 performances, closing on the day of her death, January 22, 1965.

Hansberry's other completed works include *The Drinking Gourd, What Use Are Flowers,* and *Les Blancs,* which had a short run on Broadway in 1970. *To Be Young, Gifted, and Black,* a theatrical collage based on Hansberry's writings, was the longest-running drama of the 1968–1969 off-Broadway season. Though Hansberry's writing was to some extent overshadowed in the 1970s by more militant writers, in recent years there has been a renewed interest in her work, partly because it has been praised by such authors as Amiri Baraka and August Wilson, and partly because of successful revivals of *A Raisin in the Sun* in theatres and on television.

Civil Rights and African American Militancy: 1960–1970

In the 1960s, African American theatre was strongly influenced by the civil rights movement. Theatre aimed at improving the rights and opportunities of minorities became especially important to black Americans.

The actor-playwright Ossie Davis (1917–2005) wrote *Purlie Victorious* (1961), a comedy satirizing the traditional racial stereotypes of the south, and 9 years later it returned to Broadway as a musical. A drama of southern racism by James Baldwin, *Blues for Mister Charlie* (1964), was also produced, though it closed quickly.

Perhaps the outstanding example of theatre inspired by civil rights at the grassroots level was the Free Southern Theatre, established in 1963 by Tom Dent, Gilbert Moses, and Richard Schechner (Schechner would later champion environmental theatre). Based in New Orleans, the company toured Louisiana's rural communities with plays and skits about freedom.

By the middle to late 1960s, it was clear that African American playwrights had found their voice in both realism and departures from realism. Playwrights like Adrienne Kennedy (1931–) in *Funnyhouse of a Negro* (1964), Lonne Elder III (1932–1996) in *Ceremonies in Dark Old Men* (1969), and Charles Gordone (1925–1995) in *No Place to Be Somebody* (1969) proved themselves masters at placing characters in true-to-life settings and using dialogue to make accurate observations about life. Many other African American playwrights used highly imaginative techniques which broke with realistic tradition. Douglas Turner Ward (1930–), for example, had black men play in whiteface—a reversal of the minstrel show—in his play *Day of Absence* (1970). Possibly the most controversial African American playwright of the 1960s, both for his subject matter and for his theatrical techniques, was Amiri Baraka.

AMIRI BARAKA

A prolific and provocative dramatist, Amiri Baraka (1934–) has well over thirty plays to his credit. Before Baraka, black protest drama had been solely realistic; by infusing allegory and lyricism into his vivid depictions of racially torn America, Baraka changed the shape of this protest drama and inspired a whole school of writing.

Baraka was born in Newark, New Jersey; his original name was Everett LeRoi Jones. He attended Rutgers University and then Howard University. After serving briefly in the Air Force, he moved to New York, where he attended Columbia University and earned an M.A. in German literature from the New School of Social Research. During this time, he became associated with the "beat" poets of the 1950s.

(© Christopher Felver/Corbis)

Amiri Baraka.

Two of Baraka's earlier plays—*A Good Girl Is Hard to Find* (1958) and *Dante* (1961)—had been produced, but it was *Dutchman* (1964) that brought him to the forefront of American theatre. Set in a steamy subway car in New York City, *Dutchman* is a verbal and sexual showdown between a middle-class assimilated black man and a white temptress. Their conflict becomes a metaphor for political, sociological, and psychological dilemmas confronting African Americans. *Dutchman* earned Baraka a Guggenheim Fellowship and an Obie Award for the Best American Play of 1963–1964. It is also credited with beginning a renaissance of African American theatre in the 1960s and 1970s and with demonstrating a need for a new aesthetic for contemporary black works.

Baraka's *The Slave* and *The Toilet,* a double bill of one-act plays, opened off-Broadway in 1965. *The Slave* is a domestic battle involving an interracial couple, set against the background of a race war; *The Toilet,* set in a washroom in an inner-city high school, is an impassioned work in which teenage gang members pummel a boy to death. These plays foreshadowed the urban violence that was soon to engulf the United States. Baraka's next notable work, *Slave Ship* (1970), used a number of ritualistic devices.

After Baraka rose to success in New York theatre, he left to form his own performing company in the black community. The Black Arts Repertory Theatre and School in Harlem was his first endeavor. He then returned to Newark, where he became founder and director of the Spirit House Movers and Players.

In addition to being a dramatist, Baraka is also a poet, novelist, musicologist, essayist, critic, and editor. In the 1980s, he returned to Marxist philosophy and published a controversial autobiography. He continues to write plays; his *Meeting Lillie* was produced off-off-Broadway in 1993. Baraka also writes a great deal of poetry and music criticism, and lectures at universities. This prolific author published *The Autobiography of Leroi Jones/Amiri Baraka* in 1984. Baraka was a professor in the Africana Studies Department at State University of New York at Stony Brook from 1985 to 1999.

Among his numerous awards are fellowships from the Guggenheim Foundation and the National Endowment for the Arts as well as the PEN/Faulkner Award and the Rockefeller Foundation Award for Drama. Baraka was appointed the state

(Sara Krulwich/The New York Times)

AFRICAN AMERICAN PLAYWRIGHTS
In the period following World War II a number of talented African American playwrights emerged, beginning with Lorraine Hansberry. Among them was Charles Fuller, whose drama *Soldier's Play* won the Pulitzer Prize in 1982. Shown here is a scene from a revival of the play with (from the left): Teagle F. Bougere, James McDaniel, and Anthony Mackie. It was presented by the Second Stage Theatre in New York.

of New Jersey's poet laureate in 2002. His controversial poem "Somebody Blew Up America," which some claimed was anti-Semitic, led the New Jersey legislature to eliminate the honorary position in 2003.

African American Producing Organizations

By 1970, the Black Theatre Alliance listed over 125 producing groups in the United States. Only a few of these survived the decade, but many had a significant impact. For example, the New Lafayette Theatre, founded in 1966, operated until 1972; it introduced the playwright Ed Bullins (1935–), experimented with black ritual, and published the journal *Black Theatre.*

Among production organizations, the Negro Ensemble Company (NEC) became the oldest professional African American company in continuous production. It was conceived and administered by Douglas Turner Ward, originally with assistance from Robert Hooks and Gerald Krone. Beginning in 1967, it produced many significant original plays, including some which moved to Broadway, among them *The River Niger* (1973) by Joseph Walker (1935–), *The First Breeze of Summer* (1975) by Leslie Lee (1935–), and *A Soldier's Play* (1981) by Charles Fuller (1939–), which won the Pulitzer Prize. In the 1990s, the Negro Ensemble Company had serious financial difficulties and at least once nearly ceased operating. In 1993, it produced in a theatre at LaGuardia Community College in the borough of Queens, since it could not afford either Broadway or off-Broadway houses.

Movements in theatre between 1945 and 1975 both continued traditions from the past and forced audiences and artists to reevaluate earlier forms of drama and earlier staging practices. In the years that followed, these experiments would have an impact on commercial as well as avant-garde theatre.

Summary

A number of theatrical movements were in evidence between 1945 and 1975. The absurdist dramas of Samuel Beckett, Eugène Ionesco, and Harold Pinter have had a profound influence on contemporary playwriting. Other movements included the "angry young men" in England and documentary drama. The two leading American dramatists, Arthur Miller and Tennessee Williams, continued to work in a more conventional realistic style but also used "selective realism."

Happenings, multimedia, environmental theatre, and poor theatre—as in the productions of Jerzy Grotowski's Polish Laboratory Theatre—forced theatregoers to reevaluate their traditional expectations about the actor–audience relationship and other aspects of drama. Many significant eclectic directors, including Peter Brook, had an international impact.

In the United States, off-Broadway, off-off-Broadway, and regional theatre attempted to break away from commercialism. Producers such as Joseph Papp and Ellen Stewart introduced new playwrights and practitioners. Regional professional theatres became firmly established in many American cities. African American theatre artists wrote plays and organized production companies that focused on civil rights issues of the 1950s and 1960s.

MILESTONES CHAPTER 14 THEATRES FROM 1945 TO 1975

Theatre History

- Jean-Paul Sartre (1905–1980), *No Exit*
- Samuel Beckett (1906–1989), *Waiting for Godot*
- Roger Blin (1907–1984)
- Jean-Louis Barrault (1910–1994)
- Tennessee Williams (1911–1983), *A Streetcar Named Desire (below)*

- Eugène Ionesco (1912–1994), *The Chairs*
- Arthur Miller (1915–2005) *(below)*, *Death of a Salesman*

- Peter Weiss (1916–1982), *The Investigation*
- Alan Schneider (1917–1984)
- Jean Genet (1920–1986), *The Maids*
- Josef Svoboda (1920–2002)
- Ellen Stewart (c. 1920–)
- Joseph Papp (1921–1991)
- Giorgio Strehler (1921–1997)
- Franco Zeffirelli (1923–)

Cultural and Historical Developments

- Albert Camus's *L'Étranger* (1942)
- World War II ends; United Nations founded (1945)
- Nuremberg trials (1946)
- India achieves independence from British rule (1947)
- Independent state of Israel established (1948)
- George Orwell's *1984*; Germany divided (1949)
- People's Republic of China established (1949)
- Jackson Pollock's *Autumn Rhythm* (1950)
- Cold war; Rock 'n' roll era begins (1950s)
- Korean war (1950–1953)
- Stalin dies (1953)
- McCarthy-Army hearings; hydrogen bomb tested (1954)
- Vladimir Nabokov's *Lolita* (1955)
- Russia crushes Hungarian revolt; Suez crisis (1956)
- Sputnik I and II; Jack Kerouac's *On the Road* (1957)
- Jasper John's *Three Flags* (1958)
- Fidel Castro becomes premier of Cuba (1959)
- Belgian Congo granted independence; the Beatles (1960)
- Berlin Wall constructed (1961)
- Cuban missile crisis; James Baldwin's *Another Country* (1962)
- Warfare escalates between North and South Vietnam; John F. Kennedy, president of the United States, assassinated (1963)
- Betty Friedan's *Feminine Mystique* (1963)
- Russian president Nikita Khrushchev resigns (1964)
- Martin Luther King, Jr., assassinated (1968)
- Andy Warhol's *Cambell's Soup Can I (Tomato)* (1968)

continued

Photo Credits: Marlon Brando and Jessica Tandy in *A Streetcar Named Desire.* (Theatre Collection, The Museum of the City of New York) / Arthur Miller. (AP Images)

- Peter Brook (1925–)
- Edward Albee (1928–), *Who's Afraid of Virginia Woolf?*
- John Osborne (1929–1994), *Look Back in Anger*
- Lorraine Hansberry (1930–1965) *(below), A Raisin in the Sun*

- Harold Pinter (1930–), *The Birthday Party*
- Peter Hall (1930–)
- Jerzy Grotowski (1933–1999), *The Constant Prince*
- Amiri Baraka (1934–), *Dutchman*
- Off-Broadway and off-off-Broadway movement (1940s)
- Professional regional theatre companies develop in the United States (1940s)
- Rodgers and Hammerstein's *Oklahoma!* (1943)
- The Living Theatre (1946)
- Happenings, multimedia, and environmental theatre develop (1960s; 1970s)
- New Lafayette Theatre (1966)
- Negro Ensemble Company (1967)
- *Apollo 11* lands on the moon *(below);* Woodstock festival, New York (1969)

- Administration of Richard Nixon initiates policy of détente (1970s)
- Joseph Beuys's *Coyote, I Like America and America Likes Me* (1974)
- Nixon resigns U.S. presidency after Watergate scandal (1974) *(below)*

- Vietnam war ends; Saul Bellow's *Humboldt's Gift* (1975)

PHOTO CREDITS: Lorraine Hansberry. (UPI/Corbis) / Apollo astronauts walk on moon. (NASA) / Richard Nixon resigns. (© Wally McNamee/Corbis)

CHAPTER 15

Contemporary Theatre in the United States: 1975 to the Present

Breakthrough Play: Angels in America

A play that struck a chord with many audience members in the early 1990s was *Angels in America* by Tony Kushner. At once fanciful and terrifyingly realistic, it was a definitive treatment of the AIDS epidemic and many other challenges facing America. Seen here are Ellen McLaughlin as the angel and Stephen Spinella in one section of the play, entitled *Angels in America: Millennium Approaches.* This photo is from the original Broadway production in 1993.

(© Joan Marcus)

It is difficult to assess the social, political, and economic upheavals of the years from 1975 to the present; we are too close to these developments to evaluate their significance for western society. We can, however, look at certain key events.

Background: Worldwide Changes since 1975

The years since 1975 have seen continued turmoil around the world. Although the war in Vietnam ended in the early 1970s, there were many conflicts in the 1980s and 1990s, including a war in Afghanistan initiated by the Soviet Union, interventions by the United States in Grenada and Panama, and a war in the Persian Gulf in which United Nations forces expelled Iraqi troops from Kuwait. Nonetheless, this region remained unstable, and in late 1998 Iraq was bombed by the United States and Britain. In 2003 the United States and Britain invaded and occupied Iraq.

There were early hopes for peace in the Middle East, after Israel and Egypt signed a nonaggression agreement at Camp David in 1977, but then these hopes were dimmed by turmoil over Israel's occupation of the West Bank, by the Islamic fundamentalist movement, and by continued terrorism. The release of long-held American hostages in Lebanon and the alliance formed by the United States and several Arab nations during the Gulf War revived optimism again, and in September 1993 Israel and the Palestine Liberation Organization signed an agreement respecting each other's right to exist. Additional agreements followed, including the Wye Agreement of 1998, in which Israel relinquished West Bank territory in return for recognition of its existence. However, the Palestinians rejected the final offer made by the Israelis. The violence in the Middle East escalated. Suicide bombers terrorized Israeli civilians, while the Israelis continued to send military forces into occupied Palestinian territories, destroying homes, bombing terrorist targets (and causing civilian casualties), and curtailing Palestinian citizens' rights to travel and congregate. With the Israelis' unilateral departure from Gaza and the election of Hamas by the Palestinians in 2006, the turmoil in the region has not abated.

The culmination of this instability was the terrorist attack on the United States on September 11, 2001. On that date, four airplanes were hijacked by Middle Eastern terrorists. Two were flown into New York City's World Trade Center, destroying both towers; another was flown into the Pentagon; the fourth crashed in Pennsylvania, after its passengers resisted the terrorist hijackers. The United States proclaimed a war on terror and toppled the fundamentalist Islamic regime in Afghanistan. An additional impetus for the war on terror was the mailing of deadly anthrax spores soon after the September 11 attacks. While no one claimed responsibility for these attacks, they unnerved the American public. Still, some of the tactics of the United States government concerning security at home provoked outcries that civil liberties were being curtailed.

There were radical changes in what had been the communist world in both Europe and Asia. By 1990, eastern Europe was being democratized as the communist regimes collapsed. One of the most vivid images of that year was the demolishing of the Berlin Wall, which had symbolized the cold war. In Czechoslovakia, the playwright Václav Havel (1936–)—who had been attacked and even imprisoned by the communist regime and whose politically charged works had been banned in his own country—was elected president in 1989. However, the democratization of communist Europe has not been tranquil. In Russia, Poland, and Czechoslovakia, the new governments proved unstable. In what was once Yugoslavia, there has been an ongoing civil war between Muslims and Christians, in which the attacks on Muslims are reminiscent of the genocide directed against Jews under Nazism. The reunification of Germany weakened its economy and also brought a neo-Nazi movement and terrorist attacks on immigrants. In addition, the Russian economy has been highly unstable, leading to political unrest.

In China, there has been a remarkable change in economic policies since the 1980s. With the opening of relations with the west a few years earlier, the Chinese communist government allowed more capitalist ventures and the introduction of western businesses. However, the Chinese government viciously crushed democratic demonstrations in 1989—in scenes which were televised across the world. While it is still not clear how soon the Chinese government will allow political liberalization, the Chinese economy continues to grow unabated.

There has also been worldwide economic turmoil, though some European and Asian economies have flourished. In the late 1970s and again in the late 1980s, recessions had a significant impact on the American economy, which had at best been sluggish. Fiscal uncertainty was one reason Bill Clinton was elected president in 1992, defeating the incumbent, George Bush, and ending a 12-year reign by the Republicans which had begun with Ronald Reagan in 1980. In the 1990s, the American economy saw remarkable growth; however, there were difficulties with the economy early in the twenty-first century as a result of 9/11. However, the economy again rebounded. A historically stunning occurrence at the close of the century was the highly controversial impeachment of President Clinton, in which Americans confronted a convergence of political and moral issues. In 2000, the United States saw the closest election in its history. The Supreme Court was required to make a decision affecting the final outcome, and George W. Bush won, even though he lost the popular vote. He won a second, close election in 2004.

Throughout these years, there have been conservative movements which attempted to counter the advances made by gays, feminists, and other minorities. Gay groups, for instance, had become more vocal politically, partly because of AIDS, which was killing many homosexuals. (AIDS is a disease that destroys the body's natural immune system. It began to reach epidemic proportions in the 1980s, and a significant number of theatre figures have died of it, including the Broadway musical director Michael Bennett and the founder of the Ridiculous Theatrical Company, Charles Ludlam. In the 1990s, there was a decrease in the number of AIDS cases in the western world, and some new drugs that could arrest its development were being used.) Conservative politicians worldwide also questioned government support of the arts.

There have also been other worries regarding the spread of new illnesses. Bacteria immune to antibiotics have developed. There was fear of the spread of SARS (severe acute respiratory syndrome) from Asia. More recently, the world has tried to prepare itself for a possible deadly pandemic of avian (bird) flu.

Technological innovations have continued to change the way we live, and particularly the way we communicate. Microcomputers, popularized in the late 1970s, have become more and more advanced: laptops and powerbooks—portable computers—are now as powerful as some of the early mainframes. "Faxes" allow documents to be sent around the world instantaneously over telephone lines; and telephone lines themselves may eventually be replaced by wireless communication. E-mail messages are sent from microcomputers across networks. The Internet has also changed the way we distribute information, shop, and interact; iPods and similar devices allow us to carry our music and video entertainment with us.

What is the state of theatre as it develops in the new millennium? Where is it headed? We cannot be certain about the answer to the second question, but we can draw some reasonable conclusions about the first. A good way to consider theatre in the twenty-first century is to look at some key examples from the past decades. In this chapter we will look at a variety of American developments.

During the past four decades, a significant number of playwrights and theatre companies throughout the world have attacked what they see as oppressive social and political institutions and have used unique theatrical techniques.

Some of these companies and dramatists have worked in what is described as a *postmodernist* style. This term suggests that "modernist" interest in antirealism is no longer central, and that art has moved beyond abstraction. Contemporary playwrights—and other theatre artists—combine abstraction and realism, so that their work cannot be easily classified. Also, the distinction between "high" art and popular art is no longer entirely clear: postmodernists use both "artistic" and popular concerns and techniques.

We will begin our review of contemporary theatre by focusing on major dramatists, companies, and individual artists in the United States whose work reflects the diversity of this nation and the diversity of its theatrical styles, as well as the diverse political and social debates during the past quarter of a century.

Dramatists of Diversity

Gender Diversity

In the United States, many female playwrights have questioned traditional gender roles and the place of women in American society. Representative works include *'night, Mother* (1983) and *Getting Out*, by Marsha Norman (1947–); *Crimes of the Heart* (1977), *The Miss Firecracker Contest* (1981), *The Debutante Ball* (1997), and *Impossible Marriage* (1998) by Beth Henley (1952–); and *Isn't it Romantic* (1981), *The Heidi Chronicles* (1988), *The Sisters Rosensweig* (1992), *An American Daughter* (1997), and *Third* (2005) by Wendy Wasserstein (1950–2006). Like many other contemporary playwrights, Wasserstein also wrote screenplays; one of hers is *The Object of My Affection*. Paula Vogel (1951–) is another award-winning playwright; she received the Obie for best play for *Baltimore Waltz* (1992) and the Pulitzer Prize for *How I Learned to Drive* (1997).

Feminist theatre companies have also forced audiences to reexamine gender biases. Some scholars estimate that more than 100 feminist companies have been founded in the United States; these companies include the Omaha Magic Theatre in Nebraska, headed by Megan Terry (1932–), a well-known off-Broadway playwright of the 1960s; the Spiderwoman Collective in New York; At the Foot of the Mountain in Minneapolis; Women's Experimental Theatre; and the Women's Project in New York.

One of the most political and most prolific of female playwrights is Maria Irene Fornes, whose long and distinguished career goes back to the off-off-Broadway movement of the 1960s.

(© T. Charles Erickson)

FEMINIST THEATRE COMPANIES
Women playwrights of all types have come to the forefront in recent decades. They include mainstream writers as well as many others whose work is more avant-garde. Many focus on strong feminist or lesbian concerns. A production that included five women dramatists and five women directors was *The Antigone Project* presented by the Women's Project. In this piece, different views of the Greek heroine Antigone were featured, creating a mosaic. The scene here shows Jeanine Serralles (right) as the embodiment of one of the Antigones.

MARIA IRENE FORNES

Maria Irene Fornes (1930–) is among the avant-garde dramatists who began the off-off-Broadway movement. Unlike many of her contemporaries, she has continued to work off-off-Broadway and shows no sign of wanting to leave noncommercial theatre.

Fornes was born in Havana, Cuba, in 1930, and came to the United States in 1945 with her mother and one sister. After becoming a naturalized citizen in 1951, she went to Europe for 3 years and pursued her original goal of becoming a painter. In 1954, in Paris, she saw Roger Blin's production of *Waiting for Godot*. Even though she spoke no French, she was so moved by the experience that she decided to devote her life to playwriting.

(Sara Krulwich/The New York Times)

Maria Irene Fornes.

She returned to New York in 1957 and worked as a textile designer. In 1960 she started to write plays, and in 1964 she had her first important production, *Tango Palace*. In 1965 she won two Obie awards, one for *The Successful Life of 3: A Skit for Vaudeville*, and one for the musical *Promenade* (written in collaboration with Al Carmines), perhaps the best-known of her early works. During the course of her career, Fornes has won nine Obies.

(© Gerry Goodstein/Yale Repertory Theatre)

FORNES: A PIONEER PLAYWRIGHT
A Latina playwright who paved the way for many feminist playwrights was Maria Irene Fornes. Her play *Fefu and Her Friends,* about a gathering of like-minded women, had an ingenious structure, with a second act in which the audience was divided into sections, each seeing a different scene in a different location. The audience was reunited in the third act in the main theatre space. Shown here are Julianna Margulies (Emma) and Joyce Lynn O'Connor (Fefu). The production was at the Yale Repertory Theatre.

Fornes's plays are unconventional in structure, dialogue, and staging. They are fundamentally symbolic and often include both brutality and slapstick humor. Her work of the 1960s showed a strong absurdist influence and was full of linguistic tricks and deliberately fanciful incongruities of time, space, and character. In the 1970s, Fornes continued to search for her own unique voice, and many critics believe she found it in *Fefu and Her Friends* (1977), which took a more realistic approach. In the 1970s, she also began working with INTAR, the Hispanic American Arts Center in New York City. In the 1980s, she wrote a number of plays, including *Mud* (1983, revised 1985), *The Conduct of Life* (1985), and *Abingdon Square* (1984). In 1992, her epic opera *Terra Incognita,* a revisionist treatment of Columbus, had its premiere in Italy. In 1998, the Women's Project in New York presented Fornes's *Summer in Gossensass,* a dramatization of the attempt to stage the first English production of Ibsen's *Hedda Gabler;* the text draws parallels between the actress who wished to perform Hedda, Ibsen's fictional Hedda, and contemporary feminist issues. Among Fornes's other works are *Oscar and Bertha* (1991), *The Audition* (1998), and *Letters from Cuba* (2000). Since 1968, Fornes has directed many of the productions of her plays.

Because of the unique nature of her work, Fornes has not achieved the kind of national recognition typically associated with success in American theatre. Her plays embody the ethic of off-off-Broadway and strike a unique balance between concern with human relationships and social and political consciousness.

Diversity of Cultural and Sexual Orientation

Maria Irene Fornes is not only a significant female playwright but also a significant Hispanic playwright: her work often reflects her cultural background as well as her concerns with issues of gender. One key development in American theatre during the past quarter of a century has been an explosion of theatres that reflect the cultural as well as the sexual diversity of the United States.

(© T. Charles Erickson)

KIA CORTHRON'S BREATH, BOOM

One talented, prolific young African American playwright is Kia Corthron, who has written at least two dozen plays, won numerous awards and commissions, and been produced by many of the best not-for-profit theatres in the United States. One of her recent plays is *Breath, Boom*. In the scene shown here, Kellee Stewart (left) and Jan Leslie Harding appear in a production by the Huntington Theatre, directed by Michael John Garcés.

Contemporary African American Playwrights

Suzan-Lori Parks (1964–), Pearl Cleage (1948–), and Cheryl West (1956–) are three contemporary African American female playwrights whose works deal with issues of racism and feminism and have been produced in regional and alternative theatres. Parks's *Venus* (1996), for example, depicts the life of a nineteenth-century black woman who was exhibited in England as the Venus Hottentot, a sideshow freak. Parks's other critically acclaimed plays include *The America Play* (1993), *The Death of the Last Black Man in the Whole Entire World* (1990), and *Topdog/Underdog*, which won a Pulitzer Prize in 2002.

Pearl Cleage's best-known plays are the one-act *Chain* (1992) and *Flyin' West* (1992), which was produced by Atlanta's Alliance Theatre Company; she has also created a number of performance pieces, a form that will be discussed later in this chapter. Cheryl West, trained as a social worker, deals with domestic crises in such works as *Before It Hits Home* (1989) and *Holiday Heart* (1994).

Two additional female African American dramatists whose works are politically charged are Kia Corthron (1961–) and Lynn Nottage (1964–). Corthron's works, which include *Seeking the Genesis* (1996) and *Force Continuum* (2000), have been commissioned by leading regional and off-Broadway companies. Nottage's best-known works are *Crumbs from the Table of Joy* (1996); *Mud, River, Stone* (1997); and *Intimate Apparel* (2003).

African American theatre and drama continue to be a vital force, not only in New York but in all the major cities of the United States. In the past decade, African American artists have continued to make an impact on commercial and noncommercial theatres. For example, George C. Wolfe (1955–), author-director of *The Colored Museum* (1986), *Spunk* (1990), *Jelly's Last Jam* (1992), and *Bring in da' Noise, Bring in da' Funk* (1996), also directed both parts of the award-winning *Angels in America.* In 1993, Wolfe was appointed artistic director of the Public Theatre, the renowned off-Broadway theatre founded by the New York producer Joseph Papp. At that theatre, Wolfe directed many significant productions, including a revival of the musical *On the Town* in 1997, as well as the musical *Caroline or Change* (2003), with a book by Tony Kushner.

Another African American director, Kenny Leon (1955–), in 2002 founded the True Colors Theatre in Atlanta. Leon also served as artistic director of Atlanta's Alliance Theatre for over 10 years. He has also directed at many significant regional theatres, including the Oregon Shakespeare Festival, the Goodman Theatre, and Arena Stage. In 2004, Leon directed a Broadway revival of *A Raisin in the Sun,* with Sean ("Puff Daddy") Combs.

One of the most significant contemporary playwrights in the United States, August Wilson, was an African American whose work focused on the issues that have confronted African Americans throughout the history of this nation.

AUGUST WILSON

The critical and popular success of the plays of August Wilson (1945–2005) makes it clear that he was one of the major American dramatists of the twentieth century. Wilson evokes the African American experience at various times in history through richly poetic texts.

The son of a white father and a black mother, Wilson grew up in a two-room apartment behind a grocery store on Bedford Avenue in Pittsburgh. He attended Catholic schools until, at the age of 15, he left school when a teacher erroneously accused him of plagiarism. To keep his mother from worrying, Wilson spent his afternoons in the public library, completing his education on his own. During his hours in the library, he developed a love of poetry, in particular the works of Dylan Thomas. Following a brief enlistment in the army, Wilson moved into a boardinghouse, resolved to become a poet.

(Sara Krulwich/The New York Times)

August Wilson.

In 1968, Wilson helped found the Black Horizons Theatre Company in Pittsburgh. In the late 1970s and early 1980s, he struggled to establish himself as a poet and held various odd jobs in Minneapolis. At the same time, he became interested in playwriting and wrote a number of dramas, including *The Homecoming* (1979), *The Coldest Day of the Year* (1979), *Fullerton Street* (1980), *Black Bart and the Sacred Hills* (1981), and *Jitney* (1982); which was successfully revived in New York in 2000.

When Wilson submitted a draft of *Ma Rainey's Black Bottom* to the Eugene O'Neill Center in Waterford, Connecticut—a workshop devoted to new plays—his work came to the attention of Lloyd Richards, the artistic director. Richards had directed the original production of *A Raisin in the Sun* and was also the head of the Yale Drama School and the Yale Repertory Theatre. With Richards directing, *Ma Rainey's Black Bottom* opened at the Yale Rep in April 1984, and six months later it moved to Broadway. (Wilson had to borrow a tuxedo for the Broadway opening.) From *Ma Rainey's Black Bottom* through *Two Trains Running,* Richards was Wilson's mentor, directing all his plays at the Yale Rep or at other regional theatres before bringing them to New York.

Wilson's play *Fences,* a family drama set in the 1950s, was produced in New Haven in 1985; in 1987, it opened in New York, where it received rave notices and went on to win the Pulitzer Prize. *Joe Turner's Come and Gone,* which deals with an African American searching for his lost wife, also opened in New York in 1987, while *Fences* was still running. In *Joe Turner*—more than his two preceding plays—Wilson uses a heavily poetic style of realism.

The Piano Lesson won Wilson his second Pulitzer Prize in 1990. *Two Trains Running* (1992), a play that deals with the turmoil of the 1960s, was more comedic than his earlier works but was received less enthusiastically by the New York critics when it opened on Broadway in 1992. Among Wilson's recent works are *Seven Guitars* (1995) and *King Hedley II*, which opened on Broadway in April 2001. (Like his earlier plays, this one was also staged at regional theatres prior to its New York production.) Wilson's final two plays were *Gem of the Ocean* (2003) and *Radio Golf* (2005).

Wilson's major plays are part of a cycle of ten dramas—one for each decade of the twentieth century—tracing the African American experience. Wilson's work is not political in the usual rhetorical sense: it remains poetic rather than polemical. Wilson argues that in order to know who you are now, you must know who you were in the past. His characters are universal figures, standing for everyone who has ever struggled with himself or herself and with social forces. Wilson once said, "I write about the black experience in America and try to explore in terms of the life I know best those things which are common to all cultures." Wilson died of liver cancer, after completing his historic cycle, on October 8, 2005. The Virginia Theatre in New York's Broadway district was renamed in his honor soon after his death. He is the first African American theatre artist to receive this honor.

JOE TURNER'S COME AND GONE Wilson's play *Joe Turner's Come and Gone* is set in Pittsburgh in 1911, a time when there was a mass exodus by African Americans from the south to the north. Harold Loomis, the play's central character, arrives with his daughter, Zonia, at a boardinghouse in Pittsburgh run by Bertha and Seth Holly. Loomis, a Southern church deacon kidnapped by whites and forced into a seven-year period of servitude, is now seeking his wife, Martha. Martha had been staying at the boardinghouse but has moved out to serve in another town's church. A white traveling salesman, Rutherford Selig, finds Martha for Loomis, who leaves his daughter with her, realizing that they cannot reunite.

Among the other boarders at the Holly home are Bynum, a conjurer; Jeremy Furlow, a young Southern black who hopes to make his fortune playing the guitar; Mattie Campbell, a woman searching for her husband whom Jeremy persuades to move into the boardinghouse but then abandons; and Molly Cunningham, the woman with whom Jeremy leaves.

On the surface, Wilson's play seems to follow the traditions of realism. The boardinghouse is populated by a cross section of individual African Americans struggling and searching early in the twentieth century. Wilson, through the realistic plotline, shows his audience that for blacks, freedom is an illusion. Seth wants to start his own business but cannot get financing without turning his home over to a white man. Loomis, supposedly a free southerner, was forced into servitude, which destroys his family. Jeremy loses his job because he will not pay part of his salary to a white man.

However, Wilson's play deviates from realism in significant ways. The structure of the play, for example, violates the traditional European model. Rather than developing each act in a straight dramatic line, he divides each into a series of short scenes. There is a secondary plotline, which is not clearly integrated and seems extraneous to the main action: Zonia and Reuben develop a childhood romance. But the tale of the children is again one of a search for identity, and their discussions echo, almost like a chorus, the concerns of the adults in the play.

(© Peter Cunningham/Time Life Pictures/Getty Images)

THE PLAYWRIGHT AUGUST WILSON One of the most important playwrights of the past half century is the African American dramatist August Wilson. During the course of his career he wrote a monumental series of plays about the black experience in America. There were ten in all, one for each decade of the twentieth century. Shown here in a scene from one of his plays, *Joe Turner's Come and Gone,* are Delroy Lindo (right) and Ed Hall (left).

Joe Turner's Come and Gone is also highly metaphorical, with many of the symbolic elements, according to the playwright, rooted in African ritual. Throughout the play, Bynum, who functions as an African healer, tells characters that they need to find their own "song," which will give them their self-identity. (Wilson frequently uses music as a metaphor for freedom in his dramas.) Bynum is also searching for a Shiny Man, a godlike figure who will bring him his own song.

In Act I, scene 4, the boardinghouse residents dance the juba, which Wilson says should be "as African as possible," when suddenly Loomis speaks in tongues and then recounts a dream in which he sees the bones of his ancestors and unites himself with them. At the end of the play, Loomis cuts his chest in a blood ritual, purifying himself and setting himself free.

Wilson's play clearly presents the marginalization of African Americans in white society. However, Wilson also argues that blacks should search for their unique identity, an identity rooted in the African past. His characters cannot find themselves through identities established by white America—as is seen in Seth's inability to succeed financially even though he willingly throws off his southern and African heritage—but can find themselves only in finding their own songs.

Latino-Latina American Theatre

In American theatre since 1975, many other playwrights—and many theatre companies—have focused on multicultural concerns: the special concerns of racial and ethnic groups and other cultures within American society. For example, many theatre artists have dramatized issues connected to peoples with a Spanish-speaking heritage.

Contemporary Latino-Latina American theatre, also known as Hispanic American theatre, in America can be divided into three major groups: Chicano theatre, Cuban American theatre, and Puerto Rican or Nuyorican theatre. All of these address the experiences of Spanish-speaking peoples living in the United States, and the plays are sometimes written in Spanish but are usually in English.

(© Stephanie Maze/Corbis)

Luis Valdéz (center) flanked by his brother Daniel, who wrote the music *Zoot Suit* and also appears in it, and another actor from the production.

CHICANO THEATRE Chicano theatre, which originated primarily in the west and southwest, came to prominence during the time of the civil rights movements of the 1960s. El Teatro Campesino ("Farmworkers' Theatre") grew out of the work of Luis Valdéz, who joined Cesar Chavez in organizing farmworkers in California. Valdéz wrote *actos,* short agitprop pieces dramatizing the lives of workers.

El Teatro Campesino became the prototype for other groups such as Teatro de la Gente ("People's Theatre"), founded in 1967; and Teatro de la Esperanza ("Theatre of Hope"), begun in 1971 in Santa Barbara, California. Also in 1971, a network of these theatres across the United States was established. In the 1990s, a well-known theatre, Teatro Vista, performed for Mexican and Hispanic audiences in Chicago.

Other plays about the Chicano experience followed. One of the most notable was *Roosters* (1987) by Milcha Sanchez-Scott (1955–), in which cockfighting is a metaphor used to explore Chicano concerns and family conflicts. Among other writers who have dealt with Chicano as well as wider themes is Arthur Giron (1937–), an American from Guatemala.

LUIS VALDÉZ

Luis Valdéz (1940–) was born in Delano, California. His parents were migrant farmworkers, and he was the second of their ten children. While in high school, Valdéz appeared on local television shows. He graduated from San Jose State College, where his first play was produced, in 1964. Immediately after graduation, he joined the San Francisco Mime Troupe, a company noted for its political theatre, improvisatory technique, and use of found spaces.

In 1965, Valdéz founded El Teatro Campesino, to support a strike that farmworkers had organized in Delano. Valdéz described El Teatro Campesino as "somewhere between Brecht and Cantinflas." (Cantinflas was a well-known Mexican slapstick comic film actor.) Critics compared the company's early work to modern, political commedia dell'arte. Valdéz characterized this early work as follows: "Instead of Arlecchinos, Pantalones, and Brighellas, we has Esquiroles (scabs), Contratistas (contractors), Patroncitos (growers), and Huelgistas (strikers)." El Teatro Campesino performed on a flatbed truck, traveling from town to town.

By the late 1960s and early 1970s, Valdéz and El Teatro Campesino began treating aspects of Chicano life other than farmwork, and their performance texts became more structured and somewhat less improvisational. Recognition for the company also grew; for example, El Teatro Campesino won an Obie award in 1968. In 1971, the company moved to its permanent location in San Juan Batista in California.

In 1978, Valdéz was commissioned by the Mark Taper Forum, a leading regional theatre in Los Angeles, to write *Zoot Suit*. Coproduced with El Teatro Campesino, the play, which was directed by Valdéz, ran for 46 weeks, winning the Los Angeles Critics' Circle Award for Distinguished Production. Valdéz also directed *Zoot Suit* in New York on Broadway, where it had a less successful 4-week run. A film version was written and directed by Valdéz in 1981.

The financial success of *Zoot Suit* allowed El Teatro Campesino to purchase an old packing house in San Juan Batista and convert it into a theatre. Since the success of *Zoot Suit,* Valdéz has continued to write plays and direct plays with El Teatro Campesino, and he has become a noted figure in film and television. In 1987, he directed the popular film *La Bamba,* and in 1994 he directed the television film *The Cisco Kid,* in which he revised the stereotypical representation of the title character. He also adapted and directed two of his plays for PBS.

Among Valdéz's other well-known dramas are *Dark Root of a Scream* (1967), *Bernabe* (1970), *Soldado Razo* (*Buck Private,* 1970), *La Carpa de los Rasquachis* (*The Tent of the Underdogs,* 1973), *Bandido!* (1982), *Corridos* (1983), and *I Don't Have to Show You No Stinking Badges* (1986). Valdéz has received many awards and honors, including: an Obie, the Los Angeles Drama Critics Award, and an Emmy.

ZOOT SUIT In 1978, Valdéz's play *Zoot Suit,* a Brechtian musical about racial violence in Los Angeles in 1943, opened in Los Angeles to critical acclaim; it later moved to Broadway in 1979 (the first and only Chicano play to do so). *Zoot Suit* ostensibly deals with an occurrence in the history of Mexican Americans. The play focuses on the arrest for murder, trial, imprisonment, and eventual vindication of a group of Chicanos who belong to the 38th Street gang in Los Angeles in the 1940s. The title of the play refers to a type of suit they wear, popular with young Chicanos. The protagonist is Henry Reyna, the leader of the gang, who is arrested the day before his induction into the navy to serve in World War II.

While *Zoot Suit* is based on an actual historic event, Valdéz does not strive for a realistic re-creation. Instead, he uses dramatic strategies that he developed in working with his company, El Teatro Campesino, which agitated for political and economic justice for migrant workers. El Teatro Campesino was best-known for its *actos,* short pieces that propagandized for better lives for the workers. These pieces were often broadly comic in style and characterization, used representational characters, and were highly theatrical.

(© Liz Lauren)

A MILESTONE IN LATINO-LATINA THEATRE
A significant event in the emergence of Latino-Latina theatre was the production of *Zoot Suit* by Luis Valdéz. It was a Brechtian musical based on a real event, but it was given a highly theatrical treatment. It began in Los Angeles and moved to Broadway. The scene here with Marco Rodriguez as Pachuco was staged at the Goodman Theatre in Chicago.

Zoot Suit is reminiscent of the actos. The play uses a narrator, Pachuco, who stands for all Chicanos throughout history, and who literally controls the dramatic action, setting the scenes and sometimes stopping the action and interacting with Henry and the audience. Another representational character is the Press, standing for all the newspapers that sensationalized tales of Chicano violence to increase sales. The setting is also highly theatrical, using the image of the controlling newspapers throughout.

The theatricality of *Zoot Suit* is also reminiscent of many earlier forms of dramatic literature and theatre. Valdéz uses a number of popular techniques to engage the audience. For example, like a musical, *Zoot Suit* uses song to further the action, to comment on characters, and to set up spectacular scenes of music and dance. In addition, the play has the feel of a melodramatic prison film of the 1940s, with some of the characterizations being exaggerated in a manner reminiscent of that genre.

But Valdéz is interested in making a political statement and has been clearly influenced by many Brechtian techniques. The play is episodic, and each scene is titled to underscore its sociopolitical meaning. The author always reminds audiences that they are in the theatre and that they are watching actors portray characters; this is clearly the case with El Pachuco, the narrator. Music is used to comment on the action, and in this play—unlike the traditional musical comedy—it also underscores Valdéz's political message. As Brecht suggested, history is used by the author not simply to educate and inform the audience about a forgotten past event but to draw parallels with contemporary issues. It is evident that Valdéz is also influenced by the "living newspapers" of the 1940s, in which actual events were used to make a political comment.

Valdéz's play clearly asks questions about the marginalization of Chicanos. He points out that they are both indigenous peoples—as is highlighted in the scene in which the Pachuco is stripped to clothing reminiscent of his Aztec origins—and contemporary Americans, interested in the "Anglo" music of Glenn Miller and willing to serve in World War II. Still, American society is closed to them and to their traditions. Even well-meaning liberals are chided by the playwright for using Chicanos for their own political agenda rather than for meeting them on equal ground. Only when Alice Bloomfield—a liberal news reporter—admits her discomfort with Chicanos do she and Henry begin to communicate honestly. Valdéz's vision presents the possibility of an America that can embrace all cultures only if it allows the uniqueness of all cultures to flourish side by side.

(© T. Charles Erickson/The McCarter Theatre Center)

LATINO-LATINA PLAYWRIGHTS TAKE THE STAGE
During recent decades a number of talented Latino-Latina playwrights have appeared on the scene. One of them, Nilo Cruz, won a Pulitzer Prize for his play *Anna in the Tropics,* about a group of Cuban Americans who work in a cigar factory in Florida in the late 1940s. The performers in the scene shown here are David Zayas, Jimmy Smits, John Ortiz, Vanessa Aspillaga, and Daphne Rubin-Vega. The production was at the McCarter Theatre Center and Broadway.

Cuban American and Nuyorican Theatre Cuban American theatre developed chiefly in Florida. The Federal Theatre Project of the 1930s resulted in fourteen Cuban American productions in 1936 and 1937. We have already discussed a highly regarded Cuban American playwright, Fornes. Among recent Cuban American dramatists who have emerged in the past quarter-century are Manuel Martin, Mario Pena, Dolores Prida, Ivan Acosta, and Omar Torres. (Torres's work is centered in Miami and New York.) Another Cuban-American playwright, Nilo Cruz, won the 2003 Pulitzer Prize for his play *Anna in the Tropics.* A new play by Cruz, *Beauty of the Father,* opened in 2006.

Nuyorican is a term that refers to Puerto Rican culture, mostly in New York but elsewhere as well. Works by playwrights with a Puerto Rican orientation began to be produced in the 1960s and 1970s by groups such as the Teatro Repertorio Español, the Puerto Rican Traveling Theatre, and the New York Public Theatre. The Nuyorican Poets' Café presented plays by a number of Puerto Rican playwrights, including Miguel Pinero (1947–1988), an ex-convict whose drama *Short Eyes,* a harshly realistic portrayal of prison life, proved to be very successful and won a number of awards in the 1973–1974 season. In recent years, a new group of Puerto Rican playwrights

(© Joan Marcus)

ASIAN AMERICAN THEATRE
Among the diverse multicultural forms to emerge strongly in the latter part of the twentieth century was Asian American theatre. One of its best-known playwrights is David Henry Hwang, whose *M. Butterfly* is shown here. This play is about an American diplomat in China who falls in love with a Chinese actress and has a long affair with her, only to discover later that the performer is really a man. The scene here is from the Broadway production with Alec Mapa and Tony Randall.

has come to prominence, including Yvette Ramirez, Candido Tirado, Edward Gallardo, and Juan Shamsul Alam.

Asian American Theatre

For most of the nineteenth century and the first half of the twentieth century, Asians appeared in American dramatic offerings strictly as stereotypes. With the coming of greater cultural and ethnic awareness in the 1960s and 1970s, this began to change. In 1965, several Asian American performers and directors founded the East West Players in Los Angeles. In 1973, two more groups were formed—the Asian Exclusion Act in Seattle and the Asian-American Theatre Workshop in San Francisco—and in 1977 the director-actor Tsia Chang (1945–) founded the Pan Asian Repertory Theatre in New York. These groups employed Asian American performers, produced dramas from the Asian cultural heritage, and emphasized new plays written by and for Asian Americans.

A number of plays by Asian American writers were produced in the 1970s and 1980s, including a memory play by Philip Kan Gotanda (1950–) called *Song for a Nisea Fisherman* (1980). A playwright who came to prominence in the 1980s was

David Henry Hwang (1957–), whose parents immigrated from China to California. Hwang wrote several plays that won wide recognition, beginning with *FOB,* produced in 1980; and *The Dance and the Railroad,* produced in 1981. Later in the decade, in 1988, Hwang's *M. Butterfly* opened successfully on Broadway. Based on a true story, *M. Butterfly* deals with a French diplomat who meets and falls in love with a Chinese opera singer who he thinks is a woman but who turns out to be a man and a spy. The play uses its plotline, and references to the opera *Madame Butterfly,* to underscore themes related to western imperialism and sexism. Hwang's *Golden Child* (1996) premiered off-Broadway and then, after revisions, had a less successful Broadway run. In 2003, he collaborated with the composer Philip Glass on *The Sound of a Voice.* Hwang also cowrote the book of the musical *Flower Drum Song* for a production in 2001. In 2006, Hwang contributed the book for the Broadway musical *Tarzan,* which was produced by Disney, and had music by the pop composer Phil Collins.

There has been a movement to have more Asian Americans employed as performers in appropriate roles. Hwang and the actor B. D. Wong, who played the Chinese opera singer in the original production of *M. Butterfly,* led a vigorous protest against the hiring of an English actor to play the leading role in the musical *Miss Saigon.* That battle was lost; but in 1996, when a revival of *The King and I* opened on Broadway, it had a large proportion of Asian American performers.

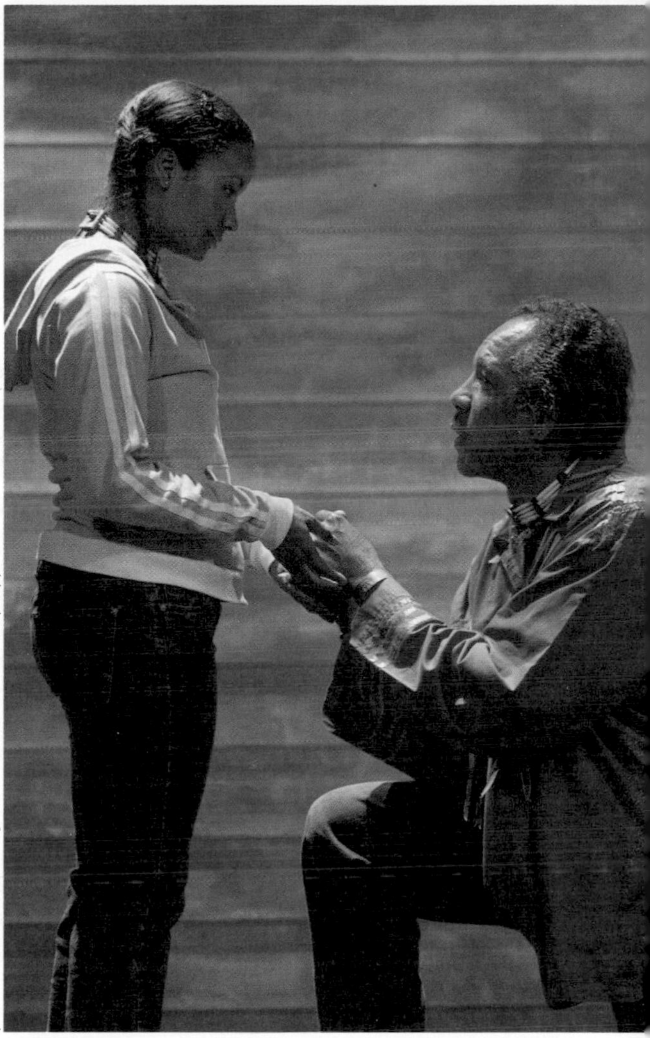

(Photo: Ann Marsden, 2005, at Penumbra Theatre Company.)

NATIVE AMERICAN THEATRE
Another important theatre that has gained prominence in recent years is Native American theatre. The playwrights celebrate and reexamine the experience of Native Americans, as well as the rituals and ceremonies that were part of their society. A particularly prolific Native American playwright is William S. Yellow Robe, Jr. His play *Grandchildren of the Buffalo Soldiers* concerns a homecoming that leads to the examination of crucial racial and intergenerational questions. Shown here are Maya Washington (August Jackson) and James Craven (Craig Robe) in a scene from a coproduction by Penumbra Theatre Company and Trinity Repertory Company, directed by Lou Bellamy.

Native American Theatre

Strictly speaking, there was not a Native American theater tradition; rather, there were spiritual and social traditions that had theatrical elements. These were found primarily in ancient rituals and communal celebrations, which were often infused with cosmic significance. Also, in these events, unlike traditional western theater, there was no audience as such: those observing were considered participants just as much as the principal performers. Many of these ceremonies and the like were outlawed by the American government in the nineteenth century. Thus, the legacy of rituals and ceremonies, which had strong theatrical components—not to mention significant spiritual and cultural value—was forced to go "underground" if it continued at all.

The American Indian Religious Freedom Act of 1972 made it legal once again for certain ceremonies, such as the sun dance, to resume. The increased awareness of these rituals and celebrations contributed to the emergence of a Native American theatre. Two groups that led the way in the past three decades were the Native American Theatre Ensemble and Spiderwoman.

The Native American Theatre Ensemble, which was originally called the American Indian Theatre Ensemble, was founded by Hanay Geiogamah. (It is important to note that those familiar with Native American theatre invariably identify theatre companies and theatre artists not with the generic term Native American theatre, but in terms of their nations. Thus, Geiogamah is identified as Kiowa/Delaware.) Geiogamah's organization gave its premiere performance at La Mama in New York City in 1972, and later toured widely, not only in North America but also in Europe and elsewhere.

Spiderwoman Theatre comes under the headings of both Native American theatre and feminist theatre. Founded in 1975, it is the longest continually running women's theatre in North America, as well as the longest-running Native American theatre. Three of its founding members, Lisa Mayo, Gloria Miguel, and Muriel Miguel, draw on storytelling and other theatrical traditions to celebrate their identities as American Indian women and to comment on stereotypes of women in general.

What is important to note about Native American theatre today is that it is not primarily historical or ceremonial. Though elements of tribal traditions may be incorporated, the emphasis among playwrights and producers is really on contemporary work, fusing the problems and aspirations of today's Native Americans with their heritage. The challenges and preoccupations of young Native American playwrights are similar to those addressed by their Euro-American counterparts.

Several Native American playwrights have recently published single-author anthologies of their works. These include William F. Yellow Robe, Jr. (Assiniboine), Diane Glancy (Cherokee), and E. Donald Two-Rivers (Anishinabe). Another important contemporary playwright is Bruce King (Turgle Clan, Hodenausaunee-Oneida). King and Yellow Robe are also directors who have founded their own companies in the recent past and have taught playwriting and performance at the Institute of American Indian Arts in Santa Fe, New Mexico, an organization that nurtures the next generation of Native American theater artists.

Gay and Lesbian Theatre

A number of plays and performers introduced gay and lesbian themes into the American theatre before the 1960s. For example, in the nineteenth century and the early twentieth century, there was considerable cross-dressing in performances, raising questions about sexual orientation and gender roles. Also, plays included material on this subject matter; one good example is Lillian Hellman's *The Children's Hour* (1934), in which a presumed lesbian relationship between two schoolteachers was presented.

However, the play that first brought gay life to the forefront in American theatre was *The Boys in the Band* (1968) by Mart Crowley (1935–). Crowley depicted a group of men living an openly gay life. In 1969, the year after it opened, gay patrons at the Stonewall Inn in New York's Greenwich Village fought against police officers who were attempting to close the bar. This uprising, considered the beginning of the modern gay rights movement, changed the attitudes of gay activists, who now rejected what they considered stereotypical depictions in Crowley's play. However, a

(© Joan Marcus)

GAY AND LESBIAN THEATRE
Among the many alternative theatres that emerged in the last part of the twentieth century was theatre centering on the gay and lesbian experience. An important company in this kind of theatre calls itself the Five Lesbian Brothers. One of its recent plays is *Oedipus at Palm Springs*, written by four members of the troupe. It is a modern, transgender view of the Greek myth of Oedipus. In the scene here Dominique Dibbell is Prin and Peg Healey is Terri. The production was at the New York Theatre Workshop in 2005.

significant New York revival for its thirtieth anniversary led to a reevaluation of the play's significance in the history of gay and lesbian theatre in the United States.

In the 1970s and 1980s, complex gay characters were presented unapologetically, often in plays by gay writers. These included *The Ritz* (1975) by Terrence McNally (1939–) and *Torch Song Trilogy* (1983) by Harvey Fierstein (1954–). Since then more and more plays have dealt expressly with gay and lesbian issues. The AIDS crisis of the 1980s and 1990s engendered a number of dramas, including *The Normal Heart* (1985) by Larry Kramer (1935–), *As Is* (1985) by William M. Hoffman (1939–), the two-part play *Angels in America: A Gay Fantasia on National Themes* (1990–1993) by Tony Kushner (1957–), *Love! Valour! Compassion!* (1995) by McNally, and *Take Me Out* by Richard Greenberg (1958–), which won a Tony in 2003.

Groups that use cross-dressing to break stereotypes of gender and sexual orientation have also been extremely important in the past three decades. Among the early "gender bender" groups were the Cockettes and the Angels of Light in San Francisco and Centola and Hot Peaches in New York. A lesbian theatre company that is known for its drag performances and satirical use of classical literature is Split Britches, founded in 1980 by Lois Weaver (1949–), Peggy Shaw (1944–), and Deborah Margolin (1953–). Split Britches is probably best known for its production *Belle Reprieve* (1991), which made satiric references to Tennessee Williams's *A Streetcar Named Desire. Belle Reprieve* was created collaboratively with an English gay company, Bloolips, founded in 1977 and also known for its drag cabaret-like performances and cross-dressed presentations of well-known dramas.

A major gay theatre company, which forced audiences to consider their own attitudes toward homosexuality, was the Ridiculous Theatrical Company, founded in 1967 by Charles Ludlam; this company burlesqued classical works and traditional dramatic forms by presenting them in drag. Furthermore, it used its burlesque drag versions of classical literature to draw parallels to contemporary gay issues. Even after Ludlam's death, the Ridiculous Theatrical Company continued to perform successfully for a decade.

CHARLES LUDLAM

Charles Ludlam (1943–1987) was a complete theatre artist, functioning at various points in his career as playwright, actor, director, and designer. The goal of his work, ironically, was to poke fun at the theatre, its representation of gender, and its portrayal of gays. His work with the Ridiculous Theatrical Company was honored with many awards, including numerous Obies, a Drama Desk Award, a Guggenheim Fellowship, and grants from the National Endowment for the Arts and the New York State Council of the Arts.

(Anita and Steve Shevett)

Charles Ludlam.

Ludlam was attracted to theatre at a very young age. His early experiences with theatre include attending a Punch and Judy puppet show at the Mineola Fair on Long Island in 1949, constant filmgoing with his mother, and appearances in elementary school plays. In 1958, Ludlam served an apprenticeship at the Red Barn Theatre, a summer stock company on Long Island. The next year, he attend performances of Pirandello's *Tonight We Improvise* and Gelber's *The Connection* by the Living Theatre, one of the seminal avant-garde companies of the 1950s and 1960s, which he later said left a lasting impression on him and his view of theatre. The Living Theatre also inspired him to found the Students' Repertory Theatre in Northport, Long Island, at the age of 17; he directed and acted there.

In the early 1960s, Ludlam studied at Hofstra University, receiving an acting scholarship. There he wrote his first play, *Edna Brown,* which he later destroyed. Ludlam's acting style at Hofstra, however, was criticized as being excessive.

After leaving Hofstra, he moved to New York City and became immersed in the avant-garde and gay theatre scenes. He began his professional career in 1966 with the Play-House of the Ridiculous, as both a performer and a playwright. He made his New York debut in 1966 playing Peeping Tom in Ronald Tavel's *The Life of Lady Godiva,* which was directed by John Vaccaro. The Play-House of the Ridiculous experimented with many of the techniques that became part of Ludlam's repertoire: cross-dressing, exaggerated performance style, and burlesquing of popular and classical literature. Ludlam staged his play *Big Hotel* (1967) at the Play-House of the Ridiculous, but he was fired by Vaccaro during rehearsals for Ludlam's second play, *Conquest of the Universe.*

Many of Vaccaro's actors left with Ludlam, who formed his own company, The Ridiculous Theatrical Company. They presented *Conquest of the Universe* under the title *When Queens Collide* in 1967, using an alternative title because Vaccaro's troupe was also staging the play. Between 1967 and 1987, Ludlam was a prolific playwright and actor with the Ridiculous Theatrical Company, often playing lead roles in drag.

Ludlam's plays and the company's outrageous performance style helped the Ridiculous achieve cult status in New York and international recognition. Still, while

(© Anita and Steve Shevett)

THE MYSTERY OF IRMA VEP
The playwright-performer Charles Ludlam's takeoff on a Victorian melodrama illustrates many elements of postmodern theatre. One element is a drastic reworking of theatre from the past. Another is a consciousness of gender considerations, illustrated by the cross-dressing of the two actors who play all the roles: Stephen DeRosa and Everett Quinton. The production was at the Westside Theatre.

the company attracted grants and awards and leased a permanent theatre space, the Ridiculous was always on the fringe of even the avant-garde, and its finances were often uncertain. Because of financial and artistic difficulties, the Ridiculous Theatrical Company was reorganized in 1980, with some of the longtime members leaving.

Among Ludlam's most notable plays during these two decades were *Bluebeard* (1970), *Camille* (1973, and revived posthumously in 1990), *Stage Blood* (1975), *Der Ring Gott Farblonjet* (1977), *Le Bourgeois Avant-Garde* (1982), *The Mystery of Irma Vep* (1984), *Medea* (1984), *Salammbo* (1985), and *The Artificial Jungle* (1986).

All of Ludlam's works exhibit his "ridiculous" dramatic techniques: satirizing stereotypes based on gender and sexual orientation through the use of cross-dressing, heightened theatricality, burlesquing of popular and serious literature, recognition of the audience, and a larger-than-life acting style. While Ludlam's work is campy on the surface, his plays clearly deal with gay politics in a serious and sometimes poignant fashion.

During the 1980s, Ludlam developed a career apart from the Ridiculous Theatrical Company, acting in films, including *The Big Easy, Imposters,* and *Forever Lulu;* and appearing on television, in episodes of *Miami Vice* and *Tales from the Crypt.* He also played the title role in *Hedda Gabler* at the American Ibsen Theatre in Pittsburgh in 1984. In addition, he taught playwriting at Yale University.

Ludlam died from complications due to AIDS on May 28, 1987. His Ridiculous Theatrical Company, under the artistic direction of Everett Quinton, continued to perform for another decade until Quinton disbanded the company in 1997. Ludlam's complete plays as well as an anthology of critical and theoretical writings were published posthumously. His most popular work was *The Mystery of Irma Vep.*

THE MYSTERY OF IRMA VEP Ludlam's *The Mystery of Irma Vep* is subtitled "a penny dreadful." This was a Victorian form of literature that mixed sensationalism, melodrama, foreign locales, and romance. Ludlam is clearly satirizing the traditions of that form in this comic send-up, which ostensibly deals with discovering who killed Lord Edgar's first wife and son. *Irma Vep* has monsters, mysterious deaths, eerie settings, a scene in Egypt, and stereotypical Victorian characters, all of which are made fun of through exaggeration. Ludlam is also burlesquing the horror films of the 1940s that were similar in plotline to the "penny dreadfuls." In addition, there are subtle comic references to classics, such as Ibsen's *Little Eyolf.*

While Ludlam's work is enjoyable purely on the level of literary and film satire, the playwright is also poking fun at theatre as well as representing gender and gay issues. As Ludlam indicates in his opening stage direction: "*The Mystery of Irma Vep* is a full-length quick-change act. All roles are portrayed by two performers." (In its original staging, Ludlam and his longtime lover, Everett Quinton, played all the parts.) Throughout the production, the spectators are constantly reminded that they are watching theatre. The quick changes force the audience to laugh at accepted conventions of realistic theatre, such as actors playing individualized characters and changing costumes. Furthermore, we are always aware that two men are playing all the roles, male and female.

Ludlam's dramatic strategy, however, goes beyond making fun of literature and theatrical convention. Through his campy, comic use of cross-dressing, he makes the audience confront the stereotypical representations of gender that have been part of theatre history. All the male and female characters in the play are parodies of the stereotypical gender types found in melodrama: the threatened Lady Enid, the noble and heroic Lord Edgar, and the servants.

In addition, Ludlam makes his audience deal with issues of sexual orientation by never letting the spectators forget that both actors are men. When men and women kiss in *Irma Vep,* the audience recognizes that two men—one cross-dressed—are engaging in an act of passion. Ludlam wants us to question all our biases about gender and sexual orientation. That he does so through the accessible forms of camp and burlesque won a wide audience for *The Mystery of Irma Vep,* a play that is frequently revived in university, regional, and community theatres. In 1998, the Ridiculous Theatrical Company staged an immensely successful revival of this play.

Other American Dramatists

Many young off-Broadway and off-off-Broadway playwrights of the 1960s have made major contributions to American theatre during the past quarter-century. Examples are *Talley's Folly* (1979), *The Fifth of July* (1980), *Burn This* (1987), *Redwood Curtain* (1993), *Sympathetic Magic* (1997), and *Book of Days* (1998) by Lanford Wilson (1937–); as well as *The House of Blue Leaves* (1970), *The Landscape of the Body* (1977), *Bosoms and Neglect* (1979), *Lydie Breeze* (1982), *Six Degrees of Separation* (1991), and *Lake Hollywood* (1999) by John Guare (1938–). Possibly the two most acclaimed American dramatists of the past 25 years have been Sam Shepard and David Mamet.

SAM SHEPARD

Sam Shepard (1943–), whose dramas adroitly blend images of the American west, pop motifs, science fiction, and other elements of popular and youth culture, is one of the most inventive American playwrights. He has won dozens of awards, including Obies for eleven plays (more than any other author). Many critics consider him the dominant American playwright of his generation. Having written forty-two plays in just about 22 years, he is surely among the most prolific.

(Laurent Emmanuel/AP Images)
Sam Shepard.

Shepard's father was in the army, and Shepard spent his childhood on military bases. His original ambition to become a veterinarian came to an end after a single year in college, and in 1963 he arrived in New York at the age of 19 determined to become an actor. Shepard early on became involved in both the rock-and-roll community and the avant-garde theatre scene. For that matter, he toured with Bob Dylan and later wrote a book about the experience, *Rolling Thunder Logbook* (1977). Two years after his arrival in New York, the *New York Times* called him the "acknowledged 'genius' of the off-off-Broadway circuit"—not as an actor, however, but as a playwright. In 1966 Shepard became the first dramatist to receive three Obies in one year, winning awards for *Chicago, Icarus's Mother,* and *Red Cross.* Other major works of the 1960s included *The Rock Garden* (1964) and *La Turista* (1966).

Shepard lived in England from 1971 to 1974. Two notable plays of this period—*The Tooth of Crime* (1972) and *Geography of a Horse Dreamer* (1974)—premiered in London. In late 1974, he became playwright in residence at the Magic Theatre in San Francisco, where most of his subsequent plays of the 1970s were first produced.

Shepard's characters are storytellers, and his plays are characterized by long monologues. While his characters tell many stories, though, the truth of any particular story is never verified. The audience is invited to speculate, to form opinions about the dynamics of a person or family. Shepard's best-known works belong to what he calls his "family trilogy": *Curse of the Starving Class* (1977), *Buried Child* (1978), and *True West* (1980). *Fool for Love* (1983), which Shepard also directed, and *A Lie of the Mind* (1985) explored many of the same themes as the trilogy, including the death of traditional family structure, inability to establish lasting relationships, the violence of American society, and a longing for a simpler time. He wrote the book for a one-act musical entitled *The Sad Lament of Pecos Bill on the Eve of Killing His Wife* (1983), with music and lyrics by Catherine Stone.

In the 1990s, Shepard did less dramatic writing. His play *States of Shock* (1991), which deals allegorically with the Persian Gulf war, was not well received, nor was *Simpatico* (1994). He revised *Buried Child* for a production by the Steppenwolf Theatre in Chicago; it was transferred unsuccessfully to New York in 1997 but was the first of his plays staged in a Broadway theatre. Shepard has also cowritten theatre pieces with the renowned American director Joseph Chaikin, including *Tongues* and *When the World Was Green (A Chef's Fable)* for the Olympic Arts Festival in Atlanta in 1996.

Shepard has also turned his attention to screenwriting, film directing, and acting, appearing in many films and television dramas, including *Days of Heaven* (1978), *Frances* (1982), *The Right Stuff* (1983), *Fool for Love* (1985), *Crimes of the Heart* (1986), *Baby Boom* (1987), *Steel Magnolias* (1989), *Voyager* (1991), *Thunderheart* (1992), *The Pelican Brief* (1993), *Snow Falling on Cedars* (1999), *The Pledge* (2001), *The Notebook* (2004), and *Stealth* (2005). He also wrote the acclaimed film *Paris, Texas* (1984) for the German director Wim Wenders.

Shepard has led a reclusive life with his wife, the film star Jessica Lange. In an interview in 1999, he remarked that he was working on a play he had begun a decade earlier, entitled *The Late Henry Moss. Moss* was directed by Shepard at San Francisco's Magic Theatre in December 2000 with an all-star cast. Joseph Chaikin directed the New York premier in 2001. Shepard's *God of Hell* (2004), a comedy in three scenes, focuses on contemporary political issues. In 2004, Shepard also appeared off-Broadway in a production of Caryl Churchill's *A Number.*

DAVID MAMET

David Mamet (1947–) has over the past three decades established himself as a mainstay of American theatre. He has written more than twenty full-length plays, a number of short plays, and several original and adapted screenplays. He has won numerous awards, including three Chicago Jefferson Awards for best new play of the season, two Obies, two New York Drama Critics Circle Awards, and the Pulitzer Prize for *Glengarry Glen Ross* (1984).

Mamet was born in Chicago and was brought up in the Jewish area of the South Side. His mother was a teacher and his father a labor lawyer and amateur semanticist. After his parents divorced, Mamet lived with his mother and attended a private school in a Chicago suburb, Olympia Fields. Mamet's uncle was the director of broadcasting for the Chicago Board of Rabbis, and for a time Mamet appeared on television playing Jewish children with various religious problems.

Mamet attended Goddard College in Vermont, majoring in literature and theatre. From 1968 to 1969, he took an 18-month break from formal studies to work at the Neighborhood Playhouse, a Stanislavski-oriented program under the direction of Sanford Meisner, who had been an actor with the Group Theatre in the 1930s. Mamet completed his degree in 1969. For a short time, he tried to work as an actor, but his ambition diminished after he worked for one season in a summer stock theatre. After a succession of jobs, he returned to Goddard College as an instructor and began writing plays for use in his drama classes.

(© Kevin Winter/Getty Images)

David Mamet.

In 1972, he returned to Chicago, where his one-act play *Sexual Perversity in Chicago* won a Jefferson Award as best new play of the year. In 1975, *Sexual Perversity* and another one-act play, *Duck Variations,* opened in New York and won the Obie for best play. In 1977, *American Buffalo* opened on Broadway and was voted best new play by the New York Drama Critics Circle. In 1983, Mamet was a founding member of the Atlantic Theatre Company, which has become one of New York's leading off-Broadway theatre venues.

Glengarry Glen Ross (1983), which opened at the National Theatre in London and was dedicated to Harold Pinter, brought Mamet international attention and in 1992 was adapted as a film. The Broadway production of *Speed-the-Plow* (1988) featured the rock star Madonna. In 1992, *Oleanna,* which Mamet also directed, stirred up a controversy because of its handling of the subject of sexual harassment—it involves charges made by a woman student against a college professor. His most recent plays are *The Cryptogram* (1994), *The Old Neighborhood* (1998), *Boston Marriage* (1999), and *Romance* (2005).

Mamet, like Shepard, has also written a number of films, including *Spartan* (2004), *Heist* (2001), *Lakeboat* (2000), *State and Main* (2000), *Wag the Dog* (1998), *The Spanish Prisoner* (1998), *The Edge* (1997), *Oleanna* (1994), *Homicide* (1991), *Things Change* (1988), *House of Games* (1987), and *The Verdict* (1982). He also directed *Heist, State and Main, The Spanish Prisoner, Oleanna, Things Change,* and *House of Games.*

Mamet's plays are very reminiscent of Pinter. They have naturalistic language and settings and down-and-out characters whose struggles are clearly recognizable, but they do not provide the clear-cut exposition or dramatic resolutions of traditional realism. Mamet's plays question the ability of humans to communicate and interact honestly.

MUSICAL THEATRE

We should bear in mind that in all the world's major cities, commercial theatre continues to be prominent. A good example is the sustained popularity of musical theatre. Though the musical has undergone significant changes, it remains primarily a commercial enterprise. As we pointed out in Chapter 14, *Fiddler on the Roof* (1964), a traditional American musical, is often considered the end of a "golden era." The rock musical *Hair* (1967)—by Galt McDermott (1928–), Gerome Ragni (1942–), and James Rado—marked a significant change: it had no real story line and was a celebration of the antiestablishment lifestyle of the 1960s.

After *Hair,* the musical scene became increasingly fragmented. Fewer and fewer book musicals were written; instead, there were other approaches. One new approach was the concept musical, in which a production is built around an idea rather than a story. Two examples, both composed by Stephen Sondheim and directed by Harold Prince (1928–), are *Company* (1970) and *Follies* (1971). Three of Sondheim's later works—*Sunday in the Park with George* (1985), *Into the Woods* (1988), and *Assassins* (1991)—can also be considered concept musicals. In *Passion* (1994) Sondheim returned to the traditional book musical.

Another significant trend, which started in the 1960s and then began to dominate musical theatre in the 1970s and 1980s, was the choreographer-turned-director—an artist who provides the vision for a musical. Two significant director-choreographers were Gower Champion (1920–1980), who was responsible for *Hello Dolly!* (1964) and *42nd Street* (1980); and Bob Fosse (1927–1989), who directed *Sweet Charity* (1966) and *Pippin* (1972). Jerome Robbins is generally recognized as the leading American director-choreographer, and a retrospective revue of his major work—*Jerome Robbins's Broadway*—was the only successful musical of the 1988–1989 season. *A Chorus Line* (1975), which is so far the longest-running American musical, was developed by the director-choreographer Michael Bennett (1943–1987). Tommy Tune has continued the tradition of the choreographer-director with such productions as *Nine* (1982), *Grand Hotel* (1989), and *The Will Rogers Follies* (1991). Two other examples of the choreographer-director are Susan Stroman (1960–), responsible for *The Producers* (2001); and Kathleen Marshall (1963–), who directed and choreographed the Broadway revival of *The Pajama Game* in 2006.

Another trend in musical theatre in the last quarter of a century has been the emergence of British composers and lyricists. The leading figure in this trend is the composer Andrew Lloyd Webber (1948–), who wrote *Jesus Christ Superstar* (1971) and *Evita* (1979) with the lyricist Tim Rice (1944–). Webber, working with others, has also written the immensely popular *Cats* (1982), *The Phantom of the Opera* (1987), and *Sunset Boulevard* (1993). Two other lavish musicals originating in Britain are *Les Misérables* (1987) and *Miss Saigon* (1989).

There has also been a trend toward revivals of earlier musicals—an indication that the output of new work has diminished, though also an indication that these earlier works form part of an important heritage and have lasting value. However, in the late 1990s there was a sense that the American musical was rebounding. The popularity of George C. Wolfe's *Bring in da' Noise, Bring in da' Funk* (1994) and the huge success of *Rent* by Jonathan Larson (1960–1996), first off-Broadway in 1995 and then on Broadway in 1996, seemed to reawaken interest in the American form. *Rent,* an adaptation of the opera *La Bohème,* uses many musical forms (rock, jazz, Latin, opera) to tell a story about starving artists in the East Village of New York; it won the Pulitzer Prize for drama and the Tony Award for Best Musical in 1996.

Disney's musicals have also been highly successful; they include *The Lion King* (1997), *Aida* (1999), and *Tarzan* (2006). The extremely popular *The Lion King* was produced in 1997 by Disney, a company whose presence has spurred on the economic revitalization of the Broadway theatre district in New York City; this musical was based on the popular Disney animated film and has music by the rock composer Elton John. The director of *The Lion King,* as well as the designer of the masks and puppets, is Julie Taymor (1952–). Taymor, who is a designer, adapter of literature for the stage, and director, is well known for her avant-garde puppet techniques borrowed from Asian theatres. For example, she used puppets in staging Shakespeare's *The Tempest* (1986)

(© Joan Marcus)

AMERICAN MUSICAL THEATRE MEETS THE AVANT-GARDE
Julie Taymor—who had spent most of her career working with experimental and avant-garde theatre groups, and had also absorbed theatrical techniques from southeast Asia—was chosen to direct the musical *The Lion King*. The result was a Broadway musical that had many elements of the avant-garde—a mixture that met with great success. Shown here is Tsidii Le Loka in the Broadway production.

at New York's off-off-Broadway Theatre for a New Audience, in her frequently revived adaptation of a short story *Juan Darien* (1988), in a Tokyo production of Igor Stravinsky's opera *Oedipus Rex* (1992), and in a production of *The Green Bird* (1996), an eighteenth-century comedy by Carlo Gozzi. The huge commercial success of *The Lion King*, however, clearly reflects a merging of popular and experimental theatre.

In addition, there seem to be indications of a weakening of the British musical imports. Three failures were Andrew Lloyd Webber's *Sunset Boulevard,* which lost $30 million worldwide; *Whistle Down the Wind,* which had a tryout in Washington, D.C., but never reached New York; and *The Woman in White,* which failed on Broadway in 2005.

However, there is also a blurring of the line between what is an American musical and what is a British musical. Disney, for example, continued its tradition of successful Broadway musicals with *Aida,* with music by the British rock star Elton John (1947–) and directed by Robert Falls (1954–), who was well known for his productions at the Victory Gardens Theatre and the Goodman Theatre in Chicago. Falls had also won critical acclaim for his revival of *Death of a Salesman* in 1999. *Aida* opened on Broadway in 2000, after being repeatedly reworked out of town.

The continuing popularity of revivals also reflects the blurring of the distinction between British and American musical theatre. While there have been many significant American musical revivals, including *Into the Woods,* there have also been a number of British revivals that used American personnel.

For example, the Broadway revival of *Oklahoma!* in 2002 was directed by Trevor Nunn, following his successful production for the Royal National Theatre, and choreographed by Susan Stroman, a leading American musical theatre artist, who directed the award-winning *The Producers, Contact* (2000), and the Broadway revival of *The Music Man* (2000). The New York producer was Cameron Macintosh, who had been the leading financial figure in British musical theatre in the 1980s.

Still, there are several noticeable trends in recent musicals in the United States. As mentioned, one that continues is the flow of revivals of established musicals from the past. Another is the adaptation of films into stage musicals such as *The Producers* (2001), *Hairspray* (2003), *Monty Python's Spamalot* (2005), and *Dirty Rotten Scoundrels* (2005), among others. Still another trend has been the "jukebox" or "songbook," musical in which the well-known songs of composers or singers are the basis for the show. Two examples are *Mamma Mia* (2001), featuring the music of the Swedish group ABBA; and *Jersey Boys* (2005), based on music made popular by the singer Frankie Valli. Scattered among these kinds are original musicals: some more traditional, like *Wicked* (2003) and *Light in the Piazza* (2005); and others unconventional and somewhat irreverent, such as *Urinetown* (2001), *Avenue Q* (2003), and *The Drowsy Chaperone* (2005), which originated in Canada.

STEPHEN SONDHEIM

The American musical composer and lyricist Stephen Joshua Sondheim (1930–) is critically regarded as possibly the most important figure in the American musical theatre of the past four decades. Sondheim's musicals combine complicated lyrics, ingenious characters, intriguing subject matter, and complex music and lyrics.

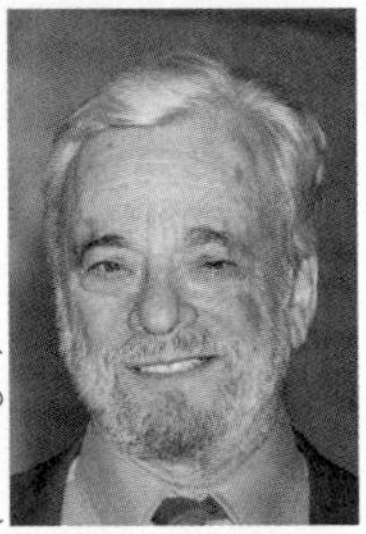

(AP Images)

Stephen Sondheim.

Sondheim was born in New York City. After his parents divorced, he moved to Pennsylvania, where his next-door neighbor, Oscar Hammerstein II, taught him how to write lyrics. Sondheim wrote musicals while attending Williams College, where he won the Hutchinson Prize for Music Composition, allowing him to study theory and composition with Milton Babbitt.

Early in his career, Sondheim wrote for television and created incidental music for Broadway productions. In 1957, he was the lyricist for Leonard Bernstein's *West Side Story;* in 1959, he collaborated with Jule Styne on *Gypsy.* In 1962, Sondheim wrote the music and lyrics for the musical *A Funny Thing Happened on the Way to the Forum,* which won him his first Tony Award.

From the 1960s through the 1990s, Sondheim became America's best-known composer of musicals. His most famous works are *Passion* (1994), *Assassins* (1991), *Into the Woods* (1987), *Sunday in the Park with George* (1984), *Merrily We Roll Along* (1981), *Sweeney Todd* (1979), *Pacific Overtures* (1976), *The Frogs* (1974), *A Little Night Music* (1973), *Follies* (1971), *Company* (1970), and *Anyone Can Whistle* (1964).

Sondheim has also contributed to many other theatre productions and films. He wrote the lyrics for *Do I Hear a Waltz?* (1965), as well as additional lyrics for *Candide* (1973). *Side by Side by Sondheim* (1976), *Mary Me a Little* (1981), *You're Gonna Love Tomorrow* (1983), and *Putting It Together* (1992) are theatrical revues of his music and lyrics. Sondheim also composed the scores for the films *Stavisky* (1974) and *Reds* (1981) and wrote the songs for *Dick Tracy* (1990), which earned him an Academy Award. The multitalented Sondheim was also a coauthor of the movie *The Last of Sheila* (1973) and the drama *Getting Away with Murder* (1996).

Stephen Sondheim's musical work has received many honors, including Tony Awards for *Passion, Into the Woods, Sweeney Todd, A Little Night Music, Follies,* and *Company*. All these musicals, along with *Pacific Overtures* and *Sunday in the Park with George,* also received the New York Drama Critics Circle Award. *Sunday in the Park with George* was awarded the Pulitzer Prize for drama in 1985. In 1993, Sondheim was honored by the Kennedy Center in Washington, D.C., for his lifelong contribution to the arts.

While Sondheim's work has been critically acclaimed, many of his musicals have not attained widespread popularity. *Follies, Passion, Pacific Overtures,* and *Assassins* have sometimes been characterized as too idiosyncratic for popular tastes. *Assassins,* which deals with the lives of people who killed America's presidents, has not had a Broadway production. It was scheduled to be revived in the fall of 2001, but it was canceled after the events of September 11 of that year. There was a successful revival on Broadway in 2004.

Sondheim's great contribution to musical theatre history has been recognized through a number of revivals. *Follies* was staged again on Broadway in 2001. *Into the Woods* received the Tony Award for best musical revival in 2002. The ingenious revival of *Sweeney Todd,* staged by John Doyle, was a hit in New York City, where it was restaged in 2005, after productions in England. The Kennedy Center in Washington, D.C., presented a unique celebration of Sondheim's work, reviving six of his musicals in repertory from May to August 2002.

Alternative Theatre

In the past two decades, many theatre artists have explored new ways of breaking away from mainstream theatre. This is evident in the United States, where theatre artists have tried to find outlets for their work outside commercial Broadway theatre, and even outside the larger regional theatres, which have become more reliant on commercial success for their own financial survival. (The trend has also been international: a number of significant avant-garde theatre companies have been established in European cities—in Germany and France, for example. Possibly the best-known is the Théâtre du Soleil, a French company founded by Ariane Mnouchkine, who is discussed in Chapter 16.)

Alternative theatres in the United States, and internationally, also reflect postmodernist points of view. Postmodernist artists question categorizations of works. Postmodernism questions the idea of an accepted "canon" of classics; postmodernists also ask why certain artists and certain groups should have held positions of power and privilege throughout theatre history.

Accordingly, postmodernists rebel against traditional readings of texts, arguing that theatre productions may have a variety of "authors," including directors and individual audience members; they argue that each individual audience member creates his or her own reading. Postmodernist directors are noted for deconstructing classic dramas—that is, taking the original play apart, developing a new, individual conceptualization, and trying to represent onstage the issues of power embedded in the text. Postmodernism also suggests that the modernist interest in realism and abstraction, popular art and high art, is no longer relevant. (Refer back to our earlier discussion of *The Lion King,* a production that breaks down the distinction between popular art and high art as well as commercial and experimental theatre.)

Among the most significant groups that have developed off-off-Broadway since 1970 are the Performance Group, the Wooster Group, and Mabou Mines. All have experimented with striking theatrical images, physical performance techniques, improvisation, texts created by performers and directors, and environmental staging.

Richard Schechner and the Performance Group

The Performance Group was founded in 1968 by Richard Schechner and used a remodeled garage called the Performing Garage. The company was known for its environmental stagings of *Dionysus in '69* (1969), *The Tooth of Crime* (1973), *Mother Courage* (1975), and *The Balcony* (1979). In directing *Mother Courage,* Schechner had the audience move from time to time and reconfigure itself so that its relationship to the stage action continually changed.

After the Performance Group disbanded in 1980, Schechner remained a significant theorist, educator, and practitioner. In the 1980s, he wrote about the relationship between anthropology and theatre and was a leading teacher and theorist of performance. In 1993, he directed *Faust Gastronome,* a reworking of the Faust story, loosely based on Marlowe and Goethe, in which Faust was presented as obsessed with and surrounded by images of food. For this production, Schechner worked with a new company, East Coast Artists. In Schechner's version, Hitler and other anachronistic figures inhabit Faust's world. Schechner used outrageous and grotesque devices: Mephistopheles—the devil—had a tail shaped like a phallus, and the piece closed with a naked Faust being covered with Chinese food and boiled in a large vat. Schechner also commented on gender stereotypes by casting women as men and vice versa.

The Wooster Group

Out of the Performance Group grew The Wooster Group, under the artistic direction of Elizabeth LeCompte (1944–). The Wooster Group, which gained international renown in the 1980s, is noted for "deconstructing" well-known texts—that is, taking them apart and commenting on them—in performance pieces which tackle controversial social issues. (Arthur Miller sued the company to keep it from using parts of his play *The Crucible.*) The Wooster Group's best-known productions are *Route 1 & 9* (1981), which used sections of *Our Town; L.S.D.* (1983); and *Brace Up* (1991), a performance adaptation of *The Three Sisters,* which commented on the text through narration and video. In 1997, the Wooster Group presented a highly theatrical, highly physical version of Eugene O'Neill's *The Hairy Ape,* in a run-down theatre in the Times Square area. As with many of the Wooster Group's works, *The Hairy Ape* had been "workshopped" before this presentation, the performers adopted a highly presentational style, microphones and amplification were used to create unsettling

(© Paula Court)

THE EMPEROR JONES REINTERPRETED
The Wooster Group was one of several organizations that often turned conventional theatre upside-down. Their version of *The Emperor Jones* by Eugene O'Neill featured the title character played in black face. Here, Scott Shepherd and Kate Valk appear in *The Emperor Jones,* as revived by the Wooster Group in 2006.

sounds, and video was also used. The production starred a film actor, Willem Dafoe (1955–), who began his acting career with this company and who has frequently returned to work with it. The Wooster Group has also worked extensively on an alternative reading of O'Neill's *The Emperor Jones.* The company presented its adaptation of Racine's *Phaedra,* entitled *To You, the Birdie* (2002) and *Poor Theater* (2004).

Mabou Mines

Mabou Mines was organized in 1970, originally under the artistic direction of Lee Breuer (1937–), and is well known for staging the plays of Samuel Beckett. This company has a highly visual style and has developed many theatre pieces using imagery and techniques from popular culture, including cartoons. One of its early works, *The B. Beaver Animation* (1974), brought the audience into a world of cartoon-like beavers constructing a dam; it was part of a series of works Breuer referred to as "animations." Like *The Birds* by Aristophanes—a Greek Old Comedy—*B. Beaver* used the animal kingdom to reflect comically on the human condition. Breuer's most controversial production was *Lear* (1990), which reversed the gender

(© Beatriz Schiller)

RED BEADS, BY MABOU MINES
Described as a combination fairy tale, puppet play, and chamber opera, *Red Beads,* created by the avant-garde troupe Mabou Mines, mixes music, dance, puppetry, and other theatrical elements to tell the story of a 13 year old girl coming of age. With a strong Asian influence, the story is presented in fragments, and features such elements as characters suspended in air and floating cloth such as seen here. Presented in New York City in 2005.

of the characters in Shakespeare's play: thus Lear was played by a woman. One of Mabou Mines's productions, which was workshopped and restaged frequently in the late 1990s, is *Peter and Wendy,* which retells the Peter Pan story using puppets with other experimental techniques and was presented at the New Victory theatre in New York in 1997. In 2003, the company presented *Mabou Mines DollHouse,* a new reading of Ibsen's text, in which the males are played by actors between 3 feet 4 inches and 4 feet 5 inches tall and the women are both six feet tall. In 2005, the company presented *Red Beads.*

Breuer has also directed a number of works on his own, including *Gospel at Colonus* (1983), an adaptation of Sophocles' tragedy which uses African American music, and which he has revived many times.

Another significant director with Mabou Mines was Joanne Akalaitis (1937–). Akalaitis not only directed for Mabou Mines but also created many intriguing Shakespearean productions with the Public Theatre, including *Cymbeline* (1989) and *Henry IV, Parts I and II* (1991). She has directed works for many other theatres as well, including *Endgame* (1984) at the American Repertory Theatre in Boston, Genet's *The Screens* at the Guthrie Theatre (1989), *'Tis Pity She's a Whore* (1990) and *The Iphigenia Cycle* (1997) at the Goodman Theatre in Chicago, and *In the Summer House* (1993) by Jane Bowles at Lincoln Center in New York. Akalaitis served as artistic director of the New York Public Theatre and artist in residence at Chicago's Court Theatre. She has also taught at the Juilliard School and Bard College.

Other Alternative Groups and Playwrights

A number of newer off-Broadway companies became noted for introducing dramatists and plays. Two of the most significant were the Circle Repertory Company (founded in 1969), which introduced many of Lanford Wilson's plays of the 1970s and 1980s; and the Manhattan Theatre Club (founded in 1970), which presented new works by American and European playwrights.

Other off-off-Broadway companies in the 1970s and 1980s developed a reputation for staging alternative works. Among them was The Theatre for the New City, which was founded in 1971 in New York's East Village. This organization is dedicated to presenting new texts and companies as well as building a sense of community through performing in other boroughs of the city and staging an annual Halloween theatre event.

Among the groups established in the 1980s were the Cucaracha Theatre, under the artistic direction of Richard Caliban, who also directs at many other off-off-Broadway venues; and En Garde Arts, organized by Anne Hamburger, which had authors write plays for specific sites, such as an abandoned warehouse or a vacant automobile showroom. Hamburger shut down En Garde Arts in 1999 to become the artistic director of San Diego's regional theatre, La Jolla Playhouse. She stayed there for only one season, leaving to become executive vice president of Creative Entertainment for Disney's theme parks and resorts.

Maria Irene Fornes wrote her short play *Hunger* (1988) for En Garde Arts, as part of an evening of works entitled *Three Pieces for a Warehouse.* One of the more successful productions by En Garde Arts was *Crowbar* (1990) by Mac Wellman (1945–), the author of more than thirty avant-garde plays. It is set in a run-down theatre where ghosts of the theatrical past confront socioeconomic realities of the present; Richard Caliban, the director, used an actual theatre scheduled for demolition on 42nd Street as the environmental setting. Among Wellman's other plays are *Bad Penny* (1989), *Terminal Hip* (1990), *Sincerity Forever* (1990), *Hyacinth Macaw* (1994), and *Swoop* (1994).

There have been many other playwrights whose works have been introduced by off- and off-off-Broadway theatres as well as theatres outside New York. Romulus Linney (1930–) is a highly poetic dramatist whose works, which include *The Sorrows of Frederick* (1967), *Holy Ghosts* (1976), *Tennessee* (1976), *Three Poets* (1989), and *2: Göring at Nuremberg* (1992), have most often been staged outside New York. In 1991, an off-Broadway company in New York, Signature Theatre, which is dedicated to presenting a season of works by a single playwright in residence, chose Linney as the playwright for its initial season. In the years since then, Signature has focused on the works of Edward Albee (premiering *Three Tall Women*), Adrienne Kennedy, Sam Shepard, Arthur Miller, Lanford Wilson, and other leading American dramatists.

Another playwright featured by Signature Theatre is Horton Foote (1916–), whose works were staged in the 1994–1995 season. Foote began writing plays in the 1940s but did not achieve significant recognition until after 1975. Foote's best-known dramas are *Texas Town* (1942), *The Trip to Bountiful* (1953), *Dividing the Estate* (1989), *Talking Pictures* (1990), and the *The Young Man from Atlanta,* which won a Pulitzer Prize in 1995. Foote is also an accomplished screenwriter whose films include *To Kill a Mockingbird* (1962), *The Chase* (1966), *Tender Mercies* (1983), and *The Trip to Bountiful* (1985). Foote's works, frequently produced in regional and off-Broadway theatres, focus on southern life in a poetically realistic fashion, reminiscent of Tennessee Williams.

Wallace Shawn (1943–) is an actor and playwright whose works, such as *Our Late Night* (1975), *Aunt Dan and Lemon* (1985), and *The Fever* (1991), focus on sex, violence, and cruelty. Paula Vogel, mentioned earlier, is known for dramas that focus on dysfunctional families, domestic violence, and gender issues. Among her most frequently produced works are *Desdemona: A Play about a Handkerchief* (1979), *The Baltimore Waltz* (1982), and her award-winning *How I Learned to Drive* (1997).

A current playwright whose work has been staged by leading off-Broadway theatres is Richard Greenberg (1958–). His best-known plays include *Eastern Standard* (1988), *Three Days of Rain* (1998), *Take Me Out* (2002), and *A Naked Girl on the Appian Way* (2004).

Other off-Broadway companies that introduced significant playwrights are the Manhattan Theatre Club, Atlantic Theatre Company, New Group, and Second Stage.

Alternative American Directors

A number of American directors continue to experiment with alternative styles of production. Many base their work on the theories of avant-garde artists of the early twentieth century, such as Meyerhold, Brecht, and Artaud. Others create a highly individual and personal aesthetic, in work that is often autobiographical.

RICHARD FOREMAN AND ROBERT WILSON

Two experimental directors in the United States whose works were initially seen off-off-Broadway are Richard Foreman (1937–) and Robert Wilson (1944–). Their work is often unified by a theme or point of view which they determine, and the material is often organized as units analogous to the frames of television or film. Often, stunning theatrical images are a key to, and contain the essence of, the ideas that interest them.

Richard Foreman's work is autobiographical and self-reflexive—that is, it always makes the audience aware of watching a theatrical work which is commenting on itself. Foreman has staged most of his productions with the Ontological-Hysteric Theatre, which he founded in 1968. As the name of his company suggests, his theatrical pieces focus on inability to communicate through language. His works use a number of repeated theatrical devices, including voice-overs to comment on the stage action, exaggerated physical and vocal techniques, and visual elements such as clotheslines strung across a setting. Foreman has directed and designed more than thirty of his own plays. Among Foreman's works are *Film Is Evil, Radio Is Good* (1987); *Lava* (1990); *Eddie Goes to Poetry City* (1991); *My Head Was a Sledgehammer* (1994); *I've Got the Shakes* (1995); *Pearls for Pigs* (1997); *Paradise Hotel* (1999); *Bad Boy Nietzsche* (2000); *Now That Communism Is Dead, My Life Feels Empty* (2001); *Maria del Bosco* (2002); *Panic* (2003); and *The Gods Are Pounding My Head* (2005).

(Sara Krulwich/The New York Times)

AVANT-GARDE THEATRE IN AMERICA

Three alternative theatres that came to prominence in the 1970s and 1980s and remain active today are the Ontological Hysteric Theatre, the Wooster Group, and Mabou Mines. All three take a daring, experimental approach both to the classics and to contemporary theatre pieces. They often deconstruct a text from the past, or put together a collage or montage of bits and pieces of theatre, film, and movement to create an original piece. Shown here is Richard Foreman, originator and artistic director of the Ontological Hysteric Theatre, on the set of *Zomboid!*

In 1988, the Ontological-Hysteric and the Wooster Group coproduced his *Symphony of Rats*. In 1992 the company moved into a new home in Saint Mark's Church in New York City, where Foreman created a new piece each year. In 2004, Foreman announced a new focus on digital video and film in his presentations.

Robert Wilson often creates huge, extremely long epic productions which revolve around intensely theatrical images and are frequently accompanied by music in an operatic style. Among his best-known works are *Deafman Glance* (1970), *The Life and Times of Joseph Stalin* (1972), *A Letter to Queen Victoria* (1974), *The $ Value of Man* (1975), *Einstein on the Beach* (1976), *Death Destruction & Detroit* (1979), *The Man in the Raincoat* (1981), *The Golden Windows* (1982), *CiVil warS* (1983–1984), and *Death Destruction & Detroit II* (1987). Theatrical images woven into *Death Destruction & Detroit II* underscored Wilson's thematic interests: these images included ancient Chinese warriors, a mythological monster, a fat dwarf, a woman who cuts her baby open and eats salad from its belly, terrorists, a black panther, and giant rats.

(Nicole Bengiveno/The New York Times)

THE DIRECTOR PREPARES
The avant-garde experimental director Robert Wilson is a designer as well as a director who works in both theatre and opera, around the world as well as in the United States. He has a theatre lab at the Watermill Center on Long Island. He is seen here working on a concept while he balances a Shaker chair (dating from 1836) on its back legs in the main building of the Watermill Center.

In the late 1980s and 1990s, Wilson also brought his technique of striking images to productions of existing texts. He staged Euripides' *Alcestis* (1986) in Europe; Ibsen's *When We Dead Awaken* (1991) for the American Repertory Theatre; and Büchner's *Danton's Death* (1993), starring the well-known television and theatre actor Richard Thomas, for the Alley Theatre in Houston.

Wilson's work has found more support, critically and financially, in Europe than in the United States. For example, *The Black Rider,* an extremely visual piece based on a German folktale, premiered in Germany in 1992 and ran there for over a year; it was presented at the Brooklyn Academy of Music in 1993. In 1995, Wilson staged a one-person *Hamlet* in which he starred. He liberally took Shakespeare's speeches for the protagonist and several characters and reworked them into his performance piece. One of his avant-garde operas, *Time Rocker* (1997), has music by the rock star Lou Reed.

Since the 1990s, Wilson has focused on opera productions. Two examples are *Parsifal,* which he staged in Hamburg (1991), Houston (1992), and Los Angeles (2005); and *Lohengrin,* which he directed for New York's Metropolitan Oprea House in 1998 and 2006. While Wilson also spends much of his time reviving his earlier works, in 2005 he staged *I La Galigo,* based on an epic Indonesian poem.

(© Craig Schwartz/Center Theatre Group; Ahmanson Theatre)

THE VISION OF ROBERT WILSON
The director Robert Wilson has followed his own path in approaching theatre. In both his epic works and his smaller-scale experimental productions, he has emphasized strong visual imagery rather than text. It is not surprising that he has also been active in directing opera. The piece shown here—*The Black Rider: The Casting of the Magic Bullets*—is an artistic collaboration of Wilson, the songwriter Tom Waits, and the text writer William S. Burroughs. With deep roots in beat-era literature; honky-tonk rhythm and blues; and expressionist theatre, film, and cabaret, the show retells the tale of Wilhelm, a clerk who sells his soul to the devil in exchange for magic bullets that will make him a champion hunter in the eyes of his future father-in-law. This scene features, left to right, Richard Strange (Kuno), Mary Margaret O'Hara (Käthchen), and Matt McGrath (Wilhelm).

DES MCANUFF, PETER SELLARS, AND ANNE BOGART

A number of major American directors have had an impact on American and international theatre; many of them have also had a transforming impact on the United States's established regional theatres. They include Des McAnuff (1952–), Peter Sellars (1958–), and Anne Bogart (1951–).

Des McAnuff, who was born in Princeton, Illinois, was one of the founders of Dodger Productions in 1978 and was a key director for this new organization. Dodger was housed first at the Brooklyn Academy of Music and then at Joe Papp's

Public Theatre. McAnuff directed the group's initial presentation *Gimme Shelter* and then went on to direct for many leading off-Broadway and regional theatres, including the Public and Canada's Stratford Shakespeare Festival. In 1983, McAnuff revived the regional La Jolla Playhouse in San Diego. As has been true for most of his career, his work at this theatre was highly eclectic, ranging from experimental new plays to musicals (such as *The Who's Tommy*) to revivals of classics. McAnuff served as artistic director until 1994. He returned in 2001. The La Jolla has won over 200 theatre awards during McAnuff's tenure. He directed the Tony Award–winning Best Musical, *Jersey Boys* (2005), which premiered a year earlier at La Jolla. McAnuff also directed Billy Crystal in his one-person show, *700 Sundays* (2004).

Peter Sellars was born in Pittsburgh, Pennsylvania, and attended Harvard University. By the time Sellars was 27, he had directed over 100 productions, beginning with *The Inspector General* for the 1980–1981 season of the American Repertory Theatre in Boston. Sellars served unsuccessfully as artistic director of the Boston Shakespeare Company and the American National Theatre at the Kennedy Center in Washington, D.C., in the mid-1980s. He has directed for many of the leading regional theatres, including the Guthrie and the Goodman. Sellars is most noted for his modern readings of classic texts; for example, setting a Mozart opera in the Trump Tower or Shakespeare's *The Merchant of Venice* in contemporary California. Sellars organized the Olympic Arts Festival events for the Los Angeles Olympics of 1984, focusing on that city's multicultural tradition. Since November 1990, when he was appointed the Los Angeles Philharmonic's creative consultant, Sellars has achieved international recognition for his opera productions. They include Stravinsky's *Histoire du Soldat* (1992), the contemporary setting of Debussy's *Pelléas et Mélisande* (1995), and Hindemith's *Mathis der Maler* (1995). Sellars has also staged new operatic works. His productions of John Adams's *Nixon in China* (1987), *The Death of Klinghoffer* (1991), and *Doctor Atomic* (2005) were highly acclaimed. In 2002, he served as the artistic director of the Adelaide Festival of the Arts. Sellars has used classical texts to comment on contemporary political and social issues. His production of Aeschylus's *The Persians* (1993) was meant to draw parallels to the first U.S. war in Iraq. He staged Euripides' *Children of Herakles* (2002) to reflect on how wars cause heartbreaking human displacement.

Anne Bogart is known for her collaborative works, which use highly vocal and physical techniques. Bogart has also worked at a number of regional theatres and from 1989 to 1991 was the artistic director of the Trinity Repertory Company, a regional theatre which was founded in Providence, Rhode Island, in 1964 and which had been under the artistic direction of Adrian Hall from then until 1989. Bogart is the co-artistic director of the Saratoga International Theatre Institute, which she founded with the Japanese director Tadashi Suzuki (1939–) in an effort to revitalize contemporary American theatre through international collaboration. (Suzuki is himself noted for having started a performance company in Toga, Japan, that focuses on intense physical and vocal training, with influences from traditional Japanese theatres.) Bogart is also a cofounder of Via Theatre, which is dedicated to the support of young theatre artists.

Bogart frequently conceives and directs the theatrical pieces she stages. For example, for the 1997–1998 season at the Saratoga International Theatre Institute she conceived and directed *The Medium; Small Lives, Big Dreams; Going, Going, Gone; Culture of Desire;* and *Bob* (a one-person piece that focuses on the career of the avant-garde director Robert Wilson). In 1998, she staged two short musical works—*The Seven Deadly Sins* and *Carmina Burana*—at the New York City Opera. Other works directed by Bogart include *Cabin Pressure* (1999), *Room* (2000), *War of the Worlds* (2000), *La Dispute* (2003), *Nicholas and Alexandra* (2003), and *Death and the Ploughman* (2004).

Bogart is also well known for her theoretical approach to directing, known as *viewpoints.* Based on ideas from the avant-garde choreographer Merce Cunningham and the experimental director Jerzy Grotowski, viewpoints was originally incorporated into performance training at the Experimental Theatre Wing of New York University/Tisch School of the Arts. It combines elements of dance and stage movement with concepts of time and space. Initially viewpoints had six components on which performers, teachers, and directors concentrated: space, time, shape, movement, story, and emotion. Bogart has since subdivided the element of time into four separate segments, and space into five segments. Viewpoints, therefore, mixes many differing acting techniques and refuses to suggest that one element or approach is more significant than any other.

Established Theatre Companies

Since 1975, many theatres that had become historically important institutions found themselves confronting the same questions as alternative theatres. In the face of dwindling audiences; competition from commercial theatre, film, and television; and, in many cases, diminished government support, these established theatres began to ask what their mission was and what artistic direction they should take in order to survive into the twenty-first century. Some of these companies turned to alternative artists to regain the sense of experimentation that had originally been important to them. At the same time, however, these theatres had economic problems, which limited their ability to experiment and often threatened their very existence.

American Regional Theatres: Traditional and New

An important development in American theatre is that an equivalent of off-off-Broadway emerged in other major cities across the country—Washington, Chicago, Minneapolis, Los Angeles, San Francisco, Seattle. Small groups performed as alternatives to the larger regional theatres which had been established in the 1940s, 1950s, and 1960s.

In Chicago, for example, a number of smaller theatres, including Wisdom Bridge, Victory Gardens, Body Politic, and Steppenwolf, were founded in the 1970s. Steppenwolf has brought many productions to New York, including *The Grapes of Wrath,* which won the 1990 Tony Award; and, in 1993, *The Song of Jacob Zulu.* Steppenwolf was founded in 1976, and its original acting company included many performers who went on to become media stars, including John Malkovich (1953–   ), Gary Sinise (1955–   ), and Laurie Metcalf (1955–   ).

The 1970s saw many other major off-Loop Chicago theatres, including Wisdom Bridge, where Robert Falls, currently artistic director of the Goodman, began his directing career; the Organic; the Body Politic; St. Nicholas; and Victory Gardens.

(© T. Charles Erickson)

REGIONAL THEATRE: A VITAL RESOURCE
Regional theatres have been an important part of the American theatre scene for the past several decades. Generally these are not-for-profit theatres. Some are large and well established; others are middle-size; still others are small, often experimental groups. A work emerging from regional theatres was Mary Zimmerman's *The Secret in the Wings,* based on classic children's tales. It originated at the Lookingglass Theatre in Chicago and was also performed at the Berkeley Repertory Theatre, the Seattle Repertory Theatre, and the McCarter Theatre Center. Pictured here are three whimsically costumed suitors and the princess in a scene from the production at the McCarter Theatre in Princeton, New Jersey.

These theatres also introduced successful actors, including Joe Montegna (1947–), and many significant playwrights.

Lookingglass Theatre was founded in Chicago in 1988 and has received praise for its productions of literary adaptations that use intriguing staging devices. (The star of the television series *Friends,* David Schwimmer, is a founding member of the company.) In 2002, Lookingglass's artistic director, Mary Zimmerman, won the Tony Award for best direction, after her production of *Metamorphoses* (1998) moved to New York City.

The La Jolla Playhouse in San Diego, under the artistic direction of Des McAnuff, had many commercial successes, including its adaptation in 1993 of The Who's rock musical *Tommy,* which moved to Broadway, and *Jersey Boys* in 2004 and 2005. The Actors Theatre of Louisville became known for introducing new plays and playwrights; one of its most intriguing endeavors was a competition for 5-minute plays. A number of productions by the Actors Theatre were transferred to Broadway in the late 1970s. The American Repertory Theatre (ART), founded in 1979 by Robert Brustein (1927–) in conjunction with Harvard University, became noted for productions of classical plays by avant-garde directors. Brustein, before his work with ART, was the head of the Yale Drama School and founder of the Yale Repertory Theatre in 1966.

Transformations in Established American Theatre Companies

Some of the established theatres in the United States have undergone significant changes in the last three decades. Many of these theatres made changes by hiring new artistic directors, often replacing figures who had been instrumental in founding them. Two examples are the Guthrie Theatre in Minneapolis and the Public Theatre in New York.

The Guthrie Theatre hired the Romanian Liviu Ciulei (1923–) as artistic director in 1981. Ciulei brought an approach that included practices of many alternative directors; under his artistic direction and that of Garland Wright (1945–1998), who followed him from 1986 to 1994, the Guthrie became known for developing a strong permanent acting ensemble and for controversial stagings of historic plays. In 1993, for example, Wright staged a nineteenth-century Russian comedy, *Too Clever by Half* (1858), in a highly expressionistic style. After Garland Wright announced his resignation in 1994, a search for his successor began. In February 1995, the Guthrie's board of directors named Joe Dowling (1948–) the theatre's seventh artistic director. Dowling is an internationally known director who had a long association with the Abbey Theatre, Ireland's national theatre. Dowling also oversaw the construction of the Guthrie's new multistage facility, which opened in 2006.

The Public Theatre in New York experienced a tumultuous period after the death of its founder, Joseph Papp. Joanne Akalaitis, who succeeded Papp, brought in avant-garde companies and performance artists; however, the theatre's board said that she had been unable to generate audiences or to give enough productions, and in 1993 (as we noted in Chapter 14) replaced her with George C. Wolfe (1955–). Wolfe, an African American, was the author-director of *The Colored Museum* and *Spunk*—critically acclaimed productions that had been presented at the Public in the late 1980s—and of the hit Broadway musical *Jelly's Last Jam* (1992). At the time of his appointment, Wolfe was directing Tony Kushner's *Angels in America: Millennium Approaches,* for which he won the Tony award for best direction in 1993. Later in the same year, Wolfe directed the second half of this epic work, *Angels in America: Perestroika;* the two halves were then running in repertory on Broadway. He also directed a public television production of Anna Deavere Smith's *Fires in the Mirror.* Wolfe stepped down as the Public Theatre's artistic director in 2004. Oskar Eustis, who has served as artistic director of the regional Trinity Repertory Company in Providence, Rhode Island, assumed the post in 2005.

Performance Art

In the past quarter-century, a number of artists have experimented with forms that force audiences to confront the issues of what is "performance," what is "theatre," and what is the "subject" of theatrical representation. *Performance art* is a recent form that poses these questions and then some. In many ways performance art returns us to a question in the Introduction: what is theatre and from what forms did it originate?

Performance art has two important antecedents: first, earlier avant-garde experiments of the twentieth century—such as dada, surrealism, and happenings, which stressed the irrational and attacked traditional artistic values and forms—and second, the theories of Antonin Artaud and Jerzy Grotowski.

During the past 30 years, the term *performance art* has stood for various things. In its earliest manifestations, performance art was related on one hand to painting and on the other hand to dance. In the 1970s, one branch of performance art emphasized the body as an art object: some artists suffered self-inflicted pain, and some went through daily routines (such as preparing a meal) in a museum or in a theatre setting. Another branch focused on "site-specific" or environmental pieces in which the setting or context was crucial: performances were created for specific locations such as a subway station, a city park, or a waterfront pier.

In some of these earliest forms of performance art, story, character, and text were minimized or even eliminated. The emphasis was not on narrating a story or exploring recognizable characters but rather on the visual and ritualistic aspects of performing. This type of theatre was often the work of an individual artist who incorporated highly personal messages, and sometimes political and social messages, into the event. Often, the overall effect was like a continually transforming collage. As might be expected, there was, as mentioned earlier, an affinity between this kind of theatre—with its emphasis of the visual picture formed onstage—and painting. Often, stage movement in performance art was also closely related to dance.

In an article in *Artsweek* in 1990, Jacki Apple explained how the emphasis of performance art shifted in the 1970s and 1980s:

> In the 1970's performance art was primarily a time-based visual art form in which text was at the service of image; by the early 80's performance art had shifted to movement-based work, with the performance artist as choreographer. Interdisciplinary collaboration and "spectacle," influenced by TV and other popular modes ... set the tone for the new decade.[1]

The tradition of performance art as a form influenced by movement and dance is best seen in the work of a leading performance artist, Martha Clarke (1944–), who began her career in dance and has continued to stage dance performances. Clarke's presentations combine dance, popular entertainment, and stunning visual effects. Among her best-known productions are *Garden of Earthly Delights* (1984), *Vienna Lusthaus* (1986), *Miracolo d'Amore* (1988), and *Endangered Species* (1990). She directed two Mozart operas, *The Magic Flute* and *Cosi Fan Tutte,* in 1992 and 1993 at Glimmerglass Opera in upstate New York, incorporating many of the techniques of her visual style.

In recent years the connotation of the term *performance art* has changed yet again. It is now often associated with individual artists who present autobiographical material onstage. Several such artists—Karen Finley (1956–) is one of the most visible—became a cause of controversy when their work was seized on by ultraconservative religious groups and members of Congress as a reason to oppose funding the National Endowment for the Arts. These artists often espouse such causes as feminism and civil liberties for lesbians and homosexuals. Often, they use nudity or other controversial representations of gender, sexuality, or sexual orientation to confront audiences. Such was the case in *Alice's Rape* (1989), in which Robbie McCauley performed as her great-great grandmother, a nude slave on the auction block. Other performance artists whose works are highly politicized include Rachel Rosenthal (1926–), Laurie Anderson (1947–), Holly Hughes (1951–), and Tim Miller (1959–).

Off-off-Broadway has been the initial home of many performance artists. Two artists who began performing solo pieces in alternative spaces but have now received commercial productions are Spalding Gray (1941–2004) and Bill Irwin (1950–). Gray, a monologuist who discussed issues that ranged from his own personal concerns to politics, was reminiscent of ancient storytellers who created a theatrical environment single-handedly. Gray, who began as a member of the Performance Group and the Wooster Group, was best-known for *Swimming to Cambodia* (1984) and *Monster in the Box* (1991).

Bill Irwin's performances are mimelike, and he uses popular slapstick techniques to reflect on the contemporary human condition. Irwin appeared on Broad-

[1]Jacki Apple, "Art at the Barricades," *Artsweek,* vol. 21, May 3, 1990, p. 21.

way in 1989 in *Largely New York* and in 1993 in *Fool Moon* (revived several times in the 1990s). Irwin's work is often referred to as *new vaudeville.* New vaudevillians, such as Irwin, combine popular techniques such as mime, clowning, and stand-up comedy with serious subject matter, creating performances which are not easy to categorize. Irwin starred in a speaking role in 2005 in the broadway revival of *Who's Afraid of Virginia Woolf?*

A number of other solo performance artists have also become more commercially mainstream. They include Eric Bogosian (1953–) and Danny Hoch (1970–), each of whom creates performance pieces in which he plays multiple ethnic characters from his own New York background. Bogosian's best-known solo performances are *Drinking in America* (1987); *Sex, Drugs, and Rock and Roll* (1990); and *Pounding Nails in the Floor with My Forehead* (1994). Hoch received critical notice for *Some People* (1994) and *Jails, Hospitals, and Hip Hop* (1997). Another leading performance artist, John Leguizamo (1965–), became popular in the 1990s for his performance pieces, including *Spic O'Rama* and *Mambo Mouth,* which deal with Hispanic social and political life in the United States. His *Freaks* was presented to critical and audience acclaim on Broadway in 1998, and in 2001 he presented his show *Sexaholic.* In 2006, Sarah Jones (1973–) won a special Tony Award for her one-person, multicharacter performance *Bridge and Tunnel.* Jones's first performance work, *Surface Transit* (1998), was staged at the Nuyorican Café in New York City.

(Sara Krulwich/The New York Times)

PERFORMANCE ART: THE ONE-PERSON SHOW

A branch of contemporary performance art is the one-person show, in which a single artist presents material that is sometimes autobiographical, sometimes invented, sometimes a combination of the two. A good example is Sarah Jones, who in her one-woman show *Bridge & Tunnel* plays many roles representing various people coming to New York City. She portrays a wide range of characters, and reveals the problems and challenges faced by those people in today's urban world.

ANNA DEAVERE SMITH

(© Evan Agostini/Getty Images)

Anna Deavere Smith.

Anna Deavere Smith (1950–) is the most prominent African American performance artist in the United States. The eldest of five children, she was born to a middle-class family in Baltimore and was raised in that city. Smith remembers that her family were the first African Americans in the neighborhood where she lived. Smith attended Beaver College, a women's school in Pennsylvania, graduating in 1971 and then going on to complete an M.F.A. in acting at the American Conservatory Theatre in San Francisco.

After completing her graduate work, Smith pursued a career as a performer and acting instructor, teaching at Carnegie Mellon University, Yale University, the University of Southern California, and Stanford University. Smith spent 1996 in residence at New York University. Smith has also had an active stage and film career, appearing in stage productions of *Mother Courage* (1980) and *Tartuffe* (1983) as well as in the movies *Dave* (1993), *Philadelphia* (1993), *The American President* (1995), *The Human Stain* (2003), and *The Manchurian Candidate* (2004), and the television series *The West Wing* (2000–2006).

Smith is best-known for her series of one-woman works, *On the Road: A Search for American Character*. In this series, she portrays many real people she has met and interviewed; as a performer she crosses gender and racial lines to represent all the people with whom she has talked and to ask pointed questions about racial and gender identity. She usually tape-records her conversations with the many people she interviews and creates a mosaic of diverse characters, attitudes, and voices. Her performance style captures the person she is representing with both a great sense of actuality and an exaggerated demonstration of his or her idiosyncrasies. Smith has remarked that she is influenced by Brecht's theory of the performer as demonstrator.

Some of Smith's earliest works were developed at universities, where she was invited to stage workshops. Smith's two best-known works of this series focus on racial explosions. *Fires in the Mirror* was critically acclaimed when it was presented at Joseph Papp's Public Theatre in New York in 1992 and televised on PBS in 1993. In *Fires in the Mirror,* Smith portrayed individuals involved in and reflecting on the racial conflict between Hasidic Jews and the black population of Crown Heights, Brooklyn. *Twilight Los Angeles 1992* premiered at the Mark Taper Forum in Los Angeles in 1993, under the direction of Emily Mann (1952–). *Twilight* was then produced as a work in progress at the McCarter Theatre in Princeton, New Jersey, where Mann is artistic director. George C. Wolfe directed its New York production in 1994 at the Public Theatre and on Broadway. In *Twilight,* Smith presented people affected by the Los Angeles uprising that followed the acquittals in the first trial of the police officers charged with brutalizing Rodney King.

In 1997, Smith premiered a new work, *House Arrest: First Edition,* which was based on interviews recorded during the presidential campaign of 1996. In this work, however, Smith herself did not appear; instead, she directed fourteen performers in her performance style. It was not well received critically when it was staged in Washington, D.C. Her work *Piano* premiered in 2000.

Trying to describe the key influence on her performance work and style in an interview for *George Magazine* in 1995, Smith quoted a statement by Malcolm X: "It's not truth unless it's spoken." Smith received a MacArthur Fellowship in 1996 and is the recipient of many honorary doctorates.

DEBATES IN THEATRE HISTORY | Can Theatre Survive in the New Millennium?

A recurrent contemporary debate is whether live theatre can survive in the twenty-first century. The cost of producing theatre—even for alternative groups—declining audiences, and competition from film, television, computers, and other digital media lead some analysts to argue that theatre will not be as vital an art form in this new century as it has been in the past, and that it will probably become an art appealing only to a very specialized audience, much like opera today.

Others, however, argue that theatre is a unique art form, that it has been and still is able to incorporate other arts into its aesthetic makeup, and that these factors will keep it alive and healthy. These analysts point out that a significant number of alternative theatres continue to spring up in major cities throughout the world. They also argue that theatre will survive and be vigorous despite challenges from electronic and digital media, because in the future modern technology will play an important role in theatre. There will be continuing experiments with multimedia, fusing theatre with film, television, and dance.

With all these innovations, though, the people who believe that theatre will remain vital argue that in certain ways the theatre of the future will be an extension of the theatre of the past. Theatre will be enacted by women and men, in person, before an audience. The works these performers present will deal primarily with the hopes, fears, agonies, and joys of human beings. Even the most radical alternative artists deal with the same human issues that have always been part of theatre. A television critic in a popular national newspaper, reviewing a Public Broadcasting System special on the Broadway production of *Angels in America,* remarked, "What this demonstrates is how the theatre can seize a moment with immediacy, with a bolder impact than the more dominant, yet less visionary, entertainment media of films and TV."*

*Matt Roush, "*Angels* and the '80s: Tony Winner Soars in Its Social Context," *USA Today,* June 11, 1993, section D, p. 3.

A performance artist who continues to mix various media in his intensely visual works is Ping Chong, a Chinese American theatre director, choreographer, video artist, and installation artist. In 1998, Chong created *Kwaidan,* which incorporated puppets and shadow effects with live actors. In 2005, Chong cocreated, with the Shaanxi Folk Art Theatre of Xian, China, *Cathay: Three Tales of China,* a work for puppet theatre.

A number of spaces have become highly recognized for their presentation of performance artists. These include PS 122, a converted public school in the East Village of Manhattan; and the Kitchen, also located in downtown New York City. In addition, many museums throughout the United States are known for presenting series of performance artists, including the Walker Museum in Minneapolis and the Museum of Contemporary Art in Chicago. The fact that performance art is most often presented in converted, found spaces or museums again reflects the diversity of the form and its relationship to earlier avant-garde movements and the visual arts.

In our final chapter, we will turn our attention to contemporary international developments.

SUMMARY

American theatre from 1975 to the present reflects the great diversity of the nation. Diverse artists, dealing with issues of gender, race, and sexual orientation, have had an impact on contemporary theatre in the United States. Dramatists and directors influenced by postmodernist theory, along with contemporary performance artists, have led audiences to reevaluate the nature of theatre. Regional theatres and alternative theatre companies have brought the art to audiences throughout the country.

Theatre History

- Maria Irene Fornes (1930–), *Fefu and Her Friends*
- Stephen Sondheim (1930–)
- Mart Crowley (1935–), *The Boys in the Band*
- Richard Foreman (1937–)
- Luis Valdéz (1940–) *(below)*, *Zoot Suit*

- Charles Ludlam (1943–1987), *The Mystery of Irma Vep*
- Sam Shepard (1943–), *True West*
- August Wilson (1945–2005), *Joe Turner's Come and Gone*
- Mac Wellman (1945–), *Crowbar*
- Miguel Pinero (1947–1988), *Short Eyes*
- David Mamet (1947–), *American Buffalo*
- Pearl Cleage (1948–), *Chain*
- Andrew Lloyd Webber (1948–)
- Wendy Wasserstein (1950–2006), *The Heidi Chronicles*
- Anna Deavere Smith (1950–) *(below)*, *Fires in the Mirror*

- Paula Vogel (1951–), *How I Learned to Drive*
- Directors Robert Wilson (1944–); Anne Bogart (1951–); Julie Taymer (1952–); Des McAnuff (1952–); George C. Wolfe (1955–); Peter Sellars (1958–)

Cultural and Historical Developments

- Introduction of microcomputers (1970s)
- Jimmy Carter elected president (1976)
- George Lucas's *Star Wars* (1977)
- Camp David accord reached between Israel and Egypt (1979) *(below)*

- Judy Chicago's *Dinner Party* (1979)
- American hostages held by revolutionaries in Tehran (1979–1981)
- Rap music (1980s)
- Norman Mailer's *The Executioner's Song* (1980)
- Ronald Reagan elected president (1980)
- AIDS epidemic (1980s)
- "Star Wars" initiative launched (1983–1993)
- Alice Walker's *The Color Purple* (1983)
- Space shuttle *Challenger* disaster (1986)
- Iran-contra scandal; "black Monday" on Wall Street (1987)
- Toni Morrison's *Beloved;* George Bush elected president (1988)
- *Exxon Valdez* oil spill in Alaska; United States intervention in Panama (1989)
- Persian Gulf war (1990–1991)
- Los Angeles riots following acquittal of police in Rodney King case (1992)
- Bill Clinton elected president (1992); reelected (1996)

continued

PHOTO CREDITS: Luis Valdéz. (© Stephanie Maze/Corbis) / Anna Deavere Smith. (© Evan Agostini/Getty Images) / Camp David accords, 1979. (Bob Daugherty/AP Images)

MILESTONES CHAPTER 15 CONTEMPORARY THEATRE IN THE UNITED STATES: 1975 TO THE PRESENT

- Cheryl West (1956–), *Before It Hits Home*
- David Henry Hwang (1957–), *M. Butterfly*
- Tony Kushner (1957–), *Angels in America*
- Jonathan Larson (1960–1996), *Rent*
- Suzan-Lori Parks (1964–), *The America Play*
- John Leguizarno, *Sexaholic*
- East West Players (1965)
- The Performance Group (1968)
- Ontological-Hysteric Theatre (1968)
- Nuyorican Poets' Café (1970s)
- Mabou Mines (1970)
- Asian Exclusion Act (1973)
- Asian-American Theatre Workshop (1973)
- Pan Asian Repertory Theatre (1977)
- Split Britches (1980)
- Wooster Group (1980s)
- Denver Center Theatre Company's *Black Elk Speaks* (1993) *(below)*

- United States sends troops to Somalia (1993)
- North American free trade agreement (1994)
- Federal Building in Oklahoma City bombed; United States sends peacekeeping troops to Bosnia and Herzegovina; World Trade Organization created (1995)
- Frank Gehry's Guggenheim Museum Bilbao opens (1997) *(below)*

- George W. Bush becomes president in contested election (2000); reelected (2004)
- Vermont authorizes civil unions (2000)
- Terrorist attacks, September 11, 2001
- Military invasion in Afghanistan (2001)
- Space shuttle *Columbia* disaster (2002)
- U.S.-led coalition invades and occupies Iraq (2003)
- Christos and Jeanne-Claude's *The Gates,* Central Park, New York (2005)
- Hurricane Katrina devastates gulf coast region (2005) *(below)*

PHOTO CREDITS: *Black Elk Speaks.* (Terry Shapiro/Denver Theatre Center) / Guggenheim Bilbao. (© Eberhard Streichan/zefa/Corbis) / New Orleans flooded by hurricane Katrina, 2005. (David J. Phillip/AP Images)

CHAPTER 16

Global Theatres

Théâtre du Soleil

Among the more important international theatres of the past half century is Théâtre du Soleil, founded in 1964 by Ariane Mnouchkine. Based in Paris, France, the theatre presents classics that have been made contemporary, or revitalized in other ways. Also featured is strikingly original work. Shown here is a scene from *Le Dernier Caravanserail (Odyssées)*, presented in Paris in 2003. This particular production was developed from visits to refugee camps and detention centers in many parts of the world over a period of years by the thirty-six members of the troupe, and lasts six hours. The scenery is stored in cargo containers and wheeled about the stage, as shown here, to reinforce the continual flight of the refugees.

(© Martine Franck/Magnum)

As was noted in the introduction to Chapter 15, the tumultuous world events since 1975 have had a significant impact on theatre throughout the world. The political upheavals in Europe, Asia, Latin America, and the Middle East continue to affect international theatre artists. In this chapter, we will not be able to offer a comprehensive overview of all international theatre artists or movements; instead, we will highlight and summarize some of the key developments.

Globalization and Theatre

Thomas Friedman, in his acclaimed book *The World Is Flat,* analyzes how globalization has affected business and industry in contemporary society. One can no longer tell whether a product is made by a company of a specific country, since most major corporations are multinational. The automobile industry clearly reflects the trend toward industrial globalization, as does the personal computer industry. A car created today by a Japanese, Korean, or German manufacturer may be assembled in the United States. A PC may be assembled in the United States, but the 24-hour help desk may be located in India.

The same is true in today's theatre. Many diverse groups influence one another to create the contemporary theatrical landscape. Theatre artists cross national boundaries to stage their works with artists of other countries. Popular works tour the world and cross-pollinate other theatrical ventures. International theatre festivals bring artists of various nationalities to interact with those in the host community.

Casts and production companies are made up of individuals of various nationalities and ethnicities. A classic American musical staged in London with British performers—the recent revival of *Oklahoma!* first staged at London's Royal National Theatre in 1999—was remounted in New York City in 2002, by the original English director, Trevor Nunn, and producer, Cameron Macintosh, along with the American choreographer Susan Stroman, but with American actors.

An Israeli playwright, Joshua Sobol, collaborated with a Viennese director, Paulus Manker, beginning in 1995, and also directed a production of Shakespeare's *Merchant of Venice* at the Illinois Shakespeare Festival in the United States in 2002.

Experimental artists appropriate the styles and techniques of traditional theatres from around the world. Artists mix and match all sorts of styles, historical antecedents, materials, and techniques. An experimental theatre director from Minneapolis, Leslie Mohn, for example, applied traditional Chinese techniques from Peking opera in a unique adaptation of a late-nineteenth-century realistic drama by the Norwegian playwright Ibsen, *White Boned Demon.* The original production was presented in 1986 at the Red Eye Theatre. The director, three years later, restaged this work at an experimental, noncommercial theatre space in New York City and then again with college students at an Illinois university.

What these examples suggest is that we can no longer easily classify theatre productions and artists by specific national designations. Ease of travel, electronic communication, and the commerce of theatre have all led to a blurring of national theatres. Instead, like the global economy, theatre is a global activity. Still, in order to try to bring some structure to our discussion, we will organize this chapter along traditional national boundaries. However, we will frequently point to the global interplay and impact of the various theatre artists and companies.

European Theatres

British and Irish Playwrights

In English theatre, a significant number of new "angry" playwrights attack traditional political, social, and economic institutions while also creating works that reflect postmodernist sensibilities. Among the best-known of these authors are David Hare (1947–), Howard Brenton (1942–), and David Edgar (1948–). David Hare's work gained considerable visibility, particularly after a number of his works were transferred from London to

Broadway in the 1980s and 1990s. Hare's dramaturgy mixes political interests with a strong focus on human relationships. Among the plays that have brought him recognition are *Fanshen* (1975), a collaboration with the Joint Stock Company, *Teeth 'n' Smiles* (1975), *Plenty* (1978), *A Map of the World* (1983), *Pravda* (1985, cowritten with Howard Brenton), *The Secret Rapture* (1989), *Racing Demon* (1990), *Murmuring Judges* (1991), *Absence of War* (1993), *Skylight* (1995), *Amy's View* (1997), *The Judas Kiss* (1998), *Via Dolorosa* (1998), *The Blue Room* (1998), *The Permanent Way* (2003), and *Stuff Happens* (2004), an attack on the United States' invasion of Iraq. Hare has also directed. More contemporary sociopolitically-oriented British playwrights include Patrick Marber (1964–), author of *Dealer's Choice* (1995) and *Closer* (1997); and Jez Butterworth (1969–), author of *Mojo* (1995).

There is also a new generation of young Irish playwrights who dramatize social, political, and historical issues. One of the best-known is Martin McDonagh (1970–), whose works include *The Beauty Queen of Leenane* (1996), *The Cripple of Inishmaan* (1996); *A Skull in Connemara* (1997), *The Lonesome West* (1997), *The Lieutenant of Inishmore,* and *The Pillowman* (2003). Conor McPherson (1971–) has gained international attention for *St. Nicholas* (1996), *The Weir* (1997), *Dublin Carol* (2000), *Shining City* (2004), and *The Seafarer* (2006).

A number of female English playwrights have achieved considerable recognition, including Timberlake Wertenbaker (1946–) and Pamela Gems (1925–). Sarah Kane (1971–1999) received considerable attention after she committed suicide. Her works include *Blasted* (1995), *Cleansed* (1998), and *Crave* (1998). A British playwright who has achieved immense worldwide recognition for politically charged feminist plays is Caryl Churchill.

CARYL CHURCHILL

Caryl Churchill (1938–) was born in London. From 1948 through 1955, her family lived in Montreal, Canada; in 1957, she returned to England to study at Oxford University, where she completed her B.A. in English language and literature in 1960. While at Oxford, she wrote her first play, *Downstairs,* which was produced there and at the National Union of Students/Sunday Times Student Drama Festival. During the 1960s, she married, had three sons, and spent a long apprenticeship writing radio plays.

(© Martha Swope)

Caryl Churchill.

As the women's movement began to gather momentum in the 1970s, Churchill had her first major success with *Owners* (1973). Since then she has become famous for a number of plays including *Cloud Nine* (1979), *Top Girls* (1982), *Fen* (1983), *Serious Money* (1985), *Mad Forest* (1990), *The Skriker* (1996), *Blue Heart* (1998), *Far Away* (2000), and *A Number* (2002). Many of her early plays were created with the Joint Stock Company or the English Stage Company; frequently, she developed these dramas by working closely with the actors, who suggested changes, additions, and deletions.

Churchill's work is characterized by a unique fluidity of structure. She often mixes chronological and anachronistic events. She also double-casts roles in many of her plays, and she reverses gender roles, forcing audiences to explore generally accepted sexual stereotypes. (In *Cloud Nine,* for example, she has men play some of the female roles and women play some of the male roles.) She is brilliant at mixing

(© Geraint Lewis)

CARYL CHURCHILL'S TOP GIRLS
One of the most innovative and purposeful voices in the contemporary English-speaking theatre is the British playwright Caryl Churchill. In play after play she has challenged preconceptions about both society and dramatic form. One of her most striking dramas is her inventive piece about role playing, *Top Girls*. The characters seen here are in costumes from different time periods because part of the plot has to do with women from various eras meeting at a dinner table.

theatricality with reality to create a unique postmodernist blend in plays that are extremely political.

Churchill has received numerous awards, including the Susan Smith Blackburn Prize, which she won twice.

German and Italian Dramatists

Three Germans who have received significant attention in the United States for plays that question the traditional values of western society are Peter Handke (1942–), Franz Xaver Kroetz (1946–), and Heiner Müller (1929–1995). Handke's plays—including *Offending the Audience* (1966), *Self-Accusation* (1966), *Kaspar* (1968), *Ride across Lake Constance* (1970), *They Are Dying Out* (1973), and *Slow Homecoming* (1982)—focus on the shortcomings of language as a tool for communication and are surreal and symbolic in style.

Kroetz's plays, with their stichomythic language and grotesque relationships, are reminiscent of Mamet and Shepard. Kroetz's best-known works include *Farm Yard* (1972) and *Mensch Meier* (1978). Two of his most poignant works are *Request Concert* (1971), a short play with only one character and no dialogue which carefully details the last night of a lonely woman's life before her suicide; and *Extended Forecast* (1993), which deals with a woman preparing to enter an old-age home. *Extended Forecast* had its New York premiere in 1993 at Café La Mama.

Müller, who began his career in communist East Germany in the 1950s, became known for the short plays he wrote in the late 1970s and 1980s—explosions of images ridiculing traditional values and institutions. His most famous play is *Hamletmachine* (1977), an Artaud-like scenario. Müller directed many of his own works.

The Italian playwright Dario Fo (1926–) is known for his satirical political comedies, which attack capitalist institutions and are reminiscent of Aristophanes. Among his best-known works are *The Accidental Death of an Anarchist* (1970); *We Won't Pay, We Won't Pay* (1974); and with the actress Franca Rame (1929–), his wife, *Female Parts* (1981). Fo, with Rame, has run his own theatre companies, directing and acting in his plays. Fo won the Nobel Prize for literature in 1997.

European Directors

In Europe, as in the United States, many directors have radically reinterpreted classical plays to make these texts speak more directly to contemporary audiences. These directors are also postmodernist in their outlook: they believe that they can find unique "readings" of plays, and they use techniques of both "high" and "low" art. Often, their works are condemned by critics and audiences who believe that these directors are perverting classical texts.

The German director Peter Zadek (1926–) staged controversial readings of Shakespeare in the 1970s and 1980s. Zadek's productions, which he developed out of improvisations with his company, included a vaudevillean *King Lear* and an *Othello* with the title character performed in blackface. Zadek was artistic director of the theatre in Bochum from 1972 to 1985 and then of the Deutsches Schauspielhaus in Hamburg from 1985 to 1990. From 1993 to 1995, he was a codirector of the Berliner Ensemble. Since that time, he has worked as a director throughout Germany and Europe. In 1999, Zadek restaged, at Berlin's Schaubühne, his acclaimed 1977 production of *Hamlet.* His most recent productions include Ibsen's *Rosmersholm* (2000), Marlowe's *The Jew of Malta* (2001), Tennessee Williams's *Night of the Iguana* (2002), Ibsen's *Peer Gynt* (2004) at the Berliner Ensemble and Edinburgh Festival, Strindberg's *Dance of Death, I and II* (2005), and Delaney's *A Taste of Honey* (2006).

Peter Stein (1937–) became known in the 1970s for postmodernist productions in which he reworked classical texts to heighten ideological statements he felt were inherent in them and to express his own political viewpoints. He often used techniques of Brecht, Artaud, and naturalism. Among Stein's early productions were Edward Bond's *Saved* (1967), Weiss's *Vietnam Discourse* (1968), Brecht's *The Mother* (1970), Ibsen's *Peer Gynt* (1971), and Aeschylus's *Oresteia* (1980). From 1970 to 1985, Stein was the artistic director of Berlin's Schaubühne Theatre; the German government recognized his stature as a theatrical innovator by building the new Schaubühne am Lehniner Platz in Berlin in 1981. In the mid-1980s Stein departed from his earlier experimentation and began to stage more traditional productions, including *The Three Sisters* (1984), *Phaedra* (1987), and *The Cherry Orchard* (1989). In 1987, he directed an expressionistic production of *The Hairy Ape* at London's National Theatre. He still directs at the Schaubühne and often stages operas at European theatres.

After giving up his position as artistic director of the Schaubühne, Stein has directed throughout Europe. From 1992 to 1997, he was in charge of the theatre presentations at the Salzburg Festival. Among his most recent productions are a Russian *Oresteia,* with actors from the Moscow Art Theatre (1994); a 20-hour production of both parts of Goethe's *Faust* (2000); Chekhov's *The Seagull* (2003) with Fiona Shaw; Sophocles' *Medea* at the 2005 Epidaurus Festival in Greece; and *Blackbird* in 2005 at the Edinburgh Festival in Scotland and then at London's National Theatre, Stein has also directed a number of innovative opera productions, including *Otello* (1986), *Falstaff* (1988), and *Pelléas et Mélisande* (1992).

Andrei Serban (1943–) was born in Romania and emigrated to the United States in 1969; Ellen Stewart introduced him to American audiences at Café La Mama in 1970. Among his best-known productions in the United States are a farcical *Cherry Orchard* (1977) at Lincoln Center, a postmodernist *Marriage of Figaro* (1982) at the Guthrie Theatre, *Uncle Vanya* (1983) at La Mama with Joseph Chaikin in the cast, and *The King Stag* (1984) at the American Repertory Theatre (ART) in Boston. In 2003 he staged Shakespeare's *Pericles* at the ART. Serban has also directed a number of highly theatrical operas. Like Wilson and Foreman, he uses striking visuals to help convey his viewpoint on a text he is staging. For Serban, image and mood are frequently more important than the spoken word. For example, his postmodern production of *The Marriage of Figaro* featured characters dressed in trench coats and sunglasses who were pushed around a shiny, mirror-like stage in a shopping cart; another character rode a skateboard wherever he went; and Figaro himself flew over the heads of the audience on a huge swing while making his most famous speech.

Yuri Lyubimov (1917–) took over the artistic direction of the Taganka Theatre in the Soviet Union in 1964. The Taganka was considered a home of experimentation, and its productions were reminiscent of Meyerhold's antirealistic work. Because of its experiments with form, however, the theatre and Lyubimov were constantly under attack by the Soviet government. Eventually, the government took away Lyubimov's control of the Taganka, and he was not allowed to return from a western tour in 1984. Lyubimov then directed in Europe, the United States, and Israel, receiving a great deal of attention for his experiments with theatrical style. His best-known works are his adaptations of Dostoyevsky's novels *Crime and Punishment* and *The Possessed.* The Arena del Sol, a nineteenth-century outdoor stone theatre in Bologna, Italy, hosted two seasons, 1984–1985 and 1985–1986, under Lyubimov's artistic direction. In 1989, after the democratization of what was then still the Soviet Union, Lyubimov was reinstalled as artistic director of the Taganka. In the early 1990s, he directed Ibsen's *The Wild Duck* at the Arena Theatre in Washington, D.C. He now focuses almost exclusively on his work at the Taganka.

Two other well-known European directors are Luca Ronconi (1933–) and Ingmar Bergman (1918–). Ronconi began as an actor but since 1963 has made his reputation as a director. Since the 1980s, he has been best-known for his direction of opera. Among his opera productions are The *Turn of the Screw* (1995), *Tosca* (1997), *Lohengrin* (1999), and *Ariadne auf Naxos* (2000). In 1997, he staged *Toward Peer Gynt,* an abridged version of Ibsen's play.

Ingmar Bergman, outside Sweden, is probably best-known as a film director and screenwriter. (His film scripts are often compared to the plays of Ibsen and Strindberg.) However, since the 1940s he has staged over 100 productions, most of them at major theatres in Sweden. He has also directed in other European countries, including Germany and England, and has toured many of his productions. Among the best-known since the 1970s are *Hedda Gabler,* staged at London's National

Theatre in 1970; *A Dream Play* (1970); *Nora and Julie* (1981); *A Doll's House* (1989); *Peer Gynt* (1991); *The Winter's Tale* (1994); *Ghost Sonata* (2000); *Maria Stuart* (2000); and *Ghosts* (2002).

Two other widely admired Europeans are the Polish director Tadeusz Kantor, who became noted in the United States in the 1980s for his avant-garde productions; and Ariane Mnouchkine, a French director of Russian extraction.

TADEUSZ KANTOR

Tadeusz Kantor (1915–1990) was a Polish director who also worked as a scene designer and visual artist. He graduated from the Kraków Academy in 1939, and during the Nazi occupation he founded the underground Independent Theatre. After the war, he became known as an avant-garde stage designer, creating designs for such productions as *Saint Joan* (1956) and *Measure for Measure* (1956).

(AP Images)

Tadeusz Kantor during a performance of *Let the Artists Die*, Warsaw, 1986.

Kantor became disenchanted with the growing institutionalization of the avant-garde and formed his own theatre, Cricot 2, in 1955 with a group of visual artists. In the 1960s he became widely known for staging happenings, and he traveled widely with his theatre. He also became particularly interested in the work of the absurdists and the Polish surrealist Stanislaw Ignacy Witkiewicz. Kantor's best-known productions of this period included *The Cuttlefish* (1956) and *The Water Hen* (1968).

In the 1970s, Kantor began creating his own theatre pieces; the most famous of these was *Dead Class* (1970), in which a teacher (played by Kantor himself) presided over a séance-like world where seemingly dead characters confronted their younger selves, represented by mannequins. The use of mannequins with live actors was a technique he had begun to experiment with as early as the 1950s.

During the next two decades, Kantor toured the world with his company and his productions, among them *Wielpole, Wielpole* (1980); *Where Are the Snows of Yesteryear* (1982); *Let the Artists Die* (1985); *I Shall Never Return* (1988); and *Today Is My Birthday* (1990). These later works have been described as very personal reflections in which Kantor reveals his deepest, inmost thoughts through stunning theatrical imagery. In some of these works, as in *Dead Class*, he represented himself onstage. Kantor's work became well known in the United States through presentations at Ellen Stewart's Café La Mama in the 1980s.

(© Martine Franck/Magnum Photos)

THE DIRECTOR AT WORK
Here we see Ariane Mnouchkine directing the actors Juliana Carneiro da Cunha (Dorina) and Brontis Jodorowsky (Orgon) in *Tartuffe,* at the Théatre du Soleil, Paris, 1995.

ARIANE MNOUCHKINE

Since her founding of the avant-garde Théâtre du Soleil in Paris in 1964, Ariane Mnouchkine (1940–) has become one of the most widely admired directors in Europe. Although strongly influenced by Copeau, Brecht, Artaud, and Meyerhold, she is also known for her effective use of nonwestern dramatic techniques, especially those of Japan and India.

Ariane Mnouchkine was born in Boulogne-sur-Seine, near Paris. She was the eldest daughter of Alexandre Mnouchkine, a well-known film producer who came originally from Russia. As a child, Mnouchkine was fascinated by film work and often visited her father on his sets. While studying psychology at Oxford University, she became involved with the Oxford University Drama Society. On returning to Paris in 1959, she joined a group of like-minded students at the Sorbonne to form the Association Théâtrale des Étudiantes de Paris and was elected its first president. In the early 1960s, Mnouchkine scraped together enough money to realize a lifelong dream of traveling to the far east. In Japan, Cambodia, and other parts of Asia, she found a beauty of form and a sense of ritual that she considered indispensable to theatre.

When she returned to Paris in 1963, Mnouchkine and several of her friends established a "theatrical community" which was to become the Théâtre du Soleil.

The company has produced everything from loose collections of improvised materials to acclaimed versions of Shakespeare's works to a powerful 10-hour staging of the *Oresteia,* the cycle of Greek tragedies about the house of Atreus.

Among the best-known collectively created productions of the Théâtre du Soleil are *The Clowns* (1969); *1789* (1970), which environmentally dramatized the historical background of the French Revolution; *The Age of Gold* (1975); and *Les Atrides* (1991), the adaptation of the *Oresteia.* Among its text-based productions were a stage adaptation of the novel *Mephisto* (1979); Shakespeare's *Richard II* (1981), *Twelfth Night* (1982), and *Henry IV, Part I* (1984); and two plays by a leading French feminist theorist, Hélène Cixous.

Mnouchkine gained significant attention in the United States through presentations by the Théâtre du Soleil at the Olympics Art Festival in Los Angeles in 1984 and at the Brooklyn Academy of Music in 1992. Her presentation of *Les Atrides* at the Brooklyn Academy of Music won a special Obie award in 1993. Among her other productions are *The Treacherous Town or the Awakening of the Furies* (1994); *And Suddenly Sleepless Nights,* (1997), which deals with the plight of illegal immigrants; and the two-part, 6-hour *The Last Caravan Stop* (*Odysées,* 2003), which deals with the horrors of refugees and which Mnouchkine restaged in tents in a New York City park in 2005.

Transformations in Government-Subsidized European Theatres

Some of the national theatres of Europe have also incorporated avant-garde techniques and artists, though others have been forced to become more commercial to avert financial crises. The Comédie Française, the Royal Shakespeare Company, and the Royal National Theatre are representative of the kinds of changes that occurred in many government-subsidized theatres throughout Europe.

Antoine Vitez (1930–1990) ran the Comédie Française from 1988 until his death. Under his brief direction, this 300-year-old theatre began to present radical reinterpretations of many historically important French writers. Vitez was greatly influenced by Grotowski's "poor theatre," by Marxism, by Brecht's theories, by his own background in mime, and by unique postmodernist readings of texts. Vitez's early work was in Marseille in the 1960s; later, in the 1970s, he brought productions to the meeting halls and schools of working-class Paris. In 1968, he was appointed director and leading teacher of the Conservatoire, the renowned acting school affiliated with the Comédie Française. From 1972 to 1974, he was a co-artistic director of the Théâtre National de Chaillot, and he took over complete artistic direction of this theatre in 1981. Many French critics believe that his early death robbed the Comédie Française, France's oldest government-supported theatre, of an artistic director who could have transformed it. Since then, the Comédie Française has had three artistic directors: Jacques Lassalle (1936–), who served from 1990 to 1993; Jean Pierre Miquel, who served for the next eight years (1937–2003); and Marcel Bozonnet (1944–), who took over in 2001.

In England, the Royal Shakespeare Company (RSC) and the Royal National Theatre suffered from increased costs—incurred partly by new buildings—and from reduced government support. In the 1980s, under the artistic direction of Trevor Nunn (1940–) and Terry Hands (1941–), the Royal Shakespeare Company experienced financial and artistic crises, especially after it moved into its new facility. The RSC's Barbican Center was built in 1982 and has two theatres: the Barbican, with a seating capacity of 1,162; and a small theatre called The Pit, with a seating capacity of 185. In addition, the RSC continued to stage productions in Stratford, England, the birthplace of William Shakespeare. (In 2003 the RSC gave up the Barbican as its base in London.) Nunn was especially criticized for staging productions that were as commercial as those of the West End—London's equivalent of Broadway. These attacks were fiercest following the company's highly successful musical *Les Misérables.* Among the productions that were best received, artistically and commercially, during this period was an epic adaptation of Charles Dickens's novel *Nicholas Nickelby* (1980).

Adrian Noble (1950–) is a director who revitalized the Royal Shakespeare Company in the 1980s with his unique conceptualizations of classic texts. Among his best-known productions for this company were *King Lear* (1982), done in a Beckett-like style; *Antony and Cleopatra* (1982); *The Comedy of Errors* (1983); *Henry* V (1984); *The Winter's Tale* (1984); *As You Like It* (1985); and *Mephisto* (1986). Noble was made an associate director of the RSC in 1982. In 1988, he was made artistic director of the Stratford season. After leaving the Royal Shakespeare Company in 1989, Noble returned to become its artistic director in 1991. He then directed a number of significant productions, including *A Midsummer Night's Dream* (1994), *Travesties* (1994), *The Cherry Orchard* (1995), *Cymbeline* (1996), and *Little Eyolf* (1997).

In 2003, Michael Boyd succeeded Noble as artistic director of the RSC. Boyd's productions of *Henry VI, Parts I, II, and III* and *Richard III* (2000–2001), which formed part of the RSC's *England: The Histories* cycle, were acclaimed. Between 2006 and 2007, the Royal Shakespeare Company produced the complete works of Shakespeare, including his poetry. The RSC staged some of the works and brought in international artists. A series of productions that were contemporary responses to Shakespeare, such as *The Baghdad Richard,* by the Kuwaiti writer-director Sulayman Al-Bassam, were also commissioned.

In 1992, Noble had directed *Hamlet* for the RSC, with Kenneth Branagh (1960–) in the title role. Branagh was a leading performer who gained significant visibility performing with the RSC in the mid-1980s. He opened the Royal Shakespeare Company's 1984 season at Stratford-upon-Avon playing the title role in *Henry V* (directed by Adrian Noble), followed by Laertes in *Hamlet,* and the King of Navarre in *Love's Labours Lost.* He also played Mike in *Golden Girls* by Louise Page at the Other Place. In 1985 Branagh played at the Barbican Theatre in London in *Henry V, Love's Labours Lost,* and *Hamlet.* Branagh left the Royal Shakespeare Company to form the Renaissance Theatre Company, which not only specialized in the classics but also encouraged its actors to direct. Branagh also made a significant international reputation for himself by directing films and using star movie performers to bring Shakespeare to mass audiences. His best-known film work includes *Henry V* (1989), *Dead Again* (1991), *Peter's Friends* (1993), *Much Ado about Nothing* (1994), *Mary Shelley's Frankenstein* (1994), and *Hamlet* (1996). He performed Iago opposite Laurence Fishburne in the film version of *Othello* (1996).

The Royal National Theatre ran into controversy under the artistic direction of Peter Hall, who became its artistic director in 1973, and his successor Richard Eyre (1943–), who took over in 1988. Much of this controversy developed because a huge amount of governmental support was required to operate its new facility. The Royal National Theatre, however, maintained its reputation for employing England's most important actors and for reviving historically significant but forgotten dramas. During the London season of 1992–1993, one of the most successful productions—artistically and commercially—was the National's revival of the Rodgers and Hammerstein musical *Carousel,* directed by Nicholas Hytner (1956–). This was a revival of a neglected work, with a new interpretation that underscored an inherent theme—the dark side of the class struggle. It was then staged in New York City at Lincoln Center. The Royal National also staged Tony Kushner's *Angels in America,* before it received its New York production. There have been continued changes in recent years at the Royal National. Richard Eyre served as artistic director until 1997, when he was succeeded by Trevor Nunn. Hytner was announced as the new director of the National effective April 2003.

Both the Royal Shakespeare Company and the Royal National Theatre continue to support new innovative theatre artists. One example is Deborah Warner (1959–), an English director who has used a more experimental style of production, along with reinterpretations of texts that focus on feminist, gender, and other sociopolitical issues. Warner began her career with an alternative London troupe, the Kick Theatre Company, which she founded in 1980, when she was 21. She has since directed unique interpretations of the classics for the Royal Shakespeare Company and the Royal National in London. She is best-known for the many productions she has directed starring the actress Fiona Shaw (1959–), including Shakespeare's *Richard II,* with Shaw in the title role; Beckett's *Footfalls,* in which Beckett's precise stage directions were ignored and lines were transposed, leading to a lawsuit by the Beckett estate; and a site-specific staging of T. S. Eliot's *The Waste Land,* which used a variety of spaces, including a disco in Brussels, a fort in Dublin, an old movie theatre in Montreal, a medical lecture hall in Paris, and a dilapidated theatre in New York's Times Square area. In the summer of 2000 and again in the winter of 2001, Warner directed Shaw in an adaptation of *Medea.* Originally an Abbey Theatre production, *Medea* was staged in New York City in 2002, first at the Brooklyn Academy of Music and then on Broadway. In 2002, Warner also directed the adaptation of the novel *The Powerbook* for the National Theatre. The production was created by and starred Shaw.

Simon McBurney, a founding member of England's Theatre de Complicite, also directed at the Royal National Theatre, staging Brecht's *Caucasian Chalk Circle* in 1997. The invitation for McBurney to direct at the National is a reflection of respect for the alternative theatre produced by Theatre de Complicite, which was founded in 1983 and adapts literature using a very theatrical style of performance and staging. Among the company's best-known productions are *The Street of Crocodiles* (1992–1994), *The Three Lives of Lucy Cabrol* (1994–1996), a production of Ionesco's *The Chairs* (1997), and *The Noise of Time* (2000). The company has toured more than 25 productions to over 180 cities in 41 countries. *Cabrol* and *The Chairs* were both pre-

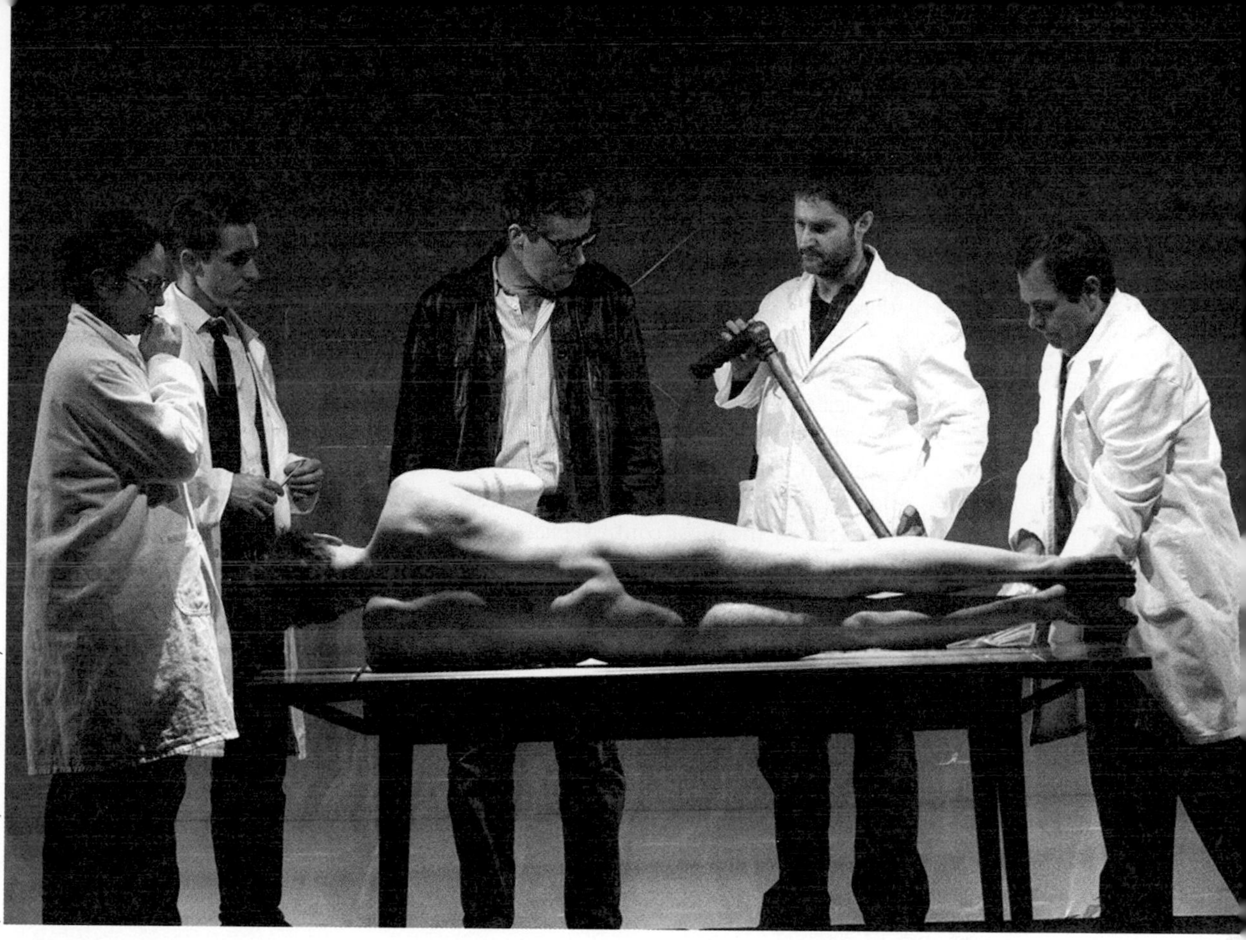

(Sara Krulwich/The New York Times)

THEATRE DE COMPLICITE
An English theatre company that offers highly original work is Theatre de Complicite, under the leadership of Simon McBurney. A typical piece, and a good example of contemporary avant-garde theatre, is *Mnemonic*. The central image of the play is a body from 5200 years ago, preserved in ice. It serves as a point of departure for a fantasia on memory, time, the distortions of history, and the way in which we exhume the past in order to examine the present. The scene here shows McBurney on the gurney, surrounded by members of the company.

sented in New York City. Recently, Complicite announced that it was working on its first original screenplay.

Sam Mendes (1965–) is also a director who has worked with the Royal Shakespeare Company and the Royal National. After studying at Cambridge University Mendes began his theatre career in 1987, at the Chichester Festival Theatre. In 1990, he began working at the Royal Shakespeare Company, staging successful productions of *Troilus and Cressida*, Ben Jonson's *The Alchemist*, and *Richard III*. He has directed a number of works at the Royal National Theatre, including Edward Bond's *The Sea*, Jim Cartwright's *The Rise and Fall of Little Voice*, and a production of *Othello* (1997) that has toured internationally.

From 1992 through 2002, Mendes was the artistic director of the Donmar Warehouse, where he staged a range of eclectic productions, including Stephen Sondheim's *Assassins,* Brian Friel's *Translations, The Glass Menagerie,* Kander and Ebb's *Cabaret* (which was restaged by the Roundabout Theatre in New York City), and David Mamet's *Glengarry Glen Ross.* In 2003 he directed a revival of the muscial *Gypsy* on Broadway. Mendes is also the director of the films *American Beauty* (1999) and *The Road to Perdition* (2002).

The Donmar Warehouse is a 250-seat nonprofit theatre that stages an eclectic mix of works, including contemporary approaches to classics, new works, and small-scale musicals. Donmar has supported innovative new directors, and many renowned film and stage actors have appeared in productions, including Nicole Kidman (1967–), Gwyneth Paltrow (1972–), and Ian McKellan (1939–). When Mendes stepped down as artistic director, Michael Grandage (1962–) succeeded him.

One of the most controversial events in the London theatre was the reopening of the Old Vic in 2004 as a producing house, with the American film and stage actor Kevin Spacey (1959–) as its artistic director. Spacey also acts in productions, including *Richard II* (2005), directed by Trevor Nunn; and *A Moon for the Misbegotten* (2006), directed by Howard Davies, who directed a number of award-winning shows at the Royal National and Almeida Theatres.

The Almeida Theatre was founded by Pierre Audi, its first artistic director, in 1980 in a run-down part of North London. The actor Ian McDiarmid (1944–) and the director Jonathan Kent (1950–) became artistic directors in 1990 and served in that capacity until 2002, when Michael Attenborough (1960–) succeeded them. The Almeida produces new plays and revivals, frequently transferring productions to London's West End and to Broadway.

Canada and Australia since World War II

As was pointed out in Chapter 13, Canadian and Australian theatres, before World War II developed commercially, presenting popular forms of entertainments that also reflected national identity. Two Australian examples are *The Squatter's Daughter, or, The Land of the Wattle* (1907), which focused on the Australian outlaw known as the bushranger; and the pantomime *The Bunyip, or The Enchantment of Fairy Princess Wattle Blossom* (1916), which included a mythological Aboriginal character.

During the same period, Australia and Canada developed "little theatres"—some professional and some amateur—that presented noncommercial, and often politically charged, works. In Australia, three such companies were Sydney's New Theatre League, established in 1936; Melbourne's New Theatre Club, founded in 1937; and Brisbane's Unity Theatre, which also opened in 1937. Hart House Theatre, founded on the campus of the University of Toronto in 1919, was one example of the Canadian "little theatre" movement. It presented many of Canada's most important theatre artists in the two decades before World War II. After World War II, the Hart House became a venue for university productions, reflecting the vitality of university theatre across Canada.

Since World War II, the theatres of Canada and Australia have seen developments that parallel the complexity of the international theatre scene. For example, in Canada in the 1950s and 1960s, many regional theatres were established. One of the most famous is the Stratford Shakespeare Festival in Stratford, Ontario. This festival, established in 1952 under the artistic direction of Tyrone Guthrie, continues to produce classics, musicals, and contemporary works, in multiple venues. Australia also saw the development of theatres across the nation from the 1950s through the 1970s.

Both Australia and Canada also developed avant-garde companies and theatres from the late 1960s through the present. In 1967, Betty Burstall (1926–) established Melbourne's La Mama theatre, based on New York's famous experimental theatre. La Mama continues to function. Company B, which was established in Sydney in 1985 and is still producing, is known for presenting contemporary works and unique readings of classics. Among the stars who have recently appeared with the company are the film actors Geoffrey Rush (1951–) and Cate Blanchett (1969–).

Playwrights and theatre artists have dealt with the issues related to these countries' diverse populations. Possibly the best-known of the playwrights is Michel Tremblay (1942–), who was born in Montreal. His French-language plays focus on working-class Canadians and gay issues. Buddies in Bad Times, established in 1979 and still producing in Toronto, is committed to gay and lesbian theatre. In the 1980s, feminist theatres in Australia included Home Cooking Theatre (1981) and Vital Statistix (1984). The Australian musical *Bran Nue Dae* (1990) dealt with Aboriginal life.

There are also Canadian and Australian artists who present performance art and multimedia works. The French-Canadian Robert Lepage (1957–) is a well-known director, creator of theatrical productions, and actor. In 1993, he founded Ex Machina, a multimedia performance center in Quebec City. Among Lepage's other well-known productions are a postmodernist version of Shakespeare's *A Midsummer Night's Dream* at the Naion Theatre in London in 1993 and his own *Far Side of the Moon* (2000), in which he played both of the work's two characters. Lepage is probably best-known for KÁ, the Cirque du Soleil production he staged in Las Vegas in 2005.

African Theatres and Drama

It is not possible for us to review the complete history of worldwide theatre in this survey. However, it is important to note the significant theatrical contributions of African civilizations and their influence on western traditions. As we noted in the Introduction, early African societies had many traditional performances that were connected to ceremonies and rituals and used music, song, and dance. African theatre artists in the twentieth century used these traditional forms and subverted forms of popular western theatre in order to create work that reflects anticolonial struggles as well as attacks against totalitarian regimes in the newly independent African nations.

Contemporary African theatre and society are divided into English-speaking Africa, French-speaking Africa, and Portuguese-speaking Africa. In all these nations, which were originally defined by nineteenth-century colonial powers, there are also attempts to experiment with the indigenous languages of the peoples of Africa.

In Portuguese-speaking Africa, which includes Angola, Cape Verde, Guinea-Bissau, Mozambique, and São Tomé and Principe, missionaries introduced religious drama in order to spread Catholicism. Before independence in 1975, much of the theatre of this part of Africa was vaudeville-like in nature, although some anticolonial dramas were written. After independence, there was a greater focus on theatre that would arouse social consciousness, and plays followed the model of agitprop dramas; theatrical companies created collaborative works that focused on political and social issues. In Angola, for example, the National School of Theatre was founded in 1976 and staged works that focused on African liberation.

Among the best-known works from Portuguese-speaking Africa are *The Devil's Skin* (Angola, 1977) by Manuel Santos Lima; *Bombo's Chalk Circle* (Angola, 1979) by Henrique Guerra; *The Old Man Is Untouchable* (Angola, 1980) by Costa Andrade; *Shameless* (Cape Verde, 1979) by Donald Pereira de Macedo; and the plays by the Mozambican author Orlando Mendes.

French-speaking (francophone) Africa includes areas south of the Sahara as well as nations in northern Africa. There is a vital theatre in the sub-Saharan nations, influenced by traditional forms of storytelling and music as well as by French theatre traditions. Many of the plays written in this part of French-speaking Africa have been produced in festivals organized in Paris. In addition, some of these African plays were also read and performed in New York during the 1990s by the off-off-Broadway Ubu Repertory Theatre. The plays of this region usually focus on historical chronicles, social concerns, and political circumstances. Among the most significant playwrights of this region are Senegal's Cheik Ndao (1933–), the Ivory Coast's Bernard Dadié (1916–), the Congo's Sony Labou Tansi (1947–) and Felix Tchicaya U'Tamsi (1931–1988), Cameroon's Guillaume Oyono-Mbia (1939–), and Togo's Senouvo Zinsou (1946–). Theatre in French-speaking Africa also received international attention when such well-known contemporary directors as Roger Blin and Peter Brook employed actors from this region in some of their productions.

English-speaking (anglophone) Africa, which includes Nigeria, South Africa, Uganda, and Zambia, has had a significant international impact. Anglophone theatre became more highly developed in the 1950s because of the influence of universities in this region. Universities encouraged the work of dramatists and also organized traveling theatre troupes.

Among the influences on the theatre of English-speaking Africa are traditional forms, popular theatre, and the indigenous languages of the peoples; in fact, there has been considerable debate over whether theatre should be created in the language of the African peoples or in English. Among the leading theatre artists from anglophone Africa are the Nigerians Hubert Ogunde (1916–1990), the playwright who is often cited as the founder of modern Nigerian theatre; Moses Olaiya Adejumo (1936–), an actor-manager; and Olu Obafemi (1951–), a playwright, director, and actor. Among the leading playwrights in Zimbabwe are S. J. Chifunyise (1948–), Ben Shibenke (1945–), and Thompson Tsodzo (1947–). In Kenya, the playwright Ngugi wa Thiong'o (1938–), who has created individual and col-

(© Joan Marcus)

A SOUTH AFRICAN PLAYWRIGHT: ATHOL FUGARD
Fugard, a South African playwright whose work deals primarily with racial relationships and inequality in his native country, has won international recognition for his penetrating dramas. Shown here is a scene from one of his best-known plays, *Master Harold . . . and the Boys,* with Michael Boatman, Christopher Denham, and Danny Glover in the Broadway production.

laborative works in Kenyan languages, was arrested by the oppressive government between 1977 and 1978 and then forced to live in exile. South Africa produced many significant playwrights and theatre companies in the 1970s, including the Market Theatre, People's Space Theatre, and Junction Avenue Theatre Company; these companies frequently produced works that questioned South Africa's apartheid.

Concern for political and social equality is at the heart of the works of the South African playwright Athol Fugard (1932–) and the Nigerian playwright Wole Soyinka, and these two authors have become the most internationally renowned of all contemporary African playwrights.

Fugard, who is white, attacked apartheid in such plays as *The Blood Knot* (1964), *Sizwe Banzi Is Dead* (1973), *Master Harold . . . and the Boys* (1982), *A Lesson from Aloes* (1987), and *Playland* (1992). Some of Fugard's early works, such as *Sizwe Banzi* and *Statements after an Arrest under the Immorality Act* (1972), were written in collaboration with black actors. Fugard sometimes stages and acts in his own works. His works are in the tradition of the plays of Henrik Ibsen and Arthur Miller, so he has sometimes been criticized for taking a simplistic liberal point of view. Nonetheless, his dramas clearly represent the racial turmoil of South Africa during apartheid and postapartheid. His postapartheid works include *Valley Song* (1996) and *The Captain's Tiger* (1998).

WOLE (OLUWOLE AKINWANDE) SOYINKA

The Nobel Prize–winning author Wole Soyinka (1934–) has spent much of his productive life in exile from his Nigerian homeland, as a result of political oppression and his unwillingness to remain silent in the face of totalitarianism. Soyinka was born Oluwole Akinwande Soyinka on July 13, 1934, in Ijebu Isara in western Nigeria. His father, Ayo Soyinka, was an Anglican schoolmaster; and his mother, Eniola, was a shopkeeper.

(François Mori/AP Images)

Wole Soyinka.

After studying Greek, English, and history from 1952 to 1954 at the University of Ibadan in Nigeria, an institution affiliated with the University of London, Soyinka traveled to England to attend the University of Leeds. There he was a member of the university theatre group. He earned his bachelor's degree in English literature with honors in 1957 and then began work on his M.A. degree, also at Leeds, but quit his studies in order to work full-time in professional theatre. In 1957, Soyinka was employed as a play reader for the Royal Court Theatre, London.

In 1958, Soyinka began his playwriting career, writing *The Swamp Dwellers* for the University of London Drama Festival. In 1959, *The Swamp Dwellers* and *The Lion and the Jewel* were produced in Ibadan. That same year, Soyinka wrote, produced, and acted in *An Evening without Decor,* a compilation of works which attacked racism and colonialism; it was staged at the Royal Court in London.

In 1960 Soyinka returned to Nigeria to study west African drama. Throughout the 1960s, Soyinka wrote plays, films, and radio dramas while teaching English and theatre at a number of African universities. In addition, his work began to receive international attention. In 1966, his *Trials of Brother Jero* was produced by the Hampstead Theatre Club in London and *The Lion and the Jewel* was staged at the Royal Court. That same year Soyinka shared with Tom Stoppard the John Whiting Award for promising new playwrights. At the same time, Soyinka's plays were also being staged in New York theatres. *Trials of Brother Jero* and *The Strong Breed* were presented at the off-Broadway Greenwich Mews Theatre in 1967, and the following year *Kongi's Harvest* was produced by the Negro Ensemble Company.

Throughout the 1960s, Soyinka was under attack by the Nigerian government, particularly because of his political writings. In 1965, after being falsely accused of conspiring against the government, he was imprisoned. Many renowned authors protested, including the Americans William Styron and Norman Mailer, and their protests eventually led to his release.

But two years later, at the outset of the Nigerian civil war, Soyinka was accused of aiding the newly independent Biafra. He was arrested and imprisoned for more than two years in solitary confinement. During his imprisonment, Soyinka wrote his jail memoirs secretly, on any scraps of paper he could acquire. These writings were published in 1972 as *The Man Died: The Prison Notes of Wole Soyinka.*

In the fall of 1969, after Soyinka was released from prison, he became chair of the department of theatre arts at the University of Ibadan. However, the following

(© ArenaPAL/Topham/The Image Works)

WOLE SOYINKA: NOBEL PLAYWRIGHT
A remarkable playwright from Nigeria, Wole Soyinka, is an outspoken playwright who has faced many hardships, including being jailed for his beliefs. Undeterred, he has continued to write plays, and in 1986 he was awarded the Nobel Prize for literature. The scene shown here is from his play *The Road*, produced by Talawa Theatre Company, the flagship black company in Britain.

year he escaped from Nigeria and went into exile for five years. During that time, he continued to write many works. His adaptation of *The Bacchae* was commissioned in 1973 by the Royal National Theatre in London. Also, two collections of his plays were published during his exile.

Soyinka returned to Nigeria in 1975, and in 1976 he became a professor of English at the University of Ife. During the 1970s and 1980s, he was an outspoken political figure; at the same time, his international reputation was heightened by visiting professorships at prestigious universities in England and America—including Harvard, Yale, Cornell, and Cambridge—as well as by his continued prolific writing. He wrote possibly his best-known play, *Death and the King's Horseman,* in 1976.

In 1986, Soyinka was awarded the Nobel Prize for literature—the first African writer to receive this award. The Swedish Academy described him as "one of the finest poetical playwrights that have written in English." Soyinka wrote almost no new plays after winning this prestigious award, but he continued to write poetry, fiction, and literary essays.

In 1994, Soyinka published his memoirs, subtitled *Memories of a Nigerian Childhood.* Ironically, just a year later he was again forced to flee Nigeria, fearing that he might be imprisoned by the current government. In 1996, in response to the political turmoil in his homeland, he wrote *The Open Sore of a Continent: A Personal Narrative of the Nigerian Crisis.* The next year, he was charged with treason in absentia by the military dictatorship. Soyinka was appointed to a distinguished visiting professorship at Emory University in Atlanta in 1997.

Soyinka is a highly prolific author who has worked in many literary genres. Among his other well-known plays are *Before the Blackout* (1965), *The Detainee* (1965, a radio play), *The Road* (1969), *Madmen and Specialists* (1970), and *Opera Wonyosi,* an adaptation of Brecht's *Threepenny Opera* (1981). He has also published many volumes of poetry, memoirs, and fiction. His work has introduced contemporary African theatre to western audiences and at the same time has raised political awareness of the horrors of colonialism and totalitarianism in Africa.

Latin American Theatres

As was discussed in Chapter 13, in the twentieth century, there was a development of realistic drama, experimental theatre, radical sociopolitical drama, and popular forms, all existing side by side in Latin America. While there have been economic, political, and social problems, including periods of censorship and governmental repression (for example, in Chile during the dictatorship of Pinochet from 1973 to 1989), all the countries in Latin America have significant theatres and playwrights. Frequently these artists have responded to the political and social turmoil in their societies.

At the beginning of the twentieth century, for instance, many comedies were written throughout Latin America—and especially in Argentina—that dealt with the unique local customs of each of the Latin American nations. In the period between the world wars, the dramatists of Latin America were clearly influenced by such European styles as surrealism and expressionism but often touched on nationalistic issues.

Following World War II, many Latin American dramatists began to focus on the unique national issues and concerns that confronted their individual countries. Some of Latin America's most developed and politically active playwrights and theatre companies can be found today in Argentina, Brazil, Chile, Mexico, and Peru. The theatre artists of these countries have fused the popular styles of their peoples onto the modernist styles of modern western theatre, including realism, expressionism, absurdism, and performance art.

Among the most significant of the postwar Latin American dramatists are the Mexican Elena Garro (1920–), the Chilean Alejandro Sieveking (1935–), the Colombian Guillermo Maldonado (1945–), the Peruvian Mario Vargas Llosa (1936–), and the Brazilian Plinio Marcos (1935–).

AUGUSTO BOAL

South America produced many significant politically active theatre artists in the twentieth century. The most internationally renowned is the Brazilian playwright, director, and theorist Augusto Boal (1931–). Boal, who initially was a chemistry student, studied theatre in New York, where he was influenced by both Brechtian epic theatre and Stanislavsky's realism. Boal was a playwriting student under John Gassner, who encouraged him to pursue his inventive mingling of these disparate techniques. Upon his return to his native country, Boal worked for the Arena Theatre in São Paulo as a resident director and playwright, writing such works as *Lean Wife, Mean Husband* (1957); *Revolution in South America* (1961); and *Joe, From the Womb to the Tomb* (1962). In the 1960s, Boal created works about historical figures, theatrical and revolutionary. Because of his Marxist beliefs, and the increased threat of censorship at the Arena Theatre, Boal was forced into exile in 1971.

In exile, traveling throughout South America and other parts of the world, Boal experimented with different styles of theatre. He created a documentary-like drama that focused on current political issues and used environmental staging, presenting performances in public spaces to surprised audiences. Boal became best-known internationally for his theoretical work *Theatre of the Oppressed* (1975), which became a dominant manifesto for revolutionary and socially conscious theatre. In it, Boal argues that at its conception, theatre was a form shared by all people. During the course of its long history, theatre evolved into a form in which some participants (the audience) passively watched, and others (the actors) performed. Boal's politicized theatrical theories stress the audience's involvement and awareness, without a sharp distinction between performers and spectators. For example, Boal called for *simultaneous dramaturgy,* in which the audience suggests changes to the script to the actors, who then incorporate them into the production. Boal's *forum theatre* allows the audience to break into the performance if they disagree at any point with the unfolding drama.

Augusto Boal tours internationally and has published several other works, including *Games for Actors and Non-Actors* (1992) and *The Rainbow of Desire* (1995). Boal's autobiography, *Hamlet and the Baker's Son: My Life in Theatre and Politics* (2001), resonated with theatergoers as well as those interested in his socially engaged life. Boal continues to teach, give workshops, and lecture throughout the world.

Cultural Interchange in Asian Theatres

As was noted in Chapters 12 and 13, the period at the end of the nineteenth century and the beginning of the twentieth saw increasing interchange between Asian and western theatres. Particularly, western theatre had a growing influence on the modern theatres of India, China, and Japan. In all three countries, traditional theatre continued: kathakali in India, Peking opera in China, and nō and kabuki in Japan. But awareness of western theatre was widening.

As in Latin America, Asian countries were influenced in the early twentieth century by western dramatic forms, particularly the modernist traditions of realism and departures from realism. The colonial influence also led to a weakening of the traditional forms of theatrical practice, both popular and classical.

Following World War I, there was a politicization of Asian theatres. Some theatre artists opposed western influences and the colonial mentality. In the past four decades, there has been a unique return of traditional forms blended into the sociopolitical sensibilities of Asian theatre artists. This return to traditional forms, in itself, is a rejection of colonial and postcolonial western intrusions into the continent.

(© Jeremy Horner/Corbis)

KATHAKALI: INDIAN FOLK DANCERS
Asian theatre has formal, long-standing traditions as well as folk traditions that have always been popular with the average audience member. Seen here are kathakali dancers in Kerala, India. This form of theatre requires quick footwork and complex movements coordinated with the exact time of the music. It also features elaborate costumes, as shown.

Theatres in India, China, and Japan since World War II

In India several changes occurred a few decades into the twentieth century. For one thing, World War I was disruptive. Perhaps more pervasive, though, was the advent of cinema. In India, film became extremely popular, from the standpoint of both producers and consumers. Films began to be produced in great numbers, and audiences flocked to them. At mid-century, this trend, plus World War II, led to a great dropping off of professional theatre in many parts of India.

The theatre that emerged in the latter half of the twentieth century was primarily an amateur theatre. It is estimated that Calcutta has as many as 3,000 registered amateur theatre groups, Bombay perhaps has as many as 500, and Madras has at least 50. Many of these theatres do not have a permanent home, but some do. Also, some of them present professional-quality theatre. Moreover, these theatres keep alive plays written by Indian playwrights, past and present, as well as plays from other nations.

In China after the civil war and Mao Zedong's rise to power following World War II in 1949, spoken drama continued to be written, but additional emphasis was given to traditional forms of popular theatre. These traditional forms were familiar in the countryside and became a medium for carrying messages of the government to remote corners of the nation. During the cultural revolution, which began in 1966, theatrical activity—particularly spoken drama—was more restricted; increasing emphasis was placed on a few dance-dramas, elaborately staged and performed, that had very heavy ideological or propagandistic content. For the most part, theatre artists, along with intellectuals, were seen as subversive and suffered greatly during this era in Chinese history.

Since the death of Mao, and the opening up of China to the west in the late 1970s, there has been cross-fertilization between the Chinese traditions and western drama. Theatre artists from the United States and Europe have visited and performed in China. Arthur Miller, for example, directed a production of *Death of a Salesman* in Beijing in 1983.

In addition, popular traditional forms, such as Peking opera and other forms of classic music-drama, which were demeaned during Mao's rule, are becoming popular again. While much of the drama still remains socialist in point of view and realistic in style, there have been a number of artists who push the boundaries of subject matter and style, fusing classical traditions with contemporary forms and issues. Ping Chong's puppet theatre production with the Shaanxi Folk Art Theatre of Xian, China, *Cathay: Three Tales of China* (2005), is just one example of the merging of avant-garde and traditional forms in contemporary China.

Since the end of World War II, contemporary theatre in Japan has been in a healthy state. A number of truly gifted playwrights have emerged, chief among them Kinoshita Junji (1914–), whose work combines social concerns with humor and, when appropriate, elements from Japanese folk tradition.

In the second half of the twentieth century there were three main branches of theatre in Japan. One was traditional theatre—nō, bunraku, and kabuki, of which the most active was kabuki.

A second branch consisted of various manifestations of *shingeki,* a word that means "new theatre." Shingeki began in the late nineteenth century and in one form or another continued throughout the twentieth century. Broadly speaking, it was a modern theatre, in contrast to the traditional classic theatres. For one thing, it was more realistic than the traditional theatres. In addition, at the beginning it

EAST MEETS WEST: DEATH OF A SALESMAN
Eastern theatre has had a strong influence on western theatre, and in turn Asian theatre has embraced much of western drama. A good example was a Chinese production of Arthur Miller's *Death of a Salesman,* shown here. Miller went to China to oversee the presentation.

was influenced by such western playwrights as Ibsen and Chekhov. In the early twentieth century, shingeki banished the gods and the fantastic from theatre, partly because they had played such a large role in classic theatre. Later, after World War II, nonrealistic elements were admitted to shingeki dramas. Overall, shingeki has undergone changes of its own and has at times been influenced by western theatre. In general, it remains a theatre in which the playwright is a central figure; in recent years it has included female playwrights, who were almost nonexistent in earlier times.

The third strain of modern Japanese theatre has been avant-garde or experimental theatre. A good example of this movement is the work of Tadashi Suzuki, who began his work at Waseda University in Tokyo and then developed a theatre community in the mountains at Toga. Following the models of men such as Jerzy Grotowski and Peter Brook, Suzuki led a director-centered theatre that was international in its ideas and its reach. Theatre pieces were developed by the company under the guidance of the director, and there was an emphasis on ensemble playing, on physical movement, and on combining the old and the new, the traditional and the experimental. Other theatre figures created their own brand of avant-garde work, some of it paralleling that being done in the west, but some distinctly Japanese. One example is the performance artist Issei Ogata (1952–).

(© Jack Vartoogian)

JAPANESE AVANT-GARDE: TADASHI SUZUKI
A Japanese director who has been in the forefront of experimentation and the updating of the classics is Tadashi Suzuki. The modern avant-garde has been international in scope, with artists in different parts of the world influencing one another. Suzuki emphasizes physical movement and body training for his actors. Shown here is Yukiko Saito in Suzuki's version of *Electra*.

Theatres in the Middle East

Contemporary theatre in the Arab world is greatly affected by the politics of the region. While the Islamic religion has strong prohibitions against theatre, there have always been storytelling, folkloric, and popular comic traditions throughout the middle east, before Islamic times and since. As in Asia and Latin America, the close of the nineteenth century and the beginning of the twentieth century saw a rise in western colonial influence on the theatres of the Arab middle east.

(© Stephanie Berger)

AN ISLAMIC MUSICAL DRAMA: TA'ZIYEH

The word *Ta'ziyeh* means mourning. At a festival at Lincoln Center, three plays in a series were presented by a company of eighteen Iranian performers along with four camels, four horses, and six sheep. The event was very spiritual and partook of ritual, devotion, and pageantry as well as theatre. The basis for the plays was the battle of Kerbala in 680, during which Iman Hussein, the grandson of Muhammad, and his followers were killed. The scene shown here was from this epic passion play, which was presented in Farsi.

Three early playwrights who are often said to be responsible for the introduction of western dramatic techniques into the Arab world are the Lebanese author Marun al-Naqqash (1817–1855); Abu Khalil al-Qabbani (1851–?), a Syrian who came to Egypt after his theatre was closed in Damascus; and Ya'qub Sannu (1839–1912), a Jewish-Egyptian dramatist. Western influence was particularly prevalent in the years following World War I.

Another tradition in Arab dramaturgy at the close of the nineteenth century and the beginning of the twentieth century was the adaptation of historic events into plays. Three Lebanese playwrights who were noted for their history dramas were Al-Ahdab (1826–1921), Al-Hadad (1867–1899), and Father Hanna Tannous (1866–1946).

After World War II and through the 1970s, there was significant development of professional theatrical activity throughout the middle eastern region, including Egypt, Iran, Syria, Lebanon, and Iraq. The theatres of these countries continued to be influenced by western practices and artists, but there also developed a good deal of theatrical cross-fertilization. Iran, for example, was host to a significant international festival of avant-garde artists in the early 1970s. The festival featured works by such notable western artists as Peter Brook, Jerzy Grotowski, and Robert Wilson, and many of these works clearly reflected the influence of middle eastern theatre and literature.

However, the works of many Arab theatre artists were highly nationalistic during this era and returned to traditional folk materials; examples are the works by the Iraqi playwright-director Qassim Mohammed (1935–).

With the rise of Islamic fundamentalism and totalitarianism in many of these countries, theatrical activities have been halted, significantly curtailed, or rigidly controlled by the state. For example, the theatrical infrastructure in Iraq was severely damaged by Iraq's war with Iran in the 1980s, by economic hardships after the Persian Gulf War in the early 1990s, and then again with the invasion and occupation of Iraq by the United States and Britain in 2003. In Saudi Arabia, the state-sponsored Saudi Society for Culture and Arts, established in 1972, oversees much theatrical activity; however, there is great controversy over the support of theatrical art.

There are currently a number of significant theatre artists who deal with the contemporary political turmoil of the middle east, including the ongoing battles with Israel, particularly in Egypt and in the Palestinian territories.

Three internationally recognized contemporary Egyptian playwrights are Alfred Farag (1929–), Lenin El-Ramley (1945–), and Gamal Abdel Maqsoud (1942–). In Jordan, the ministry of culture has sponsored annual theatre festivals, and there have also been independent festivals that bring together theatre artists from many parts of the Arab world.

While there has been Palestianian theatre since the 1850s, historians have focused most on theatrical activities since the Israeli occupation in 1967. Many companies and playwrights have created theatrical works that express the Palestinian point of view in relationship to Israel's control of the West Bank and, until recently, Gaza. A Palestinian company that is gaining international recognition from its visits to the Royal Court Theatre in London is Al-Kasaba Theatre, originally founded in Jerusalem in 1970 but now located in Ramallah in the occupied West Bank. In 2001, Al-Kasaba staged *Alive from Palestine: Stories behind the Headlines,* which consists of a series of monologues dealing with the intifada, the Palestinian uprising against Israel. The company's artistic director is George Ibrahim.

Two other productions that reflect the Palestinians' existence under Israeli occupation are *The Alley* (1992), a one-women production written and performed by Samia Qazmouz al-Bakri, which focuses on the lives of Palestinian women since 1948; and *We Are the Children of the Camp* (2000) by al-Rowwad Theatre for Children in the Aida refugee camp near Bethlehem. This production, performed primarily by children, toured the United States in 2005.

Israeli theatre has also developed since the founding of the state of Israel in 1948. Israeli drama has been influenced by the eastern European origins of many of its founders as well as the middle eastern traditions of those Jews who left Arab nations to settle in the Jewish state.

One national theatre of Israel is the Habimah, which was established in Russia in the early twentieth century and settled in what was then British-controlled Palestine in 1931. The other large national theatre in Israel is the Tel Aviv Municipal Theatre, referred to as the Cameri, founded in 1944 by the director Yossef Milo (1916–). There are many other active Israeli theatres throughout the country—in Tel Aviv, Jerusalem, Haifa, and elsewhere. As in Europe and the United States, there are also smaller fringe theatrical groups, which experiment with avant-garde techniques, and performance artists. Most of the theatres in Israel receive some governmental subsidy.

Israeli drama also reflects the tumultuous history of the nation. Early drama dealt with the establishment of the state and nationalism. More recent dramatic works explore the complexities of middle eastern politics, including Israel's relationship with the Palestinians.

In the 1950s, Israel's best-known playwrights were Aharon Megged (1920–) and the poet Leah Goldberg (1915–1970). Nissim Aloni (1926–1998), in the 1950s and 1960s, was Israel's first author to focus exclusively on theatre. In the 1970s and 1980s, Hanoch Levin (1943–1999) was the prominent playwright and director.

The most internationally recognized Israeli dramatist is Joshua Sobol (1939–), whose play *Ghetto* (1984) was produced throughout the world; Peter Zadek and Nicholas Hytner were among the producers. In the 1980s, Sobol served as an artistic director with the Municipal Theatre in Haifa, frequently combining Israeli and Palestinian actors in controversial productions. Sobol is also a director; in 2002, he staged a production of *The Merchant of Venice* for the Illinois Shakespeare Festival that used cross-gender casting.

Summary

Throughout the world, many new companies and established theatres confronted new aesthetic and political issues. Traditional non-European forms mingle with western dramatic forms in many parts of the world.

The complexity of contemporary international theatre makes it difficult to draw conclusions. Future historians, however, will undoubtedly consider worldwide theatre a clear reflection of concerns that confronted our global society. As theatre develops in the twenty-first century, one thing seems certain: the globalization that emerged in the twentieth century will have set the stage for whatever is to come.

Theatre History

- Cao Yu (1910–1996), *The Thunderstorm*
- Cricot 2, Tadeusz Kantor (1915–1990)
- Taganka Theatre, Yuri Lyubimov (1917–)
- Dario Fo (1926–), *The Accidental Death of an Anarchist*
- Directors Peter Zadek (1926–); Peter Stein (1937–); Andrei Serban (1943–)
- Egyptian playwrights: Alfred Farag (1929–), Lenin El Ramley (1945–), Gamal Abdel Maqsoud (1942–)
- Heiner Müller (1929–1995), *Hamletmachine*
- Athol Fugard (1932–), *Master Harold ... and the Boys*
- Wole Soyinka (1934–) *(below)*, *Death and the King's Horseman*

- Caryl Churchill (1938–), *Blue Heart*
- Joshua Sobol (1939–), *Ghetto*
- Tadashi Suzuki (1939–)
- Théâtre du Soleil, Ariane Mnouchkine (1940–) *(below)*

- Peter Handke (1942–), *Kaspar*

Cultural and Historical Developments

- Camp David accord reached between Israel and Egypt; Shah of Iran deposed by regime of Ayatollah Khomeini
- Mother Teresa awarded Nobel Peace Prize (1979)
- Iran-Iraq war; Soviet intervention in Afghanistan; John Maxwell Coetzee's *Waiting for the Barbarians* (1980)
- Anwar al-Sadat assassinated in Cairo; Polish labor union Solidarity suppressed (1981)
- Anselm Kiefer's *Nuremberg* (1982)
- Mikhail Gorbachev begins political reforms in Soviet Russia (1985)
- Salman Rushdie's *The Satanic Verses* (1988)
- Vaclav Havel, Czechoslovakian playwright, elected president; Berlin Wall taken down; Chinese government crushes pro-democracy demonstration in Tiananmen Square (1989) *(below)*

- Eastern Europe democratized; apartheid ends in South Africa (1990)
- Persian Gulf war (1990–1991)
- Soviet Union dissolves (1991)
- Wars of Yugoslav succession (1991–1995)
- Gerhard Richter's *Abstract Picture* (1992)
- European Union established (1993)
- Nelson Mandela *(right)* elected president of South Africa; North American Free Trade Agreement; Israel-Jordan peace accord (1994)

continued

Photo Credits: Wole Soyinka (François Mori/AP Images) / Ariane Mnouchkine. (© Martine Franck/Magnum Photos) / Lone Chinese protestor facing tank in Beijing, June 5, 1989. (Jeff Widener/AP Images) / President Mandela dancing at inaugural concert, May 10, 1994. (John Parkin/AP Images)

MILESTONES CHAPTER 16 GLOBAL THEATRES [1975–PRESENT] *continued*

- Franz Xaver Kroetz (1946–), *Farm Yard*
- David Hare (1947–), *Plenty*
- Issei Ogata (1952–), performance artist
- Patrick Marber (1964–), *Dealer's Choice*
- Jez Butterworth (1969–), *Mojo*
- Martin McDonagh (1970–), *The Beauty Queen of Leenane (below)*

- Sarah Kane (1971–1999), *Blasted*
- Conor McPherson (1971–), *St. Nicholas* (1996), *The Weir*
- Augusto Boal's *Theatre of the Oppressed* (1975)
- George Ibrahim's Al-Kasaba, Palestinian theater company

- J. K. Rowling's *Harry Potter and the Philosopher's Stone*; José Saramago's *Blindness* (1997)
- European Central Bank created (1998)
- Euro adopted as single European currency (1999) *(below)*

- Escalating violence in the Middle East; Gao Xingjian's *Soul Mountain* (2000)
- U.S.-led coalition invades and occupies Iraq (2003)
- Tsunami strikes Sumatra, Thailand, Sri Lanka, and southern India; terrorist attack, Madrid (2004)
- Terrorist attack, London; death of Pope John Paul II; Israeli withdrawal from Gaza (2005)

PHOTO CREDITS: Anna Manahan, Marie Mullen, and Brian F. O'Byrne in *The Beauty Queen of Leenane*. (Sara Krulwich/The New York Times) / Euros. (Punchstock)

Glossary of Theatrical Terms

Afterpiece In eighteenth- and nineteenth-century theatre, an entertainment staged after the main play.

Agon In Greek Old Comedy, a scene with a debate between the two opposing forces in the play, each representing one side of a social or political issue.

Agonthetes In Hellenistic Greece, the government official responsible for producing plays for festivals.

Alienation An aspect of Bertolt Brecht's theory of epic theatre: the concept that audiences' emotional involvement should be minimized so that they will instead be involved intellectually with the political or social message.

Allegory Representation of an abstract theme or themes through symbolic use of character, action, and other concrete elements of a play. In its most direct form—for example, the medieval morality play—allegory uses personification to present characters representing abstract qualities, such as virtues and vices, in action that spells out a moral or intellectual lesson.

Alojero In corrales, the theatres of the Spanish golden age, a stand from which refreshments—food and drinks—were sold.

Amphitheatre (1) Large oval, circular, or semicircular outdoor theatre with rising tiers of seats around an open playing area; *also,* an exceptionally large indoor auditorium. (2) In French neoclassical theatre, an undivided gallery at the rear with inexpensive, bleacher-like seating.

Angle perspective Use of two or more vanishing points, frequently at the sides of a painted design. Ferdinando Bibiena is usually credited with introducing angle perspective early in the eighteenth century.

Angry young men Group of antiestablishment English playwrights of the 1950s who dealt with the dissolving British empire, class conflict, and political disillusionment.

Antagonist Character who is the chief opponent of the main character (the protagonist) in a drama. In some cases there may be several antagonists.

Aposentos In the Spanish golden age, the boxes in a corral.

Apprentice In Elizabethan England, a young performer in an acting company who was taught the art of acting through actual experience and who received room and board from a key member of the troupe.

Apron Stage space in front of the curtain line or proscenium; also called the *forestage.*

Archon Athenian government official appointed to oversee the staging of drama at the City Dionysia festival.

Arena Type of stage that is surrounded by the audience on all four sides; also called *theatre-in-the-round.*

Aside In a play, thoughts spoken aloud by one character without being noticed by others onstage.

Atellan farce Form of Roman theatre: improvised comedic pieces dealing with exaggerated family situations or satirizing historical or mythological figures.

Auleum In Roman theatre, a front curtain that was raised and lowered on telescoping poles.

Autos sacramentales In the Spanish golden age, religious dramas combining characteristics of mystery and morality plays.

Avant-garde Term applied to plays of an experimental or unorthodox nature, which attempt to go beyond standard usage in form, content, or both.

Backdrop Large drapery or painted canvas, which provides the rear or upstage masking of a set.

Backstage Stage area behind the front curtain; also, the areas beyond the setting, including wings and dressing rooms.

Ballad opera Eighteenth-century English form that burlesqued opera: there was no recitative, songs were set to popular tunes, and characters were drawn from the lower classes. John Gay's *The Beggar's Opera* is the most famous example.

Batten A length of pipe or a pole hung parallel to the stage floor and suspended from above the stage on which scenery or lighting instruments are hung.

Benefit Tradition begun in eighteenth-century theatre whereby the profits from an evening's performance were given to a performer or group of performers.

Biomechanics An aspect of Vsevelod Meyerhold's theory of acting: the idea that an actor's body should be machinelike and that emotion can be represented externally.

Blocking Arrangement of actors' movements onstage with respect to each other and the stage space.

Bookholder In Elizabethan theatre, the prompter who gave actors their lines.

Border Strip of drapery or painted canvas hung across the top of the stage from a batten to mask the area above the stage; *also,* a row of lights hung from a batten.

Boulevard theatres In eighteenth-century France, theatres located on Boulevard du Temple in Paris, catering to popular tastes.

Box Small, private compartment for a group of spectators, built into the walls of a traditional proscenium-arch theatre.

Box set Interior setting using flats to form the back and side walls and often the ceiling of a room.

Breeches roles Male roles played by females, particularly popular in Restoration and eighteenth-century English theatre.

Bunraku Japanese puppet theatre. The puppets are two-thirds life-size and are manipulated by men in black robes who are conventionally regarded as being invisible to the audience.

Burlesque Ludicrous imitation of a dramatic form or a specific play. Closely related to satire, but usually lacking the moral or intellectual purposes of reform typical of satire.

Burletta Eighteenth-century English dramatic form resembling comic opera and defined by the lord chamberlain as a play with no more than three acts, each of which had to include at least five songs.

Business Obvious and detailed physical movement of actors to reveal character, aid action, or establish mood; e.g., pouring drinks at a bar, opening a gun case.

Canon Set of literary works believed to be universally accepted as important and historically significant. Today, many critics argue that certain groups are underrepresented in the canon, and that it therefore does not adequately reflect human accomplishments.

Capa y espada Literally, "cape and sword": full-length Spanish plays that revolved around intrigue and duels over honor.

Carros In the Spanish golden age, pageant wagons on which autos sacramentales were staged.

Catharsis see *Katharsis.*

Cavea In Roman theatre, the seating area.

Cazuela In the Spanish golden age, the gallery located above the tavern in the back wall of a theatre; the area in which women were segregated.

Chiaroscuro In painting, emphasis of contrasts between light and shadow, associated with Giambattista Piranesi and others.

Choral odes In classical Greek drama, songs chanted by the chorus between the episodes.

Choregus In ancient Greece, a wealthy person who underwrote most of the expenses for the production of an individual playwright's works at a dramatic festival.

Chorodidaskalos In ancient Greek theatre, the person who trained and rehearsed the chorus.

Chorus (1) In ancient Greek drama, a group of performers who sang and danced, sometimes participating in the action but usually simply commenting on it. (2) Performers in a musical play who sing and dance as a group rather than individually.

City Dionysia The most important Greek festival in honor of the god Dionysus; it was staged in Athens in the spring and was the first to include dramatic activities.

Claque People in the audience who are hired to applaud; the tradition of the claque began in Roman theatre.

Climatic Drama See *Crisis Drama.*

Combination company In the nineteenth century, a complete touring production, including supporting players, scenery, and costumes.

Comedia In the Spanish golden age, a three-act full-length nonreligious play.

Comédie larmoyante "Tearful comedy": in eighteenth-century France, a form of drama meant to evoke sentimental tears.

Comedy Category of drama that is generally light in tone; it is concerned with issues that are not serious, has a happy ending, and is designed to amuse and provoke laughter. (See also *Old Comedy, New Comedy, Comedy of humours, Comedy of manners, Farce, Satire, Slapstick.*)

Comedy of humours Form of comedy developed by Ben Jonson in the early seventeenth century. It is based on Roman comedy and stresses ridicule directed at characters who are dominated by a single trait (or "humour") to the point of obsession.

Comedy of manners Form of comic drama that became popular in the latter half of the seventeenth century in France and among English playwrights during the Restoration. It emphasizes a cultivated or sophisticated atmosphere, witty dialogue, and characters whose concern with social polish is charming, ridiculous, or both.

Comic opera (opéra comique) In eighteenth-century France, an entertainment in which action was mimed by the performers and dialogue was often sung by the audience. Later, French comic opera became more like ballad opera.

Commedia dell'arte Form of comic theatre, originating in Italy in the sixteenth century, in which dialogue was improvised around a loose scenario involving a set of stock characters, each with a distinctive costume and a traditional name.

Compañias de partes In the Spanish golden age, acting troupes organized according to the sharing system.

Complication The introduction in a play of a new force, which creates a new balance of power and makes reaching a resolution more difficult and more complicated.

Confidant (confidante) Minor character in whom a major character or the protagonist confides.

Conflict Tension between two or more characters, leading to a crisis or a climax. The basic conflict is the fundamental struggle or imbalance underlying the play as a whole. May also be a conflict of ideologies, actions, and the like.

Constructivism Following World War I, a movement in scene design in which sets were created to provide greater opportunities for physical action. The sets, which were frequently composed of ramps, platforms, and levels, were nonrealistic. The Russian director Vsevelod Meyerhold used many constructivist settings.

Continental seating Auditorium arrangement in which audience members enter and exit at the ends of rows; there is no center aisle.

Contract system System under which performers are hired for a specific period of time and paid a set salary.

Corral In the Spanish golden age, a theatre usually located in the courtyard of a series of adjoining buildings.

Crisis drama Dramatic structure, developed in classical Greece and popular with modern realists, in which the dramatic action begins near the climax, with the characters in the midst of their struggles. Usually, crisis drama has few characters, few locales, much exposition, and only one main action, and covers a short span of time.

Curtain-raiser In nineteenth-century theatre, a short play staged before a full-length drama.

Cycle plays See *Mystery plays.*

Cyclorama Large curved drop used to mask the rear and sides of the stage; painted a neutral color or blue to represent sky or open space. It may also be a permanent stage fixture made of plaster or a similar durable material.

Dada Movement in twentieth-century art between World War I and World War II which was based on deliberate presentation of the irrational and on attacks against traditional artistic values.

Deconstructionism In theatre history, an approach based on the concept that a text has no stable reference. It questions historical assumptions about the ability of language to represent reality.

Decorum Neoclassical rule, developed in the Italian Renaissance, that dramatic characters must behave in set ways based on their social class and background.

Denouement The moment when suspense is finally satisfied and the "knot is untied." The term is from the French and was used to refer to the working out of the resolution in a well-made play.

Desvanes "Attics": in the Spanish golden age, cramped, low-ceilinged boxes located on the fourth floor of a corral.

Deus ex machina Literally, "god from a machine." In ancient Greek theatre, the convention of bringing in gods on a mechane—that is, a crane or lever suspended from the top of the scene house. The term now applies to any unjustified or arbitrary dramatic device used to resolve a plot, usually in the final moments.

Director In American usage, the person who is responsible for the overall unity of a production, coordinating the efforts of the contributing artists. The director is in charge of rehearsals and supervises the actors in the preparation of their parts. The American *director* is the equivalent of the French *metteur en scène.* For many years in Britain, the director was known as the *producer.*

Dithyramb In ancient Greece, a choral song describing the adventures of a god or heroic figure.

Documentary drama Term encompassing different types of twentieth-century drama that presented material in the fashion of journalism or reporting. *Living newspaper* drama of the 1930s used signs and slide projections to deal with broad social problems; other documentary dramas use a more realistic approach.

Domestic drama Also known as *bourgeois drama.* Domestic drama deals with problems of the middle and lower classes, particularly problems of the family and home.

Dominus Leader of a Roman acting troupe.

Double-entendre Word or phrase in comedy that has a double meaning, the second meaning often being sexual.

Doubling Having an actor play more than one role in a play. Doubling was common in Greek and Elizabethan theatre.

Downstage Front of the stage toward the audience.

Doyen In the Comédie Française, the head of the company and the actor with the longest service.

Drame Eighteenth-century French term usually denoting a serious drama that dealt with middle-class characters. Some critics suggest that drame included such eighteenth-century forms as domestic tragedy, middle-class tragedy, and tearful comedy (comédie larmoyante).

Drolls In seventeenth-century England, short dramas that were either excerpts from or condensations of longer plays. Drolls were presented during the Commonwealth and at the beginning of the Restoration.

Drop Large piece of fabric, generally painted canvas, hung from a batten to the stage floor, usually to serve as backing.

Eclectic Theatre artist who works in a variety of modes and does not identify with one particular artistic movement.

Ekkyklema In ancient Greek theatre, a wagon used to bring characters onstage—often to reveal the results of offstage violence.

Elevator stage Stage which allows the entire floor or sections of the floor to be raised and lowered automatically.

Emotional recall Stanislavski's exercise to assist the actor in presenting realistic emotions. The performer thinks of the circumstances surrounding an event in his or her own life that led to an emotion similar to what the character is supposed to feel in the play. By mentally re-creating these circumstances, the performer will feel the emotion.

Ensemble playing Acting that stresses the total artistic unity of a performance rather than the individual performances of specific actors.

Entremeses In the Spanish golden age, interludes during the intermissions of comedias; these could be comic sketches, songs, or dances.

Environmental theatre A type of theatre production in which the total environment—the stage space and the audience arrangement—is emphasized. A form of environmental theatre came to the forefront in experimental theatre of the 1960s. Among its aims are elimination of the distinction between audience space and acting space, a more flexible approach to interactions between performers and audience, and substitution of a multiple focus for the traditional single focus.

Epic theatre Twentieth-century form of presentation associated with the German dramatist Bertolt Brecht, its chief advocate and theorist. Epic theatre is aimed at the intellect rather than the emotions, seeking to present evidence regarding social questions in such a way that they may be considered objectively and an intelligent conclusion may be reached.

Epilogue Speech addressed to the audience after the conclusion of a play and spoken by one of the actors.

Episkenion In Hellenistic Greece, the second story of the skene or scene house.

Episodic drama Dramatic structure—extremely popular in the English Renaissance and the Spanish golden age—in which the dramatic action begins early in the story. Episodic drama has little exposition, many characters, frequent changes of time and place, and subplots.

Existentialism Set of philosophical ideas whose principal modern advocate was Jean-Paul Sartre. The term *existentialist* is applied to plays by Sartre and others that illustrate these views. Sartre's central thesis was that there are no fixed standards or values by which one can live, and that each individual must create his or her own code of conduct regardless of conventions imposed by society.

Exodos In classical Greek drama, the final scene, in which all the characters exit from the stage.

Exposition Imparting of information that is necessary for an understanding of the story but will not be covered by the action onstage: events or knowledge from the past, or occurring outside the play, which must be introduced if the audience is to understand the characters or the plot. Exposition is almost always a challenge in drama because relating or conveying information is static; the dramatist must find ways to make expository scenes dynamic.

Expressionism Movement that developed and flourished in Germany during the period immediately preceding and following World War I. Expressionism in drama was characterized by an attempt to depict subjective states through distortion; striking, often grotesque, images; and lyric, unrealistic dialogue.

Farce One of the major genres of drama, sometimes regarded as a subclass of comedy. It aims to entertain and to provoke laughter, and its humor is a result primarily of physical activity and visual effects.

Feminism In theatre history, an approach based on the belief that woman's place in theatre has not been sufficiently explored.

Flat Single piece of scenery, usually of standard size, combined with similar units to create a set. Formerly made of canvas stretched over a wooden frame, but now frequently made of a hard substance such as luan; a hard flat is sometimes called a *Hollywood* or *movie* flat.

Fly loft or flies Space above the stage where scenery may be lifted out of sight by means of ropes and pulleys when it is not needed.

Footlights Row of lights in the floor along the edge of the stage or apron; once a principal source of stage light but now rarely used.

Forestage See *Apron.*

Found space Space not originally intended for theatre which is converted for productions. Avant-garde artists often produce theatre events in found spaces.

Fourth-wall convention Pretense that in a proscenium-arch theatre the audience is looking into a room through an invisible fourth wall. The term is often attributed to the eighteenth-century French philosopher Denis Diderot.

Futurism Art movement begun in Italy about 1905 which idealized mechanization and machinery.

Gallery In traditional proscenium-arch theatres, the undivided seating area cut into the walls of the building.

Gesamtkunstwerk Richard Wagner's term for a unified operatic work of art, in which all elements—music, words, story, scenery, costumes, orchestra, etc.—form a total piece.

Glories In the Italian Renaissance, flying machines used for special effects.

Gradas In the Spanish golden age, benches placed along the side walls of the patio or pit area in a corral.

Groove system System in which there were tracks on the stage floor and above the stage to allow for the smooth movement of flat wings on and off the stage; usually there were a series of grooves at each stage position. The system was developed during the Italian Renaissance and was used through the nineteenth century in England, the United States, and the Netherlands.

Groundlings In Elizabethan theatre, audience members who stood in the yard.

Hamartia Ancient Greek term usually translated as "tragic flaw." The literal translation, however, is "missing the mark," and this suggests to some scholars that hamartia is not so much a flaw in character as an error in judgment made by the protagonist.

Hanamichi In kabuki theatre, the bridge from behind the audience (toward the left side of the audience) on which actors can enter to the stage. Important scenes are also played on the hanamichi.

Happenings Form of theatrical event that was developed out of experimentation by certain American abstract artists in the 1960s. Happenings are nonliterary, replacing the script with a scenario which provides for chance occurrences, and are performed (often only once) in such places as parks and street corners.

Hashigakari In nō theatre, the bridge on which actors make their entrance from the dressing area to the platform stage.

Heavens Also called *shadows.* In the English Renaissance, a roof protecting the stage of a public theatre, often painted on the underside to represent the heavens literally. (For French neoclassical usage, see *Paradis.*)

Hireling A member of an Elizabethan acting company who was paid a set salary and was not a shareholder.

History play In the broadest sense, a play that is set in a historical milieu and deals with historical events and personages; but the term is usually applied only to plays which deal with vital issues of public welfare and are nationalistic in tone.

Householders In Elizabethan England, star members of an acting company who were given part-ownership of its playhouse; *also,* people who owned buildings and rented them to acting companies.

Hubris Ancient Greek term usually translated as "excessive pride"; hubris is a common tragic flaw.

Hypokrite Greek term for "actor."

Innamorata In commedia dell'arte, the stock female lover.

Innamorato In commedia dell'arte, the stock male lover.

Inner stage Area at the rear of the stage that can be cut off from the rest by means of curtains or scenery and revealed for special scenes.

Interludes In medieval England, short dramatic pieces, usually presented between courses of a banquet.

Intermezzi In the Italian Renaissance, entertainments performed between the acts of operas and full-length plays.

Irony Condition that is the reverse of what we have expected; also, a verbal expression whose intended implication is the opposite of its literal sense. Irony is a device particularly suited to theatre and found in virtually all drama.

Joruri In Japanese puppet theatre, chanted texts.

Kabuki The most eclectic and theatrical of the major forms of Japanese theatre. Roles of both sexes are performed by men in a highly theatrical, nonrealistic style. Kabuki combines music, dance, and dramatic scenes with an emphasis on color and movement. The plays are long and episodic, consisting of loosely connected dramatic scenes which are often performed independently.

Kathakali In southwestern India, a form of dance drama presented by torchlight, dealing with clashes of good and evil.

Katharsis Greek word, usually translated as "purgation," which Aristotle used in his definition of tragedy. For some, it refers to the vicarious cleansing of certain emotions in the audience through their representation onstage.

Kothornus In Hellenistic Greek theatre, the platform boot worn by actors.

Kyōgen In nō theatre, farcical interludes presented between plays.

Lazzi In commedia dell'arte, comic pieces of business repeatedly used by characters.

Lehrstücke "Learning pieces": short dramas written by Bertolt Brecht in the early 1930s.

Liturgical drama Any religious drama, usually sung or chanted, that relates to the Bible and is presented in Latin inside a church sanctuary. The form was highly developed in the medieval period.

Living newspapers The Federal Theatre Project's dramatizations of newsworthy events in the 1930s.

Local color Inclusion in scenery of locations that audience members will recognize from their own community. Use of local color in settings became more common in the eighteenth century.

Loges In French neoclassical theatre, boxes.

Long run In commercial theatre, presentation of a drama for as long a period of time as it remains popular with the public. In nineteenth-century American and English theatre, the long run replaced repertory.

Lords' rooms In English Renaissance theatre, boxes frequented by wealthy patrons.

Ludi Romani Roman festival in honor of Jupiter into which drama was first introduced.

Luñetas In the Spanish golden age, semicircular benches located in the front of the pit.

Magic if Stanislavski's acting exercise which requires the actor to ask, "How would I react *if* I were in this character's position?"

Mansion Medieval scenic unit, often presented as an individual house or locale.

Masking Scenery or draperies used to hide or cover.

Masque Lavish form of private theatrical entertainment which developed in Renaissance Italy and spread rapidly to the courts of France and England. The masque combined poetry, music, elaborate costumes, and spectacular effects of stage machinery.

Mechane In ancient Greek theatre, a crane used for flying characters into the playing area.

Medieval drama Range of plays that make up the religious and folk drama developed during the Middle Ages. (See *Liturgical drama, Mystery plays, Morality play.*)

Melodrama Historically, a distinct form of drama popular throughout the nineteenth century which emphasized action, suspense, and spectacular effects; generally melodrama used music to heighten the dramatic mood. Melodrama had stock characters and clearly defined villains and heroes, and it presented unambiguous confrontations between good and evil.

Mime In ancient Greece and Rome, a form of theatrical entertainment that consisted of short dramatic sketches characterized by jesting and buffoonery.

Minstrelsy Type of nineteenth-century production featuring white performers made up in blackface.

Mise-en-scène Arrangement of all the elements in a stage picture, either at a given moment or dynamically throughout a performance.

Morality play Medieval drama designed to teach a lesson. The characters were often allegorical and represented virtues or faults, such as good deeds, friendship, or avarice. The most famous example is *Everyman.*

Mosqueteros Literally, "mosquitos": in the Spanish golden age, the noisy groundlings in the corrales.

Moving panorama In the nineteenth century, a setting painted on a cloth which was unrolled by spools to create an illusion of movement and changing locales.

Multiculturalism In theatre history, an approach focusing on diverse cultural, social, and ethnic groups that have traditionally been underrepresented.

Multimedia Use of electronic media, such as slides, film, and videotape, in live theatre.

Multiple setting Form of stage setting, common in the Middle Ages, in which several locations are represented at the same time; also called *simultaneous setting.* Used also in various forms of contemporary theatre.

Musical theatre Broad category which includes opera, operetta, musical comedy, and other musical plays (the term *lyric theatre* is sometimes used to distinguish it from pure dance). It includes any dramatic entertainment in which music and lyrics (and sometimes dance) are integral and necessary.

Musicians' gallery In English Renaissance theatre, the third level of the tiring house, where the accompanying musicians were located.

Mystery plays Also called *cycle plays.* Short medieval dramas presented in western Europe and England, based on events of the Old and New Testaments. Many such plays were organized into historical cycles which told the story of human history from the creation to doomsday.

National theatre A theatre dedicated to the drama of a specific country and usually subsidized by the government.

Naturalism Special form of realism. The theory of naturalism came to prominence in France and elsewhere in Europe in the latter half of the nineteenth century. The French playwright Émile Zola advocated theatre that would follow the scientific principles of the age: drama should look for the causes of "disease" in society the way a doctor looks at disease in an individual, and theatre should expose social "infection" in all its ugliness. Naturalism attempts to achieve the verisimilitude of a documentary film, conveying the impression that everything about the play—the setting and the way the characters dress, speak, and act—is exactly like everyday life.

Naumachia In ancient Rome, sea battles staged in a flooded amphitheatre or on a lake.

Neutral platform stage Unlocalized stage which allows for easy shifts of locale through the use of properties, entrances, and exits. It was used first in the Middle Ages and later in the English Renaissance.

New Comedy Hellenistic Greek and Roman comedies that deal with romantic and domestic situations.

Nō Also spelled *noh.* Rigidly traditional Japanese drama which in its present form dates back to the fourteenth century. Nō plays are short dramas combining music, dance, and lyrics with a highly stylized and ritualistic presentation. Virtually every aspect of a production—including costumes, masks, and a highly symbolic setting—is prescribed by tradition.

Objective Stanislavski's term for that which is urgently desired and sought by a character, the desired goal which propels a character to action.

Obstacle That which delays or prevents the achieving of a goal by a character. An obstacle creates complication and conflict.

Off-Broadway Movement developed in the late 1940s as a reaction to Broadway commercialism; its primary goal was to provide an outlet for experimental and innovative works, unhindered by commercial considerations. Off-Broadway theatre spaces are small (usually holding about 200 spectators), and many have thrust or arena stages. Many American actors and directors began their careers off-Broadway.

Off-off-Broadway Center for experimentation in New York theatre that developed when off-Broadway became commercialized in the 1960s. Off-off-Broadway is dedicated to introducing and showcasing new talent, experimenting with new styles of production, and avoiding the limitations of commercial theatre.

Offstage Areas of the stage, usually in the wings, which are not in view of the audience.

Old Comedy Classical Greek comedy that pokes fun at social, political, or cultural conditions and at individuals. The only surviving examples are by Aristophanes.

Onkos In Hellenistic Greece, the high headdress of a mask.

Onnagata In Japanese kabuki, women's roles played by male actors.

Orchestra (1) Ground-floor seating in an auditorium. (2) In ancient Greek theatre, the circular playing space.

Pageant master In the Middle Ages, a professional stage manager who oversaw the production of a cycle of mystery plays.

Pantomime Originally, a Roman entertainment in which a narrative was sung by a chorus while the story was acted out by dancers. Now used loosely to cover any form of presentation that relies on dance, gesture, and physical movement without speech.

Parabasis In Greek Old Comedy, a scene in which the chorus directly addressed the audience members and made fun of them.

Paradis "Heavens": in French neoclassical theatre, the third tier of galleries along the side walls.

Parados In classical Greek drama, the scene in which the chorus enters. *Also,* the entranceway for the chorus in Greek theatre.

Parasite In Roman New Comedy, a stock character who is motivated purely by sensual needs, e.g., gluttony.

Paraskenia In ancient Greek theatre, the wings of the skene.

Parterre In French neoclassical theatre, the pit where audience members stood.

Pastoral Idealized dramatization of rural life, often including mythological creatures, popular during the Italian Renaissance.

Patio In the Spanish golden age, the pit area for the audience.

Peking opera Popular theatre of China that developed in the nineteenth century.

Pensionnaire Hireling in a French acting troupe.

Performance art Alternative form of theatre. Performance art often uses elements of the visual arts, dance, and popular entertainment in unique configurations. Also, personal, individual, autobiographical presentations.

Periaktoi In ancient Greek theatre, a three-sided scenic piece which could be revolved to show the audience three different scenes.

Perspective Illusion of depth in painting; introduced into scene design during the Italian Renaissance.

Pinakes In ancient Greek theatre, painted flats.

Pit Floor of the house in a traditional proscenium-arch theatre. The pit was originally a standing area; later, backless benches were added.

Platea In medieval theatre, an unlocalized playing area.

Plot (1) As distinct from *story,* a patterned arrangement of events and characters for a drama. The incidents are selected and arranged for maximum dramatic impact. A plot may begin long after the beginning of the story and may refer to information regarding the past in flashbacks or exposition. (2) In Elizabethan theatre, an outline of the dramatic action which was posted backstage so that actors could refresh their memory during a performance.

Point of attack The moment in a story when a play actually begins. The dramatist chooses a point in time along the continuum of events which he or she judges will best start the action and propel it forward.

Pole-and-chariot system Giacomo Torelli's mechanized means of changing sets made up of flat wings.

Poor theatre Term coined by Jerzy Grotowski to describe his ideal of theatre stripped to its barest essentials. According to Grotowski, the lavish sets, lights, and costumes usually associated with theatre reflect only base, materialistic values and must be eliminated.

Positivism In theatre history, the idea that history can be chronicled objectively and explained logically.

Postmodernism Theory that division of artworks into modernist categories, such as realism and departures from realism, is artificial. Postmodernist works mix realistic and nonrealistic elements as well as techniques from both "high" and "low" art.

Preparation (1) Previous arranging of circumstances, pointing of character, and placing of properties in a production so that the ensuing actions will seem reasonable. (2) Actions taken by a performer getting ready for a performance.

Private theatres In Elizabethan and Jacobean England, indoor theatres.

Proagon In classical Greece, an initial event of a festival; performers and playwrights appeared in presentations intended to announce and advertise the coming plays.

Processional staging In the Middle Ages, a form of staging popular in England and Spain. Though there is much debate about how it actually worked, apparently each mystery play was set up on a wagon which moved from locale to locale within a town, so that the play would be presented separately at each stop—each audience area—along its route.

Producer In American usage, the person responsible for the business side of a production, including raising money. In British usage, a *producer* was the equivalent of an American *director.*

Proedria In ancient Greek theatres, front-row seats reserved for political and religious dignitaries.

Prologos In classical Greek drama, the opening scene which sets the action and provides the necessary background information.

Prologue Introductory speech delivered to the audience by one of the actors or actresses before a play begins.

Props *Properties;* objects that are used by performers onstage or are necessary to complete a set.

Proscenium Arch or frame surrounding the stage opening, like a picture frame; developed during the Italian Renaissance.

Proskenion In Hellenistic Greece, the bottom level of the skene, or stage house.

Protagonist Principal character in a play; the one whom the drama is chiefly about.

Psychological gesture According to the twentieth-century Russian acting theorist Mikhail Chekhov, a characteristic movement or activity which would sum up a character's motives and preoccupations.

Public theatres In Elizabethan England, outdoor theatres.

Pulpitum In Roman theatre, a raised platform stage.

Rake To position scenery on a slant or angle other than parallel or perpendicular to the curtain line; *also,* an upward slope of the stage floor away from the audience.

Raked stage Stage that slopes upward away from the audience toward the back of the stage.

Realism Broadly speaking, the attempt to present onstage people and events corresponding to those observable in everyday life.

Regional theatre (1) Theatre whose subject matter is specific to a particular geographic region. (2) Theatres situated outside major theatrical centers.

Régisseur Continental term for *theatre director;* it often denotes a dictatorial director.

Rejas In the Spanish golden age, windows, protected by grills and overlooking a corral, from which the play could be seen.

Repertory or repertoire Acting company that at any given time has a number of plays it can perform alternately; *also,* the plays themselves.

Restoration drama English drama after the restoration of the monarchy, from 1660 to 1700. Presented for an audience primarily of aristocrats who gathered about the court of Charles II, Restoration drama consisted largely of heroic tragedies in neoclassical style and comedies of manners which took a cynical view of human nature.

Reversal Sudden switch or turnaround of circumstances or knowledge which leads to a result contrary to expectations. Called *peripeteia* or *peripety* in Greek drama.

Revisionism In theatre history, an approach based on the belief that history is usually told from the viewpoint of a social, political, or cultural elite; that it is therefore usually distorted; and that in consequence it needs to be rewritten.

Revolving stage Large turntable on which scenery is placed so that as it moves, one set turns out of sight while a new one is brought into view.

Ritual Specifically ordered, ceremonial religious, personal, or social event.

Romanticism Nineteenth-century literary and dramatic movement that developed as a reaction to the strictures of neoclassicism. Imitating the loose, episodic structure of Shakespeare's plays, the romantics sought to free the writer from all rules and considered the unfettered inspiration of artistic genius the source of all creativity. They laid more stress on mood and atmosphere than on content, but one of their favorite themes was the gulf between human beings' spiritual aspirations and physical limitations.

Sacra rappresentazioni "Sacred representations": in the late Middle Ages and early Renaissance, Italian religious dramas in medieval style, based on biblical stories and lives of saints.

Satire In theatre, drama that uses techniques of comedy—such as wit, irony, and exaggeration—to expose and attack folly and vice.

Satyr play One of the three types of classical Greek drama. A satyr play was usually a ribald takeoff on Greek mythology and history and included a chorus of satyrs, mythological creatures who were half-man and half-goat.

Scaena In Roman theatre, the stage house.

Scaena frons In Roman theatre, the ornate three-dimensional facade of the stage house.

Scene (1) Stage setting. (2) One of the structural units into which a play or an act of a play is divided. (3) Location of a play's action.

School drama In the English Renaissance, plays written at the universities and presented at schools rather than to the general public.

Script Written or printed text of a play or some other theatrical representation; a script consists of dialogue, stage directions, descriptions of characters, and the like.

Secrets In medieval theatre, special effects.

Semiotics In theatre history, an approach based on the argument that historians need to focus on audiences' responses to elements of a production in which function and signs have a specific meaning for viewers.

Sentimental comedy In eighteenth-century England, comedy that reaffirmed middle-class morality: the virtuous characters were rewarded and the wicked punished.

Set Scenery, taken as a whole, for a scene or an entire production.

Set piece Piece of scenery that stands independently in a scene.

Shadow play Play in which the audience sees shadows of puppets or actors on a screen; developed most fully in southeast Asia.

Shareholders In Elizabethan acting troupes, members who received part of the profits as payment.

Shite In nō theatre, the leading actor.

Shutters Two large flat wings that close off a perspective setting in back.

Sides A single actor's own lines and cues. Elizabethan actors learned their roles from sides.

Simultaneous setting Medieval convention of presenting more than one locale onstage at the same time; also called *multiple setting.*

Siparium In Roman theatre, a backdrop curtain at the rear of the stage.

Skene In ancient Greek theatre, the scene house behind the orchestra.

Slapstick Type of comedy or comic business that relies on ridiculous—often violent—physical activity for its humor.

Sociétaire Shareholder in a French acting troupe.

Soliloquy Speech in which a character who is alone onstage utters inner thoughts.

Sottie In the Middle Ages, a short, satirical French farce.

Spine In the Stanislavski method, the dominant desire or motivation of a character; usually thought of as an action and expressed as a verb.

Stage convention An understanding, established through custom or usage, that certain devices will be accepted or assigned specific meaning or significance arbitrarily—that is, without requiring that they be natural or realistic.

Stanislavski method Set of techniques for and theories about acting which promotes a realistic style stressing psychological gestures and emotional truth as opposed to conventional theatricality.

Stationary staging In the Middle Ages, a form of staging popular on the European continent. A series of small scenic mansions were set up side by side, usually in conjunction with a large platform stage, so that all the plays of a cycle could be presented in one location.

Stock characters Stereotypical characters, usually not fully developed as unique individuals. In the Italian Renaissance, commedia dell'arte had many popular stock characters, including servants, masters, and young lovers. Modern melodrama has stock characters such as heroes and villains.

Stock set Standard setting for a locale used in every play which requires that environment.

Storm and stress An antineoclassical movement in eighteenth-century Germany which was a forerunner of romanticism.

Street theatre Generic term for groups that perform in the open and attempt to relate to the needs of a specific community or neighborhood; *also,* their presentations.

Subtext Meaning and movement of a play below its surface; that which is implied but never stated. Sometimes more important than surface activity.

Surrealism Movement attacking formalism in the arts which developed in Europe after World War I. Seeking a deeper and more profound reality than the rational or the conscious, the surrealists replaced realistic action with the strange logic of dreams and cultivated such techniques as automatic writing and free association of ideas.

Symbolism In drama, a movement of the late nineteenth century and early twentieth century which sought to replace realistic representation of life with the expression of inner truth. Symbolist drama used myths, legends, and symbols in an attempt to reach beyond everyday reality; it was closely linked to symbolist poetry.

Taburetes In the Spanish golden age, a row of stools or a few benches at the front of the patio (pit) of a corral, near the stage.

Tan In Peking opera, a female role.

Tetralogy In classical Greek theatre, four plays—three tragedies and one satyr play—written by a single author for a festival.

Theatre of cruelty Antonin Artaud's visionary concept of theatre based on magic and ritual which would liberate deep, violent, erotic impulses. He wanted to reveal the cruelty which he saw as existing beneath all human action—the pervasiveness of evil and violent sexuality.

Theatre of the absurd Term first used by Martin Esslin to describe the works of certain playwrights of the 1950s and 1960s who expressed a similar point of view regarding the absurdity of the human condition. In theatre of the absurd, rational language is debased and replaced by clichés and trite or irrelevant remarks. Realistic psychological motivation is replaced by automatic behavior which is often absurdly inappropriate to the situation. Although the subject matter is serious, the tone of these plays is usually comic and ironic.

Theatricalism Style of production and playwriting that emphasizes theatricality for its own sake. Less a coherent movement than a quality found in the work of many artists rebelling against realism, it frankly admits the artifice of the stage and borrows freely from the circus, the music hall, and similar entertainments.

Theatron In ancient Greek theatre, the seating area, carved into a hillside.

Theme Central thought of a play; the idea or ideas with which the play deals and which it expounds.

Thespian Synonym for "actor"; the term is derived from Thespis, who is said to have been the first actor in ancient Greek theatre.

Thingspielen In Nazi Germany, massive propagandistic theatrical spectacles staged outdoors.

Thrust stage Platform stage surrounded on three sides by the audience.

Thymele In ancient Greek theatre, the altar in the center of the orchestra.

Thyromata In Hellenistic Greece, large openings into the second story of the skene.

Tiring house In English Renaissance theatre, a three-story stage house behind the raised platform stage.

Total theatre In Asia, a synthesis or complete integration of all elements—acting, mime, music, dance, and text. Some twentieth-century avant-garde theatre artists have also called for the creation of total theatre.

Tragedy One of the most fundamental forms of western drama. Tragedy involves a serious action of universal significance and has important moral and philosophical implications. Following Aristotle, most critics agree that a tragic hero or heroine should be an essentially admirable person whose downfall elicits our sympathy while leaving us with a feeling that there has in some way been a triumph of the moral and cosmic order which transcends the fate of any individual. The disastrous outcome of a tragedy should be seen as the inevitable result of the character and his or her situation, including forces beyond the character's control. Traditionally, tragedy was about the lives and fortunes of people of stature—kings, queens, and the nobility—and there has been a great deal of debate about whether or not modern tragedy, tragedy about ordinary people, is possible.

Tragic flaw The factor that is a character's chief weakness and makes him or her most vulnerable; it often intensifies in time of stress. At times, an abused and incorrectly applied theory from Greek drama.

Tragicomedy In the Renaissance, plays that had tragic themes and noble characters yet ended happily. Modern tragicomedy combines serious and comic elements.

Many plays of this type involve comic or ironic treatment of a serious theme.

Trap Opening in the stage floor, normally covered, which can be used for special effects, such as having scenery or performers rise from below, or which permits the construction of a staircase that ostensibly leads to a lower floor or cellar.

Trilogy In classical Greece, three tragedies written by the same playwright and presented on one day; they were usually connected by story or thematic concerns.

Tropes In the early Middle Ages, lyrics added to musical passages in religious services; these interpolations were often structured like playlets and evolved into liturgical drama.

Tsure In nō theatre, a secondary role.

Übermarionette "Superpuppet": term coined by Edward Gordon Craig in the early twentieth century to describe what he considered the ideal performer—one who would allow the director to control the performance totally.

Unities Term referring to the rule that a play should occur within one day (unity of time), in one place (unity of place), and with no action irrelevant to the plot (unity of action). Contrary to widespread opinion, Aristotle insisted only on unity of action. Certain neoclassical critics of the Renaissance insisted on all three unities.

Unit setting Single setting, developed by Edward Gordon Craig, that can be made to represent various locales by moving basic elements and adding properties.

University wits In the English Renaissance, university graduates and professional dramatists who wrote plays based on Roman models but incorporating some medieval elements.

Vomitoria In Roman theatre, covered exits for the performers.

Waki "Explainer": in Japanese nō, the second most important character.

Well-made play Type of play popular in the nineteenth century and early twentieth century which combined apparent plausibility of incident and surface realism with a tightly constructed and contrived plot.

Wings (1) Left and right offstage areas. (2) Narrow standing pieces of scenery, or "legs," more or less parallel to the proscenium, which form the sides of a setting.

Yard In Elizabethan public theatres, the pit, or standing area.

Zanni In commedia dell'arte, comic male servants.

Zarzuela In the Spanish golden age, a court entertainment; usually, a short, stylized musical drama based on mythology and with ornate scenic effects, influenced by Italian opera and intermezzi.

Zibaldoni In the Italian Renaissance, manuscripts compiled by actors in commedia dell'arte, containing jokes, comic business, and repeated scenes and speeches; some of these manuscripts survive today.

Pronunciation Guide

Theatrical Terms and Names

Note: This is a list of phonetic spellings to assist in the pronunciation of technical terms, place names, names of theatrical figures—actors, directors, designers, playwrights—and names of characters in plays. (The stress is put on the syllable that is in capital letters.)

Abydos .... ah-BEE-dohs
Academia dei Confidenti .... ak-uh-DEE-mee-uh day-ee cohn-fee-DAHN-tee
Accesi .... a-CHAY-see
Aeschylus .... EHS-kih-luhs
Aesopus .... EH-soh-pus
Agamemnon .... ag-uh-MEHM-nahn
agon .... AG-ohn
agonthetes .... ag-ohn-THEH-tees
Alcestis .... al-SEHS-tis
Aleotti .... ah-lee-AH-tee
Aminta .... ah-MEEN-tah
Amphitryon .... am-FIH-tree-ahn
Andreini .... an-DREE-nee
Andromache .... an-DRAHM-uh-kee
Andromède .... AN-droh-mehd
Antigone .... an-TIHG-uh-nee
aposentos .... a-pos-SEHN-tohs
Aragoto .... ah-rah-GAH-toh
architettura .... ahr-kih-teh-TOOR-ah
archon .... AHR-kahn
Arion .... uh-RYE-uhn
Aristophanes .... ar-ih-STAH-fuh-nees
Aristotle .... AR-ih-stah-tuhl
Arlecchino .... ar-leh-KEE-noh
Artaud .... ar-TOH
Atipho Phaedria .... a-TEE-fo FAY-dree-ah
Atreus .... AY-tree-uhs
auleum .... AW-lee-uhm

Aulis .... AW-lihs
autos sacramentales .... AW-tohs sa-crah-mehn-TAH-lehs
avant-garde.. ah-VAHNT-GAHRD

Bacchae .... BAK-ee
Beaumarchais .... boh-mar-SHAY
Bharata.. buh-RUHT-uh
Bibiena .... bib-ee-AY-nuh
biwa... BEE-wah
Bourges .... BOORZH
Brecht.. BREKHT
Büchner .... BOOKH-nuhr
bunraku .... buhn-RAH-koo

Calderón .... KAWL-deh-rohn
Capek, Karel .... CHAH-pehk, KAR-ehl
Cao, Yu.. KOW, YOO
carros .... KAH-rohs
Castelvetro, Lodovico.......................... kas-tehl-VEHT-roh, loh-duh-VEE-koh
cavea... KAH-vee-uh
Centlivre .... sehn-LEE-vruh
Champmeslé... sham-MAY-zlay
chiaroscuro .... kee-ow-roh-SKOO-roh
Chikamatsu Monzaemon .... CHEE-kah-MAHT-soo MOHN-zah-eh-MOHN
Choephori .... koh-EHF-uh-ree
choregus... koh-REE-gus
choregoi .... koh-REE-gaw-ee
chorodidaskalos .... koh-roh-dih-DAHS-kah-los
Comédie Française.............................. koh-may-DEE frahn-SEYZ
comédie larmoyante............................ koh-may-DEE lahr-moy-AHNT
commedia dell'arte.............................. koh-MAY-dee-ah dehl-AHR-teh
compañias de parte .... kahm-pa-NYEE-ahs day PAHR-teh
confraternities .... kohn-FRAH-tuhr-nih-tees
Copeau.. kah-POH
Coquelin, Constant-Benoît .... kohk-LAIN, kawn-STAHN beh-NWAH
Corneille .... kawr-NAY
Creon .... KREE-ahn

denouement .... deh-noo-MAHN
deus ex machina.................................. DEH-ews eks MAH-kih-nah
Diderot... DEE-deh-roh

Dionysia	dye-uh-NEE-see-uh
Dionysus	dye-uh-NYE-suhs
dithyrambic	dihth-ih-RAM-bik
dominus	DOH-mih-nuhs
doyen	doy-EHN
Dottore	doh-TOH-reh
drame bourgeois	DRAM boor-ZHWAH
Drottningholm	DROT-nihng-holm
Duse	DOO-zuh
ekkyklema	eh-KIH-kleh-mah
Epidamnus	eh-pih-DAM-nuhs
episkenion	eh-pih-SKEH-nee-uhn
Erotium	eh-rah-TEE-um
Eteocles	eh-TEE-uh-klees
Etruria	ee-TROO-ree-uh
Eumenides	yoo-MEHN-ih-dees
Euripides	yuh-RIH-pih-dees
Farnese	Fahr-NEH-seh
Festspielhaus	FEHST-shpeel-haus
Francesco	fran-CHEHS-koh
Freie Bühne	FRYE-eh BOO-neh
Gao Ming	GAH-oh MIHNG
Gesamtkunstwerk	geh-zamt-KOONST-verk
Giraudoux	jih-rah-DOO
Gloucester	GLAW-stehr
Godot	guh-DOH
Goethe	GEHR-teh
Goldoni	gohl-DOH-nee
Gottsched	GAHT-shed
Gozzi	GAH-tzee
gradas	GRAH-dahs
Grein	GRYNE
Grotowski	gruh-TUHV-skee
Gyubal Wahazar	gee-OO-bahl wah-HAH-zahr
hanamichi	hah-nah-MEE-chee
Harlequin	HAHR-luh-kwihn
hamartia	hah-MAHR-tee-ah

hashigakari .... hah-shee-gah-KAH-ree
hegemonic .... heh-jeh-MAHN-ik
Hernani.. ehr-NAN-nee
Hippolytus.. hih-PAH-lih-tuhs
Hôtel de Bourgogne........................... oh-TEHL deh bohr-GOH-nyeh
Hrosvitha.. rohs-VEE-tah
hubris.. HYOO-bris

I Gelosi.. EE jel-OH-see
Ikhernofret .... ih-KEHR-noh-freht
innamorata .... ihn-nah-moh-RAH-tah
intermezzi.. ehn-tehr-MEH-tzee
Ionesco... yuh-NEHS-koh
Iphigenia.. ih-fih-jeh-NYE-uh
Isis .... EYE-suhs
Ismene.. is-MEE-nee

Jocasta.. yoh-KAHS-tuh
jorui .... joh-ROO-ree
Junji, Kinoshita.................................. juhn-jee kee-NOH-shee-tah

kabuki .... kah-BOO-kee
Kalidasa.. ka-leh-DAH-sah
Kan'ami.. KAHN AH-MEE
kathakali .... kah-thah-KAH-lee
katharsis... kuh-THAHR-sihs
Kawatake Mokumai .... KAH-wah-TAH-kay MOH-koo-MAH-ee
Kitano .... kee-TAH-noh
Komachi Sotoba .... koh-MAH-chee soh-TOH-bah
kothornoi.. koh-THOR-noy
kothornus .... koh-THOR-nuhs
Kunio, Kishida.................................... KOO-nee-oh kee-SHEE-dah
kyogen.. kee-OH-gehn

Le Gallienne....................................... leh GAH-lee-ehn
Li Yu .... LEE YOO
Lope de Vega...................................... LOH-pay deh VEY-geh
Ludi Florales....................................... LOO-dee floh-RAH-lehs
Lugné-Poë.. LOO-nyeh poh-AY
luñetas.. LOO-nyee-tahs
Lysistrata.. lih-sih-STRAH-tuh

Mahabharata .... muh-HAH-BAH-rah-tuh
Mahabhasya... muh-HAH-BAH-see-yuh
Marais .... ma-RAY
Marinetti.. mah-ruh-NEH-tee
mechane... MEH-kah-neh
de Medici .... deh MEHD-ih-chee
Mei Lanfang.. MAY LAHN-fahng
Menaechmus .... mih-NEK-mahs
Menaechmi... mih-NEK-mee
Messenio .... meh-SEE-nee-oh
Methexis .... Meh-THEX-is
Meyerhold, Vsevelod Emilievich........ Mye-her-hohld, ZEH-veh-lohd eh-MEE-lee-eh-vihtch
Miles Gloriosus .... MEE-lehs gloh-ree-OH-suhs
mimesis.. MYE-MEE-sihs
Minturno, Antonio .... mihn-TOOR-noh, an-TOH-nee-oh
Mnouchkine .... noosh-KEEN
Molière... moh-lee-AIR
motomasa .... moh-toh-MAH-sah

Natyasastra .... nat-yuh-SAHS-truh
naumachia .... naw-MAH-kee-uh
Neuber .... NOY-ber
Nietzsche.. NEE-tsheh

Oedipus .... EHD-uh-puhs
Oeta... oh-EH-tah
Okuni... uh-KOO-nee
Olimpico... oh-LIHM-pee-koh
onkos.. AHN-kohs
Oresteia.. oh-reh-STEE-uh
Orbecche.. Orh-BEHK-eh
Osiris.. oh-SYE-rihs
Oxenstierna .... UHK-sehn-SHTEHR-nah

Pantalone... pan-tah-LOH-nay
parabasis .... puh-RAB-uh-sihs
parados .... PAR-uh-dohs
paraskenia.. pa-ra-SKEE-nee-ah
Pathelin .... pa-the-LAIN
Peniculus.. peh-NIH-kyoo-luhs
pensionnaires .... pehn-see-ohn-AYRES

periaktoi... peh-ree-AHK-toy
Peruzzi, Baldassare .... peh-ROOT-zee, BAHL-dah-SAH-reh
Philoctetes .... fih-luhk-TEE-tees
Phormio... FOHR-mee-oh
pinakes .... pih-NAH-kehs
platea... PLAH-tay-ah
plebians... pleh-BEE-ahns
Plutus .... PLOO-tuhs
Polyneices .... pohl-eh-NEE-sees
Poquelin, Jean-Baptiste .... poh-kah-LAIN, ZHAHN bap-TEEST
proagon... proh-AH-gohn
proedria .... proh-EH-dree-ah
prologos .... proh-LOH-gohs
Prometheus... pruh-MEE-thee-uhs
Pseudolus .... SOO-dah-luhs
pulpitum.. PUHL-pih-tuhm

Qi Rushan .... KEE roo-SHAHN
Quem quaeritis................................... KWEHM KWAY-rih-tihs

Ramayana .... rah-mah-YAH-nah
recitative .... reh-sih-tah-TEEVE
régisseur .... ray-zhee-SUHR
Richelieu .... REESH-loo
Roscius .... ROHSH-ee-uhs

Sabbioneta .... sah-bee-ohn-NEH-tah
Salle des Machines .... SALLE day MAH-sheen
Salmacida Spolia .... sahl-mah-SEE-dah SPOH-lee-ah
santería .... san-tah-REE-ah
satyr .... SAY-tuhr
scaena.. SKAY-nuh
Scaliger .... SKAL-ih-juhr
Scamozzi .... skah-MOH-zee
Serlio .... SEHR-lee-oh
Shakuntala .... shah-KUHN-tah-lah
shaman.. SHAY-mehn (or) SHAH-mehn
shamisen .... SHAH-mee-sehn
Shii No Shosho .... SHEE-eh NOH SHOH-shoh
shite .... SHEE-tay
siparium .... sih-PAH-ree-uhm

skene .... SKEE-nee
Sofonisba .... soh-fohn-NIHS-bah
Sophocles .... SAH-feh-klees
Sotoba Komachi .... Soh-TOH-bah koh-MAH-chee
sottie .... SAH-tee
Svoboda .... SVOH-boh-dah
Tagore, Rabindranath .... teh-GOHR, reh-BEEN-dreh-nath
taburetes .... tah-boo-REH-tehs
Tasso, Torquato .... TAH-soh, tawr-KAW-toh
Taziya .... Tah-ZEE-yuh
Téatro Farnese .... tay-AH-troh fahr-NEH-seh
Teiresias .... tye-REE-see-uhs
tetralogy .... teh-TRAH-loh-jee
Théâtre du Marais .... tay-AH-truh doo mah-RAY
Théâtre Libre .... tay-AH-truh LEE-bruh
theatron .... thee-AY-trahn
Thebes .... THEEBS
Thérèse Raquin .... teh-RAYS rah-KAN
thespian .... THEHS-pee-ehn
Thespis .... THEHS-pihs
Thyestes .... thye-EHS-tees
thymele .... THYE-meh-lee
thyromata .... thye-ROH-mah-tah
Torelli .... toh-REHL-ee
Trachiniae .... treh-KIHN-ee-ay
tsure .... TSUH-ray
Tsurya Namboku .... TSUH-roo-yah NAHN-boh-koo
Turandot .... TOO-rahn-daht
Tzara .... TSAH-rah

Uruashi .... oo-roo-AH-shee

verisimilitude .... veh-rih-sih-MIHL-ih-tood
Vikrama .... vih-KRAH-mah
vodun .... VOH-dun

Wang Shifu .... WAHNG SHEE-foo
Witkiewicz, Stanisław Ignacy .... viht-KEH-vihch, stan-HIS-wahv ihg-NATS
Woyzeck .... VOY-tsek

Yeats .... YAYTS
Yuan .... yoo-AHN
yugen .... YOO-jihn

Zeami .... zay-AH-mee
zibaldoni .... zih-bahl-DOH-nee

Selected Bibliography

GENERAL THEATRE HISTORIES

Banham, Martin, et al., *The Cambridge Guide to African and Caribbean Theatre.* Cambridge University Press, New York, 1994.

Banham, Martin (ed.), *The Cambridge Guide to the Theatre,* 2d ed., Cambridge University Press, New York, 1995.

Beadle, Richard (ed.), *The Cambridge Companion to Medieval English Theatre,* Cambridge University Press, New York, 1994.

Berthold, Margot, *A History of World Theatre: From the Beginnings to the Baroque,* Felicia Londrè (trans.), Ungar, New York, 1972.

Brandon, James R. (ed.), *Cambridge Guide to Asian Theatre,* Cambridge University Press, New York, 1993.

Brockett, Oscar, with Franklin J. Hildy, *History of the Theatre,* 9th ed., Allyn and Bacon, Boston, 2003.

_______, and Robert Findlay, *Century of Innovation: A History of European and American Theatre and Drama since the Late Nineteenth Century,* 2d ed., Allyn and Bacon, Boston, 1991.

Brown, John Russell (ed.), *The Oxford Illustrated History of Theatre,* Oxford University Press, New York, 1997.

Carlson, Marvin A., *Places of Performance: The Semiotics of Theatre Architecture,* Cornell University Press, Ithaca, N.Y., 1989.

_______, *Theories of the Theatre: A Historical and Critical Survey from the Greeks to the Present,* expanded ed., Cornell University Press, Ithaca, N.Y., 1993.

Note: This is a list of significant general historical works for and specific works for each period covered in the textbook. It is of course, only a selected bibliography of the many works available in English.

Cole, Toby, and Helen K. Chinoy (eds.), *Actors on Acting,* rev. ed., Crown, New York, 1980.

_______, *Directors on Directing: A Source Book of the Modern Theatre,* Macmillan, New York, 1986.

Gillespie, Patti P., and Kenneth M. Cameron, *Western Theatre: Revolution and Revival,* Macmillan, New York, 1984.

Hartnoll, Phyllis, and Peter Found (eds.), *The Concise Oxford Companion to the Theatre,* new ed., Oxford University Press, New York, 1993.

Londrè, Felicia, *The History of World Theatre: From the English Restoration to the Present,* Continuum, New York, 1991.

Londrè, Felicia Hardison, and Daniel J. Watermeier, *The History of North American Theater: From Pre-Columbian Times to the Present,* Continuum, New York, 1998.

Nagler, Alois M., *Sources of Theatrical History,* Theatre Annual, New York, 1952.

Partnow, Elaine T., *The Female Dramatist: Profiles of Women Playwrights from the Middle Ages to Contemporary Times,* Facts on File, New York, 1998.

Roberts, Vera M., *On Stage: A History of the Theatre,* 2d ed., Harper and Row, New York, 1974.

Rubin, Don (ed.), *World Encyclopedia of Contemporary Theatre,* 5 vols., Routledge, New York, 1995–1999.

Watson, Jack, and Grant F. McKernie, *A Cultural History of Theatre,* Longman, New York, 1993.

Wickham, Glynne, *A History of the Theatre,* Cambridge, Cambridge University Press, 1992.

Wilmeth, Don B., and Tice L. Miller (eds.), *Cambridge Guide to American Theatre,* 2d ed., Cambridge University Press, New York, 1996.

Witham, Barry (ed.), *Theatre in the United States: A Documentary History,* Cambridge University Press, New York, 1996.

Zarrilli, Phillip B., Bruce McConachie, et al., *Theatre Histories: An Introduction,* Routledge, New York, 2006.

INTRODUCTION

Bratton, Jacky, *New Readings in Theatre History,* Cambridge University Press, Cambridge, 2003.

Brown, Ivor, *The First Player: The Origin of Drama,* Morrow, New York, 1928.

Case, Sue-Ellen, and Janelle Reinelt (eds.), *The Performance of Power: Theatrical Discourse and Politics,* University of Iowa Press, Iowa City, 1991.

Dolan, Jill, *The Feminist Spectator as Critic,* University of Michigan Press, Ann Arbor, 1991.

Gainor, J. Ellen (ed.), *Imperialism and Theatre,* Routledge, New York, 1995.

Hunningher, Ben, *The Origin of the Theater,* Hill and Wang, New York, 1961.

Kirby, E. T., *Ur-Drama: The Origins of Theatre,* New York University Press, New York, 1975.

Postlewait, Thomas, and Bruce McConachie (eds.), *Interpreting the Theatrical Past: Essays in the Historiography of Performance,* University of Iowa Press, Iowa City, 1989.

Ridgeway, William, *The Drama and Dramatic Dances of Non-European Races,* Cambridge University Press, Cambridge, 1915.

Solomon, Alisa, *Re-Dressing the Canon: Essays on Theatre and Gender,* Routledge, New York, 1997.

Turner, Victor, *From Ritual to Theatre,* Performing Arts Journal Publications, New York, 1982.

Wiles, David, *A Short History of Western Performance Space,* Cambridge University Press, Cambridge, 2003.

Wise, Jennifer, *Dionysus Writes: The Invention of Theatre in Ancient Greece,* Cornell University Press, Ithaca, N.Y., 1998.

CHAPTER 1: GREEK THEATRE

Arnott, Peter D., *The Ancient Greek and Roman Theatre,* Random House, New York, 1971.

———, *Public and Performance in the Greek Theatre,* Routledge, New York, 1991.

Aylen, Leo, *The Greek Theater,* Associated University Presses, London, 1985.

Bieber, Margarete, *The History of Greek and Roman Theater,* 2d ed., Princeton University Press, Princeton, N.J., 1961.

Butler, James H., *The Theatre and Drama of Greece and Rome,* Chandler, San Francisco, Calif., 1972.

Csapo, Eric, and William J. Slater, *The Context of Ancient Drama,* University of Michigan Press, Ann Arbor, 1995.

Dearden, C. W., *The Stage of Aristophanes,* London, Athlone, 1976.

Easterling, P. E., *The Cambridge Companion to Greek Tragedy,* Cambridge University Press, Cambridge, 1997.

Edmunds, Lowell, and Robert W. Wallace (eds.), *Poet, Public, and Performance in Ancient Greece,* Johns Hopkins University Press, Baltimore, Md., 1997.

Flickinger, Roy C., *The Greek Theatre and Its Drama,* 4th ed., University of Chicago Press, Chicago, Ill., 1936.

Green, J. R., *Theatre in Ancient Greek Society,* Routledge, New York, 1995.

O'Higgins, Laurie, *Women and Humor in Classical Greece,* Cambridge University Press, Cambridge, 2003.

Pickard-Cambridge, A. W., *The Dramatic Festivals of Athens,* reissued ed., Oxford University Press, New York, 1988.

Rehm, Rush, *Greek Tragic Theatre,* Routledge, New York, 1992.

Scott, William C., *Musical Design in Aeschylean Theatre,* University Press of New England, Hanover, N.H., 1984.

_______, *Musical Design in Sophoclean Theatre,* University Press of New England, Hanover, N.H., 1996.

Stone, Laura, *Costume in Aristophanic Comedy,* Arno, New York, 1981.

Taaffe, Lauren K., *Aristophanes and Women,* Routledge, New York, 1994.

Taplin, Oliver, *Greek Tragedy in Action,* Routledge, London, 1993.

Vince, Ronald W., *Ancient and Medieval Theatre: A Historiographical Handbook,* Greenwood, Westport, Conn., 1984.

Walton, J. Michael, *Greek Theatre Practice,* Greenwood, Westport, Conn., 1980.

_______, *Living Greek Theatre: A Handbook of Classical Performance and Modern Production,* Greenwood, Westport, Conn., 1987.

Webster, T. B. L., *S,* 2d ed., Methuen, London, 1970.

Wiles, David, *The Masks of Menander: Sign and Meaning in Greek and Roman Performance,* Cambridge University Press, New York, 1991.

_______, *Tragedy in Athens: Performance Space and Theatrical Meaning,* Cambridge University Press, New York, 1997.

_______, *Greek Theatre Performance,* Cambridge University Press, Cambridge, 2000.

CHAPTER 2: ROMAN THEATRE

Allen, James T., *Stage Antiquities of the Greeks and Romans and Their Influence,* McKay, New York, 1927.

Arnott, Peter D., *The Ancient Greek and Roman Theatre,* Random House, New York, 1971.

Beacham, Richard C., *The Roman Theatre and Its Audience,* Harvard University Press, Cambridge, Mass., 1992.

_______, *Spectacle Entertainments of Early Imperial Rome,* Yale University Press, New Haven, Conn., 1999.

Beare, William, *The Roman Stage: A Short History of Latin Drama in the Time of the Republic,* Methuen, London, 1968.

Bieber, Margarete, *The History of Greek and Roman Theater,* 2d ed., Princeton University Press, Princeton, N.J., 1961.

Butler, James H., *The Theatre and Drama of Greece and Rome,* Chandler, San Francisco, Calif., 1972.

Csapo, Eric, and William J. Slater, *The Context of Ancient Drama,* University of Michigan Press, Ann Arbor, 1995.

Duckworth, George E., *The Nature of Roman Comedy,* 2d ed., University of Oklahoma Press, Norman, 1994.

Forehand, Walter E., *Terence,* Twayne, Boston, Mass., 1985.

Slater, William J. (ed.), *Roman Theatre and Society,* University of Michigan Press, Ann Arbor, 1995.

Vince, Ronald W., *Ancient and Medieval Theater: A Historiographical Handbook,* Greenwood, Westport, Conn., 1984.

Wiles, David, *The Masks of Menander: Sign and Meaning in Greek and Roman Performance,* Cambridge University Press, New York, 1991.

Zagagi, Netta, *The Comedy of Menander: Convention, Variation, Originality,* Indiana University Press, Bloomington, 1995.

CHAPTER 3: EARLY ASIAN THEATRES

Arnott, Peter, *The Theatres of Japan,* Macmillan, New York, 1969.

Bowers, Faubion, *Theatre in the East: A Survey of Asian Dance and Drama,* Grove, New York, 1969.

Dolby, William, *A History of the Chinese Drama,* Harper and Row, New York, 1976.

Ernst, Earle, *The Kabuki Theatre,* Oxford University Press, New York, 1957.

Fei, Faye Chunfung (ed. and trans.), *Chinese Theories of Performance from Confucius to the Present,* University of Michigan Press, Ann Arbor, 2002.

Gargi, Balwant, *Theatre in India,* Theatre Arts, New York, 1962.

Jain, Nemi Chandra, *Indian Theatre: Tradition, Continuity, and Change,* Vikas, New Delhi, 1992.

Keene, Donald, and Kaneko Hiroshi, *No and Bunraku: Two Forms of Japanese Theatre,* Columbia University Press, New York, 1990.

Howard, Roger, *Contemporary Chinese Theatre,* Heinemann Educational, London, 1978.

Leiter, Samuel L., *The Art of Kabuki: Famous Plays in Performance,* University of California Press, Berkeley, 1979.

_______, *New Kabuki Encyclopedia,* Greenwood, Westport, Conn., 1997.

Ortolani, Benito, *The Japanese Theatre: From Shamanistic Ritual to Contemporary Pluralism,* rev. ed., Princeton University Press, Princeton, N.J., 1995.

Richmond, Farley, et al., *Indian Theatre: Traditions of Performance,* University of Hawaii Press, Honolulu, 1990.

Scott, A. C., *The Classical Theatre of China,* Allen and Unwin, London, 1957.

Waley, Arthur, *The No Plays of Japan,* Knopf, New York, 1922.

CHAPTER 4: MEDIEVAL THEATRES IN EUROPE

Butterworth, Philip, *Theatre of Fire: Special Effects in Early English and Scottish Theatre,* Society for Theatre Research, London, 1998.

Case, Sue-Ellen, "Re-Viewing Hrosvit," *Theatre Journal,* 35, December 1983, pp. 533–542.

Chambers, E. K., *The Medieval Stage,* 2 vols., Clarendon, Oxford, 1903.

Davidson, Clifford, *Technology, Guilds, and Early English Drama,* Medieval Institute Publications, Kalamazoo, Mich., 1996.

Dunbar, Ogden H., *The Staging of Drama in the Medieval Church,* Associated University Presses, Cranbury, N.J., 2001.

Enders, Jody, *Death by Drama and Other Medieval Urban Legends,* University of Chicago Press, Chicago, Ill., 2002.

_______, *The Medieval Theatre of Cruelty,* Cornell University Press, Ithaca, N.Y., 1999.

_______, *Rhetoric and the Origins of Medieval Drama,* Cornell University Press, Ithaca, N.Y., 1992.

Hanawalt, Barbara A., and Michal Kobialka (eds.), *Medieval Practices of Space,* University of Minnesota Press, Minneapolis, 2000.

Hardison, O. B., *Christian Rite and Christian Drama in the Middle Ages,* John Hopkins Press, Baltimore, Md., 1965.

Kobialka, Michal, *This Is My Body: Representational Practices in the Early Middle Ages,* University of Michigan Press, Ann Arbor, 1999.

Mills, David, *Recycling the Cycle,* University of Toronto Press, Toronto, 1998.

Muir, Lynette, R., *The Biblical Drama of Medieval Europe,* Cambridge University Press, New York, 1995.

Nagler, Alois M., *Medieval Religious Stage: Shapes and Phantoms,* George C. Schoolfield (trans.), Yale University Press, New Haven, Conn., 1976.

Nelson, Alan H., *The Medieval English Stage: Corpus Christi Pageants and Plays,* University of Chicago Press, Chicago, Ill., 1974.

Normington, Katie, *Gender and Medieval Drama,* Brewer, Rochester, N.Y., 2004.

Tyedeman, William, *English Medieval Theatre, 1400–1500,* Routledge and Kegan Paul, London, 1986.

_______, Michael J. Anderson, and Nick Davis (eds.), *The Medieval European Stage, 500–1550,* Cambridge University Press, Cambridge, 2001.

Vince, Ronald W., *Ancient and Medieval Theatre: A Historiographical Handbook,* Greenwood, Westport, Conn., 1984.

Vince, Ronald W. (ed.), *A Companion to the Medieval Theatre,* Greenwood, Westport, Conn., 1989.

Wickham, Glynne, *The Medieval Theatre,* Weidenfeld and Nicolson, London, 1974.

Young, Karl, *The Drama of the Medieval Church,* 2 vols., Clarendon, Oxford, 1933.

CHAPTER 5: THE THEATRE OF THE ITALIAN RENAISSANCE

Andrews, Richard, *Scripts and Scenarios: The Performance of Comedy in Renaissance Italy,* Cambridge University Press, Cambridge, 1993.

Bjurstrom, Per, *Giacomo Torelli and Baroque Stage Design,* Nationalmuseum, Stockholm, 1961.

Cairns, Christopher (ed.), *The Renaissance Theatre: Texts, Performance, and Design,* Ashgate, Brookfield, Vt., 1999.

_______ (ed.), *Scenery, Set, and Staging in the Italian Renaissance,* Edwin Mellon Press, Lewiston, N.Y., 1996.

Ducharte, Pierre, *The Italian Comedy,* R. T. Weaver (trans.), Dover, New York, 1966.

Henke, Robert, *Performance and Literature in the Commedia dell'Arte,* Cambridge University Press, Cambridge, 2003.

Hewitt, Barnard (ed.), *The Renaissance Stage: Documents of Serlio, Sabbatini, and Fürttenbach,* University of Miami Press, Coral Gables, Fla., 1958.

Kennard, Joseph S., *Italian Theatre,* B. Blom, New York, 1964.

Lazzi: The Comic Routines of the Commedia dell'Arte, Mel Gordon (ed. and trans.), Performing Arts Journal, New York, 1992.

Mullin, Daniel C., *The Development of the Playhouse: A Survey of Architecture from the Renaissance to the Present,* University of California Press, Berkeley, 1970.

Mulryne, J. R., and Margaret Shewring, *Theatre of the English and Italian Renaissance,* St. Martin's, New York, 1991.

Oosting, J. Thomas, *Andrea Palladio's Teatro Olimpico,* UMI Research Press, Ann Arbor, 1981.

Richards, Kenneth, and Laura Richards, *The Commedia dell'Arte: A Documentary History,* Blackwell, New York, 1990.

Vince, Ronald W., *Renaissance Theatre: A Historiographical Handbook,* Greenwood, Westport, Conn., 1984.

CHAPTER 6: THE THEATRE OF THE ENGLISH RENAISSANCE

Adams, John C., *The Globe Playhouse: Its Design and Equipment,* Barnes and Noble, New York, 1966.

Astington, John, *English Court Theatre, 1558–1642,* Cambridge University Press, New York, 1999.

Beckerman, Bernard, *Shakespeare at the Globe, 1599–1602,* Macmillan, New York, 1962.

Bentley, Gerald E., *The Profession of Player in Shakespeare's Time, 1590–1642,* Princeton University Press, Princeton, N.J., 1984.

Callaghan, Dympna, *Shakespeare without Women: Representing Gender and Race on the Renaissance Stage,* Routledge, New York, 2000.

Chambers, E. K., *The Elizabethan Stage,* 4 vols., Clarendon, Oxford, 1965.

Eccles, Christine, *The Rose Theatre,* Routledge, New York, 1990.

Graves, R. R., *Lighting the Shakespearean Stage, 1567–1642.* Southern Illinois University Press, Carbondale, 1999.

Gurr, Andrew, *Playgoing in Shakespeare's London,* 2d ed., Cambridge University Press, New York, 1996.

_______, *The Shakespearean Playing Companies,* Oxford University Press, New York, 1996.

_______, *The Shakespearean Stage, 1574–1642,* Cambridge University Press, Cambridge, 1970.

_______, and John Orrell, *Rebuilding Shakespeare's Globe,* Routledge, New York, 1989.

Hildy, Franklin J. (ed.), *New Issues in the Reconstruction of Shakespeare's Theatre: Proceedings of the Conference Held at the University of Georgia,* February 16–18, 1990, vol. 1, *Artists and Issues in the Theatre,* Lang, New York, 1990.

Hodges, C. W., *The Globe Restored: A Study of the Elizabethan Theatre,* Coward, McCann, and Geoghegan, New York, 1953.

Hodges, C. Walter, *The Staging of Shakespeare's Plays, 1576–1616,* Cambridge University Press, New York, 1999.

Ingram, William, *The Business of Playing: The Beginning of the Adult Professional Theatre in Elizabethan London,* Cornell University Press, Ithaca, N.Y., 1993.

Knutson, Roslyn Lander, *Playing Companies and Commerce in Shakespeare's Time,* Cambridge University Press, Cambridge, 2001.

Leggatt, Alexander, *Jacobean Public Theatre,* Routledge, New York, 1992.

McMillin, Scott, *The Queen's Men and Their Plays,* Cambridge University Press, New York, 1998.

Mulrayne, J. R., and Margaret Shewring, *Theatre of the English and Italian Renaissance,* St. Martin's, New York, 1991.

Nagler, Alois M., *Shakespeare's Stage,* Yale University Press, New Haven, 1958.

Orgel, Stephen, *Impersonations: the Performance of Gender in Shakespeare's England,* Cambridge University Press, New York, 1996.

Orrell, John, *The Human Stage: English Theatre Design, 1567–1640,* Cambridge University Press, New York, 1988.

Peacock, John, *The Stage Designs of Inigo Jones,* Cambridge University Press, New York, 1995.

Shapiro, Michael, *Gender in Play on the Shakespearean Stage: Boy Heroines and Female Pages,* University of Michigan Press, Ann Arbor, 1995.

Smith, Irwin, *Shakespeare's Blackfriar's Playhouse: Its History and Its Design,* New York University Press, New York, 1964.

Stern, Tiffany, *Rehearsal from Shakespeare to Sheridan,* Oxford University Press, Oxford, 2000.

Thomson, Peter, *Shakespeare's Theatre,* Routledge, New York, 1992.

Vince, Ronald W., *Renaissance Theater: A Historiographical Handbook,* Greenwood, Westport, Conn., 1984.

White, Martin, *Renaissance Drama in Action,* Routledge, New York, 1998.

Wickham, Glynne, Herbert Berry, and William Ingram, *English Professional Theatre, 1530–1660,* Cambridge University Press, Cambridge, 2000.

CHAPTER 7: THE THEATRE OF THE SPANISH GOLDEN AGE

Allen, John J., *The Reconstruction of a Spanish Golden Age Playhouse: El Corral del Principe, 1583–1744,* University Presses of Florida, Gainesville, Fla., 1983.

Crawford, J. P. W., *Spanish Drama before Lope de Vega,* Lippincott, Philadelphia, Pa., 1937.

Ganelin, Charles, and Howard Mancing (eds.), *The Golden Age Comedia: Text, Theory, and Performance,* Purdue University Press, West Lafayette, Ind., 1994.

McKendrick, Melveena, *Theatre in Spain, 1490–1700,* Cambridge University Press, Cambridge, 1989.

Shergold, N. D., *A History of the Spanish Stage from Medieval Times until the End of the 17th Century,* Clarendon, Oxford, 1967.

Stoll, Anita K., and Dawn L. Smith, *Gender, Identity, and Representation in Spain's Golden Age,* Bucknell University Press, Lewisburg, Pa., 2000.

_______, and _______, *The Perception of Women in Spanish Theater of the Golden Age,* Associated University Presses, Cranbury, N.J., 1991.

Vince, Ronald W., *Renaissance Theater: A Historiographical Handbook,* Greenwood, Westport, Conn., 1984.

CHAPTER 8: FRENCH NEOCLASSICAL THEATRE

Arnott, Peter D., *An Introduction to the French Theatre,* Rowman and Littlefield, Totowa, N.J., 1977.

Clarke, Jan, *The Guénégaud Theatre in Paris (1673–1680),* Mellon, Lewiston, N.Y., 2001.

Herzel, Roger W. *The Original Casting of Molière's Plays,* University of Michigan Press, Ann Arbor, 1981.

Howarth, William D., et al. (eds.), *French Theatre in the Neo Classical Era, 1550–1789,* Cambridge University Press, New York, 1997.

Lawrenson, T. E., *The French Stage in the 17th Century: A Study in the Advent of the Italian Order,* rev. ed., AMS, New York, 1986.

Lough, John, *Paris Theatre Audiences in the Seventeenth and Eighteenth Centuries,* Oxford University Press, Oxford, 1957.

Ravel, Jeffrey S., *The Contested Parterre: Public Theatre and French Political Culture, 1680–1791,* Cornell University Press, Ithaca, N.Y., 1999.

Scott, Virginia, *The Commedia dell'Arte in Paris, 1644–1697,* University of Virginia Press, Charlottesville, 1990.

Tollini, Paul, *Scene Design in the Court of Louis XIV: The Work of the Vigarini Family and Jean Berain,* Mellon, Lewiston, N.Y., 2003.

Turnell, Martin, *The Classical Moment: Studies in Corneille, Molière, and Racine,* New Directions, New York, 1963.

Vince, Ronald W., *Renaissance Theater: A Historiographical Handbook,* Greenwood, Westport, Conn., 1984.

Wiley, W. L., *The Early Public Theatre in France,* Harvard University Press, Cambridge, Mass., 1960.

CHAPTER 9: THE THEATRE OF THE ENGLISH RESTORATION

Fisk, Deborah Payne (ed.), *The Cambridge Companion to English Restoration Theatre,* Cambridge University Press, Cambridge, 2000.

Hotson, Leslie, *The Commonwealth and Restoration Stage,* Russell and Russell, New York, 1962.

Howe, Elizabeth. *The First English Actresses: Women and Drama, 1660–1700,* Cambridge University Press, New York, 1992.

Hume, Robert D. (ed.), *The London Theatre World, 1660–1800,* Southern Illinois University Press, Carbondale, 1980.

Johnson, Odai, *Rehearsing the Revolution: Radical Politics in the English Restoration,* University of Delaware Press, Newark, 2000.

Kenny, Shirley Strum (ed.), *British Theatre and the Other Arts, 1660–1800,* Folger, Washington, D.C., 1984.

The London Stage, 1660–1800, 11 vols., Southern Illinois University Press, Carbondale, 1960–1968.

McCollum, John I. (ed.), *The Restoration Stage,* Houghton Mifflin, Boston, Mass., 1961.

Milhous, Judith, and Robert D. Hume, *Producible Interpretation: Eight English Plays, 1675–1707,* Southern Illinois University Press, Carbondale, 1985.

Southern, Richard, *Changeable Scenery: Its Origin and Development in the British Theatre,* Faber and Faber, London, 1952.

Summers, Montague, *The Restoration Theatre,* Macmillan, New York, 1934.

Vince, Ronald W., *Neoclassical Theatre: A Historiographical Handbook,* Greenwood, Westport, Conn., 1988.

CHAPTER 10: THEATRES IN THE EIGHTEENTH CENTURY

Baur-Heinhold, Margarete, *The Baroque Theatre: A Cultural History of the 17th and 18th Centuries,* McGraw-Hill, New York, 1967.

Brandt, George W. (ed.), *German and Dutch Theatre, 1600–1848,* Cambridge University Press, New York, 1993.

Brown, Frederick, *Theater and Revolution: The Culture of the French Stage,* Viking, New York, 1980.

Brown, Jared, *The Theatre in America during the Revolution,* Cambridge University Press, New York, 1995.

Bruford, W. H., *Theatre, Drama, and Audience in Goethe's Germany,* Greenwood, Westport, Conn., 1974.

Carlson, Marvin, *Goethe and the Weimar Theatre,* Cornell University Press, Ithaca, N.Y., 1978.

Carlson, Marvin, *The Italian Stage: From Goldoni to D'Annunzio,* McFarland, Jefferson, N.C., 1981.

Donkin, Ellen, *Getting into the Act: Women Playwrights in London, 1776–1829,* Routledge, New York, 1995.

Donohue, Joseph (ed.), *The Cambridge History of the British Theatre,* Vol. 2, Cambridge University Press, Cambridge, 2004.

Hemmings, F. W. J., *Theatre and State in France, 1760–1905,* Cambridge University Press, New York, 1994.

Hughes, Leo, *The Drama's Patrons: A Study of the 18th Century London Audience,* University of Texas Press, Austin, 1971.

Johnson, Odai, William J. Burling, and James A. Coombs, *The Colonial American Stage, 1665–1774: A Documentary Calendar,* Fairleigh Dickinson University Press, Madison, N.J., 2002.

Kennedy, Emmet, et al., *Theatre, Opera, and Audiences in Revolutionary Paris: Analysis and Repertory,* Greenwood, Westport, Conn., 1996.

Leach, Robert, and Victor Borovsky (eds.), *A History of Russian Theatre,* Cambridge University Press, Cambridge, 1999.

Moody, Jane, *Illegitimate Theatre in London, 1770–1840,* Cambridge University Press, Cambridge, 2000.

Nathans, Heather S., *Early American Theatre from the Revolution to Thomas Jefferson: Into the Hands of the People,* Cambridge University Press, Cambridge, 2003.

Nicoll, Allardyce, *The Garrick Stage,* University of Georgia Press, Athens, 1980.

Pedicord, Harry W., *The Theatrical Public in the Time of Garrick,* King's Crown, New York, 1954.

Price, Cecil, *Theatre in the Age of Garrick,* Rowman and Littlefield, Totowa, N.J., 1973.

Prudhoe, John, *The Theatre of Goethe and Schiller,* Blackwell, Oxford, 1973.

Stone, George Winchester, Jr. (ed.), *The Stage and the Page: London's "Whole Show" in the Eighteenth-Century Theatre,* University of California Press, Berkeley, 1981.

Vince, Ronald W., *Neoclassical Theatre: A Historiographical Handbook,* Greenwood, Westport, Conn., 1988.

Wilmeth, Don B., and Christopher Bigsby (eds.), *The Cambridge History of American Theatre,* Cambridge University Press, New York, 1998.

CHAPTER 11: THEATRES FROM 1800 TO 1875

Bank, Rosemarie K., *Theatre Culture in America, 1825–1860,* Cambridge University Press, New York, 1997.

Booth, Michael, *English Melodrama,* Jenkins, London, 1965.

Brandt, George W. (ed.), *German and Dutch Theatre, 1600–1848,* Cambridge University Press, New York, 1993.

Brown, Frederick, *Theater and Revolution: The Culture of the French Stage,* Viking, New York, 1980.

Carlson, Marvin, *The French Stage in the 19th Century,* Scarecrow, Metuchen, N.J., 1972.

_______, *The German Stage in the 19th Century,* Scarecrow, Metuchen, N.J., 1972.

———, *The Italian Stage,* McFarland, Jefferson, N.C., 1981.

Davis, Tracy C., *Actresses as Working Women: Their Social Identity in Victorian Culture,* Routledge, New York, 1991.

_______ . *The Economics of the British Stage, 1800–1914,* Cambridge University Press, Cambridge, 2000.

_______, and Ellen Donkin, *Women and Playwriting in Nineteenth-Century Britain,* Cambridge University Press, New York, 1999.

Donkin, Ellen, *Getting into the Act: Women Playwrights in London, 1776–1829,* Routledge, New York, 1995.

Durham, Weldon B., ed., *American Theatre Companies, 1749–1887,* Greenwood, Westport, Conn., 1986.

Engle, Ron, and Tice L. Miller (eds.), *The American Stage: Social and Economic Issues from the Colonial Period to the Present,* Cambridge University Press, New York, 2001.

Frick, John W., *Theatre, Culture, and Temperance Reform in Nineteenth-Century America,* Cambridge University Press, New York, 2003.

Gies, David Thatcher, *The Theatre in Nineteenth-Century Spain,* Cambridge University Press, New York, 1994.

Grimstead, David, *Melodrama Unveiled: American Theatre and Culture, 1800–1850,* University of Chicago Press, Chicago, Ill., 1968.

Hatch, James V., *Black Playwrights, 1823–1977: An Annotated Bibliography of Plays,* Bowker, New York, 1977.

Hemmings, F. W. J., *The Theatre Industry in Nineteenth-Century France,* Cambridge University Press, New York, 1993.

_______, *Theatre and State in France, 1760–1905,* Cambridge University Press, Cambridge, 1994.

Marshall, Herbert, and Mildred Stock, *Ira Aldridge: The Negro Tragedian,* Southern Illinois University Press, Carbondale, 1968.

McConachie, Bruce, *Melodramatic Formations: American Theatre and Society, 1820–1870,* University of Iowa Press, Iowa City, 1992.

McCormick, John, *Popular Theatres of Nineteenth-Century France,* Routledge, New York, 1993.

Mackerras, Colin, *The Chinese Theatre in Modern Times: From 1840 to the Present,* University of Massachusetts Press, Amherst, 1975.

Powell, Kerry, *Women and Victorian Theatre,* Cambridge University Press, New York, 1997.

_______ (ed.), *The Cambridge Companion to Victorian and Edwardian Theatre,* Cambridge University Press, Cambridge, 2003.

Rowell, George, *The Victorian Theatre: A Survey,* Oxford University Press, New York, 1956.

Roy, Donald (ed.), *Romantic and Revolutionary Theatre, 1789–1860,* Cambridge University Press, New York, 2003.

Schoch, Richard W. *Shakespeare's Victorian Stage: Performing History in the Theatre of Charles Kean,* Cambridge University Press, Cambridge, 1998.

Vardac, A. Nicholas, *Stage to Screen: Theatrical Methods from Garrick to Griffith,* Harvard University Press, Cambridge, Mass., 1949.

Wilmeth, Don B., and Christopher Bigsby (eds.), *The Cambridge History of the American Theatre,* Vol. 1, *Beginnings to 1870,* Cambridge University Press, Cambridge, 1998.

Williams, Simon, *German Actors of the Eighteenth and Nineteenth Centuries: Idealism, Romanticism, and Realism,* Greenwood, Westport, Conn., 1985.

______, *Richard Wagner and Festival Theatre,* Greenwood, Westport, Conn., 1994.

Witham, Barry B., *Theatre in the United States: A Documentary History,* Vol. 1, *1750–1915, Theatre in the Colonies and the United States,* Cambridge University Press, Cambridge, 1995.

CHAPTER 12: THEATRES FROM 1875 TO 1915

Appia, Adolphe, *Essays, Scenarios, and Designs,* Walther R. Volbach (trans.), Richard C. Beacham (ed.), UMI Research Press, Ann Arbor, 1989.

Beacham, Richard C., *Adolphe Appia: Artist and Visionary of the Modern Theatre,* Harwood Academic, Philadelphia, Pa., 1994.

Benedetti, Jean. *Stanislavski and the Actor,* Routledge/Theatre Arts Books, New York, 1998.

Bentley, Eric, *The Playwright as Thinker: A Study of Drama in Modern Times,* Reynal and Hitchcock, New York, 1946.

Brown, Frederick, *Theater and Revolution: The Culture of the French Stage,* Viking, New York, 1980.

Davis, Tracy C., *George Bernard Shaw and the Socialist Theatre,* Greenwood, Westport, Conn., 1994.

Deak, Frantisek, *Symbolist Theater,* Johns Hopkins University Press, Baltimore, Md., 1993.

Gardner, Vivien, and Susan Rutherford (eds.), *The New Woman and Her Sisters: Feminism and Theatre, 1850–1914,* University of Michigan Press, Ann Arbor, 1992.

Garten, Hugh, *Modern German Drama,* Grove, New York, 1962.

Hatch, James V., *Black Playwrights, 1823–1977: An Annotated Bibliography of Plays,* Bowker, New York, 1977.

———, and Ted Shine, *Black Theater, U.S.A.,* Free Press, New York, 1974.

Innes, Christopher, *Edward Gordon Craig,* Cambridge University Press, New York, 1983.

———, *Avant-Garde Theatre, 1892–1992,* Routledge, New York, 1993.

Isaacs, Edith J., *The Negro in the American Theatre,* Theatre Arts, New York, 1947.

Kershaw, Baz (ed.), *The Cambridge History of British Theatre,* Vol. 3, Cambridge University Press, Cambridge, 2004.

Koller, Ann Marie, *The Theatre Duke: Georg II of Saxe-Meiningen and the German Stage,* Stanford University Press, Palo Alto, Calif., 1984.

Leach, Robert, *Revolutionary Theatre,* London, Routledge, New York, 1994.

Miller, Anna Irene, *The Independent Theatre in Europe: 1887 to the Present,* Long and Smith, New York, 1931.

Mitchell, Loften, *Black Drama: The Story of the American Negro in the Theatre,* Hawthorn, New York, 1967.

Morash, Chris, *A History of Irish Theatre, 1601–2000,* Cambridge University Press, Cambridge, 2002.

Patterson, Michael, *The Revolution in the German Theatre, 1900–1933,* Routledge and Kegan Paul, London, 1981.

Piches, Jonathan, *Vsevolod Meyerhold,* Routledge, London, 2003.

Roose-Evans, James, *Experimental Theatre: From Stanislavsky to Peter Brook,* 2d ed., Routledge, New York, 1996.

Schuler, Catherine, *Women in Russian Theatre: The Actress in the Silver Age,* Routledge, New York, 1996.

Schumacher, Claude (ed.), *Naturalism and Symbolism in European Theatre, 1850 to 1918,* Cambridge University Press, New York, 1996.

Shattuck, Roger, *The Banquet Years: The Arts in France, 1885–1918,* Harcourt, Brace, New York, 1961.

Slonim, Marc, *Russian Theatre from the Empire to the Soviets,* Collier, Cleveland, Ohio, 1962.

Styan, J. L., *Max Reinhardt,* Cambridge University Press, New York, 1982.

Valency, Maurice, *The Flower and the Castle: An Introduction to Modern Drama,* Macmillan, New York, 1963.

Volbach, Walther R., *Adolphe Appia, Prophet of the Modern Theatre,* Wesleyan University Press, Middletown, Conn., 1968.

Whitton, David, *Stage Directors in Modern France: Antoine to Mnouchkine,* Manchester University Press, Manchester, 1987.

Worrall, Nick, *The Moscow Art Theatre,* London, Routledge, 1996.

CHAPTER 13: THEATRES FROM 1915 TO 1945

Abramson, Doris, *Negro Playwrights in the American Theatre, 1925–1959,* Columbia University Press, New York, 1969.

Aronson, Arnold, *American Avant-Garde: A History,* Routledge, New York, 2000.

Artaud, Antonin, *The Theatre and Its Double,* M. C. Richards (trans.), Grove, New York, 1958.

Brecht, Bertolt, *Brecht on Theatre,* John Willett (trans.), Hill and Wang, New York, 1964.

Carter, Huntly, *The New Spirit in the European Theatre, 1914–1924,* Doran, New York, 1926.

Chansky, Dorothy, *Composing Ourselves: The Little Theatre Movement and the American Audience,* Southern Illinois University Press, Carbondale, 2004.

Clunes, Alec, *The British Theatre,* Cassell, London, 1964.

Elam, Harry, and David Krasner, *African American Performance and Theatre History: A Critical Reader,* Oxford University Press, Oxford, 2000.

Eyre, Richard, and Nicholas Wright, *Changing Stages: A View of British and American Theatre in the Twentieth Century,* Bloomsbury, London, 2000.

Fearnow, Mark, *American Stage and the Great Depression,* Cambridge University Press, New York, 1997.

Fraden, Rena, *Blueprints for a Black Federal Theatre, 1935–1939,* Cambridge University Press, New York, 1994.

Fuegi, John, *Brecht and Company,* Grove, New York, 1994.

Gadberry, Glen (ed.), *Theatre in the Third Reich, The Prewar Years: Essays on Theatre in Nazi Germany,* Greenwood, Westport, Conn., 1995.

Goldberg, RoseLee, *Performance Art: From Futurism to the Present,* Abrams, New York, 1988.

Hatch, James V., *Black Playwrights, 1823–1977: An Annotated Bibliography of Plays,* Bowker, New York, 1977.

Houghton, Norris, *Moscow Rehearsals,* Harcourt, Brace, New York, 1936.

Isaacs, Edith J., *The Negro in American Theatre,* Theatre Arts, New York, 1947.

Kuhns, David F., *German Expressionist Theatre: The Actor and the Stage,* Cambridge University Press, New York, 1997.

Leach, Robert, *Vsevelod Meyerhold,* Cambridge University Press, Cambridge, 1993.

Mitchell, Loften, *Black Drama: The Story of the American Negro in the Theatre,* Hawthorn, New York, 1967.

Patterson, Michael, *The Revolution in the German Theatre, 1900–1933,* Routledge and Kegan Paul, London, 1981.

Rabkin, Gerald, *Drama and Commitment: Politics in the American Theatre of the Thirties,* Indiana University Press, Bloomington, 1964.

Richard, Shaun (ed.), *The Cambridge Companion to Twentieth-Century Irish Drama,* Cambridge University Press, Cambridge, 2004.

Roose-Evans, James, *Experimental Theatre: From Stanislavsky to Peter Brook,* 2d ed., Routledge, New York, 1996.

Rovit, Rebecca, and Alvin Goldfarb (eds.), *Theatrical Performance during the Holocaust: Texts, Memoirs, and Documents,* Johns Hopkins University Press, Baltimore, Md., 1999.

Rudlin, John, *Jacques Copeau,* Cambridge University Press, New York, 1986.

Rudnitsky, Konstantin, *Russian and Soviet Theatre: Tradition and the Avant-Garde,* Roxane Permar (trans.), Thames and Hudson, New York, 2000.

Schuler, Catherine, *Women in Russian Theatre: The Actress in the Silver Age,* Routledge, New York, 1996.

Wainscott, Ronald Harold, *The Emergence of the Modern American Theater, 1914–1929,* Yale University Press, New Haven, Conn., 1997.

Whitton, David, *Stage Directors in Modern France: Antoine to Mnouchkine,* Manchester University Press, Manchester, 1987.

Willett, John, *Expressionism,* McGraw-Hill, New York, 1970.

CHAPTER 14: THEATRES FROM 1945 TO 1975

Abramson, Doris, *Negro Playwrights in the American Theatre, 1925–1959,* Columbia University Press, New York, 1969.

Bigsby, C. W. E., *Modern American Drama, 1945–1990,* Cambridge University Press, New York, 1992.

Bradby, David, *Modern French Drama, 1940–1990,* 2d ed., Cambridge University Press, New York, 1991.

Brook, Peter, *The Empty Space,* Atheneum, New York, 1982.

Chinoy, Helen Krich, and Linda Walsh Jenkins (eds), *Women in American Theatre,* 3d ed., Theatre Communications Group, New York, 2001.

Cohn, Ruby, *Currents in Contemporary Drama,* Indiana University Press, Bloomington, 1969.

Cook, Judith, *The National Theatre,* Harrap, London, 1976.

Doty, Gresdna, and Billy J. Harbin (eds.), *Inside the Royal Court Theatre, 1956–1981,* Louisiana State University Press, Baton Rouge, 1990.

Elam, Harry J., *Taking It to the Streets: The Social Protest Theater of Luis Valdez and Amiri Baraka,* University of Michigan Press, Ann Arbor, 1997.

Elsom, John, *Post-War British Theatre,* Routledge and Kegan Paul, Boston, 1981.

Esslin, Martin, *The Theatre of the Absurd,* Anchor, Garden City, N.Y., 1969.

Grotowski, Jerzy, *Towards a Poor Theatre,* Simon and Schuster, New York, 1969.

Hatch, James V., *Black Playwrights, 1823–1977: An Annotated Bibliography of Plays,* Bowker, New York, 1977.

Kolin, Philip C. (ed.), *American Playwrights since 1945: A Guide to Scholarship, Criticism, and Performance,* Greenwood, Westport, Conn., 1989.

Maufort, Marc (ed.), *Staging Difference: Cultural Pluralism in American Theatre and Drama,* Lang, New York, 1995.

Mitchell, Loften, *Black Drama: The Story of the American Negro in the Theatre,* Hawthorn, New York, 1967.

Poggi, Jack, *Theater in America: The Impact of Economic Forces, 1870–1967,* Cornell University Press, Ithaca, N.Y., 1968.

Schechner, Richard, *Public Domain: Essays on the Theatre,* Discus, New York, 1970.

Smeliansky, Anatoly, *The Russian Theatre after Stalin,* Cambridge University Press, Cambridge, 1999.

Svoboda, Josef, *The Secret of Theatrical Space: The Memoirs of Josef Svoboda,* Jarka Burian (trans.), Applause, New York, 1993.

Weales, Gerald, *American Drama since World War II,* Harcourt, Brace, and World, New York, 1962.

Whitton, David, *Stage Directors in Modern France: Antoine to Mnouchkine,* Manchester University Press, Manchester, 1987.

CHAPTERS 15 AND 16: CONTEMPORARY AMERICAN THEATRE; GLOBAL THEATRES

Banham, Martin, *African Theatre Today,* Pitman, London, 1976.

_______ (ed.), *A History of Theatre in Africa,* Cambridge University Press, Cambridge, 2004.

Banham, Martin, James Gibbs, and Femi Osofisan (eds.), *African Theatre in Development,* Indiana University Press, Bloomington, 1999.

_______, _______, and _______ (eds.), *African Theatre: Playwrights and Politics,* Indiana University Press, Bloomington, 2001.

Beardsell, Peter, *A Theatre for Cannibals: Rudolfo Usigli and the Mexican Stage,* Fairleigh Dickinson University Press, Rutherford, N.J., 1992.

Bigsby, C. W. E., *Contemporary American Playwrights,* Cambridge University Press, New York, 1999.

_______, *Modern American Drama, 1945–1990,* Cambridge University Press, New York, 1992.

Blau, Herbert, *The Dubious Spectacle: Extremities of the Theater, 1976–2000,* University of Minnesota Press, Minneapolis, 2002.

Bottoms, Stephen J., *The Theatre of Sam Shepard,* Cambridge University Press, New York, 1998.

Bradby, David, *Modern French Drama, 1940–1990,* 2d ed., Cambridge University Press, New York, 1991.

_______, and Annie Sparks, *Mise en Scène: French Theatre Now,* Methuen Drama, London, 1997.

Brater, Enoch (ed.), *Feminine Focus: The New Women Playwrights,* Oxford University Press, New York, 1989.

Calandra, Denis, *New German Dramatists: A Study of Peter Handke, Rainer Werner Fassbinder, Heiner Müller, Thomas Bernhard,* Macmillan, New York, 1983.

Canning, Charlotte, *Feminist Theaters in the U.S.A.: Staging Women's Experience,* Routledge, New York, 1996.

Case, Sue-Ellen (ed.), *Split Britches: Lesbian Practice/Feminist Performance,* Routledge, New York, 1996.

Clark, Fred, and Ana Lúcia Gazolla de Garcia (eds.), *Twentieth-Century Brazilian Theatre,* Estudios de Hispanófila, Chapel Hill, N.C., 1978.

Conteh-Morgan, John, *Theatre and Drama in Francophone Africa,* Cambridge University Press, 1995.

Crespy, David, *Off-Off-Broadway Explosion: How Provocative Playwrights of the 1960s Ignited a New American Theatre,* Back Stage, New York, 2003.

Elam, Harry J., *Taking It to the Streets: The Social Protest Theater of Luis Valdez and Amiri Baraka,* University of Michigan Press, Ann Arbor, 1997.

_______, and David Krasner (eds.), *African-American Performance and Theatre History,* Oxford University Press, New York, 2001.

Etherton, Michael, *The Development of African Drama,* Hutchison University Library for Africa, London, 1982.

George, David Sanderson, *The Modern Brazilian Stage,* University of Texas Press, Austin, 1992.

Goldberg, RoseLee, *Performance Art: From Futurism to the Present,* Abrams, New York, 1988.

Goodman, Lizbeth, *Contemporary Feminist Theatres,* Routledge, New York, 1993.

Graham-White, Anthony, *The Drama of Black Africa,* Samuel French, New York, 1974.

Griffin, Gabriele, *Contemporary Black and Asian Women Playwrights in Britain,* Cambridge University Press, Cambridge, 2003.

Holland, Peter, *English Shakespeares: Shakespeare on the English Stage in the 1990s,* Cambridge University Press, New York, 1997.

Howard, Roger, *Contemporary Chinese Theatre,* Heinemann Educational, London, 1978.

Huerta, Jorge A., *Chicano Theater: Themes and Forms,* Bilingual, Ypsilanti, Mich., 1982.

Jacob, Paul, *Contemporary Indian Theatre: Interviews with Playwrights and Directors,* Sangeet Natak Akademi, New Delhi, 1989.

Jones, John Bush, *Our Musicals, Ourselves: A Social History of the American Musical Theatre,* Brandeis University Press, Medford, Mass., 2003.

Kantor, Tadeusz, *A Journey through Other Spaces: Essays and Manifestos, 1944–1990,* Michal Kobialka (trans.), University of California Press, Berkeley, 1993.

Kolin, Philip C. (ed.), *American Playwrights since 1945: A Guide to Scholarship, Criticism, and Performance,* Greenwood, Westport, Conn., 1989.

Kritzer, Amelia Howe, *The Plays of Caryl Churchill,* St. Martin's, New York, 1991.

Lamb, Ruth, *Mexican Theatre of the Twentieth Century,* Ocelot, Claremont, Calif., 1975.

Mackerras, Colin, *The Chinese Theatre in Modern Times,* University of Massachusetts Press, Amherst, 1975.

Marranca, Bonnie, *The Theatre of Images,* Drama Book Specialists, New York, 1977.

Martin, Carol (ed.), *A Sourcebook of Feminist Theatre and Performance,* Routledge, New York, 1996.

McConachie, Bruce, *American Theatre in the Culture of the Cold War: Producing and Contesting Containment, 1947–1962,* University of Iowa Press, Iowa City, 2003.

McDonough, Carla J., *Staging Masculinity: Male Identity in Contemporary American Drama,* McFarland, Jefferson, N.C., 1997.

Mottram, Ron, *Inner Landscapes: The Theatre of SamShepard,* University of Missouri Press, Columbia, 1984.

Moy, James S., *Marginal Sights: Staging the Chinese in America,* University of Iowa, Iowa City, 1993.

Patterson, Michael, *Peter Stein: Germany's Leading Theatre Director,* Cambridge University Press, New York, 1981.

Pereira, Kim, *August Wilson and the African-American Odyssey,* University of Illinois Press, Urbana, 1995.

Perkins, Kathy, and Roberta Uno, *Contemporary Plays by Women of Color: An Anthology,* Routledge, New York, 1996.

Peterson, Jane T., and Suzanne Bennett, *Women Playwrights of Diversity: A Bio-Bibliographical Sourcebook,* Greenwood, Westport, Conn., 1997.

Pottlitzer, Joanne, *Hispanic Theater in the United States and Puerto Rico,* Ford Foundation, New York, 1988.

Powell, Brian, *Japan's Modern Theatre: A Century of Change and Continuity,* Japan Library, Kent, 1994.

_______, *Kabuki in Modern Japan: Mayama Seika and His Plays,* St. Martin's Press, New York, 1990.

Ramirez, Elizabeth C., *Footlights across the Border: A History of Spanish-Language Professional Theatre on the Texas Stage,* Lang, New York, 1990.

Reinelt, Janelle G., *After Brecht: British Epic Theater,* University of Michigan Press, Ann Arbor, 1994.

Roemer, Rick, *Charles Ludlam and the Ridiculous Theatrical Company,* McFarland, Jefferson, N.C., 1998.

Savran, David, *The Wooster Group, 1975–1985: Breaking the Rules,* UMI Research Press, Ann Arbor, 1986.

Sebald, W. G. (ed.), *A Radical Stage: Theatre in Germany in the 1970s and 1980s,* St. Martin's, New York, 1988.

Senda, Akihiko, *The Voyage of Contemporary Japanese Theatre,* J. Thomas Rimer (trans.), University of Hawaii Press, Honolulu, 1997.

Shafer, Yvonne, *August Wilson: A Research and Production Sourcebook,* Greenwood, Westport, Conn., 1998.

Shyer, Laurence, *Robert Wilson and His Collaborators,* Theatre Communications Group, New York, 1989.

Whitton, David, *Stage Directors in Modern France: Antoine to Mnouchkine,* Manchester University Press, Manchester, 1987.

Williams, Mance, *Black Theatre in the 1960s and 1970s,* Greenwood, Westport, Conn., 1985.

INDEX

Note: (illus.) indicates an illustration; (n.) indicates a note.